THE STATE OF
NONPROFIT AMERICA

THE STATE OF
NONPROFIT AMERICA

LESTER M. SALAMON
Editor

BROOKINGS INSTITUTION PRESS
Washington, D.C.

Published in collaboration with the Aspen Institute

ABOUT BROOKINGS

The Brookings Institution is a private nonprofit organization devoted to research, education, and publication on important issues of domestic and foreign policy. Its principal purpose is to bring knowledge to bear on current and emerging policy problems. The Institution maintains a position of neutrality on issues of public policy. Interpretations or conclusions in Brookings publications should be understood to be solely those of the authors.

ABOUT ASPEN

Founded in 1950, the Aspen Institute is a global forum for leveraging the power of leaders to improve the human condition. Through its seminar and policy programs, the Institute fosters enlightened, morally responsible leadership and convenes leaders and policymakers to address the foremost challenges of the new century.

Copyright © 2002
Lester M. Salamon

All rights reserved. No part of this publication may be reproduced or transmitted in any form or by any means without permission in writing from the Brookings Institution Press, 1775 Massachusetts Avenue, N.W., Washington, DC 20036 (www.brookings.edu).

Library of Congress Cataloging-in-Publication data

The state of nonprofit America / Lester M. Salamon, editor.
    p.   cm.
Includes bibliographical references and index.
  ISBN 0-8157-0624-3 (alk. paper)
  ISBN 0-8157-0623-5 (pbk. : alk. paper)
  1. Nonprofit organizations—United States. I. Salamon, Lester M.

HD62.6 .S734 2003
338.7'4—dc21   2002015521

9 8 7 6 5 4 3 2 1

The paper used in this publication meets minimum requirements of the American National Standard for Information Sciences—Permanence of Paper for Printed Library Materials: ANSI Z39.48-1992.

Typeset in Adobe Garamond

Composition by Cynthia Stock
Silver Spring, Maryland

Printed by R. R. Donnelley and Sons
Harrisonburg, Virginia

This book is dedicated to the memory of
William A. Díaz
scholar, activist, colleague, and friend,
whose courage in the face of a crippling illness
and dedication to the cause of human rights and social justice
embodied the spirit of nonprofit America at its best

Contents

Preface

The literature on America's nonprofit sector has burgeoned in recent years. Long an obscure academic backwater inhabited by a small band of dedicated mavericks, the field of nonprofit studies has swelled into a mighty stream fed by growing doubts about the capabilities of government, political and ideological resistance to expanded public spending, and concerns about America's civic health.

While this increased attention has substantially expanded the base of information available about America's nonprofit organizations, it has not yet generated the clear understanding that is needed of the sector's changing position and role. For one thing, nonprofit organizations continue to be caught up in the long-standing political conflict over the relative roles of the state and the market in responding to public problems, creating a heavy ideological overlay that distorts our view and systematically blocks out uncomfortable facts. Beyond this, the sheer outpouring of information creates its own confusion. Once starved for information, nonprofit practitioners are now deluged by it. Fitting the bits and pieces together into an integrated understanding thus becomes a full-time occupation, something that few harried practitioners or volunteer board members have the luxury to pursue.

This book was conceived as a response to this dilemma. It seeks to provide a comprehensive, but readable, assessment of the state of America's nonprofit sector at what turns out to be a pivotal moment in its development. More than a compilation of facts and figures, the book seeks to interpret what is going on and make it understandable to the broad cross section of informed opinion on which the future of this sector ultimately depends.

To be sure, this is no mean undertaking, which may explain why it has never been attempted before. Nonprofit organizations are almost infinitely varied. They come in different sizes, operate in widely diverse fields, perform numerous functions, and support themselves in many ways. What is more, all of these features are in flux. Unlike the elephant in the ancient tale, this beast thus appears different depending not only on who touches it and where, but also when.

To assist me in this mission impossible, I was fortunate enough to forge a partnership with the Aspen Institute's Nonprofit Sector and Philanthropy Program and to recruit an extraordinary group of colleagues. Together we have worked over the past two-and-a-half years to produce a portrait of America's nonprofit sector, and its component parts, that is factually grounded and sensitive to the sector's diversity, while still reaching for the broad interpretive judgments that are needed to make sense of the swirling crosscurrents of daily events.

When this project began, the American stock market was at historic highs, the central political question was what to do with a burgeoning federal surplus, dot.com entrepreneurs were transforming philanthropy with the windfall profits of their ingenuity, and America was bursting with a confidence born of apparent omnipotence. The resulting book appears, however, in the wake of September 11, following the precipitous collapse of the dot.com bubble, in the midst of a continuing economic slump, and with growing concerns about escalating government deficits both nationally and in most states.

While we have attempted to accommodate many of these developments, inevitably it has not been possible to make this account as current as yesterday's newspaper. Far from diminishing the value of this book, however, these shifts make it clear why the kind of interpretive perspective we have sought to produce is so useful. Readers can judge for themselves whether the trends and developments we have highlighted are the ones that will prevail in the years immediately ahead, but we are convinced that the central themes identified will meet the test of time and prove every bit as germane today as they were when the project was originally conceived. Those themes emphasize the enormous resilience that the American nonprofit sector has displayed over the past two decades, the significant re-engineering the sector has undergone as a consequence, and the vast opportunities and corresponding risks that this process has brought in its wake. Not only are these trends important for the future of the nonprofit sector, but also they hold enormous implications for the society of which these institutions are so pivotal a part.

In addition to the colleagues who contributed chapters to this volume and who put up with the extensive consultations required to fashion it into an integrated book, I want to express my appreciation as well to Alan Abramson,

Winnifred Levy, and Scott Walsberger of the Aspen Institute's Nonprofit Sector and Philanthropy Program, and to Kathryn Nelson, formerly of Aspen, who collaborated with me on every step of the design and execution of this project; to the advisory committee that helped us shape the project from the outset, including Sara Engelhardt of the Foundation Center; Peter Goldberg of the Alliance for Children and Families, Valerie Lies of the Donors Forum of Chicago, Geraldine Mannion of the Carnegie Corporation of New York, Jon Pratt of the Minnesota Council of Nonprofits, Jan Masaoka of CompassPoint Nonprofit Services, Susan Saxon-Harrold formerly of the Independent Sector, Edward Skloot of the Surdna Foundation, Henry Ramos of Mauer Kunst Consulting, and Elizabeth Boris of the Urban Institute; to the numerous other colleagues who reviewed and commented on drafts of the chapters; to Christopher Kelaher, our editor at Brookings Institution Press, and his colleagues Janet Walker, Rebecca Clark, and copyeditor Elizabeth Forsyth; and to the Carnegie Corporation of New York, the Nathan Cummings Foundation, the John D. and Catherine T. MacArthur Foundation, the Charles Stewart Mott Foundation, the David and Lucille Packard Foundation, and the Rockefeller Brothers Fund for the financial support that made this work possible. Needless to say, however, the opinions and interpretations offered here are those of the authors and editor only and may not represent the views of any of the organizations with which we may be affiliated or that have supported or published the work.

Finally, this book is dedicated to the memory of William A. Díaz, a colleague and friend who contributed a chapter to this book but who died before it could appear in print. Bill's work on this project was the final professional act of his life, and he brought to it all the determination and conviction he demonstrated in all of his important work in the third sector. Indeed, Bill Díaz's courage in the face of a crippling illness and his dedication to the cause of human rights and social justice symbolize for me the spirit that underlies the nonprofit sector and that makes it so crucial a part of American life to understand and preserve.

LESTER M. SALAMON

PART I

Overview

1

The Resilient Sector:
The State of Nonprofit America

LESTER M. SALAMON

When three hijacked planes crashed into the World Trade Center and the Pentagon on the morning of September 11, 2001, the police, fire, and military organs of New York City, Washington, D.C., and the U.S. government were not the only entities to respond with heroism and élan. The events of that horrific morning also triggered a spirited response from the vast, uncharted network of private voluntary institutions that forms the unseen social infrastructure of American life. In small towns and large cities, from the Florida Keys to northernmost Alaska, people rushed to offer assistance. In part, the responses were spontaneous and unstructured. But in far larger part, they were organized and orchestrated, mobilized by the vast assortment of organizations and institutions that compose what is increasingly recognized as a distinct, if not wholly understood, sector of our national life known variously as the nonprofit, the charitable, or the civil society sector.

Like the arteries of a living organism, these organizations carry a life force that has long been a centerpiece of American culture—a faith in the capacity of individual action to improve the quality of human life. They thus embody two seemingly contradictory impulses that form the heart of American character: a deep-seated commitment to freedom and individual initiative and an equally fundamental realization that people live in communities and consequently have responsibilities that extend beyond themselves. Uniquely among American institutions, those in the nonprofit sector blend these competing impulses,

3

creating a special class of entities dedicated to mobilizing *private initiative for the common good.*

The terrorists who crashed civilian jetliners into unarmed buildings on that fine September morning did not, therefore, assault a nation without the capacity to respond. That capacity extended well beyond the conventional and visible institutions of government. It embraced as well a largely invisible social infrastructure of private, charitable groups and the supportive impulses to volunteer and give that it has helped to nurture.

And respond it did. Within two months, individuals, corporations, and foundations had contributed $1.3 billion in assistance to a wide array of relief efforts. Blood donations alone were estimated to have increased between 250,000 and 400,000 pints in the wake of the disaster.[1] Some of the institutions involved in mobilizing this response were household words—the Red Cross, the Salvation Army, and United Way. Others were established but less-well-known institutions like the New York Community Trust, the Community Service Society of New York, the Chicago Mercantile Exchange Foundation, and many more. Still others were created especially to deal with this crisis—the September 11 Fund, the Twin Towers Fund, Trial Lawyers Care (to assist victims with legal issues), and the Alaska Culinary Association (to benefit families of restaurant workers killed in the World Trade Center collapse). Altogether, some 200 charitable organizations reportedly pitched in to help directly with the relief and recovery effort in New York alone, and countless others were involved more indirectly. According to one recent survey, an astounding 70 percent of all Americans made some kind of contribution to this response.[2]

Revealing though this episode has been of the remarkable strengths of America's "third," or nonprofit, sector, however, it simultaneously revealed the sector's limitations as well. Private voluntary groups, though highly effective in mobilizing individuals to act, are far less equipped to structure the resulting activity. In short order, the fragile systems of nonprofit response were severely challenged by the enormity of the crisis they confronted in the aftermath of September 11. Individual agencies, concerned about their autonomy, resisted efforts to coordinate their responses, either with each other or with government authorities. Individuals in need of assistance had to navigate a multitude of separate agencies, each with its own eligibility criteria and targeted forms of aid. Inevitably, delays and inequities occurred; many individuals fell through the slats, while others benefited from multiple sources of assistance. What is more, misunderstandings arose between the donors, most of whom apparently intended their contributions to be used for immediate relief, and some agencies, most notably the Red Cross, that hoped to squirrel the funds away for longer-term recovery, general institutional support, and other, less-visible, disasters down the road. What began as an inspiring demonstration of the power of America's charitable community thus became a demonstration of its shortcomings as well.

In this, the story of the nonprofit sector's response to the crisis of September 11 is emblematic of its position in American life more generally. Long celebrated as a fundamental part of the American heritage, America's nonprofit organizations have suffered from structural shortcomings that limit the role they can play. This juxtaposition of strengths and limitations, in turn, has fueled a lively ideological contest over the extent to which we should rely on these institutions to handle critical public needs, with conservatives focusing laser-like on the sector's strengths and liberals often restricting their attention to its weaknesses instead. Through it all, though largely unheralded and perhaps unrecognized by either side, a classically American compromise has taken shape. This compromise was forged early in the nation's history, but it was broadened and solidified in the 1960s. Under it, nonprofit organizations in an ever-widening range of fields were made the beneficiaries of government support to provide a growing array of services—from health care to scientific research—that Americans wanted but were reluctant to have government directly provide.[3] More than any other single factor, this government-nonprofit partnership is responsible for the growth of the nonprofit sector as we know it today.

During the past twenty years, however, that compromise has come under considerable assault. At the same time, the country's nonprofit institutions have faced an extraordinary range of other challenges as well—significant demographic shifts, fundamental changes in public policy and public attitudes, new commercial impulses, massive technological developments, and changes in lifestyle, to cite just a few. Although nonprofit America has responded with creativity to many of these challenges, the responses have pulled it in directions that are, at best, poorly understood and, at worst, corrosive of the sector's special character and role.

Despite the significance of these developments, little headway has been made in tracking them systematically, in assessing the impact they are having both generally and for particular types of organizations, and in getting the results into the hands of nonprofit practitioners, policymakers, the press, and the public at large. This book is intended to fill this gap, to offer an overview of the state of America's nonprofit sector, and to identify the changes that might be needed to promote its long-term health. To do so, the book assembles a set of original essays prepared by leading authorities on key components of the American nonprofit scene and on the key trends affecting their evolution. The result is the first recent integrated account of a set of institutions that we have long taken for granted, but that the Frenchman Alexis de Tocqueville recognized more than 175 years ago to be "more deserving of our attention" than any other part of the American experiment.[4]

This chapter summarizes the basic story that emerges from this assessment. Given the diversity of America's nonprofit institutions and the multitude of forces impinging on its various parts, this is no mean task. From my perspective, however, a dominant, if hardly universal, impression clearly emerges from the separate brush strokes of analysis offered in this book's chapters. Fundamentally, it is an impression of *resilience*, of a set of institutions and traditions facing enormous challenges but also important opportunities and finding ways to respond to both with considerable creativity and resolve. Indeed, nonprofit America appears to be well along in a fundamental process of "reengineering" that calls to mind the similar process that large segments of America's business sector have undergone since the late 1980s.[5] Faced with an increasingly competitive environment, nonprofit organizations have been called on to make fundamental changes in the way they operate. And that is just what they have been doing.

What is involved here, moreover, is not simply the importation of "business methods" into nonprofit organizations, although that is sometimes how it is portrayed.[6] While nonprofits are becoming more "business-like," the business methods they are adopting have themselves undergone fundamental change in recent years, and many of the changes have involved incorporating management approaches that have long been associated with nonprofit work—such as the emphasis on organizational mission, the ethos of service to clients, and the need to imbue staff with a sense of purpose beyond the maximization of profit. In a sense, these longtime nonprofit management principles have now been fused with business management techniques to produce a blended body of management concepts that is penetrating business and nonprofit management alike.

Like all processes of change, this one is far from even. Some organizations have been swept up in the winds of change, while others have hardly felt a breeze or, having felt it, have not been in a position to respond. What is more, it is far from clear which group has made the right decision or left the sector as a whole better off, since the consequences of some of the changes are far from certain and at any rate are mixed.

Any account of the "state of nonprofit America" must therefore be a story in three parts, focusing first on the challenges and opportunities America's nonprofit sector is confronting, then examining how the sector's institutions are responding to these challenges and opportunities, and finally, assessing the consequences of these responses both for individual organizations and subsectors and for nonprofit America as a whole. The balance of this chapter offers such an account. To set the stage, however, it may be useful to explain more fully what the nonprofit sector is and why it deserves our attention.

What Is the Nonprofit Sector and Why Do We Need It?

The nonprofit sector is a vast and diverse assortment of organizations. It includes most of the nation's premier hospitals and universities, almost all of its orchestras and opera companies, a significant share of its theaters, all of its religious congregations, the bulk of its environmental advocacy and civil rights organizations, and huge numbers of its family service, children's service, neighborhood development, antipoverty, and community health facilities. It also includes the numerous support organizations, such as foundations and community chests, that help to generate financial assistance for these organizations, as well as the traditions of giving, volunteering, and service they help to foster.

More formally, we focus here on organizations that are eligible for exemption from federal income taxation under Section 501(c)(3) of the tax code, plus the closely related "social welfare organizations" eligible for exemption under Section 501(c)(4) of this code. Included here are organizations that operate "exclusively for religious, charitable, scientific, or educational purposes" and that do not distribute any profits they may generate to any private shareholder or individual. Alone among the twenty-six types of organizations exempted from federal income taxation, the 501(c)(3) organizations are also eligible to receive tax-deductible contributions from individuals and businesses, a reflection of the fact that they are expected to serve broad public purposes as opposed to the interests and needs of the members of the organization alone.[7]

Scale

No one knows for sure how many such nonprofit organizations exist in the United States, since large portions of the sector are essentially unincorporated and the data available on even the formal organizations are notoriously incomplete. A conservative estimate puts the total number of formally constituted 501(c)(3) and (c)(4) organizations at 1.2 million as of the mid-1990s, including an estimated 350,000 churches and other religious congregations.[8] As of 1998, these organizations employed close to 11 million paid workers, or over 7 percent of the U.S. work force, and enlisted the equivalent of another 5.7 million full-time employees as volunteers.[9] This means that paid employment alone in nonprofit organizations is three times that in agriculture, twice that in wholesale trade, and nearly 50 percent greater than that in both construction and finance, insurance, and real estate, as shown in figure 1-1. With volunteer labor included, employment in the nonprofit sector, at 16.6 million, approaches that in all branches of manufacturing combined (20.5 million).[10]

Most of this nonprofit employment is concentrated in three fields—health (43 percent), education (22 percent), and social services (18 percent). With volunteers included, the distribution of employment changes significantly, with the religious share swelling to 23 percent and health dropping to 34 percent (figure 1-2).

These large categories disguise, however, the huge array of separate services and activities in which nonprofit organizations are involved. A classification system developed by the National Center for Charitable Statistics, for example, identifies no fewer than twenty-six major fields of nonprofit activity and sixteen functions—from accreditation to fundraising—in each. Each of the major fields

Figure 1-1. *Nonprofit Employment in Relation to Employment in Major U.S. Industries, 1998*

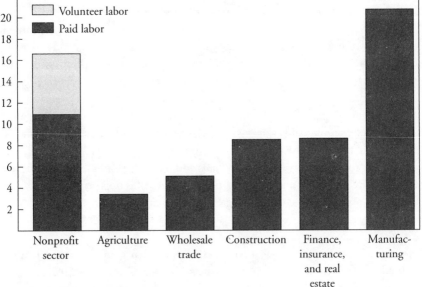

Workers (millions)

Legend:
Volunteer labor
Paid labor

Categories (x-axis):
Nonprofit sector | Agriculture | Wholesale trade | Construction | Finance, insurance, and real estate | Manufacturing

Source: Murray S. Weitzman, Nadine Tai Jalandoni, Linda M. Lampkin, and Thomas H. Pollack, *The New Nonprofit Almanac and Desk Reference* (San Francisco: Jossey-Bass, 2002), pp. 33, 23, 80; U.S. Census Bureau, *Statistical Abstract of the United States,* 120th ed. (Washington: U.S. Government Printing Office, 2000), p. 420.

is then further subdivided into subfields. Thus, for example, the field of arts, culture, and humanities has fifty-six subfields, and the field of education has forty-one. Altogether, this translates into several thousand potential different types of nonprofit organizations.[11]

Even this fails to do justice to the considerable diversity of the nonprofit sector. Most of the employment and economic resources of this sector are concentrated in large organizations. However, most of the organizations are quite small, with few or no full-time employees. Of the nearly 670,000 organizations recorded on the Internal Revenue Service's list of formally registered 501(c)(3) organizations (exclusive of religious congregations and foundations) in 1998, only about a third, or 224,000, filed the information form (Form 990) required of all organizations with expenditures of $25,000 or more. The remaining two-thirds of the organizations were thus either inactive or below the $25,000 spending threshold for filing.[12] Even among the filers, moreover, the top 4 percent accounted for nearly 70 percent of the reported expenditures, while the

Figure 1-2. *Distribution of Nonprofit Employment, Paid and Volunteer, by Field, 1998*

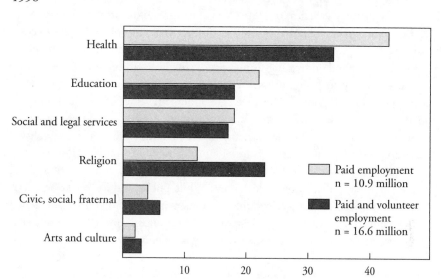

Source: Author's estimates based on data in Weitzman and others, *The New Nonprofit Almanac and Desk Reference* (San Francisco: Jossey-Bass, 2002); Virginia B. Hodgkinson and Murray S. Weitzman, *Nonprofit Almanac: 1996/97* (San Francisco: Jossey-Bass, 1996).

bottom 40 percent, with expenditures of less than $100,000 each, accounted for less than 1 percent of the total.[13]

Roles and Functions

Quite apart from their economic importance, nonprofit organizations make crucial contributions to national and community life.[14]

THE SERVICE ROLE. In the first place, nonprofit organizations are *service providers*: they deliver much of the hospital care, higher education, social services, cultural entertainment, employment and training, low-income housing, community development, and emergency aid services available in our country. More concretely, this set of organizations constitutes:

—Half of the nation's hospitals,

—One-third of its health clinics,

—Over a quarter of its nursing homes,

—Nearly half (46 percent) of its higher education institutions,

—Four-fifths (80 percent) of its individual and family service agencies,

—70 percent of its vocational rehabilitation facilities,

—30 percent of its daycare centers,

—Over 90 percent of its orchestras and operas,

—The delivery vehicles for 70 percent of its foreign disaster assistance.

While disagreements exist over how "distinctive" nonprofit services are compared to those provided by businesses or governments, nonprofits are well known for identifying and addressing unmet needs, for innovating, and for delivering services of exceptionally high quality. Thus nonprofit organizations pioneered assistance to AIDS victims, hospice care, emergency shelter for the homeless, food pantries for the hungry, drug abuse treatment efforts, and dozens more too numerous to mention. Similarly, many of the premier educational and cultural institutions in the nation are private, nonprofit organizations—institutions like Harvard, Princeton, Johns Hopkins, the Metropolitan Museum of Art, and the Cleveland Symphony, to name just a few. While public and for-profit organizations also provide crucial services, there is no denying the extra dimension added by the country's thousands of private, nonprofit groups in meeting public needs that neither the market nor the state can, or will, adequately address.

THE ADVOCACY ROLE. In addition to delivering services, nonprofit organizations also contribute to national life by identifying unaddressed problems and bringing them to public attention, by protecting basic human rights, and by giving voice to a wide assortment of social, political, environmental, ethnic, and community interests and concerns. Most of the social movements that have animated American life over the past century or more operated in and through the nonprofit sector. Included here are the antislavery, women's suffrage, populist, progressive, civil rights, environmental, antiwar, women's, gay rights, and conservative movements. The nonprofit sector has thus operated as a critical social safety valve, permitting aggrieved groups to bring their concerns to broader public attention and to rally support to improve their circumstances. This advocacy role may, in fact, be more important to the nation's social health than the service functions the sector also performs.

THE EXPRESSIVE ROLE. Political and policy concerns are not the only ones to which the nonprofit sector gives expression. Rather, this set of institutions provides the vehicles through which an enormous variety of other sentiments and impulses—artistic, religious, cultural, ethnic, social, recreational—also find expression. Opera companies, symphonies, soccer clubs, churches, synagogues, fraternal societies, book clubs, and Girl Scouts are just some of the manifestations of this expressive function. Through them, nonprofit organizations enrich human existence and contribute to the social and cultural vitality of community life.

THE COMMUNITY-BUILDING ROLE. Nonprofit organizations are also important in building what scholars are increasingly coming to call social capital—

those bonds of trust and reciprocity that seem to be crucial for a democratic polity and a market economy to function effectively.[15] Alexis de Tocqueville understood this point well when he wrote in *Democracy in America*:

> Feelings and opinions are recruited, the heart is enlarged, and the human mind is developed, only by the reciprocal influence of men upon one another . . . these influences are almost null in democratic countries; they must therefore be artificially created and this can only be accomplished by associations.[16]

By establishing connections among individuals, involvement in associations teaches norms of cooperation that carry over into political and economic life.

VALUE GUARDIAN.[17] Finally, nonprofit organizations embody, and therefore help to nurture and sustain, a crucial national value emphasizing individual initiative in the public good. They thus give institutional expression to two seemingly contradictory principles that are both important parts of American national character: the principle of *individualism*—the notion that people should have the freedom to act on matters that concern them—and the principle of *solidarity*—the notion that people have responsibilities not only to themselves but also to their fellow human beings and to the communities of which they are part. By fusing these two principles, nonprofit organizations reinforce both, establishing an arena of action through which individuals can take the initiative not simply to promote their own well-being but to advance the well-being of others as well. This is not simply an abstract function, moreover. It takes tangible form in the more than $200 billion in private charitable gifts that nonprofit organizations help to generate from the American public annually and in the 15.8 billion hours of volunteer time they stimulate for a diverse array of purposes.

Challenges and Opportunities

Despite the important contributions they make, nonprofit organizations find themselves in a time of testing at present. To be sure, they are not alone in this. But the challenges facing nonprofit organizations are especially daunting, since they go to the heart of the sector's operations and raise questions about its very existence.

Nonprofit organizations have generally responded energetically and creatively to these pressures. What is more, they have taken ample advantage of the opportunities they also enjoy. But the responses have been uneven and not without risks. It is therefore necessary to look more closely at these challenges and opportunities and at the way nonprofit organizations have responded to them.

Key Challenges

Fundamentally, nonprofit America has confronted six critical challenges over the recent past. From all indications, moreover, these challenge seem likely to persist—and in some cases to intensify—in the years ahead.

THE FISCAL CHALLENGE. In the first place, America's nonprofit organizations have suffered from a persistent fiscal squeeze. To be sure, that squeeze was relieved in part in the aftermath of World War II, and particularly during the 1960s, thanks to a significant infusion of government support. Although it is not widely recognized, the government efforts to stimulate scientific advance and overcome poverty and ill health during this period relied heavily on nonprofit organizations for their operation.[18] By the late 1970s as a consequence, federal support to American nonprofit organizations outdistanced private charitable support by a factor of two to one, while state and local governments provided additional aid. What is more, this support percolated through a wide swath of the sector, providing needed financial nourishment to universities, hospital, clinics, daycare centers, nursing homes, employment and training organizations, family service agencies, and many more. Indeed, much of the modern nonprofit sector as we know it took shape during this period as a direct outgrowth of expanded government support.

This widespread government support to nonprofit organizations suffered a severe shock, however, in the early 1980s. Committed to a policy of fiscal restraint, and seemingly unaware of the extent to which public resources were underwriting private, nonprofit action, the Reagan administration attacked federal spending in precisely the areas where federal support to nonprofit organizations was most extensive—social and human services, education and training, community development, and nonhospital health. Although the budget cuts that occurred were nowhere near as severe as originally proposed, federal support to nonprofit organizations, outside of Medicare and Medicaid, declined by approximately 25 percent in real dollar terms in the early 1980s and returned to its 1980 level only in the late 1990s.[19] Although some state governments boosted their own spending in many of these fields, the increases were not sufficient to offset the federal cuts. Nonprofit organizations in the fields of community development, employment and training, social services, and community health were particularly hard-hit by these reductions. Although the government's fiscal pressure significantly eased in subsequent years, the experience of the 1980s and early 1990s has left a residue of anxiety that new budget pressures are now reviving.

Not just the amount, but also the form, of public sector support to the nonprofit sector changed during this period, moreover. Where earlier government offered grants and contracts to nonprofit organizations and gave nonprofits the inside track, during the 1980s and 1990s government program managers were encouraged to promote for-profit involvement in government contract work, including that for human services.[20] More significantly, the use of grants and contracts itself gave way increasingly to forms of assistance such as vouchers and tax expenditures that channel aid to consumers rather than producers, thus requiring nonprofits to compete for clients in the market, where for-profits have traditionally had the edge.[21] Already by 1980, the majority (53 percent) of federal assistance to nonprofit organizations took the form of such consumer subsidies, much of it through the Medicare and Medicaid programs. By 1986 this stood at 70 percent, and it continued to rise into the 1990s.[22] In part, this shift resulted from the concentration of the budget cuts of the 1980s on the so-called discretionary spending programs, which tended to be supply-side grant and contract programs, while Medicare and Medicaid—both of them demand-side subsidies—continued to grow.[23] In part also, however, it reflected the ascendance of conservative political forces that favored forms of assistance that maximized consumer choice. The price of securing conservative support for new or expanded programs of relevance to nonprofit organizations in the late 1980s and 1990s, therefore, was to make them vouchers or tax expenditures. The new Childcare and Development Block Grant enacted in 1990 and then reauthorized and expanded as part of the welfare reform legislation in 1996 specifically gave states the option to use the $5 billion in federal funds provided for daycare to finance voucher payments to eligible families rather than grants or contracts to daycare providers, and most states have pursued this option.[24] In addition, another $2 billion in federal daycare subsidies is delivered through a special childcare tax credit. Nonprofit daycare providers, like their counterparts in other fields, have thus been thrown increasingly into the private market to secure even public funding for their activities. As a result, they have been obliged to master complex billing and reimbursement systems and to learn how to "market" their services to potential "customers."

Not only did government support to nonprofit organizations change its form during this period, but so did important elements of private support. The most notable development here was the emergence of "managed care" in the health field, displacing the traditional pattern of fee-for-service medicine. Medicare provided an important impetus for this development by replacing its cost-based reimbursement system for hospitals in the early 1980s with a system of fixed payments for particular procedures. Corporations, too, responded to the rapid escalation of health care benefits for their workers by moving aggressively during the 1980s to replace standard fee-for-service insurance plans with managed care plans that featured up-front "capitation" payments to managed care providers. These providers then inserted themselves between patients and health care providers, negotiating rates with the providers and deciding which procedures were truly necessary. By 1997, close to 75 percent of the employees in medium and large establishments, and 62 percent of the employees in small establishments, were covered by some type of managed care plan.[25] More recently, managed care has expanded into the social services field, subjecting nonprofit drug treatment, rehabilitation service, and mental health treatment facilities to the same competitive pressures and reimbursement limits as hospitals have been confronting.

Adding to the fiscal pressure nonprofits face has been the inability of private philanthropy to offset cutbacks in government support and finance expanded nonprofit responses to community needs. To be sure, private giving has grown considerably in recent years. Between 1977 and 1997, for example, total private giving grew by 90 percent after adjusting for inflation, roughly equivalent to the growth of gross domestic product. However, this lumps the amounts provided for the actual operations of charities in a given year with large endowment gifts to foundations, universities, and other institutions that are typically not available for use in a given year, as well as with gifts to religious congregations, most of which go to the upkeep of the congregations and clergy, as Mark Chaves shows in chapter 8 of this volume. When we focus on the private gifts available to support nonprofit human service, arts, education, health, and advocacy organizations in a given year, the growth rate was closer to 62 percent, still impressive but well below the 81 percent growth rate of gross domestic product.[26] Indeed, as a share of personal income, private giving has been declining steadily in the United States: from an average of 1.86 percent in the 1970s, down to 1.78 percent in the 1980s, and to 1.72 percent in the early 1990s. Especially distressing, as Virginia Hodgkinson notes in chapter 12, has been the disappointing rate of giving by the well-off, which has fallen considerably as a share of their income over the past decade or more, perhaps as a result of tax changes that lowered the tax rates of the wealthy and hence their financial incentives to give.[27] While giving as a share of personal income increased somewhat in the late 1990s, it did not return to its 1970s level; and the stock market sell-off and recession of 2000–02 have constrained its further growth despite the outpouring of support in response to September 11.

Although giving has grown in absolute terms, therefore, it accounted for only 8 percent of the growth of the nonprofit sector outside of religion between 1977 and 1997. As a share of total sector income, private giving actually lost ground, falling from 18 percent of the total in 1977 to 12 percent in 1997, and there is little evidence that this has changed substantially in recent years.[28] Indeed, many types of nonprofit organizations fear that September 11 may bring a decline in charitable support as resources are shifted to post-disaster relief and recovery.

THE COMPETITION CHALLENGE. In addition to a fiscal challenge, nonprofit America has also faced a serious competitive challenge as a result of the striking

Table 1-1. *Nonprofit and For-Profit Roles in Select Fields, 1982–97*

Field	Percentage nonprofit		Percentage change in relative nonprofit share
	1982	1997	
Employment			
Child daycare	52	38	–27
Job training	93	89	–4
Individual and family services	94	91	–3
Home health	60	28	–53
Kidney dialysis centers	22	15	–32
Facilities, participation			
Dialysis centers	58[a]	32	–45
Rehabilitation hospitals	70[a]	36	–50
Home health agencies	64[a]	33	–48
Health maintenance organizations	65[a]	26	–60
Residential treatment facilities for children	87[b]	68	–22
Psychiatric hospitals	19[a]	16	–16
Hospices	89[c]	76	–15
Mental health clinics	64[b]	57	–11
Higher education enrollments	96	89	–7
Nursing homes	20[b]	28	+ 40
Acute care hospitals	58[a]	59	+ 2

Source: U.S. Census Bureau, *U.S. Economic Census* (Washington: U.S. Census Bureau, 1999); Bradford Gray and Mark Schlesinger, chapter 2 of this volume, fig. 2-1; National Center for Education Statistics, *Digest of Education Statistics 2000* (Washington: Department of Education, National Center for Education Statistics, 2000), pp. 202–03, 209.

a. Initial year for data is 1985, not 1982.

b. Initial year for data is 1986, not 1982.

c. Initial year for data is 1992.

growth of for-profit involvement in many traditional fields of nonprofit activity, from health care and welfare assistance to higher education and employment training. This, too, is not a wholly new development. But the scope of competition appears to have broadened considerably in recent years, and in an increasing range of fields nonprofits have been losing "market share." Thus, as shown in table 1-1, the nonprofit share of daycare jobs dropped from 52 to 38 percent between 1982 and 1997, a decline of some 27 percent. Similarly sharp declines in the relative nonprofit share occurred among rehabilitation hospitals, home health agencies, health maintenance organizations, kidney dialysis centers, mental health clinics, and hospices. In many of these fields, the absolute number of nonprofit facilities continued to grow, but the for-profit growth outpaced it. And in at least one crucial field—acute care hospitals—while the nonprofit *share* increased slightly, a significant reduction occurred in the *absolute number* of nonprofit (as well as public) facilities, so that the for-profit share of the total increased even more.

The range of for-profit firms competing with nonprofits has grown increasingly broad, moreover. For example, the recent welfare reform legislation has attracted defense contractors like Lockheed-Martin into the social welfare field because it puts a premium on the information-processing and contract management skills they have developed as master contractors on huge military systems. Under many of these new arrangements, in fact, nonprofit providers are serving as subcontractors to for-profit firms hired by states or local governments to manage the welfare reform process. Even the sacrosanct field of charitable fundraising has recently experienced a significant for-profit incursion in the form of financial service firms such as Fidelity and Merrill Lynch, as Leslie Lenkowsky and Virginia Hodgkinson report in chapters 11 and 12, respectively, of this volume. By 2000, the Fidelity Charitable Gift Fund, established in 1991, had attracted more assets than the nation's largest community foundation and distributed three times as much in grants.[29]

The reasons for this striking pattern of for-profit success are by no means clear and vary from field to field. The shift in forms of public funding mentioned earlier has very likely played a role, however, forcing nonprofits to compete for subsidized customers in the marketplace, where for-profit firms have a natural advantage. The rise of health maintenance organizations and other "third-party payment" methods has had a similar effect, as Bradford Gray and Mark Schlesinger argue in chapter 2 of this volume, since such organizations emphasize price rather than quality or community roots in choosing providers, thus minimizing the comparative advantages of nonprofits. Technological developments have also given for-profit firms a strategic edge because technology puts a premium on access to capital and nonprofits have an inherent difficulty generating capital because their nonprofit status makes it impossible for them to sell shares in the equity markets. Nonprofits are therefore at a particular disadvantage in fields where rapid increases in demand or new technological innovations necessitate increased capital expenditures.[30]

THE EFFECTIVENESS CHALLENGE. One consequence of the increased competition nonprofits are facing has been to intensify the pressure on them to perform and to demonstrate that performance. The result is a third challenge: the effectiveness challenge. As management expert William Ryan has written, "Nonprofits are now forced to reexamine their reasons for existing in light of a market that rewards discipline and performance and emphasizes organizational capacity rather than for-profit or nonprofit status and mission. Nonprofits have no choice but to reckon with these forces."[31] This runs counter to long-standing theories in the nonprofit field that have emphasized this sector's distinctive advantage precisely in fields where "information asymmetry" makes it difficult to demonstrate performance and where "trust" is consequently needed instead. Because they are not organized to pursue profits, it was argued, nonprofits are more worthy of such trust and therefore are more reliable providers in such difficult-to-measure fields.[32]

In the current climate, however, such theories have few remaining adherents, at least among those who control the sector's purse strings. Government managers, themselves under pressure to demonstrate results because of the recent Government Performance and Results Act, are increasingly pressing their nonprofit contractors to deliver measurable results, too. Not to be outdone, prominent philanthropic institutions have jumped onto the performance bandwagon. United Way of America, for example, thus launched a bold performance measurement system in the mid-1990s complete with website, performance measurement manual, and video in order to induce member agencies to require performance measurement as a condition of local funding. Numerous foundations have moved in a similar direction, increasing their emphasis on evaluation both of their grantees and of their own programming.[33] Indeed, a new foundation affinity group, Grantmakers for Effective Organizations, has been formed, and a new "venture philanthropy" model is attracting numerous adherents.[34] The key to this model is an investment approach to grantmaking that calls on philanthropic institutions to invest in organizations rather than individual programs, to take a more active hand in organizational governance and operations, and to insist on measurable results.

The resulting "accountability environment" in which nonprofits are having to operate will doubtless produce many positive results. But it will also increase the pressures on hard-pressed nonprofit managers to demonstrate progress in ways that neither they, nor anyone else, may be able to accomplish, at least not without far greater resources than are currently available for the task. What is more, as Evelyn Brody shows in chapter 15, accountability expectations often fail to acknowledge the multiple stakeholders whose demands for accountability nonprofits must accommodate. The risk is great, therefore, that the measures most readily at hand, or those most responsive to the market test, will substitute for those most germane to the problems being addressed. That, at any rate, is the lesson of public sector experience with performance measurement, and the increased focus on price rather than quality or community benefit in third-party contracting with nonprofit health providers certainly supports this observation.[35]

THE TECHNOLOGY CHALLENGE. Pressures from for-profit competitors have also accelerated the demands on nonprofits to incorporate new technology into their operations. Indeed, technology has become one of the great wild cards of nonprofit evolution. Like the other challenges identified here, technology's impact is by no means wholly negative. As Elizabeth Boris and Jeff Krehely argue in chapter 9 of this volume, new information technology is increasing the capacity of nonprofits to advocate by reducing the costs of mobilizing constituents and connecting to policymakers and allies. This observation finds confirmation in Jeffrey Berry's careful analysis of the growing influence of citizen groups, which he attributes in important part to access to television news.[36] Technology is also opening new ways to tap charitable contributions. The September 11 tragedy may well have marked a turning point in this regard, since some 10 percent of the funds raised came via the Internet.[37]

Nonprofit education, health, and arts institutions are also benefiting from technological change. As Atul Dighe shows in chapter 16 of this volume, medical practice has already been transformed by new technology, but genetic engineering and the new field of bionics linking biosciences with electronics promise even more dramatic breakthroughs, making it possible to deliver medical services not only in one's home, but in one's body through the implantation of biosensors that can think and react. Digitization is having a similar effect in the arts world, as Margaret Wyszomirski points out in chapter 5 of this volume. Three on-site classical music websites are already in operation, providing live, streaming transmissions of orchestral concerts from around the world, and this is just the beginning. A project of the Mellon Foundation is digitizing the collections of hundreds of museums at a level of technical sophistication unmatched by anything even imagined before. Cultural institutions sit on vast stockpiles of cultural raw material that is potentially available for exploitation in the new digital era, and many institutions are taking advantage of the opportunities.

But enticing as the opportunities opened by technological change may be to the nation's nonprofit institutions, they pose equally enormous challenges. Most obvious, perhaps, are the financial challenges. As one recent study notes, "Information technologies are resource intensive. They entail significant purchase costs, require significant training and upkeep, and yet become obsolete quickly."[38] Because of the structural disadvantages nonprofits face in raising capital due to their inability to enter the equity markets, however, the massive intrusion of new technological requirements into their work puts them at a distinct disadvantage vis-à-vis their for-profit competitors. We have already seen the consequences of this in the health maintenance organization industry, where the lack of capital following the discontinuation of government funding led to the rapid loss of market share to for-profit firms, which were better able to capitalize the huge investments in information-processing equipment required to manage the large risk pools that make managed care viable. Similar pressures are now at work in the social services industry, where managed care is also taking root.

Not only does technology threaten to alter further the balance between nonprofits and for-profits, but also it threatens to alter the structure of the nonprofit sector itself, advantaging larger organizations over smaller ones. This is due in part to the heavy fixed costs of the new technology. Already, concerns about a "digital divide" are surfacing within the sector, as survey after survey reveals the unequal distribution of both hardware and the capacity to adapt the hardware to organizational missions.[39] Although initially stimulating competition by giving even small upstarts access to huge markets, information technology also creates "network effects" that accentuate the advantages of dominant players.[40] Significant concerns have thus surfaced that e-philanthropy will allow large, well-known national nonprofits to raid the donor bases of local United Ways and operating charities and that information technology more generally will give exceptional advantages to large nationally prominent agencies in the competition for business partners, government funding, and foundation grants.

But the challenges posed by technology go far beyond financial or competitive considerations. Also at stake are fundamental philosophical issues that go to the heart of the nonprofit sector's mission and modes of operation. As Wyszomirski shows in chapter 5, such issues have surfaced especially vividly in the arts arena where the new technology raises fundamental questions of aesthetics, creative control, and intellectual property rights. Similar dilemmas confront educational institutions that are tempted by the new technologies to "brand" their products and package them for mass consumption, but at the risk of alienating their professorate, losing the immediacy of direct student-faculty contact, and giving precedence to the packaging of knowledge rather than to its discovery. How these technological dilemmas are resolved could well determine how the nonprofit sector evolves in the years ahead.

THE LEGITIMACY CHALLENGE. The moral and philosophical challenges that American nonprofit organizations are confronting go well beyond those posed by new technology, however. Rather, a serious fault line seems to have opened in the foundation of public trust on which the entire nonprofit edifice rests. This may be due in part to the unrealistic expectations that the public has of these institutions, expectations that the charitable sector ironically counts on and encourages. Also at work, however, has been the strident indictment that conservative politicians and commentators have lodged against many nonprofit organizations over the past decade. The central charge in this indictment is that nonprofit charitable organizations have become just another special interest, regularly conspiring with government bureaucrats to escalate public spending and doing so not so much out of real conviction about the needs being served as out of a desire to feather their own nests. Heritage Foundation president Edward Fuelner put this case especially sharply in 1996, criticizing charities for urging Congress to expand social welfare spending, while themselves "feeding at the public trough."[41] Entire organizations have been formed, in fact, to "de-halo" the nonprofit sector in this way, charging that a "new kind of nonprofit organization" has emerged in recent years "dedicated not to voluntary action, but to an expanded government role in our lives."[42] To remedy this, advocates of this view rallied behind the so-called Istook amendment, which sought to limit the advocacy activity of nonprofit organizations by prohibiting any non-profit organization receiving government support from using any more than 5 percent of its *total* revenues, not just its public revenues, for advocacy or lobby-ing activities.

Similar challenges to the legitimacy of nonprofit organizations have arisen from critics who take nonprofits to task for becoming *overly* professional and thus losing touch with those they serve. This line of argument has a long lineage in American social science, as evidenced by the brilliant analysis by historian Roy Lubove of the professionalization of social work, which led social workers away from social diagnosis, community organizing, and social reform toward a client-focused, medical model of social work practice.[43] More recently, critics on the left have charged nonprofit organizations generally with contributing to the over-professionalization of social concerns. By redefining basic human needs as "problems" that only professionals can resolve, these critics contend, this over-professionalization alienates people from the helping relationships they could establish with their neighbors and kin.[44] By embracing professionalism, non-profit organizations destroy community rather than building it up, the critics note. On the right, critics have been equally derisive of the professionalized human service apparatus, charging it with inflating the cost of dealing with social problems by "crowding out" lower-cost alternative service delivery mecha-nisms that are at least as effective.[45]

These sentiments echo loudly in the Bush administration's 2001 proposal to privilege "faith-based charities" in the distribution of federal assistance. A princi-pal appeal of this idea is the prospect of replacing formal, professionalized non-profit organizations with informal church groups staffed by dedicated volun-teers. This reinforces a quaint nineteenth-century image of how charitable organizations are supposed to operate, an image that competitive pressures, accountability demands, and technological change have made increasingly untenable.

Coupled with a spate of high-profile scandals in the early 1990s, these criti-cisms seem to have shaken public confidence in charitable institutions. Surveys taken in 1994 and 1996 find only 33 and 37 percent of respondents, respec-tively, expressing "a great deal" or "quite a lot" of confidence in nonprofit human service agencies, well behind the proportions expressing similar levels of confidence in the military and small business (see table 1-2).[46] This improved considerably in the late 1990s, perhaps as a consequence of the perceived success of welfare reform. Yet, even at this latter date, while a substantial majority of respondents agreed that "charitable organizations play a major role in making our communities better places to live," only 20 percent "strongly agreed" with this statement. And only 10 percent were willing to agree "strongly" that most charities are "honest and ethical in their use of donated funds." All of this sug-gests that America's nonprofit institutions are delicately balanced on a knife-

Table 1-2. *Public Attitudes toward Charitable and Other Organizations in the United States, 1992–99*

| | 1992–96 | | | 1999 | |
| | Percent expressing a great deal or quite a lot of confidence | | | Percent expressing confidence | |
Institutions	*1992*	*1994*	*1996*	*A great deal*	*A great deal or quite a lot*
Youth development	48	47	50	33	72
Human services	37	33	37	29	68
Religious organizations	47	50	55	32	61
Private higher education	49	48	57	23	59
Military	49	49	54	22	57
Small business	46	53	56	16	55
Health organizations	40	36	39	15	43
Local government	24	23	31	9	33
State government	19	21	26	8	31
Federal government	18	19	23	8	27
Major corporations	19	22	24	7	29

Source: Independent Sector, *Giving and Volunteering in the United States, 1999* (Washington: Independent Sector, 1999), pp. 3, 5.

edge of public support, with most people willing to grant them the benefit of the doubt, but with a strong undercurrent of uncertainty and concern.[47] As a consequence, a relative handful of highly visible scandals—such as the United Way scandal of the early 1990s, the New Era Philanthropy scandal of the mid-1990s, or the Red Cross difficulties in the wake of September 11—can have an impact that goes well beyond their actual significance.

HUMAN RESOURCE CHALLENGE. Inevitably, fiscal stress and public ambivalence toward the nonprofit sector have taken their toll on the sector's human resources. Experts in the child welfare field, for example, have recently identified "staff turnover" as "perhaps the most important problem" facing the field, citing "stress, . . . overwhelming accountability requirements, and concern over liability" as the principal causes.[48] As Shepard Forman and Abby Stoddard show in chapter 7, similar problems afflict the international relief field due to the explosion of complex humanitarian crises that blend enormous relief challenges with complicated political and military conflicts.

Especially difficult has been the recruitment and retention of frontline service workers for whom salary, benefit, and safety issues are particularly important, but retention of managerial personnel has also grown increasingly problematic. One study of graduates of public policy programs reports, for example, that the proportion of these public-spirited young people who take their first job in non-profit organizations doubled between the early 1970s and the early 1990s. However, the nonprofit sector's retention rate for these personnel has declined over time, with more turning to the for-profit sector as an alternative.[49] Of special concern is the turnover of talent and burnout at the executive director level. Executive directors who came into the field to pursue the social missions of their agencies find themselves expected to function instead as aggressive entrepreneurs leading outward-oriented enterprises able to attract paying customers, while retaining the allegiance of socially committed donors and boards, all of this in a context of growing public scrutiny and mistrust. According to one recent study, a surprising two-thirds of the executive directors in a national sample of nonprofit agencies were in their first executive director position, and over half of these had held the job for four years or less. Although most reported enjoying their job, a third indicated an intention to leave it within two years, and even among those likely to take another job in the nonprofit sector, only half indicated that their next job was likely to be as an executive director.[50] As Wyszomirski reports in chapter 5, leadership recruitment has become a particular challenge in the arts field, where the vacancy rate for art museum directors hit a fifteen-year high in 1999.

SUMMARY. In short, nonprofit America has confronted a difficult set of challenges over the recent past. Fiscal stress, increased competition, rapidly changing technology, and new accountability expectations have significantly expanded the pressures under which these organizations must work, and this has affected the public support these organizations enjoy and their ability to attract and hold staff.

Opportunities

But challenges are not all that nonprofit America has confronted in the recent past. It has also had the benefit of a number of crucial opportunities, many of which seem likely to persist. Four of these in particular deserve special attention.[51]

SOCIAL AND DEMOGRAPHIC SHIFTS. In the first place, recent social and demographic shifts have created new demands for nonprofit services and new prospects for attracting the personnel these organizations will need. Included among these shifts are the following:

—The doubling of the country's elderly population between 1960 and 2000 and the prospect that there will be four times as many elderly Americans in 2025 as there were in 1960,

—The jump in the labor force participation rate for women, particularly married women, from less than 20 percent in 1960 to 64 percent in 1998,[52]

—The doubling of the country's divorce rate since the 1960s and the resulting sharp jump in the number of children involved in divorces,[53]

—A fivefold increase in the number of out-of-wedlock births, from roughly 225,000 in 1960 to more than 1.25 million per year by the mid-1990s,[54]

—The doubling of refugees admitted to the United States, from 718,000 between 1966 and 1980 to 1.6 million during the next fifteen years.[55]

Taken together, these and other sociodemographic changes have expanded the demand for many of the services that nonprofit organizations have traditionally provided, such as child daycare, home health and nursing home care, family counseling, foster care, relocation assistance, and substance abuse treatment and prevention. What is more, the demand for these services has spread well beyond the poor and now encompasses middle-class households with resources to pay for them, a phenomenon that one analyst has called "the transformation of social services."[56] Indeed, the acceleration of modern life and the pressures on two-career families have led, as Dighe notes in chapter 16, to the "outsourcing" of key aspects of family life, from child daycare to tutoring and party arranging. Since nonprofit organizations are actively engaged in many of these fields, they stand to gain from this trend.

Equally important is the emergence of what Dighe, following demographer Paul Ray, calls the Cultural Creatives, a growing subgroup of the population that now numbers as many as 50 million people.[57] Cultural Creatives differ from both "Moderns" and "Traditionalists," the two other dominant population groups in America, by virtue of their preference for holistic thinking, their cosmopolitanism, their social activism, and their insistence on finding a better balance between work and personal values than the Moderns seem to have found. Although they have yet to develop a full self-consciousness, Cultural Creatives are powerfully attracted to the mission orientation of the nonprofit sector and could well help to resolve some of the sector's human resource challenges.

THE NEW PHILANTHROPY. Also working to the benefit of the nonprofit sector is a series of developments in private philanthropy. The first of these is the *intergenerational transfer of wealth* between the depression-era generation and the postwar baby boomers that is anticipated over the next forty years. Estimated to range anywhere from $10 trillion to $40 trillion or more, this wealth accumulated in the hands of the depression-era generation as a consequence of their relatively high propensity to save, their fortuitous investment during the 1950s and 1960s in relatively low-cost houses that then escalated in value, and the stock market surge of the 1980s and 1990s, which substantially boosted the value of their investments.[58]

A second development is the *new wealth* created by the dot-com economy and other powerful economic trends and policies during the 1980s and 1990s, substantially increasing income levels at the upper end of the income scale. Between 1979 and 1992, for example, the share of the nation's wealth controlled by the top 1 percent of households climbed from 20 percent to over

40 percent. Indeed, one-third of the projected intergenerational transfer is expected to go to 1 percent of the baby boom generation, for an average inheritance of $1.6 million per person among this select few.[59]

To be sure, lengthening life expectancy may dissipate much of this wealth in heavy health care and nursing home expenses. What is more, the stock market meltdown of 1999–2002 provides a powerful reminder of the ephemeral quality of much of the presumed new wealth. Nevertheless, with so much money "in play," substantial opportunities likely exist for the expansion of charitable bequests. The fact that 60 percent of the mid-size and larger foundations in existence as of 1999 were created in the 1980s and 1990s certainly lends credence to this belief, although the phase-out of the estate tax enacted in 2001 may put a damper on the extent to which philanthropy will benefit from these developments by eliminating the major financial incentive for forming foundations.[60]

Also encouraging for nonprofit prospects are the new strategies of corporate social involvement that have surfaced in recent years and the *greater corporate willingness to engage in partnerships and collaborations with nonprofit organizations* that has resulted from them. Although corporate giving has proved far more disappointing than many hoped in the early 1980s, numerous corporations have begun integrating social responsibility activities into their overall corporate business strategies. This has been done in part out of altruistic motives, but in part also out of a recognition that such relationships can serve corporate strategic goals—by winning consumer confidence, ensuring corporations a "license to operate" in the face of increasingly mobilized consumer, environmental, and worker movements, and promoting employee loyalty and morale.[61] As such, they have a more secure base than altruism alone can provide. The result has been to make corporate managers available to nonprofit organizations, not simply as donors, but as allies and collaborators in a wide range of socially important missions, from improving the well-being of children to protecting natural resources. Although nonprofit reputations may be put at risk through such relationships, there are also intriguing possibilities for extremely productive partnerships.

GREATER VISIBILITY AND POLICY SALIENCE. Also working to the advantage of nonprofit organizations has been a spate of political developments that have substantially increased their visibility. For one thing, the policy environment ushered in by the elections of Margaret Thatcher in the United Kingdom and Ronald Reagan in the United States brought nonprofit organizations out of the obscurity to which the rise of the welfare state had consigned them over the previous half-century. Conservative politicians like Thatcher and Reagan needed an explanation for how social problems would be handled once government social welfare protections were cut, and the nonprofit sector offered a highly convenient one. Suddenly, attention to the nonprofit sector and philanthropy became a central part of the policy dialogue, even though conservative politicians had to overlook the inconvenient fact that the nonprofit organizations they were championing were funded largely by the very government social welfare programs they were cutting. When the policy pendulum swung back to the left, as it did with the election of Tony Blair in the United Kingdom and Bill Clinton in the United States, nonprofit organizations remained very much on the policy screen, as evidenced by the "third way" rhetoric in the United Kingdom and similar formulations in Europe, which view active partnerships between government and the civil society sector as an alternative to relying solely on either the market or the state.[62]

Nonprofit organizations have also gained visibility as a result of the collapse of communism in Central Europe in the late 1980s and the proliferation of complex humanitarian crises in much of the developing world.[63] In both cases, nonprofit organizations have been prominently involved, stimulating change and offering alternative mechanisms of response. More recently, these organizations have benefited from growing concerns about the state of civic engagement in the United States. This is so because nonprofit organizations have been identified as crucial contributors to "social capital," to the bonds of trust and reciprocity thought to be necessary to sustain civic involvement. Encouragement of a vital nonprofit sector thus has come to be seen as a critical prerequisite for a healthy democracy.[64]

Finally, the events of September 11 also increased the public's recognition of the nonprofit sector. As noted earlier, nonprofit organizations were visible participants in the response to this tragedy. Beyond this, the September 11 events seem to have reawakened Americans to the importance of the functions that nonprofit institutions perform, functions such as serving those in need, building community, and encouraging values of care and concern.

GROWTH OF GOVERNMENT SOCIAL WELFARE SPENDING. Finally, and perhaps most important, government social welfare spending, which had stalled and in some cases reversed course in the early 1980s, resumed its growth in the late 1980s and into the 1990s. As noted in table 1-3, total public social welfare spending increased 36 percent in real, inflation-adjusted dollars between 1985 and 1995 compared to a 24 percent increase in the country's real gross domestic product.[65] Particularly notable was the 69 percent growth in health spending, but significant increases were recorded in housing, education, and social service spending as well—trends that have continued in more recent years.

As reflected in the chapters by Steven Smith, Margaret Wyszomirski, Avis Vidal, and Bradford Gray and Mark Schlesinger, five factors seem to have been responsible for this growth:

—*Broadening of federal entitlement spending.* In the first place, spending under the basic government entitlement programs for health and income assistance

Table 1-3. *Growth in Real Government Social Welfare Spending*
Percentage change, 1985–95

Function	Total	Federal	State and local
Pensions	18	13	40
Income assistance	27	34	7
Health	69	67	73
Education	40	9	43
Elementary, secondary	–34	–34	–34
Higher	36	–23	31
Housing	54	63	–10
Social services	23	5	49
Total	36	30	45
Total without pensions, health	37	29	40

Source: U.S. Social Security Administration, *Annual Statistical Supplement to the Social Security Bulletin* (Washington: U.S. Department of Health and Human Services, Social Security Administration, 2000), pp. 119–222.

grew rapidly during this period, largely due to the steady broadening of eligibility. For example, coverage under the federal Supplemental Security Income (SSI) program, which was originally created to provide income support to the elderly poor, ballooned from 4.1 million recipients in 1980 to 6.6 million by 1999, largely as a result of aggressive efforts to enroll disabled people, including children and youth, in the program. The number of children covered by SSI increased from 71,000 in 1974 to over 1 million in 1996 as a consequence, boosting expenditures in real terms from $16.4 billion in 1980 to $30.2 billion in 1999.[66] And since SSI entitles participants to coverage under Medicaid—the federal health care financing program for the poor—this increase translated into Medicaid growth as well.

But this was not the only source of Medicaid eligibility expansion. Medicaid coverage was extended to fifty distinct subgroups during the late 1980s and early 1990s, including the homeless, newly legalized aliens, AIDS sufferers, recipients of adoption assistance and foster care, as well as broader categories of the disabled and the elderly. Between 1980 and 1998 as a consequence, Medicaid coverage jumped from 21.6 million people to 40.6 million.[67]

At the same time, the range of services these programs cover also expanded dramatically. Thus skilled nursing care, home health care, hospice care, and kidney dialysis services became eligible for Medicare coverage, while intermediate care for the mentally retarded, home health care, family planning, clinic care, child welfare services, and rehabilitation services were added to Medicaid. These changes, coupled with state options to add additional services (for example, physical therapy, medical social worker counseling, case management, trans-

Table 1-4. *Growth in Federal Entitlement Program Spending, 1980–99*

Program	Spending (in billions of constant 1999 U.S. dollars)[a]		Percentage change, 1980–99
	1980	1999	
Medicare	79.9	212.0	+165
Medicaid[b]	56.8	189.5	+222
Supplemental Security Income[b]	9.5	30.9	+225
Total	146.2	432.4	+196
U.S. gross domestic product	4,900.9	8,856.5	+81

Source: U.S. House of Representatives, Committee on Ways and Means, *2000 Green Book: Background Material and Data on Programs within the Jurisdiction of the Committee on Ways and Means,* 106 Cong. 2 sess. (Washington, October 6, 2000), pp. 100, 912, 214; Council of Economic Advisers, *Economic Report of the President, 2002* (Washington: Executive Office of the President, Council of Economic Advisers, 2002), table B-2.

a. Based on chain-type price deflators for the service component of personal consumption expenditures.

b. Includes both federal and state spending.

portation),[68] transformed Medicaid from a relatively narrow health and nursing home program into a veritable social service entitlement program.

Reflecting these changes, as shown in table 1-4, spending on the major federal entitlement programs jumped nearly 200 percent in real terms between 1980 and 1999, more than twice the 81 percent real growth in the U.S. gross domestic product. Although reimbursement rates often still were not sufficient to cover the full costs of the services, the expansion in the pool of resources available was substantial.

—*New federal initiatives.* In addition to expanding existing programs, federal policymakers also created a variety of new programs to address long-standing or newly emerging social ills. For example, four federal childcare programs were enacted in 1988 and 1990 alone, and special programs were added as well for homeless people, AIDS sufferers, children and youth, people with disabilities, voluntarism promotion, drug and alcohol treatment, and home health care. Federal spending on the homeless, for example, went from virtually zero in 1986 to $1.2 billion in fiscal 2000.[69]

—*Greater state activism.* Renewed federal activism was mirrored, and in some cases anticipated, by activism at the state and local level. In some cases, as Wyszomirski shows in the case of the arts, state and local governments replaced cuts in federal spending with their own new or expanded programs. In other cases, states found new veins of federal funding to tap as old ones ran dry. Under the "Medicaid maximization strategy," for example, programs formerly funded entirely by the states, or by federal discretionary programs subjected to Reagan-era budget cuts, were reconfigured to make them eligible for funding under the more-lucrative Medicaid or SSI programs. As Steven Smith reports in chapter 4 of this volume, mental health, mental retardation, maternal and child health rehabilitation, and AIDS services were special targets for this strategy, particularly as Medicaid expanded eligibility for pregnant women and children, and SSI (and hence Medicaid) expanded coverage for AIDS patients and the disabled.[70] Finally, a growing number of states opted to exploit the flexibilities built into the Medicaid program to extend care beyond the required minimum in order to address key social problems, such as teen pregnancy and drug abuse.[71] Taken together, these changes explain why state and local social welfare spending grew even faster than federal spending between 1985 and 1995 (45 versus 30 percent), as reflected in table 1-3.[72]

—*The welfare reform windfall.* A fourth factor contributing to the recent expansion of government spending in fields where nonprofits are active was the passage of the federal welfare reform legislation in 1996 and subsequent change in the welfare caseload. The Personal Responsibility and Work Opportunity Reconciliation Act (PRWORA) of 1996 essentially replaced the existing program of entitlement grants to states to help cover welfare payments to dependent children and families with a fixed federal grant that was guaranteed for six years, during which states were required to move welfare recipients into paying jobs. As part of this legislation, states were permitted to use a portion of these funds to finance not simply welfare payments but also a variety of work readiness, childcare, and human service activities. The result was to transform the existing welfare program into "a broad human services funding stream."[73] When welfare rolls began to fall sharply in the late 1990s, thanks to the economic boom then in progress and the stringent work requirements built into the new law, states found themselves with a fiscal windfall since their welfare grants from the federal government were locked in at the preexisting levels, while their payments to recipients declined. States were thus able to invest the savings in a variety of service programs designed to prepare even more welfare recipients for work. By 1999, for example, spending on cash and work-based assistance under the welfare program had fallen to 60 percent of the total funds available, leaving 40 percent for a variety of childcare, work readiness, drug abuse treatment, and related purposes. As a result, the social welfare system was awash with funds.[74]

—*New tools.* Finally, given the prevailing climate of tax cuts and hostility to expanded government spending throughout the 1980s and early 1990s, policymakers increasingly responded to social welfare and related needs by relying more heavily on unconventional tools of government action, such as loan guarantees and tax subsidies, which do not appear as visibly on the budget.[75] The use of such tools is by no means entirely new, of course. The deduction for medical expenses and the exclusion of scholarship income, for example, have long been established features of the tax code. But the use of such tools in fields where nonprofits are active expanded considerably over the past decade or more with the addition or extension of programs such as the childcare tax credit, the credit for student loan interest payments, the low-income housing tax credit, and the new market tax credit. As Kirsten Grønbjerg and Lester Salamon show in chapter 14, these alternative tools represented another $315.2 billion in federal assistance in fields where nonprofits are active as of fiscal 2001. This represents a 123 percent increase in constant dollars over what was available through these tools a decade earlier, a rate of increase that exceeds even that achieved by the spending programs in these same fields. In many fields, such as daycare, the indirect subsidies available through the tax system now easily exceed those available through outright spending programs.[76] What is more, as noted earlier, the new tools generally deliver their benefits to consumers rather than producers, making it necessary for nonprofits to market their services in order to benefit from them.

To be sure, the expansion of government spending that occurred over the past decade did not affect all fields in which nonprofits are active. Public spending on higher education, for example, lost ground, although the creation of a direct student loan program and the continued expansion of tax and credit programs for higher education softened some of the blow. In addition, the shift in the character of public sector support from producer- to consumer-side subsidies meant that access to it grew more difficult, necessitating more intensive marketing efforts. Nevertheless, the increase that took place in government spending in fields where nonprofits are active has been striking, creating another important opportunity for the sector.

The Nonprofit Response: A Story of Resilience

How has nonprofit America responded to the extraordinary combination of challenges and opportunities it has faced over the past decade and a half? Has the sector been able to cope with the challenges and take advantage of the opportunities? To what extent and with what consequences for its current health and character, and for its likely future evolution? It is to these questions that we now turn.

Based on the conventional wisdom about the responsiveness of nonprofit organizations, we should not expect very much. "Profit-making organizations are more flexible with respect to the deployment and redeployment of resources," management experts Rosabeth Moss Kanter and David V. Summers wrote in 1987. "But the centrality of mission for nonprofit organizations places limitations on their flexibility of action."[77] Nonprofits are not to be trusted, Professor Regina Herzlinger similarly explained to readers of the *Harvard Business Review* in 1996, because they lack the three basic accountability measures that ensure effective and efficient business operations: the self-interest of owners, competition, and the ultimate bottom-line measure of profitability.[78]

Contrary to these conventional beliefs, however, the past ten to fifteen years have constituted a period of extraordinary resilience and adaptability on the part of America's nonprofit sector. Although largely unheralded, nonprofit America has undergone a quiet revolution during this period, a massive process of reinvention and reengineering that is still very much under way. To be sure, the resulting changes are hardly universal: change has been more pronounced in some fields than in others, and even within fields substantial variation exists among agencies of different sizes and orientations. What is more, there are serious questions about whether the resulting changes are in a wholly desirable direction or whether they have exposed the sector to unacceptable risks. Although important shadings are needed to do justice to the considerable diversity that exists, however, there is no denying the dominant picture of extraordinary resilience, adaptation, and change. More specifically, ten threads of change are apparent.

Overall Sector Growth

Perhaps the most vivid evidence of the nonprofit sector's resilience is the striking record of recent sector growth. Between 1977 and 1997, as shown in table 1-5, the revenues of America's nonprofit organizations increased 144 percent after adjusting for inflation, nearly twice the 81 percent growth rate of the nation's economy. Nonprofit revenue growth was particularly robust among arts and culture organizations, social service organizations, and health organizations, in each of which the rate of growth was at least twice that of the U.S. economy. However, even the most laggard components of the nonprofit sector (education and civic organizations) grew at a rate that equaled or exceeded the economy total.[79]

Table 1-5. *Real Growth in Nonprofit Revenue, by Subsector, 1977–97*

Field	Percentage of total, 1977	Percentage change, 1977–97	Share of change, 1977–97
Health	47	167	55
Education	25	82	14
Social services	9	213	14
Civic, social	4	79	2
Arts, culture	2	280	3
Religion	13	135	12
Total	100	144	100
U.S. gross domestic product		81	

Source: Data on nonprofit organizations adapted from Weitzman and others, *The New Nonprofit Almanac and Desk Reference* (San Francisco: Jossey-Bass, 2002), pp. 96–97; data on U.S. gross domestic product from Council of Economic Advisers, *Economic Report of the President, 2002* (Washington: Executive Office of the President, Council of Economic Advisers, 2002).

Evidence of the vibrancy of the nonprofit sector extends well beyond financial indicators, which are heavily influenced by the performance of the largest organizations. Equally revealing is the record of recent organizational formation. Between 1977 and 1997, the number of 501(c)(3) and 501(c)(4) organizations registered with the Internal Revenue Service increased 115 percent, or about 23,000 organizations a year.[80] By comparison, the number of business organizations increased only 76 percent during this same period. Moreover, the rate of nonprofit organization formation accelerated in more recent years, jumping from an average of 15,000 a year between 1977 and 1987 to more than 27,000 a year between 1987 and 1997, and this despite increased pressures for organizational mergers. Evidently, Americans are still finding in the nonprofit sector a convenient outlet for a wide assortment of social, economic, political, and cultural concerns.[81]

Marketing to Paying Customers

What accounts for this record of robust growth? One of the central explanations appears to be the success with which American nonprofits took advantage of the favorable demographic and social trends to market their services to a clientele increasingly able to afford them. Reflecting this, even with religious congregations included, fees and charges accounted for nearly half (47 percent) of the growth in nonprofit revenue between 1977 and 1997—more than any other source (see table 1-6).

To be sure, not all components of the nonprofit sector relied equally heavily on fees and charges to finance their operations during this period, as shown in table 1-7. What is striking about the past two decades of nonprofit development, however, is how extensively reliance on fee income has spread throughout the sector. After adjusting for inflation, fee income jumped 272 percent for arts and culture organizations, 220 percent for civic organizations, and over 500

Table 1-6. *Changing Structure of Nonprofit Revenue, 1977–97*

| | | Share of total | | | | Share of revenue growth, 1977–97 | |
| | Percentage change, 1977–97 | 1977 | | 1997 | | | |
Revenue source		All	Without religion	All	Without religion	All	Without religion
Fees, charges	145	46	51	47	51	47	51
Government	195	27	31	33	37	37	42
Philanthropy	90	27	18	20	12	16	8
Total	144	100	100	100	100	100	100

Source: See table 1-5.

Table 1-7. *Growth of Nonprofit Fee Income, by Subsector, 1977–97*

Field	Percentage change, 1977–97	Share of total revenue		Share of revenue growth, 1977–97
		1977	*1997*	
Education	77	67	65	63
Social services	587	13	28	35
Civic	220	19	34	53
Arts, culture	272	47	46	46
Religion	163	14	16	17
Total	145	46	47	47
Total without religion	144	51	51	51

Source: See table 1-5.

percent for social service organizations between 1977 and 1997, thus account-ing for 46, 53, and 35 percent, respectively, of the growth of these agencies. Even religious organizations boosted their commercial income during this period, largely, as Chaves shows in chapter 8 of this volume, through the sale or rental of church property.

Not only did nonprofits boost their fee revenues from existing clients, they also apparently pursued middle-class clientele into the Sun Belt and the sub-urbs. This is evident in the growing suburbanization of philanthropy during the 1980s reported by economist Julian Wolpert and in the geographic spread of nonprofit employment reported by the Johns Hopkins Nonprofit Employment Data Project.[82] Seventy percent of the substantial growth in nonprofit employ-ment in the state of Maryland between 1989 and 1999, for example, took place in the Baltimore and Washington suburbs, whereas the city of Baltimore, which started the period with nearly half of the state's nonprofit employment, accounted for only 17 percent of the growth.

Clearly, market forces have penetrated into the nonprofit sector well beyond the fields of health and higher education to which they were formerly mostly confined. And the organizations in this broader array of fields have demon-strated an equal capacity to respond to them.

Successful Pursuit of Public Funds

Not only have nonprofit organizations managed to adapt themselves to the new market opportunities they are facing, but also they have proved adept at coping with the new public funding terrain that has evolved in recent years. As a result, despite the rhetoric of retrenchment that characterized this period, one of the most striking recent developments has been an enormous growth in nonprofit revenue from public sector sources. As noted in table 1-6, government support

Table 1-8. *Growth in Nonprofit Revenue from Government, by Subsector, 1977–97*

Field	Percentage change, 1977–97	Share of total revenue		Share of revenue growth, 1977–97
		1977	1997	
Health	248	32	42	48
Education	94	18	19	21
Social services	200	54	52	51
Civic	8	50	30	5
Arts, culture	214	12	10	9
Religion	0	0	0	0
Total	195	27	33	37
Total without religion	195	31	37	42

Source: See table 1-5.

to the nonprofit sector increased 195 percent in real terms between 1977 and 1997, proportionally more than any other source, and these figures do not include the windfall from welfare reform discussed earlier. Government accounted for 37 percent of the sector's substantial growth during this period, boosting its share of the total from 27 percent in 1977 to 33 percent in 1997. And with religious congregations excluded (since they do not receive much government support), the government contribution to sector growth came to 42 percent, boosting government's share of the sector's revenue from 31 percent in 1977 to 37 percent in 1997.

Not all segments of the sector benefited equally from this expanding government support, of course. The major beneficiaries were nonprofit health, social service, and arts organizations, all of which received increased government support by 200 percent or more after adjusting for inflation (table 1-8). Government revenue growth was less robust for education organizations, although it still exceeded the overall growth of the domestic economy, while for civic organizations it barely kept pace with inflation, perhaps confirming fears that the real thrust of the budget cutting of the 1980s and early 1990s was to "defund the left."

The proximate cause of this extraordinary growth in nonprofit revenue from government was, of course, the expansion in government spending that occurred in fields where nonprofits are active. At least as important, however, has been the skill with which nonprofit organizations have adapted to the shifts they faced in the *forms* of public support. As Smith shows in chapter 4, social service agencies had to be particularly nimble in adjusting to the new realities as states shifted their social service spending from stagnant or declining discretionary grant programs to the rapidly growing Medicaid and SSI programs, both of which deliver their benefits to clients and therefore require agencies to master new marketing, billing, and reimbursement management skills. That they did so is evident in the sizable 200 percent increase in public funding they achieved.

Similarly impressive was the success of nonprofit housing and community development organizations in taking advantage of the new low-income housing tax credit designed to stimulate the flow of private investment capital into low-income housing. As recounted by Avis Vidal in chapter 6 of this volume, this success was largely due to the role that a skilled set of nonprofit intermediary organizations played in packaging the resulting tax credits and marketing them to for-profit financial institutions, generating in the process a substantial flow of private capital into the hands of community-based organizations in this field. In view of the capital deficiencies facing nonprofit organizations in many fields, this record holds important lessons for the sector in general.

This significant expansion of government support has had its downsides, of course. Particularly problematic has been the tendency for Medicaid (and to some extent Medicare) reimbursement rates to fall behind the actual costs of delivering the services they are intended to support.[83] For-profit vendors can respond to these cuts by pulling out of the affected lines of business, but non-profits often find this difficult. As a consequence, nonprofit organizations often end up using scarce private charitable resources to subsidize federally funded services.

Even so, the success with which nonprofit organizations have adapted to the new government funding realities is another demonstration of the sector's recent resilience and adaptability. More than that, it provides another indication of the sector's growing "marketization," since so much of the government aid now takes the form of "consumer-side" subsidies. When this voucher-type government support is added to the fee income that nonprofits receive, as it is in the data on "program service revenue" that nonprofit organizations report to the Internal Revenue Service, it turns out that two-thirds (67 percent) of the reported income of nonprofit 501(c)(3) organizations as of 1998 came from such "commercial" sources. And with investment income included as well, the commercial total is over 75 percent. Even among human service nonprofits, the combination of consumer-side government subsidies and fee income accounted for over half (54 percent) of total revenue in 1998.[84]

The Revolution in Charitable Fundraising

Accompanying the growing sophistication that nonprofit organizations have demonstrated in pursuing fee income and tapping government support has been the increased creativity they have displayed in raising charitable contributions. As the chapters by Hodgkinson, Lenkowsky, and Young and Salamon show in more detail, the past twenty years have witnessed a growing professionalization of charitable fundraising and, with it, a proliferation of mechanisms for generating charitable resources. One reflection of this is the emergence and growth of specialized organizations catering to the new fundraising profession—the National Society of Fund-Raising Executives, now the Association of Fund-Raising Professionals (AFP), the Council for the Advancement and Support of Education, the Association for Healthcare Philanthropy, and the National Committee for Planned Giving. As recently as 1979, AFP, the largest of these organizations, boasted only 1,899 members. By 1999 it claimed more than 20,000, and the National Committee for Planned Giving, a more specialized body, itself had 11,000.

This growth of a fundraising profession has had the fortuitous result, as Hodgkinson shows in chapter 12, of helping to democratize charitable giving, moving it from an almost exclusive focus on the wealthy to a much broader base. The vehicle for this has not been individual solicitors standing on street corners in the old Salvation Army model. Rather, the technology of charitable giving has been transformed through the development of devices such as workplace solicitation, telethons, direct mail campaigns, telephone solicitation, and, most recently, e-philanthropy. Entire organizations have surfaced to manage this process of extracting funds. Included here are entities such as United Way, various health appeals (for example, the American Cancer Society, the American Heart Association), and the nation's growing network of community foundations. As noted, for-profit businesses also have gotten into the act.[85] The new actors have been financial service companies that have capitalized on their mastery of finance to popularize a variety of relatively new "planned giving" mechanisms. These instruments allow donors to earn tax-sheltered income on funds deposited in special "split income" or "charitable remainder" trusts during their lifetime or the lifetime of designated beneficiaries and then to contribute the remaining assets to charities at their death without having to pay estate taxes. The for-profit investment firms have also actively promoted a variety of "donor-advised funds," which give donors the opportunity to retain control over assets deposited for charitable purposes, while securing tax advantages at the full appreciated value of the contributed assets at the time of contribution. By 2000, the largest of these operations, the Fidelity Charitable Gift Fund managed by the Boston-based for-profit investment firm Fidelity Investments, reported assets of $2.4 billion. Partly in response to this competition, nonprofit community foundations and federated funding organizations have also intensified their use of these instruments, boosting the reported assets in donor-advised funds to an estimated $10.4 billion as of 2000.[86] Along with new "donor option" arrangements in traditional federated charitable appeals like United Way and the new "venture philanthropy," this explosion of donor-advised funds suggests the emergence of what Lenkowsky in chapter 11 of this volume sees as an alternative entrepreneurial model of institutional philanthropy modeled on the decentralized, entrepreneurial firms that have been the source of much of the new-economy wealth now being channeled into charitable activity. As such, it

differs from the more bureaucratic forms found in the larger staffed foundations, which grew out of the hierarchic enterprises of an earlier era.

This revolution in the technology of charitable fundraising doubtless boosted
charitable giving above what it might otherwise have been. It did not, however,
counter the effects of other developments, including tax and other policies,
working to dampen the growth in giving. For one thing, the new forms of charitable fundraising are often more costly, requiring heavier administrative expenditures to raise a given quantity of charitable resources. For another, some of the
new vehicles delay the transfer of wealth into charitable uses. Donor-advised
funds and charitable remainder trusts are essentially holding vats for charitable
dollars, and some in the charitable community bewail the resulting reduction in
direct contributions to operating charities and in direct contact between donors
and recipient organizations that these devices also produce.[87] Whatever the reason, despite the innovations in fundraising techniques, the growth of private
charitable giving, while substantial, has not kept pace with the growth of nonprofit revenue more generally. Thus, as shown in table 1-6, charitable giving
increased 90 percent between 1977 and 1997, well below the growth rate for
the other major sources of nonprofit revenue. Philanthropy accounted for only
16 percent of the growth of the sector as a consequence, and much of this was
due to the growth of contributions to religious congregations. With that portion
of private giving excluded, philanthropy accounted for only 8 percent of the sector's growth, and its share of sector income declined from 18 to 12 percent.[88]

As with the other sources of income, the growth in giving varied by subsector,
as shown in table 1-9. Especially notable was the above-average growth of private
giving in the fields of religion, civic activity, and arts and culture, where private
giving accounted for over 40 percent of total revenue growth during this twenty-
year period. By contrast, philanthropic support to the nation's social service agencies grew much more slowly. As a result, the philanthropic share of social service
organization income fell from 33 percent in 1977 to 20 percent twenty years
later. Philanthropy, it appears, became even more amenities-oriented over this
twenty-year period, a trend that is potentially troubling, as Diaz argues in chapter
17 of this volume. Although the events of September 11 may ultimately reverse
this trend, the evidence as of this writing is hardly encouraging.

Expanded Venture Activity

A fifth manifestation of the nonprofit sector's recent resilience has been its
increased involvement in commercial ventures. Such ventures differ from the
collection of fees for standard nonprofit services in that they entail the creation
and sale of products and services primarily for a commercial market. Examples
here include museum gift shops and on-line stores, church rentals of social halls,
and licensing agreements between research universities and commercial firms.
Existing law has long allowed nonprofit organizations to engage in such com-

Table 1-9. *Growth in Nonprofit Revenue from Philanthropy, by Subsector,*
1977–97

Field	Percentage change, 1977–97	Share of total revenue		Share of revenue growth, 1977–97
		1977	1997	
Health	3	14	6	0
Education	91	15	16	17
Social services	91	33	20	14
Civic	106	31	36	42
Arts, culture	307	41	44	45
Religion	131	86	84	83
Total	90	27	20	16
Total without religion	62	18	12	8

Source: See table 1-5.

mercial activities so long as they do not become the primary purpose of the organization. Since 1951 the income from such ventures has been subject to corporate income taxation unless it is "related" to the charitable purpose of the organization.

Solid data on the scope of this activity are difficult to locate since much of it is considered "related" income and buried in the statistics on fees, but the clear impression from what data exist suggests a substantial expansion over the past two decades. One sign of this is the growth in so-called "unrelated business income" reported to the Internal Revenue Service. Although the Internal Revenue Service has been notoriously liberal in its definition of what constitutes unrelated, as opposed to related, business income, the number of charities reporting such income increased 35 percent between 1990 and 1997, and the amount of income they reported more than doubled.[89] As of 1997, gross unrelated business income reported by nonprofit organizations reached $7.8 billion, an increase of 7 percent over the previous year, following increases of 30 percent a year over the previous two years.

Cultural institutions seem to have been especially inventive in adapting venture activities to their operations, perhaps because they have the clearest "products" to sell. The Guggenheim Museum has even gone global, with franchises in Italy, Germany, and Spain, while elaborate touring exhibitions and shows have become standard facets of museum, orchestra, and dance company operations. Cultural institutions are also actively exploiting the new digitization technologies, often in collaboration with commercial firms. In the process, as Wyszomirski notes, arts organizations are being transformed from inward-oriented institutions focused primarily on their collections to outward-oriented enterprises competing for customers in an increasingly commercial market.

Other types of nonprofit organizations are also increasingly involved in commercial-type ventures. Thus hospitals are investing in parking garages, universities are establishing joint ventures with private biotechnology companies, and social service agencies are operating restaurants and catering businesses. The business activities of nonprofit hospitals have grown especially complex, with elaborate purchasing and marketing consortia linking hospitals, medical practitioners, insurance groups, and equipment suppliers.[90]

Perhaps the most interesting facet of this development is the recent tendency of some nonprofit organizations to utilize business ventures not simply to generate income but also to carry out their basic charitable missions. This reflects a broader transformation in prevailing conceptions of the causes of poverty and distress from one focused on providing individuals with needed services to one focused on getting them to work. Thus, as Dennis Young and Lester Salamon discuss in chapter 13 of this volume, rather than merely training disadvantaged individuals and sending them out into the private labor market, a new class of "social-purpose enterprises," or "social ventures," has emerged to employ former drug addicts, inmates, or other disadvantaged persons in actual businesses as a way to build skills, develop self-confidence, and teach work habits. Examples here include the Greyston Bakery in Yonkers, New York, which trains and hires unemployable workers in its gourmet bakery business; Pioneer Human Services, a nonprofit in Seattle, Washington, that operates an aircraft parts manufacturing facility, food buying and warehousing services, and restaurants;[91] and Bikeable Communities in Long Beach, California, which promotes bicycle use by offering valet and related services to cyclists. The result is a thoroughgoing marriage of market means to charitable purpose and the emergence of a new hybrid form of nonprofit business.

Adoption of the Enterprise Culture

These developments point, in turn, to a broader and deeper penetration of the market culture into the fabric of nonprofit operations. Nonprofit organizations are increasingly "marketing" their "products," viewing their clients as "customers," segmenting their markets, differentiating their output, identifying their "market niche," formulating "business plans," and generally incorporating the language, and the style, of business management into the operation of their agencies. Management expert Kevin Kearns argues that nonprofit executives are now "among the most entrepreneurial managers to be found anywhere, including the private for-profit sector."[92]

How fully the culture of the market has been integrated into the operations, as opposed to the rhetoric, of the nonprofit sector is difficult to determine. Certainly the appetite for materials has been robust enough to convince commercial publishers like John Wiley and Sons to invest heavily in the field, producing a booming market in "how-to" books offering nonprofit managers training in "strategic planning," "financial planning, "mission-based management," "social entrepreneurship," "streetsmart financial basics," "strategic communications," "high-performance philanthropy," and "high-performance organization," to cite just a handful of recent titles.[93] The Drucker Foundation's *Self-Assessment Tool*, with its market-oriented stress on the five questions considered most critical to nonprofit-organization performance (What is our mission? Who is our customer? What does the customer value? What are our results? What is our plan?), was reportedly purchased by more than 10,000 agencies in the first five years following its publication in 1993, suggesting the appetite for business-style management advice within the sector.[94]

More concretely, there is growing evidence that the market culture is affecting organizational practices, organizational structures, and inter-organizational behavior. Hospitals, for example, are increasingly advertising their capabilities, universities are investing in off-campus programs, museums and symphonies are establishing venues in shopping centers, and even small community development organizations are engaging in complex real estate syndications. Significant changes are also occurring in the basic structure and governance of nonprofit organizations. Boards are being made smaller and more selective, substituting a corporate model for a more community-based one. Similarly, greater efforts are being made to recruit business leaders onto boards, further solidifying the dominant corporate culture. In addition, the internal structure of organizations is growing more complex. To some extent this is driven by prevailing legal restrictions. Thus, as Boris and Krehely note in chapter 9, many nonprofit advocacy organizations have created 501(c)(4) subsidiaries to bypass existing restrictions on their lobbying activity as 501(c)(3) charities. Similarly, nonprofit residential care facilities are segmenting their various programs into separate corporate entities to build legal walls around core operations in case of liability challenges. And universities, freed by the Bayh-Dole act and subsequent legislation to patent discoveries developed with federal research funds, are turning to complex consortium arrangements to help market the products of university-based scientific research.[95] Behind the comforting facade of relatively homey charities, nonprofit organizations are being transformed into complex holding companies, with multiple nonprofit and for-profit subsidiaries and offshoots, significantly complicating the task of operational and financial management and control.

New Business Partnerships

As the culture of the market has spread into the fabric of nonprofit operations, old suspicions between the nonprofit and business sectors have significantly softened, opening the way for nonprofit acceptance of the business community not simply as a source of charitable support but also as a legitimate partner for a wide range of nonprofit endeavors. This perspective has been championed by charismatic sector leaders, such as Billy Shore, who urge nonprofits to stop thinking about how to get donations and start thinking about how to market the considerable assets they control, including particularly the asset represented by their reputations.[96] This has meshed nicely with the growing readiness of businesses to forge strategic alliances with nonprofits in order to generate "reputational capital." The upshot has been a notable upsurge in strategic partnerships between nonprofit organizations and businesses.

One early manifestation of this approach was the American Express invention of "cause-related marketing" in the early 1980s. Under this technique, a nonprofit lends its name to a commercial product in return for a share of the proceeds from the sale of that product. Research has demonstrated that such arrangements bring substantial returns to the companies involved, boosting sales, enhancing company reputations, and buoying employee morale. Coca Cola, for example, experienced a 490 percent spurt in the sales of its products at 450 Wal-Mart stores in 1997 when it launched a campaign promising to donate 15 cents to Mothers Against Drunk Driving for every soft drink case it sold. More generally, a 1999 Cone/Roper survey finds that two-thirds of Americans have greater trust in companies aligned with a social issue and that more than half of all workers wish their employers would do more to support social causes. This evidence has convinced a growing number of corporations to associate themselves and their products with social causes and the groups actively working on them. Apparel retailer Eddie Bauer thus has entered cause-related marketing arrangements with American Forests, Evian with Bill Shore's Share our Strength, Liz Claiborne with the Family Violence Prevention Fund, Mattel with Girls Incorporated, Timberland with City Year, and many more. By 1998, such arrangements were generating $1.5 billion in marketing fees for the nonprofit organizations involved.[97]

Increasingly, moreover, cause-related marketing relationships have evolved into broader partnerships that mobilize corporate personnel, finances, and know-how in support of nonprofit activities. The most successful of these efforts deliver benefits to both the corporation and the nonprofit. Thus, for example, when the Swiss pharmaceutical manufacturer Novartis contributed $25 million to the University of California at Berkeley for basic biological research, it secured in the bargain the right to negotiate licenses on a third of the discoveries of the school's Department of Plant and Microbial Biology, whether it paid for these discoveries or not.[98] Management expert Rosabeth Moss Kanter even argues that businesses are coming to see nonprofits not simply as sources of good corporate images, but as the "beta site for business innovation," a locus for developing new approaches to long-standing business problems, such as how to recruit inner-city customers to the banking system or how to locate and train entry-level personnel for central-city hotels.[99] In these and countless other ways, nonprofit organizations and businesses have begun reaching out to each other across historic divides of suspicion to forge interesting collaborations of value to both, leading the Aspen Institute's Nonprofit Sector Strategy Group to "applaud the new strategic approach that businesses are bringing to societal problem-solving and the expansion of business partnerships with nonprofit groups to which it has given rise."[100]

Building a Nonprofit Infrastructure

In addition to absorbing significant aspects of the dominant market culture, however, nonprofit America has been busy developing its own institutional infrastructure, building on the solid base established by the Charity Aid Societies of the late nineteenth century and the subsector organizations representing particular industries (for example, hospitals, higher education, museums) created in the early part of the twentieth century. But as Alan Abramson and Rachel McCarthy point out in chapter 10, the past twenty to twenty-five years have witnessed a considerable filling out of this structure and a fundamental change in its character with the emergence of a new class of infrastructure organizations devoted not to a particular nonprofit industry, but to the nonprofit sector as a whole. This has reflected the enormous growth of the sector, the growing pressures for professionalization of the sector's operations, and the sector's increased involvement with government, which has necessitated more effective representation. Indeed, according to historian Peter Hall, the nonprofit sector was literally "invented" as a concept during this period.[101]

The result has been a substantial enlargement of the organizational apparatus providing services, support, and representation for the nonprofit sector as a whole. Independent Sector, the largest and most visible of the sectorwide infrastructure groups, created in 1980, now numbers more than 700 foundations, corporations, and nonprofit umbrella organizations among its members. Other organizations have been formed to represent organized philanthropy (for example, the Council on Foundations, the Association of Small Foundations, the National Network of Grantmakers, the Forum of Regional Associations of Grantmakers), nonprofit organizations in particular states (for example, the Maryland Association of Nonprofit Organizations), and organizations serving low-income and disfranchised populations (for example, the National Committee for Responsive Philanthropy). In addition, the research and educational apparatus of the sector has filled out remarkably, with nonprofit research centers established at Yale University, Johns Hopkins University, Indiana University, Harvard University, the Urban Institute, and elsewhere; nonprofit degree or certificate programs created in close to 100 colleges and universities; and more than 700 unaffiliated management support organizations offering nondegree instruction and technical assistance to nonprofit managers. To serve this expanding network of experts, new professional associations have come into existence or been enlarged (for example, the Association for Research on Nonprofit Organizations and Voluntary Action), professional journals have been launched or revamped (for example, *Nonprofit and Voluntary Sector Quarterly, Nonprofit Management and Leadership*); special nonprofit sections have been added to existing journals (for example, the *Harvard Business Review*); and a nonprofit press has been created (*The Chronicle of Philanthropy, Nonprofit Times, The Nonprofit Quarterly*). What was once a scatteration of largely overlooked institutions has thus become a booming cottage industry dedicated to the proposition that nonprofit organizations are distinctive institutions with enough commonalities, despite their many differences, to be studied, represented, networked, serviced, and trained as a group.

Meeting the For-Profit Competition

Nonprofits have also begun to hold their own in the face of the rising tide of for-profit competition. To be sure, the credit for this does not belong to nonprofits alone. Rather, the for-profit sector has proved to be far less formidable a competitor in many of the spheres where both operate than initially seemed to be the case. As Gray and Schlesinger point out in chapter 2 of this volume, a "life cycle" perspective is needed to understand the competitive relationship between nonprofit and for-profit organizations in the health field, and a similar observation very likely applies to other fields as well. For-profit firms have distinct advantages during growth spurts in the life cycles of particular fields, when new services are in demand as a result of changes either in government policy or in consumer needs. This is so because these firms can more readily access the capital markets to build new facilities, acquire new technology, and attract sophisticated management. In addition, they are better equipped to market their services and achieve the scale required to negotiate favorable terms with suppliers (for example, pharmaceutical companies). However, once they become heavily leveraged, the continued success of these enterprises comes to depend heavily on the expectation of continuing escalation of their stock prices. When this expectation is shaken, as it often has been thanks to shifts in government reimbursement policies for Medicare and Medicaid, the results can be catastrophic and precipitous. In such circumstances, for-profit firms have shown a distressing tendency to engage in fraudulent practices. In the 1990s, for example, for-profit nursing homes, squeezed by new state policies designed to reduce Medicaid costs, turned to misleading billing practices to sustain their revenues and ultimately got caught. A similar scenario played out in the hospital field twice in the past two decades—first in the late 1980s and again in the mid-1990s. In both cases, overly optimistic for-profit entrepreneurs found it impossible to sustain the growth paths that their stock valuations required and ended up being discredited when government agencies and private insurers found that they had fraudulently inflated their costs and overbilled for services.[102] This boom and bust cycle seems to operate as well in the social service field, particularly where government support is a crucial part of the demand structure of agencies. For-profit involvement grows in response to increased public funding, but then suffers a shakeout when government reimbursement contracts.

All of this demonstrates why nonprofit involvement is so crucial, especially in fields where the public has a vital stake in maintaining a reasonable level of quality care. At the same time, such involvement is far from guaranteed, even where nonprofits pioneer the service. Given the intensity of competition at the present time and the expanded access of for-profits to government support, nonprofits can hold their own only where they have well-established institutions, where they can secure capital, where they manage to identify a meaningful market niche and a distinctive product, where they respond effectively to the competitive threat, and where individual consumers or those who are paying on their behalf value the special qualities that nonprofits bring to the field. The fact that nonprofits have continued to expand substantially in the face of competition suggests that many nonprofits have been up to this challenge, although recent reports indicating problems for nonprofit hospitals in generating capital to respond to a surprising spurt in admissions make it clear that serious challenges remain.[103]

Meeting the Political Competition

In addition to fending off for-profit competition in the economic sphere, nonprofit organizations have also demonstrated unusual, and growing, effectiveness in the political sphere. This achievement is especially surprising in view of the role that money has come to play in American politics, the serious economic pressures under which organizations are operating, and the apparent decline in civic participation identified by scholars such as Robert Putnam.[104] It is all the more remarkable in light of the legal limitations on nonprofit political action—limitations that bar nonprofit organizations from engaging in electoral activity, from contributing to political campaigns, and from devoting more than a limited share of their resources to "lobbying."[105] Indeed, as Boris and Krehely report in chapter 9, only 1.5 percent of all nonprofit 501(c)(3) organizations that filed the required Form 990 with the Internal Revenue Service in 1998 reported any expenditures on lobbying, and the amount they spent represented less than one-tenth of 1 percent of their expenditures.

Despite these limitations, however, nonprofits have amassed an extraordinary recent record of advocacy achievements. One manifestation of this has been the sizable number of social and political "movements" that have taken form within the nation's nonprofit institutions. More generally, the past twenty to thirty years have witnessed the growing capacity of a variety of citizen groups to influence the policy process, as reflected in Jeffrey Berry's careful analysis of the role of such groups in shaping the congressional agenda between the early 1960s and the early 1990s.[106] With only 7 percent of the Washington interest group universe throughout this period, these groups accounted for anywhere from 24 to

32 percent of the congressional testimony, generated between 29 and 40 percent of the press coverage of pending legislation, and were nearly 80 percent as effective in passing legislation they favored as the business lobbies against which they were often arrayed. As Berry points out,

> In every measurement taken so far, liberal citizen groups have demonstrated that they are effective and tenacious Washington lobbies. . . . Even if business remains more powerful, liberal citizen groups have proved that they are worthy adversaries capable of influencing policymakers.[107]

Not only have nonprofit citizen groups proved effective in national political advocacy, but also these organizations have recently extended their reach upward to the international level and downward to states and localities. The same new communications technologies that have facilitated the rise of global corporations have permitted the emergence of transnational advocacy networks linking nonprofit citizen groups across national borders. This "third force" is rapidly transforming international politics and economics, challenging government policies on everything from land mines to dam construction and holding corporations to account in their home markets for environmental damage or labor practices they may be pursuing in far-off lands.[108] Indeed, the recent eagerness that multinational corporations have shown for cause-related marketing arrangements and broader strategic partnerships with nonprofit organizations has been driven in important part by the threat these networks pose to their "license to operate" and to their reputations among both consumers and their own staff. Similarly, nonprofits have forged advocacy coalitions at the state level to make sure that devolution does not emasculate policy gains achieved nationally. The expansion of state social welfare and arts spending cited earlier can probably be attributed in important part to this nonprofit policy advocacy at the state level.

That nonprofit citizen groups have been able to develop such clout is due in part to changes in public attitudes and in political circumstances—the declining influence of political parties, the growing public concern for amenities such as a healthy environment, and the end of the cold war. But at least as important has been the capacity and effectiveness of the citizen organizations themselves—their ability to attract resources and talented personnel, the dedication and seriousness with which they have approached their work, and the effectiveness they have shown in utilizing the resources at their command. As Boris and Krehely show in chapter 9, nonprofit advocacy organizations have blossomed into highly complex organizations commanding millions of dollars of resources. The Sierra Club, for example, has sixty-five chapters throughout the United States, with 550,000 members, a separate Sierra Club Foundation, and a Sierra Club Political Action Committee. The Nature Conservancy is now a holding company for five nonexempt and four exempt organizations, including a Nature Conservancy Action Fund, and oversees 300 state and local organizations. Not only are many of these organizations large and complex, however, they also seem to be increasingly well managed. As Berry shows, these groups have built substantial donor bases, earned a reputation for doing their homework, and enjoy at least as much credibility as their business opponents.[109]

Summary and Implications

Nonprofit America has thus responded with extraordinary creativity and resilience to the challenges and opportunities it has confronted over the past twenty years. The sector has grown enormously as a consequence—in numbers, in revenues, and in the range of purposes it serves. In addition, it seems to have expanded its competencies and improved its management, although these are more difficult to gauge with precision. To be sure, not all components of the sector have experienced these changes to the same degree or even in the same direction. Yet what is striking is how widespread the adaptations seem to have been.

In large part, what allowed nonprofit organizations not only to survive, but to thrive, during this period was that they moved, often decisively, toward the market. Nonprofit organizations took active advantage of the growing demand for their services, expanded their fee income, launched commercial ventures, forged partnerships with businesses, adopted business-style management techniques, mastered new consumer-side forms of government funding, reshaped their organizational structures, incorporated sophisticated marketing and money-management techniques into even their charitable fundraising, and generally found new ways to tap the dynamism and resources of the market to promote their organizational objectives. This move toward the market has by no means been universal. Nor is it entirely new. What is more, it did not exhaust the range of responses the sector made to the challenges it faced. Yet it has clearly been the dominant theme of the decade, and its scope and impact have been profound, affecting all parts of the sector to some extent. As a result, the nonprofit sector that is entering the twenty-first century is not "your father's nonprofit sector." Rather, it has been substantially reengineered, and this process is still very much under way, although it has yet to be fully appreciated by the sector itself or by the nation at large.

On balance, these changes seem to have worked to the advantage of the nonprofit sector, strengthening its fiscal base, upgrading its operations, enlisting new partners and new resources in its activities, and generally improving its reputation for effectiveness. But they have also brought significant risks, and the risks may well overwhelm the gains. Before drawing the final balance sheet on the state of nonprofit America, therefore, it is necessary to weigh the gains against these risks.

The Risks

More specifically, the nonprofit sector's response to the challenges of the past twenty years, creative as it has been, has exposed the sector to at least five important risks.

GROWING IDENTITY CRISIS. In the first place, the nonprofit sector is increasingly confronting an identity crisis as a result of a growing tension between the market character of the services it is providing and the continued nonprofit character of the institutions providing them. As Gray and Schlesinger show in chapter 2, this tension has become especially stark in the health field, where third-party payers, such as Medicare and private health maintenance organizations, refuse to consider values other than actual service cost in setting reimbursement rates, and where bond rating agencies discount community service in determining what nonprofit hospitals have to pay for the capital they need to expand. Left to their own devices, nonprofit institutions have had little choice but to adjust to these pressures, but at some cost to the features that make them distinctive. Under these circumstances, it is no wonder that scholars have been finding it so difficult to detect real differences between the performance of for-profit and nonprofit hospitals and why many nonprofit health maintenance organizations and hospitals have willingly surrendered the nonprofit form or sold out to for-profit firms.[110] Private universities are similarly experiencing increasing strains between their mission to propagate knowledge and the expansion of their reliance on corporate sponsorship, which has brought with it demands for exclusive patent rights to the fruits of university research.[111] Marketing pressures are also intruding on the operations of nonprofit arts and cultural institutions, limiting their ability to focus on artistic quality and transforming them, as Wyszomirski notes in chapter 5, into social enterprises more attentive to market demands. So intense has the resulting identity crisis become, in fact, that at least some scholars are beginning to reject the long-standing notion that nonprofits are reluctant participants in the market, providing only those "private goods" needed to support their "collective goods" activities, and are coming to see many of them functioning instead as essentially commercial operations dominated by "pecuniary rather than altruistic objectives."[112]

INCREASED DEMANDS ON NONPROFIT MANAGERS. These tensions have naturally complicated the job of the nonprofit executive, requiring these officials to master not only the substantive dimensions of their fields but also the broader private markets within which they operate, the numerous public policies that increasingly affect them, and the massive new developments in technology and management with which they must contend. They must do all this, moreover, while balancing an increasingly complex array of stakeholders that includes not only clients, staff, board members, and private donors but also regulators, government program officials, for-profit competitors, and business partners and while also demonstrating performance and competing with other nonprofits and with for-profit firms for fees, board members, customers, contracts, grants, donations, gifts, bequests, visibility, prestige, political influence, and volunteers.[113] No wonder that burnout has become such a serious problem in the field, despite the excitement and fulfillment the role entails.

INCREASED THREAT TO NONPROFIT MISSIONS. Inevitably, these pressures pose threats to the continued pursuit of nonprofit missions. Nonprofit organizations forced to rely on fees and charges naturally begin to skew their service offerings to clientele who are able to pay. What start out as sliding fee scales designed to cross-subsidize services for the needy become core sources of revenue essential for agency survival. Organizations needing to raise capital to expand are naturally tempted to locate new facilities in places with a client base able to finance the borrowing costs. When charity care, advocacy, and research are not covered in government or private reimbursement rates, institutions have little choice but to curtail these activities.

How far these pressures have proceeded is difficult to say with any precision. As Diaz shows in chapter 17, support for the poor has never been the exclusive, or the primary, focus of nonprofit action. Nor need it be. What is more, many of the developments identified above have usefully mobilized market resources to support genuinely charitable purposes. Yet the nonprofit sector's movement toward the market is creating significant pressures to move away from those in greatest need, to focus on amenities that appeal to those who can pay, and to apply the market test to all facets of their operations.[114] The move to the market may thus be posing a far greater threat to the nonprofit sector's historic social justice and civic mission than the growth of government support before it.

DISADVANTAGING SMALL AGENCIES. A fourth risk resulting from the nonprofit sector's recent move to the market is to put smaller agencies at an increasing disadvantage. Successful adaptation to the prevailing market pressures increasingly requires access to advanced technology, professional marketing, corporate partners, sophisticated fundraising, and complex government reimbursement systems, all of which are problematic for smaller agencies. Market pressures are therefore creating not just a digital divide, but a much broader "sustainability chasm" that smaller organizations are finding it increasingly difficult to bridge. Although such agencies can cope with these pressures in part through collaborations and partnerships, these devices themselves often require sophisticated management and absorb precious managerial energies.[115] As the barriers to entry, and particularly to sustainability, rise, the nonprofit sector is thus at risk of losing one of its most precious qualities—its ease of entry and its availability as a testing ground for new ideas.

POTENTIAL LOSS OF PUBLIC TRUST. All of this, finally, poses a further threat to the public trust on which the nonprofit sector ultimately depends. Thanks to the pressures they are under and the agility they have shown in responding to them, American nonprofit organizations have moved well beyond the quaint Norman Rockwell stereotype of selfless volunteers ministering to the needy and supported largely by charitable gifts. Yet popular and press images remain wedded to this older image, and far too little attention has been given to bringing popular perceptions into better alignment with the realities that now exist and to justifying these realities to a skeptical citizenry and press. As a consequence, nonprofits find themselves vulnerable when highly visible events, such as the September 11 tragedy, let alone instances of mismanagement or scandal, reveal them to be far more complex and commercially engaged institutions than the public suspects. The more successfully nonprofit organizations respond to the dominant market pressures they are facing, therefore, the greater the risk they face of sacrificing the public trust on which they ultimately depend. This may help to explain the widespread appeal of the Bush administration's faith-based charities initiative. What makes this concept so appealing is its comforting affirmation of the older image of the nonprofit sector, the image of voluntary church groups staffed by the faithful solving the nation's problems of poverty and blight, even though, as Chaves shows in chapter 8, this image grossly exaggerates both the capacity and the inclinations of most congregations to engage in meaningful social problem solving.

Resetting the Balance: The Task Ahead

What all of this suggests is that a better balance may need to be struck between what Gray and Schlesinger term the nonprofit sector's "distinctiveness imperative"—the things that make nonprofits special—and the sector's "survival imperative"—the things nonprofits need to do in order to survive. To be sure, these two imperatives are not wholly in conflict. Nevertheless, the tensions between them are real, and there is increasing reason to worry that the survival imperative may be gaining the upper hand. To correct this, steps will be needed in both domains, and the steps will require support from many different quarters.

THE DISTINCTIVENESS IMPERATIVE. Actions to address the nonprofit sector's distinctiveness imperative are perhaps the most urgent. Several different types of action may be useful here.

—*Rethinking community benefit and charitable purpose.* In the first place, action is needed in the realm of values and ideas. In a sense, nonprofit organizations have been so busy coping with the powerful market forces they are facing that they have allowed the market definitions of value to dominate the public discourse and even their own behavior. Largely lacking, as *The Nonprofit Quarterly* recently noted, is "agreement around a powerful affirmation of identity distinguishing [the nonprofit sector] from the other two social sectors." To the extent that any consensus exists on this point, as reflected in court decisions, legislative proposals, and popular accounts, it focuses on care for the poor as the chief, or exclusive, rationale justifying nonprofit status. But this is far too narrow a ground for the sector to defend successfully given the survival demands it also confronts and the other functions it performs. Nonprofits must therefore develop a broader and more coherent statement of "the nature of [their] game."[116] This will require a serious rethinking of the central concepts of charitable purpose and community benefit that justify the nonprofit sector's existence, a task that, Abramson and McCarthy point out in chapter 10, the sector's infrastructure organizations have not yet adequately addressed.

Illustrative of the direction this might take is the suggestion by Gray and Schlesinger in chapter 2 to extend the concept of community benefit for nonprofit hospitals to embrace not only charity care but also a broader commitment to community health and to the production of collective goods such as trained medical professionals and scientific advance. Similar insights can be found in Forman and Stoddard's discussion in chapter 7 of the recent efforts of nonprofit humanitarian assistance agencies to forge new principles of humanitarian aid that take account of the complex humanitarian and military crises increasingly common around the world. More generally, nonprofit America must give broader and more concrete meaning to its claims to serve the public good by stressing the sector's commitments to reliability, to trustworthiness, to quality, to equity, to community, and to individual and community empowerment. These are powerful rationales in a society that values pluralism and freedom but wishes to balance them with a sense of solidarity and responsibility for others. But they must be more forcefully and concretely articulated and then be more fully interpreted and applied in the context of particular agencies and fields.

—*Improving public understanding.* As efforts go forward to clarify the nonprofit sector's vision and rationale, parallel efforts must be made to communicate this vision to the public and reconcile it with how the sector actually works. This must go beyond the ritualistic celebrations of charitable giving and voluntarism that currently form the heart of the sector's public relations effort, important though these may be. Rather, the public must be introduced to the broader realities of current nonprofit operations, to the remarkable resilience that the sector has shown in recent years, and to the full range of special qualities that make nonprofit organizations worth protecting. This will require a better public defense of the sector's long-standing partnership with government, clarification of the special ways in which nonprofits are enlisting market means to promote nonprofit ends, and the further development and dissemination of codes of conduct to help nonprofits and the public understand the delicate balance nonprofits have to strike between their survival and their distinctiveness.

—*Policy shifts.* Changes may also be needed in public policy to make sure that the sector's commitments to community benefit and charitable purpose are given effective incentives and are reinforced. This may require challenging the narrow conceptions of charitable purpose embodied in some legal opinions. But it may also require some tightening of the legal provisions under which nonprofits operate. At a minimum, this could involve more stringent policing of the existing unrelated business income tax provisions to ensure that nonprofit organizations pay income taxes on business activities that stray too far from their charitable purposes. Beyond this, it could involve shifting from the current system of tax-exempt *organizations* to a system of tax-exempt *activities* under which organizations earn exemptions from taxes only for those activities that support valid public, or community, purposes. Under such a system, nonprofit organizations would have to justify their exemptions in annual tax filings that identify the share of their income that goes to support such purposes. Such a system would provide more regular reinforcement of the community benefits that nonprofits are supposed to provide and help to reassure the public that these benefits are actually being provided.

THE SURVIVAL IMPERATIVE. For this effort to promote the "distinctiveness imperative" of nonprofit organizations to work, however, steps will also be needed to ease the survival imperative under which they labor. Three of these deserve particular mention here.

—*Capitalizing the sector.* In the first place, additional steps are needed to correct the structural impediments the nonprofit sector faces in generating investment capital because of its lack of access to the equity markets. More than any other single cause, these impediments explain the difficulty nonprofit organizations have faced in responding to technological change and maintaining their market niche during periods of rapid expansion of demand. The experience of nonprofit hospitals and higher education institutions demonstrates, however, that nonprofit organizations can often hold their own in such circumstances when they can gain access to the needed capital at competitive rates. In both of these cases, special tax incentives were provided to subsidize bonds issued to finance nonprofit facilities. The recent example of nonprofit involvement in low-income housing described by Vidal in chapter 6 tells a similar story in a context characterized by smaller-scale institutions. Here the provision of special tax advantages for investors was supplemented by the emergence of nonprofit intermediary institutions that package the tax breaks for sale to investors.

Many nonprofit organizations, particularly in the human service field, still lack access to such tax breaks and the capital funds they can leverage, however. As a consequence, they are at a competitive disadvantage in keeping up with rapid technological change and meeting increases in demand. To correct this, a broader nonprofit investment tax credit could usefully be enacted. Such a measure would create a more level playing field for nonprofit agencies, ease the survival pressures they face, and thus allow them to continue performing their distinctive roles.

—*Buy-in by third-party payers.* By itself, improved access to capital for nonprofit organizations will still not give nonprofits the financial leeway they need to address their distinctive missions unless steps are also taken to relieve the fiscal squeeze these organizations face. That squeeze, in turn, is increasingly shaped by the reimbursement policies of third-party payers—private insurance companies, health maintenance organizations, corporate benefit administrators, and government voucher programs like Medicare and Medicaid. Whether nonprofit hospitals can continue to support their teaching and research functions, for example, is significantly affected by whether Medicare considers this function vital enough to justify an adjustment in the normal hospital reimbursement rate. Increasingly, third-party payers have been ratcheting down the kinds of functions they are willing to support in this way, requiring the providers of health care, clinic care, nursing home care, drug abuse treatment, and many other services to shave costs to the bone. To reverse this trend, nonprofit organizations, possibly with help from the public sector, will have to convince third-party payers that these activities are both worthy of support and able to be supported. Blue Shield of California's recent adoption of an incentive system that takes account of quality, and not just cost, in setting hospital reimbursement rates is promising in this regard, but there clearly is still a long way to go.[117]

—*Encouragement of private giving for priority community benefits.* The nonprofit survival imperative can also be eased through continued and expanded encouragement of charitable giving and volunteering, particularly that targeted on community benefit activities. One way to do this would be to replace the existing tax deduction system with one based on tax "credits." Unlike deductions, which deliver more tax benefits per dollar of contribution to upper-income taxpayers than to lower-income ones, tax credits provide the same tax benefits to all taxpayers regardless of their income.[118] What is more, the scale of the credits can be geared to the particular community benefits being promoted simply by varying the share of the contribution that can be used to offset taxes for various types of contributions. American charitable giving has been stuck below 2 percent of personal income for some time. It is worth considering radical approaches that might boost this level in the future, and a system of tax credits instead of deductions might well be one of those worth trying.

Conclusions

It has been said that the quality of a nation can be seen in the way it treats its least advantaged citizens. But it can also be seen in the way it treats its most valued institutions. Americans have long paid lip service to the importance they attach to their voluntary institutions, while largely ignoring the challenges these institutions face. During the past decade and a half, these challenges have been extraordinary. But so, too, has been the nonprofit sector's response. As a result, the state of nonprofit America is surprisingly robust as we enter the new millennium, with more organizations doing more things more effectively than ever before.

At the same time, the movement to the market that has made this possible has also exposed the sector to enormous risks. What is more, the risks go to the heart of what makes the nonprofit sector distinctive and worthy of public support—its basic identity, its mission, and its ability to retain the public's trust.

Up to now, nonprofit managers have had to fend for themselves in deciding what risks it was acceptable to take in order to permit their organizations to survive. Given the stake that American society has in the preservation of these institutions and in the protection of their ability to perform their distinctive roles, it seems clear that this must now change. Americans need to rethink in a more explicit way whether the balance between survival and distinctiveness that nonprofit institutions have had to strike in recent years is the right one for the future and, if not, what steps might now be needed to shift this balance for the years ahead.

The argument here is that some adjustments are needed, that America's nonprofit institutions require broader support in preserving the features that make them special. Whether others agree with this conclusion remains to be seen. What seems clear, however, is that better public understanding of the state of nonprofit America is needed if such judgments are to be possible. Our hope is that this book will contribute to such understanding. That, at any rate, is our goal.

Notes

1. Gilbert M. Gaul and Mary Pat Flaherty, "Red Cross Collected Unneeded Blood: Resources Lacking to Freeze Surplus," *Washington Post,* November 11, 2001, p. A1.

2. AAFRC Trust for Philanthropy, "What Do Crises Mean for Philanthropy?" *Giving USA Update,* vol. 4 (2001), p. 3.

3. For a fuller discussion of this partnership, see Lester M. Salamon, "Partners in Public Service," in Walter W. Powell, ed., *The Nonprofit Sector: A Research Handbook* (Yale University Press, 1987), pp. 99–117; and Lester M. Salamon, *Partners in Public Service: Government-Nonprofit Relations in the Modern Welfare State* (Johns Hopkins University Press, 1995).

4. Alexis de Tocqueville, *Democracy in America,* vol. 2, the Henry Reeve text as revised by Francis Bowen (New York: Vintage Books, 1945 [1835]), p. 118.

5. On the reengineering movement in the corporate sector, see Michael Hammer and James Champy, *Reengineering the Corporation: A Manifesto for Business Revolution,* rev. ed. (London: Nicholas Brealey, 1994); Michael Hammer and James Champy, *Reengineering the Corporation: A Manifesto for Business Revolution* (London: Nicholas Brealy, 1993); David K. Carr and Henry J. Johnson, *Best Practices in Reengineering: What Works and What Doesn't in the Reengineering Process* (New York: McGraw-Hill, 1995).

6. See, for example, Kevin P. Kearns, *Private Sector Strategies for Social Sector Success: The Guide to Strategy and Planning for Public and Nonprofit Organizations* (San Francisco: Jossey-Bass, 2000).

7. Section 501(c)(4) organizations share these basic purposes but are permitted to pursue them more extensively through "lobbying" efforts, something 501(c)(3) organizations can do only to a limited extent. However, contributions to the 501(c)(4) organizations are not tax deductible. This distinction between 501(c)(3) and 501(c)(4) organizations is a notoriously slippery one, depending on the definition of the term "lobbying" and the meaning of the restriction on the former organizations not to engage in such activity to a substantial extent. Recent laws have attempted to clarify this distinction by specifying more precisely what falls within the domain of lobbying and what exactly is meant by "substantial." Fundamentally, lobbying means direct or indirect efforts to influence the passage of particular pieces of legislation or particular administrative rules, whereas "substantial" has come to mean roughly 20 percent or more of agency expenditures. In addition to sections 501(c)(3) and 501(c)(4), the U.S. tax code contains over twenty other subsections under which organizations can be granted tax exemptions. These include business associations, labor unions, and social clubs. None of these types of organizations is eligible to receive tax-deductible gifts, however, because they primarily serve their members rather than the public at large. See Bruce R. Hopkins, *The Law of Tax Exempt Organizations,* 6th ed. (New York: John Wiley and Sons, 1992), pp. 327–52.

8. Based on data presented in Lester M. Salamon, *America's Nonprofit Sector: A Primer,* 2d ed. (New York: Foundation Center, 1999), pp. 22 and 41, note 2. Religious congregations are not required to register for tax-exempt status, although many do.

9. Murray S. Weitzman, Nadine Tai Jalandoni, Linda M. Lampkin, and Thomas H. Pollack, *The New Nonprofit Almanac and Desk Reference* (San Francisco: Jossey-Bass, 2002), p. 21.

10. U.S. Census Bureau, *Statistical Abstract of the United States: 2000,* 120 ed. (Washington: U.S. Government Printing Office, 2000), p. 420.

11. Virginia B. Hodgkinson and Murray S. Weitzman, *Nonprofit Almanac: 1996/1997* (San Francisco: Jossey-Bass, 1996), pp. 271–309.

12. Weitzman and others, *New Nonprofit Almanac,* p. 125. See also Internal Revenue Service, *Statistics of Income Bulletin,* Publication 1136 (Washington: Internal Revenue Service, February 1997), table 21.

13. Elizabeth Boris, "The Nonprofit Sector in the 1990s," in Charles T. Clotfelter and Thomas Ehrlich, eds., *Philanthropy and the Nonprofit Sector in a Changing America* (Indiana University Press, 1999), pp. 16–17.

14. The discussion here draws heavily on Salamon, *America's Nonprofit Sector,* pp. 15–17.

15. See, for example, James S. Coleman, *Foundations of Social Theory* (Harvard University Press, 1990), pp. 300–21; Robert Putnam, *Making Democracy Work: Civic Traditions in Modern Italy* (Princeton University Press, 1993), pp. 83–116, 163–85.

16. De Tocqueville, *Democracy in America,* vol. 2, p. 117.

17. This term was first used by Ralph Kramer to describe one of the crucial roles of nonprofit organizations. Kramer used it to refer most squarely to volunteering, but it has a broader meaning as well. Ralph Kramer, *Voluntary Agencies in the Welfare State* (University of California Press, 1981), pp. 193–211.

18. For a more complete analysis of this system of government-nonprofit relations and the broader pattern of "third-party government" of which it is a part, see Salamon, "Partners in Public Service," pp. 99–117; and Salamon, *Partners in Public Service.* For a discussion of the federal government's support of nonprofit research universities, see Don K. Price, *The Scientific Estate* (Harvard University Press, 1965). This pattern of government support to nonprofit organizations did not begin in the postwar period, however. Rather, its roots lie deep in American history. For example, Harvard College, the first nonprofit, was financed in important part by an earmarked tax on corn levied by the colonial government of Massachusetts beginning in the seventeenth century. Similarly, subsidies for nonprofit human service were a standard feature of American urban life in the 1880s and 1890s. By the mid-1890s, in fact, more public welfare aid in New York, Pennsylvania, Connecticut, Maryland, and even the District of Columbia went to support private institutions than to public ones, and far more of the income of private nonprofit organizations in a wide variety of fields came from government than from private philanthropy. One early study showed, for example, that in New York City, 69 percent of the income of a group of prominent nonprofit children's agencies came from public subsidies. On higher education, see John S. Whitehead, *The Separation of College and State: Columbia, Dartmouth, Harvard, and Yale* (Yale University Press, 1973), pp. 3–16. On social services, see Amos Warner, *American Charities: A Study in Philanthropy and Economics* (New York: Thomas Y. Crowell, 1894), pp. 400–05.

19. Lester M. Salamon and Alan J. Abramson, "The Federal Budget and the Nonprofit Sector: Implications of the *Contract with America,*" in Dwight F. Burlingame, William A. Diaz, Warren F. Ilchman, and Associates, eds., *Capacity for Change? The Nonprofit World in the Age of Devolution* (Indianapolis: Indiana University Center on Philanthropy, 1996), pp. 8–9; Alan J. Abramson, Lester M. Salamon, and C. Eugene Steurle, eds., "The Nonprofit Sector and the Federal Budget: Recent History and Future Directions," in Elizabeth T. Boris and C. Eugene Steurle, eds., *Nonprofits and Government Collaboration and Conflict* (Washington: Urban Institute, 1999), pp. 110–12.

20. Office of Management and Budget, *Enhancing Governmental Productivity through Competition: A New Way of Doing Business within the Government to Provide Quality Government at Least Cost* (Washington: Office of Management and Budget, August 1988), p. 15, quoted in Donald Kettl, *Shared Power: Public Governance and Private Markets* (Washington: Brookings, 1993), p. 46.

21. Vouchers essentially provide targeted assistance to eligible recipients in the form of a certificate or a reimbursement card that can be presented to the provider of choice. The provider then receives payment for the certificate or reimbursement from the government. Tax expenditures use a similar method, except that no actual certificate is used. Rather, eligible taxpayers are allowed to deduct a given proportion of the cost of a particular service (for example, daycare) either from their income (tax deduction) or from the taxes they owe (tax credit). For a discussion of vouchers, tax expenditures, and other tools of public action, see Lester M. Salamon, ed., *The Tools of Government: A Guide to the New Governance* (New York: Oxford University Press, 2002).

22. Salamon, *Partners in Public Service*, p. 208. Both Medicare and Medicaid are essentially voucher programs since consumers are entitled to choose the provider they wish and the government then reimburses the provider for the cost.

23. Spending on Medicaid, for example, swelled more than fourfold in real dollar terms between 1975 and 1998, while discretionary spending stagnated or declined. Computed from data in U.S. House of Representatives, Committee on Ways and Means, *2000 Green Book: Background Material and Data on Programs within the Jurisdiction of the Committee on Ways and Means,* 106 Cong. 2 sess. (Washington, October 6, 2000), pp. 912, 923.

24. U.S. House of Representatives, Committee on Ways and Means, *2000 Green Book*, pp. 599, 617. As of 1998, well over 80 percent of the children receiving daycare assistance under this program were receiving it through such voucher certificates.

25. Of these, 40 percent of the large-establishment employees and 35 percent of the small-establishment employees were covered by preferred provider plans, and the balance of employees were covered by true health maintenance organizations. U.S. Census Bureau, *Statistical Abstract of the United States, 2000* (Washington: U.S. Census Bureau, 2000), table 180, p. 119.

26. Author's estimates based on data in Weitzman and others, *New Nonprofit Almanac*, pp. 96–97.

27. Generally speaking, the higher the rate of tax, the lower the out-of-pocket "cost" of a gift since the taxpayer would have to pay more to Uncle Sam if he or she chose not to give. Paradoxically, therefore, higher tax rates increase the financial incentive to give, and lower tax rates reduce this incentive.

28. Computed from data in Weitzman and others, *Nonprofit Almanac*, pp. 96–97. These figures exclude giving to religious organizations for religious purposes but include the portion of religious giving that goes to support other charitable purposes, such as social welfare and education. With all religious giving included, the decline in giving's total share of sector income was slightly less pronounced—from 26 percent in 1977 to 18.5 percent in 1997. See chapter 16 by Atul Dighe.

29. The Fidelity Gift Fund recorded assets of $2.2 billion as of early 2000 and made grants of $374 million in the 1998–99 fiscal year. By comparison, the New York Community Trust reported assets of $2.0 billion as of the end of 1999 and grants during 1999 of $130.7 million. AAFRC Trust for Philanthropy, *Giving USA 2001: The Annual Report on Philanthropy for the Year 2001* (Indianapolis Center on Philanthropy, 2001), p. 53; Foundation Center, *Foundation Yearbook of Facts and Figures on Private, Corporate, and Community Foundations, 2001,* Foundation Today Series (New York: Foundation Center, 2001), pp. 67–68.

30. For a discussion of recent problems that nonprofit hospitals have encountered in generating capital, see Reed Abelson, "Demand, but No Capital, at Nonprofit Hospitals," *New York Times,* June 21, 2002, p. B1.

31. William P. Ryan, "The New Landscape for Nonprofits," *Harvard Business Review,* vol. 77 (January/February 1999): 128.

32. Henry Hansmann, "The Role of Nonprofit Enterprise," *Yale Law Journal,* vol. 89, no. 5 (April 1980): 835–901.

33. See, for example, Michael Porter and Mark R. Kramer, "Philanthropy's New Agenda: Creating Value," *Harvard Business Review,* vol. 77 (November/December 1999): 121–30; Gar Walker and Jean Grossman, "Philanthropy and Outcomes," in Clotfelter and Ehrlich, eds., *Philanthropy and the Nonprofit Sector in a Changing America,* pp. 449–60.

34. Christine W. Letts, William Ryan, and Allen Grossman, "Virtuous Capital: What Foundations Can Learn from Venture Capitalists," *Harvard Business Review,* vol. 75 (March/April 1997): 36–44, especially pp. 2–7.

35. H. George Frederickson, "First There's Theory. Then, There's Practice," *Foundation News and Commentary,* vol. 42, no. 1 (March/April 2001): 38. See also Doug Easterling, "Using Outcome Evaluation to Guide Grant Making: Theory, Reality, and Possibilities," *Nonprofit and Voluntary Sector Quarterly,* vol. 29, no. 3 (September 2000): 482–86; Walker and Grossman, "Philanthropy and Outcomes."

36. Jeffrey Berry, *The New Liberalism: The Rising Power of Citizen Groups* (Washington: Brookings, 1999), especially pp. 12–130.

37. Nicole Wallace, "Online Giving Soars as Donors Turn to the Internet Following Attacks," *Chronicle of Philanthropy*, October 4, 2001, p. 22.

38. Andrew Blau, *More than Bit Players: How Information Technology Will Change the Ways Nonprofits and Foundations Work and Thrive in the Information Age*, a report to the Surdna Foundation (New York: Surdna Foundation, May 2001), p. 10.

39. A survey by the Association of Arts Agencies cited by Margaret Wyszomirski in chapter 5, for example, found that 34 percent of arts organizations had only one or no computers and 46 percent had no website. See, more generally, Stephen Greene, "Astride the Digital Divide: Many Charities Struggle to Make Effective Use of New Technology," *Chronicle of Philanthropy*, January 11, 2001.

40. Andrew Blau, *More than Bit Players*, p. 9.

41. Edwin Feulner, "Truth in Testimony," Heritage Foundation Testimony (Washington: Heritage Foundation, August 22, 1996).

42. Capital Research Center, "Our Mission," available at www.capitalresearch.org [November 1996].

43. Roy Lubove, *The Professional Altruist* (Harvard University Press, 1965).

44. John McKnight, *The Careless Society: Community and Its Counterfeits* (New York: Basic Books, 1995), p. 10.

45. Stuart Butler, *Privatizing Federal Spending* (New York: Universe Books, 1985); Martin Anderson, *Imposters in the Temple: American Intellectuals Are Destroying Our Universities and Cheating Our Students* (Englewood Cliffs, N.J.: Simon and Schuster, 1992).

46. Independent Sector, *Giving and Volunteering, 1999* (Washington: Independent Sector, 1999), chap. 3, pp. 3, 5.

47. Similar evidence of public ambivalence emerges from a survey conducted for the Maryland Association of Nonprofit Organizations. Only 38 percent of the respondents in this survey indicated that they think private charitable organizations are "very trustworthy," only 29 percent "strongly agree" that the money they donate to charities is being used as they expect it to be, and 87 percent expressed worry that they are being "scammed" by telephone solicitations. Maryland Association of Nonprofit Organizations, *Protecting the Public Trust: Revisiting Attitudes about Charities in Maryland* (Baltimore: Maryland Association of Nonprofit Organizations, 2002).

48. Phillip Howe and Corinne McDonald, "Traumatic Stress, Turnover, and Peer Support in Child Welfare" (Washington: Child Welfare League of America, 2001), available at www.cwla.org/programs/trieschman/2001 fbwPhilHowe.htm [August 14, 2002].

49. Thus among public policy program graduates in the classes of 1973, 1974, 1978, and 1979, an average of 14 percent took their first job in the nonprofit sector and 14 percent remained employed in the nonprofit sector in the mid-1990s. By contrast, an average of 16 percent of these graduates took their first job in the private business sector, and 33 percent were employed in the business sector as of the mid-1990s. Computed from data in Paul Light, *Making Nonprofits Work: A Report on the Tides of Nonprofit Management Reform* (Washington: Brookings, 2000), p. 10.

50. Jeanne Peters and Timothy Wolfred, *Daring to Lead: Nonprofit Executive Directors and Their Work Experience* (San Francisco: CompassPoint Nonprofit Services, August 2001), pp. 13–14, 20–21.

51. The discussion here draws heavily on Salamon, *America's Nonprofit Sector*.

52. U.S. Census Bureau, *Statistical Abstract of the United States, 2000*, pp. 408–09.

53. U.S. Census Bureau, *Statistical Abstract of the United States, 2000*, table 144, p. 101.

54. 1960 and 1980 figures from U.S. Census Bureau, *Statistical Abstract of the United States, 1982/3*, table 97, p. 66; figures for 1990s from U.S. Census Bureau, *Statistical Abstract of the United States, 2000*, table 88, p. 71.

55. U.S. House of Representatives, Committee on Ways and Means, *2000 Green Book*, p. 1363.

56. Neil Gilbert, "The Transformation of Social Services," *Social Services Review*, vol. 51, no. 4 (December 1977): 624–41.

57. Paul Ray and Sherry Ruth Anderson, *Cultural Creatives: How 50 Million People Are Changing the World* (San Francisco: Harmony, 2000).

58. Robert V. Avery and Michael S. Rendell, "Estimating the Size and Distribution of the Baby Boomers' Prospective Inheritances" (Cornell University, Department of Consumer Economics, 1990). For more recent estimates, see John J. Havens and Paul G. Schervish, "Millionaires and the Millennium: New Estimates of the Forthcoming Wealth Transfer and the Prospects for a Golden Age of Philanthropy" (Boston College, Social Welfare Research Institute, October 1999).

59. *Top Heavy* (New York: Twentieth Century Fund, 1995), table A-1. For a summary of the thinking on this intergenerational wealth transfer, see Harvey D. Shapiro, "The Coming Inheritance Bonanza," *Institutional Investor*, vol. 38, no. 6 (June 1994): 143–48.

60. Foundation Center, *Foundation Yearbook, 2001*, p. 43.

61. Craig Smith, "The New Corporate Philanthropy," *Harvard Business Review*, vol. 72 (May/June 1994): 105–16, especially p. 107; Jane Nelson, *Business as Partners in Development: Creating Wealth for Countries, Companies, and Communities* (London: Prince of Wales Business Leaders Forum, 1996); Reynold Levy, *Give and Take: A Candid Account of Corporate Philanthropy* (Harvard Business School, 1999).

62. As "third way" theorist Anthony Giddens has put it, "The fostering of an active civil society is a basic part of the politics of the third way." Anthony Giddens, *The Third Way: The Renewal of Social Democracy* (Cambridge, U.K.: Polity, 1998), p. 78.

63. The number of natural disasters tripled between the 1960s and the 1990s, while the number of armed conflicts, many of them civil wars, jumped from an average of twenty-three per year in the 1960s to over forty per year in the 1990s. See chapter 7 by Shepard Forman and Abby Stoddard.

64. Robert Putnam, *Bowling Alone: The Collapse and Revival of American Community* (New York: Simon and Schuster, 2000).

65. U.S. Social Security Administration, *Annual Statistical Supplement to the Social Security Bulletin* (Washington: U.S. Department of Health and Human Services, Social Security Administration, 2000), pp. 119–22.

66. U.S. House of Representatives, Committee on Ways and Means, *2000 Green Book*, p. 214. Expenditures are adjusted for inflation and expressed in 1999 dollars.

67. U.S. House of Representatives, Committee on Ways and Means, *2000 Green Book*, pp. 892–93; Teresa A. Coughlin, Leighton Ku, and John Holahan, *Medicaid since 1980: Costs, Coverage, and the Shifting Alliance between the Federal Government and the States* (Washington: Urban Institute Press, 1994), p. 2.

68. U.S. House of Representatives, Committee on Ways and Means, *2000 Green Book*, pp. 924, 927.

69. U.S. House of Representatives, Committee on Ways and Means, *2000 Green Book*, pp. 597, 953–54.

70. Coughlin, Ku, and Holahan, *Medicaid since 1980*, p. 87. For further detail, see chapter 4 by Stephen Smith.

71. As of 1998, for example, thirty-five states as well as the District of Columbia had agreed to extend coverage to the so-called "medically needy"—that is, individuals who are otherwise eligible for Medicaid coverage but who exceed the Medicaid income limits; twenty-two agreed to offer hospice care, twenty-six agreed to cover skilled nursing facilities for individuals under twenty-one, and thirty-one agreed to provide rehabilitative

services. U.S. House of Representatives, Committee on Ways and Means, *2000 Green Book*, p. 927.

72. Computed from data in U.S. Social Security Administration, *Social Security Bulletin* (Washington: U.S. Department of Health and Human Services, Social Security Administration, 1997 and 1990).

73. U.S. House of Representatives, Committee on Ways and Means, *2000 Green Book*, p. 354.

74. The number of people on "welfare" fell by half between 1994 and 1999, from 14.2 million in 1994 to 7.2 million in 1999. In addition, the portion of those remaining on the rolls requiring full cash grants also declined because more of them were working. States were guaranteed federal grants under the new temporary assistance for needy families (TANF) program at their peak levels of the early 1990s and were also obligated to maintain their own spending on needy families at 75 percent of their previous levels. U.S. House of Representatives, Committee on Ways and Means, *2000 Green Book,* pp. 376, 411.

75. For a general discussion of these "alternative tools" of public action, see Lester M. Salamon, "The New Governance and the Tools of Public Action: An Introduction," in Salamon, ed., *Tools of Government*, pp. 1–47. For a discussion of tax expenditures and loan guarantees, see Christopher Howard, "Tax Expenditures," in Salamon, ed., *Tools of Government*, pp. 410–44; and Thomas H. Stanton, "Loans and Loan Guarantees," in Salamon, ed., *Tools of Government*, pp. 381–409.

76. The $3.56 billion in subsidies made available to middle-income and lower-middle-income families through the daycare tax credit thus exceeds the roughly $3 billion in subsidies provided to poor families through the childcare and development block grant.

77. Rosabeth Moss Kanter and David V. Summers, "Doing Well While Doing Good: Dilemmas of Performance Management in Nonprofit Organizations and the Need for a Multiple-Constituency Approach," in Walter W. Powell, ed., *The Nonprofit Sector: A Research Handbook* (Yale University Press, 1987), p. 154.

78. Regina Herzlinger, "Can Public Trust in Nonprofits and Governments Be Restored?" *Harvard Business Review,* vol. 9 (March/April 1996): 98.

79. Data assembled by Independent Sector, the national umbrella organization representing the nonprofit sector, suggest a considerable slowing of the rate of revenue growth for most components of the nonprofit sector during the most recent 1992–97 period. However, data generated from Form 990s filed by nonprofit organizations fail to confirm this slowdown. Thus, for example, while the Independent Sector data indicate real, inflation-adjusted growth rates of 2.7, 1.8, and 3.8 percent a year for all nonprofit organizations, for health organizations, and for social service organizations, respectively, during 1992–97, the Form 990 data show real increases of 4.4, 2.9, and 7.2 percent a year, or nearly twice as great, for similar classes of organizations during virtually the same period, 1992–98. See Weitzman and others, *New Nonprofit Almanac*, pp. 102–03, 144–45.

80. Internal Revenue Service, *Data Book* (Washington: Internal Revenue Service, various years); Weitzman and others, *New Nonprofit Amanac*, pp. 4–5. Nonprofit organizations are not required to incorporate or register with the Internal Revenue Service unless they have annual gross receipts of $5,000 or more and wish to avail themselves of the charitable tax exemption. Religious congregations are not required to register even if they exceed these limits, although many do. It is therefore likely that more organizations exist than are captured in Internal Revenue Service records. It is also possible that some of the new registrants are organizations that have long existed but have chosen to register only in recent years. Because the legal and financial advantages of registration are substantial, however, it seems likely that the data reported here represent real growth in the number of organizations despite these caveats.

81. This same picture of organizational vitality emerges from detailed scrutiny of the Form 990s that registered nonprofit organizations are obliged to file with the Internal Revenue Service. Because these forms are only required of organizations with $25,000 or more in revenue, it might be assumed that older and larger organizations would dominate the reporting agencies. Yet a recent analysis of these reporting organizations reveals that most of those in existence as of 1998 had been founded since 1985, and half of these had been founded since 1992. Weitzman and others, *New Nonprofit Almanac*, p. 129.

82. Julian Wolpert, *Patterns of Generosity in America: Who's Holding the Safety Net?* (New York: Twentieth Century Fund, 1993), pp. 7, 27, 39–40. Sarah Dewees and Lester M. Salamon, "Maryland Nonprofit Employment: 1999," Johns Hopkins Nonprofit Employment Bulletin 3 (Baltimore, Johns Hopkins University, Institute for Policy Studies, Center for Civil Society, May 2001).

83. See, for example: Raymond Hernandez, "A Broad Alliance Tries to Head off Cuts in Medicare," *New York Times*, May 13, 2001, p. Al.

84. Weitzman and others, *New Nonprofit Almanac*, 2002, pp. 136, 168.

85. In one of the special ironies of the nonprofit field, the principal generator of data on private charitable giving in the United States has long been the trade association representing the nation's leading *for-profit* fundraising firms, the American Association of Fund-Raising Counsel.

86. Harvy Lipman, "Survey Finds Rapid Rise in Assets and Grants of Donor-Advised Funds," *Chronicle of Philanthropy*, May 31, 2001, p. 10.

87. See, for example, Thomas J. Billitteri, "A Run for the Money: Growth in Donor-Advised Accounts Spurs Fierce Competition for Funds," *Chronicle of Philanthropy*, April 20, 2000, p. 1.

88. Philanthropy did better in the most recent period (1992–97) than earlier, and there is some hope that this more recent pattern will hold, although the stock market decline of 2000–02 makes this somewhat doubtful.

89. Harvey Lipman and Elizabeth Schwinn, "The Business of Charity: Nonprofit Groups Reap Billions in Tax-Free Income Annually," *Chronicle of Philanthropy*, October 18, 2001, p. 25.

90. See, for example, Mary Williams Wals, "Hospital Group's Link to Company Is Criticized," *New York Times*, April 27, 2002, p. B1; Walt Bogdanich, "Two Hospital Fundraising Groups Face Questions over Conflicts," *New York Times*, March 24, 2002, p. A1.

91. Roberts Enterprise Development Fund, *Social Purpose Enterprises and Venture Philanthropy in the New Millennium* (San Francisco: Roberts Enterprise Development Fund, 1999); www.independentsector.org/pathfinder [August 29, 2002], a website created by the Pathfinder Project of Independent Sector and the University of Maryland.

92. Kearns, *Private Sector Strategies for Social Sector Success*, p. 25.

93. Based on recent offerings from John Wiley and Sons' website, www.wiley.co.uk/products/subject/business/nonprofit/management.html [August 14, 2002].

94. Frances Hesselbein, "Foreword," in Peter Drucker, *The Drucker Foundation Self-Assessment Tool*, rev. ed. (San Francisco: Jossey-Bass, 1999), p. vi.

95. See, for example, Walter W. Powell and Jason Owen-Smith, "Universities as Creators and Retailers of Intellectual Property," in Burton Weisbrod, ed., *To Profit or Not to Profit: The Commercial Transformation of the Nonprofit Sector* (Cambridge University Press, 1998), pp. 169–93.

96. Tracy Thompson, "Billy Shore Wants to Help Nonprofit Institutions Link Their Charitable Works with Profit-Making Enterprises," *Washington Post Magazine*, December 19, 1999, pp. 7–22; Bill Shore, *Revolution of the Heart: A New Strategy for Creating Wealth and Meaningful Change* (New York: Riverhead Books, 1995).

97. Susan Gray and Holly Hall, "Cashing in on Charity's Good Name," *Chronicle of Philanthropy,* July 20, 1998, p. 26; Business for Social Responsibility Education Fund, *Cause-Related Marketing* (San Francisco: Business for Social Responsibility Education Fund, 1999).

98. Eyal Press and Jennifer Washburn, "The Kept University," *Atlantic Monthly* (March 2000): 39–40.

99. Rosabeth Moss Kanter, "Innovation and Change: From Spare Change to Real Change: The Social Sector as Beta Site for Business Innovation," *Harvard Business Review,* vol. 77, no. 3 (May/June 1999): 122–32.

100. Aspen Institute, Nonprofit Sector Strategy Group, *The Nonprofit Sector and Business: New Visions, New Opportunities, New Challenges* (Washington: Aspen Institute, 2001).

101. According to Hall, this invention was undertaken to protect the institution of the private foundation and other charitable institutions supported by wealthy individuals from the onslaught of populist reformers worried about the antidemocratic influence these institutions wielded over the national economy and national life. Peter Hall, *Inventing the Nonprofit Sector and Other Essays on Philanthropy, Voluntarism, and Nonprofit Organizations* (Johns Hopkins University Press, 1992), pp. 66–80.

102. See, for example, Kurt Eichenwald, "Columbia/HCA Fraud Case May Be Widened, U.S. Says," *New York Times,* February 28, 1998; and chapter 2 in this volume by Bradford Gray and Mark Schlesinger.

103. Since the beginning of 2000, Moody's Investors Service has downgraded the bonds of 121 nonprofit hospitals, affecting $24 billion in bonds. See Reed Abelson, "Demand, but No Capital, at Nonprofit Hospitals," *New York Times,* June 12, 2002, p. B1.

104. Putnam, *Bowling Alone.*

105. As detailed more fully in chapter 9 by Elizabeth Boris and Jeff Krehely, lobbying differs from advocacy in that it is directed at specific pieces of legislation or regulatory actions.

106. Berry, *The New Liberalism.*

107. Berry, *The New Liberalism,* p. 119.

108. See, for example, Margaret E. Keck and Kathryn Sikkink, *Activists beyond Borders: Advocacy Networks in International Politics* (Cornell University Press, 1999); Anne M. Florini, ed., *The Third Force: The Rise of Transnational Civil Society* (Washington: Japan Center for International Exchange and the Carnegie Endowment for International Peace, 2000).

109. Berry, *The New Liberalism,* pp. 119–52.

110. A classic statement of this tension, focusing on a much earlier period, can be found in David Rosner, *A Once Charitable Enterprise: Hospitals and Health Care in Brooklyn and New York, 1885–1915* (Princeton University Press, 1982). For more recent analyses, see Regina Herzlinger and William S. Krasker, "Who Profits from Nonprofits?" *Harvard Business Review,* vol. 65 (January/February 1987): 93–106; David S. Salkever and Richard G. Frank, "Health Services," in Charles T. Clotfelter, ed., *Who Benefits from the Nonprofit Sector?* (University of Chicago Press, 1992), pp. 24–54.

111. Press and Washburn, "The Kept University." See also Donald Stewart, Pearl Rock Kane, and Lisa Scruggs in chapter 3 of this volume.

112. Estelle James, "Commercialism among Nonprofits: Objectives, Opportunities, and Constraints," in Weisbrod, ed., *To Profit or Not to Profit,* p. 273. For the alternative theory, see Burton Weisbrod, "Modeling the Nonprofit Organization as a Multiproduct Firm: A Framework for Choice," in Weisbrod, ed., *To Profit or Not to Profit,* pp. 47–64.

113. Evelyn Brody, "Agents without Principals: The Economic Convergence of the Nonprofit and For-Profit Organizational Forms," *New York Law School Law Review,* vol. 40, no. 3 (1996): 457–536. See also chapter 15 in this volume by Evelyn Brody.

114. James, "Commercialism among Nonprofits," p. 279.

115. Chapin Hall Strategic Restructuring Study.

116. "Please, Allow Us to Introduce Ourselves," *Nonprofit Quarterly,* vol. 8, no. 3 (July 2001): 3, quoting a Rolling Stones 1968 refrain.

117. Milt Freudenheim, "Quality Goals in Incentives for Hospitals," *New York Times,* June 24, 2002, p. C1.

118. Under the existing tax deduction system, taxpayers are allowed to subtract their charitable contributions from their taxable income if they itemize their deductions. Since higher-income taxpayers face higher tax rates, however, the resulting deductions are "worth" more to them than to lower-income taxpayers or those who do not itemize their deductions. Tax credits, however, are deducted from the actual taxes a taxpayer owes. Credits can be set equal to the contribution or at some fraction of the contribution (for example, 40 percent of the contribution can be deducted from the tax bill).

PART II

Major Fields

2

Health

BRADFORD H. GRAY AND MARK SCHLESINGER

The American health care system is characterized by paradox. At its best, it offers technological care at a level that is unmatched in the world, yet the United States ranks far down the list of countries in basic measures of population health such as infant mortality and life expectancy. Hundreds of state laws require health insurers to provide coverage for particular types of services (for example, fertility treatment) or types of providers (for example, chiropractors), yet some 44 million Americans have no health insurance at all. Although health care is widely recognized as a social good that places a substantial claim on public resources, public policy in recent decades has sought to make health care a market good based on *individual* choices. Although American health care is extraordinarily expensive, it is still thought of as a charitable field, since the organizations that absorb the largest share of the expenditures—hospitals—are predominantly nonprofit, tax-exempt organizations.

Health care must occupy a central place in any account of the American nonprofit sector. Organizations that provide health services account for just over half of the revenues of the entire nonprofit sector, and their share has been increasing.[1] For many Americans, hospitals may be the most readily recognized nonprofit institutions, because of the vital services they provide to community residents, their visible physical presence, and their history as an object of civic commitment. Nonprofit organizations also provide virtually every other kind of health-related service.

Nevertheless, there is great disquiet in the nonprofit health care sector today. In recent years, financial pressures have caused some well-established nonprofit hospitals to choose between merging with a competitor, selling to a for-profit company, or closing. Entire categories of health care organizations (home health agencies, managed care plans, rehabilitation hospitals) have gone from predominantly nonprofit to mostly for-profit in just a few years. Major health care institutions that have long been viewed as pillars of their community have suddenly faced demands from state and local officials to document that they are sufficiently charitable to deserve their tax exemptions. Academics have published learned articles doubting the rationale for tax exemptions for nonprofit organizations whose revenues come mostly from the sale of services (so-called commercial nonprofits), as is the case with most health care organizations.[2]

Thus, despite its size, vitality, and enormous historical importance, the nonprofit sector in health care faces serious financial, competitive, regulatory, and intellectual challenges. These challenges are neither superficial nor transitory but instead are rooted in ambiguities and changes in how Americans interpret the meaning of health care and in their expectations regarding the performance of nonprofit organizations in medical care. An important source of ambiguity regarding expectations of nonprofits is the diversity of the health care sector itself. Health care is a highly heterogeneous field made up of many kinds of organizations—hospitals, nursing homes, health maintenance organizations (HMOs), drug treatment centers, and so forth. These subfields or *domains*, as we term them, differ from each other in many important ways. They each have their own histories, meet particular kinds of needs, and have their own regulatory and payment regimes.

The experiences of nonprofit enterprises in the different health care domains have been quite varied in recent decades. The presence of nonprofits has declined sharply over the past fifteen years in several domains but remained stable in others. For a few services, the market share of nonprofit providers actually increased over the past fifteen years. This chapter suggests that these patterns can be understood by viewing services from a life-cycle perspective that takes account of the highly policy-sensitive context in which American health care organizations operate. As particular services move through different stages from innovation to institutionalization, the relative potential for nonprofit and for-profit involvement changes.

In addition to developments that have shaped particular service domains, a broader set of institutional changes has swept through American health care over the past two decades. Some of these threaten the viability of the nonprofit sector. Others create new, potentially valuable niches for nonprofit enterprise, albeit with characteristics that are different from those that the authorities historically have recognized as justifications for tax exemptions. This chapter seeks to identify systematically the factors that are influencing today's health care organizations, to analyze how nonprofit health care providers have responded to them, and to consider future options.

The discussion falls into four parts. The first section examines the role of nonprofits in health care and the context within which nonprofit health care organizations operate. The goal is to establish why a concern about the future of the nonprofit form is so crucial in this field. Against this backdrop, the second section takes up some of the central challenges that confront nonprofit organizations in health care. These challenges revolve around the fundamental tension between the market character of health services and the nonprofit character of many of the institutions that provide them. The third section then examines how nonprofits have been responding to these challenges. These responses have taken two rather different forms: first, a slow but steady incorporation of essentially commercial practices and, second, a rearguard effort to preserve the distinctiveness of the nonprofit form. The final section considers alternative approaches that nonprofit organizations in health care might use to protect or enhance their distinctive contributions.

Prevailing Realities about the Role of Nonprofits in Health Care

Notwithstanding the diverse domains that compose health care, a number of broad generalizations can be made about the field. This section emphasizes six realities.

Reality 1: A Major but Varied Role for Nonprofits

Nonprofit organizations occupy a major place in the health field. Table 2-1 shows the ownership composition of twelve major service domains in two recent periods—the mid-1980s and the late 1990s. Nonprofit organizations are the predominant providers in six of these domains (outpatient mental health clinics, acute care hospitals, residential treatment facilities for emotionally disturbed children, multiple-service mental health organizations, hospice programs, and community health centers). Nonprofit organizations account for one-quarter to one-third of most other health institutions, including HMOs, home health agencies, dialysis centers, and rehabilitation hospitals. In most areas where for-profits now predominate (nursing homes being the exception), the early innovators that identified emerging needs and developed initial responses to them were nonprofits.

Table 2-1 also demonstrates that the nonprofit share of fields cannot be assumed to be fixed. The stability of the nonprofit share has varied markedly among health care domains in recent years. For-profit firms have become predominant in several domains in which nonprofits predominated as recently as fifteen to twenty years ago. (The seeming anomalies in the categories in table 2-1 are addressed in a later discussion of growth trends.)

Table 2-1. *Ownership Trends, by Health Care Domain*

Domain	Mid-1980s			Late 1990s			Percentage change
	Year	Number	Percent	Year	Number	Percent	
Domains of for-profit expansion							
Dialysis centers	1985			1997			
For profit		616	42		2,322	68	277
Nonprofit		847	58		1,101	32	30
Subtotal, dialysis centers		1,463	100[a]		3,423	100[a]	134
Rehabilitation hospitals	1985			1998			
For profit		11	15		119	58	982
Nonprofit		51	70		71	35	39
Government		11	15		14	7	27
Subtotal, rehabilitation hospitals		73	100[b]		204	100[c]	179
Home health agencies	1985			1997			
For profit		2,055	36		6,290	67	206
Nonprofit		3,653	64		3,123	33	−15
Subtotal, home health agencies		5,708	100[d]		9,413	100[d]	65
Health maintenance organizations	1985			1997			
For profit		137	35		481	74	251
Nonprofit		256	65		167	26	−35
Subtotal, health maintenance organizations		393	100[e]		648	100[f]	65
Outpatient mental health clinics	1986			1997			
For profit		45	6		322	18	616
Nonprofit		502	64		1,007	57	101
Government		242	31		426	24	76
Subtotal, outpatient mental health clinics		789	100[g]		1,755	100[g]	122
Hospice programs	1992			1999			
For profit		151	13		593	28	293
Nonprofit		957	82		1,365	65	43
Government		63	5		146	7	132
Subtotal, hospice programs		1,171	100[h]		2,104	100[h]	80
Domains of nonprofit resurgence or for-profit decline							
Nursing homes	1986			1997			
For profit		14,300	75		11,250	65	−21
Nonprofit		3,800	20		4,792	28	26
Government		1,000	5		1,134	7	13
Subtotal, nursing homes		19,100	100[i]		17,176	100[i]	−10
Private psychiatric hospitals[j]	1985			1998			
For profit		233	67		275	73	18
Nonprofit		117	33		102	27	−13
Subtotal, psychiatric hospitals		350	100[b]		377	100[c]	8

Domain		Mid-1980s			Late 1990s		Percentage change
	Year	Number	Percent	Year	Number	Percent	
Domains of nonprofit stability							
Community health centers	n.a.			1997			
For profit		n.a.	n.a.		0	0	n.a.
Nonprofit		n.a.	n.a.		641	100	n.a.
Government		n.a.	n.a.		0	0	n.a.
Subtotal, community health centers			100		641	100[k]	n.a.
Multiservice mental health organizations	1988			1998			
For profit		13	1		69	8	431
Nonprofit		863	67		590	68	−32
Government		381	30		211	24	−45
Subtotal, multiservice mental health organizations		1,257	100[l]		870	100[l]	−31
Residential treatment facilities for emotionally disturbed children	1986			1997			
For profit		31	7		69	8	123
Nonprofit		378	87		590	68	56
Government		27	6		211	24	681
Subtotal, residential treatment facilities for emotionally disturbed children		436	100[m]		870	100[l]	100
Acute care hospitals	1985			1997			
For profit		805	14		797	16	−1
Nonprofit		3,349	58		3,000	59	−10
Government		1,578	28		1,260	25	−20
Subtotal, acute care hospitals		5,732	100[b]		5,057	100[n]	−12

n.a. Not available.

a. U.S. Department of Health and Human Services, Centers for Medicare and Medicaid Services, Office of Clinical Standards and Quality, data from the Program Management and Medical Information System, 1985–97, Baltimore.

b. American Hospital Association, *Hospital Statistics 1986 Edition,* tables 2A and 2B (Chicago, 1986).

c. American Hospital Association Resource Center, *American Hospital Association Annual Survey* (Chicago, 1998).

d. Health Care Financing Administration, *1998 Profile of Medicare Chart Book* (www.hcfa.gov/stats/stats. htm/98datacmp.pdf).

e. InterStudy Publications, *InterStudy 1985 Guide to National Firm HMOs* (St. Paul, Minn.).

f. InterStudy Publications, *InterStudy Competitive Edge 8.1* (Excelsior, Minn.).

g. U.S. Department of Health and Human Services, Substance Abuse and Mental Health Services Administration, data as reported to the Center of Mental Health Services, Rockville, Md.

h. General Accounting Office, *Medicare: More Beneficiaries Use Hospice but for Fewer Days of Care.* GAO/ HEHS-00-182 (Washington: GAO, September 2000).

i. National Center for Health Statistics, *National Nursing Home Survey* (Hyattsville, Md., 1997).

j. Not revealed in the table is an increase (from 24 to 27 percent) in nonprofits' market share that occurred between 1991 and 1998. During that period, the number of for-profit psychiatric hospitals declined from 405 to 275.

k. U.S. Department of Health and Human Services, Health Resources and Services Administration, Bureau of Primary Health Care (www.bphc.hrsa.dhhs.gov/databases/fqhc/default.htm).

l. U.S. Department of Health and Human Services, Substance Abuse and Mental Health Services Administration, Center for Mental Health Services, Survey and Analysis Branch, Inventory of Mental Health Organizations, unpublished data, 1988, Rockville, Md.

m. U.S. Department of Health and Human Services, Substance Abuse and Mental Health Services Administration, data as reported to the Center for Mental Health Services, Rockville, Md.

n. American Hospital Association, *Hospital Statistics 1999 Edition* (Chicago, 1999).

Reality 2: Importance of Trustworthiness and Professional Values

Trustworthiness is particularly salient in health care because the receipt of timely, skillful, and appropriate services may be a matter of life and death for patients who are often poorly situated to judge the appropriateness or quality of needed services. Such patients are vulnerable to unscrupulous or incompetent service providers, who may misdiagnose symptoms, provide unnecessary services, or skimp on quality of care. Third-party payers are also quite vulnerable to fraud and abuse.

Because nonprofit health care organizations are prohibited from distributing profits to those who control the organization, they have been posited to be less likely than for-profits to exploit the vulnerabilities of patients for economic gain.[3] There is some evidence that nonprofit health care providers are more trusted by patients and are, at least under certain conditions, more trustworthy in their behavior than are for-profits.[4] The question of comparative trustworthiness, however, has received little attention from researchers or policymakers. Although assuring the trustworthiness of care is a major purpose of the extensive regulatory framework under which health care organizations operate, trustworthiness has never been offered as a reason for granting nonprofit organizations tax-exempt status.

It has been suggested that the supposed trustworthiness advantage of nonprofit organizations is largely irrelevant in health care since patients have a physician whose training and professional values convey a sense of responsibility for protecting the patient and who will presumably deter organizational actions that do not serve the patient's interests.[5] However, for several reasons, professionalism is quite incomplete as a protector of vulnerable patients in health care settings. Many patients have no identified physician. Physician autonomy has declined in the face of managed care, and concern has grown about physicians' economic and organizational entanglements that create the appearance of conflicts of interest.[6] Moreover, many decisions that affect patient care are organizational in nature and outside the physician's control (such as the ratio of nurses to patients on a hospital floor). Finally, health care organizations that provide highly routinized services (such as clinical labs, dialysis centers, insurance claims processing, and custodial long-term care) may not have to accommodate to professional values. For all of these reasons, *organizational* as well as professional values may be important when services are being provided to vulnerable populations.

It has also been suggested that nonprofit ownership promotes organizational objectives that are more compatible with professional norms than is for-profit ownership.[7] This, too, might make nonprofits more trustworthy from the patient's standpoint. However, as noted later, evidence about this is quite limited and mixed.

Trustworthiness concerns are not confined to the patient's circumstances. Because expensive medical services are impossible for individuals to plan and budget for, systems of third-party payment are necessary in medical care. But third-party payers are poorly situated to assess the necessity and quality of the services for which they are asked to pay, so third-party payment systems have also relied heavily on trust and are vulnerable to fraud.[8] With health care costs threatening to break the budget among both public and private purchasers, fraud has become a serious problem.[9] Although some fraudulent activities have occurred among nonprofit providers, experience suggests that fraud as a large-scale *organizational* strategy for generating profits is most likely to occur among for-profit organizations.[10] Indeed, in recent years leading investor-owned companies from the hospital, psychiatric hospital, nursing home, and dialysis industries all have agreed to pay penalties in the hundreds of millions of dollars to settle Medicare fraud charges.[11] Four such settlements occurred in 2000 alone. Moreover, there is evidence that nonprofit hospitals are less aggressive in seeking to maximize revenues generated from third-party payers than are their for-profit counterparts,[12] although it is not clear whether this pattern holds across all nonprofit services.

In short, there is reason to believe that the nonprofit form offers advantages in the health arena due to the special need for trust in this field and the inadequacy of alternative ways to provide it.

Reality 3: An Extremely Dynamic Arena

The health care field is characterized by specialized knowledge, high client expectations, extensive technological development, and rapid change embodied in the development of new services, new treatment capacities, and new organizational infrastructure. A continued push for innovation involves cycles of new technologies, changing concepts of appropriate care, and new or expanded government and private funding programs that open or expand the market for particular services (for example, in recent decades, hemodialysis and hospice care). Cost containment pressures have created a different source of change, leading to new payment methods and organizational arrangements (for example, managed care plans). The dynamism of health care places enormous pressures on the organizations that provide health services to adapt to changing technologies and expectations. This, in turn, means that hospitals and other health care organizations are very capital intensive, requiring regular infusions of capital.

Reality 4: A Capital-Intensive Market Good

To fund their operating costs, America's nonprofit health care institutions for more than a century have relied heavily on—and competed for—revenues generated from the sale of services.[13] Charitable contributions now account for only a very few percentage points of most nonprofits' revenues. Institutions that once competed primarily on the basis of their reputation, location, and the historical loyalty of doctors and patients find third-party purchasers emphasizing price when selecting among providers of services. For nonprofits in health care, survival requires commercial success in a crowded marketplace that often includes for-profit competitors.

The capital needs of health care organizations lend additional significance to this competitive reality. Most of today's nonprofits meet their capital needs with retained earnings and borrowed money. The availability and the cost of debt are a direct function of an organization's creditworthiness, evaluated in cold economic terms. Bond-rating firms on Wall Street do not take favorable notice of an institution's service to the community.[14] Their concern is sound financial performance, measured in terms of keeping costs lower than the revenues generated through the sale of services. Depending on private capital while selling services in the marketplace means that nonprofit health care organizations face the same constraints that any business does.

Reality 5: Charitable Roots Matter

The historical roots of today's health care organizations lie in eighteenth- and nineteenth-century charitable initiatives created to serve the poor and infirm.[15] It is no coincidence that nonprofit health care organizations are tax-exempt under federal law as *charitable* organizations. The need for charity care has never disappeared. The early hospital insurance programs were not created until the 1930s, but this private insurance was tied to employment and thus did not cover large groups where health care needs were high and ability to pay was low, including the elderly, the disabled, and poor women with dependent children. These groups were not covered until Medicare and Medicaid were passed in 1965, and it was only then that health care began to attract interest from serious investors. But the system of health insurance remains incomplete, with 15 percent of the population (44 million people) uninsured and millions more with seriously inadequate health insurance. Notwithstanding the commercial, competitive nature of today's health care, expectations of charitability continue to apply to nonprofit health care organizations. The coherence and strength of these expectations vary by type of institution and locale, and some institutions clearly feel them more strongly than others. Not all nonprofits have meaningful charitable origins. But understanding the modern meaning of health care's charitable roots is a key challenge for particular institutions and for the field itself.

Reality 6: A Policy-Sensitive Field

Although operating in a market context, American health care is shaped by government policy. Dozens of local, state, and federal agencies have regulatory oversight of the standards of quality and business practices of health care organizations. In addition, the federal and state governments influence the health care system through their requirements as purchasers of care; the Medicare and Medicaid programs pay for a combined 28 percent of all medical care. Public policy also affects countless other important matters, such as the terms in which relationships between providers and private insurers are negotiated. Both new funding programs and relatively small and obscure changes in regulatory details can produce important changes in organizational behavior or even cause shifts in the mix of ownership in a particular domain within health care. Over the past decade, public policy has shown substantially more concern about issues pertaining to the ownership of health care organizations—particularly the justification of nonprofits' tax exemption and the sale of nonprofits to for-profit purchasers.

Recent Challenges

The realities we just described shape and intensify the challenges that face today's nonprofit organizations in health care. Four of the most important arise from (a) institutional change and growing constraints on the services that non-profit health care organizations provide, (b) the changing nature of for-profit competition, (c) new expectations regarding accountability, and (d) changing ideas about health and health care. This section examines each of these challenges in turn.

Fiscal Pressures and Institutional Constraints

Health care organizations have been shaped in many ways by the means of paying for medical care. Once the Medicare and Medicaid programs were added in 1965 to the existing system of employment-based health insurance and provided coverage to the elderly, disabled, and many of the poor, more than 85 percent of Americans had an arrangement whereby someone else paid for some or all of their medical services. This system of third-party payment facilitated the rapid growth in health care expenditures that brought U.S. health care costs from 5 percent of gross national product (GNP) in 1960 to 14 percent by the mid-1990s.

The system of third-party payment has another side, however. Because a small number of third-party payers (a term that includes insurance companies, HMOs and managed care organizations, and Medicare and Medicaid) generally account for the bulk of health organizations' revenues, these purchasers have great influence, and changes in their policies and practices can quickly change the circumstances of providers.

Recently, such changes have been significant. Prior to the 1980s, Medicare, Medicaid, and the health insurance industry had very inadequate means of controlling what they paid for, how much they paid for it, or both. Medicare reimbursed hospitals for allowable costs and had difficulty because of the resulting incentive to generate more costs. Medicaid paid via a fee schedule but had little means of controlling the provision of unnecessary care. Payments to institutions from insurance companies were based on the institutions' *bills*, so there was no constraint on cost there. Denying payment for "unnecessary" services that had been rendered to a beneficiary was difficult because the bill would then be sent to the insured person who could be expected to complain to his or her employer, the insurance commissioner, or both. As a Wall Street analyst reportedly said of the investor-owned hospital companies in the 1970s, it would have been difficult *not* to make money in this industry.

Several institutional changes occurred in response to this untenable situation. They included new payment methods, new oversight and accountability methods, new organizational forms, and consolidation among payers. For example, in 1983 Medicare replaced cost-based reimbursement with a per case payment methodology, enabling annual decisions to be made regarding whether and how much rates would be changed. New types of managed care organizations came into being that had capacities to carry out various forms of utilization review functions, including prior authorizations of elective hospitalizations and specialty referrals, and reviews of the appropriateness of services and patterns of care.[16] Denial of payment for services deemed to be medically unnecessary became possible and provoked the now familiar outrage among providers and patients. Consolidation took place in two broad forms. First was the enrollment of insured populations into health plans that both provided managed care functions and negotiated terms with providers. Second was the consolidation among insurers and managed care organizations themselves.

These changes had several consequences:

—Providers lost much of their power to pass along cost increases. Medicare sets its own rates, and managed care plans have consolidated in many markets and are tough negotiators.

—The effective decisions regarding where certain services will be purchased moved into different and fewer hands and have resulted in revenue losses for some providers. For example, a large health plan may contract with a single provider to do all of its CAT scans or all of its laboratory work, thereby eliminating that source of revenue for other providers.

—Obtaining payment for services already provided became a complex process for many institutions, with the validity of claims for payment being subject to challenge on many grounds. Provider complaints about slow payment and unjustified denials of payment led several states in recent years to impose penalties on payers for nonpayment of "clean" claims within a certain interval (for example, ninety days).

Concern has also grown that the various constraints introduced by third-party payers threaten the ability of nonprofit providers to finance charitable or community-benefit activities that have been supported in part from the flow of patient care dollars. Studies have shown, for example, that relatively few managed care plans are willing to pay for activities related to research or medical education.[17] Plans that focus on the profitability of their operations may avoid contracting with providers who treat many indigent or expensive patients. Recent studies have documented that in areas with the most extensive managed care penetration, the amount of uncompensated medical care that is provided declines, and dumping (economically motivated discharges) of unprofitable patients increases.[18]

But the institutional changes brought about by managed care also represent a potentially new and important role for nonprofit health care. Because managed care organizations can have a profound impact on the delivery of medical services, questions have been raised about risks associated with the exercise of this powerful role by organizations motivated primarily by the profit motive. Industry surveys continue to show that nonprofit plans are the highest rated, and the only available systematic comparison of data on plan performance shows that nonprofit plans tend to outperform for-profit plans.[19] To date, however, policymakers remain uncertain about whether these differences justify preferential treatment for nonprofit enterprise in this arena of American medicine.

Expanded For-Profit Competition

A second major challenge facing nonprofit health care organizations stems from for-profit competition. The nature of competition from for-profits has changed in several ways over the past twenty to thirty years. For-profit firms have become much more prominent in health care. A different form of organization has become dominant among them, with investor-owned corporations replacing local proprietors as the typical owners. And for-profits have introduced competition in the public policy arena as well as in the marketplace.

DOMAINS OF FOR-PROFIT EXPANSION. Of the domains within the health care field that are shown in table 2-1, seven experienced substantial for-profit expansion over the past fifteen years. In several domains, for-profit firms displaced nonprofits as the predominant form of ownership. Among HMOs, the for-profit share expanded from 35 percent in 1985 to 74 percent in 1997. Among home health centers, it went from 36 to 67 percent, with similar figures seen among dialysis centers. And among rehabilitation hospitals, the for-profit share jumped from 15 percent in 1985 to 58 percent in 1998. For-profits gained significant ground on nonprofits in a number of additional fields, such as outpatient mental health clinics, hospice programs, and psychiatric hospitals.

The growing prominence of the for-profit sector in health care has presented several challenges for the nonprofit sector.[20] For many individual nonprofits, there has been a *competitive* challenge from organizations that are frequently much more active and sophisticated in marketing. In some fields, the for-profits also have presented a *takeover* challenge, with for-profit organizations aggressively seeking to gain market share through the purchase of existing nonprofit firms. Finally, the growth of for-profits has sometimes presented a *legitimacy* challenge to nonprofits, as some research has shown that the measurable charitable activities of tax-exempt nonprofits differ little from those of their tax-paying for-profit counterparts.

THE SHIFT TO INVESTOR OWNERSHIP. Until recent decades, for-profit health care organizations were generally locally owner-operated facilities, as with the doctor-owned hospitals and mom-and-pop nursing homes. The creation of Medicare and Medicaid in 1965 created incentives that led to the establishment and growth of hospital and nursing home companies owned by investors, most of whom had little or no contact with or personal knowledge of the facilities owned by their company.[21] Publicly traded, investor-owned companies that own multiple facilities have become typical of the for-profit sector in virtually all domains within health care, including hospitals, nursing homes, HMOs, dialysis centers, and even hospices.

The shift from proprietary to investor ownership has had several important consequences for nonprofits. These new organizations are generally much better capitalized than the proprietary organizations were, and they compete much more effectively. The sale of a marginal proprietary facility to an investor-owned company that then renovated or replaced it has been a common event. Moreover, companies that own multiple facilities are able to bring in more sophisticated management than was typical of proprietary institutions and are able to gain some advantages of scale and scope. Finally, in some domains, particularly those pertaining to managed care, size is important both in gaining access to certain markets (for example, national corporations) and in negotiating favorable terms with suppliers (for example, service providers).

Investor ownership also changes the dynamics of for-profit involvement. The stock price of publicly traded companies is a function of both the company's earnings and investors' expectations of future earnings. Growth is therefore rewarded. Since a company's access to capital and the wealth of its executives are a function of stock price, investor-owned corporations have strong incentives to grow. The most rapid path toward earnings growth is from acquisitions, and many of the publicly traded health care companies have gone through periods of omnivorous growth, fed by high stock prices, which were fed, in turn, by further growth. In some domains, strong pressures and enticements for nonprofits to sell have resulted when companies were in such a growth period. However, when that growth is curtailed by stagnant demand, scandal, or other barriers to acquiring new facilities, the stock value of the corporation can decline precipitously.[22] Within just the past two decades, virtually all investor-owned health service companies have experienced this boom-bust cycle. It has led to the resale, closure, or conversion back to nonprofit status of many for-profit facilities, particularly hospitals. A similar phenomenon has been evident in the massive withdrawal in 2000 and 2001 of for-profit HMOs from participation in Medicare, as they did from Medicaid in the late 1990s. When continuity of medical care is important for patients, the closure of facilities during the bust periods can seriously disrupt treatment and threaten patient well-being.

COMPETITION IN THE PUBLIC POLICY ARENA. The shift to investor-owned corporations has also increased the political influence of the for-profit sector. Large corporations can and do use their financial resources to influence regulatory actions, policy decisions, and even electoral outcomes at the local, state, and national levels.[23] In many areas, the interests of for-profit and nonprofit organizations diverge. In our own research, we have learned of lobbying activities encouraging state and local attacks on nonprofit hospitals' tax exemptions and against new state laws to regulate the sale of nonprofit hospitals to for-profit purchasers. At the federal level, the trade association of for-profit hospitals has sought rule changes to obtain, from a fixed pot of money from which all hospitals are paid, reimbursement to for-profit hospitals from Medicare for the costs of local property tax payments. Multiple-state corporations often can circumvent state regulation, either by shifting certain activities to less regulated states or by threatening to avoid a state entirely if regulations are enforced against them.

New Expectations for Accountability

In addition to experiencing heightened competition and financial pressures, many types of nonprofit health care organizations are also facing increased accountability pressures, with demands mounting for documentation to justify the tax and other benefits they receive as nonprofit institutions.

This new demand for accountability has arisen from several sources. Legal scholars have challenged the rationale for tax exemptions, with hospitals often cited as a case in point.[24] A body of empirical research developed in the 1980s showed only modest and inconsistent differences between for-profit and nonprofit hospitals regarding the amount of uncompensated care that they provided.[25] This all occurred in the context of a growing American sense of distrust in all social institutions,[26] with the public expecting to see evidence to back up institutional claims about social benefits. Within the health care field, the demand for accountability has been embodied in the growing use of report cards for grading the performance of various organizations, particularly HMOs. The expansion of for-profit involvement in the health field has helped to stimulate this demand, raising awareness of providers' mixed motives and also creating an organized political interest with a stake in raising doubts about nonprofits' tax exemptions or other forms of preferential treatment that create "unfair" competition.[27] Beneficiaries of nonprofits' charitable and community service activities (indigent patients, those with the most complex and costly cases, those in need of unprofitable services, those who benefit from experimental techniques) rarely have an equivalent capacity to organize and voice their concerns in a politically effective manner. Thus, ironically, arguments about the need to eliminate tax exemptions so as to create a level playing field in the provision of health services have often been made in the absence of a level playing field in political representation.

Several efforts have been launched in recent years to increase the accountability of nonprofit health care providers, particularly regarding their presumed charitable mission. At the federal level, a congressionally mandated study by the General Accounting Office in 1990 compared the amount of charity care provided by hospitals in five states with the value of their federal tax exemptions.[28] Although most passed this test, it was apparent that not all hospitals met this standard. Three pieces of federal legislation that would have toughened the standards for tax exemptions for hospitals were proposed in 1990, but none passed. Less demanding standards were incorporated in President Clinton's ill-fated health reform proposals in 1994.

More meaningful change has occurred at the state level. New requirements pertaining to charitable status have been implemented in some twenty states in recent years and debated in several others.[29] Primarily applying to hospitals, these state regulations use one or both of two approaches. One requires nonprofits to assess community needs and develop plans for addressing them. The other requires reporting on the amount of charity care that is provided.

THE CHANGING DEFINITIONS OF CHARITY. Underlying the debates over the accountability of nonprofit health providers has been a growing confusion about what should constitute charitability and community service for nonprofits in the health care arena. As noted, nonprofits in health care have a history of providing free or reduced-price care to people who lack the means to pay. Moreover, many of today's nonprofit hospitals benefited from federal Hill-Burton construction funds, which came attached with obligations (often poorly enforced) that hospitals provide a certain level of free care. Nonprofit health care organizations have always been tax-exempt as *charitable* organizations.

But the definition of charity in the health care field has undergone important changes over the years. First, after the enactment of Medicare and Medicaid in 1965, the number of Americans without health insurance declined dramatically, and the expectations applied to nonprofit health care facilities changed. In 1969 the Internal Revenue Service (IRS) changed the criteria for tax exemption for hospitals (and, by extension, for other health care organizations) from a definition that emphasized serving the poor (a so-called relief-of-poverty definition of charity) to a definition that emphasized providing health services to the community at large (the community-benefit standard). The community-benefit definition did not reference service to patients who were unable to afford medical services. The new public programs—particularly Medicaid—often reimbursed treatment at a sufficiently low rate that health care providers could lose money even on ostensibly insured patients. Serving such patients could be seen as providing a partially charitable activity, although one that is difficult to document in a satisfactory way.

Second, health care is different from many other services in that the cost of the service depends to a great extent on the idiosyncratic characteristics of the individual patient. Patients with more complex conditions and multiple co-morbidities are generally much more expensive to treat. But per case payment systems typically do not adjust, or adjust only partially, for complexity of conditions. Consequently, patients with the most complex cases may be unprofitable, even when they have insurance. Serving them may again be a form of charitable activity that is difficult to document effectively.[30]

Complicating matters further is the fact that health care institutions do not necessarily have a pool of funds available for charity care. Charitable contributions have become a small part of the average nonprofit hospital's revenues, and many other types of nonprofit health care organizations may receive lesser charitable contributions than do hospitals. While private contributions accounted for 18 percent of the revenues of the nonprofit sector as a whole (including religious congregations), only 4 percent of the revenues of organizations that provide health services came from contributions, less than half of the share fifteen years earlier.[31] For many institutions, surplus revenues from paying patients have been a source of funds for subsidizing research, education, and charity care. But this source has been vulnerable to changes in the economic environment brought about by the strategies of large purchasers of care.

COMPETING DEMANDS FOR ORGANIZATIONAL SURPLUS. With community benefit defined broadly enough to include a variety of health promotion and disease prevention activities that have nothing to do with providing free care to the needy, judgments about whether health institutions are operating in a way that serves the community, and therefore whether they deserve their tax-exempt status, become increasingly difficult. Many legitimate demands compete for the limited surplus that organizations are able to generate. In an academic medical center, for example, a surplus might be used to pay for the care of indigent patients, to cover the expenses associated with high-cost, complex treatments, to support research or medical education, to develop new services that are not yet covered by insurance, or to engage in a host of other activities in the community that have health-related consequences. These activities might all be seen as community benefits. Only some would be viewed as charity care. Moreover, only some might count under the community-benefit criteria established by state legislatures or attorneys general, and only some might benefit the community within which the hospital is located, as opposed to the broader health care system or country as a whole. No established criteria in law or the academic literature make it clear which, if any, of these activities are most compatible with a nonprofit mission.

Beyond this, there is a tension between approaches to accountability that rely on *countable* forms of community benefit and many of the newly emerging concepts of community benefit.[32] Counting the number of indigent patients who have received treatment is easy compared to measuring the benefits that result from greater trustworthiness, preserving professional ethics in patient care, or addressing the social determinants of health. Yet these forms of community benefit may be just as important.

THE GOALS OF THIRD-PARTY PURCHASERS. Even if a consensus were achieved within a health care institution about the appropriate types of community-benefit activities to support, it is not clear that the third-party payers who finance health care institutions would be agreeable. Indeed, the ability of institutions to generate a surplus depends crucially on the objectives of third-party purchasers. If purchasers value community service and see nonprofit enterprises as making distinctive contributions to the community, they might prefer to contract with nonprofits for services, perhaps even at prices that exceed those that would be paid to a for-profit firm that is less oriented toward community benefit. Conversely, if a purchaser were indifferent to community benefit, it would be unwilling to pay nonprofits a premium on market prices. In other words, the objectives of purchasers—more specifically, their expectations for nonprofit behavior—may play a crucial role in sustaining ownership-related differences in performance. Yet almost nothing is known about these expectations or how they might be influenced.

Changing Interpretations of Health and Health Care

Finally, nonprofit health care providers have been affected by a broader set of changes in American medicine over the past two decades. These changes have altered the nature of health services and the norms of performance against which those services are judged.

THE GROWTH OF CONSUMER CHOICE IN MEDICAL CARE. One of these changes has been the change in public policies and private practices to encourage individuals to assume greater responsibility for choosing among health insurance plans. For example, the federal HMO Act encouraged employers to offer employees choices among plans. Public programs such as Medicare and Medicaid began to incorporate similar choices in the mid-1980s, and the role of consumer choice was expanded considerably in the 1990s.[33]

Consumer choice is lauded as empowering individuals by providing them with control over the types of medical care they consider most important. But consumer empowerment also creates the potential for misinformed choices and problematic consequences if individuals act on insufficient or inaccurate information about the options they face. To the extent that nonprofit organizations have less incentive to misrepresent their performance, a larger nonprofit presence may enhance the odds that consumers can make effective decisions.

THE DEPROFESSIONALIZATION OF MEDICAL SERVICES. The professional training of health providers, particularly physicians, has always emphasized the vulnerability of patients and hence the need to instill not only technical competence but also a fiduciary ethic, a concern for protecting the well-being of patients.[34] To the extent that these professional norms held, the influence of professionals within health care organizations could mitigate some of the dangers that the profit motive could pose to patients.[35] Nonprofit ownership has been depicted as promoting organizational objectives that are more compatible with such professional norms than is for-profit ownership,[36] although the evidence on this is mixed. Some studies find that nonprofit health care providers allow for greater professional *autonomy* (for example, the freedom to practice without organizational constraints),[37] although others suggest that there are few ownership-related differences in professional *authority* (influence over organizational policies).[38]

Some three decades ago cracks began to appear in the foundation on which claims to the authority of medical professionals had been erected. "Medicine, like many other American institutions, suffered a stunning loss of confidence in the 1970s."[39] By the mid-1980s, both sociologists and doctors themselves were writing about the "deprofessionalization" of medicine, as practitioners lost autonomy under the oversight of managed care plans,[40] and public confidence in the motives of the profession continued to erode.[41] By the mid-1990s, a sociologist studying the professions in a number of different countries would write, "No profession in our sample has flown quite as high in guild power and control as American medicine, and few have fallen as fast."[42]

The challenge to professionalism in American medicine holds two potential implications for the role of nonprofit enterprise in this field. First, if professionals become less willing or able to act as effective agents for their patients (or are so perceived by those patients), the trustworthiness of health care *organizations* becomes increasingly important for protecting patients from exploitation. Second, as professional autonomy and authority are circumscribed by managed care arrangements, the motives of managed care plans become increasingly important. If, as some limited evidence suggests, nonprofit plans are more likely to preserve professional prerogatives, ownership may play an important, albeit indirect, role in safeguarding patient welfare.[43]

NEW UNDERSTANDING OF THE DETERMINANTS OF POPULATION HEALTH. A third important change in the practice of medicine has involved a change in our understanding of the causes of ill health. Since the beginning of the twentieth century, public health advocates have recognized the importance of nonclinical factors, including economic, social, and environmental conditions, in shaping the health of populations.[44] But these perspectives have been incorporated only episodically into health policy, which remained focused on the delivery of medical care and the ways in which individual behaviors affect the prospects for health, downplaying the role of community infrastructure, corporate practices, or other social factors.[45]

This omission has begun to change as policymakers have become more aware of evidence linking health to societal characteristics and grown increasingly frustrated by the modest returns from high levels of spending on medical care.[46] For example, the recent literature contains a compelling accumulation of evidence that community characteristics exert a powerful, independent influence on the health of residents.[47] The important role of community resources has been reinforced by the growing prevalence of chronic conditions.[48] The success of interventions for people with chronic conditions often depends on the availability of social and other health-related services in the community as well as on the willingness of family caregivers to help meet relatives' needs.[49]

Recognizing these social determinants suggests avenues for redirecting the resources that nonprofit health care agencies devote to community-benefit activities. For example, the most effective approach to improving the health of residents in low-income communities may not involve the provision of charitable medical services to the infirm. Instead, it may require the allocation of resources to programs designed to improve the nutritional content of the meals in neighborhood restaurants, reducing the prevalence of local traffic accidents, or installing smoke detectors in residences whose inhabitants cannot otherwise afford them.[50]

Nonprofit Responses to the Challenges They Face

How have these challenges affected the role of nonprofits in the health field? Broadly speaking, three sets of responses are evident. First, the role of nonprofits in various domains of the health field has shifted in response to the entry of well-financed for-profit organizations, although this has varied greatly by domain. Second, changes have taken place in the structure and practices of nonprofit providers, mostly in the direction of convergence with for-profit providers. And third, efforts have been made to maintain a distinctive role for nonprofits. Each of these responses is considered in the following subsections.

Shifts in the Nonprofit Role

As shown in table 2-1, several domains within health care have undergone a rapid transformation from predominantly nonprofit to predominantly for-profit ownership. This pattern is unusual within the nonprofit sector, and it is important to understand what drove this shift and what it might portend for the future of nonprofit involvement in this field and potentially in others.

Having worked in the health field for roughly two decades, we think that such understanding cannot be derived from any existing general theory about the role of nonprofit organizations or about the types of social needs that nonprofit organizations meet, whether these be theories focusing on the "public goods" character of the services, the asymmetries of information between client and service provider,[51] or the inability of organizations to distribute their surplus. Nor does the record support the view that the entry or growth of a for-profit element in a nonprofit field initiates a cascade that leads to the elimination of the presence of nonprofits. To the contrary, table 2-1 shows that, while for-profits are replacing, or at least outdistancing, nonprofits in a number of health domains, in other domains—for example, nursing home care and general hospitals—nonprofits have been either holding their own or increasing their market share. Even in most of the fields in which the share of nonprofits has been declining, the absolute number of nonprofit organizations has been increasing.

All of this suggests a need to complement theoretical explanations about the reasons for the presence of nonprofit or for-profit organizations in a field with a more careful understanding of the varying contexts within which services are provided, the factors that have accounted for the rapid growth of the for-profit sector in several domains, and the reasons for the persistence or even resurgence of nonprofits in others.

Our examination of the health care experience suggests that patterns of ownership appear to be influenced by a combination of three contextual factors—the historical era in which a service first emerges, prevailing market conditions, and government policies that may intentionally or unintentionally advantage certain types of providers.

DOMAINS OF FOR-PROFIT EXPANSION. The interplay of historical origins, market conditions, and government policies can be seen vividly in the experience of the four health care domains in which for-profits came to outdistance nonprofits between the mid-1980s and the late 1990s—dialysis centers, rehabilitation hospitals, home health agencies, and HMOs. In part, these four domains lend credence to a view advanced by scholars fifteen years ago that for-profit growth is a result of the inability or failure of nonprofit providers (as a result of either restricted access to capital or weak entrepreneurial incentives) to respond quickly to substantial increases in demand for their services.[52] All of the health care domains that experienced dramatic for-profit expansion in the 1980s and 1990s did so in the context of a large growth in the total number of organizations, which reflected a substantial increase in the number of patients with resources to pay for services.

Several of these domains were also affected by a second factor that has influenced ownership patterns in recent decades—the adoption by federal policymakers of explicit policies that either inhibited the growth of nonprofit organizations or stimulated the expansion of their for-profit competitors. These policies reflected insensitivity, or perhaps even skepticism, among policymakers about the merits of nonprofit enterprise in medical care.[53]

Dialysis centers provide a clear example of the pattern of for-profit expansion following policy reforms that stimulated demand for services. As of 1970, less than 5 percent of all dialysis—which was then a very new technology—was provided under for-profit auspices.[54] In 1972, patients suffering from chronic kidney failure gained coverage for treatment under Medicare through passage of the federal end-stage renal disease program. The number of patients whose care was paid for by this program immediately surged and has increased since then at a relatively steady 7–9 percent a year.[55] As the number of providers of dialysis services grew, the market share of for-profit agencies reached 20 percent by 1977 and continued to grow, reaching 68 percent by 1997.

For *rehabilitation hospitals*, the rapid increase in demand was partially a product of technology and partially a result of policy change. Technological improvements in physical medicine had led over many years to much more concerted efforts to rehabilitate patients with severe head and spinal cord injuries. Once Medicare shifted to paying hospitals on a per case basis in 1983, patients requiring rehabilitation services began to be transferred out of acute care beds and into rehabilitation units (often in the same hospital) or into rehabilitation hospitals. This led to almost a tripling in the number of rehabilitation hospitals over the next fifteen years and a corresponding increase in the market share of for-profit facilities.

For *home health care*, higher demand was again in part the result of new technology, which made it possible to provide services in the home that had once required hospitalization. New drug infusion equipment was high on this list. In addition, Medicare's prospective payment system for hospitals stimulated demand by creating powerful incentives for the rapid discharge of hospitalized patients; many of these patients still needed services, which could be provided at home. Demand was stimulated further by a 1989 court case that required the Health Care Financing Administration (the agency that administered the Medicare and Medicaid programs) to apply less restrictive standards for qualifying Medicare beneficiaries for home care.

Ownership mix among home health care providers was also affected by policies that were targeted to form of ownership. Prior to 1981, for-profit home care agencies were required to have state licensure in order to participate in Medicare. This quality-of-care protection was not required of nonprofit agencies. Many states did not have licensure procedures for home care agencies, so this regulation inhibited the expansion of for-profit home care. It was repealed early in the Reagan administration, opening the market to rapid entry by for-profit agencies at the same time that changes in the rules for hospital payment were stimulating demand.

In the case of *health maintenance organizations*, the expansion of the for-profit role that occurred in the 1980s was a product of a number of policy decisions. One was the discontinuance of a federal program that had provided start-up capital for nonprofit HMOs, making it difficult for the nonprofit sector to respond to growing demand. Coupled with this were IRS reservations about whether nonprofit HMOs deserved tax exemptions; in the IRS view, HMOs provided *private* benefits (either to the enrolled population or to physicians) rather than benefits to the community at large, as exemption required. Whereas the developers of new plans in the 1970s had reasons to choose the nonprofit form (to secure funding under the HMO Act), in the 1980s the federal government had become an obstacle to the creation of new nonprofit plans since any initiative to create a new plan faced considerable uncertainty about whether it would be able to obtain a tax exemption. Finally, lax oversight at the state level facilitated the conversion of plans from nonprofit to for-profit. Approximately one-third of nonprofit HMOs converted to for-profits in the 1980s, either by selling their assets to a for-profit purchaser or by reorganizing the corporation.[56] For-profit conversions of HMOs were motivated both by their need for capital to facilitate growth and by insiders' ability to acquire the assets at bargain prices. Few states had experience with for-profit conversions, and most had little or no regulatory staff to review such transactions, which apparently often occurred for much less than fair market value.[57]

DOMAINS OF NONPROFIT PERSISTENCE OR RESURGENCE. Although powerful forces are at work in the health field to encourage the growth of for-profit involvement, often at the expense of nonprofit providers, these forces are by no means irresistible or inevitable. The cases of general hospitals, hospice programs, nursing homes, and psychiatric hospitals provide examples of periods of nonprofit persistence, nonprofit resurgence, and for-profit decline. The patterns exhibited here are instructive.

General hospitals constitute a domain in which nonprofit providers have resisted the pressures of for-profit incursion. Despite fears in the past two decades that these facilities would be swallowed by the capacious maws of large for-profit hospital corporations,[58] hospitals continue to be approximately 60 percent under private nonprofit auspices, a figure that has remained roughly constant for more than thirty years, even as the number of hospitals in the country has shrunk substantially.

Hospitals have had mixed ownership since the first surveys were conducted early in the twentieth century. The first surveys reported that about half of all hospitals were for-profit—mostly small hospitals owned by individual doctors and operated as an adjunct to their offices.[59] As the technology of health care developed through the century and as quality and life safety rules became more demanding, operation of these small-scale hospitals became increasingly difficult. In each survey that was done, the for-profit sector was smaller—36 percent in 1928, 25 percent in 1941, 18 percent in 1950, and 12–14 percent when the Medicare law passed in 1965.[60] Toward the end, part of this decline can be attributed to the Hill-Burton program, a postwar federal initiative that subsidized the construction of nonprofit hospitals.

As with several other domains, equity capital was attracted to hospitals by the investment opportunity resulting from the passage of Medicare and Medicaid. Not only did these programs provide health insurance for the elderly and the poor, but Medicare also included provisions that facilitated access to capital for hospitals and nursing homes, treating capital costs (interest, depreciation, and, for for-profits, return on equity) as reimbursable expenses under the cost-based reimbursement system of paying for services. Investor-owned hospital companies began to be formed in the middle to late 1960s.[61]

The ability of for-profit organizations to grow in the acute care hospital field was limited by several factors, however. First, no shortage of hospital beds appeared after the Medicare and Medicaid programs came on line.[62] After almost twenty years of federal Hill-Burton program support for hospital construction, the country's ample stock of hospitals and beds was easily able to absorb the 5–10 percent increase in utilization that occurred. Second, the new programs enhanced the financial health of nonprofit hospitals and facilitated their access to debt as a source of capital. Their boards of trustees had little reason to consider the sale of their hospitals. Third, by the time that the initial set of investor-owned companies began to develop some real size and heft in the mid-1970s, the federal government and the states had put in place a health planning program under which a certificate of need had to be obtained before a new hospital could be constructed.

Thus, although the Medicare and Medicaid programs created a stimulus for demand, even well-capitalized companies faced limited paths for growth in the hospital domain. Nevertheless, new investor-owned hospital companies did grow: they (a) signed contracts to manage nonprofit and public hospitals, (b) acquired most of the remaining proprietary hospitals owned by physicians, (c) built specialized institutions such as psychiatric facilities, and (d) built new community hospitals in parts of the country that were experiencing rapid population growth and had a relatively underdeveloped nonprofit infrastructure. As a consequence, the share of hospital beds that were for-profit increased, roughly doubling (from 6 to 11 percent) between the mid-1960s and the mid-1990s, with a corresponding decline in public (but not nonprofit) hospitals.

To be sure, twice in the past twenty years, changes in the economic environment produced a degree of panic among nonprofit hospitals and prompted the sale of some nonprofit hospitals to for-profit purchasers. The first wave occurred in the early 1980s when Medicare's prospective payment system was coming into place. Deeply worried about their institutions' ability to cope with the new payment method, which contained no assurances that a hospital's costs of caring for Medicare patients would be covered, the trustees of some nonprofit hospitals sold out to the rapidly growing investor-owned hospital companies, which had high stock prices and abundant capital. So dire were the predictions that hospital care in the United States would go entirely for-profit that the Institute of Medicine (IOM) at the National Academy of Sciences appointed an expert panel to assess the likely consequences.[63] When the IOM report was published in 1986, however, the majority of the panel concluded that the risk of a for-profit takeover was seriously overstated. By then, the hospital companies had experienced serious setbacks.[64] Having learned well the tricks of maximizing revenues under the cost-based reimbursement system, for-profit companies struggled under the new payment system. The companies' high stock prices came back to earth as a result, and some of their hospitals closed, while some reverted to nonprofit control.

The second wave of panic selling by nonprofit hospitals occurred in the mid-1990s. Again there was a serious threat to the hospitals' economic well-being. This time it was the growth and increasing aggressiveness of managed care. And, again, some investor-owned companies (most notably, Columbia/HCA and Tenet) grew rapidly by acquiring the remnants of the struggling companies from the 1980s and, as a consequence, had high stock prices and abundant capital. These companies became active purchasers of nonprofit hospitals, and Richard Scott, chief executive officer of Columbia/HCA, launched outspoken attacks on the legitimacy of tax exemptions for nonprofit hospitals. Then, in early 1997, Columbia/HCA became enmeshed in a series of major investigations by government agencies and insurance companies into allegations of fraud involving over-billing and charging for unnecessary services.[65] The company's stock price tumbled, Scott was fired, and the company became a net seller of hospitals, some of which again became nonprofit. The company made a $745 million payment to settle the federal fraud case in 2000, and it also followed the strategy used by previously discredited companies of changing its name.

These two waves of highly publicized acquisitions of nonprofit hospitals by for-profit companies attracted considerable controversy, and by the late 1990s some twenty-five states had adopted legal reforms regarding sales of nonprofit hospitals. These reforms were designed to increase public scrutiny and mitigate conflicts of interest. Yet despite all the concern about the activities of investor-owned hospital companies, the overall composition of the hospital domain changed very little.[66] Some for-profit acquisitions eventually turned into closures, and some conversions occurred in the opposite direction.[67]

Legislation created a growth opportunity for *hospice services* in the early 1980s that appears similar to examples where rapid for-profit expansion ensued, particularly renal dialysis services. As with dialysis, the legal change provided Medicare payment (beginning in 1983) for a service in a new field that was almost entirely nonprofit (only 2 percent of hospice programs were operating under for-profit auspices in the early 1980s).[68] Yet this new source of payment for services led to a much more limited initial for-profit increase among hospice providers than had occurred for dialysis services.

Two factors appear to account for the difference. First, in contrast to the dialysis case, more than 1,000 nonprofit hospice programs were already in operation by the time Medicare coverage was enacted. The hospice concept came to this country from England in the late 1970s and struck a chord. Through grassroots charitable and voluntary activity, hospice programs were created all over the country before third-party payment was available to pay for services. Some were independent organizations; some were creations of other organizations, such as nonprofit hospitals. Second, because of concerns about cost and quality and the desire of leaders of the hospice movement to assure that hospice services were distinctly different from existing hospital services, the law set stringent requirements for hospice programs to be eligible for funding.[69] This created a barrier to entry. Moreover, some of the requirements themselves—the provision of ministerial, bereavement, and volunteer services that were not directly reimbursable—signaled that entrepreneurs were not welcome. Combined, these two factors enabled the nonprofit sector to absorb most of the expanding demand, leaving a smaller market opportunity for new for-profit competitors. Thus, even nine years later (in 1992) the total number of Medicare-certified hospice providers was 1,208, of which only 13 percent were for-profit.

The use of hospice services grew much more rapidly in the 1990s, with the number of persons using Medicare hospice benefits alone doubling (from 143,000 to 295,000) between 1992 and 1996 and continuing to grow thereafter. No single cause can be identified, but there are several indications that a consensus had developed—among the health professions, the public, and policymakers—that our growing technological ability to prolong life was creating needless suffering at very high cost. For example, the Patient Self-Determination Act was enacted in 1991, requiring health care organizations to educate patients and staff about end-of-life treatment and to document patients' wishes. A palliative care physicians' group was established in the early 1990s. In any event, the increasing demand for hospice services was accompanied by growing numbers of hospice programs, with for-profits increasing most rapidly (from 151 to 623 in 1998, an increase of more than 300 percent).[70] The much larger nonprofit sector also grew, but at a slower rate (50 percent over the same time period). The growth trend stopped at that point, when new restrictions on Medicare payments were introduced. The number of hospice programs declined in 1999, with the decline being slightly more rapid among the for-profits (4.8 percent) than the nonprofits (4.2 percent).

The hospital and hospice examples suggest circumstances under which new funding in a domain does not change its nonprofit character. The nursing home and psychiatric hospital examples show that the growth of the for-profit sector within a domain is not immutable.

Between 1986 and 1997, the market share of for-profit *nursing homes* (measured either by number of facilities or by number of beds) fell from 75 to 65 percent. Both the share and absolute number of nonprofit facilities increased markedly during this same time. This situation contrasts sharply with earlier historical periods, when, as in other health fields, the for-profit market share increased dramatically. Among nursing homes, the first increase predated World War II, a largely unforeseen and probably unintended consequence of the Social Security Act of 1935, which established a new cash assistance program to enable the elderly poor who needed it to purchase institutional care.[71] The act stipulated that such funds could not be paid to any "inmate of a public institution," thereby opening a marketing opportunity to proprietors. By the time the earliest survey of ownership was done among nursing homes (in this case, skilled nursing facilities) in 1954, the pattern was set: 71 percent were for-profit, many of them essentially boarding houses, 14 percent were nonprofit, and the rest were public.[72]

The market share of for-profit nursing homes subsequently declined during the 1950s, as nonprofit nursing homes gained access to federal construction subsidies.[73] But demand for services (and thus the market share of for-profit nursing homes) received a second boost in the 1965 legislation that created Medicare and Medicaid. The Medicaid program, which became the largest purchaser of nursing home care, stimulated a major growth in nursing home capacity. The total number of beds roughly doubled between 1963 and 1971, and the for-profit share of nursing home beds grew from 60 to 72 percent.[74]

By the 1990s, however, the growth dynamic in the nursing home industry was reversed, as state and federal governments began to pay for more home health care and states enacted various policies designed to reduce institutionalization of the elderly and disabled. With demand stagnant, the number of for-profit facilities began to decline. This reflects in part the dynamics associated with stock valuation in investor-owned corporations, a process described earlier in this chapter. Also at work, however, was the tendency of some for-profit entrepreneurs to try to sustain revenue growth through fraudulent practices. This pattern, which has been documented as well among psychiatric hospitals,[75] involved everything from inappropriate billing to repurchasing arrangements through which homes were sold multiple times to overstate the capital costs on which their reimbursement was partially based.[76]

As with general hospitals, there has long been a small proprietary sector among *psychiatric hospitals*. The for-profit sector began to grow in the 1960s as great changes were taking place in psychiatric care. As the de-institutionalization movement was emptying out many beds in state and county psychiatric hospitals, a growing number of states began to require that private insurance plans include coverage for mental health care. There had long been epidemiological evidence of unmet need for psychiatric services, especially among the poor, the elderly, and children. Thus a combination of factors in the late 1960s and 1970s stimulated demand for psychiatric services.[77] Public hospitals continued to house the chronically mentally ill who were public charges. Private psychiatric hospitals served the growing market of insured "short stay" patients.

Investor-owned companies that owned multiple facilities appeared in the late 1960s. The number of for-profit psychiatric hospitals grew 80 percent (from 81 to 146) between 1969 and 1979, while the number of nonprofits increased 8 percent, from 87 to 94.[78] The pace of for-profit growth quickened in the 1980s. One reason was that Medicare exempted psychiatric hospitals from the prospective payment system that was introducing new cost constraints. Another reason was that managed care did not have effective tools with which to distinguish appropriate from inappropriate psychiatric admissions. Investor money moved into psychiatric hospitals, and at least two of the major hospital companies, National Medical Enterprises and Hospital Corporation of America, shifted their corporate focus in that direction. The number of for-profit psychiatric hospitals increased to 233 by 1995 and peaked at 405 in 1991. By comparison, there were 130 nonprofit hospitals in that year.

The rapid increase signified by those numbers—from 146 to 405 hospitals in twelve years—is characteristic of the for-profit sector when new demand appears. But what followed is another side of the for-profit sector in health care. By 1998, there were only 275 for-profit psychiatric hospitals. The nonprofits had declined too—to 102—but this was far less dramatic than on the for-profit side. Two factors prompted the decline. One affected all psychiatric hospitals— the increased effectiveness of the cost containment methods of managed care and health benefit design. The other affected all of the major for-profit companies— widespread fraud investigations followed by successful prosecutions and settlements. The charges include unnecessary admissions, hospital stays involving high charges and little treatment until insurance benefits were used up, and kickbacks to referring physicians. With all of the leading companies—National Medical Enterprises, Community Psychiatric Centers, Charter Medical, Hospital Corporation of America—engaged in some or all of these practices, investor money fled this field. Nonprofit market share grew in the 1990s.

A LIFE CYCLE PERSPECTIVE ON THE ROLES OF NONPROFIT AND FOR-PROFIT MEDICAL CARE. We have described several forces that have encouraged the expansion of for-profit involvement in the health care market. The most important appears to have been public policies that expanded demand for services, demand that was not met by existing nonprofit agencies. For-profit expansion has been most dramatic when demand has expanded rapidly in undeveloped domains. In many instances, the public policies that changed the ownership composition of health care domains did so only inadvertently, as with Medicare's original capital payment rules that facilitated the creation and growth of the investor-owned sector among hospitals. But there are also examples in which public policies directly targeted to ownership contributed to the for-profit shift, as in the home health and HMO domains, where preferential policies that had favored nonprofit agencies were stripped away or policies that favored their for-profit competitors were implemented. The lack of recognition of a distinctive role of nonprofit enterprise in health care has contributed to a policy environment in which nonprofits have a diminishing overall share in the delivery of services.

But the for-profit expansion is far from inevitable or universal. The stability of the nonprofit sector among community hospitals, even after passage of the demand-stimulating Medicare and Medicaid programs, is a prime example. It is noteworthy that public policies for more than half a century have facilitated nonprofit hospitals' access to capital, that an ample supply of hospital beds was consequently in place when the Medicare/Medicaid legislation was passed, and that the Medicare law included provisions to pay hospitals for their capital costs.

The growth of for-profit health care in any given domain also appears to have limits. The very sensitivity to profitability that attracts investor capital quickly to arenas of increased demand also makes investor-owned facilities particularly likely to leave markets that are no longer profitable. Because third-party payment concentrates purchasing decisions in a few hands in health care, and because two of the largest purchasers are government programs, the profitability of health care providers is monitored and responded to. Moreover, the aggressive pursuit of profit provides incentives within companies that may induce illegal or unethical behavior, which in a whole series of well-publicized cases has induced stigmatized corporations to downsize, drop lines of business, or merge into other companies and disappear.

A life cycle of development thus seems to exist in the health field. In the initial stage of service development, fledgling organizations experiment with new approaches, responding to emerging needs or making use of newly available technologies. This initial experimentation stage in health care has occurred almost exclusively in the nonprofit sector, with support from philanthropy, government grants, or existing nonprofits. The earliest hospitals, the original forms of third-party health insurance, the first HMOs, the first renal dialysis facilities, the earliest drug treatment centers, and the pioneering forms of hospice were all operated under private nonprofit auspices.[79] None of the early examples was motivated by perceptions of potential financial returns. The nonprofit form provided the mechanism that facilitated pioneering experiments that antedated formal government funding programs.

The availability of government funding for services opens a new stage in the life cycle. A stable source of revenues is essential to the survival and growth of a nascent field, but the clear pattern is that when a government program begins to pay for a service, investor capital is immediately attracted and the composition of the field changes. However, the conditions that favor the expansion of the for-profit sector do not eliminate the role for nonprofit organizations, even for the most completely commercialized services. The for-profit expansion is checked in part by payers' ability to react when providers become too profitable. Moreover, there will always be some patients (for example, the most complex and costly cases), some communities (typically the most geographically isolated or economically deprived), or some circumstances under which treatment proves unprofitable.[80] And as noted, the for-profit rôle is further circumscribed by the tendency to succumb to incentives for fraudulent behavior, resulting in a loss of legitimacy and capital for investor-owned enterprise in the domain. Trustworthiness may come to be seen as an important factor in preserving a nonprofit role in health care after all.

Toward Convergence: Shifts in Organizational Practices and Structure

Even where nonprofits have maintained their role, they have often found it necessary to respond to the challenges confronting them in the health care field by becoming more like commercial enterprises. Three sets of changes have been particularly notable here: (a) changes in organizational practices, (b) changes in organizational structure, and (c) interorganizational linkages.

CHANGES IN ORGANIZATIONAL PRACTICES. Nonprofit health care providers today engage in advertising, marketing, and other business practices that previously were characteristic primarily of the for-profit sector. One symbolically powerful example involves the efforts of some hospitals to attract affluent patients by establishing plush concierge floors with private chefs and antique furniture. Many nonprofit institutions in health care have invested some of their surplus revenues in commercial enterprises chosen for their profit-generating potential. Some of these investments bear some relationship to the core mission (as with a hospital's parking garage), but not all do so. Such practices do not necessarily undermine the organization's focus on community benefits; indeed, the revenues from profitable services may be used to subsidize community-benefit activities. But they can induce a subtle shift in the perceptions of consumers and third-party purchasers, who may come to consider nonprofit health care agencies as indistinguishable from their for-profit counterparts.

CHANGES IN ORGANIZATIONAL STRUCTURE. A second set of converging practices involves changes in organizations themselves. An example is the composition of the *governing boards* of nonprofit health care organizations. Historically, nonprofits had large boards, selected to facilitate fundraising in the community. Many still do, but nonprofit boards have been coming to resemble those in the for-profit world—smaller in size and selected in a manner that emphasizes strategic planning and technical expertise in areas such as finance and marketing.[81] This change is attributed to the demands of the competitive environment. The consequences for the charitable side of nonprofit enterprise are poorly understood.

Changes in the basic organizational structure of many nonprofit health care organizations also include the creation of for-profit subsidiaries to develop new service areas. Joint ventures with proprietary physician groups or other specialized for-profit companies are common. Some of these joint ventures involve services that were once provided within hospitals and are now provided on an outpatient basis in specialized facilities or in patients' homes. These joint ventures are intended to capture revenues that would otherwise be lost. Another form of hybrid ownership involves managed care plans. Many joint ventures link hospitals with other kinds of providers, particularly physicians, who are seeking to achieve either economies or bargaining power in the face of managed care. Many of these entities have failed, and the growing conventional wisdom seems to be that hospitals do best by maintaining their core focus.

INTERORGANIZATIONAL LINKAGES. A third type of convergence involves interorganizational linkages. In response to the entry of large, investor-owned corporations, many nonprofits have sought to gain comparable economies of scale by banding together in one of several ways. One way has been through cooperative purchasing arrangements such as that operated by a for-profit consortium labeled the Voluntary Hospitals of America. In other cases, multiple facilities are integrated under a single national or regional parent corporation. A 1999 survey by the trade magazine *Modern Healthcare* obtained data from 185 nonprofit, multiple-hospital systems with a total of 1,448 hospitals, approximately half of all of the nonprofit hospitals in the country.[82] Multiple-hospital systems are also found among many other types of nonprofits, including HMOs and nursing homes.

The creation of joint ventures and multiple-facility systems requires changes in governance structures. Commonly, a system-level board is created, which may include representatives from the component institutions; the institutions' boards typically have only limited powers. In these arrangements, many important types of decisions (for example, regarding capital investments) are commonly removed from the community served by the facility, creating a challenge for meeting community needs.[83]

Another form of convergence stemming from interorganizational linkages involves trade associations. In some domains, trade associations that once gave moral shape to their industry and were exclusively nonprofit or dominated by nonprofits have now integrated and avoid taking positions that might alienate members on the other side of the for-profit/nonprofit divide. The leadership on social issues that once came from the dominant trade associations is increasingly passing to smaller associations made up of segments from within the nonprofit side of the domains, such as the Catholic Health Association or the Alliance of Community Health Plans.

Efforts to Maintain a Distinctive Nonprofit Role

While many responses to the challenges facing nonprofit health providers have moved nonprofits toward convergence with their for-profit competitors, efforts intended to maintain or enhance the distinctiveness of the nonprofit providers are also evident. These have taken two principal forms. Most visible have been projects to encourage nonprofits to provide more public goods and engage in more community-benefit activities. In response to growing disquiet among scholars, policymakers, and even their own members about the drift toward commerciality and the justification for granting tax exemptions to nonprofit hospitals, and in an effort to avoid reliance for guidance on the piecemeal decisions of the IRS tax courts and state regulators, the American Hospital Association, the Catholic Hospital Association, and the Voluntary Hospitals of America all undertook initiatives in the late 1980s to define an appropriate and measurable scope for community-benefit activities.[84] All three definitions emphasized community participation in determining the appropriate mix of community benefits for each nonprofit. Implicitly, this suggested that health needs vary substantially across communities and that more standardized notions of community benefit would not be sensible. Beyond this commonality, however, there was little agreement among the three approaches.[85] And none was particularly compatible with the sort of community-benefit standards being developed by state officials.

Beyond these collective efforts are numerous less visible efforts made within the boards of trustees of particular institutions to adhere to their institution's historical mission or adapt to changing community expectations. Even so, and even in states that require community-benefit reporting, it appears that far more time and energy are devoted in most nonprofit organizations to the sort of practices that represent a convergence between nonprofit and for-profit sectors in health care than to policies and practices that make nonprofit health care distinctive.

Paths toward the Future

A significant and potentially dangerous drift is evident in the health field toward diminished nonprofit distinctiveness and convergence toward the for-profit form. Whatever benefits may arise from this trend—for example, regarding ability to compete and to gain access to capital—our analysis suggests that much that is important would be lost if nonprofit institutions were to disappear from the health care field or surrender their distinctive features too completely. Among other things, the potential losses would include a commitment to the more intangible aspects of quality, an important degree of institutional stability, a significant element of trustworthiness, and support for community benefit, broadly conceived.

To date, however, inadequate steps have been taken to avoid this outcome. The community-benefit standards that have been developed are most applicable for hospitals and have serious shortcomings when applied to other service domains.[86] Individual organizations acting on their own seem more enamored of approaches that move them in the direction of convergence than ones that establish their distinctive characteristics. An approach is needed that takes into account the sort of tensions and complexities that characterize the contemporary role of nonprofit enterprise in American medicine.

Practically speaking, this will involve simultaneously addressing the two principal imperatives that nonprofit organizations in the health field currently confront: first, what we term the survival imperative and, second, what we refer to as the distinctiveness imperative. Let us examine each of these in turn and the steps that are needed to address them.

The Survival Imperative

Nonprofit organizations confront two challenges to economic sustainability: establishing the value of nonprofit services and responding to expansions in demand. This section examines each of these in turn.

ESTABLISHING THE VALUE OF NONPROFIT SERVICES. Nonprofits in health care will not survive if large purchasers do not want to contract with them. To date, public programs like Medicare and Medicaid (with exceptions) have not contracted selectively, but private sector purchasers do. And there are growing pressures for public programs to adopt selective contracting to save money. In this sort of environment, it is imperative that nonprofit agencies establish that the services they offer are a reasonable value.

For some services, such as hospitals and managed care plans, past research suggests that nonprofit services are no more costly than those provided by for-profit agencies.[87] In these cases, if nonprofit providers can establish that their services are better in quality or more reliable, they would have a real competitive advantage. For other services, such as nursing home care, nonprofit services are consistently more expensive than services under for-profit auspices.[88] In these cases, establishing that additional benefits are associated with nonprofit services is vital to maintaining the long-term viability of the nonprofit sector.

Nonprofit providers can make this case most obviously in terms of the quality and reliability of the services they provide (for example, trustworthiness).

These matters are increasingly subject to measurement and public reporting. Nonprofits also need to make the case that broader community benefits are associated with their enterprise. For this appeal to be effective, nonprofits must have a story to tell, and purchasers must be convinced that it is *their* responsibility to care about community benefits. Certainly some employers and some state Medicaid agencies that contract selectively have accepted these responsibilities.[89] Even if there is an effective campaign to broaden this commitment, nonprofit providers will have to document their comparative advantages more effectively on both community-benefit and quality grounds. Some past research suggests that modest ownership-related differences in quality do exist, albeit in different forms in different service domains. Our comprehensive review of the comparative research literature is forthcoming.[90]

RESPONDING TO EXPANSIONS IN DEMAND. The second challenge to economic sustainability involves the rapid expansion of for-profit market share in domains that experience large increases in demand for services. Although a nonprofit sector persists in these domains—even the ones with the longest history of extensive commercialization—it is clear that the rapid transformations of ownership that occur in times of service expansion threaten the legitimacy of the nonprofit sector in the eyes of policymakers. The inability of the sector to respond to increasing demand, particularly when this growth in demand is the result of a change in public policy, raises questions about the reliability of the nonprofit sector as a source of vital services.

However, as documented earlier in the chapter, the greater responsiveness of investor-owned corporations carries certain liabilities. One involves the boom-bust cycle associated with stock valuation. This produces waves of hyperexpansion, followed by a collapse in capacity. The resulting turbulence in the delivery system disrupts continuity of services for patients and communities. As the prevalence of chronic illness increases with the aging of the American population, the costs of disrupted care-giving relationships become more problematic. An additional liability involves the risks of fraudulent behavior associated with the relentless pressures for growth in investor-owned health care. The more we rely on a system involving consumer choice, the more vulnerable will patients be to potential exploitation. This exact pattern appeared in the psychiatric hospital industry in the late 1980s, when thousands of patients were unnecessarily hospitalized or inadequately treated under for-profit auspices.[91]

Although these liabilities are not sufficient to justify—or convince policymakers of the need for—a prohibition on investor ownership, they could be used to justify government programs to subsidize the capital investments of nonprofit health care organizations. In domains where such subsidies once existed, nonprofit organizations had the capacity to expand to meet rather sizable increases in demand. Such public policies can lessen the pressures that produce hyperexpansion in the for-profit sector, stabilizing both sectors simultaneously.

The Distinctiveness Imperative

The second imperative facing nonprofits in health care is not simply to survive, but to retain their distinctiveness in doing so. Here, a fundamental tension exists between the growing demands for accountability, which encourage quantifiable forms of community benefit that can be applied in a consistent manner throughout the nonprofit health care sector, and the considerable heterogeneity of the institutions that compose this sector.

Although this central tension cannot be fully resolved, it can be addressed more successfully if policymakers and other key decisionmakers take account of two fundamental attributes of the contemporary health scene identified earlier: first, the presence of multiple concepts of community benefit in the health field and, second, the different stages of development that health organizations go through. It is possible that the standards of community benefit that are appropriate for different institutions vary depending on their stage of development. The task of ensuring institutional distinctiveness may therefore differ at different stages of the process.

ALTERNATIVE CONCEPTIONS OF COMMUNITY BENEFIT. One of the fundamental difficulties in rationalizing the nonprofit role in the health field is the tendency to define the community-benefit contributions of nonprofit agencies rather narrowly. The forms of community benefit that have been identified in IRS rulings, tax court decisions, and state legislation tend to treat care for the indigent as the primary (in some cases, the sole) criterion for tax exemption. This represents only a small portion of the possible beneficial pathways. Some services are at stages in their developmental cycle for which charity care is simply not the appropriate standard for community benefit. Instead, attention should focus on three alternative paradigms of community benefit in health care that go beyond these conventional legal-historical definitions.[92]

The first we term the community health orientation.[93] It has emerged largely from the efforts of clinicians concerned about how to respond to the broader social determinants of health and has been embodied to varying degrees in past policies associated with neighborhood health centers, community mental health centers, and community-oriented primary care.[94] At its core, this approach emphasizes different aspects of responsibility that health care professionals and organizations might have to the community: responsibility to inform the community about their practices and performance, responsibility to share their resources and expertise to address local needs, as well as responsibility to assume a fair share of the costs of unprofitable patients and services.

A second perspective we refer to as the healthy community paradigm.[95] This approach draws its criteria for community benefit from the conceptual frameworks of sociology and social epidemiology, again with an emphasis on the various social and environmental factors that affect population health.[96] Perhaps best reflected in the World Health Organization's healthy cities program, this paradigm calls not simply for health care organizations to be responsive to community needs but also to help build each community's own capacity to respond to those needs. This might entail placing the resources of health care organizations under the control of the community and subordinating professional prerogatives to the preferences of community residents.[97] It also places greater emphasis on the need to redistribute resources and political voice to disenfranchised portions of the community, encouraging health care organizations to act as catalysts to enhance the capacity of community groups and agencies to determine for themselves the appropriate priorities for health care spending and policies.

The third perspective can be termed the market failures interpretation.[98] It derives its conclusions from economic models of markets applied to the delivery of medical services, highlighting those circumstances under which the costs and benefits that face a health care organization differ from the impact that their decisions have on society as a whole. In contrast to the other perspectives, this paradigm emphasizes, for example, both the harms and the benefits that managed care plans may generate for community residents who are not enrolled in the plan.[99] It also directs attention to the role of various public goods, such as training certain medical professionals or supporting clinical research, that generate substantial collective benefits beyond local geographic boundaries.

STAGES IN THE LIFE CYCLE. Which of these community-benefit standards makes the most sense in a particular service domain depends to some extent on its stage of development. In the first stage, when services are largely experimental in nature, the knowledge building that occurs almost exclusively in the nonprofit sector is itself an important public good. Organizations that are a locus of research and innovation should be recognized as important sources of community benefit, albeit benefit that is not limited to any one locality but instead extends to the health system as a whole.

In the second stage of the life cycle, private demand for the service expands, while third-party coverage remains incomplete. At this stage, patients with limited financial means often lack financial access to treatment. Charity care, in its traditional sense, becomes the primary priority for the nonprofit sector.

In the third stage of the life cycle, third-party coverage becomes more complete, and some services have achieved near universal coverage. Under these circumstances, charity care in the sense of treatment of indigent patients becomes a less relevant standard for assessing community benefit for many institutions. In most cases, however, it has not yet become entirely irrelevant, because a large and growing number of Americans are without health insurance.[100] Subsidizing treatment for this population remains an important part of the nonprofit mission in health care. Needs vary, however. In many communities the portion of the population that is both uninsured and unhealthy is quite small, and many communities have publicly funded institutions whose explicit mission is to serve the poor and uninsured. However, many insured patients may be unprofitable to treat if their third-party payers are penurious in their payments or if their cases are complex and more costly than average. Under these circumstances, organizations that avoid creaming the most profitable cases on admission and discourage the dumping (early discharge) of unprofitable patients to other facilities are providing an important community benefit.

For populations that are fully and adequately insured for coverage, other forms of community benefit are more relevant, such as those suggested by the community health orientation. The propensity of nonprofit organizations to behave in a more trustworthy fashion or to protect professional values may prove an important safeguard for patient welfare, particularly when third-party purchasers are unwilling or unable to effectively monitor the welfare of the population whose treatment they are financing. Such trustworthiness is difficult to document by conventional methods. But it is possible to develop new measures for report cards on organizational performance, measures that focus on the extent to which patients are fully and adequately informed or that assess the extent to which health care providers have the autonomy to represent patients' interests effectively.

In the final stage of the life cycle, demand stagnates and may even decline, as happened with hospitals. This creates a difficult challenge for existing nonprofit organizations. Boards of trustees typically see their responsibilities in terms of building or at least sustaining their institution. It is out of character for a board to step back and assess whether their community would be better off with less capacity.

At this stage, community benefits can be best served by incorporating our emerging understanding of the social determinants of health. As long as trustees see their organization's mission as locked into a particular set of clinical services, they have little flexibility to respond to declining demand. However, if they instead see its mission as addressing the health *needs* for which those services are relevant, other opportunities emerge. For example, if the market for renal dialysis has excess capacity, it will benefit the community to have some nonprofit agencies shift their resources to address nutritional issues, health education programs, or other community-based interventions that can reduce health problems related to kidney failure. At this stage, the challenge for accountability becomes less one of measuring the organization's commitment to these activities and more one of assessing how those activities actually affect health outcomes.

This life cycle perspective can assist policymakers to consider the sorts of community-benefit activities that are appropriate for particular service domains. In reality, of course, this assessment will be more complicated than suggested here. But this is not inconsistent with notions of accountability. It simply calls for nonprofit organizations to be clear about the needs that they are addressing through their community-benefit activities and to accept responsibility for documenting them. And it requires that community benefits be viewed more broadly than has been true in the past. How this comports with the constraints of the marketplace and the new demands for public accountability are great challenges for the future.

Conclusions

As organizations that are simultaneously commercial and charitable entities, nonprofit health care organizations must play to two audiences. The first looks at them as fee-collecting, service-providing organizations. The second sees them as tax-exempt charitable organizations. The future of nonprofit health care depends on satisfactory reconciliation of these two roles.

On the commercial side, nonprofits in health care are judged by the people they serve, by third-party purchasers, and by the providers of capital. They must operate successfully in business terms, often in competition with for-profit organizations. Notably, even as the field has undergone a growth-driven shift toward for-profit control, it is rare to see a decline in both absolute numbers and market share of the nonprofit sector.

Will nonprofits continue to maintain positions in the various competitive domains within health care? We believe that this will depend on their ability to be part of the solution to the many difficult problems that confront the numerous stakeholders in the system. From the patient's standpoint, will nonprofits be more trustworthy regarding quality, and will they not exploit patient vulnerabilities? From the physician's standpoint, will nonprofits operate in ways that are compatible with professional values regarding quality and service? From the payer's standpoint, will nonprofits provide greater value and fewer propensities for fraud and abuse? There are theoretical reasons to expect superior performance by nonprofits on these dimensions, and there is some supportive empirical evidence. But market trends will not turn on the work of scholars. Key questions for the future will be whether (a) nonprofits behave differently than for-profits, (b) purchasers detect these differences, and (c) purchasers care about the differences enough to influence their purchasing decisions. Too little is known about these matters to be confident of the results.

As regards charitable expectations, health care nonprofits must meet the expectations of the public, actual and potential donors and volunteers, policymakers, and regulators. They face growing pressure to demonstrate that they deserve the tax benefits that they receive from government. Because these tax benefits can be stated in numerical terms, there has been a tendency to demand evidence of community benefit in similar terms. Yet many important health promotional activities in which organizations can engage are not readily quantifiable. Nonprofits in health care will therefore face the dual challenge of (a) educating policymakers about the types of activities that are appropriately viewed as meeting organizations' community-benefit obligations and (b) demonstrating that they are indeed engaged in such activities.

A final challenge facing the nonprofit sector in health care comes from an ironic confluence of trends regarding expectations and regulations. In the era prior to substantial federal involvement in both the financing and regulation of health care, the system operated substantially on trust. Physicians and hospitals were expected to take care of people who could not afford such care, and providers were trusted to provide the services for which they were billing insurance plans. Undoubtedly, these expectations and this trust were not always well founded, but they had a degree of plausibility because of their consistency with prevailing beliefs about the meaning of professionalism and the nonprofit nature of medical institutions.

The growing prevalence of for-profit organizations has been accompanied by a stream of regulatory actions aimed at blocking negative excesses in the pursuit of profits, excesses that are not necessarily limited to for-profits. Thus legislation was passed in 1986 requiring hospitals to provide emergency services without regard to ability to pay, waves of cost containment and anti-fraud legislation have been implemented, and several types of managed care reforms have been passed. There also has been stopgap legislation to fill some of the worst holes in insurance coverage left after the passage of Medicare and Medicaid, most notably expanded coverage in the late 1980s and mid-1990s to cover additional poor children and pregnant women. Eventually some form of universal health insurance may even be passed.

Taken together, these legislative and regulatory changes are addressing dimensions of performance that were once managed largely through reliance on the nonprofit form. Thus nonprofits are being challenged to justify their distinctiveness at a time when public policy is forcing their for-profit competitors to act in accord with the same high ideals that nonprofits were expected to exhibit automatically. Ironically, therefore, these formal requirements may ultimately undermine the very distinctiveness of the institutions that once best embodied them.

Notes

1. *Nonprofit Almanac: Dimensions of the Independent Sector, 1996–1997* (Washington: Independent Sector, 1996). In terms of employment, health services organizations are even more dominant, accounting for 57 percent of the wages and salaries paid in the nonprofit sector in 1994, again having grown substantially (from 49 percent) since 1977.

2. Henry B. Hansmann, "The Role of Nonprofit Enterprise," *Yale Law Journal,* vol. 89 (1980): 835–901; Frank A. Sloan and others, "Hospital Ownership and Cost and Quality of Care: Is There a Dime's Worth of Difference?" *Journal of Health Economics,* vol. 20 (2001): 1–21; M. G. Bloche, "Should Government Intervene to Protect Nonprofits?" *Health Affairs,* vol. 17 (1998): 7–25.

3. Hansmann, "The Role of Nonprofit Enterprise"; Richard Steinberg and Bradford H. Gray, "'The Role of Nonprofit Enterprise' in 1992: Hansmann Revisited," *Nonprofit and Voluntary Sector Quarterly,* vol. 22 (1993): 297–316.

4. Andreas Ortmann and Mark Schlesinger, "Trust, Repute, and the Role of Nonprofit Enterprise," *Voluntas,* vol. 8 (1997): 97–119.

5. John Kultgen, *Ethics and Professionalism* (University of Pennsylvania Press, 1988); Hansmann, "Role of Nonprofit Enterprise."

6. Bradford H. Gray, *The Profit Motive and Patient Care* (Harvard University Press, 1991), pp. 111–51. Marc Rodwin, *Medicine, Money, and Morals: Physicians' Conflicts of Interest* (Oxford University Press, 1993), pp. 204–41.

7. Giandomenico Majone, "Professionalism and Nonprofit Organizations," *Journal of Health Politics, Policy, and Law,* vol. 8 (1984): 639–59.

8. Bradford H. Gray, "Trust and Trustworthy Care in the Managed Care Era," *Health Affairs,* vol. 16 (1997): 34–49.

9. Theda Skocpol, *Boomerang: Health Care Reform and the Turn against Government* (New York: W. W. Norton, 1997); Malcolm Sparrow, *License to Steal* (Boulder, Colo.: Westview, 2000).

10. Gray, *Profit Motive and Patient Care,* pp. 111–51.

11. Mark Schlesinger and Bradford H. Gray, "Nonprofit Organizations and Health Care: Burgeoning Research, Shifting Expectations, and Persisting Puzzles," in W. W. Powell and Richard Steinberg, eds., *The Nonprofit Sector: A Research Handbook,* 2d ed. (Yale University Press, forthcoming).

12. Constance M. Baker and others, "Hospital Ownership, Performance, and Outcomes," *Journal of Nursing Administration,* vol. 30 (2000): 227–40; Gray, *Profit Motive and Patient Care,* pp. 93–96.

13. Rosemary Stevens, *In Sickness and in Wealth: The American Hospital in the Twentieth Century* (New York: Basic Books, 1988); Paul Starr, *The Social Transformation of American Medicine* (New York: Basic Books, 1982).

14. Gray, *Profit Motive and Patient Care,* pp. 20–22.

15. Charles E. Rosenberg, *The Care of Strangers: The Rise of America's Hospital System* (New York: Basic Books, 1987).

16. Mark Schlesinger, Bradford H. Gray, and Elizabeth Bradley, "Charity and Community: The Role of Nonprofit Ownership in a Managed Health Care System," *Journal of Health Politics, Policy, and Law,* vol. 21 (1996): 697–752.

17. Robert E. Mechanic and Allen Dobson, "The Impact of Managed Care on Clinical Research: A Preliminary Investigation," *Health Affairs,* vol. 15 (1996): 72–89.

18. Peter Cunningham and others, "Managed Care and Physicians: Provision of Charity Care," *Journal of the American Medical Association,* vol. 281 (1999): 1087–92; Mark Schlesinger and others, "The Determinants of Dumping: A National Study of Economically Motivated Transfers Involving Mental Health Care," *Health Services Research,* vol. 32 (1997): 561–90.

19. David U. Himmelstein and others, "Quality of Care in Investor-Owned and Not-for-Profit HMOs," *Journal of the American Medical Association,* vol. 282 (1999): 159–63.

20. Bradford H. Gray, "Tax Exemptions as Health Policy," *Frontiers of Health Services Management,* vol. 12 (1996): 37–42.

21. Gray, *Profit Motive and Patient Care*, p. 32.

22. Gray, *Profit Motive and Patient Care,* p. 24.

23. Gray, *Profit Motive and Patient Care,* pp. 152–65.

24. John D. Colombo and Mark A. Hall, *The Charitable Tax Exemption* (Boulder, Colo.: Westview, 1995); Hansmann, "Role of Nonprofit Enterprise"; Robert C. Clark, "Does the Nonprofit Form Fit the Hospital Industry?" *Harvard Law Review,* vol. 93 (1980): 1416–89.

25. Gray, *Profit Motive and Patient Care.*

26. Robert D. Putnam, *Bowling Alone* (New York: Simon and Schuster, 2000); Orlando Patterson, "Liberty against the Democratic State: On the Historical and Contemporary Sources of American Distrust," in M. E. Warren, ed., *Democracy and Trust* (Cambridge University Press, 1999), pp. 151–207.

27. Small Business Administration, *Unfair Competition by Nonprofit Organizations with Small Business: An Issue for the 1980s* (Washington: Small Business Administration, 1983).

28. *Nonprofit Hospitals: Better Standards Needed for Tax Exemption* (Washington: General Accounting Office, 1990).

29. Coalition for Nonprofit Health Care, *State Law Approaches to Ensuring the Social Accountability of Nonprofit Health Care Organizations* (Washington: Coalition for Nonprofit Health Care, 1999).

30. Nancy Wolff and Mark Schlesinger, "Risk, Motives, and Styles of Utilization Review: A Cross-Condition Comparison," *Social Science and Medicine,* vol. 47 (1998): 911–26.

31. *Nonprofit Almanac,* pp. 160, 165.

32. For a systematic analysis of four different frameworks within which the meaning of community benefit might be defined, see Mark Schlesinger and others, "A Broader Vision for Managed Care, Part 2: A Typology of Community Benefits Provided by HMOs," *Health Affairs,* vol. 17 (1998): 26–49.

33. Amy Bernstein and Anne Gauthier, "Choices in Health Care: What Are They and What Are They Worth?" *Medical Care Research and Review,* vol. 56, supplement 1 (1999): 5–23.

34. Kultgen, *Ethics and Professionalism.*

35. Hansmann, "Role of Nonprofit Enterprise."

36. Majone, "Professionalism and Nonprofit Organizations."

37. Schlesinger, Gray, and Bradley, "Charity and Community."

38. Institute of Medicine, "The Changing Nature of Physician Influence in Medical Institutions," in Bradford H. Gray, ed., *For-Profit Enterprise in Health Care: A Report of the Institute of Medicine* (Washington: National Academy Press, 1986), pp. 171–81.

39. Starr, *Social Transformation of American Medicine,* p. 379.

40. Dahlia K. Remler and others, "What Do Managed Care Plans Do to Affect Care? Results from a Survey of Physicians," *Inquiry,* vol. 34 (1997): 196–204; Mark Schlesinger, Bradford H. Gray, and Kristin Perreira, "Medical Professionalism under Managed Care: The Pros and Cons of Utilization Review," *Health Affairs,* vol. 16 (1997): 106–24.

41. Robert J. Blendon, T. S. Hyams, and J. M. Benson, "Bridging the Gap between Expert and Public Views on Health Care Reform, " *Journal of the American Medical Association,* vol. 269 (1993): 2573–78.

42. Elliot A. Krause, *Death of the Guilds: Professions, States, and the Advance of Capitalism: 1930 to the Present* (Yale University Press, 1996), p. 36.

43. Wolff and Schlesinger, "Risk, Motives, and Styles of Utilization Review"; Schlesinger, Gray, and Bradley, "Charity and Community."

44. Thomas McKeown, *The Role of Medicine: Dream Mirage or Nemesis?* (Princeton University, 1979); Richard Meckel, *Save the Babies* (Johns Hopkins University Press, 1991); Benjamin Amick and others, "An Introduction," in Benjamin Amick and others, eds., *Society and Health* (Oxford University Press, 1995).

45. Deborah Lupton, *The Imperative of Health: Public Health and the Regulated Body* (London: Sage Publications, 1995); Deborah Stone, "The Resistible Rise of Preventive Medicine," in Lawrence Brown, ed., *Health Policy in Transition* (Duke University Press, 1987), pp. 103–28.

46. Sally MacIntyre, "The Black Report and Beyond: What Are the Issues?" *Social Science and Medicine,* vol. 44 (1997): 723–45.

47. Ichiro Kawachi and others, "Social Capital, Income Inequality, and Mortality," *American Journal of Public Health,* vol. 87 (1997): 1491–98; Roderick Wallace and Deborah Wallace, "A U.S. Apartheid and the Spread of AIDS to the Suburbs: A Multi-City Analysis of the Political Economy of Spatial Epidemic Threshold, "*Social Science and Medicine,* vol. 41 (1995): 333–45; Thomas A. LaViest, "The Political Empowerment and Health Status of African-Americans: Mapping a New Territory," *American Journal of Sociology,* vol. 97 (1992): 1080–95; Donald Patrick and Thomas Wickizer, "Community and Health," in Amick and others, eds., *Society and Health,* pp. 46–92.

48. Catherine Hoffman, Dorothy Rice, and Hai-Yen Sung, "Persons with Chronic Conditions: Their Prevalence and Costs," *Journal of the American Medical Association,* vol. 276 (1996): 1473–79.

49. Susan M. Allen and Vincent Mor, "Unmet Need in the Community: The Springfield Study," in Stephen L. Isaacs and James R. Knickman, eds., *To Improve Health and Health Care, 1998–1999* (San Francisco: Jossey-Bass, 1997), pp. 132–60; Dorothy Rice and others, "The Economic Burden of Alzheimer's Disease Care," *Health Affairs,* vol. 12 (1993): 164–76.

50. John McKnight, *The Careless Society: Community and Its Counterfeits* (New York: Basic Books, 1995).

51. Helmut K. Anheier and Avner Ben-Ner, eds., "Economic Theories of Non-Profit Organizations: A *Voluntas* Symposium," *Voluntas,* vol. 8 (1997): 93–96.

52. Theodore R. Marmor, Mark Schlesinger, and Richard W. Smithey, "Nonprofit Organizations and Health Care," in W. W. Powell, ed., *The Nonprofit Sector: A Research Handbook* (Yale University Press, 1987), pp. 221–39.

53. Schlesinger, Gray, and Bradley, "Charity and Community."

54. Mark Schlesinger, *Public, For-Profit, and Private Nonprofit Enterprises: A Study of Mixed Industries,* Ph.D. dissertation (University of Wisconsin-Madison, 1984).

55. Richard A. Rettig and Norman G. Levinsky, eds., *Kidney Failure and the Federal Government* (Washington: National Academy Press, 1991), p. 111.

56. Ari Ginsberg and Ann Buchholtz, "Converting to For-Profit Status: Corporate Responsiveness to Radical Change," *Academy of Management Journal,* vol. 33 (1990): 445–77.

57. Anne L. Bailey, "Charities Win, Lose in Health Shuffle," *Chronicle of Philanthropy,* June 14, 1994, p. 1.

58. Robert Kuttner, "Columbia/HCA and the Resurgence of the For-Profit Hospital Business," *New England Journal of Medicine,* vol. 335 (1996): 362–67, 446–51.

59. Bruce Steinwald and Duncan Neuhauser, "The Role of the Proprietary Hospital," *Law and Contemporary Problems,* vol. 35 (1970): 817–38; Stevens, *In Sickness and in Wealth.*

60. Steinwald and Neuhauser, "Role of the Proprietary Hospital," p. 819. Different sources report slightly different percentages.

61. Gray, *Profit Motive and Patient Care,* pp. 32–37.

62. Herman Somers and Anne Somers, *Medicare and the Hospitals: Issues and Prospects* (Washington: Brookings, 1967).

63. Gray, ed., *For-Profit Enterprise in Health Care.*

64. Gray, *Profit Motive and Patient Care*, pp. 37–48.

65. Lucette Lagnado, Anita Sharpe, and Greg Jaffe, "States Review Columbia/HCA Billing Practices," *Wall Street Journal*, July 22, 1997; Lucette Lagnado, "Insurance Companies Start an Independent Probe into Billing Practices," *Wall Street Journal*, July 31, 1997.

66. Cutler and Horwitz count 330 conversions of nonprofit hospitals between 1970 and 1995. David M. Cutler and Jill R. Horwitz, "Converting Hospitals from Not-for-Profit to For-Profit Status: Why and What Effects?" in David M. Cutler, ed., *The Changing Hospital Industry: Comparing Not-for-Profit and For-Profit Institutions* (University of Chicago Press, 2000).

67. Jack Needleman, Deborah J. Chollet, and JoAnn Lamphere, "Hospital Conversion Trends," *Health Affairs*, vol. 16 (1997): 187–95.

68. Vincent Mor, *Hospice Care Systems: Structure, Process, Costs, and Outcome* (New York: Springer, 1987).

69. Mor, *Hospice Care Systems.*

70. U.S. General Accounting Office, *Medicare: More Beneficiaries Use Hospice but for Fewer Days of Care* (Washington: U.S. General Accounting Office, 2000).

71. Cathy Hawes and Charles D. Phillips, "The Changing Structure of the Nursing Home Industry and the Impact of Ownership on Quality, Cost, and Access," in Gray, ed., *For-Profit Enterprise in Health Care*, pp. 492–541.

72. Schlesinger, "Public, For-Profit, and Private Nonprofit Enterprises."

73. Bruce Vladeck, *Unloving Care: The Nursing Home Tragedy* (New York: Basic Books, 1980).

74. Schlesinger, "Public, For-Profit, and Private Nonprofit Enterprises."

75. Mark Schlesinger and Bradford H. Gray, "Institutional Change and Its Consequences for the Delivery of Mental Health Services," in Allan V. Horwitz and Teresa L. Scheid, eds., *A Handbook for the Study of Mental Health: Social Contexts, Theories, and Systems* (Cambridge University Press, 1999), pp. 427–48.

76. Vladeck, *Unloving Care.*

77. Robert A. Dorwart and Mark Schlesinger, "Privatization of Psychiatric Services," *American Journal of Psychiatry*, vol. 145 (1988): 543–53.

78. Alan I. Levenson, "The Growth of Investor-Owned Psychiatric Hospitals," *American Journal of Psychiatry*, vol. 139 (1982): 902–07.

79. Many early hospitals that are considered nonprofit organizations today were established before today's distinction between public and private nonprofit organizations existed.

80. Nancy Wolff and Mark Schlesinger, "Access, Hospital Ownership, and Competition between For-Profit and Nonprofit Institutions," *Nonprofit and Voluntary Sector Quarterly*, vol. 27, no. 2 (1998): 203–36.

81. Brian J. Weiner and Jeffrey Alexander, "Corporate and Philanthropic Models of Hospital Governance: A Taxonomic Evaluation," *Health Services Research*, vol. 28 (1993): 325–55.

82. Deanna Belliandi, Barbara Kirchheimer, and Ann Saphir, "Profitability a Matter of Ownership Status," *Modern Healthcare*, vol. 30 (2000): 24–44.

83. Jeffrey A. Alexander, Bryan J. Weiner, and Melissa Succi, "Community Accountability among Hospitals Affiliated with Health Care Systems," *Milbank Quarterly*, vol. 78 (2000): 157–84.

84. Bradford H. Gray, "The Future of the Nonprofit Form for Hospitals," *Frontiers of Health Services Management*, vol. 8 (Summer 1992): 3–32.

85. Robert Sigmond and J. David Seay, "In Health Care Reform, Who Cares for the Community?" *Journal of Health Administration Education,* vol. 12 (1994): 259–68; Daniel R. Longo, "The Measurement of Community Benefit: Issues, Options, and Questions for Further Research," *Journal of Health Administration Education,* vol. 12 (1994): 291–318.

86. Schlesinger and others, "A Broader Vision for Managed Care, Part 2."

87. Gray, *Profit Motive and Patient Care,* pp. 92–96.

88. Schlesinger, "Public, For-Profit, and Private Nonprofit Enterprises."

89. Raymond J. Baxter and Robert E. Mechanic, "The Status of Local Health Care Safety Nets," *Health Affairs,* vol. 16 (1997): 7–23.

90. Mark Schlesinger and Bradford H. Gray, "Nonprofit Organizations and Health Care: Burgeoning Research, Shifting Expectations, and Persisting Puzzles"; Bradford H. Gray, Gerard Carrino, Sara R. Collins, and Michael K. Gusmano, "The Empirical Literature Comparing For-Profit and Nonprofit Hospitals, Managed Care Organizations, and Nursing Homes: Updating the Institute of Medicine Study," New York Academy of Medicine, Division of Health and Science Policy website (www.nyam.org/divisions/healthscience/publications.shtml).

91. Schlesinger and Gray, "Institutional Change and Organizational Performance."

92. Schlesinger and others, "A Broader Vision, Part 2."

93. Jonathan Showstack and others, "Health of the Public: The Private Sector Challenge," *Journal of the American Medical Association,* vol. 276 (1996): 1071–74; David R. Lairson and others, "Managed Care and Community-Oriented Care: Conflict or Complement," *Journal of Health Care for the Poor and Underserved,* vol. 8 (1997): 36–55.

94. Eileen Connor and Fitzhugh Mullan, eds., *Community-Oriented Primary Care: New Directions for Health Services Delivery* (Washington: National Academy Press, 1983); Alice Sardell, *The U.S. Experiment in Social Medicine* (University of Pittsburgh Press, 1988).

95. This is enunciated most clearly in David G. Whiteis, "Unhealthy Cities: Corporate Medicine, Community Economic Underdevelopment, and Public Health," *International Journal of Health Services,* vol. 27 (1997): 227–42. Some aspects also are captured in Kevin Barnett, *The Future of Community Benefit Programming: An Expanded Model for Planning and Assessing the Participation of Health Care Organizations in Community Health Improvement Activities* (Berkeley, Calif.: Public Health Institute, 1997).

96. Amick and others, "An Introduction."

97. McKnight, *Careless Society.*

98. This has been applied explicitly to notions of community benefit by Mark V. Pauly, "Health Systems Ownership: Can Regulation Preserve Community Benefits?" *Frontiers of Health Services Management,* vol. 12 (1996): 3–34; Carolyn Madden and Aaron Katz, *Community Benefits and Not-for-Profit Health Care: Policy Issues and Perspectives,* a report prepared for the Catholic Health Association (University of Washington, School of Public Health and Community Medicine, 1995); Schlesinger, Gray, and Bradley, "Charity and Community"; and Susan Sanders, "The Common Sense of the Nonprofit Hospital Tax Exemption: A Policy Analysis," *Journal of Policy Analysis and Management,* vol. 14 (1995): 446–66.

99. Generally, the focus has been on community benefit. A modest literature on the impact of organizational practices on the community-wide costs of medical care is summarized in Harold Luft, "Health Services Research as a Scientific Process," in Gordon Defriese, Thomas Ricketts, and Jane Stein, eds., *Methodological Advances in Health Services Research* (Ann Arbor: Health Administration, 1995): pp. 341–62.

100. Catherine Hoffman and Alan Schlobohm, *Uninsured in America: A Chart Book* (Washington: Kaiser Commission on Medicaid and the Uninsured, 2000).

3

Education and Training

DONALD M. STEWART, PEARL ROCK KANE, AND LISA SCRUGGS

Currently, there are 1,694 private, nonprofit colleges and universities educating roughly 20 percent of all students in American higher education and 27,402 private, nonprofit elementary and secondary schools educating about 10 percent of the kindergarten through twelfth grade (K–12) student population.[1] With 29,096 institutions in all, private, nonprofit education is a significant part of both America's independent sector and its educational infrastructure. There are no precise figures for the number of nonprofit organizations engaged in pre-employment training and placement. Yet, all together, these organizations are major contributors to the formation of the nation's human capital. They are important to the economy and to the democratic process.

Sustained by income earned from tuition and fees as well as from gifts, contracts, and grants, these institutions continue to exist in large part thanks to Section 501(c)(3) of the U.S. tax code, which exempts them from federal taxes. This chapter seeks to explain how these nonprofit entities function, the purposes they serve, and the forces that help to shape them. More specifically,

The authors thank John Cummins (Grinnell College, 2001) who did a masterful job of editing, rewriting, assembling, and formatting the vast amount of information provided by three authors to create a comprehensive and coherent chapter. We are greatly indebted to him for his fine work, good humor, and keen eye. We also would like to thank John P. Chalmers of the Chicago Community Trust for his meticulous and thoughtful review of the final draft and Derek Bok, president emeritus of Harvard University, for his wrap-up review and suggestions.

focusing on higher education, K–12 education, and employment training, it seeks to answer several questions: What is the state of nonprofit education and training in the United States today? Is it viable? What are the major challenges it is facing? How is it responding and how should it respond to these challenges at this time?

The chapter argues that the private, nonprofit sector in education and training, while small, fragile, and under attack, has survived in the past by being both responsive and resilient and that it is important for America that it be so in the future. However, its survival is not a foregone conclusion. Its institutions can only survive in a highly competitive environment if they continue to be adaptive, serve as sources of innovation, set high standards of quality to justify their price structure, and finally, offer greater choice and opportunity to an increasingly diverse population.[2]

Higher Education

America's genius has long resided in its ability to balance the strengths of private enterprise in its for-profit mode with public (government) as well as voluntary, nonprofit action in a constantly shifting "mixed economy" of institutions that seek to serve both the public and private good.[3] Nowhere are the inevitable tensions in such an arrangement more evident than in the field of American higher education, where a number of private, nonprofit colleges and universities face serious financial challenges. These institutions—which include major research universities, elite liberal arts colleges, as well as small nonselective liberal arts colleges—have historically been important sources of opportunity, experimentation, and innovation; yet some, particularly the small, nonelite colleges, now face the prospect of closings and mergers due to declining enrollments and insufficient alternative sources of income, such as endowments.[4]

Historically, the balance of enrollment between public and private, nonprofit institutions of higher education shifted to the former as American higher education grew and matured. In the words of University of Pennsylvania president emeritus Martin Meyerson some thirty years ago, the financial consequences of this shift made private, nonprofit liberal arts colleges and universities "an endangered breed."[5] If indeed that was a major challenge in the early 1970s when Mr. Meyerson made his observation, is it true today? If so, why do some private liberal arts colleges face extinction, while others thrive? Is "excess capacity" the fundamental issue to be addressed as we consider the challenges and accomplishments of private, nonprofit colleges and universities in the twenty-first century?

To answer these questions, we look first at the scale, contours, and historical origins of the nonprofit role in higher education. We then turn to some of the challenges that nonprofit higher education faces today and its responses to them.

The Nonprofit Role

In the fall of 1997, 14.9 million students were enrolled in approximately 4,064 higher education institutions in the United States.[6] While close to half of those institutions were private and nonprofit, 80 percent of all students were enrolled in public institutions. Yet the roughly 1,694 four-year private, nonprofit institutions of higher education in America have an aggregate enrollment of approximately 3 million and are distinctive in their diversity, resilience, commitment to moral values, and ability to respond to and serve changing social needs. Thus, for example, 904 are religiously affiliated (237 Roman Catholic), 47 are historically black, and 77 are women's colleges. Many are small, rural, and residential, offering small classes and nurturing environments. Often, these institutions have enrollments of fewer than 1,000 students. Good teaching, not research, is the primary goal of their faculty, and they do not practice selective admission.[7] Others are elite (that is, selective) colleges and universities that remain important teaching and research centers, setting standards of achievement and access for public and private institutions alike. While most of these "pacesetters" of higher education are doing well financially, they also face tremendous pressure to compete for students, faculty, and financial resources.[8]

BACKGROUND. It all started with Harvard College. Founded in 1636 under the aegis of the Massachusetts Bay Colony, Harvard—like the other eight "colonial colleges" created before 1770—sought to provide a classical education to prepare the clergy and "new world" leadership in law and medicine.[9] Modeled after Oxford and Cambridge, the colonial colleges were small and built on humanistic liberal arts traditions with heavy emphases on classical languages (Greek and Latin), ancient and medieval philosophy, history, art, and religion, with only a modicum of math and science. These colleges were focused more on preserving the past than on addressing practical needs of the day. Although at the outset they were governed largely by the clergy, each of the colleges received some form of needed assistance from the local colonial government and, later, state authorities. As Frederick Rudolph comments cynically in *The American College and University: A History*, "One great barrier to determining who paid the bills of the American college is the myth of the privately endowed independent college, a myth that was not encouraged until the colleges discovered that they could no longer feed at the public trough and had in one sense, indeed, become private."[10] At that point in time, American higher education and private, nonprofit higher education were, for all practical purposes, synonymous.

Hundreds of small colleges like these institutions were founded from 1770 until just after the Civil War. Often they were religiously inspired, denominationally related, and part of the country's western expansion. They were also all private and all poor.

Although the lines between public and private often get blurred in the history of American higher education, the Dartmouth College case decided by the U.S. Supreme Court in 1819 helped to lay the foundation for the legal distinction between a "public" and "private" college. This decision made clear the inability of the State of New Hampshire to encroach on Dartmouth's name or set policy regarding its leadership since the college was not a public entity supported by funds from the state's treasury. The practical upshot of the decision was the cessation of instate subsidies for Dartmouth and for private colleges in other states as well. The price paid for institutional autonomy was often penury on the part of independent (private) institutions.[11]

THE GROWTH OF GOVERNMENT INVOLVEMENT. After the Civil War, as Rudolph notes, states discovered more appealing outlets for their public largess than the "old-time" colleges with their religious orientation and adherence to a classical course of study.[12] With the passage of the first Morrill Act in 1862 and the second in 1890, state legislatures turned to state universities and federally endowed agricultural and mechanical colleges to develop practical and applied studies and to provide trained manpower for the agricultural, scientific, and industrial revolutions taking place at the dawn of the twentieth century.

In the process, public higher education began its growth and expansion in earnest. State colleges or "normal schools" were also opened to train public school teachers. Of special note in the 1890 Morrill Act was the provision that black Americans, in accordance with the 1890 Supreme Court decision of *Plessy v. Ferguson*,[13] would attend "separate but equal institutions of higher education," thus opening the way for the creation of public historically black colleges and universities (many private, nonprofit black colleges were started earlier in the nineteenth century, such as Spelman College in 1881).

Private colleges, with their large number of institutions spread across the country, held their own competitively for the first half of the twentieth century against the increasing number of state-supported public institutions. At the close of World War II until the early 1950s, enrollment was evenly divided between the two sectors. From 1950 through 1967, however, both public and private institutions experienced exponential growth in enrollment, but the public sector grew far more rapidly than the private. In 1968, private enrollment leveled off at slightly more than 2 million students, while public enrollment reached 5 million and continued to grow, reaching 9 million by 1977 and 11.2 million by 1997.[14]

A major engine for this growth was the expansion that occurred in state and federal support. Following World War II, the G.I. bill of rights, or Servicemen's Readjustment Act of 1944 (Public Law 78-346 and amendments), injected massive resources into the higher education sector. Returning G.I.s flooded university and college campuses with their "vouchers," which could be used at both private and public institutions. Initially, the federal government was willing to pay additional dollars to meet the higher tuition of private schools. However, competition for students between tuition-dependent private, nonprofit institutions and state-subsidized public institutions, coupled with complaints from state congressional delegations as well as governors, culminated in the early equalization of payments between public and private institutions. Since tuition at the public institutions was lower, an increasing number of G.I.s went to public institutions, and that trend only accelerated during the Korean War's G.I. bill period. Over time, private institutions found it difficult to attract and hold large numbers of veterans because of the cost-price differential.[15]

The structure of American higher education expanded further following the report in 1947 of the President's Commission on Higher Education, which recommmended that education through the fourteenth grade be made available to all students in the same way that high school by then was available.[16] Here was the opening wedge for the community college movement, which picked up momentum through the 1950s, 1960s, and early 1970s in states and cities all over the country. Public higher education's greatest growth has largely taken place in the community college subsector, which now accounts for half of all public sector students.[17]

Additional public support was provided to private institutions through the National Defense Education Act (Public Law 85-864 as amended), which was enacted in response to Sputnik in 1958 and provided scholarships, training grants, as well as federally subsidized loans for academically able students demonstrating financial need. Subsequently, the Higher Education Act of 1965 (Public Law 89-329) provided education opportunity grants of up to $1,500 in federal funds to students with "exceptional need." The funds were allocated to the institution, not the individual student, as was the case with G.I. bill payments. In neither case, however, did the aid offset the financial advantage that public institutions enjoyed.

With passage of the 1972 amendments to the Higher Education Act of 1965, Congress shifted the focus of its college aid from institutions to students, creating the basic education opportunity grant (BEOG) to target poor students. Although the "means-tested" BEOG was large enough to pay tuition at both public institutions and a number of private institutions in 1972–73, rising costs and prices meant that they barely covered the costs of tuition at community colleges a decade later, when BEOGs were renamed Pell grants.[18] Federal grant aid to students continued to decline during the 1980s and 1990s, reaching its lowest level since the 1980s in 1995–96, by which time federal aid had largely shifted from grants to loans.[19]

THE STRUCTURE OF PRIVATE HIGHER EDUCATION. This pattern of public and private development has produced a diverse structure of private higher education institutions. Most numerous are the small, nonselective undergraduate institutions that are the descendants of the early private colleges that emerged in the nineteenth century. These institutions usually rely overwhelmingly on tuition revenues for their survival and appeal to students on the basis of special religious, geographic, ethnic, or value affinities. Although these institutions are not strong in any one or combination of revenue sources, they continue to benefit from the strong commitment in American culture and society to the importance of choice. There may be brand loyalty, even if it is not for a major brand, and not all students want to attend public institutions even if they are cheaper.[20]

At the opposite extreme are the elite private colleges and universities. The thirty-two members of the Consortium on Financing Higher Education (COFHE), for example, have strong endowments, world-class faculty, and the most talented students in the United States as measured by SAT/ACT scores.[21] They are considered the medallion institutions of private higher education in America. Their major competitors are one another and flagship public institutions like the University of California at Berkeley, University of California, Los Angeles, as well as the universities of Michigan and Virginia. These institutions stand at the head of the food chain in the highly stratified system of private higher education in the United States based on selectivity and research productivity.[22]

Within this group are the elite research universities. In fact, the most notable development in private, nonprofit higher education at the turn of the twentieth century was the creation of the modern research university. Johns Hopkins University (1876), modeled after the graduate research universities of nineteenth-century Germany, was among the first along with Harvard, Yale, Princeton, Columbia, Brown, Cornell, Rutgers, and Penn. Beginning graduate and graduate professional programs at almost the same time were the University of Chicago in the late nineteenth century, supported by John D. Rockefeller Sr., and the Massachusetts Institute of Technology, which still remains the nation's one private land grant institution.[23] Stanford University was not far behind. State land grant universities quickly followed (for example, Michigan, Illinois, Minnesota, and California) and gained status comparable to that of the private universities, but the premier research universities in the private sector were already at the forefront of technological innovation and change.

In between these two poles of the continuum are several hundred other private colleges and universities that lie outside the top tier but nevertheless remain "selective." These so-called Baccalaureate I (liberal arts) institutions regularly lead the lists in the *U.S. News and World Report's* ratings of America's best colleges. Thus, for example, the top fifty schools out of 228 national universities offering a full range of undergraduate majors in addition to master's and Ph.D. degrees as well as 162 national liberal arts colleges that award at least 40 percent of their degrees in the liberal arts are all private, nonprofit institutions. In addition, with a few exceptions, the top fifty out of 505 "regional" universities that offer a full range of undergraduate liberal arts offerings and some graduate programs, along with 428 "regional liberal arts colleges" that grant fewer than 40 percent of their degrees in liberal arts disciplines, are also predominantly private.[24] The most selective are COFHE members, and most (but not all) of them have the resources to grant need-based as well as merit-based admission and support.[25] These institutions are also considered financially strong by Moody's. A recent study prepared by Moody's Investors Service of some 240 of these selective, private, nonprofit colleges and universities (including the COFHE institutions) finds that they remain creditworthy, even though "longer-term divergence in credit quality is likely."[26]

Challenges

While significant segments of private higher education remain financially viable, however, all segments face an increasing range of challenges that have put institutional survival in question for some and institutional mission in question for others. Five of these challenges deserve special mention here.

AFFORDABILITY. Perhaps the most basic challenge facing private higher education has been the escalation of costs and the increased reliance on tuition income to cover them. Cost increases in higher education have exceeded those elsewhere in the economy, apparently because of the labor-intensive nature of teaching and research; the competitive battles among elite institutions for the best faculty, top students, and research funding; as well as library costs and the heavy expense of technology.[27] With a faculty culture that expects excellence, full participation in all decisions, and a self-perpetuating board (often made up of alumni) not able to exercise corporate-like top-down decisionmaking, cost containment is difficult to achieve. Quality, demonstrated by new programs, prestigious professors, and the most competitive students, is expensive—the latter often due to need-based admission and scholarship support. Yet faculty salaries, followed by student aid and technological improvements, constitute the largest expenses of private universities.[28]

With the decline in government financial aid in the 1980s and 1990s, and its shift from grants to loans, institutions have had to rely increasingly on tuition revenue to cover their costs. Although this has been true of all institutions, it has been particularly true of private institutions. Thus, for example, in 1995–96, the major source of income for public institutions of higher education was state government (35.9 percent), with tuition income a mere 18.8 percent and endowment income only 0.6 percent (local government, federal government, private sources, and sales and services made up the rest).[29] It is a very different picture for private, nonprofit institutions of higher education, where, according to McPherson and Schapiro, net tuition revenue composes 55 percent of all revenues at private research and doctorate-providing universities, 76 percent of revenues at private liberal arts colleges, and 85 percent of revenues at private comprehensive universities.[30]

To keep this revenue growing sufficiently to cover costs, institutions have had to boost their tuition. As a consequence, tuition increases in higher education in the 1980s and 1990s outpaced the country's rate of inflation (the consumer price index, CPI, as measured in real dollars), causing severe affordability problems for middle- and lower-income families. As the National Commission on the Cost of Higher Education reported in January 1998,

> Rising college tuitions are real. In the twenty years between 1976 and 1996, the average tuition at public universities increased from $642 to $3,151, and the average tuition at private universities increased from $2,881 to $15,581. Tuitions at public two-year colleges, the least expensive of all types of institution, increased from an average of $245 to $1,245 during this period.[31]

Costs per student rose particularly fast in private research universities during the 1970s (as compared to modest increases in state-supported institutions during that same period). Increases in the net cost of attending private universities exceeded not only the overall rate of inflation, but also inflation in medical costs.[32] According to the most recent analyses performed by the College Board, tuition has increased more than 100 percent of the CPI since 1981, while median family income has risen only 27 percent in real terms.[33]

In this environment, private, nonprofit higher education is less attractive than public higher education to the middle class as well as to the more affluent. "Middle-class melt" is the phrase most often used by private institutions as they see students and families "who can pay" choose lower-priced public institutions.[34] With the federal government providing the bulk (three-quarters) of the $75 billion in available student aid in the form of loans through the Federal Family Education Loan Program (FFELP) and the Ford Direct Student Loan Program, college has become even less affordable to families and students unwilling to incur increasing amounts of debt. It remains to be seen what impact the Taxpayer Relief Act of 1997 (Public Law 105-34), which created non-need-based support through Hope scholarships and Lifetime Learning tax credits, will have on consumer choice vis-à-vis public versus private colleges and universities. In any event, its benefits will accrue to the middle class, leaving poor students still unable to increase their access to higher-priced colleges and universities, whether private or public.

CHALLENGE TO THE LIBERAL ARTS COLLEGES. A second challenge facing private higher education has been the assault on the tradition of liberal arts education. At the core of the academy, the arts and science disciplines as they have evolved from the classical curricula of the colonial colleges and developed into the graduate departments and professional schools of our major research universities provide the intellectual rigor and knowledge that define higher learning and are at the heart of traditional liberal arts institutions.[35]

According to Breneman and Finn, of the 2,827 colleges included in the 1970 classification system of the then Carnegie Commission on Higher Education, over half (1,514) were private, and the selective private institutions dominated the four-year liberal arts categories.[36] However, Bok notes, "As the search for jobs grew more difficult in the stagnant economy of the 1970s, students shifted en masse from the liberal arts toward vocationally oriented studies."[37] Faced with mounting competition for a dwindling student population, some private liberal arts colleges appear to have responded by relaxing academic standards, adding vocational majors, increasing student-faculty ratios, and requiring fewer liberal arts courses. The less selective liberal arts colleges, most vulnerable to public sector competition, were caught in this "crunch," and their quality diminished accordingly.[38] Thus, defining a liberal arts college as an institution that awards at least 40 percent of its degrees in arts and science disciplines (versus degrees awarded in occupational or professional areas), David Breneman found that only 212 of the 540 institutions classified as liberal arts colleges by the Carnegie Commission in 1970 deserved that designation as of 1994.[39] This shift threatens to emasculate one of the defining rationales for the preservation of private, nonprofit education.

CHALLENGE TO THE RESEARCH UNIVERSITIES. Where private, nonprofit higher education has held its own distinctive competence, and continues to do so today, is with the research university model, which it planted in American soil before the turn of the twentieth century. Yet, while many of these universities remain viable, challenges abound. Indeed, the private, nonprofit research university faces "its most serious long-term financial challenge since World War II and probably its most momentous in history."[40] The golden age of federal support for academic research in the physical sciences and engineering ended along with the cold war in 1989. Federal and state appropriations for research and graduate education in the country's 100 major research institutions are virtually stagnant and, in some fields, declining.[41] The exception is the National Institutes of Health (NIH), particularly in the biomedical and biotechnology fields. NIH funding has continued to increase for the last four years, fueling research in the fields of genomics, embryonics, stem cell regeneration, AIDS, and oncology.[42] Of the 100 major research universities receiving the bulk of NIH funding, thirty are private and seventy are public. However, the private institutions have long received a disproportionate share of the federal funds.[43]

Research universities with academic health centers have a particular set of challenges. Their major collective challenges are cost containment and cost reimbursement under the Medicaid program (Public Law 89-97). Caught by surprise in the early 1990s by increased economic competition from managed care companies working on behalf of cost-conscious employers and private insurance companies, these academic health centers find themselves in a cost-price squeeze that they cannot control, matching the general woes of private higher education today.[44] Often serving large, uninsured, and poor communities, these centers also depend on state-provided Medicaid reimbursement in order to provide primary care and graduate medical education that can never be delivered in a strictly cost-effective manner. In addition, the recent advent of reduced Medicare reimbursement rates and reduced fees from privately insured patients have made it virtually impossible to cross-subsidize Medicaid patients for whom states rarely cover full costs, thereby adding one more cost burden to the academic health centers of private research universities.[45] This cost pressure in research universities with academic health centers applies not only to patient care, but also to teaching and research.

Due to the balanced budget amendment of 1997 (S.274), which capped payments for medical procedures regardless of cost as well as cut funding for graduate medical education, teaching hospitals are no longer the "cash cows" for research universities that they were in the 1970s, 1980s, and early 1990s. The situation is compounded by increased pressure from federal agencies such as the National Institutes of Health to reduce the reimbursement rates for indirect costs while increasing productivity.[46] NIH support for both direct and indirect research costs is therefore no longer able to cross-subsidize—to the extent it did in the past—the teaching and research functions of the research institutions' medical education program.[47] Basic scientific research support for the academic health centers and their medical faculties must increasingly come from the university's tuition income and, when appropriate, patient-care revenues. Yet tuition covers only a fraction of the total cost of educating undergraduates at most research universities, thereby causing disparities that not even Arthur Andersen might hide.[48]

FOR-PROFIT COMPETITION. A fourth challenge facing American private education results from new technological advances that have opened the way to growing competition from for-profit providers of educational services. To be sure, computer-based and on-line education offers new opportunities to improve academic effectiveness and efficiency, as the case of Ohio Dominican College reported by Allen Splete shows.[49] But it also generates more competition from for-profit or other non-campus-based providers of educational services, particularly for part-time, working adult students. Such nontraditional students helped to relieve many private colleges of their financial difficulties by enrolling in their continuing education programs during the enrollment trough of the 1970s, 1980s, and early 1990s, when there were insufficient numbers of traditional eighteen- to twenty-one-year-olds to fill available spaces at many of these institutions. The University of Phoenix, today the nation's largest for-profit private university, offers on-line, complete degree programs in business management, technology, education, and nursing to more than 35,000 students.[50] Using an asynchronous format much like e-mail, the part-time learner is able to access the Internet courses of choice (for a price), any time or place, to follow the curriculum. The University of Phoenix is fully accredited by the North Central Association, as are Harvard, Princeton, and Yale.

Western Governors' University, the Learning Odyssey, Argosy University, and California Virtual University are other for-profit institutions that offer distance-learning opportunities that appeal to the part-time student who might well have attended a private, nonprofit institution instead. Although less than 2 percent of this type of student is involved in "cyber learning" delivered by a for-profit entity, this area will continue to grow. A number of nonprofit universities have moved into this market and have sought to deliver on-line distance education through for-profit subsidiaries.[51] For example, NYU On-line, established by New York University, sought to provide career-focused courses and certified programs. E-Cornell, at Cornell University, was established to deliver on-line courses. Fathom, part of Columbia University, brought up an "interactive knowledge site." Duke Corporate Education, established by Duke University's Fuqua School of Business, provides consulting advice on-line to corporations. Babson Interactive, at Babson College in Boston, offers nondegree business courses.

Many questions arise, however, as to how private, nonprofit higher education institutions will manage these for-profit entities and whether they will be successful financially. Many of these undertakings have already proven to be unsuccessful financially.[52] As in the case of many dot-com commercial undertakings, there is insufficient demand in the field of private, higher education by traditional and adult students to justify the cost of developing expensive courseware for delivery over the Internet. The fascination with technology seems unable to sustain a viable market for on-line college-level courses, and many universities have lost millions of dollars in start-up costs for distance-learning programs as a result. Samples of failed on-line university ventures, as reported recently by *The New York Times*, include:

—California Virtual University, a clearinghouse of existing on-line courses offered by all of the public and private colleges in the State of California, was initiated in 1997 and abandoned in April 1999.

—Western Governors' University, a clearinghouse of existing American on-line degree and nondegree programs, was scaled back to just teacher education.

—Virtual Temple, a wholly owned, profit-making corporation based at Temple University and designed to provide a "global university," was abandoned in July of 2001.

—E-Cornell, from Cornell University, was reorganized to focus solely on nondegree programs in medical education and hotel administration.

—NYU On-line was abandoned in December of 2001, after investments in excess of $20 million.

—Fathom Consortium, which includes Columbia University (its largest investor), the London School of Economics, the University of Chicago, and the New York Public Library, is reconsidering the program after expenditures in excess of $25 million and, one assumes, very little return.[53]

Opportunities to use computer-based information systems to mount new distributed instructional programs will continue to present themselves to private, nonprofit universities as they seek to remain financially viable by finding new revenue streams.[54] Few private four-year colleges have the capacity to mount such Internet-based efforts. Partnerships with other nonprofit organizations, with public organizations, and with for-profit organizations may still offer new marketing possibilities, but for now, they remain elusive.[55] Yet computer-based distributed education is here to stay, and whether it supplements the residential college experience for the traditional undergraduate or is part of the professional training of a corporate executive, it will continue to transform private higher education by making new relationships and partnerships between private, nonprofit, and for-profit institutions part of business as usual.[56]

SHIFTING PRIORITIES OF PRIVATE PHILANTHROPY. A fifth concern facing private higher education is an apparent shift in priorities on the part of private charitable institutions, especially foundations. Education has traditionally been valued and well supported by philanthropy. In the early twentieth century, the era of big foundations commenced with the Rockefeller Foundation, which supported schools of medicine and public health. Andrew Carnegie followed by establishing free public libraries. Philanthropic support has continued to the present day, with giving to higher education in fiscal 2000–01 reportedly growing 4.3 percent over the previous twelve-month period in spite of a depressed stock market.[57] According to the Council for Aid to Education's annual survey, "Voluntary Support of Education," private contributions to American colleges and universities for the fiscal year ending June 30, 2001, reached $24.2 billion, yet the rate of increase was much lower than the previous year's (1999–2000) increase of 12.7 percent. Annual voluntary support for higher education has doubled since 1994, when it reportedly totaled $12 billion. The largest share of support comes from alumni (28 percent), with private research universities receiving, on average, the largest share per institution—about twice the amounts received, on average, by public research universities. Harvard University, with its $18.3 billion endowment, held the number one position in gifts received last year ($683 million), with Stanford University a close second.

Yet, in spite of its success, many view with alarm the decrease in educational giving to colleges and universities, particularly from foundations. Many of the largest foundations, such as Gates, Pew, and Atlantic Philanthropies, are focusing on K–12 education, prompting Bob Weisbuch, president of the Woodrow Wilson Foundation in Princeton, to ask, "Are we in the liberal arts failing to make a case for ourselves?"[58] Undergraduate education continues to receive the largest share of foundation giving (35 percent), but elementary and secondary education is a close second.

The most vulnerable institutions, given the shifting priorities of foundations and the need for both an endowment and a strong base of alumni giving, are the small, often nonselective, unendowed, private liberal arts colleges.[59] Shortfalls in enrollment at small regional colleges, like Ripon in Wisconsin (with a modest endowment of $35 million), mean financial disaster, with tuition the only real source of income. Institutions like Ripon make up the vast majority of the 1,600 private liberal arts colleges in the United States. Only thirty-one have endowments greater than $1 billion, with an overall median endowment of $12 million. Many of these institutions may be forced to close their doors. The trustees of Notre Dame College in New Hampshire and Marycrest International University in Iowa have already decided to follow this path rather than face mounting faculty and staff layoffs along with growing accumulated debt.

How serious the shift in priorities of major funders is for private higher education is by no means clear. Private support for private colleges continues to rise, increasing by 68 percent to almost $7 billion for support from alumni between 1995 and 2000.[60] During the same period, private support increased 64 percent to $5.5 billion from individuals other than alumni, 44 percent to $4 billion from corporations, 9 percent to $5 billion from foundations, and 9 percent to $370 million from religious organizations. Given the pattern of distribution between elite and nonelite institutions, only a small amount of these contributions went to the vast majority of small, private liberal arts colleges in the United States.

The strong economy of the 1990s, which both created great private wealth and added to existing fortunes, resulted in numerous gifts to higher education. It is now predicted that between $40 trillion and $136 trillion will migrate between the generations over the next fifty years, depending on the state of the economy.[61] A significant portion of this money will find its way into American higher education. What proportion of this great transfer of wealth will find its way into private colleges and universities, particularly the endangered breed of small, private liberal arts colleges? It is hard to predict, but if some of it is not so directed, many of these fine institutions will cease to exist. Herein lies one of philanthropy's major challenges for the twenty-first century.

Nonprofit Responses

In the face of these challenges, nonprofit higher education institutions have shown considerable resourcefulness. Several different types of responses are thus in evidence.

MARKETING TO STUDENTS. In the first place, institutions have aggressively marketed themselves to potential students in order to overcome their cost-price problems. Many private institutions have used "merit" awards, "gap" awards, partial payments, discounts on the "sticker price," and aggressive marketing to help gain market share, although the public-private price differential continues to give public institutions a competitive edge. The most common marketing technique used today by private institutions is discounting, using so-called merit aid to attract the middle-income student with at least partial ability to pay. Discounting tuition helps private institutions to negotiate with students and their families around the full cost or sticker price in order to reach agreement on tuition amounts the family can afford or is willing to pay. However, by continuing to reduce their tuition charges in order to attract middle-income students, private institutions—particularly small nonselective colleges with enrollments fewer than 850 students—are reducing income needed for institutional maintenance and therefore survival.[62]

Given the complex array of public and private colleges and universities with tuition and fee charges (prices) that range between $27,000 and above (which 6 percent of the student population attend) and $4,000 and below (which 22 percent of all students attend), the discounting of prices is an important marketing strategy of enormous importance to institutional cash flow.[63] Particularly among small colleges that charge low tuition, there is a desperate effort to diversify and strengthen revenue streams as they compete with large and selective institutions, but they can only discount so much before putting themselves out of business. Business officers focus on discounting because of its critical role in revenue generation. Today, private higher education is retaining an average of only 62 cents on each dollar charged as it lowers its sticker price in order to attract more students.[64] Several small, little-known, low-tuition private, nonprofit colleges crossed the equilibrium point and gave away far more potential income than they needed to run the institution and simply ran out of money. Bradford College in Massachusetts could not give its product away at any price and closed its doors. Discounting has its limitations, although today the average tuition discount in private higher education is 38 percent.

COMMERCIALIZATION OF RESEARCH. A second broad approach to funding higher education, available mostly to large research universities, is the commercialization of university research, frequently in partnership with the for-profit sector. The patent and trademark amendments, better known as the Bayh-Dole act (Public Law 96-517), passed in 1980, grant ownership rights to universities and their faculty principal investigators for research results supported with federal funds. As a consequence, commercial ties through licenses and patents have been proliferating, with interesting implications for traditional systems of academic values and rewards, particularly in private research universities.[65] Peer review is one such value, and its practice has now been threatened by the increasing involvement of research universities both in commercial transactions as well as in the political process.

The new commercialization has given a new twist to the long-standing tension between what Donald E. Stokes calls "general understanding," that is, knowledge for the sake of knowledge, and "applied use," that is, the solution of practical problems (for example, cancer) through the application of technological innovation.[66] Under the framework put in place by President Roosevelt's wartime director of the Office of Scientific Research and Development, Professor Vannevar Bush of the Massachusetts Institute of Technology (MIT), in his pivotal 1944 report, *Science, the Endless Frontier*, federal policy consciously sidestepped this distinction and committed itself to funding basic research in the confident expectation that practical consequences eventually would flow from it.[67] Under this structure, the autonomy of faculty and rigor of proposal review for those seeking grants from NSF (National Science Foundation) and NIH were to be safeguarded through a peer review process. In recent years, however, this confidence has been frayed, and greater attention has been given to stimulating applied research. This is particularly evident in the life sciences, where important new connections have formed with the commercial fields of medicine, pharmaceuticals, and biotechnology. The Bayh-Dole act has intensified this reorientation by giving universities a strong incentive to treat "knowledge as property," according to Powell and Owen-Smith, with academic entrepreneurship encouraged and rewarded.[68] New for-profit subsidiaries and partnerships get formed, as does a new culture within the university, where values such as discovery and peer recognition in refereed journals leading to promotion and tenure based on merit are challenged by the promise of greater financial rewards generated by a commercial venture. New companies are being formed by universities for purposes of technology transfer, and the universities themselves are being described as engines of economic progress (for example, job creation) rather than as centers of academic excellence.

Such may have been the intent of Bayh-Dole, but such is not the intent of most major private research universities as they seek to balance the values of intellectual curiosity, collegiality, and rigor against the need for increased revenue. Yet 19 percent of all university research is now conducted in conjunction with private industry, and university patenting has grown quite rapidly, particularly in the life sciences.[69] Four out of the ten leading research universities with the most contractual agreements with biotechnology companies are private: MIT, Harvard, Stanford, and Johns Hopkins (where gene splicing got started).[70] These same ten institutions receive the largest share (21 percent) of federal support ($13 billion in 1992) for research and are in the forefront of commercialization. Their institutional structures and outreach efforts all reflect this area of emphasis (for example, all have comparable offices of technology transfer, offices of patent administration, and offices of sponsored research).

Like the boundaries that, in theory, once separated basic from applied research and technology, as well as the boundaries that separated the disciplines of the life sciences, the boundaries that separate private, nonprofit research universities from for-profit, commercial operations that seek to use research results for commercial purposes (for example, drug companies) are becoming blurred. The federal government, through the Bayh-Dole legislation, has seen fit to make research universities, once important instruments for national defense, instruments for enhancing American economic competitiveness at a time when the institutions need added financial support. Although the academic benefits of commercialization of research remain unclear, the financial rewards are obvious, though only a small handful of institutions seem to make significant profits on patents.[71] Meanwhile, however, important academic values are being threatened.

POLITICIZATION OF RESEARCH FUNDING. Another response to the pressures on higher education has been the growth of what has sometimes been called "academic pork-barreling," that is, the earmarking of research grants through the federal appropriations process, bypassing the mechanisms of peer review. From 1980 to 1993, congressional earmarking for universities and colleges amounted to more than $3 billion.[72] In fiscal 2000 alone, such earmarks had risen to $1.7 billion. Although public institutions have been especially active in the pursuit of such earmarks, arguing that the peer review system gives unfair advantage to the established private institutions through an academic "old boys' network," private institutions have also gotten into the act as well. Many academics consider congressional earmarks undesirable since they are based on political considerations.[73]

OTHER RESPONSES. Colleges and universities around the nation are using a wide range of coping strategies, as nonselective, underendowed private institutions struggle to survive through aggressive marketing and redefinition of missions.[74] An interesting collection of presidential essays edited by Allen P. Splete, former president of the Council of Independent Colleges (which represents many such "invisible colleges," as once characterized by Clark Kerr), describes the successful marketing responses employed by thirteen private, nonprofit institutions of higher education to deal with mounting enrollment challenges. They include:

—San Antonio's former Roman Catholic college, University of the Incarnate Word, diversified its graduate course offerings to become a university and increased its enrollment of Hispanic students as the result of aggressive bilingual advertising throughout the Southwest.[75]

—Pittsburgh's all-female Chatham College bolstered enrollment by reaffirming its gender orientation while admitting part-time male students into much-expanded graduate programs, all the while emphasizing academic rigor and measurable outcomes through institutional assessment.[76]

—Park College in Parkville, Missouri, facing a diminishing pool of potential white students, changed its curricular offerings and the racial and ethnic composition of its faculty in order to build its enrollment successfully from the surrounding African American and Hispanic communities.[77]

—College of Mount St. Joseph in Cincinnati, Ohio, moved from being a staid Roman Catholic women's college to embrace coeducation and, through its strategic planning process (Visions 2000), created a new culture of participation and a new curriculum to attract new students.[78]

—Drury University (formerly Drury College), located in scenic Springfield, Missouri, while maintaining its grounding in the liberal arts, added a business program (Breeds School of Business) and a five-year professional degree in architecture to strengthen its professional offerings in order to increase sagging enrollment.[79]

All five of these institutions adopted modern management techniques with a strong marketing orientation and, save for Chatham in Pittsburgh, redefined their basic mission in order to widen their market appeal. All continue to consider themselves essentially liberal arts institutions, and all five stress the importance of building ethical character.

As these cases suggest, private, nonprofit higher education institutions in the United States, particularly those that are nonselective, have had to work hard to avoid the Meyersonian label of an "endangered breed." But as a whole, the private, nonprofit sector of American higher education seems to be doing just that. In all of their diversity—from major private research universities, to elite liberal arts colleges, to small regional four-year colleges serving special populations such as African Americans, Hispanics, women, and sectarian groups—private, nonprofit institutions, large and small, hold a special place in American higher education as well as in the nonprofit sector. Facing the constant challenge of maintaining and enhancing academic quality, while remaining price competitive, these institutions nevertheless have been holding their own, with one-fifth of the nation's higher education student population since the 1970s. Although somewhat outdated, a list compiled by the National Association of Independent Colleges and Universities indicates that twenty-five accredited private, nonprofit undergraduate institutions offering baccalaureate liberal arts degrees have closed since 1986, but only eight of those closings took place after 1993, the last one being West Coast University in Los Angeles in 1997.[80]

Indeed, enrollment at private institutions is projected to grow at an annual average rate of 1.7 percent between 2004 and 2010, which is 0.1 percent higher than the projected 1.6 percent growth rate of four-year public institutions.[81]

This projected increase in enrollment at private, nonprofit colleges and universities is an outgrowth of the overall projected increase in undergraduate enrollment—an estimated increase of 2.6 million students between 1995 and 2015.[82] Demographics tell us that this growth spurt, following almost no growth for twenty years since the "baby boomers" hit campuses in the 1960s, reflects the students born between 1982 and 1996—that is, the post–World War II baby boom "echo." They will be joined by a growing number of adults, including the "boomers" (much subdued since the 1960s) as well as foreign students, in our graduate and professional schools. Of the 2.6 million new students, 80 percent are projected by 2015 to be minorities: African American, Hispanic, and Asian-Pacific Islanders. Overall, minority enrollment is anticipated to rise by 2 million in absolute numbers, or a rise of 29.4 percent, to 37.2 percent of undergraduate enrollment. What does this 16 percent increase in the overall student population, one-third of which will be minority students, mean for private colleges and universities? Is this the new and expanded market that they need? Probably not: since many of these students will be first-generation, poor, and victims of substandard urban and rural school systems, they will likely go to community colleges. The absence of grant aid and growing trend of private colleges—selective and nonselective—to provide merit-based rather than need-based aid (like the federal and state governments) preclude the possibility that poor minority students will ever have greater representation in private higher education.[83] Yet private colleges can make a difference, as in the case of the Associated Colleges of Illinois, with their precollegiate talent identification and mentoring programs as well as teacher training.[84]

Conclusion

In spite of the challenges it faces, the private, nonprofit higher education sector is growing, however modestly. The research universities and highly selective colleges (that is, the elite institutions) lead the way, getting more applicants than ever before. Well-to-do families still want the "insurance policy" of an Ivy League education.[85] The institutions at all tiers continue to survive and offer access, choice, diversity, innovation, and postsecondary education experiences of overall quality. Quality teaching and learning remain at the heart of the enterprise, at the undergraduate, graduate, and graduate professional levels, with research an important stimulus for all three. In addition, these institutions are affordable to many middle-income families when appropriate financial aid, tax credits, or discounting arrangements are made available. Yet many middle-income families are opting for public rather than private institutions as a consequence of changing values, improved public higher education, and limited discretionary income. While stopping this loss is a challenge, private institutions are not an endangered breed, but a special breed of institution that is well worth preserving and eminently preservable.

Elementary and Secondary Education

Not only does the nonprofit sector play a significant role in the field of higher education, but it maintains a significant presence in elementary and secondary education as well. This section describes private elementary and secondary education in America, beginning with the background, types, and demographics of private schools. It then turns to the challenges facing private schools. As a context for the discussion, we examine two prominent types of private schools— Catholic and independent.

Background

The first schools in America were private, often relying on a combination of funding from tuition and taxes for their existence. Long before Horace Mann championed free public education for the towns of Massachusetts, a variety of private schools existed to serve a diversity of family orientations and preferences. Some schools were rooted in Puritan traditions; others were operated by churches, chartered corporations, or enterprising individuals. These schools competed for the students who could afford the cost of tuition.

A small number of private schools that were supported by philanthropy educated students who were excluded from other school options, such as students of color.[86] In fact, the Protestant ethos of mass education in America felt culturally alienating to some groups, who, believing their survival at stake, did what "beleaguered or dissenting" minorities have done throughout history: they built their own schools, resisting state intervention.[87] In the landmark *Pierce v. Society of Sisters* Supreme Court decision of 1925, Justice McReynolds notes, "The liberty of parents and guardians to direct the upbringing and education of children under their control is vital to the health of America."[88] Often called the Magna Carta of private schools, this decision established the private school's right to exist and a parent's right to choose a private school.[89]

The Diversity of Private Schools

In 1899, the first year that the federal government collected statistics on private schools, approximately 11 percent of all elementary and secondary school students attended private schools. Despite minor fluctuations, private school enrollment hovered at roughly 10 percent during most of the twentieth century, and today some 11 percent of all American students (5,076,199) attend 27,402 private (nonpublic) elementary and secondary schools.[90] Fully 83 percent of private school students attend religious schools, half of which are Catholic. The most rapidly growing religious sector is conservative Christian. Another 17 percent of private school students attend nonsectarian schools.[91] Often not reflected in these statistics are types too difficult to count, such as home schools, which are estimated to include 500,000 to 750,000 children.[92]

Catholic and independent schools provide useful lenses for examining the status of American private schooling. Catholic schools serve the largest population of private school students. Independent schools are a small group of private, nonsectarian schools that educate 8 percent of all students who attend private schools; they are often referred to as "prep schools."[93] In spite of their small numbers, these schools have exerted significant influence, for they rank among the most prestigious institutions in the country. As different as these schools may be in terms of clientele and economics, Catholic and independent schools face similar threats to their stability.

CATHOLIC SCHOOLS. In the nineteenth century, waves of Catholic immigrants, many uneducated and impoverished, precipitated militant anti-Catholic bias in the heavily Protestant American society and Protestant-oriented public schools.[94] Catholic leaders responded by developing their own school system, mandating "a Catholic school for every parish" dedicated to placing "every Catholic child in a Catholic school."[95] Reaching peak enrollments in the mid-1960s, Catholic schools served half of elementary-age Catholic children and one-third of secondary school-age Catholics.

As the number of teachers available from religious orders decreased and the upward mobility of Catholics made religious schools less appealing to them, Catholic school enrollments declined. Then, in the mid-1960s, the Second Vatican Council proclaimed an enlarged mission for Catholic schools, identifying the schools as instruments of social justice focused on building communities and fostering emotional, as well as academic, development. As a result, the schools have been welcoming an increasing number of racial minorities and non-Catholic students.[96]

Catholic schools today are characterized by a focused academic curriculum, small size, decentralized governance, the concept of the school as a community, and inspirational ideology. Requiring the same curriculum for all, the focused program in Catholic schools results in higher academic achievement than in public schools.[97]

INDEPENDENT SCHOOLS. Beginning in the seventeenth century, a variety of quasi-private schools existed in the United States. Although most depended on public funds for survival, these schools were private in their governance and ownership. Some were maintained by churches as adjuncts of religious programs. Others were private ventures run by individuals or groups of teachers. Still others, known as academies, were founded by self-perpetuating boards of trustees to offer instruction that went beyond rudimentary literacy and computation. Most of these schools were also public in the sense that they were open to children with the desire and means to attend.[98]

With the evolution of common schools—free schools providing basic education for all—many of these private schools lost constituents and public support. Yet families willing to pay for education reflecting their own values remained. These private schools evolved into independent boarding and day schools. Independent boarding schools, which grew out of the academy movement, were shaped after the European upper-class model. Emphasizing physical, intellectual, and moral education, independent boarding schools included both classical and modern curricula. Independent day schools developed from proprietary schools or schools operated for profit, town and church schools, and country day schools, which were designed to provide an education comparable to that of the boarding schools.[99]

Today's independent boarding and day schools reflect this range of origins. Some are traditional, some progressive, some single sex, some coeducational, some highly selective, some designed to offer struggling students a second chance, some with impressive endowments, some reliant on tuition, some fully reliant on philanthropy to educate disadvantaged children. The defining characteristic of an independent school is its "self-selecting and thus self-perpetuating board of trustees [that] bears ultimate responsibility for [its] philosophy, resources, and programs."[100] Mission-driven, independent schools are mostly small and self-supporting, avoiding public monies to protect against government interference. They determine their own curricula, devise their methods for selecting faculty and students, and strive for personalized environments.

The schools in the National Association of Independent Schools, an affiliation of 1,100 independent schools, serve approximately 500,000 students.[101] These schools, which are among the most costly private schools, are known as prep schools, for their purpose is to prepare students for college. Requiring a rigorous curriculum, independent prep schools enjoy influence disproportionate to their numbers due to the quality of their programs, the success their graduates have matriculating at competitive colleges, and the substantial social, economic, and political capital of their alumni.

Challenges to Private Schools

In recent years, both Catholic and independent schools have broadened their missions to serve more racially and economically diverse populations. Supported by philanthropy during the late twentieth-century prosperity, these schools have served many who might otherwise have attended public schools. Success in educating diverse populations has made Catholic and independent schools notable contributors to the common good. However, commitment to diversity, which often means a commitment to low tuition or financial aid, means a greater reliance on donors, making the schools more vulnerable to external conditions.

The uncertain economy of the twenty-first century presents a number of challenges to Catholic and independent schools, which will have to confront the issues of diversity, teacher shortages, competition, and their own affordability.

DIVERSITY. Both Catholic and independent schools recognize the need to enroll a more diverse population for philosophical and pragmatic reasons. Not only are the schools responding to a moral imperative to promote social justice by educating *all* Americans, but they are reacting to economic and demographic realities. More than 12 million American children live in poverty; another 16.7 million live in low-income families.[102] Children of color compose one-third of five- to seventeen-year-olds in the United States; twenty-five years from now, almost half of American children will be children of color.[103]

Efforts to educate a more diverse student body have played out differently in Catholic and independent schools. Catholic schools, already established in inner cities to educate European immigrants, continue to focus on educating the poor, both Catholic and non-Catholic. Independent schools have made more modest attempts to recruit economically and racially diverse students, often choosing those with high potential from neighborhoods outside of the schools' immediate locations.

The changing Catholic school demographics have created both financial pressures and challenges to the definition of Catholic education. Today, students of color compose 25 percent of Catholic school enrollment, and 13 percent of students are non-Catholic.[104] Since more than one-third of urban Catholic schools are situated in inner cities (1,020 of the 3,752 schools), these figures belie the reality that many schools serve 90 to 100 percent students of color, frequently a predominantly non-Catholic clientele.[105] At Edmund Rice High School in Harlem, New York, for example, where all students are African American or Latino, 79 percent are non-Catholic; 69 percent receive financial aid. Suburban Catholic schools, which typically serve largely white populations, report an increase in enrollments, attributable in part to the schools becoming "a little less Catholic," thereby attracting more non-Catholic children.[106]

Ever since national interest in social justice emerged in the 1960s, independent schools have sought more religious, racial, and economic diversity. At independent schools today, religious prejudice appears a thing of the past, and the enrollment of students of color, from the full economic spectrum, has increased to 17 percent. About 16 percent of all students at independent schools receive need-based financial aid, although only 43 percent of those receiving aid are students of color.[107]

Independent schools, which pride themselves on preparing students for leadership, must consider that their graduates will live in a diverse society. Yet the extent and nature of diversity in any school depends on the availability of resources, as well as on the disposition of trustees and parents. At Phillips Academy at Andover, Massachusetts, a school with a large endowment where there is a serious commitment to diversity, 31 percent of students are students of color, and 39 percent of all students receive financial aid. Schools with more limited resources must decide the extent to which their populations should reflect the broader society.

FACULTY RECRUITMENT. Private schools rely heavily on capable faculty to provide a challenging academic program and promote school values. Characteristically, private schools—even the most well-endowed schools—offer lower salaries than public schools. Private school teachers forgo higher income for the opportunity to work with motivated students in safe environments, and some seek work in atmospheres that reflect their religious or moral values.

A looming teacher shortage may soon make it difficult for private schools to hire able faculty. The National Center for Education Statistics predicts that, nationwide, 1.7 million to 2.7 million teachers will be needed by the end of the decade because of teacher attrition, retirement, and increased student enrollment.[108] State and local governments are attracting teachers, particularly to urban areas, by offering incentives like sign-on bonuses, tuition forgiveness plans, and alternative certification arrangements that allow teachers to earn credentials while teaching. As entry into public school teaching becomes easier and more financially appealing, Catholic and independent schools will find it more difficult to recruit able teachers.

The diminishing number of clerics working in Catholic schools has exacerbated the need for hiring lay teachers. Lay faculty, which has increased from 85 percent to the current 93 percent in the past decade, creates a demand for higher wages and better benefits. Since most teachers in Catholic schools hold state certification, hiring incentives in public schools may lure these teachers away from Catholic schools.[109]

Distinguishing between "qualified" and "certified," independent schools have traditionally drawn from a large pool of teachers who hold liberal arts degrees, but not necessarily teaching licenses. Whereas independent schools have attracted those unwilling to undergo teacher education programs, curtailed requirements for public school teachers may lure teachers from independent schools to higher-paying public schools.[110] The current compensation at independent schools, which may include housing subsidies and tuition waivers for faculty children, may have to be more competitive with public schools, especially in hard-to-staff areas such as mathematics and computer science.[111]

SCHOOL CHOICE AND COMPETITION. Public school reform efforts that depend on choice and competition are also affecting private schools, which have always been influenced by market forces. Designed to offer low-income families escape from low-performing public schools and to spark improvement through competition, vouchers and charter schools are currently the most significant school choice alternatives.

Thirty-six states and the District of Columbia have passed laws allowing individuals or groups to set up autonomous public schools under state charters. Charter schools, numbering more than 2,000 in America, must follow state guidelines and are not permitted to select their students. Yet they choose their instructional approaches freely; they make financial and hiring decisions without bureaucratic intervention. Usually run as nonprofit organizations, charter schools resemble private schools because they are usually small, have specific curriculum goals, and attract like-minded families, creating value communities characteristic of private schools. In urban areas, many charter schools resemble Catholic schools, for they require uniforms, stress disciplined behavior, and teach a focused curriculum.

Vouchers, another instrument of school choice, are given to families, who use them to offset the cost of tuition at the school of their choice. Privately funded vouchers have served more than 13,000 low-income families in thirty-three states.[112] Publicly funded vouchers, the most hotly debated choice option, allow parents to use taxpayer money for private school tuition. Voucher programs in Milwaukee, Cleveland, and Florida, which allow vouchers to be used in religious schools, have been embroiled in the courts over their constitutionality.

What impact do these instruments have on Catholic and independent schools? Catholic schools make up the largest group of schools participating in voucher programs.[113] Catholic schools, which are a strong presence in urban areas, have proved an affordable choice for parents using vouchers. If the U.S. Supreme Court decides in favor of using taxpayer funds for religious schools, public vouchers will bolster Catholic school enrollments. Still, neither the long-term commitment of private contributors nor public funds for vouchers can be guaranteed, leaving the impact on Catholic schools uncertain.

Charter schools may attract families who would otherwise choose a Catholic school. The cost-free alternative of charter schools may be particularly attractive to families who choose a Catholic school for reasons other than religion.[114] As it stands, approximately 11 percent of charter school students come from private schools.[115] These students seem likely to have come from Catholic schools, because most charter schools are in inner cities, where there is a predominance of Catholic schools and a high percentage of non-Catholics attending.

Charter schools and vouchers are likely to have less impact on independent schools. The amount of a voucher is not significant when compared to the high tuition of most independent schools. Similarly, given the preponderance of charter schools that serve the poor, enrollments of affluent families at independent schools are unlikely to be significantly affected by charters. Yet charter schools in middle-class communities may draw families who are struggling with the costs of tuition or families of color who are seeking a more balanced racial environment.

Charter schools may also appeal to altruistic faculty from independent schools, who are attracted by a small, safe, nonbureaucratic, public environment.

AFFORDABILITY. Catholic and independent schools also face rising costs associated with the demands of educating students for the twenty-first century. For example, the demand for updated technology, along with a need for technology maintenance and personnel training, puts significant pressure on schools' resources. Although a few private schools can rely on large endowments to meet operating costs, most schools are heavily dependent on student tuition. Competing with free public schools, as well as other private schools, each school needs to be adept at determining what the market will bear for the services they offer. Furthermore, since tuition does not fully cover operating costs at most private schools, fundraising efforts will be strained by rising costs.

On average, it costs Catholic secondary schools $5,466 per year to educate each student, $1,366 less than the average tuition charged.[116] At schools serving the poor, such as Rice High School, the gap is greater. Rice's cost per student is $7,250, but the tuition charged is $3,750, creating a shortfall of $3,500 per student that must be met through external sources of support, including federal supplements, fundraising efforts, and contributions from their affiliated religious order. Parish and diocesan schools also receive community contributions, but all schools that must supplement tuition are obliged to limit their admissions to the amount of funds they are able to raise.

On average, it costs independent secondary schools $12,495 per year to educate each student, $1,499 more than the average tuition charged.[117] Independent schools seldom accept government funds for fear of intervention, relying instead on contributions, mostly from current parents and alumni, who provide the largest share of annual giving dollars, and school trustees, fully 90 percent of whom contribute to the school. Perhaps because fundraising is so time-consuming and labor intensive, most schools employ professionals who devote full time to raising funds from individuals, corporations, and foundations.

In setting tuition charges, boards of trustees struggle to meet expenses of academic programs that emphasize small classes and the capital costs of maintaining expensive facilities, while not pricing themselves out of the market for middle- and upper-middle-class families. Since many families are unaware of what independent schools offer, identifying new populations and educating them to the benefits of a private school are constant challenges for admissions officers. Success in attracting families and raising funds to balance the budget is directly linked to the state of the economy.

The Lessons of Private Education

As public education has come under fire for failing to educate a large portion of America's children, particularly in inner cities, policymakers, politicians, and business leaders have begun to look to private schools for lessons about education that works. In the past, claiming that the ability to select students is a key element of private school success, public school officials have dismissed the outcomes of private schooling, ignoring the reality that most Catholic schools are not selective and that independent schools are only modestly so.

Five important lessons are learned in Catholic and independent schools:

—Allowing families to choose schools not only offers psychological advantages but also creates a cohesive community of families attracted to the school's mission.[118]

—Expecting all students to master the curriculum produces results because, given an opportunity and high expectations, most students are likely to learn.[119]

—A nurturing environment with personal attention has a positive influence on learning.[120]

—Allowing academic and organizational decisions to be made expeditiously at the school level rather than dictating them from a centralized bureaucracy is effective.[121]

—Having a strong mission, whether based on religious ideology or moral conviction, is necessary for directing and aligning institutional action.

The private sector may be regarded as a research and development effort for public schools. Policies that employ the best models of private education to influence public education may improve education for all children. The newly created charter schools, which seem to take the five important lessons learned in private schools, may be the necessary bridge between private and public education, demonstrating what is possible for all children. The hope is that market forces will cause practices in charter schools to influence practices in district schools and that the fertile cross-pollination between the private and public sectors will gain momentum, though there is not a great deal of evidence that this is actually happening.

Conclusion

Even as public schools move toward providing a variety of choices, private schools will continue to exercise their historic role in the educational fabric of America. There will always be families who want their children educated with a particular religious or moral persuasion and families who desire more personalization and academic rigor than are found in public schools. And private schools are likely to display resilience in confronting the challenges of the twenty-first century—increased diversity, teacher recruitment, school choice, and affordability. A favorable Supreme Court decision on vouchers, while unlikely to influence independent schools, would radically alter the configuration of Catholic schools in their favor and provide a secure financial future.

Private schools serve the interests of families, but they also serve the public good because a better-educated populace is in the best interests of a democracy.

Economist Milton Friedman points to the "neighborhood effect" of schooling, in which the benefits of education are applicable not only to the individual but also to the community as a whole.[122] Private schools also provide models of what is possible for all schools to achieve.

In *Pierce* v. *the Society of Sisters*, the court held that the child is not the creature of the state.[123] The opportunity for families and students to choose a diversity of schools that fit with their values is one of the most important declarations of independence Americans can make. At the same time, this opportunity needs to be balanced against the need to teach civic education and other important common values.[124] How to preserve this balance is a constant challenge for private higher education as well as for K–12. Such is the case as well for private, nonprofit organizations involved in the third subfield of education we consider here: employment training and development. Here, too, challenges abound.

Workforce Development and Training

Nonprofit organizations play a role in the education field not only through established educational institutions at the levels of higher education and elementary and secondary education, but also through less formal institutions designed to overcome the educational disadvantages of those left behind by our educational system. Job training legislation can be traced back to the 1960s, when training programs were established for workers dislocated by changes in federal trade, environmental, space, and defense policies. Growing concerns about gender equity, the needs of the disadvantaged, and the high cost of providing welfare benefits stimulated the expansion of these programs to provide job placement and training for persons other than dislocated workers. Today, the field of workforce development and training has evolved into a substantial area of public policy, involving all levels of government and thousands of educational institutions, agencies, and nonprofit organizations.[125]

The federal government has often taken the lead in this area, providing funding and spurring the creation of supporting agencies and service providers.[126] Since Congress enacted the first piece of workforce development and training legislation, more than 160 federal programs have been created. However, both federal and state governments sponsor programs designed to provide job training and other workforce development services to those whose previous education has left them unprepared for work. Some of these state and federal programs are voluntary, while others condition receipt of government benefits on participation. However, each of them has led to the increased involvement of nonprofit organizations in workforce development and training.

The nonprofit organizations that provide workforce development and training come in a variety of forms. Each of them uses different methods to create employment opportunities for workers who face multiple barriers when entering or reentering the labor force or who seek better jobs. Some are community-based organizations. Others are workforce development agencies formed in direct response to government funding. Regardless of their form, nonprofit organizations are constantly adapting in order to respond to frequently changing workforce development and training policies and programs at the federal, state, and local levels of government.

By and large, the world of workforce development and training is characterized by an entrenched division of labor whereby programs are divided into two separate subsystems. One is the subsystem of public, nonprofit, and for-profit educational institutions; the other is the subsystem of training institutions, usually nonprofit organizations and community-based organizations, but also for-profit firms. In their 1996 study, Grubb and McConnell conclude that competition among service providers from these different subsystems is uncommon.[127] Recent studies suggest, however, that this may no longer be true. In the past, many nonprofit providers experienced only limited competition for government contracts. However, substantial changes in the federal workforce development and training policies have stimulated a movement away from this nonprofit monopoly.

In some communities, more independent program administrations and state agencies have come into being. Independent agencies coupled with legislation that calls for expanded accountability provisions and individual client choice have resulted in a newly competitive environment for nonprofit organizations. Employers and government agencies also have more options for service providers. Although historically community colleges and for-profit institutions frequently served a different purpose and a different clientele within workforce development and training services, this too is changing. Most scholars agree: "Nonprofits are competing increasingly with for-profit firms, and in an amazing variety of forms."[128]

Many employers have now joined the government as primary contractors of workforce development and training services.[129] Employers now seek out community colleges, for-profit schools, community-based organizations, and other nonprofits to assist potential employees in everything from transportation and childcare provision to basic job and social interaction skills. More and more frequently, nonprofit organizations are in direct competition with for-profit training centers and proprietary educational institutions for government contracts. Additionally, community colleges serve as a potential source of competition for community-based service providers.[130] Today, over 90 percent of community colleges provide contract training for those organizations seeking a better-prepared workforce.[131]

Changing Policy Environment: Workforce Investment Act of 1998

Changes in public policy can have a significant impact on nonprofit service providers' priorities and their ability to pursue their mission. Two basic themes in current public workforce development and training policy are increased accountability and choice, as found in the Workforce Investment Act of 1998 (WIA). WIA replaces many aspects of the Job Training Partnership Act of 1982 (JTPA) and includes provisions that stress the importance of local governance, accountability, and customer choice. Just like their counterparts in higher education and elementary and secondary education, community-based organizations and nonprofit organizations have found ways to adapt to the changing times in order to continue fulfilling their role as the principal providers of workforce development and training.

INCREASED ACCOUNTABILITY. The concept of accountability in workforce development and training is not new. As with all programs born out of legislation, the government has always conditioned funding on some demonstrable evidence that program goals are being realized. However, as legislative budgets tighten and questions about the effectiveness of workforce development and training programs arise, scholars and policymakers have begun to call for more accountability and stricter enforcement of performance standards. The WIA contains a number of provisions designed specifically to enhance the level of accountability for service providers. At the heart of WIA is a new system of performance-based contracting whereby an organization's funding is tied directly to the performance of the clients it serves. This move toward more performance-based contracting may cause some funding instability for those nonprofit organizations that traditionally receive funding commitments on the basis of reputation or politics.[132]

There is some evidence that the move toward greater accountability is warranted. One recent study finds, for example, that, while neither for-profit nor nonprofit providers were consistently successful in increasing clients' earning and employment rates, both types of organizations were more effective when performance incentives were included in a providers' contract with the government.[133]

Opponents of performance-based funding argue that tying payments and bonuses to contractors' performance on measures of short-term outcome may force nonprofit organizations to move away from their charitable mission and toward shorter-term financial goals or may otherwise affect the decisions of program administrators to terminate a client's participation. In an attempt to combat this potentially unintended effect, the WIA proposes new performance standards for JTPA programs that will require the evaluation of program outcomes over a longer post-program period. However, an enduring concern with higher-stakes accountability measures and universal access (rather than programs targeted to special populations) is that the pressure to secure or protect funding will force service providers to serve only those individuals with the fewest barriers to employment and long-term placement and will punish those organizations whose mission is to serve individuals with multiple barriers to employment.[134]

CHOICE. The WIA also introduces the concept of choice into workforce development and training programs. The WIA provides for the creation and use of individual training accounts, which come in the form of a voucher and allow adult customers to "purchase the training they determine best for them" and guarantee their access to services. Unlike their predecessors, the WIA programs are not targeted to certain populations. In addition, the individual training accounts permit clients to select the services they need from their service provider. This infusion of choice into the system affects the choices nonprofits make as to which services to offer or how best to serve their clients. The decision as to whether to use a comprehensive services approach, like Project Match, or to concentrate an organization's efforts on offering clients a single service is likely to be influenced by the demand generated by the availability of individual training accounts.

The arguments for and against more choice are complicated and varied. According to the Chicago Jobs Council executive director, Robert Wordlaw, now that individual training accounts enable individuals to contract directly with community-based organizations and other service providers, the traditional community-based organization is significantly weakened.[135] It no longer can rely on receiving the funds needed for operation from government contracts. Yet proponents of the individual training accounts suggest that perhaps that is a positive effect of choice. Julie Wilen, from the Mayor's Office of Workforce Development (MOWD) in Chicago, notes that choice is designed to encourage community-based organizations and other service providers to reexamine themselves and to streamline and improve their services. If a community-based organization is successful, clients will come and bring the funding with them. Critics of this view point out that, if success is measured by indicators that do not account for the severity of barriers facing many clients whom community-based organizations serve, those organizations dedicated to working with the long-term unemployed and other hard-to-place populations will find it very difficult to survive.

Regardless of continuing policy discussions on their merits, WIA makes individual training accounts central to the nation's system of workforce development and training. For the market forces embedded within the WIA voucher system to work as intended, clients must have better information about the quality of services available.[136] Under the new federal policies, nonprofit organizations must be proactive in developing relationships with other organizations and agencies to ensure that other service providers know about and can recommend their services to clients. In addition, where available, organizations should seek certification or accreditation to make certain that they will have access to clients with individual training accounts and can improve their capacity to meet higher performance standards.

Calls for Collaboration among Nonprofit Organizations

The pressure to compete in the face of performance-based contracting and greater choice for clients has brought about new strategies of adaptation by non-profit organizations. Encouraged by federal and state policies that promote increased coordination among service providers, many nonprofit organizations have begun to collaborate with one another to enhance their services. Two examples of coordination that have enjoyed some success are one-stop career centers and formal community alliances.

ONE-STOP CAREER CENTERS. As with choice and increased accountability measures, the emphasis on one-stop centers as mechanisms for enhancing the coordination of services stems from new provisions in WIA. One-stop centers make a variety of training and employment services available all in one place. Typically, a one-stop center will integrate programs like government unemployment insurance with state job services and public assistance and job training programs run by nonprofit organizations.[137] They combine personal and automated services to help individuals streamline the process of getting employment counseling, training, and other assistance.

In one sense, one-stop career centers may assist nonprofit service providers to become more efficient and improve their capacity to serve a client's various needs. On the other hand, some nonprofit providers may view one-stop career centers as problematic in that the client has greater control over which services he or she will receive. In many programs offered by nonprofit organizations, a caseworker designs an individualized plan for each client, and they work together to realize the goals set forth in the plan and to alter the plan when necessary. Additionally, those groups serving the hardest to employ may view the one-stop system's focus on universality as detrimental to the principal goal of many workforce development and training programs: moving people out of poverty and into self-sufficiency. As with other aspects of WIA, nonprofit organizations must look for new ways to work within the system of one-stop centers and to use choice as a tool for innovation and improvement.

COMMUNITY ALLIANCES. Despite the lack of consensus among researchers as to the benefits of collaboration and integration of services in the form of one-stop career centers, efforts to encourage collaboration among various service providers continue. Many companies are forming strategic alliances in which community leaders and community-based organizations join with employers and educators to assess employer needs and to find and hire service providers who will offer workers the necessary training and match them with employers.[138] A number of nonprofit organizations now serve as employer-employee liaisons that communicate with current and prospective employees on behalf of a company and prepare workers to compete in a particular labor market.

Government agencies also seek out opportunities for collaboration with non-profit organizations and other service providers. Oftentimes, funding mechanisms can provide incentives or disincentives to collaborate. Many policymakers have figured out that funding mechanisms can be especially influential in determining whether organizations will collaborate with others. According to Julie Wilen, the director of Adult Programs for the Chicago MOWD, in drafting requests for proposals, MOWD has a unique opportunity to foster coordination among service providers.[139] Wilen notes that, by developing proposals that require proof of ability to offer comprehensive services or of established relationships with complementary organizations, MOWD encourages organizations to form relationships with other service providers in order to enhance their overall workforce development and training program.

Response of Nonprofit Organizations to Major Developments in the Field and Likely Future Evolution

Some scholars question the overall effectiveness of this nation's workforce development and training system. They suggest that the problem may be embedded in the overall approach to service provision. Some commentators on community-based workforce development and training programs suggest that many service providers fail to connect training and education to the specific job skills that employers need. Some view this disconnection between service providers and employers as a major reason that programs have not produced sustained results for the unemployed or underemployed.[140] Edwin Melendez believes that one key to successful workforce development and training is the involvement of employers in the workforce development process. He is not alone.[141]

WIA, like its predecessor, JTPA, contains some provisions that foster the involvement of corporations and other employers in workforce development and training programs. The law created a central role for private industry in guiding job training with the advent of private industry councils (PICs). PICs include representatives from various industries within a local community who distribute and monitor JTPA contracts. These councils oversee each local training system and attempt to bring local employers together with the policymakers charged with implementing workforce development and training laws and the nonprofit organizations and other service providers who work directly with the individuals in need of assistance. A number of scholars argue that the involvement of employers through PICs does not allow for the development of true collaborative relationships that are needed to move workforce development and training programs forward.[142] However, others believe that PICs hold real promise and can be the catalyst for the creation of more employer-centered training programs. More direct involvement of employers in the provision of workforce development and training will have a significant impact on nonprofit organizations. In his study of the Center for Employment Training, a community-based organization in California, Melendez concludes that the Center for Employment Training was successful because it (1) actively sought stronger connections with local employers within the community, (2) redesigned programs to meet the needs of both trainees and employers, and (3) fostered links between community-based training operations and emerging government intermediaries like one-stop career centers and school-to-work programs.

Much of the work that nonprofit organizations do in workforce development and training focuses on the needs of the disadvantaged and persons trying to move from welfare to work. One prominent scholar, Paul Osterman, suggests that groups need to broaden their focus to include services for individuals affected by corporate reorganization and dislocation.[143] Osterman argues that the current means-tested workforce development and training system stigmatizes participants. Employers then become reluctant to hire individuals who have received counseling services or treat the system as charity.[144]

In the system Osterman proposes, nonprofit organizations' current role as provider of comprehensive workforce development services would change. Instead of serving the needs of all potential clients, most nonprofit organizations would offer remedial services that mainstream institutions "may either be loath to offer or will provide in a set of tracks that have the effect of re-stratifying the system."[145] Osterman contends that future workforce development and training programs should (1) be broadly based and able to serve a wide range of clients, (2) be employer-centered and work directly with employers and worker representatives to ensure that program participants are attaining skills needed in the workplace, and (3) view the employer community as a significant customer.

While not everyone agrees that Osterman's model for the system of workforce development and training is the right one, many do advocate a move toward more employer-centered training. Employer-centered programs refer to training programs that emphasize working directly with employers and unions, where available, and treating employers-firms as clients.[146] One scholar suggests that, to be employer-based, training should be both employer-initiated and customized to meet employer needs.[147] Providers of employer-centered programs train new hires and retrain workers to improve productivity and global competitiveness. In the past decade, there has been a trend in state and local agency employment and training programs to work directly with firms in addition to individuals.[148] As the trend toward employer-centered training programs grows, nonprofit organizations will need to adapt new strategies to respond to the demand for these types of programs.

One organization that serves as a model for many groups seeking to develop an employer-centered program is Goodwill Industries.[149] Goodwill has proven to industry that it has the capacity to train individuals by seeking and obtaining accreditation awards in the areas of employment transition and planning services, comprehensive vocational evaluation services, employee development, employment skills training, organizational and community employment services, and personal and social community support services. In addition, the organization works hard to establish a presence within the community, takes a comprehensive approach to service provision, and has forged real partnerships with employers to better understand their needs.

A strong employer-based program begins with a careful analysis of an employee's (or potential employee's) performance on the job and directly supports the employer's institutional culture and strategic goals.[150] Currently, most programs offered by traditional nonprofit service providers cater to the individual client, not employers. To sustain the important role that community-based organizations have played in the provision of workforce development and training, these nonprofit organizations will have to rethink their orientation toward individual clients. Nonprofit organizations must learn what employers need and then prepare individuals to fulfill those needs. To do so will require the development of more meaningful partnerships with employers and a willingness to move in new directions.

It is clear that the nonprofit organizations that operate workforce development and training programs will, for years to come, be forced to do their work in the face of increased accountability, tight financial budgets, greater competition from community colleges and for-profit institutions, enhanced choice for individual clients, and a more substantial role for employers in shaping workforce development and training programs. If they are to continue providing services, most organizations will need to rethink and reshape their programs. Flexibility and strategic planning will play vital roles in any successful adaptation. As the Chicago Jobs Council notes, "Recent welfare and workforce reforms have dramatically changed the role [community-based organizations] can and will play in the delivery of employment and training services. To compete in this new environment, community-based organizations will have to bolster their operations through strategic and financial planning as well as technology enhancements."[151]

Conclusion

Clearly, the private, nonprofit worlds of higher education, K–12 education, and employment training are in flux, with each facing enormous challenges. At the same time, they share certain common characteristics. All three are tax-exempt and therefore serve the public good through private action. Their organizations and institutions are part of the fascinating interplay of public and private forces that contribute to the mixed economy of our American system. Each faces extreme competition from the public as well as from the for-profit private sector. And each grapples with the need for tight financial planning and budgeting in the face of growing pressure to demonstrate quantifiable results.

Private, nonprofit organizations in education can win neither the price war with government-supported entities nor the efficiency war with for-profit entities. However, they can offer the best-quality education programs possible as well as seek new public-private or private-private partnerships that further blur the distinctions among the sectors while opening up new avenues for revenue generation. Technology may offer such opportunities, but the possibilities are still unclear.

In the final analysis, while there are no easy answers, there are new avenues coming into view. For the well-being of the independent sector and the mixed economy of our nation, these avenues are well worth exploring.

Notes

1. National Center for Education Statistics (NCES), *Digest of Education Statistics, 1999,* NCES 2000-031 (Jessup, Md.: U.S. Department of Education, National Center for Education Statistics, 2000), pp. 14, 209.

2. Inspired by a letter to the author from Derek Bok, president emeritus, Harvard University, dated October 4, 2001.

3. Martin Meyerson, "An Endangered Breed: The Private University," unpublished speech presented to the Education Writers Association of Philadelphia, February 9, 1972.

4. Martin van der Werf, "Recession and Reality Set in at Private Colleges," *Chronicle of Higher Education*, March 1, 2002, pp. A26–A28.

5. Meyerson, "An Endangered Breed."

6. National Center for Education Statistics, *Digest of Education Statistics, 1999*, p. 283. Not all of these institutions are eligible to participate in Title IV federal financial aid programs. The rest of the statistics in this paragraph come from Samuel Barbett, "Fall Enrollment in Postsecondary Institutions: 1997," *Education Statistics Quarterly*, vol. 2, no. 1 (Spring 2000): 99–104. National Center for Education Statistics, *Digest of Education Statistics 1999*, pp. 209–10, 283; see also the Women's College Coalition website, www.womenscolleges.org [July 9, 2001].

7. For a definition of selective admissions, see College Board, *The College Board Handbook, 2002* (New York: College Board, 2002), p. 923.

8. van der Werf, "Recession and Reality Set in," p. A27.

9. William and Mary, Collegiate School (Yale), New Jersey (Princeton), King's (Columbia), Philadelphia (University of Pennsylvania), Rhode Island (Brown), Queen's (Rutgers), and Dartmouth.

10. Frederick Rudolph, *The American College and University: A History* (Athens: University of Georgia Press, 1990), p. 185.

11. Rudolph, *The American College and University*, p. 188.

12. Rudolph, *The American College and University*.

13. *Plessy v. Ferguson*, 163 U.S. 537 (1896).

14. National Center for Education Statistics, *The Condition of Education 2000* (Jessup, Md.: U.S. Department of Education, Office of Educational Research and Improvement, 2000), p. 1.

15. Michael J. Bennett, *When Dreams Come True: The GI Bill and the Making of Modern America* (Washington: Brassey's, 1996), pp. 237–76.

16. Lester F. Goodchild and Harold S. Wechsler, *The History of Higher Education*, ASHE Reader Series (Needham Heights, Mass.: Simon and Schuster, 1997), p. 769.

17. National Center for Education Statistics, *Condition of Education 2000*, p. 200.

18. Named for Claiborne Pell, democratic senator from Rhode Island and former chairman of the Senate Education and Labor Committee.

19. College Board, *Trends in Student Aid, 2000* (New York: College Board, 2000), pp. 2–3.

20. In a telephone conversation, Dr. Michael McPherson, president of Macalester College, discussed how difficult it is to close a college that, for all practical purposes, has ceased to remain financially viable. Although there may be insufficient tuition and fees to cover costs, schools often continue to draw local high school graduates out of either constituency loyalty (denominational affiliation) or geographic proximity and provide local employment. In addition, boards of trustees are not sure how to close a college and are loathe to even try. Thus the question arises: To whom does a private college belong?

21. Amherst, Barnard, Brown, Bryn Mawr, Carleton, Columbia, Cornell, Dartmouth, Duke, Georgetown, Harvard, Johns Hopkins, Massachusetts Institute of Technology, Mt. Holyoke, Northwestern, Oberlin, Pomona, Princeton, Radcliffe, Rice, Smith, Stanford, Swarthmore, Trinity, University of Chicago, University of Pennsylvania, Rochester, Washington University, Wellesley, Wesleyan, Williams, and Yale.

22. Consortium on Financing Higher Education, "The Consortium: A Brief History," unpublished manuscript (Consortium on Financing Higher Education, 2000).

23. Derek Bok, personal note, August 12, 2002.

24. Consortium on Financing Higher Education, "The Consortium."

25. In a conversation with Jim Sumner, dean of admission and financial aid at Grinnell College (March 13, 2002), he stated that only fifteen private colleges and universities in the United States (eight Ivy League institutions and Grinnell among them) still offer "need-blind" admissions, where ability to pay does not influence the decision to admit.

26. Moody's Investors Service, *Private Colleges and Universities: 1990 Outlook and Medians* (New York: Moody's Investors Service, 1990), p. 1.

27. Charles T. Clotfelter, *Buying the Best: Cost Escalation in the Arts and Sciences* (Princeton University Press, 1996), p. 12; Derek Bok, personal note, August 12, 2002.

28. Clotfelter, *Buying the Best*, pp. 28, 32.

29. National Center for Education Statistics, *Condition of Education 2000*, p. 199.

30. Michael S. McPherson and Morton O. Schapiro, *The Student Aid Game: Meeting Need and Rewarding Talent in American Higher Education* (Princeton University Press, 1998), p. 11.

31. National Commission on the Cost of Higher Education, *Straight Talk about College Costs and Prices* (Phoenix: American Council on Education and the Oryx Press, 1998), p. 3.

32. Clotfelter, *Buying the Best*, pp. 2, 4.

33. College Board, *Trends in College Pricing, 2001* (New York: College Board, 2001), p. 4.

34. Michael S. McPherson, and Morton O. Schapiro, "End of the Student Aid Era? Higher Education Finance in the United States," in Michael C. Johanek, ed., *A Faithful Mirror: Reflections on the College Board and Education in America* (New York: College Board, 2001), p. 234.

35. Derek Bok, *Higher Learning* (Harvard University Press, 1986), p. 7.

36. David W. Breneman and Chester E. Finn Jr., *Public Policy and Private Higher Education* (Washington: Brookings, 1978), pp. 17–18.

37. Bok, *Higher Learning*, p. 39.

38. Breneman and Finn, *Public Policy and Private Higher Education*, pp. 195–96.

39. David W. Breneman, *Liberal Arts Colleges: Thriving, Surviving, or Endangered?* (Washington: Brookings, 1994), p. 13.

40. Roger G. Noll, "The American Research University: An Introduction," in Roger G. Noll, ed., *Challenges to Research Universities* (Washington: Brookings, 1998), p. 26.

41. Albert H. Teach, "The Outlook for Federal Support of University Research," in Noll, ed., *Challenges to Research Universities*, p. 26.

42. Here I would like to thank Michael B. Wood, president and chief executive officer of the Mayo Foundation; Robert Smoldt, vice president for administration at the Mayo Foundation; Hank Weber, vice president for community and government affairs at the University of Chicago; and Lawrence J. Furnstahl, chief finance officer, Finance and Strategic Development, University of Chicago.

43. National Institutes of Health, "NIH Support to U.S. Institutions of Higher Education, Fiscal Year 2000" (silk.nih.gov/public/cb2zoz.@www.he.inst.fy2000.dnscc [June 4, 2002]).

44. David Blumenthal, "Unhealthy Hospitals: Addressing the Trauma in Academic Medicine," *Harvard Magazine*, vol. 103, no. 4 (March/April 2001): 30.

45. Blumenthal, "Unhealthy Hospitals."

46. Roger G. Noll and William P. Rogerson, "The Economics of University Indirect Cost Reimbursement in Federal Research Grants," in Noll, ed., *Challenges to Research Universities*, pp. 111–15.

47. Commonwealth Fund, "From Bench to Bedside: Preserving the Research Mission of Academic Health Centers," in *Findings and Recommendations of the Commonwealth Fund Task Force on Academic Health Centers* (New York: Commonwealth Fund, April 1999), pp. ix–xii.

48. Derek Bok, personal note, August 12, 2002.

49. Mary Andrew Matesich, "Extending an Invitation to Tomorrow: How Integrating Technology throughout a College Led to Transforming Change," in Allen P. Splete, ed., *Presidential Essays: Success Stories,* New Agenda Series (Indianapolis: USA Group Foundation, March 2000), pp. 59–68.

50. University of Phoenix On-line (www.uopon-line.com/ [April 1, 2002]).

51. Jared L. Bleak, *Structures and Values: The Governance of For-Profit Subsidiaries of Nonprofit Universities,* Ph.D. diss. (Harvard University, Graduate School of Education, February 2001), p. 9.

52. Katie Hafner, "Lessons Learned at Dot Com U," *New York Times* (Circuits), May 2, 2002, pp. E1, E8.

53. Hafner, "Lessons Learned," p. E8.

54. Ted Marchese, "Not-So-Distant Competitors: How New Providers Are Re-making the Postsecondary Marketplace," *American Association for Higher Education Bulletin,* vol. 50, no. 9 (May 1998): 3–7.

55. Allen P. Splete, "Introduction," in Splete, ed., *Presidential Essays*, pp. 5–7.

56. Brian L. Hawkins, "Technology in Higher Education and a Very Foggy Crystal Ball," *Educause Review,* vol. 35 (November/December 2000): 65–73.

57. John L. Pulley, "Private Giving to Colleges Surpassed Expectations in 2000–1," *Chronicle of Higher Education,* April 2, 2002, p. 35. The figures in this paragraph are from this work, which quotes the Council for Aid to Education's annual survey.

58. John L. Pulley, "Crumbling Support for Colleges," *Chronicle of Higher Education,* March 29, 2002, p. A29.

59. van der Werf, "Recession and Reality Set in," p. A26. The figures in this paragraph are from this work, pp. 26–28.

60. "Donations to Colleges and Universities Rose 13.7 Percent in Fiscal 2000," *Chronicle of Philanthropy*, May 3, 2001, p. 39.

61. Stephanie Strom, "The Newly Rich Are Fueling a New Era in Philanthropy," *New York Times*, April 27, 2002, p. A10.

62. Loren Loomis Hubbell and Lucie Laponsky, "Tution Discounting in Challenging Times," *Business Officer* (Washington: NACUBO, February 2002), pp. 24–33.

63. College Board, *Trends in College Pricing*, p. 21.

64. Hubbell and Laponsky, "Tuition Discounting," p. 28. See also pp. 24, 30.

65. Wesley M. Cohen and others, "Industry and the Academy: Uneasy Partners in the Cause of Technological Advance," in Noll, ed., *Challenges to Research Universities*, pp. 111–15.

66. Donald E. Stokes, *Pasteur's Quadrant: Basic Science and Technological Innovation* (Washington: Brookings, 1997), p. 9.

67. Stokes, *Pasteur's Quadrant*, p. 2.

68. Walter W. Powell and Jason Owen-Smith, "Universities as Creators and Retailers of Intellectual Property: Life-Science Research and Commercial Development," in Burton A. Weisbrod, ed., *To Profit or Not to Profit: The Commercial Transformation of the Nonprofit Sector* (Cambridge University Press, 2000), pp. 175–82.

69. Powell and Owen-Smith, "Universities as Creators and Retailers," pp. 172–79.

70. Powell and Owen-Smith, "Universities as Creators and Retailers," pp. 184, 188.

71. Derek Bok, personal note, August 12, 2002.

72. Powell and Owen-Smith, "Universities as Creators and Retailers," p. 187.

73. Derek Bok, personal note, August 12, 2002.

74. The membership of Associated Colleges of Illinois (ACI) includes Augustana College, Aurora University, Barat College, Concordia University, Dominican University, Elmhurst College, Eureka College, Greenville College, Illinois College, Illinois Wesleyan University, Knox College, Lake Forest College, Lewis University, McKendree College, Millikin University, Monmouth College, North Central College, North Park University, Olivet Nazarene University, Principia College, Quincy University, Saint Xavier University, Trinity Christian College, and the University of St. Francis. ACI conducts numerous programs on behalf of its member colleges (for example, College Readiness) to involve high schools early in the process of preparing students for college. These programs focus on course selection, career planning, and financial aid planning. Many of these students subsequently choose to attend ACI institutions. Associated Colleges of Illinois, *Members and Leadership* (Chicago: Associated Colleges of Illinois, 2002), pp. 1–2.

75. Louis J. Agnese Jr., "Repositioning for Success," in Splete, ed., *Presidential Essays*, pp. 8–15.

76. Esther L. Barazzone, "Back from the Brink," in Splete, ed., *Presidential Essays*, pp. 21–32.

77. Donald J. Breckon, "Developing Diversity," in Splete, ed., *Presidential Essays*, pp. 31–35.

78. Frances Marie Thrailkill, "Changing the Campus Climate," in Splete, ed., *Presidential Essays*, pp. 80–85.

79. Drury University, "A History" (www.drury.edu/multinl/story.cfm?ID=117&NLID=39 [May 30, 2002]).

80. Information provided by Frank J. Baly, vice president for research and policy analysis, National Association of Independent Colleges and Universities.

81. National Center for Education Statistics, Fall Enrollment in Colleges and Universities, NCES Higher Education General Information Survey (HEGIS); Integrated Postsecondary

Education Data System, Fall Enrollment Surveys (July 2000); Higher Education Enrollment Model (March 2000).

82. Anthony P. Carnevale and Richard A. Fry, *Crossing the Great Divide: Can We Achieve Equity When Generation Y Goes to College?* (Princeton, N.J.: Educational Testing Service, 2000), pp. 8–9.

83. College Board, *Trends in Student Aid, 2000*, p. 16.

84. Associated Colleges of Illinois, *Liberal Arts for Leadership* (Chicago: Associated Colleges of Illinois, 2001), p. 1.

85. Derek Bok, personal note, August 12, 2002.

86. Diane Ravitch, *The Great School Wars, New York City, 1805–1973: A History of the Public Schools as Battlefields of Social Change* (New York: Basic Books, 1974), pp. 9–17.

87. Otto F. Kraushaar, *American Nonpublic Schools: Patterns of Diversity* (Johns Hopkins University Press, 1972), pp. 6–7.

88. *Pierce* v. *Society of Sisters of the Holy Names of Jesus and Mary,* 268 U.S. 510 (1925).

89. Kraushaar, *American Nonpublic Schools*, pp. 13–14.

90. National Center for Education Statistics, "Table 3: Enrollment in Educational Institutions, by Level and by Control of Institution: 1869–70 to Fall 2009," in National Center for Education Statistics, *Digest of Educational Statistics 1999*, p. 12.

91. This includes nonsectarian schools with special emphasis and special education schools. National Center for Education Statistics, "Number and Percentage Distribution of Private Schools, Students, and FTE Teachers, by Religious Orientation of School: United States, 1997–98," in *Private School Universe Survey, 1997–1998* (Jessup, Md.: U.S. Department of Education, National Center for Education Statistics, 1998), p. 6.

92. Patricia M. Lines, "Homeschooling: An Overview for Education Policymakers," Working Paper (U.S. Department of Education, Office of Education Research and Improvement, 1997 [rev.]), pp. 4–5; National Center for Education Statistics, *Homeschooling in the United States: 1999* (nces.ed.gov/pubsearch/pubsinfo.asp?pubid=2001033 [December 14, 2001]).

93. Council for American Private Education, "Private Education: A Changing Landscape" (www.capenet.org/facts.html [July 9, 2001]).

94. Lloyd P. Jorgenson, *The State and Non-Public School: 1825–1925* (University of Missouri Press, 1987), pp. 146–54.

95. Neil McCluskey, *Catholic Education Faces Its Future* (Garden City: Doubleday, 1969), pp. 78, 263.

96. Anthony S. Bryk, Valerie E. Lee, and Peter B. Holland, *Catholic Schools and the Common Good* (Harvard University Press, 1993), pp. 51–54.

97. For results of test scores, see National Center for Education Statistics, *Pursuing Excellence: Comparisons of International Eighth-Grade Mathematics and Science Achievement from a U.S. Perspective, 1995–1999, Initial Findings from the Third International Mathematics and Science Study* (Jessup, Md.: U.S. Department of Education, National Center for Education Statistics, December 2000), p. 30; in both mathematics and science in 1999, for example, the average achievement score of U.S. eighth-grade nonpublic school students was higher than the average of their peers in U.S. public schools; 59 percent of the nonpublic sample was composed of Catholic school students; see also "Average Mathematics Proficiency, by Age and by Selected Characteristics of Students: 1973 to 1996," table 123, p. 139 and "Average Proficiency in Reading, by Age and by Selected Characteristics of Students: 1971–1996," table 112, p. 130, both in National Center for Education Statistics, *Digest of Educational Statistics, Elementary and Secondary Education: Achievement* (Jessup, Md.: U.S. Department of Education, National Center for Education Statistics, 1999).

98. Theodore R. Sizer, ed., *The Age of the Academies* (Columbia University, Teachers College, Bureau of Publications, 1964), pp. 1–48; and Lawrence A. Cremin, ed., *The Republic and the School: Horace Mann on the Education of Free Men* (Teachers College, 1957), pp. 23–25.

99. Kraushaar, *American Nonpublic Schools*, pp. 56–68.

100. Pearl Rock Kane, ed., *Independent Schools, Independent Thinkers* (San Francisco: Jossey-Bass, 1992), p. 7.

101. National Association of Independent Schools, "Statistics 2000, for the Year 1999–2000" (Washington: National Association of Independent Schools, 2000), p. 10.

102. National Center for Children in Poverty, "Child Poverty in the States: Levels and Trends from 1979 to 1998" (cpmcnet.columbia.edu/dept/nccp/cp2method.html [July 9, 2001]).

103. U.S. Census Bureau, "Percentages of Children, Age 5–17, by Race/Ethnicity, Beginning in 1996 and Projected to 2025," *Statistical Abstract of the United States* (Washington: U.S. Census Bureau, 1996), pp. 24, 25.

104. Dale McDonald, "Exhibit 20: Catholic School Enrollment and Percentages by Ethnic Background," and Dale McDonald, "Exhibit 21: Non-Catholic Enrollment," both in *United States Catholic Elementary and Secondary School Statistics: 2001* (Washington: National Catholic Educational Association, 2001). Both are available at www.ncea.org [July 9, 2001]).

105. National Conference of Catholic Bishops and United States Catholic Conference, "U.S. Catholic Bishops—Department of Education" (nccbuscc.org/education/fedasst/statistics.htm [July 9, 2001]).

106. Nancy Trejos, "Suburban Boom Helps Revive Catholic Shools," *Washington Post*, August 13, 2000, sec. M.

107. National Association of Independent Schools, "Statistics 2000," pp. 23, 44.

108. William J. Hussar, *Predicting the Need for Newly Hired Teachers in the United States to 2008–2009* (Jessup, Md.: U.S. Department of Education, National Center for Education Statistics, 2001), available at nces.ed.gov/pubs2000/qtrlywinter/3elem/3-esq14-g.html [July 9, 2001].

109. National Center for Education Statistics, "Private Schools in the United States: A Statistical Profile, 1993–1994" (nces.ed.gov/pubs/ps/CATHOLIC.htm [July 9, 2001]).

110. Pearl Rock Kane, *Public and Independent Schools: A Comparative Study* (New York: Esther A. and Joseph Klingenstein Center for Independent School Education, 1986), p. 28.

111. Higher pay for hard-to-staff areas is already occurring, according to Jonathan Ball, senior associate director of marketing, Carney Sandoe and Associates, Boston, Mass., telephone interview by author, December 19, 2000.

112. Children's Educational Opportunity Foundation of America, *Just Doing It 4: 1998 Annual Survey of the Private Voucher Movement in America* (Bentonville, Ariz.: Children's Educational Opportunity Foundation of America, 1998), pp. 1–3.

113. Children's Educational Opportunity Foundation of America, *Just Doing It 4*, pp. 28–30.

114. Sarah Schweitzer, "Charter Schools Pull from Private," *St. Petersburg Times*, September 4, 2000, pp. 74–75.

115. Gregg Vanourek and others, "The Educational Impact of Charter Schools," in *Charter Schools in Action, Final Report, Part V* (Washington: Hudson Institute, July 1997), p. 2.

116. National Catholic Education Association, "United States Catholic Elementary and Secondary School Statistics 1999–2000: Synopsis of the Annual Report on Schools, Enrollment, and Staffing" (www.ncea.org/PubPol/databank.shtml [July 1, 2000]).

117. The figures in this paragraph are taken from National Association of Independent Schools, "Statistics 2000," pp. 57, 74.

118. James S. Coleman and Thomas Hoffer, *Public and Private High Schools: The Impact of Communities* (New York: Basic Books, 1987), pp. 6–10.

119. David Perkins, *Smart Schools: Better Thinking and Learning for Every Child* (New York: Free Press, 1992), pp. 43–72.

120. Arthur G. Powell, *Lessons from Privilege: The American Prep School Tradition* (Harvard University Press, 1996), pp. 239–47; Bryk, Lee, and Holland, *Catholic Schools and the Common Good*, pp. 274–94.

121. John E. Chubb and Terry M. Moe, *Politics, Markets, and America's Schools* (Washington: Brookings, 1990), pp. 190–91.

122. Milton Friedman, "The Role of Government in Education," *Capitalism and Freedom* (University of Chicago Press, 1982), pp. 85–86.

123. *Pierce* v. *Society of Sisters of the Holy Names of Jesus and Mary,* 268 U.S. 510 (1925).

124. Derek Bok, personal note, August 12, 2002.

125. W. Norton Grubb and Lorraine M. McDonnell, "Combating Program Fragmentation: Local Systems of Vocational Education and Job Training," *Journal of Policy Analysis and Management,* vol. 15, no. 2 (1996): 252–70.

126. Anthony P. Carnevale, "Beyond Consensus: Much Ado about Job Training," *Brookings Review,* vol. 17, no. 4 (1999): 40–43.

127. Grubb and McDonnell, "Combating Program Fragmentation."

128. Burton A. Weisbrod, "The Future of the Nonprofit Sector: Its Entwining with Private Enterprise and Government," *Journal of Policy Analysis and Management,* vol. 16, no. 4 (1997): 541–55.

129. Bill Leonard, "Welfare to Work: Filling a Tall Order," *HR Magazine,* vol. 43, no. 6 (1998): 78–80.

130. Edwin Melendez, "Matching the Disadvantaged to Job Opportunities: Structural Explanations for the Past Successes of the Center for Employment Training," *Economic Development Quarterly,* vol. 12, no. 1 (1998): 3–11.

131. Kevin J. Dougherty and Marianne F. Bakia, "Community Colleges and Contract Training: Content, Origins, and Impact," *Teachers College Record,* vol. 102, no. 1 (2000): 197–243; Robert Lynch, James C. Palmer, and W. Norton Grubb, *Community College Involvement in Contract Training and Other Economic Development Activities* (Berkeley: National Center for Research in Vocational Education, 1991).

132. See Carolyn J. Heinrich, "Organizational Form and Performance: An Empirical Investigation of Nonprofit and For-Profit Job-Training Service Providers," *Journal of Policy Analysis and Management,* vol. 19, no. 2 (2000): 233–61.

133. Heinrich, "Organizational Form and Performance."

134. Chicago Jobs Council, "Recommendations for Chicago's Local Plan Title I of the Workforce Investment Act of 1998" (Chicago Jobs Council, 2000); David M. Kennedy, "The Ladder and the Scale: Commitment and Accountability at Project Match" (Harvard University, Kennedy School of Government, 1992).

135. Robert Wordlaw, Chicago Jobs Council, telephone interview by author, December 2000. The Chicago Jobs Council is a community coalition organization dedicated to helping community-based organizations to prepare low-income Chicago residents to enter and advance in the workforce.

136. Heinrich, "Organizational Form and Performance."

137. Matthew Mariana, "One-Stop Career Centers: All in One Place and Everyplace," *Occupational Outlook Quarterly,* vol. 41, no. 3 (Fall 1997): 2–15.

138. Timothy P. Summers and Jeffrey Harrison, "Alliances for Success," *Training and Development,* vol. 46, no. 3 (1992): 69–75.

139. Julie Wilen, Mayor's Office for Workforce Development, telephone interview by author, December 2000.

140. Carnevale, "Beyond Consensus"; Paul Osterman, "Reforming Employment Training and Policies," *USA Today,* vol. 126, no. 2632 (1998): 20–21.

141. Melendez, "Matching the Disadvantaged to Job Opportunities." See Paul Osterman, "Employer-Centered Training for International Competitiveness," *Journal of Policy Analysis and Management,* vol. 12 (Summer 1998): 456–77; Robert R. Reich, *Involving Employers in Training: A Literature Review* (Washington: U.S. Department of Labor, Employment and Training Administration, 1996).

142. Dougherty and Bakia, "Community Colleges and Contract Training."

143. Paul Osterman, "The Possibilities of Employment Policy," in *Workforce Policies for the 1990s* (Washington: Economic Policy Institute, 1999), pp. 31–66.

144. Osterman, "Reforming Employment Training and Policies."

145. Osterman, "Possibilities of Employment Policy."

146. Reich, *Involving Employers in Training.*

147. Anthony P. Carnevale, "The Learning Enterprise," *Training and Development Journal,* vol. 43, no. 2 (February 1989): 26–33.

148. Paul Osterman, "New Lessons for State Training," *Spectrum,* vol. 65, no. 3 (Summer 1992): 7–14.

149. Goodwill Industries, "1999 Annual Report for Goodwill Industries of Southeastern Wisconsin and Metropolitan Chicago, Inc." (Milwaukee and Chicago: Goodwill Industries, 1999).

150. Carnevale, "Learning Enterprise."

151. Chicago Jobs Council, "Recommendations for Chicago's Local Plan Title I."

4

Social Services

STEVEN RATHGEB SMITH

For many citizens, nonprofit social service agencies *are* the nonprofit sector. The Salvation Army, Catholic Charities, homeless shelters, child welfare agencies, and soup kitchens are just a few of the many social service agencies that evoke images of private charity, community involvement, and voluntarism. The September 11, 2001, attacks on the World Trade Center and the Pentagon reinforced these images, as hundreds of millions of dollars were donated to an array of nonprofit service agencies. Nonprofit social service agencies have also entered the spotlight as a result of recent changes in public policy, including the 1996 welfare reform legislation, the devolution of some federal social welfare grant programs to state and local government, and the Bush administration's support for a more prominent role for faith-based agencies in addressing social need. Nonprofit social service agencies are receiving widespread, almost unprecedented, attention and scrutiny from policymakers and citizens. Amid this broad public interest are many concerns about the future of nonprofit social services. For-profit competitors have entered fields such as child welfare, substance abuse treatment, mental health services, and job training traditionally

The author is indebted to many people for feedback on earlier versions of this manuscript. Special thanks to Richard Belous, Susan M. Chambre, Harold W. Demone Jr., Peter Edelman, Margaret Gibelman, William Gormley, Yeheskel Hasenfeld, John Morris, Lester M. Salamon, Diane Vinokur-Kaplan, and Stephen Wernet.

149

dominated by nonprofit service providers. Many nonprofit social service agencies are small, undercapitalized, and sometimes ill equipped to respond to the growing demands of public and private funders for greater accountability. At the local level, service agencies often find it difficult to cooperate given the competition to raise grant funds and land government contracts. And the substantial reliance of social service agencies on government funds means that these agencies can be highly sensitive to government regulatory and funding priorities.

Despite these limitations, nonprofit social service agencies have a more central role in society's response to social problems than ever before. Moreover, a fundamental "transformation of nonprofit social services" has occurred in the past twenty-five years.[1] This transformation of the nonprofit role has four important dimensions. First, societal expectations for resolving community and individual problems have changed markedly. As the following pages detail, social services have expanded in scope and diversity to reflect a shift in societal expectations about the role of formal and informal service agencies. Social movements have created demands for new or expanded services such as child daycare, rape crisis centers, domestic violence programs, and AIDS services. Profound demographic changes, including big jumps in life expectancy, women's labor force participation, and immigration, have produced widespread demand for social services to cope with these changes, including more home health care, child daycare, and immigrant relocation and assistance programs. Greater sensitivity and appreciation for the profound societal costs of poverty and discrimination have helped to fuel much greater support for a diverse array of services to help disadvantaged populations.

Second, this transformed demand for social services has, in turn, tremendous implications for the role of government, especially the federal government, in responding to social need. Thus the transformation of social services has increased the scale and scope of government support. The federal government is more important in the financing of nonprofit social services today than it was during what many have considered to be the high-water mark of federal involvement in social policy, the 1960s. A big reason for this greater concentration of funding is the expansion of federal support for nonprofit social services beyond traditional grant programs. Medicaid, for example, emerged in the 1980s and 1990s as a critical source of funds for an array of social service agencies ranging from child and family service agencies to community mental health clinics. Other government support for nonprofits has grown as well. In addition to direct funding, nonprofit service agencies now receive support from other "tools of government," such as tax credits, vouchers, tax-exempt bonds, and government loans.[2] Several federal agencies beyond the Department of Health and Human Services now support community-based social services, including the Department of Agriculture, Department of Housing and Urban Development, Department of Education, and Department of Justice.

Third, the changes in societal expectations and federal policy have blurred the boundaries between traditional social services and other services, including health care, housing, corrections, and public assistance. For instance, a 100-year-old child welfare agency in Boston recently took over a for-profit health care management firm. A nonprofit job training program receives money from the federal Department of Justice's weed and seed program.[3] And the federal housing and urban development enterprise zone program funds supportive social services in target communities.

Fourth, a substantial amount of federal funding of nonprofit social service agencies occurs through intergovernmental transfers to state and local governments, which then allocate this money to local agencies. Consequently, states and, to a lesser extent, local governments have substantially increased their spending for social welfare services (as opposed to cash assistance).[4] Higher spending, combined with the push to "reinvent government,"[5] has encouraged governments at all levels to restructure their relationships with nonprofit service agencies. Evidence of this restructuring includes the introduction of managed care arrangements in child welfare, Medicaid, and mental health; renewed emphasis on accountability and performance evaluation; and the creation of new nonprofit entities with state and local support to achieve specific social welfare policy objectives, such as job training.

The changes in management and funding at the federal, state, and local levels have, in turn, promoted significant shifts in management and restructuring within nonprofit agencies. These shifts have been stimulated as well by alterations in the priorities and interests of private funders, including United Way chapters and foundations. Nonprofit executives are pressured to be more "entrepreneurial" and diversify their base of support. This emphasis on entrepreneurship is a major reason why many nonprofit social service agencies have grown substantially in the past twenty-five years. Some traditional sources of funding of nonprofit social services have declined over time (for example, the federal social services block grant and United Way funding for some agencies), but nonprofits, often in cooperation with entrepreneurial state and local government administrators, have refinanced or replaced these funds with new public grants and contracts, additional private donations or foundation grants, and fees for service.[6] This is not to suggest that some nonprofit agencies have not lost funding or experienced serious financial problems, but these difficulties tend to be related to specific circumstances of the agency and its relationship to public and private funders.

While these changes have boosted the position of nonprofit social service agencies, they also have posed profound challenges. More overall money has meant an increase in the number of agencies, intensifying the competition among them. Many of the new service agencies are small and community based, making it difficult for them to compete effectively for revenue. Even when funding is obtained, it often fails to keep pace with rising staff costs, especially in the tight labor markets of the 1990s. Also government regulations can be onerous and complicated, requiring substantial investment in management infrastructure, including new information systems, databases, and staff to cope with compliance and reporting requirements of government regulators. Government funding also can be unpredictable, especially given that many government programs reimburse nonprofit agencies on a fee-for-service basis.

The vagaries of government funding and the modest size of many agencies mean that nonprofit agencies often face serious difficulties in maintaining their financial viability. Further, welfare reform has produced a sharp drop in the number of individuals on welfare, creating new demands and expectations for nonprofit agencies. Many agencies report that they have experienced higher demand for their services due to their clients' loss of cash assistance. But the competition for resources and the programmatic constraints on public and private grants mean that agencies face many obstacles to their ability to respond adequately to clients in need.

The following pages examine in more detail the organizational and funding changes that are sweeping through the world of nonprofit social service agencies. To do so, it reviews the basic structure and relative position of nonprofit social services, examines the development of this set of organizations, outlines the key trends affecting nonprofit social service agencies, and suggests some strategies to enhance the effectiveness and operations of nonprofit social service agencies. A concluding section offers some thoughts on future directions in nonprofit social services.

Mapping the Role of Nonprofits in Social Services

The field of nonprofit social services is diverse and has many subsectors. Indeed, the makeup of this field remains a matter of dispute. The term *social services* came into widespread use in the post–World War II period, especially in the United Kingdom, where the term *personal social services* referred to the governmentally supported provision of a "wide range of services designed to promote the health and well-being of the community."[7] In the United States, the term *social services* has generally referred to those services "rendered to individuals and families under societal auspices, excluding the major independent fields of service (that is, excluding health, education, housing, and income maintenance")." [8] Thus, in practical terms, social services refer to the social care provided to deprived, neglected, or handicapped children and youth, the needy elderly, the mentally ill and developmentally disabled, and disadvantaged adults. These services include daycare, counseling, job training, child protection, foster care, residential treatment, homemakers, rehabilitation, and sheltered workshops.[9]

Especially in recent years, many scholars and policymakers would contend that this definition favors government provision over other forms of provision, such as the family, the church, and business. Consequently, the boundaries of social services have become quite contentious in terms of both the appropriate sector to provide them as well as what appropriately should be included in them. At its core, however, social services encompass an expanding array of programs designed to enhance the life of families and individuals, including programs to address domestic violence, rape, AIDS, poverty, homelessness, drug and alcohol addiction, and community living for the disabled.

Types of Organizations

Nonprofit organizations are on the front lines of the social services field. However, these organizations vary greatly in scale, character, and degree of formality. Indeed, it is possible to distinguish three broad categories of nonprofit social service agencies.

INFORMAL ORGANIZATIONS. A significant number of nonprofit social service agencies are informal, community-based groups and associations. Typically, these groups lack legal status and depend on small cash and in-kind donations to support their activities. Some also collect fees for service that vary greatly depending on the circumstances.

Classic examples of such informal associations are self-help groups such as Alcoholics Anonymous and support groups for survivors of diseases such as cancer. These informal groups usually accept no external grant funds and depend completely on volunteers, although they may receive periodic support from more formal institutions and may collaborate with established public and nonprofit institutions.[10] Other social service associations that may exist as informal organizations are soup kitchens and shelters (especially those programs affiliated with churches), daycare programs, recreational programs, and emergency assistance. Many churches also have programs that do not exist as formal organizational entities apart from the church. For instance, an interfaith soup kitchen in Seattle operates in different locations during the week and depends completely on volunteers from the member churches.

TRADITIONAL AGENCIES. At the opposite end of the continuum from the informal agencies are the older, more traditional, and professional social service organizations. Often these agencies are affiliated with the United Way and have a diversified base of funding that may include sizable private donations and endowment funds as well as substantial government funds. Agencies in this category include many long-standing child and family service agencies, the Boys and Girls Club, YWCA, American Red Cross, and Salvation Army. These agencies usually have large boards (sometimes up to forty or fifty members). They are members of larger national associations such as the Child Welfare League of America, Alliance for Families and Children, or YWCA. These organizations vary in their mix of public and private revenue, but many child and family service agencies in this category became substantially more reliant on government contracts in the past twenty-five years due to changes in public child welfare policy and increases in the number of children in foster care and the child protection system. Other organizations, such as the Salvation Army and YWCA, vary greatly in their service mix and orientation, depending on the policies of local chapters. Some Salvation Army and YWCA chapters, for instance, receive substantial government support, while other chapters refuse to accept any government funds.

RECENT ADDITIONS. A third category of agencies includes recent additions to the nonprofit social services field. Many of them reflect the impact of social movements on social services as well as new demands for social services to address urgent social problems. Many of these new agencies started as informal agencies and then became more formalized, gaining nonprofit legal status after the agency was awarded a sizable public or private grant.

This category includes many large and small agencies, especially in the following service areas: AIDS services, domestic violence, rape crisis assistance, immigrant assistance, drug and alcohol abuse treatment, mental health care, child residential treatment, and services for delinquent youth. These agencies often rely heavily on government funds (or, in some cases, on reimbursement from private insurance plans). They tend to have few volunteers, except for their boards, and receive scant private donations.

But, overall, the new additions are disproportionately small agencies with relatively small boards (eight to fifteen members). They usually are undercapitalized and face formidable challenges in attracting and recruiting talented staff and effective board members. They often are very dependent on a single revenue stream of public or private grants, creating serious imbalances in power and recurrent management problems.

Scope of the Nonprofit Social Service Sector

Because informal organizations do not have legal status, it is virtually impossible to estimate accurately how many of these informal groups exist. Available research does indicate, though, that in many service categories such as daycare, emergency assistance, and recreation for youth, informal groups and associations are very important in the overall delivery of services, even if the total amount of resources flowing through them is relatively small.

More accurate information is available on the formal social service sector. As indicated in table 4-1, in 1997, this component of the nonprofit sector employed 1,586,186 people. Most of this employment was concentrated in individual and

Table 4-1. *Nonprofit Social Services, 1997*

Service field	Establishments		Employment	
	Number	*Percent*	*Number*	*Percent*
Core social service fields				
Child daycare	18,099	18.0	239,981	12.2
Individual and family services	42,427	42.2	692,454	35.2
Job training and vocational rehabilitation	5,668	5.6	269,738	13.7
Residential care	10,869	10.8	240,732	12.2
Miscellaneous social services	15,093	15.0	143,281	7.3
Subtotal, core social service fields	92,156	91.6	1,586,186	80.5
Related service fields				
Home health	3,375	3.4	267,484	13.6
Family planning	1,365	1.4	13,820	0.7
Outpatient mental health and substance abuse centers	3,646	3.6	102,096	5.2
Subtotal, related service fields	8,386	8.4	383,400	19.5
Total service fields	100,542	100.0	1,969,586	100.0

Source: U.S. Census Bureau, *Census of Service Industries* (Washington: U.S. Census Bureau, 1997).

family service agencies, followed by job training and vocational rehabilitation and child daycare.

Individual and family services form a broad, diverse category that includes individual and family counseling, information and referral, emergency relief, and immigrant and disaster assistance. Many of the agencies are new, representing the growing demand for services to address urgent social problems. Good examples of these new agencies are rape crisis centers, AIDS-related service agencies, domestic violence shelters, and immigrant relocation programs.

Residential care is also a diverse category, including group homes for the mentally ill and developmentally disabled, residential homes for children, and halfway houses for offenders and drug abusers. The miscellaneous category largely comprises organizations that could be characterized as advocacy or social change agencies focusing on social service programs and their clients, including neighborhood change and development, welfare reform, and immigrant rights. Umbrella organizations representing different service agencies also are included in this category.[11]

As table 4-1 also shows, another 383,000 people are employed in nonprofit agencies providing services that fall on the boundary between social and health services. Most important here are home health services, which now employ more people than nonprofit child daycare centers.

While nonprofit agencies play a critical role in the social services field, they do not operate alone in this sphere. In the first place, the public sector retains an important role. Compared to the 1.6 million nonprofit employees, for example, state and local governments employed 485,000 people in social welfare activities in 1999.[12] In addition, however, in 1997 some 662,000 people worked in for-profit social service agencies, and another 708,000 worked in for-profit firms in related fields, as indicated in table 4-2. Indeed, of the 3.3 million people employed in the private sector in social services and closely related fields, 1.4 million—or 41 percent—worked in for-profit firms. For-profit employment is concentrated, however, in a relative handful of fields. As table 4-2 shows, in 1997 for-profit agencies represented a sizable percentage of employment in only three fields: child daycare (62 percent), residential care (42 percent), and home health (72 percent).

The significant presence of for-profit providers in the social service field is a product of the growth in this field over the past twenty years. As table 4-2 shows, between 1977 and 1997, overall employment in the social services field grew 163 percent.[13] Nonprofits participated in this growth, more than doubling their employment during this period. But for-profits took an even more robust part, nearly quadrupling their employment, although starting from a much smaller base. As a consequence, for-profit organizations went from 21 percent of total social service employment in 1977 to 30 percent in 1997. This increase was largely due to the rapid growth of for-profit daycare programs. In 1977, child daycare was still a predominantly nonprofit activity; but by 1997, employment in for-profit programs had reached 387,730 compared to 239,981 for nonprofit programs. Child daycare rose from 22 percent of total employment to more than 27 percent. The other noteworthy change in the for-profit/nonprofit mix is in residential care—a category composed primarily of services for children. Employment in for-profit residential programs more than tripled from 49,626 in 1977 to 172,142 in 1997. At the same time, employment in nonprofit residential programs was up only 78 percent.

The rapid growth of programs such as home health and residential mental retardation care also highlights the shift to health services from social services, partly spurred by financing. Traditional social service programs such as residential foster care or counseling have been eclipsed by the sharp escalation in health-related programs. Moreover, many traditional social service agencies, such as Catholic Charities, Lutheran Social Services, and the Jewish Family Services, now offer these health-related social services.

Census Bureau data indicate that, with the exception of child daycare, for-profit facilities tend to be concentrated in a few select states. For example, 43 percent of for-profit mental retardation facilities are in four states—California, Minnesota, Texas, and Wisconsin. Similarly, almost 50 percent of for-profit outpatient mental health and substance abuse centers are in five states: California, Florida, Minnesota, New York, and Texas.[14]

Table 4-2. *Employment Trends in Social Services, 1977–97*

Type of service	1977		1997		Percent change, 1977–97
	Number	Percent	Number	Percent	
Social services					
Child daycare	189,918	100.0	627,711	100.0	230.5
Nonprofit	102,408	53.9	239,981	38.2	134.3
For-profit	87,510	46.1	387,730	61.8	343.1
Individual and family services	182,947	100.0	762,779	100.0	316.9
Nonprofit	167,384	91.5	692,454	90.8	313.7
For-profit	15,563	8.5	70,325	9.2	351.9
Job training and vocational	151,525	100.0	301,742	100.0	99.1
Nonprofit	138,368	91.3	269,738	89.4	94.9
For-profit	13,157	8.7	32,004	10.6	143.2
Residential care	184,770	100.0	412,874	100.0	123.5
Nonprofit	135,144	73.1	240,732	58.3	78.1
For-profit	49,626	26.9	172,142	41.7	246.9
Miscellaneous social services	144,762	100.0	143,281	100.0	−1.2
Nonprofit	133,169	92.0	143,281	100.0	7.6
For-profit	11,593	8.0	n.a.	n.a.	n.a.
Subtotal, social services	853,922	100.0	2,248,387	100.0	163.3
Nonprofit	676,473	79.2	1,586,186	70.5	134.5
For-profit	177,449	20.8	662,201	29.5	273.2
Related services					
Home health	n.a.	n.a.	948,989	100.0	n.a.
Nonprofit	n.a.	n.a.	267,484	28.2	n.a.
For-profit	n.a.	n.a.	681,505	71.8	n.a.
Family planning	n.a.	n.a.	17,745	100.0	n.a.
Nonprofit	n.a.	n.a.	13,820	77.9	n.a.
For-profit	n.a.	n.a.	3,925	22.1	n.a.
Outpatient mental health and substance abuse	n.a.	n.a.	125,097	100.0	n.a.
Nonprofit	n.a.	n.a.	102,096	81.6	n.a.
For-profit	n.a.	n.a.	23,001	18.4	n.a.
Subtotal, related services	n.a.	n.a.	1,091,831	100.0	n.a.
Nonprofit	n.a.	n.a.	383,400	35.1	n.a.
For-profit	n.a.	n.a.	708,431	64.9	n.a.
Total services	n.a.	n.a.	3,340,218	100.0	n.a.
Nonprofit	n.a.	n.a.	1,969,586	59.0	n.a.
For-profit	n.a.	n.a.	1,370,632	41.0	n.a.

Source: U.S. Census Bureau, *Census of Service Industries* (Washington: U.S. Census Bureau, 1977, 1997).

n.a. Not available.

For the most part, the expansion of nonprofit and for-profit social services has not been the product of the privatization of previously public social services. Instead, this growth has been mostly in new programs and services. The exception, perhaps, is in mental health and mental retardation services. But even here, the decline in public sector involvement has been more the product of a shift in treatment mode toward community-based care in place of institutionalization than a clear-cut case of privatization.

To be sure, the growth of nonprofit social services could be said to have affected the growth rate of public employment in social services. Employment in public welfare–related activities in state and local government has been essentially flat in the past several years. In particular, the number of people employed in state and local public welfare activities in 1993 was approximately 483,000, rising only slightly to 485,000 in 1999.[15] By comparison, the growth rate in nonprofit and for-profit social services has been much more rapid.

Also state and local government agencies involved in direct social service delivery rarely offer the same services as comparable nonprofit and for-profit agencies. Public social service agencies tend to provide casework and eligibility determination, child protective services, mental health counseling, and in some cases temporary shelter. And, more recently, new public funding associated with the correctional system, including funding for drug abuse treatment and job training, has resulted in an increase in the role of public social service programs in some states.[16] As a generalization, the clients of public social service agencies tend to be more disadvantaged or distressed than are the clients of comparable nonprofit or for-profit programs. The staff of public agencies also tend to have much higher caseloads, and public programs tend to be larger—sometimes much larger—than most comparable nonprofit programs.

The Development of the Mixed Public/Private System of Social Services

The current configuration of nonprofit, public, and for-profit social service organizations has been shaped by developments and trends that go back to the earliest decades of the republic. In the colonial period, churches, voluntary organizations, neighbors, and relatives provided emergency or supplemental cash and in-kind assistance, counseling, and support for people in need. Few formal voluntary service agencies existed. But in the early 1800s, especially in the antebellum period of the 1820s and 1830s, organizations and charitable societies to care for children, mothers, and the disadvantaged proliferated throughout the country.

As the nineteenth century proceeded, more and more voluntary service organizations were founded, especially for children and youth.[17] Many of these organizations were established through religious sponsorship and affiliation, reflecting the surge of immigrants into urban America in the late nineteenth century and the concomitant need to provide them with support and social care. For instance, the major expansion of Catholic Charities occurred during this period. Many of these sectarian agencies, especially in urban areas, received public subsidies, although often these subsidies were politically controversial.[18] In the late nineteenth century, a number of other voluntary organizations with at least some faith and social care component were also established, including the YMCA, YWCA, Goodwill Industries, Volunteers of America, and Salvation Army.

With the growth of nonprofit service organizations in the nineteenth century, the structure of social care became increasingly complicated. Public organizations, including state and local institutions for the mentally ill, developmentally disabled, and delinquent youth, continued to grow in size and numbers.[19] Poor farms and almshouses were a central component of public assistance, especially for the poor elderly and disabled. Typically, these institutions were administered directly by counties and towns or "managed" under a contract to a private entrepreneur.[20] Nonprofit organizations emerged as central to service provision in child welfare (including foster care, adoption, and residential care), relief for the poor through cash and in-kind assistance (usually as a supplement to the public sector), immigrant assistance, and recreation. Public subsidies of nonprofit organizations tended to be highly targeted, with child and family service agencies the principal beneficiaries, primarily in urban areas with substantial immigrant populations.[21]

During the early part of the twentieth century, the predecessor organization to today's United Way, the Community Chest, was founded by leading members of the business and nonprofit sectors in communities across the country as a "federated" group of fundraising organizations with the goal of enhancing the overall efficiency of local services. The member agencies of the Community Chest—typically the established, elite voluntary agencies of the community, such as the YMCA, YWCA, Red Cross, Boy Scouts, Girl Scouts, and child and family service agencies—agreed to join a common fundraising campaign whose proceeds would be distributed to the member agencies. By 1929, 329 cities and towns had autonomous Community Chest chapters under the loose umbrella of the Community Chest name.[22]

The depression of the 1930s created daunting problems for nonprofit and public social service agencies. Many nonprofit agencies were forced to close or merge, and many were simply overwhelmed with the demand for help. In response, the federal government created numerous relief programs, but most of these programs were temporary. Over time, they closed, leaving the underlying structure of social services intact: large state and local institutions for specialized populations; a relatively small nonprofit sector focused primarily on child and family services, recreation, and emergency assistance; and a virtually nonexistent funding or administrative role for the federal government.

Although the structure of services began to change more permanently in the late 1940s and 1950s, the change was slow, and most new programs were small and undercapitalized. Well into the 1950s, nonprofit social service agencies that were members of the Community Chest often depended on donations from the Community Chest for 50 percent or more of their income. Agencies outside the Community Chest umbrella depended on modest private donations and fees from clients. Public funding of nonprofit agencies tended to be small scale and restricted to select agencies such as residential programs for youth. And most social services remained clustered in the category of family and child services that had characterized social services since the late 1800s.

The rediscovery of poverty and the launching of the war on poverty in the 1960s dramatically changed the funding and regulatory role of the federal government in social services. The federal initiatives of this period had profound consequences for the delivery of nonprofit social services, including the diversification of services and a shift from reliance on private donations and client fees to public financing.

Through a variety of new programs, the federal government funded an array of new social services: senior services, community mental health, community action, job training, rape crisis centers, domestic violence programs, counseling for the poor and the disabled, specialized foster care, home care for the disabled and elderly, and intensive preschool for disadvantaged children (the Head Start program).[23] This new funding allowed social services to expand beyond the traditional band of services.

The availability of federal funding for new services encouraged the establishment and growth of new nonprofit agencies outside the established network of Community Chest agencies. These new agencies usually depended heavily on government funding, although many of the established agencies benefited from the expanded government funding as well. These new agencies quickly took their place as central actors on the local social service scene, especially in service areas that more traditional agencies had largely eschewed, such as drug treatment and services for the disabled and mentally ill. Over time, these new agencies started to call for greater openness by the United Way and public grant programs that still tended to favor more traditional services such as child welfare.

Thanks to pressures from a variety of social movement organizations, federal funding permitted the expansion of social services to populations far beyond the traditional mix of child and family services. The women's movement helped to enact legislation in the 1970s providing funding for rape crisis centers, domestic violence programs, and expanded child daycare. The "deinstitutionalization movement" (particularly its legal strategies of the 1970s) revolutionized the care of the mentally ill and developmentally disabled, leading to a sharp rise in nonprofit community programs. Political advocacy around hunger and homelessness in the 1980s produced more funding for social services to address these issues.

The big rise in federal funding—in concert with the willingness of state and local governments and nonprofit agencies to tap this federal money—fundamentally altered the relative position of government and private sources in the funding of nonprofit social services. For instance, federal spending on a bundle of social services, including child welfare, vocational rehabilitation, and nutrition assistance, rose from $2.2 billion in 1970 to $8.7 billion in 1980.[24] This sharp increase in funding boosted the government share of nonprofit social agency funding to well over half. Concomitantly, the relative contribution of private fees and donations to the revenue stream of nonprofits fell dramatically.[25] The growth in public support also reduced the relative role of the Community Chest and its successor organization, the United Way, in the funding of social services. This decline continues to the present day, although local United Way chapters are increasingly important in convening key stakeholders in the community to define pressing social service priorities.[26]

Recent Trends

Against this backdrop, recent years have brought additional pressures for change in nonprofit social service agencies. These pressures have arisen from continuing shifts in federal policy, heightened competition, pressure for accountability and performance evaluation, managed care, and greater interest in faith-based services among many policymakers and community groups.

Shifts in Federal Policy

The election of Ronald Reagan as U.S. president brought at least a temporary end to the steady growth in federal social spending. Under the Omnibus Budget Reconciliation Act of 1981, funding was cut, and the states were given much broader latitude on spending decisions.[27]

These changes in federal policy (which nonprofit social service agencies almost universally opposed) prompted many state governments to cut their funding to nonprofits. These cuts were particularly severe in programs lacking substantial political support or involving controversial issues. Thus disproportionate cuts in funding hit agencies providing family planning, advocacy, legal aid, and housing services. Overall, the extent of cutbacks varied by state (and even locality, in some cases), since many state and local governments substituted their own funds for lost federal dollars. For example, a study of the impact of federal cutbacks in Buffalo revealed that state, and to a lesser extent local, government more than compensated for federal cutbacks to local human service agencies.[28] Overall, state spending on a bundle of social welfare services including child welfare increased in real terms from $4.2 billion in 1980 to more than $10 billion in 1995.[29]

But federal policy did not remain static after the Reagan initiatives, in part due to stepped-up advocacy by nonprofit executives, social policy advocates, members of Congress, and state and local administrators. Four key changes in federal policy during the 1980s and 1990s deserve special mention. First, state governments, often with the support of federal officials and nonprofit executives, refinanced social services by tapping into other sources of federal financing, especially Medicaid, the matching federal/state health insurance program for the poor and disabled. During the past two decades, Medicaid payments for services (excluding administration and other nonservice payments) grew rapidly in real terms, from $47 billion in 1980 to more than $142 billion in 1998 (in 1998 dollars).[30]

Although the reasons for the escalation of Medicaid costs are complicated,[31] an important contributing factor was cost shifting: social services previously funded primarily by state government or federal categorical grants, such as Title XX, were redefined as behavioral health services and substantially shifted to Medicaid. These services include child welfare (particularly counseling and residential treatment), mental health care, rehabilitation services, residential programs for the developmentally disabled and chronic mentally ill, and home care.[32] Indeed, one of the biggest growth areas within Medicaid has been community residential services for the mentally ill and developmentally disabled. States drastically reduced the number of people in their large public institutions and moved many of them into Medicaid-eligible, community-based programs. (Most of their support services are also financed by Medicaid.)[33] The effect of this change was to shift much of the financing of services for the mentally ill and developmentally disabled from the states to the federal government. For example, by 1996, state funds accounted for only 53 percent of all public spending on community services for the developmentally disabled; prior to the 1980s, almost all community and institutional spending was from state government.[34] This expansion and cost shifting with Medicaid also spurred the growth of nonprofit and, to a lesser extent, for-profit programs.

Changes in eligibility requirements among the poor and disabled also meant that more people were eligible for Medicaid. For example, many people with AIDS became eligible for Medicaid services in the 1990s.[35] Similarly, the number of disabled on the federal Supplemental Security Income (SSI) program rose from 2.2 million in 1980 to 5.1 million in 1999.[36] The number of children on the SSI program rose from 190,394 in 1980 to 846,784 in 2000; indeed, children were the fastest-growing subgroup of SSI recipients.[37] Since eligibility for SSI triggers eligibility for Medicaid in most states, this increase also expanded Medicaid coverage. Overall, an estimated 84 percent of all adults with severe disabilities (both emotional and physical) are covered by public insurance programs, principally Medicaid and Medicare.[38] Nationwide, the number of Medicaid recipients rose from just over 21 million in 1980 to over 40 million in 1998.[39]

Second, many new federal funding programs for social services were created, or additional funds were provided for existing programs. Child and youth services were major beneficiaries of this expansion. For instance, a survey of the nonprofit agency members of the Child Welfare League of America indicated that in the period 1979–86 the revenues of these agencies increased 240 percent, with more than 59 percent of the revenue coming directly from government.[40] Federal and state spending on childcare also has been rising, especially in recent years. For instance, total federal and state spending on childcare rose in real terms from $2 billion in 1992 to more than $5 billion in 1998.[41] In 1996 alone, $15 billion was spent on child welfare services from all levels of government, with 44 percent from federal sources.[42] The vast majority of this funding goes to nonprofit child welfare agencies. The rise in federal funding is also evident in other services where nonprofit agencies predominate, including AIDS services ($1.6 billion in 1999),[43] AmeriCorps and other volunteer service programs through the Corporation for National Service ($500 million in 2000),[44] job training, mental health,[45] and drug and alcohol abuse treatment (a projected $3.4 billion in 2001).[46] Home health care spending has also risen sharply, although this service is now dominated by large for-profit providers.[47] More specifically, home health spending rose from just $4.8 billion in 1980 to more than $29 billion in 1998 (in 1998 dollars).[48]

More generally, although spending on some federal social service programs, such as the social services block grant (SSBG) and the community services bock grant (CSBG), has declined in real terms,[49] overall real per capita non-Medicaid intergovernmental grants for public welfare have risen sharply—from $7.00 in 1988 to $43.00 in 1997.[50] This figure does not even include intergovernmental grants for nontraditional social services such as AIDS services, drug and alcohol abuse treatment, and community prevention and justice programs. SSBG, then, has been eclipsed by the expansion of other programs.[51] The rise in these intergovernmental grants has, in turn, boosted real per capita state government expenditures on noncash assistance public welfare programs from $110 in 1988 to $152 in 1997 (in 1992 dollars).[52]

Many federal departments that historically did not directly fund social services, such as the Department of Justice, Department of Education, and Department of Housing and Urban Development, emerged in the 1980s and 1990s as major funders of local social service programs. In part, this development reflected the perception that the clients of these agencies could benefit from the integration of social services such as childcare or counseling into existing categorical programs.

The third major development in federal social policy affecting nonprofit social service agencies is welfare reform, passed in 1996 and implemented in 1997. This legislation replaced the Aid to Families with Dependent Children (AFDC) program and gave states much greater flexibility in the administration and spending of federal dollars under the new program, temporary aid to needy families (TANF). Due to TANF and a burgeoning domestic economy, the number of people receiving cash benefits plummeted nationwide. Many states have spent the resulting savings on cash assistance (and additional federal aid for services) on a variety of welfare-related services, boosting overall federal and state spending on them.[53] Many nonprofit agencies have found themselves in an unusual position: after stridently opposing welfare reform and seeing at least some of their clients lose cash benefits, many agencies have received additional funding to provide job training, welfare-to-work aid, and childcare.

A final shift in federal policy affecting nonprofits has been the diversification in the tools of government support for nonprofits. Although direct funding remains the norm, new tools of support have expanded, including tax credits, loans, and tax-exempt bonds. For instance, the federal childcare tax credit has fueled the growth in demand for nonprofit (and for-profit) childcare. Tax-exempt bond financing has been used by state and local governments to help nonprofit social service agencies with their capital needs. Government loans can be politically tricky and complicated, but state and local governments as well as private foundations have used loans or revolving loan funds to help nonprofit social service agencies with various operational and capital needs.

To be sure, not all agencies have benefited equally from these changes in public funding and policy. As a consequence, some agencies have merged or closed, while others have been unable to find adequate revenues to keep pace with rising costs. Nonetheless, the shift to public financing of social services, and the subsequent expansion and diversification of that financing through a multiplicity of direct and indirect programs, has transformed social services. Prior to the 1960s, nonprofit social welfare agencies occupied a narrow niche of the market and generally lacked the financial means or organizational incentive to provide extensive services to the poor and disadvantaged. Currently, nonprofit social service agencies provide a bewildering array of services supported with public funds and complemented with other revenue sources to the poor, disadvantaged, and handicapped.

But the expansion and diversification of services also have created new and different problems for policymakers, private funders, and nonprofit staff and volunteers. The new services are often provided by new agencies that are undercapitalized and lack both political connections and a substantial base of private donors. These agencies may be able to grow because more funding is available, but they operate at the edge, scrambling for contracts and private donations to sustain their operations. Staff and volunteer burnout is a constant problem because of the time required to keep these organizations going without a broad base of resources. This situation contrasts with that of the larger, more traditional organizations that have a long history in the community and ready access to capital and political connections. Since government now relies on these new community organizations to provide vital public services, the capacity of these agencies to fulfill their public expectations has become a major policy and management issue.

Increased Competition

The expansion and transformation of federal social services policy, in turn, have precipitated, or been accompanied by, a number other changes in the external environment and internal management of nonprofits. Foremost among these changes has been a substantial increase in competition.

Prior to the 1960s, nonprofit social welfare agencies faced little direct competition. Most agencies had essentially monopoly control of services in their area—a situation reinforced by the membership rules of the Community Chest and the scarcity of resources. But the advent of federal funding dramatically changed this, prompting a big increase in the number of nonprofit service agencies in local communities and inviting for-profit competition for some services traditionally provided by nonprofit organizations, including home health care, mental health care, residential care for the developmentally disabled and mentally ill, drug and alcohol abuse treatment, hospice care, and welfare-to-work programs.

Recently, for-profit organizations have received a lot of attention in the aftermath of the 1996 welfare reform legislation. Big for-profit firms such as Maximus, America Works, and Curtis and Associates have aggressively courted state and local governments seeking to implement the TANF legislation. They have achieved some success in landing big welfare-to-work contracts in cities such as Albany (New York), Indianapolis, and New York City.[54] They also have landed contracts to manage all or part of a few state social service departments. For example, Maximus was recently awarded a contract to manage all of Connecticut's subsidized childcare slots. In this case, Maximus does not provide the childcare itself but instead manages everything from provider payments to staff training.[55]

The media attention that these high-profile contracts to Maximus and other big for-profits have attracted tends to overstate the extent to which most nonprofits face competition from for-profits. Despite growth, the total amount of direct services provided by Maximus and other big national for-profits is still small compared to the hundreds of millions of dollars being spent in services related to welfare to work.[56] (Moreover, 85 percent of the value of Maximus contracts in 2000 was in two states, Florida and Texas.)[57] As noted, for-profit social service agencies tend to be concentrated in a few service categories, such as childcare and home health care. Most nonprofit agencies are not likely to face much competition from for-profits. Even in home health care and child daycare, evidence suggests that, at least in child daycare, nonprofits and for-profits often serve different segments of the local market.[58] Far more likely in the current environment is competition from other nonprofits. The pressure on nonprofits to find new sources of revenue means that many nonprofits, especially the larger ones, are in an expansion mode and not chary about expanding into another agency's market.

Of course, this is not to understate the significance of the entry of big for-profit firms into social services. But the financial pressures on government at all levels, the spread of managed care, and new accountability and performance standards cloud the future of for-profit involvement. Given the growing diversity of many urban and suburban communities, state and local governments also have a strong incentive to respond to the emergent needs and service demands of new groups by channeling aid through community-based organizations, which tend to be nonprofit in form. This is evident, for example, in government contracting with community-based, nonprofit organizations under the new federal Workforce Investment Act of 1998.

Pressure for Accountability and Performance Evaluation

A third important trend in social service agency operations has been an expanded emphasis on accountability. This began with the initial buildup of government funding of nonprofit agencies in the 1960s. Nonprofit agencies were expected to be accountable for their expenditure of public funds. This accountability was in a line-item sense, however: Were the public funds spent according to the stipulations of the contract? This "process" accountability typically involved reporting the number of clients served or meals delivered as well as a budgetary breakdown of the allocation of various expenditures. Government also tried to increase the likelihood that the agency would deliver a quality program by requiring staff and program standards even before any money was distributed. In this initial period of the 1960s and 1970s, private foundations and the United Way tended to place very minimal accountability requirements on their grantees; usually, nonprofit agencies simply had to submit a short report at the end of their grant, stating the accomplishments achieved by the agency with the grant funds.

Over time, though, many policymakers became disenchanted with this process accountability, arguing that it provided little evidence on the effectiveness with which programs were achieving their desired outcomes. Further, public grant administrators worried about the potential mismatch between public and nonprofit service priorities. As a result, public and private funders began to demand that nonprofit agencies measure their outcomes.[59] For many nonprofit agencies, this shift to outcome evaluation involved a revolution in thinking and overall approach to service. It also required new investments in management information systems and monitoring. Funding for this management infrastructure often is scarce, putting further financial pressure on many agencies.

Outcome evaluation also increases the competitive pressure on nonprofits. In the past, nonprofits were relatively assured that their funding would continue, barring any egregious problems. But many government funding programs now tie funding to performance, raising the specter that an agency could lose funding if it did not meet specific performance targets. (Many welfare-to-work programs now have this requirement.) Financial uncertainty and competitive market pressure are further increased by the restructuring of the contracts. In order to give government agencies greater control over the performance of nonprofit contract agencies, governments have increasingly restructured contracts with nonprofit agencies from a cost-reimbursement contract to a fee-for-service contract. Nonprofit agencies now have less predictable revenues, since they will only be reimbursed when performance targets are reached.

In a major shift, local United Way chapters (to varying degrees) are adopting performance measures as a condition of funding. In the past, the United Way was a favored source of unrestricted dollars for nonprofit human service agencies. Now local United Way chapters are facing competitive pressures of their own: many United Way staff believe that they have no choice but to institute outcome evaluation and more restricted program-related funding. The impact on nonprofit agencies is substantial, since they do not have the unrestricted dollars needed to support difficult-to-fund activities such as administration.

The move to performance evaluation by government and private funders is part of what many people regard as an overdue move to increase the accountability of nonprofit agencies, both to specific program outcomes as well as more generally to their boards of directors and the community.[60] As just one indication of this attention to performance, many larger nonprofit agencies are implementing a "balanced scorecard" that includes both financial and programmatic performance measures.[61] Ultimately, the outcome of this attention to performance remains to be determined. Assessing outcomes of many social service programs is complicated and expensive. For some programs, it may be virtually impossible to evaluate outcomes given concerns about confidentiality and the difficulties involved in tracking clients after they leave a service program. Public and private funders also may find it difficult to use outcome data, however imperfect, to determine grant and contract decisions.

The Advent of Managed Care in Social Services

Managed care was pioneered in health care by health maintenance organizations (HMOs), which implemented a new payment system wherein hospitals or physicians were paid a per person rate for taking care of the health care needs of a specified number of patients. The assumption was that this would provide incentives for hospitals and doctors to be efficient and avoid unnecessary health care.

Until recently, managed care was avoided in social services, probably due to the limited funding at stake and the fragmentation of the delivery system. But the increase in public funding of social services and the much greater dependence of social services on Medicaid and other health insurance programs have provided policymakers with the rationale and opening wedge to institute managed care in social services. Typically, a state agency will select a managed care organization and pay it a per capita fee to manage the services needed by a certain class of clients (for example, the mentally ill). The managed care firm will then subcontract with local service providers—both nonprofit and for-profit—to provide the services to clients.

Managed care has spread broadly in services eligible for Medicaid such as mental health and child welfare.[62] This has a number of important implications for nonprofit social service agencies. First, managed care creates a much more uncertain funding and political environment for nonprofit agencies. In the 1960s and 1970s, government contracting with nonprofit agencies grew as a direct relationship between government and the agency.[63] This relationship had a substantial degree of predictability; agencies rarely lost their contracts, and most service providers could be assured of rate increases every year subject to the vagaries of the state budget process. Managed care makes the relationship between government and the nonprofit service provider much more indirect. A third-party intermediary—the managed care firm—is now in a position to make critical program and funding decisions. Nonprofit agencies have less ongoing, direct access to government and much more instability in their funding.

Second and related, managed care fundamentally alters the political influence of the nonprofit agency. Nonprofit service providers are now part of a web of relationships controlled by the managed care firm. These firms are not politically accountable in the same way as government, making it more difficult for nonprofit agencies to influence managed care decisions.

Third, managed care firms may be more open to new service providers due to their own pressure to hold down costs. In an interesting development, the arrival of managed care also may help to reinforce the position of community-based nonprofit organizations in service delivery. Managed care is often politically unpopular, especially in social services. Thus in return for help in pushing managed care, politicians have to agree to increase (or protect) the role of community organizations in service delivery. In Kansas, for example, where managed care was recently adopted for the state's child welfare services, all of the service providers are nonprofit.

Charitable Choice and Faith-Based Social Provision

In the 1996 welfare reform legislation, Congress included a so-called charitable choice amendment, which encouraged state and local officials charged with implementing the legislation to use faith-based organizations to provide welfare-related services.[64] Many members of Congress were concerned that faith-based organizations such as sectarian social welfare agencies and religious congregations were either barred or discouraged from providing publicly funded services because they would have to relinquish their faith identity in order to receive public funds. More recently, President George Bush proposed a faith-based and community initiative that would expand the use of faith-based organizations far beyond the welfare-related services targeted by the charitable choice amendment.

To an extent, the push for additional government support for faith-based organizations represents a backlash against the buildup of federal support for more professionalized, secularized nonprofit organizations in the past twenty-five years. These organizations often have tight linkages with government, making it difficult for newly emergent groups with less professional norms and standards, such as congregations, to obtain government funding, even if they were interested.

At this point, the future of this faith-based "movement" is quite unclear. Serious constitutional objections have been raised regarding the Bush administration's initiative. Religious conservatives and many liberals also worry that more government funding of faith-based organizations might reduce the autonomy of the organizations. And important concerns have been raised about the potential politicization of religion, since government would be placing itself in the position of evaluating the extent to which an organization is "faith-based." Regardless of the outcome of the most recent initiative, the broader interest in faith-based organizations is sure to contribute to the environmental and political uncertainty facing many nonprofit service providers.[65] Many established nonprofit service providers may now find themselves in competition with congregations and new faith-based service providers for government contracts and private donations.

New Developments in Private Philanthropy

Finally, nonprofit social service agencies have been affected by some key trends in private philanthropy, two of which in particular deserve special mention. First, private donations to nonprofit social service agencies have stagnated or declined at the same time as the number of nonprofit human service agencies has almost tripled. For example, United Way funds have hardly grown at all in the past thirty years (from $2.06 billion in 1968 to $2.16 billion in 1998, in 1998 dollars).[66] Many United Way agencies, even organizations with long-standing ties to the United Way, find that United Way funds constitute a diminishing portion of their total budget. To be sure, United Way funds remain important for many agencies. And especially for struggling community organizations, the legitimacy conferred by a United Way grant can help to leverage other grant funds.

More generally, giving to human service agencies failed to keep pace with inflation from the mid-1980s until 1998, when it increased by a significant margin.[67] Nonetheless, social services remain a very competitive environment for private donations; giving to human services as a percentage of all private giving remains only at 8.8 percent. And in 2000, giving to human services increased only 0.3 percent, adjusted for inflation.[68] The tragedy of September 11 and the resultant outpouring of donations further complicate the picture for fundraising for human services.

Obtaining private donations has also been made more complicated for human service agencies by changes within institutional philanthropy. First, unrestricted, discretionary income has become more scarce as more and more funders have chosen to support specific projects.[69] Second, many foundations and philanthropists are adopting a "venture capital" approach that entails much greater control over agency operations and much greater emphasis on performance.[70] The substantial attention given to this approach within the field of philanthropy has encouraged many established foundations to rethink their relationship with grantees and to provide grantees with more ongoing help and assistance.

Challenges Facing Nonprofit Social Service Agencies

The trends in public policy and private philanthropy have altered the social and political environment of nonprofit organizations and created new management and policy challenges. In this section, three key challenges are examined and profiled: resource development, the government-nonprofit relationship, and management infrastructure.

Resource Development

Perhaps the major challenge confronting nonprofit social service agencies at the present time is resource development. Part of the problem is that the big increase in the number of nonprofit organizations has occurred at the same time as private giving has stagnated. Public funding has increased, but it has often not kept pace with the rising costs of nonprofits. Government contracts have been restructured as fee-for-service contracts, increasing the unpredictability of an agency's public revenue. Further, many nonprofit social service agencies are woefully undercapitalized. As a result, these agencies face enormous pressure to raise capital in order to compete effectively in the current environment. The larger agencies have a greater base of capital, but also much higher overhead; paying for this overhead has become increasingly difficult given the trend toward project-related funding by foundations and the United Way.

The response of nonprofit human service agencies to the challenge of resource development has varied depending on the type of organization.

Nonetheless, a few broad trends can be discerned in private fundraising, fees and earned income, and public contracts. This section focuses on each of these key areas of nonprofit revenues.

PRIVATE FUNDRAISING. Many agencies have greatly stepped up their effort to raise private donations: development officers have been hired, new board members with fundraising potential have been appointed, and executive directors are increasingly expected to be good fundraisers. Some of the larger agencies have created affiliate entities such as Friends of the Agency to undertake special fundraising events and support campaign fund drives. In general, the big agencies with professional development staff, well-connected board members and staff, and resources for marketing and fundraising are in a much better position to compete for private donations than small or mid-size agencies. Over time, given their ability to raise private funds, big agencies probably will have a substantial edge in attracting qualified staff, new government contracts, and private grants.

The other ripple effect on private fundraising of the more competitive environment is the push to create endowments even among agencies of relatively modest size. Many agencies are undercapitalized, having started in rented space and then obtained government contracts or foundation grants. This external funding only supported operations and was generally not available for capital expenditures, however. Now many nonprofit human service agencies find themselves with aging physical structures, demands for improvements in technological capability, and intense competition with other nonprofits (and for-profits in some cases) with much better capital positions. In addition, the project-driven character of public and private grants means that nonprofit agencies have much less discretion to allocate grant funds. As a consequence, nonprofit human service agencies have a great incentive to build an endowment to provide the agency with unrestricted funding support and to improve the long-term capital position of the agency. The process of building an endowment can also have a number of positive marketing benefits for the agency.

FEES AND EARNED INCOME. The stiff competition for public contracts and private donations has encouraged nonprofit human service agencies to tap fees and earned income more extensively as a source of revenues. In the context of social services, fees and earned income can involve a variety of diverse revenue options: the payment of fees by individuals, public and private insurance companies, and corporations; the sale of services such as technical assistance or cookbooks; the receipt of money earned from client-run businesses, such as a restaurant staffed by the disadvantaged; real estate development (including parking revenue); and the sale of food at a local festival.

Substantial evidence exists that, overall, nonprofit social service agencies are more reliant on fees for their revenue than they were twenty years ago.[71] This increased reliance reflects three important developments: (a) state and local governments have restructured their contracts with nonprofit agencies on a fee-for-service basis, in part because it allows government officials to tie payment more closely to the attainment of specific performance targets; (b) nonprofit social service agencies now rely more heavily on voucher-type programs such as Medicaid, Medicare, and private insurance, all of which channel funds to consumers of services; and (c) the fastest-growing part of the nonprofit social service sector has been in daycare, which has traditionally been heavily reliant on fee income.[72]

The fee revenue received by most non-daycare social service agencies, however, usually does not represent out-of-pocket client funds; instead, it is often government or private insurance.[73] For example, a 1995 survey of nonprofit outpatient substance abuse units finds that these units received more than 67 percent of their revenues from government, 13 percent from private insurance, and 13 percent from out-of-pocket revenues.[74] Indeed, nonprofit social service agencies are substantially less dependent on out-of-pocket client fees than they were in 1960, when many agencies relied on client fees for more than half of their revenue. Many nonprofit agencies find it very difficult to raise much revenue from client fees, because most clients are poor or disadvantaged. For instance, a recent study of 106 social service agencies in high-poverty neighborhoods in Cleveland, Los Angeles, Miami, and Philadelphia finds that more than 90 percent of the clients of these agencies are low-income clients, with most on public assistance.[75] A 1999 nationwide study of welfare-to-work agencies finds that these organizations planned to use fees for service for only 1.4 percent of their revenues.[76] Further, the increased eligibility for many public programs means that nonprofits are more likely to be able to boost revenues by serving eligible clients (or expanding into growing areas) than by charging substantially higher out-of-pocket fees. For instance, a recent General Accounting Office report finds that out-of-pocket expenses as a percentage of total mental health expenditures fell from 19 to 17 percent from 1987 to 1997. At the same time, federal expenditures as a percentage of total expenditures increased from 22 to 28 percent. During this ten-year period, total expenditures on mental health increased from $37 billion to $73 billion.[77] Moreover, a substantial portion of out-of-pocket expenses for service categories such as mental health, developmental disabilities, and drug and alcohol abuse treatment are actually government income maintenance payments; out-of-pocket fees are essentially transfer payments.[78]

In a sense, the lack of reliance on out-of-pocket client fees for most nonprofit social services should be viewed as a positive step in public policy. Forty years ago, nonprofit social service agencies were heavily criticized for their failure to serve disadvantaged populations.[79] Part of the issue in serving the disadvantaged at this time was the high dependence of nonprofit social service agencies on client fees and private donations. The growth in government funding since the 1960s has substantially changed this, permitting, and often requiring, nonprofit social service agencies to increase their service to poor and disadvantaged populations.

This is not to suggest that the shift to fee income—even if it is not predominantly money directly from clients—is unimportant. The structure of fee income means that nonprofits are in an inherently more unpredictable and unstable revenue situation. Consequently, an indirect effect is to add further pressure on nonprofits to be entrepreneurial and more businesslike in order to compete effectively in the new, more unstable environment.

Another potential source of fees is earned income from the sale of products and services. Gift shops and restaurants, for example, have allowed nonprofit arts and cultural organizations to boost their income significantly in the past twenty years. Earned income also has received broad attention in recent years as an outgrowth of the social enterprise "movement," which strives to meld the values of the nonprofit and for-profit sectors by building business ventures into employment and training or social service programs. Pioneer Human Services in Seattle, for example, earns revenues in excess of $50 million in this way.

Despite the success of such organizations, most nonprofit social service agencies are not well positioned to raise much earned income. Several factors account for this situation. A sizable number of nonprofit service providers, perhaps more than half, are small and undercapitalized, with a highly targeted market niche. (Many small agencies do not even own any property.) They also are very value driven, with very little interest (or capability) in expanding their earned income. Also many agencies do not have any service that they can profitably sell on the market. For instance, an emergency shelter for youth has no marketable product. Even nonprofit programs dependent on client fees, such as childcare agencies, do not earn any significant amount of money from the sale of other services. Recent surveys of nonprofit service agencies confirm this difficulty in raising funds from earned income. A comprehensive study of social service agencies in Buffalo concluded that human service agencies were unable to raise much money in earned income; instead these agencies typically replaced lost federal funding with state and local funding.[80]

PUBLIC CONTRACTS. The diversification of government support for nonprofit service agencies, combined with stiff competition for private donations, has spurred many nonprofits to pursue new government contract opportunities. For instance, the availability of new welfare-to-work grants has encouraged even service providers that historically have not had significant contracts with public agencies to apply for this money. This is especially true of many community-based organizations.

The interest in public contracts as a revenue development strategy also affects the political posture of the agency. One trend has been the proliferation of umbrella coalitions whose primary mission is to advocate for funding and regulatory policies that support nonprofit service agencies. Further, experience with public agencies is now considered to be an asset in hiring social service agency staff and recruiting agency boards.

Relationship to Government

The growing ties between nonprofit organizations and government present nonprofit providers with important and difficult management issues. Regardless of the service category, government has increasingly detailed expectations of nonprofit performance. This includes specific outcome measures as well as complex rules on the way in which nonprofit organizations can spend public funds. In many instances, these standards are set by the federal government or state governments with little substantial input from nonprofit providers themselves. A good example is the welfare-to-work and workforce training programs. Nonprofit service providers are the principal agencies delivering these services. They are viewed as the connection between public agencies and the community. But the performance standards for these agencies are set in a top-down fashion, primarily at the federal level. This can cause conflicts with agency missions and orientations. For example, in job training programs, the federal emphasis is on job placement, whereas many community-based organizations are much more likely to emphasize "living wage" jobs and longer-term job training to achieve this goal. Government also takes a much more restricted view of eligible clients than community organizations do.[81] In these and other programs, an intricate and complex set of potentially contentious interactions between government and nonprofit agencies must be worked out on a variety of issues, including referrals, rates, allowable activities, and certification of client eligibility.[82]

This complicated, sometimes difficult, relationship with government also has mobilized nonprofit service agencies politically, especially through the formation of political coalitions to represent their interests. In general, these coalitions focus on issues of direct benefit to their member agencies, such as reimbursement rates and government regulations. There is much less incentive for these coalitions to become engaged in broader social welfare concerns such as workforce training, welfare reform, and low-income housing. In a sense, the intricacies and political sensitivities of the government-nonprofit relationship channel the political activity of providers into areas that materially affect both parties.

This is not to imply that nonprofit agencies are completely absent from involvement in important policy debates. Many nonprofit agencies, for example, opposed welfare reform. But welfare reform was an interesting issue because many people in state welfare departments also opposed it, so the opposition by nonprofit providers did not directly threaten government policymakers at the state and local level.

Where advocacy is often missing is on the more mundane implementation details of policy that reflect practice at the agency level: referral and discharge policies, eligibility criteria, performance targets, and the multiple needs of many clients seeking service. These issues are less likely to be the object of nonprofit advocacy because they pertain much more directly to the contractual relationship between government and nonprofit agencies; political advocacy might disrupt this relationship and thus threaten the revenues and programs of nonprofit agencies.

Rethinking the relationship between government and nonprofits remains one of the biggest challenges facing nonprofit service providers. The fate of these providers is tied to government policy, but the political influence needed to change government policy, whether it is policy on funding levels or regulatory policy on contracts, is often wanting. Government officials, for their part, worry that any movement away from performance standards will undermine their effort to improve outcomes and reassure the citizenry that public funds are being spent wisely.

Management Infrastructure

The growing complexity of the nonprofit social service agency environment and the escalating expectations of public and private funders for accountability and outcome evaluation have placed vastly increased demands on the management infrastructure of nonprofit service providers. In particular, nonprofit social service agencies are pressed to invest in management information systems and improved technology in order to be able to respond to the greater demands for accountability. Performance contracts require agencies to provide a lot of data on clients and programs. New accounting standards impose new record-keeping requirements on nonprofits. And the competition for funds means that nonprofit staff and boards need much better financial and program data in order to assess their present and future needs. The challenge for nonprofit social service agencies is that the expertise and resources necessary to invest adequately in new information systems is often in short supply. This is particularly true of smaller community-based agencies with roots in the informal sector.

Second, nonprofit agencies face a big challenge in attracting qualified executive leadership. Historically, many nonprofit executives rose through the ranks and were often trained as clinicians. Over time, they gradually assumed more and more administrative responsibilities. However, the emphasis on entrepreneurship and the increased external and internal complexity facing nonprofit service providers call for new types of executives or, at the very least, new training and education programs to help executives cope with a very different organizational environment. In recent years, many nonprofits have found it difficult to attract top-notch executives given the tight labor markets and their inability to pay competitive salaries.

Third, the problems of attracting qualified staff and developing a sound management infrastructure are often exacerbated by inadequate board oversight and monitoring. Board members are often attracted to serving on the board of a social service agency due to personal connections to the agency or a personal commitment to the agency's mission. But once on the board, these individuals find it very difficult to effectively monitor the work of the staff, particularly given the complexity of government performance contracts and the technical nature of many agency programs. Among smaller organizations, the problems with the board can often contribute to the already difficult challenges of attracting and keeping qualified staff, raising private donations, and developing community and political support.

Fourth, many nonprofit service agencies, especially in the area of emergency assistance and relief, rely substantially on volunteers for direct service contact with clients (even if their funding is often public or from foundations). But the competition for volunteers can be intense, and many agencies find it increasingly difficult to engage volunteers in regular volunteering, especially with complicated services or with difficult client populations. Increased liability and accountability demands also make it more imperative to have a stable source of good volunteers. To compete effectively for volunteers in this environment, nonprofit agencies are being forced to devote more resources to volunteer management, training, and oversight.

Given the increasingly restricted character of nonprofit funding, obtaining the funds to invest in management infrastructure is a major challenge for nonprofit service agencies, especially the smaller organizations. This, in turn, contributes to management instability, which then encourages funders to press agencies—notably the smaller agencies—to merge or collaborate.

Steps to Improve the Position and Effectiveness of Nonprofit Social Services

The past forty years have witnessed a fundamental "transformation of social services." In 1960, social services were limited in scope and coverage. Today, they are a sizable industry, and nonprofits are a dominant part of it. Employment in nonprofit social service agencies is at an all-time high, and the number of agencies continues to grow. Further, nonprofits are directly involved in serving the most disadvantaged members of society—from the very poor to the severely disabled—a sharp departure from forty years ago.

What is more, this development seems likely to persist. This is certainly one of the major implications of welfare reform, which shifted emphasis from income maintenance as a central feature of the welfare state to services (and work).

Yet nonprofit agencies face formidable challenges, too: in many communities, too many agencies are competing for a limited amount of public and private revenues; competition for resources often distorts the organization's mission and incentives; effective management infrastructure is often lacking; relations between government and nonprofit agencies are often problematic; outcome evaluation is complicated and difficult; and many nonprofits lack productive and useful relations with their communities. This section discusses several steps that nonprofits could take to cope with these challenges. These steps are to adopt new funding models, reinvent technical assistance, take innovative approaches to organizational governance, rethink standard setting, and generally reappraise the role of community-based organizations in delivering public services.

Solving the Funding Conundrum

Nonprofit service providers would, of course, like more money, especially given the difficulty of paying competitive wages. But more money, in and of itself, would not necessarily solve the problems of nonprofit funding, since the way in which nonprofits receive public and private funding can create incentive problems for nonprofit managers and staff by pulling them away from core missions and capabilities.

Solving this conundrum is not easy, but any solution would require placing nonprofits on a firmer financial footing. In essence, nonprofits need to be able to cross-subsidize the public goods aspect of their operations. This could entail a number of strategies: more generous rates for government-funded services, foundation funding of operational expenses, longer-term foundation grants, access to tax-exempt bond funding for capital expenses, and performance-based contracts that allow nonprofit agencies to keep surplus revenues. To be sure, these strategies need to be carefully crafted with proper accountability in place. But the creative development of these strategies could greatly help nonprofit agencies to address persistent problems in funding their core operations.

Reinventing Technical Assistance

The big increase in the number of nonprofit social service agencies has been disproportionately among smaller, more community-based organizations. Typically, these organizations were started by a committed group of people who eventually obtained external public and private grants to support their operation. But these organizations are often started with little capital or management expertise; over time, many experience significant management problems, especially in responding to heightened funder expectations for accountability.

These capacity problems have precipitated, in turn, a broad expansion of the technical assistance resources available to nonprofit organizations, especially smaller community-based organizations where the need is the greatest. However, a lot of this technical assistance is undergirded by two problematic assumptions: first, that short-term technical assistance provided by a consultant can solve the problems facing small community-based social service agencies and, second, that such agencies can become "self-sustainable." In fact, however, for many nonprofit community agencies, the issues of funding, weak boards, staff turnover, and accountability are all intertwined and cannot be solved through short-term technical assistance. And self-sustainability is unrealistic for community agencies (and many larger agencies as well). Earned income opportunities are extremely limited for such agencies, and few smaller agencies are in a position to generate substantial unrestricted donations, particularly given the current competitive environment for funding.

The emphasis on short-term technical assistance diverts attention from the longer-term funding needs of nonprofit service agencies and from a serious examination of the fit between these agencies and some of the public expectations placed on them. It also makes it difficult to develop longer-term technical assistance approaches including permanent ongoing relationships between funders and grantees on infrastructure issues. Funders and nonprofit agencies need to rethink their ongoing relationship and develop ways of working together to solve perennial issues such as board recruitment, funding, and staff-board relations. Funders need to think of themselves as investors with an ongoing commitment to the success of their grantees.

Developing new technical assistance relationships, though, is often complicated by the reluctance of many nonprofit agencies to seek assistance from funders, fearing that it might be perceived as a sign of trouble and ultimately threaten current or future funding. Public and private funders in some communities around the country are trying to overcome this problem by supporting technical assistance provided by third-party organizations, including nonprofit assistance centers. In some cases, umbrella organizations of nonprofit agencies have received support for technical assistance to their members.

Governance

The heightened expectations placed on nonprofit social service agencies and the scrutiny this has brought them from public and private funders also have intensified the pressures on nonprofit governance. However, the governance of many nonprofit agencies is poorly matched with these demands. For example, agencies may now be responsible for operating complex welfare-to-work programs but may have small boards with few people knowledgeable about government contracting. In many cases, organizations are started by groups of professional colleagues or friends who perceive a problem and form an organization to respond, but without creating links to the community. The result over time can be problems in resource mobilization and legitimacy, especially when the initial grants end, and the agency needs to find new sources of revenue.

Given the increased competition among nonprofit agencies and between nonprofits and for-profits, the continued legitimacy and political support for nonprofit social service agencies hinge on the development of creative and innovative approaches to governance that connect the agencies more directly on an ongoing basis to their communities. Although demonstrated programmatic outcomes clearly can help, building solid community roots is also crucial. Community connections can be helpful in mobilizing political support and building social capital. More generally, establishing legitimacy also involves the creative application of the idea of "community benefit," which has been employed with health care organizations. As Gray and Schlesinger note in chapter 2 of this volume, a community-benefit standard focuses attention on the overall benefits of a nonprofit organization to its community along many dimensions, including representation, hiring, and civic projects.

Many possible strategies exist to restructure the agency-community relationship, including new approaches to the nomination and election of board members, the creation of new advisory councils, and innovative ways to seek input from the community on agency programs and services. Creative programming also can promote better community-agency relationships. All of these strategies seek to develop new relationships to the community. These innovations also could increase organizational effectiveness and promote the community-building potential of these organizations.

New Approaches to Standard Setting

Despite the rhetoric of community involvement, standards for nonprofit performance are often set in a top-down fashion, with little initial input from nonprofit agencies. This is especially true for many national programs associated with welfare-to-work and job training, where the performance measures are set nationally and imposed on nonprofit service agencies. Often these standards are poorly matched with the types of clients served by nonprofits at the local level. These standards also provide nonprofit agencies with little discretion in client selection and programmatic decisions.

This approach compromises the value of nonprofit agencies in terms of their professional expertise and knowledge about community conditions and client situations. Ideally, standard setting should be a more collaborative process involving input from nonprofit organizations and government.[83] Some promising models of this type of process exist, including the Oklahoma milestone contracting initiative.[84] In the coming years, this will be one of the key issues to be resolved in the evolving relationship of nonprofit organizations to the public sector.

Concluding Thoughts

In many respects, the transformation of nonprofit social service agencies in the past thirty years typifies America's unique approach to social policy. In other countries, personal social services are championed by major political parties as an essential right of every citizen. Extensive networks of social services exist as a consequence. In this country, we have been much more reluctant to enact entitlement programs in the area of social services. Title XX in the 1970s was the first major effort to do so, and it quickly engendered congressional opposition and a funding cap. The social services block grant created in 1981 succeeded Title XX as a symbol of the federal government's commitment to social services. Its decline in real terms since 1981 demonstrates the enduring ambivalence about a major federal effort to support more universal social services.

Yet the social needs remain, so policymakers and advocates did an "end run" around SSBG. Instead of focusing on SSBG, policymakers and advocates significantly expanded federal support for social services by making technical changes to existing laws (for example, expanding Supplemental Security Income and Medicaid coverage), creating new programs for specific subsectors such as child welfare and drug abuse treatment, and reclassifying certain social services as long-term care (for example, community residences for the developmentally disabled and mentally ill) or health care (for example, counseling and drug abuse treatment). And in the past few years, nonprofit social service providers received money for new programs in part due to the political unpopularity of cash assistance. Policymakers are more apt to support expanded childcare and job training that help welfare recipients go to work than to support direct cash assistance.

This expansion carries with it great risks for nonprofit social services. Relatively modest technical changes to existing law could have a major negative impact on funding for nonprofit social services. More generally, the recently enacted Bush administration tax cut will sharply curb the revenues of the federal government in the coming years, creating a budget squeeze that will make it much more difficult to continue federal funding of many service programs. The refinancing of social services through Medicaid and, to a lesser extent, Medicare also means that the future of social services is now tied to the ongoing national debate on the role of the federal government in health care. Significant reform of Medicaid, for example, would have far-reaching effects on nonprofit social service agencies. Policy changes affecting the clients of nonprofit agencies, such as eligibility for TANF and food stamps, can have a direct impact on the demand for nonprofit services. The restrictiveness of public and private funding today makes it very difficult for many nonprofits to respond quickly to changes in client circumstances. To be sure, the overwhelming response of the American public through their donations following the tragedy of September 11 indicates that charitable support for nonprofit emergency assistance in times of national crisis can be mobilized. But barring a crisis, most nonprofit agencies find it difficult to mobilize substantial new resources in a short time frame due to the competition for public contracts and private donations. Moreover, many nonprofit agencies are dependent on the political popularity of their programs, so when an issue fades from the public agenda, the money tends to decline as well, creating serious dislocations for local nonprofit agencies.

Finally, the emphasis on performance and outcome measurement by government and private funders alike and stepped-up competition for public and private funding have made it necessary for many nonprofits to wrestle with complex issues pertaining to their mission and role in the community. This is all the more difficult given the broader debate under way in America on community service, voluntarism, and the community-building role of nonprofit organizations. Nonprofit social service agencies have a great opportunity to rebuild distressed communities, stimulate more voluntarism, and provide a locus for community service activities. But these activities may conflict with the pressure to be accountable to funders or the desire to ward off competitors who do not have the same type of community obligations. Successful nonprofit organizations will be those agencies that can use their community connections to their competitive advantage and at the same time develop the capability to be accountable to funders and their communities. These are no mean tasks.

Notes

1. The term *transformation of social services* was first used by Neil Gilbert in an influential 1977 article, "The Transformation of Social Services," *Social Service Review*, vol. 51, no. 4 (December 1977): 624–41.

2. For a discussion of these "tools," see Lester M. Salamon, ed., *The Tools of Government: A Guide to the New Governance* (Oxford University Press, 2002).

3. See General Accounting Office, *Federal Grants: More Can Be Done to Improve Weed and Seed Program Management,* GAO/GGD-99-110 (Washington: General Accounting Office, July 1999).

4. David Merriam, *What Accounts for the Growth of State Government Budgets in the 1990s?* Series A, no. A-39 (Washington: Urban Institute, July 2000); Deborah A. Ellwood and Donald J. Boyd, *Changes in State Spending on Social Services since the Implementation of Welfare Reform: A Preliminary Report* (Albany, N.Y.: Nelson A. Rockefeller Institute of Government, February 2000).

5. David Osborne and Ted Gaebler, *Reinventing Government* (New York: Plume, 1991).

6. I am indebted to Stephen Page for calling attention to the importance of entrepreneurship as a factor in the evolution of social welfare services.

7. Alfred J. Kahn, *Social Policy and Social Services*, 2d ed. (New York: Random House, 1979), p. 20.

8. Kahn, *Social Policy and Social Services*, p. 20.

9. Ralph M. Kramer, "Voluntary Agencies and the Personal Social Services," in Walter W. Powell, ed., *The Nonprofit Sector: A Research Handbook* (Yale University Press, 1987), p. 240.

10. Robert Wuthnow, *Loose Connections: Joining Together in America's Fragmented Communities* (Harvard University Press, 1998), especially chap. 2.

11. This category also includes voluntary health organizations, some grant-giving organizations focused on social policy and services, and advocacy organizations focused on the environment and human rights, among others.

12. U.S. Census Bureau, *Public Employment Data, 1993–99* (www.census.gov/govs/apes [February 4, 2002]).

13. U.S. Census Bureau, *Census of Service Industries, 1997* (Washington: U.S. Census Bureau, 1997).

14. U.S. Census Bureau, *Census of Service Industries, 1997.*

15. U.S. Census Bureau, *Public Employment Data, 1993–99.*

16. For instance, the percentage of public outpatient substance abuse treatment units rose from 26 percent in 1988 to 31 percent in 1995. John R. C. Wheeler and Tammie A. Nahra, "Private and Public Ownership in Outpatient Substance Abuse Treatment: Do We Have a Two-Tiered System?" *Administration and Policy in Mental Health*, vol. 27, no. 4 (March 2000): 198.

17. See Matthew Crenson, *Building the Invisible Orphanage* (Harvard University Press, 1998); LeRoy Ashby, *Saving the Waifs: Reformers and Dependent Children, 1890–1917* (Temple University Press, 1984), especially chap. 1.

18. Steven Rathgeb Smith and Michael Lipsky, *Nonprofits for Hire: The Welfare State in the Age of Contracting* (Harvard University Press, 1993), pp. 48–49; Crenson, *Building the Invisible Orphanage*; Amos G. Warner, *American Charities: A Study in Philanthropy and Economics* (New York: Transaction, 1989 [1894]), especially chap. 17.

19. Gerald N. Grob, *Mental Illness and American Society, 1875–1940* (Princeton University Press, 1983); Anthony M. Platt, *The Child Savers: The Invention of Delinquency*, 2d ed. (University of Chicago Press, 1977).

20. Bruce Vladeck, *Unloving Care: The Nursing Home Tragedy* (New York: Basic Books, 1980), pp. 33–35; Michael B. Katz, *In the Shadow of the Poorhouse* (New York: Basic Books, 1986); William C. Thomas Jr., *Nursing Homes and Public Policy: Drift and Decision in New York State* (Cornell University Press, 1965), chap. 2.

21. Warner, *American Charities*, chap. 17; Smith and Lipsky, *Nonprofits for Hire*, chap. 3.

22. Katz, *In the Shadow of the Poorhouse*, p. 156; Eleanor L. Brilliant, *The United Way: Dilemmas of Organized Charity* (Columbia University Press, 1990), chap. 1.

23. Senior services were also funded though the federal Administration on Aging. Funding grew from $386 million in 1975 to $788 million in 1980. From Michael F. Gutowski and Jeffrey J. Koshel, "Social Services," in John L. Palmer and Isabel V. Sawhill, eds., *The Reagan Experiment* (Washington: Urban Institute, 1982), p. 311. Most of this money was contracted or subcontracted to nonprofit agencies. Gutowski and Koshel also offer a good overview of other social service programs; see pp. 310–15.

24. Anne Kallman Bixby, "Public Social Welfare Expenditures, Fiscal Year 1995," *Social Security Bulletin*, vol. 62, no. 2 (1999): 89.

25. Lester M. Salamon and Alan J. Abramson, "The Nonprofit Sector," in Palmer and Sawhill, eds., *Reagan Experiment*, pp. 219–43. Also see Laurence E. Lynn Jr., "Social Services and the State: The Public Appropriation of Private Charity," *Social Services Review*, vol. 76, no. 1 (March 2002): 58–82.

26. Thomas J. Billitteri, "United Ways Seek a New Identity," *Chronicle of Philanthropy*, March 9, 2000, p. 23.

27. Gutowski and Koshel, "Social Services," pp. 315–22.

28. James B. Milroy, *The Impact of Federal Budget Cuts on the Community-Based Nonprofit Service Sector: A Case Study*, Ph.D. dissertation (University of New York at Buffalo, Department of Political Science, 1999).

29. Bixby, "Public Social Welfare Expenditures," p. 90.

30. U.S. House of Representatives, Committee on Ways and Means, *2000 Green Book* (www.aspe.hhs.gov/2000gb/sec15.txt [February 4, 2002]).

31. U.S. House of Representatives, Committee on Ways and Means, *2000 Green Book*. Also see John Holahan and David Liska, *Reassessing the Outlook for Medicaid Spending Growth*, Series A, no. A-6 (Washington: Urban Institute, 1997).

32. Teresa A. Coughlin, Leighton Ku, and John Holahan, *Medicaid since 1980: Costs, Coverage, and the Shifting Alliance between the Federal Government and the States* (Washington: Urban Institute, 1994), pp. 87–96. Rob Geen, Shelley Waters Boots, and Karen C. Tumlin, *The Cost of Protecting Vulnerable Children: Understanding Federal, State, and Local Child Welfare Spending*, Occasional Paper 20 (Washington: Urban Institute, 1999), especially pp. 6–17; Madeleine H. Kimmich, *America's Children: Who Cares? Growing Needs and Declining Assistance in the Reagan Era* (Washington: Urban Institute, 1985), pp. 40–41; Joshua M. Wiener and David G. Stevenson, "State Policy on Long-Term Care for the Elderly," *Health Affairs*, vol. 17, no. 3 (May/June 1998): 86.

33. Total spending on intermediate care facilities for the mentally retarded grew from $5 billion in 1981 to $10 billion in 1995 (in 1995 dollars). U.S. House of Representatives, Committee on Ways and Means, *1998 Green Book* (www.aspe.hhs.gov/1998gb/15other.htm#MEDICAID [January 2002]), p. 981. See Noel A. Mazade, Robert W. Glover, and Gail P. Hutchings, "Environmental Scan 2000: Issues Facing State Mental Health Agencies," *Administration and Policy in Mental Health*, vol. 27, no. 4 (March 2000): 174.

34. David Braddock and others, *The State of the States in Developmental Disabilities* (Washington: American Association of Mental Retardation, 1998), p. 33.

35. Jennifer Schore, Mary Harrington, and Stephen Crystal, *Serving a Changing Population: Home- and Community-Based Services for People with AIDS* (Princeton, N.J.: Mathematica Policy Research, 1998), p. 3.

36. U.S. House of Representatives, Committee on Ways and Means, *2000 Green Book* (www.aspe.hhs.gov/2000gb/sec3.txt [January 2002]).

37. U.S. Social Security Administration, "Number and Percentage of SSI Recipients, by Age, 1974–2000" (www.ssa.gov/statistics/ssi_annual_stat/2000/table2.html [February 4, 2002]).

38. U.S. General Accounting Office, *Adults with Severe Disabilities: Federal and State Approaches for Personal Care and Other Services* (Washington: General Accounting Office, 1999), p. 12.

39. U.S. House of Representatives, Committee on Ways and Means, *2000 Green Book* (www.aspe.hhs.gov/2000gb/sec15.txt [February 4, 2002]). Also Brian Bruen and John Holahan, *Medicaid Spending Growth Remained Modest in 1998, but Likely Headed Upward* (Washington: Henry J. Kaiser Family Foundation, 2001).

40. Margaret Gibelman and Harold W. Demone Jr., "How Voluntary Agency Networks Fared in the 1980s," *Journal of Sociology and Social Welfare*, vol. 17, no. 4 (1990): 6.

41. U.S. Government Accounting Office, *Child Care: States Increased Spending on Low-Income Families* (Washington: Government Accounting Office, 2001), p. 12.

42. Geen, Boots, and Tumlin, *Cost of Protecting Vulnerable Children*, p. 5. Also William T. Gormley Jr., *Everybody's Children: Child Care as a Public Problem* (Washington: Brookings, 1995), pp. 47–48. U.S. General Accounting Office, *At-Risk and Delinquent Youth: Multiple Federal Programs Raise Efficiency Questions*, GAO/HEHS-96-34 (Washington: Government Accounting Office, 1996), p. 4.

43. U.S. General Accounting Office, *HIV/AIDS: The Use of the Ryan White CARE Act and Other Assistance Grant Funds*, GAO/HEHS-0054 (Washington: Government Accounting Office, 2000), p. 8. This report also notes that $5.8 billion in Medicaid funds was spent on AIDS treatment in 1999.

44. Executive Office of the President, *Budget of the United States Government, Fiscal Year 2001, Appendix* (Washington: Government Printing Office, 2000), p. 1115.

45. U.S. General Accounting Office, *Mental Health: Community-Based Care Increases for People with Serious Mental Illness* (Washington: Government Accounting Office, 2000), p. 10.

46. Federal spending on drug abuse treatment rose from $1.8 billion in 1991 to a projected $3.4 billion in 2001. Federal spending on drug abuse prevention increased from $1.4 billion to $2.1 billion during the same period. U.S. Office of National Drug Control Policy, *National Drug Control Strategy: Budget Summary, February 2000* (Washington: Office of National Drug Control Policy, 2000), p. 11. Also U.S. General Accounting Office, *Drug and Alcohol Abuse: Billions Spent Annually for Treatment and Prevention Activities,* GAO/HEHS-97-12 (Washington: Government Accounting Office, 1996).

47. U.S. House of Representatives, Committee on Ways and Means, *2000 Green Book* (www.aspe.hhs.gov/2000gb/sec15.txt and sec2.txt [January 2002]).

48. U.S. House of Representatives, Committee on Ways and Means, *2000 Green Book* (www.aspe.hhs.gov/2000gb/appendixc [January 2002]).

49. SSBG declined in real terms $4.9 billion from 1977 to 1997. U.S. House of Representatives, Committee on Ways and Means, *1998 Green Book,* p. 713. However, Congress appropriated an extra $1 billion in 1993 to support social services in empowerment zones.

50. Merriam, *What Accounts for the Growth of State Government Budgets,* p. 5.

51. For instance, a recent Urban Institute report notes that SSBG only accounted for 12 percent of federal social service expenditures on children. See Rebecca L. Clark, Rosalind Berkowitz King, Christopher Spiro, and C. Eugene Steuerle, *Federal Expenditures on Children: 1960–1997* (Washington: Urban Institute, 2001), especially p. 7.

52. Merriam, *What Accounts for the Growth of State Government Budgets,* p. 3.

53. In California, Georgia, Missouri, and Wisconsin, for example, spending increases on childcare from 1994–95 to 1998–99 varied from 75 to 167 percent: for mental health, spending increases were from 4 to 38 percent; for employment and training services, increases ranged from 19 to 110 percent. Ellwood and Boyd, *Changes in State Spending on Social Services,* p. 17.

54. Peter Frumkin and Alice Andre-Clark, "When Missions, Markets, and Politics Collide: Values and Strategy in Nonprofit Human Services," *Nonprofit and Voluntary Sector Quarterly,* vol. 29, no. 1 (supplement 2000): 145. Also William P. Ryan, "The New Landscape of Nonprofits," *Harvard Business Review* (January/February 1999): 127–37; M. Bryna Sanger, "When the Private Sector Competes: Lessons from Welfare Reform," paper presented at the annual research conference of the Association for Public Policy Analysis and Management, Seattle, Wash., November 2–4, 2000; Mark Carl Rom, "From Welfare State to Opportunity, Inc.: Public-Private Partnerships in Welfare Reform," *American Behavioral Scientist,* vol. 43, no. 1 (September 1999): 155–76.

55. Maximus, "Welfare Reform" (www.maximus.com [August 2000]). Other big firms such as EDS and Lockheed Martin are managing parts of the TANF implementation for some states and localities.

56. Sanger, "When the Private Sector Competes"; Melissa Buis, *Welfare Policy and Federalism,* Ph.D. dissertation (Brandeis University, Department of Political Science, 2001).

57. See Sanger, "When the Private Sector Competes," p. 42.

58. Ellen Eliason Kisker, Sandra L. Hofferth, Deborah A. Phillips, and Elizabeth Farquhar, *A Profile of Child Care Settings: Early Education and Care in 1990,* vol. 1 (Washington: U.S. Department of Education, Office of Under Secretary, 1991), p. 42.

59. See, for example, Elisa Vinson, *Performance Contracting in Six State Human Service Agencies* (Washington: Urban Institute, 1999); Robert D. Behn and Peter A. Kant, "Strategies for Avoiding the Pitfalls of Performance Contracting," *Public Productivity and Management,* vol. 22, no. 4 (1999): 470–89; Harry P. Hatry, *Performance Measurement: Getting Results* (Washington: Urban Institute, 1999).

60. Christine Letts, Allan Grossman, and William Ryan, *High-Performance Nonprofit Organizations: Managing Upstream for Greater Impact* (New York: Wiley, 1999).

61. Robert S. Kaplan and David P. Norton, "Using the Balanced Scorecard as a Strategic Management System," *Harvard Business Review,* vol. 64, no. 1 (January/February 1996): 75–85.

62. Larry Friesen, "Privatized Child Welfare Services: Foster Parents' Perspectives," *Child Welfare,* vol. 80, no. 3 (May/June 2001): 309–24; State of Kansas, Department of Social and Rehabilitation Services, Division of Children and Family Policy, *Statewide Assessment: Child and Family Services Review* (Topeka: Department of Social and Rehabilitation Services, 2001).

63. Smith and Lipsky, *Nonprofits for Hire*; Kirsten A. Grønbjerg, *Understanding Nonprofit Funding* (San Francisco: Jossey-Bass, 1993).

64. For further discussion, see Mark Chaves, "Religious Congregations and Welfare Reform: Who Will Take Advantage of 'Charitable Choice'?" *American Sociological Review,* vol. 64, no. 6 (1999): 836–46; Ram A. Cnaan, *The Newer Deal: Social Work and Religion in Partnership* (Columbia University Press, 2000); Steven Rathgeb Smith and Michael Sosin, "Varieties of Faith-Related Agencies," *Public Administration Review,* vol. 61, no. 6 (November/December 2001): 651–70.

65. See Kirsten A. Grønbjerg and Steven Rathgeb Smith, "Nonprofit Organizations and Public Policies," in Charles T. Clotfelter and Thomas Ehrlich, eds., *Philanthropy and the Nonprofit Sector* (Indiana University Press, 1999), pp. 139–71.

66. Billitteri, "United Ways Seek a New Identity," p. 23.

67. AAFRC Trust for Philanthropy, *Giving USA 2000: The Annual Report on Philanthropy for the Year 1997* (New York: AAFRC Trust for Philanthropy, 2000), p. 40.

68. Janet Fix and Nicole Lewis, "Growth in Giving Cools Down," *Chronicle of Philanthropy,* May 31, 2001, pp. 1, 29–31.

69. See, for example, Richard Beaulaurier, Gilbert Contreras, Lorna Dilley, and Rebecca Joyce Kissane, *Social Service Organizations and Welfare Reform* (New York: Manpower Demonstration Research Corporation, 2001), especially pp. 34–35.

70. Letts, Grossman, and Ryan, *High-Performance Nonprofit Organizations,* especially chap. 9; Thomas J. Billitteri, "Venturing a Bet on Giving," *Chronicle of Philanthropy,* June 1, 2000, p. 1.

71. Lester M. Salamon, "The Marketization of Welfare: Changing Nonprofit and For-Profit Roles in the American Welfare State," *Social Service Review,* vol. 67, no. 1 (March 1993): 16–39.

72. For a breakdown of the revenue structure of childcare agencies, see Kisker and others, *Profile of Child Care Settings,* pp. 50–52.

73. This general trend is also evident in the study by Grønbjerg, *Understanding Nonprofit Funding,* especially chap. 4.

74. Wheeler and Nahra, "Private and Public Ownership," pp. 204–05.

75. Beaulaurier and others, *Social Service Organizations and Welfare Reform,* p. 16, sec. C. Also see Yeheskel Hasenfeld and Lisa Evans, "The Role of Non-Profit Agencies in the Provision of Welfare-to-Work Services," paper presented at the annual research conference of the Association of Public Policy Analysis and Management, Seattle, Wash., November 2–4, 2000.

76. Irma Perez-Johnson and Alan M. Hershey, *Early Implementation of the Welfare-to-Work Grants Program: Report to Congress* (Princeton, N.J.: Mathematica Policy Research, 1999), p. 19.

77. U.S. General Accounting Office, *Mental Health: Community-Based Care Increases for People with Serious Mental Illness* (Washington: General Accounting Office, 2000), p. 10.

78. See, for example, Braddock and others, *State of the States in Developmental Disabilities,* p. 33.

79. See Alfred J. Kahn, "The Social Scene and the Planning of Services for Children," *Social Work,* vol. 7, no. 3 (July 1962): 3–14; Richard A. Cloward and Irwin Epstein, "Private Social Welfare's Disengagement from the Poor: The Case of Family Adjustment Agencies," in Mayer N. Zald, ed., *Social Welfare Institutions: A Sociological Reader* (New York: John Wiley and Sons, 1965), pp. 623–44.

80. See Milroy, *Impact of Federal Budget Cuts,* p. 503.

81. See Hasenfeld and Evans, "Role of Non-Profit Agencies in the Provision of Welfare-to-Work Services." The issue is also covered more generally in Smith and Lipsky, *Nonprofits for Hire,* especially chap. 6.

82. Hasenfeld and Evans, "Role of Non-Profit Agencies in the Provision of Welfare-to-Work Services," p. 21.

83. Robert Behn, *Rethinking Democratic Accountability* (Washington: Brookings, 2001). Also see Lisbeth B. Schorr, *Common Purpose: Strengthening Families and Neighborhoods to Rebuild America* (New York: Anchor, 1997), especially chap. 4.

84. See Peter Frumkin, "Balancing Public Accountability and Nonprofit Autonomy: Milestone Contracting in Oklahoma," Working Paper (Hauser Center, Kennedy School of Government, 2001).

5

Arts and Culture

MARGARET J. WYSZOMIRSKI

The arts and culture subsector of American life is a large, heterogeneous set of individuals and organizations engaged in the creation, production, presentation, distribution, and preservation of and education about aesthetic, heritage, and entertainment activities, products, and artifacts. These individuals and organizations may be located in the commercial realm, the nonprofit sector, or the public sector. They may also be embedded in other public or private institutions such as local community centers, public or private universities, or religious institutions. The result, as the 1997 American Assembly notes, is "a large, ubiquitous, economically, and socially significant aspect of American public life." Indeed, American consumers spent an estimated $180 billion on the arts, entertainment, and communications in 1995.[1]

Although clear delineations are difficult to make in this amorphous field, nonprofit organizations constitute a critically important component of the American arts and culture scene. According to a study by Americans for the

The author is grateful to Lisa Sharamitaro, Rachel Weidinger, Christopher Caltagirone, Patricia Dewey, Tina McCalment, Celia O'Donnell, and Sue Ann Lafferty—all graduate students in the arts policy and administration program at Ohio State University—for their research assistance in gathering information about conditions in particular nonprofit fields of art. Professor James Allen Smith, senior adviser to the president of the Getty Center, made insightful suggestions on early drafts of this chapter, and Barry Szczesny, former government affairs counsel for the American Association of Museums, provided helpful comments on the section on museums.

Arts, nonprofit arts organizations spent $53.2 billion, employed 1.14 million workers, and supported 2.1 million full-time equivalent jobs.[2] According to reports to the Internal Revenue Service, around 24,000 nonprofit arts, culture, and humanities organizations are operating in the United States, including nonprofit visual art galleries; artist organizations; museums; performing arts organizations in dance, theater, opera, and music; humanities organizations and historical societies; folk art and cultural heritage groups; art education organizations; and local arts agencies and art centers.

The nonprofit arts subsector encompasses two basic types of organizations. On the one hand are organizations that engage in amateur and community-based creative activities such as community theater groups, choral groups like barbershop quartets, many craft and folk art groups, ethnic cultural societies, and art and music appreciation groups. On the other hand are professional performing, visual, literary, and media arts organizations that are managed by full-time staff and produce or present artworks that meet professional standards for quality and attract paying audiences. For the purposes of the following discussion, we concentrate on what has commonly been regarded as the nonprofit professional arts sector.

The central message of this chapter is that the professional nonprofit arts and culture sector is emerging from a decade of significant change that challenged it financially, administratively, and politically. In general, it is now stronger, more civically engaged, and more resilient than it was ten years ago. However, major and continuing challenges lie ahead as the field, its funders, and cultural policymakers continue to evolve a twenty-first-century operating paradigm.[3] As always, patterns and trends vary from one discipline to another. In addition, it has become obvious that organizational size is not only an important but also an independent factor: large, mid-size, and small cultural organizations face different challenges, with different resources and different levels of success. For the most part, large cultural organizations are thriving; small organizations are living within their means, pursuing organizational development with care, and taking strength from their link to community bases. As a group, mid-size organizations seem the most precarious, finding themselves in an increasingly competitive environment for commanding the time and attention of audiences, recruiting effective board members, and securing funding. Even some long-established organizations find themselves running deficits, destabilized by leadership successions, and occasionally even closing down.

To explore these points, the following discussion first identifies key trends and developments in the professional nonprofit arts field over the past decade. Next it looks in more detail at nonprofit arts organizations in three disciplines, focusing on the dimensions, forces, trends, and developments in these particular subsets of organizations. A final section offers some conclusions and policy implications.

A Decade of Change

Many broad changes have significantly affected the nonprofit arts sector over the past decade, challenging its mission and operations. For the most part, non-profit arts organizations have weathered these challenges and ultimately emerged more resilient and adaptable. A brief survey of significant financial, managerial, and technological changes illustrates these developments.

Finances and Funding

According to an estimate compiled by Americans for the Arts, nonprofit arts organizations, on average, receive half of their revenue from ticket and related sales, another 39 percent from individual donations, 2.5 and 3.5 percent, respectively, from corporate and foundation support, and about 5.5 percent from public funding (1 percent from the federal government, 1.5 percent from state governments, and 3 percent from local governments). During the 1990s, nonprofit arts and cultural organizations experienced substantial changes in both the patterns of their revenues and the practices of many of their financial supporters. These changes made the task of fundraising more demanding for them and shifted the allocation of time and attention many nonprofit arts organizations expended on various public funding sources. Most notable was diminished attention to the federal arts agency, the National Endowment for the Arts (NEA), both in filing fewer grant applications and in undertaking less intense advocacy efforts concerning the agency's annual budget allocation.

GOVERNMENT SUPPORT. A major source of these changes was the reduction in funding for NEA and for National Endowment for the Humanities (NEH) after 1995. Following spectacular increases during the 1970s, the 1980s consti-tuted a decade of apparent incremental growth (from $158.8 million in 1981 to $171.3 million in 1991), but actual budget erosion (in constant dollars, the agency budget dropped from $158.8 million in 1981 to $102.1 million in 1991). The NEA budget hit a historic current-dollar high of $175.9 million in 1992 and then saw three years of steady, but incremental, decline (shrinking to $162.3 million in 1995). In 1996, the budget dropped precipitously to $99.5 million, or a paltry $44.2 million in constant dollars. At that time, Congress all but eliminated the agency's ability to fund individual artists directly, except for honorific awards (such as the jazz and folk art masters) and the highly competi-tive fellowships for literary writers.

In contrast, public funding at the state and local levels has continued to rise, inverting the historic comparative roles of the national and subnational govern-ments. However, within this overall trend, the pattern is uneven, varying from state to state and from city to city. In fiscal 2000, combined appropriations for state arts agencies reached an all-time high of $396.5 million, representing an increase of 7.2 percent over the previous year. This marked the sixth aggregate rise in the past seven years, for an increase in total appropriations of 88 percent since 1993, when the combined amount was only $211 million. State arts agencies also receive funds from the NEA. In fiscal 2000, these federal block grants amounted to $29.5 million, or 6.5 percent of total state arts agency revenues. California and New York approved the largest state arts agency appropriations: $68 million and $56.7 million, respectively. Outside the U.S. territories, Wyoming committed the least: $342,000. On a per capita basis, state arts agency appropriations ranged from a high of $5.12 per person in Hawaii to a low of $0.24 per person in Texas.[4]

At the local level, local arts agencies are a primary channel of public funding. There are an estimated 4,000 local arts agencies in the country, of which 75 percent are nonprofit organizations that receive public funds and 25 percent are public agencies. The budgets of these arts agencies range from as little as $100 to the behemoth New York Department of Cultural Affairs, with a budget of $108 million. Nearly two-thirds award grants, especially among those that have budgets over $100,000 or that operate in communities with populations over 500,000. Private local arts agencies are often quite active in raising additional private funds. Nationally, the combined budgets of local arts agencies total $750 million. Virtually all local arts agencies encourage and fund collaborations with other public and community agencies, especially school districts, parks and recreation departments, libraries, convention and tourism bureaus, neighborhood groups, and chambers of commerce. Nearly one-quarter manage international programs, and a third have cultural districts.[5]

PRIVATE PHILANTHROPY. As far as private support for the arts is concerned, the early part of the 1990s was a period of unstable and disappointing financial support even as the dollar amount of contributions generally increased. Reporting on philanthropic trends in the arts at mid-decade, the President's Committee on the Arts and the Humanities painted a gloomy picture, pointing to a decline in three key indicators: the number of households contributing to the arts, the size of the average household contribution, and the share of total grant dollars received by arts organizations.[6] Concern for sustaining its essential philanthropic base led to calls for more effective efforts to cultivate cultural donors—through linking volunteering and giving, courting minority donors, and targeting new generations and new wealth.[7]

By the turn of the millennium, the picture had improved. Overall, the amount of money contributed to the arts and culture increased from just under $10 billion in 1995 to $11.1 billion in 1999. At the same time, the proportion of charitable donors contributing to the arts rose from 9 percent in 1995 to 11 percent in 1998.[8] Similarly, foundation giving to the arts, after declining from historic levels of 13–15 percent of total foundation giving to a low of 12 percent in 1995, rebounded somewhat to 13 percent in 1997, 15 percent in 1998, and 13 percent in 1999. However, even though the dollar amount increased, the sector's share of overall giving decreased from 7.6 percent in 1989 to 5.8 percent in 1999.

The 1990s also saw many foundations and corporations rethink and adapt their funding strategies and perspectives.[9] In one especially innovative gesture, a group of private foundations supported the creation of a new nonprofit organization called Creative Capital. Dedicated to funding experimental, challenging art in the performing, visual, film/video, and hybrid arts, Creative Capital began making awards in 2000.[10] In addition, the decade also saw new foundations enter the field of cultural philanthropy, notably the Lila Wallace Reader's Digest Fund, the Doris Duke Charitable Foundations, the Thomas Kenan Institute for the Arts, as well as artist-funded foundations like the Andy Warhol Foundation for the Visual Arts and the Robert Mapplethorpe Foundation.

More generally, corporate and foundation support became more dependent on the anticipated impact and outcomes of arts and cultural programming than on altruism or support of art for art's sake.[11] Many such institutional donors aimed to develop a broader systems approach, to take an ecological perspective, and to see the nonprofit arts and humanities as part of a broadly conceived culture sector. Grantmakers paid more attention to infrastructure elements, such as information and research, audience demand, and press coverage and content. Many promoted the cultivation of new relationships for arts and cultural organizations with partners outside the cultural realm or in the commercial sector. Others experimented with new program tools and expanded the role of intermediaries such as community foundations and arts service organizations.

A less positive spot in this picture concerns mid-size arts organizations, which, in contrast to both large and small organizations, have seen their revenue from contributions decline in recent years.[12] Moreover, uncertainty has clouded the philanthropic picture in the wake of the September 11 World Trade Center attack, as philanthropy generally has sought to readjust to new demands and new conditions. Although the most profound effects were centered in the New York metropolitan region, thus affecting New York cultural institutions and their funders, the effects rippled out across the country to affect cultural philanthropy and funding for nonprofit arts institutions more generally.

EARNED INCOME. Pressures to increase earned income also mounted in the arts field, resulting in changes in marketing, more emphasis on entrepreneurial activities, and a sharper concern for cultivating new audiences and new donors. Often this new entrepreneurship focused on ancillary activities such as restaurants or gift shops. Other times it involved a technologically driven strategy to digitize and, it was hoped, capitalize on an organization's intellectual property. Those cultural organizations that could also sought to build or bolster endowments—both as a hedge against shifting funding patterns and as a strategy for organizational autonomy in the face of demands from virtually all institutional funders for greater accountability and demonstrable community outcomes.

In part, the ability of nonprofit arts and cultural organizations to navigate these turbulent financial waters was facilitated by a generally strong economy and prosperous times. As the national economy weakened, and public and private funding agendas shifted in the post–September 11 environment, the nonprofit arts and culture sector faces another challenge—seeing if the accommodations made during the 1990s will be effective enough and flexible enough to sustain them in less favorable economic circumstances.

Management Concerns

During the past decade, nonprofit arts and cultural organizations confronted new variants of the enduring administrative concerns of marketing and audience development, fundraising, programming, facilities, and volunteer management. Each of these continuing demands has taken on new aspects in the face of technological innovation, globalization, demographic shifts, changes in governmental relations and public policies, and the blurring of distinctions and interactions with the commercial arts and entertainment sector. Arts and cultural organizations continue to grapple with the challenge of an increasingly heterogeneous American population and the implications of that cultural diversity for everything from marketing and audience development, to board recruitment and governance, to programming and educational activities.

Leadership took on a new urgency as generational turnover continued to ripple through the sector. Many arts organizations were established or grew to prominence during the boom years of the 1960s and 1970s. Now thirty years later, their executive and artistic directors are retiring or succumbing to age. Coinciding with the growing complexity and demands of these positions, the turnover has prompted concern about the recruitment of new leaders. As a consequence, a number of arts service organizations have instituted leadership development programs such as the American Symphony Orchestra League's orchestra management fellow program or Theatre Communications Group's new generations program for theater leadership. Nevertheless, the cultivation of a new generation of cultural policy leaders remains haphazard.

Changes in leadership at individual arts institutions sometimes cluster to effect significant change in a single community. For example, in Detroit, five of seventeen leading cultural institutions, including the orchestra and four museums, experienced a change in leadership during 1999 and 2000. Cumulatively, such change seems to be reenergizing the Detroit cultural community more generally and may lend a more popular, populist, and socially relevant cast to a hoped-for Detroit cultural renaissance.[13] Other times, succession is tempestuous or short-lived. At the Boston Museum of Fine Arts, the relatively new director,

Malcolm Rogers, won praise for his financial management, membership development, and growing community outreach, while attracting vehement criticism from curators, art critics, and scholars for what they call autocratic administration that diminishes the curatorial voice and connoisseurship.[14]

Sometimes the leadership gap is most visible from a field perspective. In 1999, at least twenty art museum directorships at prominent museums were open—for a fifteen-year-high vacancy rate. Among the museums in search of new leadership were the Whitney Museum of Art, the Detroit Institute of Arts, the St. Louis Art Museum, and the Kimbell Art Museum in Fort Worth. Primary among the reasons cited for the vacancies was a sense that the constant demands of fundraising and marketing have turned the job into a business that is driving art historians and curators from this career ladder and tarnishing the intellectual and social prestige of being a museum director.[15] Meanwhile, orchestra conductors have been engaged in a veritable international game of musical chairs, as openings appeared simultaneously at the symphonies of Berlin, New York, Philadelphia, Atlanta, Houston, Indianapolis, Cincinnati, Boston, and Cleveland.[16] In the field of dance, where turnover is exacerbated by health issues, particularly the effects of AIDS, long-established companies have been seriously destabilized by a transition in leadership. In a field like literature, which is relatively under-institutionalized, virtually all the major literary organizations are experiencing or planning for a succession of founding leadership.[17]

Nonprofit arts and cultural organizations also face a challenge, indeed a triple challenge, in the area of marketing and development. As a consequence of changing demographics, organizations must simultaneously (a) keep or increase their share of the aging baby boomers in their audience even as this cohort revises the image of retiring and invents new stages of life, (b) cultivate generations X and Y and the latest digital generation as new audiences and new donors who have different value preferences than their elders and respond to different information media, and (c) successfully position their institutions in an increasingly competitive leisure and entertainment market.[18] Most performing arts organizations have discovered that traditional subscription packages are outmoded and instead have developed flexible and tailored subscription programs.[19] For example, many arts organizations have created specific categories and events for a new generation of givers, such as the Metropolitan Museum of Art's Apollo circle for people twenty-one to thirty-nine or the Lincoln Center young patron program for theater lovers in their twenties and thirties. In addition, many cultural organizations are exploring generational marketing and brand development. The Ford Foundation started a new program called new directions/new donors with $40 million in challenge grants to arts organizations designed to "jump-start the connection [of] the new wealth and the fresh activity in the arts."[20] In the museum world, many look to the example of the Guggenheim Museum as "the first global museum brand" that has succeeded in setting up international franchises in Italy, Germany, and Spain.[21] Some organizations are beginning to explore e-development for both fundraising and as image enhancement for sponsors. For example, many orchestras now include links at their websites to their large corporate donors, thus connecting orchestra patrons directly to information about the products of corporate donors. In the face of ambitious and virtually perpetual capital and endowment campaigns, fundraisers are confronting growing and incessant demands.

In the programming area, the live performing arts, such as opera and ballet, have commissioned new works as an effort both to support creativity and to attract new audiences. Now the orchestra field is encouraging the commissioning and performance of new works. A growing number of classical music websites are offering concert experiences—often from international venues and by high-profile artists—that not only may serve classical music lovers but also may draw new audiences into a larger classical music community.[22] For presenters, the challenge of new works has combined with the new opportunities of globalization to promote greater "curatorial" activities to complement performances and presentations—as well as new administrative challenges in managing international tours and dealing with foreign artists and ensembles.[23] In both theater and dance, nonprofit companies strive to create a "hit" program that can be spun off into a touring company that will generate income that can return to the parent company as a form of cross-subsidization. The Joffrey Ballet's highly successful production of "Billboards" early in the decade is a case in point.[24] Museums too have been drawn to collaboratively mounted, touring exhibitions in which costs and collections are shared; sometimes the project is brokered by a state or regional arts agency.

Facilities management has also taken on some new dimensions. Many communities continue to renovate, enlarge, or restore historical buildings, including concert halls, opera houses, theaters, and museums. For example, in the late 1990s, the Cleveland Symphony undertook renovations of Severance Hall that cost over $20 million. A spate of construction and renovation plans in New York City will cost more than $1.5 billion over the next decade, including projects at Carnegie Hall, the Museum of Modern Art, New York Botanical Garden, Symphony Space, Museum of Jewish Heritage, and Joseph Papp Public Theater.[25] Meanwhile, the Milwaukee Art Museum just completed a $100 million expansion project, and Orchestra Place in Detroit is in the midst of a $125 million construction and renovation effort. During this period, cities also created cultural districts, spurring both renovation and new construction: among the numerous examples are those in Pittsburgh, the Philadelphia avenue of the arts, and the Denver arts and science district.

Similarly, "old" performing arts centers announced or undertook major renovation efforts even as new centers opened. The first wave of modern performing arts centers is often dated from the opening of Lincoln Center in New York

City. Such centers were built in the 1960s and 1970s and now require major expenditures on renovation and maintenance. For example, the Kennedy Center underwent considerable structural work in the late 1990s; Lincoln Center recently announced plans for $1.5 billion in renovation work, although here again September 11 has intervened.

A decade wave of cultural center building can be seen in the opening of the New Jersey Center for the Performing Arts, Getty Center in Los Angeles, and Rock and Roll Hall of Fame in Cleveland. Another facet of facilities management is being prompted by efforts to expand cultural tourism. In this regard, efforts to make cultural organizations and their programs more attractive and accessible to tourists can require greater attention to parking, signage, handicapped access, and amenities (such as cafes, childcare facilities, and restrooms). Finally, for some segments of the nonprofit arts sector—such as dance—securing and maintaining studio and administrative space in booming urban real estate markets are becoming increasingly difficult, forcing companies to build, relocate, or even close. For example, in 1999, the Brooklyn Academy of Music announced plans for a new center for dance that would provide studio space, storage area, and school facilities. The Mark Morris Company announced that it would take up residence in the new center.[26] This was a clear indication that the costs and challenges of securing studio space in Manhattan were driving even established modern dance choreographers into the other boroughs.

General Public and Governmental Interactions

Arts and cultural nonprofit organizations, in general, are finding their relationship with the general public, the government, and the community to be evolving in subtle yet significant ways. For much of the decade, controversies raged around government funding for the arts and about the nonprofit institutions that were involved in the "culture wars." Debates concerning allegedly obscene, pornographic, blasphemous, or otherwise offensive art exhibited in museums and galleries or performed on stage and in theaters raised public awareness and concern about the content of the so-called "high arts" that are generally seen as the purview of the nonprofit arts sector. The coincidence of similar debates concerning the commercial arts and entertainment industries—whether television, movies, recordings, or video games—muddied public assumptions about their ability to trust the quality of art found in many nonprofit venues as well as in the popular culture offerings of the entertainment industries. Such blurring in the public mind contributed to questions about mission legitimacy, which Salamon identifies as one of four crises challenging the nonprofit sector more generally.[27]

Nonprofit arts and cultural organizations dealt more successfully with other, less sensational, issues concerning fairness, equity, and public responsibilities. The decade opened with passage of the Americans with Disabilities Act, which brought new requirements for and placed new demands on nonprofit cultural institutions (and American society more generally) to facilitate physical accessibility for disabled citizens. The mobilization of a broad arts education movement, in tandem with the general education reform effort, highlighted the educational mission and potential of cultural organizations even as it revealed the often meager presence of arts in the schools and the frequently underdeveloped capacity of cultural organizations to contribute to a well-rounded public education. By later in the decade, the nonprofit arts community not only had risen to the general educational challenge but had extended its efforts to a targeted concern for at-risk youth, often through after-school programs.[28]

The demographic representativeness of established cultural organizations such as orchestras and museums was a major point of discussion and debate within disciplines and between specific organizations and their local communities. For example, museums began the decade with their 1992 report *Excellence and Equity* and enactment of the Native American Graves Protection and Repatriation Act.[29] Both reflected a growing concern with equity, cultural sensitivity, and the public responsibilities of museums. As the American Association of Museums report noted,

> As public institutions in a democratic society, museums must achieve greater inclusiveness. Trustees, staff, and volunteers must acknowledge and respect our nation's diversity in race, ethnic origin, age, gender, economic status, and education, and they should attempt to reflect that pluralism in every aspect of museums' operations and programs.[30]

Similarly, in the early 1990s, the American Symphony Orchestra League brought out its controversial report *Americanizing the American Symphony*.[31] Prompted in part by concern for the precarious financial state of the orchestra field, reports of aging audiences, and accusations of cultural irrelevancy, the report sought to promote change in many aspects of orchestra operations and relations with the public and local communities. These changes were both about ensuring the survival of orchestras as well as about emphasizing their public role. As the report noted,

> In order to remain a vital and relevant element of American society, the orchestra field as a whole should demonstrate greater inclusiveness and responsiveness to the demographic and cultural evolution of the United States, and individual American orchestras should reflect more closely the cultural mix, needs, and interests of their communities.[32]

This burgeoning emphasis on the public responsibilities of nonprofit cultural organizations was also evident in the 1997 reports of the National Endowment for the Arts, *American Canvas*, and of the American Assembly, *The Arts and the Public Purpose*. A theme throughout the *American Canvas* report was the disconnect between the public and the arts (specifically the arts presented by nonprofit organizations). The report noted, "Many American citizens fail to recognize the direct relevance of art to their lives . . . Some people . . . view the arts as belonging to someone else." Moreover, many Americans "are apt to look with suspicion at an 'arts world' that seems alternately intimidating, incomprehensible, expensive, alien, and . . . often disreputable."[33] The NEA specifically criticized the tendency toward elitism among its own constituency—nonprofit arts organizations:

> In enshrining art within the temples of culture—the museum, the concert hall, the proscenium stage—we may have lost touch with the spirit of art: its direct relevance to our lives . . . We may have stressed the specialized, professional aspects of the arts at the expense of their more pervasive, participatory nature.[34]

Such sentiments indicate another of Salamon's four crises of the nonprofit sector—the crisis of effectiveness and the consequences of over-professionalization.

In contrast to the National Endowment for the Arts, the American Assembly report took issue with the often implicit and sometimes explicit charge that the arts were trivial frills, largely lacking in public purpose and therefore unworthy of government support or policy attention. The consensus report of the American Assembly declared that, rather than focus on how the public sector could address the needs of the arts and artists, it was time to recognize that "the arts can and do meet the needs of the nation and its citizens . . . [that] . . . in the context of rapid technological, media, and social change, the arts [may] have special public responsibilities."[35]

It went on to point out that the "nation's founders perceived the importance of the arts both in civil society and in the marketplace," that the constitution not only provided a sense of public purpose for the arts in the copyright clause and the First Amendment, but that "today, there is a role for the arts in fulfilling some of the public purposes contained in the preamble to the constitution" and inherent to our civil society. It identified four such public mandates addressed by the arts: (a) helping to define and project an American identity, (b) contributing to the quality of life and to economic growth, (c) helping to foster an educated and aware citizenry, and (d) enhancing individual life.[36]

Finally, the nonprofit arts and culture sector dealt with questions of evaluation and accountability. Calls for evaluation, for the ability to demonstrate effectiveness, and for performance review permeated the public discourse of the 1990s. This affected nonprofit arts and culture organizations both directly and indirectly. The nonprofit sector as a whole grappled with the challenge of developing appropriate measures of its effectiveness. This, of course, included arts and cultural organizations—which may face a particularly complicated task since "process is often as important as product, and the impact of creativity and imagination [is] difficult to quantify."[37] Although arts and cultural organizations (and often their funders) are apt to regard evaluation as having a negative connotation, many are learning to see it as "part of an ongoing learning process."[38] The National Assembly of State Arts Agencies points out that performance review can contribute to good planning, improved management, effectiveness, and cost-efficiency and can bolster organizational credibility with legislators and other policymakers.[39]

In truth, cultural organizations have long been operating under a professional review system that involves critical commentary and peer review. What has become more apparent is that the arts are also operating in a system where political oversight and popular opinion are important. Each of these three evaluation perspectives—professional, political, and popular—has implicit values that are not necessarily congruent.[40] From one perspective, the current interest in evaluation and impact analysis indicates the stage of development of the cultural support system. That is, evaluation is more likely to be useful and prevalent when an old paradigm is waning and a new one is forming—a situation that seems to characterize both public and private support systems for the arts and culture. From other policy arenas, we know that evaluation that involves impact analysis is more likely to be fruitful when programs have a track record and have evolved over years of operational experience. After thirty-five years of experience with programs of direct government funding for the arts that were premised on a link between public and private funding, arts policy now has an extensive track record and thus could be regarded as capable of demonstrating policy impact.[41]

Private grantmakers feel that they are in the midst of an "accountability environment" both inside and outside their organizations. Their consequent search for impact and ways of demonstrating it are, in turn, "driving change in programs."[42] Cultural philanthropists expect a continuing emphasis on and increased use of performance review and outcome-based evaluation. Meanwhile, following the enactment of the 1993 Government Performance and Results Act, federal agencies—including cultural agencies—are required to develop five-year strategic plans with measurable goals and year-by-year indicators. Similarly, during the decade, most state governments instituted performance reviews as part of their regular budgetary and assessment process—thus affecting most state arts agencies. Indeed, the National Assembly of State Arts Agencies developed a performance measurement toolkit that identified a set of likely performance goals, operationalized a host of output measures, and demonstrated how these might be compiled into meaningful outcomes.[43] As third-party agents of both federal and state agencies, nonprofit arts organization grantees are indirectly subject to these performance measures of accountability.

Technology Effects: A Creative Quandary

A special challenge to the nonprofit arts world arises from the technological changes of recent years. The technological environment in which the nonprofit arts must function today and in the immediate future is dramatically different from what it was just a decade ago. The pace of change in the areas of information, networking, and telecommunications is dizzying. Although it is common to project the likely consequences of such technological innovations for the commercial arts and entertainment industries, or for banking, finance, and insurance services, the dawning of the information age is also propelling a rethinking of many administrative and financial assumptions, not to mention legal and policy dilemmas, for nonprofit arts organizations.

In part, such rethinking is simply inescapable. We are all living in a very different and more digital world than we were just ten years ago. For example, when Bill Clinton became president in 1992, few artists or nonprofit arts organizations had an e-mail address, websites were rare, digital information was largely a subject for scientists, and few homes owned a personal computer. Today, the best-seller nonfiction lists are populated with books about digital assets, digital capital, and a digital society. There are over 20 million websites, and 48 percent of Americans send or receive e-mail. Personal computers are as ubiquitous in the home as videocassette recorders and are indispensable in corporate, government, and academic offices.

Nonprofit arts and cultural organizations are struggling to adapt to the information age. A few examples will help to illustrate the dimensions of both the challenges and recent changes. According to a 1999 survey by the American Association of Museums, 78 percent of its members had websites, and most of those who did not either had plans to launch a website in 2000 or were considering establishing one.[44] The presence of websites rose into the ninetieth percentile for large museums as well as for living collections and natural history and science museums (with large art museums not far behind, at 85 percent). As with the digital revolution in general, this is a global phenomenon. According to one source, more than 10,000 museums in 120 countries can now be reached on-line—and more join the list every day.[45] Similarly, Opera America reports that, while few American opera companies had websites two or three years ago, now most of their members have a presence on the Internet. Three on-line classical music websites are offering live, streaming media transmissions of orchestral concerts from around the world. Individual public broadcasting stations are building or expanding on-line stores. In June 2000, the Public Broadcasting System website rolled out a new version of its on-line store—one that featured 1,500 videos, books, and compact disks.

Despite such advances, many nonprofit arts and cultural organizations continue to be ill equipped, are only partially networked, and all too often lack interactive or sophisticated websites. For example, according to a seven-state exploratory survey conducted by the National Assembly of State Arts Agencies, 34 percent of the arts organizations that responded had only one or no computers, with an equal proportion reporting that all or most of their computers were donated, which means that they were likely to be somewhat older or to exhibit compatibility problems with newer, purchased machines and software. Of the responding arts organizations in these seven states, 17 percent reported having no Internet access, while 46 percent reported not having a website. While a majority of arts organizations (59 percent) reported using their websites to share information about work or to post schedules of events, only 10 percent used their websites to sell artworks or merchandise, and a mere 6 percent could handle ticket sales on-line. Generally, organizations with smaller budgets were less likely to have Internet access and websites.[46] Clearly, the equipment and trained staff necessary to improve the technological capacity of nonprofit arts organizations will continue to be a challenge for the sector for years to come.

Artists, nonprofit arts organizations, and commercial cultural corporations are important generators of intellectual property, and in the information age, intellectual property has become a key economic resource. Today, U.S. creative industries constitute the second largest export sector of the nation (outranked only by the defense equipment industries). Nonprofit arts and cultural industries are implicated in these phenomena in many ways. They are generators of new intellectual property: sometimes these ideas get developed by commercial entertainment industries; other times these ideas and artworks constitute alternative aesthetic choices for the cultural consumer. Nonprofit arts and cultural organizations (including heritage groups and institutions) are also stewards of vast stockpiles of cultural content in the form of museum collections, historical archives, and performing arts repertoire. Such content might be called the "raw material" form of intellectual property—resources that could be converted into digital assets for the information age. But at present, and unlike their "cousins" in the commercial arts and entertainment industries, the nonprofit arts are content rich but data poor.

Thus, for nonprofit arts and cultural organizations, the creative quandary is at least fourfold.[47] First, although they have substantial intellectual property assets, many require conversion into digital formats if they are to be fully developed in the information age. Even without digitization, the task of managing intellectual property assets raises new challenges for nonprofit arts organizations. For example, it becomes a factor in labor agreements—such as the recent contract agreement involving the American Federation of Musicians and many of the nation's major symphony orchestras, opera, and ballet companies that covered both the transmission of live performances through "streaming audio" technology and prerecorded audio files that listeners can download.[48]

Second, any large-scale digital conversion is likely to incur significant financial costs, which most nonprofit arts and cultural organizations are not in a position to absorb. Furthermore, commercial arts and entertainment companies think and can act on intellectual property and technology concerns as though they were investments—and substantial investments, at that. In contrast, nonprofit arts organizations do not have the market scale or global distribution networks that help the commercial arts to recover their digital production costs, especially when the pace of technological change requires constant updating and, therefore, incurs even more costs.

Third, digitization and technological accommodation raise fundamental issues of aesthetics, management, and marketing, particularly for the performing arts. Aesthetically, going digital can divorce the live experience from some of its key elements: immediacy, immersion, fresh invention, physicality, ritual, and social interaction.[49] Thus for many in the live performing arts—most of which are situated in the nonprofit sector—a key question is whether their rather ephemeral performances should be transformed into any fixed format and whether the resultant piece becomes something other than the original. Similarly, going digital has profound implications for creative control. As Andrew Taylor points out, "Creative control by the author or artist, the carefully crafted stewardship of great works by arts organizations, and the context of a cultural work torn from its intended means of conveyance, the cultural integrity of ritual or celebratory expression . . . are all issues that lose their foothold in the information age."[50] In terms of marketing, a competing push-pull dynamic seems to be at work. There is the "pull" of looking to new, technologically based intermediaries who can help arts organizations to reach potential consumers more efficiently and conversely to direct web-surfing consumers to cultural offerings.[51] Meanwhile, there is also a "push" of trying to develop a new marketing role for nonprofit arts organizations—that of cultural experience broker—a role that is more involved and interactive with the audience than the traditional role of presenter.[52]

Finally, accurate digitization and media-distributed art from nonprofit arts and cultural organizations require continuous innovation. For example, in the case of dance preservation, to record dance choreography accurately and usefully requires both new technology to capture movement and sense motion as well as refined computer imaging techniques. Each time a new information format emerges, it raises new challenges for preservation in cultural fields. Thus nonprofit cultural organizations face the dual challenge of evolving from one technology-based information format to the next in order to keep their creative edge and to compete effectively in the world of e-commerce, while simultaneously preserving, maintaining, and facilitating public access to a legacy of cultural resources that are fixed in older technological mediums.

Technology—especially when combined with intellectual property considerations—presents the nonprofit arts and culture sector with more than an equipment and interconnectivity challenge. Rather, the nonprofit arts and culture sector finds itself in a multifaceted creative quandary over how to adapt to an information-driven, networked, digital era. While the commercial arts and entertainment industries have extensive financial resources and technological expertise that allow them to pursue and protect their interests aggressively in this new digital era, the nonprofit arts—both professional and traditional—often find themselves feeling like "poor relations," unable to match the marketing, distribution, production, or advocacy resources of the commercial arts sector. Furthermore, nonprofit arts and cultural organizations cannot confine their focus to the goal of advancing their economic interests while accommodating technological change. Rather, given their civic responsibilities, they must be concerned with advancing and protecting a variety of noneconomic interests as well as public interests in access, fair use, and preservation; the moral and creative rights of artists; and concerns for the integrity and authenticity of specific artworks and intellectual properties. Paradoxically, such concerns seem likely to increase the financial costs incurred by nonprofit arts organizations. They involve goals that are neither market driven nor market supported. Concerns for authenticity, integrity, and attribution are likely to prompt added requirements for technological protections. Finally, the digital economy and the information society require all participants to constantly reinvest to keep up with the state of public expectations, the practices of their peers and competitors, and the pace of technological innovation.

Implications for Particular Subfields

These broad shifts, changes, and trends have not affected all components of the nonprofit arts and cultural sector in the same way. It may be useful, therefore, to examine in more detail how they have affected three major types of arts institutions: museums, opera companies, and theaters. In each of the sketches that follow, attention is given to the composition of the field, revenue patterns and financial issues, audience and attendance information, and specific issues of concern.

Museums

Museums are both a field and a form of organization that encompasses the activities of many disciplines. Approximately two-thirds of museums are privately run as nonprofit organizations; the remaining third are publicly run, ranging from municipal museums and historic buildings to the Smithsonian Institution. In the United States, the entire universe of museums numbers 8,300 organizations that embrace living collections (zoos, aquariums, botanical gardens), historic sites (land and buildings), natural resources (anthropological or botanical), and works of art (presented in 2-D, 3-D, analog, digital, and virtual formats). Art museums constitute approximately 15 percent of all museums—1,214 institutions, making them the third largest category, following history museums (2,401) and historic sites (2,083). Although the American Association of Museums includes members from all of these disciplines, various museum segments also have more specialized professional organizations, such as the Association of Youth Museums, Association of Art Museum Directors, or Association of Science and Technology Centers. In addition to this segmentation by discipline, museums also differ by size. In 1989, 92 percent of all museums had an annual budget of under $100,000, with 38 percent of those working with less than $50,000 annually. Budgets of the remaining 8 percent exceeded $1 million, with some being far larger.[53]

MUSEUM FINANCES. The 1999 American Association of Museums survey[54] reported that combined museum budgets totaled $4 billion annually, split between government sources (39 percent), earned income (30 percent), private sources (19 percent), and investment income (12 percent). Although these figures include both public and private institutions, ten years later, government sources and earned income both had fallen to 28 percent, while private contributions had risen to 32 percent.[55] Among private nonprofit museums alone, these proportions are quite different, with earned income providing 35 percent of support, private contributions providing 35 percent, and government providing 15 percent. Overall, museum income has been growing. Between 1997 and 1999, median total operating income increased from $314,993 to $367,500 (with a 1999 range of $1,285 to $122 million).[56] Of the government funding awarded to art museums, the largest proportion (almost half) comes from the states, another 40 percent comes from local governments, and only 12 percent comes from the federal government. About a fifth of museums' private support comes from each of the following sources: individuals, community organizations, and parent institutions. The largest proportion of museums' earned income comes from memberships, gift shops, and publications. Endowment income accounts for about 10 percent of revenues. In 1999, 21 percent of art museums operated at a deficit (average amount of $32,000).

MUSEUM AUDIENCES. Museums in general, and art museums more specifically, are in the midst of a twenty-year trend of increasing attendance. Art museum attendance increased 8 percent between 1986 and 1988 and jumped another 15 percent between 1987 and 1999.[57] In 1997, 35 percent of the general public visited an art museum at least once annually, and 225.3 million visitors came to museums—an increase of 61.6 million over 1992.[58] Art museums were the most frequented nonprofit arts organization; attendance at historic parks was even higher at 47 percent. In terms of the age of persons attending museums, this NEA report shows that museum attendance rates are highest for persons in the thirty-five- to forty-four-year-old age range (25 percent), followed closely by twenty-five- to thirty-four-year-olds (21 percent).

To achieve and extend those gains in participation, museums are engaged in targeted efforts to reach and cultivate new generations of patrons. American

Association of Museums data show that 62 percent of art museums offer family programs in which "parents or caregivers interact with pre-school or school-aged children" and 44 percent have programming targeted to at-risk youth.[59] Children's museums are extremely popular and may be helping to socialize their young visitors to museum attendance more generally. Eighty-five percent of art museums had a web presence in 1999, and 20 percent of the art museums that have a website provide educational material formatted for use in the classroom. The Internet is also helping to expand the reach of the museum store. Recently, a coordinated museum store, museumshop.com, was created where anyone can shop at an international selection of museums ranging from the Adirondack Museum to the Louvre, the Prado, and the Museo Nacional Centro de Arte Reina Sofia in Madrid.

ISSUES FOR MUSEUMS. The decade of the 1990s began with terms like "audience development" and evolved into discussions of community and access—with access exhibiting many meanings. The Americans with Disabilities Act and the Native American Graves Protection and Repatriation Act both turned ten years old in 2000, sparking renewed attention to the evolving nature of access and the ethics of collecting. Technology brought a cluster of issues to the forefront of the museum field, including the cost and equipment required to digitize collections and protect the integrity of such images and the ways in which technology could support the educational mission of museums and facilitate their fundraising.

Other ethical issues were also of concern to the museum world. Holocaust-era assets were a hot topic. On the one hand, museum professionals struggled to devise standard practices to determine rightful ownership of items that had been acquired subsequent to being wrongfully seized during the Nazi regime. On the other hand, courts and governments both in the United States and abroad confronted claims from individuals seeking restoration or restitution for artworks originally seized during the Holocaust. By late in 2000, the museum field had developed and approved sweeping professional guidelines on this topic, calling for full disclosure and the creation of a centralized database as well as provision of advice on the handling of claims and the return of unlawfully seized artworks.[60] Another ethical issue arose from the controversial Brooklyn Museum of Art show "Sensation." In this case, a controversy originally sparked by the content of some of the pieces in the show led to the revelation of questionable relations between museums, private collectors, and commercial galleries. Indeed, many questioned the propriety of private art collectors' lending to museums artworks that become the centerpiece of exhibitions that, in turn, lent added cachet and presumably market value to these collections, particularly when the collectors not only seek to sell such works but also to exercise curatorial input into the show. In the aftermath and as part of a periodic ten-year review process, both the American Association of Museums and Association of Art Museum Directors reviewed and revised their codes of ethics to better address questions about what constitutes appropriate collector and gallery involvement in exhibition design and funding as well as post-exhibition sales of artwork.[61]

Finally, the issue of recruiting and retaining museum leadership surfaced recurrently. Frequent and numerous vacancies in directorships seem to reflect the changing—and less appealing—nature of the job. Riley and Urice report that leadership transitions are becoming increasingly difficult to navigate, the job model is changing from the curator/scholar-as-director to a more business-and-management role, and the environment is becoming more demanding.[62] Others have characterized the change in museums as fundamental: from an inward-directed establishment whose prime responsibility is its collection to an outward-oriented, outcome-based social enterprise that is accessible, unpretentious, and lively.[63]

Opera

According to Opera America, the national service organization for opera companies, the 1990s represented a decade of impressive growth for opera in North America. "Recent years have been distinguished by larger and younger audiences, more mainstage productions and performances, the emergence of an American repertoire and of American artists, and inventive educational collaborations between opera companies and their communities."[64]

Opera is an art form that intrinsically blends music and theater, often with elements of dance. Sometimes regarded as an imported and highly elite art form, opera was ranked second to last in a recent listing of public preferences for a type of music.[65] Nonetheless, opera has become "the envy of all the other performing arts, because its audiences are growing. Its appeal to the 'youth market' has astounded many. Americans are . . . finally finding out that a night at the opera can be a transcendent experience."[66] Significant crossover of artists and artistic values can be found among opera, operetta, musical theater, vocal guest artists with orchestral performances (for example, concert opera performances), church music performances (for example, oratorio), art song recitals, and even jazz performances. Phenomena such as the Three Tenors concerts have also introduced new potential audiences to opera.

Unlike many other nonprofit art forms, and perhaps due to the expense and artistic demands involved in opera production, active participation and performance of opera at the community level are rare. Thus opera in America is a relatively small discipline. Opera America counts 114 nonprofit professional companies in forty-three states in its U.S. membership. Roughly half of these companies were established after 1970, making the growth of opera throughout North America a relatively new phenomenon. In 1997–98 opera companies presented 6,078 outreach performances, an increase of 27 percent over the previous year. Opera America member companies had collective budgets of over $600 million in 1998 and employed over 20,000 people on a full-time and part-time basis. American opera companies posted over $251 million dollars in box office receipts for fiscal 1998, up 2 percent from the prior year. In 1998 the average budget of an Opera America member company was $5.9 million, up 6 percent from $5.59 million in fiscal 1997. The median budget in fiscal 1998 was $1.7 million, up 13 percent from $1.5 million in fiscal 1997, revealing particularly strong growth among the field's mid-size companies.[67]

OPERA FINANCES. Like other nonprofit arts organizations, opera companies rely on a mix of earned income, public funding, and private contributions.[68] Earned income—from ticket sales, broadcasting and recording income, investments, endowments, bank interest, and temporarily and permanently restricted income—is by far the largest source, amounting to $334 million in fiscal 1998, or 52 percent of the total. Box office receipts, which represented 40 percent of total operating income, increased 2 percent from fiscal 1997 but fell slightly as a percentage of total operating income.

Public support decreased from $20.4 million in fiscal 1997 to $17.8 million in fiscal 1998 and fell as a percentage of total income to 3 percent. Support for all programs of the National Endowment for the Arts, including a few major grants from the challenge and advancement programs, totaled $1.74 million in fiscal 1998, a 30 percent drop in funds from $2.5 million in fiscal 1997. Funding from state and local governments was slightly more than $15 million, accounting for roughly 3 percent of all income.

Private support has always been a significant source of funds for opera companies, with individual giving amounting to $161.2 million (or 26 percent of total income). The ratio of private funds to public funds has increased dramatically over recent years, rising from ten to one in fiscal 1995 to sixteen to one in fiscal 1998. At $52.8 million, foundation giving represented the second largest share of private support, composing 8 percent of total income. This represented a 6 percent increase over the previous year. Between 1997 and 1998, corporate and business giving rose 9 percent, reaching $27.6 million and accounting for 4 percent of total revenue. Combined sources of private support totaled $293 million and represented 46 percent of total income in fiscal 1998.

OPERA AUDIENCES. Paradoxically, regular operagoers may be getting older, yet the opera audience in general has been growing in numbers and growing younger. According to NEA's *Survey of Public Participation in the Arts,* opera has experienced exceptional growth among audiences in the eighteen- to twenty-four-year-old age group, as it has become infused into the popular culture and begun to resonate with the contemporary multimedia aesthetic.[69] Many opera companies aggressively market to young audiences by designing subscription programs that combine attendance at opera performances with social interaction. Although opera is still the least commonly attended of the "high" arts and is often considered "expensive" and "not for young people," creative marketing efforts have succeeded in appealing to young professionals and generation X opera neophytes alike.[70]

Overall, the U.S. opera audience has been growing since 1982, increasing 25 percent between 1982 and 1992 and another 13 percent through 1997—a growth rate greater than that of any other nonprofit art form. In 1997, 9.2 million adults (or almost 5 percent of the adult population) attended at least one opera performance. Participation in opera via broadcast and recorded media was even higher, with 15 percent of adults watching opera performances on television or video recordings, 11 percent listening to opera recordings, and 11 percent enjoying opera radio broadcasts.[71]

Opera America credits education and community programs with helping to build an appreciation for the art form and to develop audiences. Significant technological advancements, such as supertitles and seatback translations, have overcome the language barrier and made opera more accessible to opera newcomers. Successful regional companies have also been a major factor in the growth of opera, as have the creation and production of American operas. In addition, these regional opera companies have created early career opportunities for young singers. Over a decade of effort in commissioning and producing new American operas has helped to attract new audiences and keep the art form dynamic for sophisticated opera lovers as well.

ISSUES IN OPERA. Opera companies are rising to the challenge and opportunity of technology—using it to exchange information, engage in ticket sales and fundraising efforts, and enrich artistic production. For example, the Los Angeles Opera plans to engage the noted motion picture special effects firm, Industrial Light and Magic, to create the visual aspects of its production of Wagner's four-part "Ring" cycle, bringing movie production values to the opera stage. Recording and broadcast media are being used to make opera performances increasingly accessible to a larger and more diverse audience. And for a few opera companies, the income from broadcasting and recording is substantial: of the total $2.4 million earned across the field, the Metropolitan Opera received 80 percent.[72]

Nonprofit Theater

Theater in America is a cross-sectoral phenomenon, including professional nonprofit theater companies, commercial theater organizations, and nonprofit community theaters. Professional nonprofit theater companies include such well-known organizations as the Goodman Theatre (in Chicago), the Alley Theatre (in Houston), the Yale Repertory Theatre, Arena Stage (in Washington, D.C.), the Guthrie Theater (in Minneapolis), the Georgia Shakespeare Festival, and Seattle Children's Theatre. Commercial theater companies range from Broadway production companies and their touring troupes through to dinner theaters. There is also a large contingent of nonprofit community theaters. Each of these kinds of theatrical organizations may present musical as well as dramatic productions. They may operate on a regular, limited engagement, repertory, or seasonal basis. Performance spaces may be rented or owned publicly or privately, vary greatly in size, and include both indoor and outdoor venues.

Theatre Communications Group (TCG), a leading membership organization for professional nonprofit theaters in the United States, reports 375 member organizations located in forty-five states. According to the TCG's *Theater Facts 1999* survey report, professional nonprofit theaters produced 64,556 performances in 1999, sold 17.8 million tickets, and employed nearly 42,000 people in artistic (55 percent), technical (29 percent), and administrative (16 percent) positions.[73] In comparison, the American Association of Community Theatre (AACT), which serves amateur, nonprofit theater companies, lists 1,000 member groups and estimates that an additional 7,000 are operating. AACT does not collect financial or administrative information on its membership, but one can speculate that the activities of nonprofit community theaters add considerably to the picture of nonprofit theater activity that emerges from the TCG profile. Although professional theater companies probably receive the bulk of nonprofit theater revenue, community theaters account for significant numbers in terms of both attendance and active participants. Indeed, at its website, AACT notes, "Community theaters involve more participants, present more performances, offer more productions, and play to more people than any performing art in the country."[74]

Any profile of nonprofit professional theater in the United States is likely to blur the distinctions between nonprofit and commercial theaters as well as between professional and amateur productions. Actors and other theatrical personnel frequently migrate between the nonprofit and commercial sectors. Audiences seldom report an awareness of nonprofit or commercial organizational status as a factor in consumer choice or attendance preference. Bearing these caveats in mind, let us now sketch some basic dimensions of the professional nonprofit theater field using TCG figures.[75]

THEATER FINANCES. In 1999 TCG theaters contributed more than $700 million to the U.S. economy in the form of salaries, benefits, and payment for goods and services. Total expenses for nonprofit theater companies grew 16 percent between 1997 and 1999, outpacing the inflation rate and the growth of earned income. These increases in expenses were not driven by any single factor but rather occurred across the board. Nonprofit professional theaters earn approximately 60 percent of their revenues through a combination of ticket sales, concessions, endowment interest, and educational programs. The remaining 40 percent of revenues comes from contributions from individuals, corporations, foundations, and government grants. In 1999, 12 percent of nonprofit theaters reported a net deficit of 10 percent of budget or more, a slight increase since 1997—a development largely attributable to the problems facing small theaters. Even though ticket income grew 14 percent over the past three years, the ability of ticket income to support total expenses declined 2 percent. In contrast, other sources of earned income—notably income from educational and outreach programs as well as rental income—increased steadily over the past three years.

On the contributed side of the revenue sheet, individual giving accounted for approximately 13 percent of revenues, with small contributions by individual donors staying relatively steady at $260 per gift, while trustee contributions increased both in average size and in number. Corporate contributions amounted to slightly less than 6 percent of revenues, and the average corporate gift held fairly steady during the past three years. Foundation support, which amounts to about 8 percent, saw a decline in the size of the average grant, even as the number of foundation awards increased.

Public funding presented a mixed picture. Federal funding—never a large proportion of theater revenues—declined from 0.8 percent in 1997 to 0.6 percent in 1999. State funding hovered around 2.5 percent of theater revenues. Local government funding experienced substantial growth—an adjusted 18 percent increase between 1997 and 1999, with forty-five of the ninety-eight theaters reporting consistently over a three-year period enjoying an increase in local funding between 1998 and 1999. While the average endowment for individual theaters rose from $2.9 million in 1997 to $3.6 million in 1999, only 54 percent of the ninety-eight theaters reporting had any endowment. Thus nearly half of the professional nonprofit theaters lacked the safety net of an endowment; in recent years, that proportion has barely shifted despite a strong economy.

THEATER AUDIENCES. According to the NEA's *Survey of Public Participation in the Arts 1998,* almost 25 percent of the adult population, or 47.9 million people, attended a musical play, while 16 percent, or 30.9 million people, attended a nonmusical play in 1997. This was a higher public participation rate than that for other performing arts surveyed. Many of these playgoers attended multiple times, since the number of tickets sold for the year totaled 105.4 million for musicals and 77.3 million for nonmusical plays. The median age of the audience was forty-four years. About a quarter of the population also experienced theatrical offerings—whether musical or dramatic—via broadcast or recorded media. An estimated 15 million citizens personally participated in the presentation of a musical play, while approximately 5 million were involved in a nonmusical play.[76] TCG reported that, although single ticket sales decreased 15 percent over the 1997–99 period, subscription sales increased roughly 4 percent. Ticket prices increased an average of 5 percent per subscription ticket and 3 percent per single ticket. Resident attendance accounted for 89 percent of the total, with touring attendance making up the remaining 11 percent.[77]

ISSUES IN NONPROFIT THEATER. A number of issues arise at the interface of the commercial and the nonprofit theater worlds. Artists in professional nonprofit theater are woefully underpaid, and management and administrative staff earn far less than their counterparts in the for-profit world.[78] These conditions, in turn, give rise to fears of a talent drain and encourage the circulation of theatrical talent between the nonprofit and commercial sectors. Over the past twenty-five years, the professional nonprofit theater has become the primary originator and cultivator of new American drama. Recently, with encouragement from foundations and other funders, nonprofit theaters have been forming entrepreneurial partnerships with commercial producers to develop new work with commercial potential. This has given rise to concern—and considerable debate—about whether such alliances weaken the purpose of professional nonprofit theater, push it away from adventurous work, and lead trustees and supporters to equate commercial success with artistic excellence.[79] In addition, technologically enhanced production capabilities present nonprofit professional theaters with different challenges than those confronting their commercial "cousins." As audiences come to expect the spectacle and special effects they find in live commercial theater and even rock concerts (to say nothing of film and television), nonprofit theaters feel pressed to upgrade their production values through technology. However, few nonprofit theaters have the resources or opportunities to create digital assets by filming or broadcasting their performances. Thus nonprofit theaters are pushed to incur the costs of new technology but seldom reap the extensive benefits that such investments can bring to commercial theater activities.

Notes from Other Subfields

Space prohibits giving equal attention to other performing arts disciplines (notably music and dance), to the literary arts, to other nonprofit cultural organizations in the humanities, heritage, and preservation, or to public broadcasting. Nevertheless, a few observations are in order.

NONPROFIT PUBLISHING. The case of literary publishing, although not fully developed here, deserves mention because it illustrates a number of other features about nonprofit arts and culture. Distinct from commercial publishers as well as from the nonfiction and scholarly activities of many nonprofit university presses, nonprofit literary presses generally are small and often fleeting. Some are so small and under-institutionalized that they do not even acquire nonprofit status. The Council of Literary Magazines and Presses estimates that there are approximately 1,000 independent literary publishing organizations and only 50 to 60 percent of these publish regularly. More than half have no paid staff and operate with budgets of less than $35,000. In 1996 literature received only 1 percent of the grants and a mere 0.9 percent of the arts and culture funds awarded by foundations.[80] Nevertheless, the careers of writers, especially literary writers, are often propelled by a network of informal, nonprofit literary organizations as well as literary programs embedded in colleges and universities, literary centers, libraries, informal writing and reading groups, and independent literary presses and magazines. The primary role of such publishers is to work with writers; unlike many other kinds of nonprofit arts organizations, they seldom act as direct intermediaries between the author and an audience (of readers). Nonprofit publishers seldom have a public following and generally reach readers through a web of distributors, wholesalers, bookstores, and libraries.[81]

The structure of this field has many implications. As small, often embedded or informal organizations, nonprofit literary publishers have low visibility with either public or private institutional funders and generally lack the staff or resources to engage in much fundraising or marketing. Distinguishing the range and effect of nonprofit publishing organizations is extremely difficult given the way publishing statistics are gathered and categorized despite the significant research activities of the Book Industry Study Group and the American Booksellers Association. As small organizations dealing with a national, and sometimes even international, community of writers as well as a dispersed audience of literary readers, literary publishers often lack a strong profile in their own geographic community; hence as public funding has become more decentralized, literary publishers have seldom been positioned to benefit. Similarly, although web-based marketing may be a boon to commercial publishing and book sales, few nonprofit publishers have the staff or resources to create and maintain an economically profitable website.

Thus nonprofit, literary publishing as a field seems to display many similarities to voluntary arts and cultural activities in other fields, even though literary publishing would naturally fall within the professional nonprofit arena. Indeed, it draws our attention to another variant within the arts and culture sector: professional activities and organizations that are only weakly institutionalized.

THE HUMANITIES. Any discussion of the state of the arts and culture sector should give attention to the state of the humanities. Although the humanities are often appended to discussions of the arts—as in "the arts and humanities"— the structure, finances, and concerns of the two areas of cultural endeavor are not simply replicas of one another. In societal terms, the professional arts are located in both the commercial and nonprofit sectors: they are financed largely through market activity but have a significant nonprofit component that augments their commercial income with a considerable amount of contributed funds. Public funds play a relatively small role and one in which the federal government has, over time, given way to more state and local predominance. In contrast, the humanities are located primarily in the nonprofit sector, with the major distinction being between the academic-based humanities and the public humanities. Direct support of the humanities is more likely to come from public rather than private funds: in 1993 the humanities received $172.4 million from the National Endowment for the Humanities compared to approximately $100 million from private foundations. Much of the foundation money went to historical preservation and history-related museum projects, leaving only $50 million from foundations for all other humanities activity, including the academic-based humanities disciplines.[82] Thus when the NEH's budget sank to $110 million in 1996, this had an even more significant effect on the humanities than similar cuts to federal arts funding had on the arts. Although a number of other federal agencies administer policies and programs that affect the humanities (such as the Library of Congress, National Archives, Smithsonian Institution, and Department of Education), their role in the humanities is poorly understood.

Only three private foundations have distinct programs in the humanities, with the Andrew W. Mellon Foundation being the largest. While the NEA has a long history of cultivating private funding partners for its programs, the NEH was slower to do so. Particularly during the tenure of Sheldon Hackney (NEH chairman, 1993–97), this changed. Corporate support for a web-based project (EDSITEment) was solicited, an Office of Enterprise was created, and an independent 501(c)(3) organization—the National Trust for the Humanities—was established to raise private funding for NEH projects.[83] Although every state has a state humanities council, most of these are nonprofit organizations rather than state agencies. This puts them in the position of being both fundraisers and funders, unlike the state arts councils, which are predominantly funders and receive most of their money in the form of state budget appropriations. The largest proportion of humanities activity is embedded in universities and colleges—not only in departments of the humanities disciplines but also in a growing number of interdisciplinary humanities institutes.

Clearly, the funding patterns of the humanities differ from those of nonprofit arts, and the lack of sufficient data on the humanities—particularly those located within the higher educational context—makes it difficult to get a clear picture. Nevertheless, it appears that, despite the fortunes of the NEH, the 1990s "were a period of tremendous growth and prosperity for the institutional humanities . . . especially at elite universities."[84] If this momentum is to be sustained, three interrelated issues will need to be confronted. These include (a) clarifying the basic ambiguity about what is meant by the humanities, which impedes the effectiveness of fundraising efforts, (b) crafting a clearer political rationale about the public interest in the humanities, which, in turn, would make a stronger and more persuasive case about the importance of federal funding to sustain the humanities, and (c) organizing better information about the dimensions and varieties of humanities activities as well as about the range, role, and trends in both non-NEH federal and non-federal support of the humanities.

Present and Future Challenges

Clearly, the past decade has been one of considerable challenge and change for nonprofit arts and culture. It has also been a decade of significant experimentation and improvisation. Old paradigms—whether financial, administrative, or political—are noticeably in decline, and new operating paradigms are still protean. What steps might now be taken to improve the position and condition of nonprofit arts and culture as well as to strengthen their ability to make positive contributions to American society?

Certainly, nonprofit arts and culture organizations enter the twenty-first century with a heightened awareness of their public role and responsibilities. However, this awareness has not yet crystallized into an advocacy strategy, a set of stable public expectations and attitudes, or a policy agenda. Similarly, the public discourse is becoming more of a dialogue concerning both the public interest in fostering the arts and culture as well as the variety of public purposes that the arts and culture can help to advance and address.

These shifts, in turn, lead to new challenges. Financially, the language and logic of government and philanthropic support are shifting away from subsidy and toward investment and entrepreneurship. Effecting that shift requires conscious attention, targeted programs, and broadened and deepened information sharing. A decade of experimentation has taken place with regard to new funding devices and strategies, including program-related investments, a more active cultural role for community foundations, endowment-building campaigns by organizations and public trust funds for public agencies, the creation of cultural districts and earmarked taxes to support the arts, public service advertisement campaigns, and public awareness marketing campaigns. However, we have little systematic information about their effectiveness or general utility. Thus the appropriate character of emerging administrative and funding paradigms remains unclear. The same holds true for accountability mechanisms and effectiveness measures. How can a field that is still fragmented by disciplines, sector, and geography, by grantmakers and grantees, and by service organizations and scholars better share and use information, especially when it is often gathered for different institutional purposes, may be sensitive or proprietary in nature, and is built on different normative assumptions?

A broader perspective both about what the entire arts and culture sector encompasses and about what it can contribute raises different challenges. What are the dimensions and interrelations between the parts of this broadly conceived arts and culture sector? Can the nonprofit arts learn from or partner with the commercial arts when it comes to distribution and delivery systems or investment and venture capital strategies? What role do the avocational, voluntary, and community-based arts and cultural institutions play with regard to the development of talent, an audience, and a market for the professional nonprofit arts as well as for the cultural industries? If the arts and culture are both affected by and help to address other societal concerns—such as education, quality of life, and community development—how can they be included more consistently in the relevant planning and policy discussions? Nonprofit arts and culture organizations often complain that they are not "invited to the table" when tax policy is being reformed, trade or intellectual property treaties are being negotiated, or technology is being developed. And how can the arts and cultural community share knowledge and experience gained at these various "tables"? Indeed, while financing remains a necessary and persistent concern, the arts and culture sector may find that mechanisms to leverage access to the "right tables," to new players, and to better information are equal requirements of success in the information age.

The nonprofit arts and culture sector along with its public and private supporters may also need to identify new ways of targeting capacity-building efforts. Although it has been traditional to recognize that needs and practices differ from one field to another, it seems increasingly clear that needs vary by the size and age of the organizations. Certainly, the particular problems of mid-size organizations merit special attention. In addition, the organizational and professional development issues that were program targets of an earlier era might now usefully give way to technological development and entrepreneurship as areas of focus.

Finally, the nonprofit arts and cultural sector finds itself triangulated by the forces of decentralization, globalization, and the market at a time when federal support, attention, and leadership have declined. Nevertheless, a national presence is necessary: as a partner in intergovernmental affairs, as a negotiator and representative in global matters, and as a mediator and facilitator of the market. Federal cultural agencies tend to have fewer resources and less impact than they used to. Thus they must find new ways both to exercise leadership and to offer support. Arts service organizations can bring a national and sometimes even international perspective to particular issues or fields—and have the potential to assume a greater leadership and representational role. Coalitions can be assembled across fields, issue areas, sectors, and levels of community to bring together a national perspective and a capacity for effective action. Such network approaches are another consequence of decentralization, diversification, and the successes of development that the nonprofit arts and culture field experienced in the late twentieth century.

A decade of profound change, following three decades of significant growth, has brought the nonprofit arts and cultural sector to the recognition of a need for even more change and a more positive attitude about accommodating and adapting to the environment. Articulating, integrating, and routinizing the emergent financial, administrative, and political paradigms are now the task at hand.

Notes

1. American Assembly, *The Arts and the Public Purpose: Final Report of the 92nd American Assembly, May 29–June 1, 1997* (New York: American Assembly, 1997).

2. Americans for the Arts, *Arts and Economic Prosperity* (Washington: Americans for the Arts, 2002).

3. Margaret Jane Wyszomirski, "Federal Cultural Support: Toward a New Paradigm?" *Journal of Arts Management, Law, and Society,* vol. 25, no. 1 (1995): 69–83.

4. National Assembly of State Arts Agencies, *Legislative Appropriations Annual Survey: Fiscal Year 2000* (Washington: National Assembly of State Arts Agencies, 2000).

5. Randy Cohen, *Local Arts Agency Facts 1998,* Monographs, vol. 2, no. 3 (Washington: Americans for the Arts, 1998).

6. Nina Kressner Cobb, *Looking Ahead: Private Sector Giving to the Arts and the Humanities* (Washington: President's Committee on the Arts and the Humanities, 1996).

7. President's Committee on the Arts and the Humanities, *Creative America* (Washington: President's Committee on the Arts and the Humanities, 1997), pp. 18–22.

8. *Giving and Volunteering in the United States 1999* (Washington: Independent Sector, 1999).

9. Loren Renz, Steve Lawrence, and John Kendzior, *Arts Funding 2000: Funder Perspectives on Current and Future Trends* (New York: Foundation Center, 2000); Loren Renz, Steve Lawrence, and John Kendzior, *Foundation Giving 1999* (New York: Foundation Center, 1999). Also see Margaret Jane Wyszomirski, "Philanthropy and Culture: Patterns, Context, and Change," in Charles T. Clotfelter and Thomas Ehrlich, ed., *Philanthropy and the Nonprofit Sector in a Changing America* (Indiana University Press, 1999), pp. 461–80.

10. Judith H. Dobrzynski, "Private Donors Unite to Support Art Spurned by the Government," *New York Times*, May 3, 1999, pp. B1, B7.

11. Renz, Lawrence, and Kendzior, *Arts Funding 2000.*

12. American Association of Fund-Raising Counsel, *Giving USA 2000* (Indianapolis: American Association of Fund-Raising Counsel, 2000).

13. Frank Provenzano, "Cultural Countdown: 5 New Arts Leaders Prepare for Make-or-Break Period," *Detroit Free Press,* January 28, 2001.

14. Bruce Weber, "How to Make a Museum More Fun to Visit," *New York Times*, December 23, 1999, pp. E1, E5.

15. Lester M. Salamon, *Holding the Center: America's Nonprofit Sector at the Crossroads* (New York: Nathan Cummings Foundation, 1997).

16. Anthony Tommasini, "Following the Bouncing Baton," *New York Times*, June 24, 1999, pp. B1, B8.

17. Emily Redington, *Founding Director Succession in Literary Arts Organizations: A Multiple Case Study,* M.A. thesis (Ohio State University, Arts Policy and Administration, 2000).

18. Carol Scott, "Branding: Positioning Museums in the 21st Century," *International Journal of Arts Management,* vol. 2, no. 3 (2000): 35–39.

19. Rebecca Winzenried, *Symphony,* vol. 50, no. 4 (July/August 1999): 36.

20. Judith H. Dobrzynski, "Ford Devotes $40 Million More to Art," *New York Times,* May 3, 2000, p. B3.

21. Niall G. Caldwell, "The Emergence of Museum Brands," *International Journal of Arts Management,* vol. 2, no. 3 (2000): 28–34.

22. Adam Baer, "For Classical Music Lovers, the Internet Becomes a Concert Hall," *New York Times,* December 28, 2000, p. G7.

23. For example, the American Symphony Orchestra League brought out a handbook on dealing with visa, immigration, and payment issues concerning foreign artists. See Jonathan Ginsburg and Craig Etter, *Artists from Abroad: The Complete Guide to Immigration and Taxation Requirements for Foreign Guest Artists* (Washington: American Symphony Orchestra League, 2000).

24. Anna Kisselgoff, "The Joffrey Takes a Leap in a Battle for Survival," *New York Times,* March 22, 2000, pp. B1, B6.

25. Robin Pogrebin, "With Vast Cultural Projects Planned in New York, Can Donors Keep Up?" *New York Times,* January 30, 2001.

26. Jennifer Dunning, "Mark Morris Will Build Brooklyn Dance Center," *New York Times,* July 1, 1999, p. B5.

27. Salamon, *Holding the Center.*

28. Judith Humphreys Weitz, *Coming up Taller: Arts and Humanities Programs for Children and Youth at Risk* (Washington: President's Committee on the Arts and the Humanities with the National Assembly of Local Arts Agencies, 1996). Also Dian Magie and Christine E. Miller, eds., *Art Works: Prevention Programs for Youth and Communities* (Washington: National Endowment for the Arts with the Substance Abuse and Mental Health Services Administration, 1997).

29. American Association of Museums, *Excellence and Equity: Education and the Public Dimension of Museums* (Washington: American Association of Museums, 1992). Lisa Sharamitaro, *Policy Involvement through the Entire Policy Process: The American Association of Museums and the Case of the Native American Graves Protection and Repatriation Act,* Occasional Paper 14 (Ohio State University, Arts Policy and Administration Program, 2000). Also see "NAGPRA at 10: Examining a Decade of the Native American Graves Protection and Repatriation Act," *Museum News* (September/October 2000): 42–72.

30. American Association of Museums, *Excellence and Equity,* p. 8.

31. American Symphony Orchestra League, *Americanizing the American Orchestra: Report of the National Task Force for the American Orchestra: An Initiative for Change* (Washington: American Symphony Orchestra League, 1993).

32. American Symphony Orchestra League, *Americanizing the American Orchestra,* p. 37.

33. Gary O. Larson, *American Canvas* (Washington: National Endowment for the Arts, 1997), p. 13.

34. Larson, *American Canvas,* p. 57.

35. American Assembly, *Arts and the Public Purpose,* p. 11.

36. American Assembly, *Arts and the Public Purpose,* pp. 11–14.

37. Renz, Lawrence, and Kendzior, *Arts Funding 2000,* p. 30.

38. Renz, Lawrence, and Kendzior, *Arts Funding 2000,* p. 31.

39. Kelly Barsdate, *A State Arts Agency Performance Measurement Toolkit* (Washington: National Assembly of State Arts Agencies, 1996).

40. Joni M. Cherbo and Margaret J. Wyszomirski, "Mapping the Public Life of the Arts in America," in Joni M. Cherbo and Margaret J. Wyszomirski, eds., *The Public Life of the Arts in America* (Rutgers University Press, 2000), pp. 16–17.

41. Margaret Jane Wyszomirski, "The Arts and Performance Review, Policy Assessment, and Program Evaluation: Focussing on the Ends of the Policy Cycle," *Journal of Arts Management, Law, and Society,* vol. 28, no. 3 (1998): 192.

42. Renz, Lawrence, and Kendzior, *Arts Funding 2000,* pp. 29–30.

43. Barsdate, *A State Arts Agency Performance Measurement Toolkit.*

44. American Association of Museums, *1999 AAM Museum Financial Information: A Report from the National Survey* (Herndon, Va.: AWP Research, 2000), p. 37.

45. Michael S. Shapiro and Brett I. Miller, with an introduction by Christine Steiner, *A Museum Guide to Copyright and Trademark* (Washington: American Association of Museums, 1999).

46. Kelly Barsdate, Dan Martin, and Durand Pope, "Lessons from a Technology Survey of the Arts Community," paper presented at the conference Social Theory, Politics, and the Arts, Washington, October 2000.

47. Margaret Jane Wyszomirski, *Public Policy at the Intersection of the Arts, Technology, and Intellectual Property,* Occasional Paper 18, background paper prepared for the American Assembly art, technology, and intellectual property project (Ohio State University, Arts Policy and Administration Program, 2000).

48. Allan Kozin, "Classical Concerts and Audiences Seek an Audience on the Web," *New York Times,* June 13, 2000, pp. C1, C6.

49. Andrew Taylor, "Pandora's Bottle: Cultural Content in a Digital World," in Valerie B. Morris and David B. Pankratz, eds., *The Arts in a New Millennium: Research and the Arts Sector* (Greenwood Press, 2002).

50. Taylor, "Pandora's Bottle."

51. One example of this is the website for culturefinder.com, which started up in 1995, grew to a $5 million a year broker selling $3 million worth of tickets for thousands of performing arts organizations and events around the country. In effect, it became a one-stop shopping site and information provider for cultural consumers. However, even at this scale, culturefinder.com lost money and announced that it would attempt to transform itself into a nonprofit organization. See Bob Tedeschi, "E-Commerce Report: Losing Money, Culturefinder Hopes to Find Success in a Switch from dot.com to dot.org," *New York Times,* January 8, 2001, p. C10.

52. Andrew Taylor, "The Experience Brokers: The New Role for Arts Administrators in the Information Age," in *Looking Ahead: A Collection of Papers from the International Social Theory, Politics, and the Arts Conference* (Drexel University Press, 1999), pp. 66–71. See also B. Joseph Pine II and James H. Gilmore, *The Experience Economy: Work Is Theater and Every Business a Stage* (Harvard Business School, 1999).

53. American Association of Museums, *1999 AAM Museum Financial Information.*

54. American Association of Museums, *1999 AAM Museum Financial Information.*

55. This figure includes all museums, both publicly and privately run. In 1999, publicly run museums received 53 percent of their funding from government sources as compared to 16 percent for privately run museums. Conversely, privately run museums earned twice as much income as public museums (35 and 17 percent, respectively). See American Association of Museums, *1999 AAM Museum Financial Information,* p. 48.

56. American Association of Museums, *1999 AAM Museum Financial Information,* p. 62.

57. American Association of Museums, *Museums Count: A Report by the American Association of Museums* (Washington: American Association of Museums, 1994); American Association of Museums, *1999 AAM Museum Financial Information.*

58. National Endowment for the Arts, *Survey of Public Participation in the Arts: Summary Report* (Washington: National Endowment for the Arts, 1998).

59. American Association of Museums, *1999 AAM Museum Financial Information.*

60. Celestine Bohlen, "Museums Accept Proposal on Looted Arts," *New York Times*, April 13, 2000, pp. B1, B8. See also Judith H. Dobrzynski, "Museums Identify Art with Murky Pasts," *New York Times*, April 13, 2000, pp. B1, B3.

61. Dobrzynski, "Museums Identify Art with Murky Pasts."

62. Gresham Riley and Stephen Urice, "Art Museum Directors: A Shrinking Pool?" *Museum News,* vol. 75 (May/June 1996): 48–49, 64.

63. Steven Weil, "Museums in the United States: The Paradox of Privately Governed Public Institutions," *Museum Management and Curatorship,* vol. 15, no. 3 (1997): 249–57.

64. Opera America, *1998 Annual Field Report* (Washington: Opera America, 2000).

65. National Endowment for the Arts, *Survey of Public Participation in the Arts*, p. 48.

66. Opera America, *1998 Annual Field Report,* p. 9.

67. Opera America, *1998 Annual Field Report.*

68. Opera America, *1998 Annual Field Report.*

69. National Endowment for the Arts, *Survey of Public Participation in the Arts.*

70. Patrick Giles, "The Gap: Has Generation X Lost Its Way to the Opera?" *Opera News* (February 2000): 29–31.

71. National Endowment for the Arts, *Survey of Public Participation in the Arts*, p. 29.

72. Opera America, *1998 Annual Field Report,* p. 33.

73. Zannie Giraud Voss and Glenn B. Voss, with Christopher Shuff and Collette Carter, *Theater Facts 1999: A Report on Practices and Performance in the American Nonprofit Theater Based on TCG's Annual Fiscal Survey* (New York: Theatre Communications Group, 1999).

74. See AACT's website (www.aact.org [August 22, 2002]).

75. Voss and Voss, *Theater Facts 1999.*

76. National Endowment for the Arts, *Survey of Public Participation in the Arts.*

77. Voss and Voss, *Theater Facts 1999.*

78. Ben Cameron, "Broadway: Devil or Angel for Nonprofit Theater?" *New York Times*, June 4, 2000, p. 10.

79. Cameron, "Broadway."

80. Renz, Lawrence, and Kendzior, *Arts Funding 2000.*

81. Celia O'Donnell, interview with the author, Columbus, Ohio, January 2001. O'Donnell is the former executive director of the Council of Literary Presses and Magazines.

82. Cobb, *Looking Ahead*, p. 21.

83. Stanley N. Katz, "Rethinking the Humanities Endowment," *Chronicle of Higher Education,* January 5, 2001, pp. B7–B10.

84. Katz, "Rethinking the Humanities Endowment."

6

Housing and Community Development

AVIS C. VIDAL

The field of housing and community development is one in which nonprofit involvement recently has exhibited some of its most extraordinary
growth and also some of its most extraordinary creativity. Starting from virtually
nowhere thirty years ago, nonprofit organizations have established a significant
beachhead in the government-assisted portion of the American housing market.
A large part of this success can be attributed to the emergence of a unique network of nonprofit intermediary organizations that have found inventive ways to
attract private for-profit and philanthropic investment dollars into low-income
housing. In addition, nonprofit organizations contribute in a variety of other
ways to improving the living environments and economic opportunities in some
of the most distressed communities of our nation.

Impressive as the growth of nonprofit involvement in the housing and community development field has been, it also demonstrates the limits of nonprofit
action. The nonprofit achievements in this field would not have been possible
without the significant expansion that occurred in federal funding, which made
the production of affordable housing for low-income individuals and families
feasible. Although such subsidies have grown substantially over the past twenty
years, they still reach only 20 percent of the families eligible for them. Moreover,
since the supply of unsubsidized low-cost dwellings is diminishing, nonprofit
housing organizations are fighting a losing battle as the quantity of low-cost
housing they can supply falls farther behind the quantity that is needed. What is

more, the specialized skills required to develop and manage assisted housing developments make these nonprofits hard organizations to staff and put them constantly at risk of becoming alienated from the communities they are seeking to serve. For all its successes, therefore, nonprofit involvement in the housing field has had its frustrations as well.

This chapter seeks to tell this story by providing an overview of the role of nonprofits in the housing and community development field, by identifying some of the major trends in the field, and by examining how nonprofit agencies are coping with these trends and what further responses seem needed.

Role of Nonprofits in Housing and Community Development

"Housing and community development" is not a single field. Rather, "housing" and "community development" each encompasses a broad set of activities that partly overlap. This section profiles each in turn and then builds on that foundation to examine the role of nonprofits.

Structure of Housing Development and Management

Housing development and management is a large industry in which nonprofit organizations occupy a relatively small niche. This industry is commonly stratified along three basic dimensions. The most familiar ones are ownership status (owner-occupied versus rental) and type of structure (for example, single-family, duplex, multifamily). The dimension most important for the discussion here is subsidy status: that is, whether housing is market rate, public, or assisted.

Market-rate housing predominates in the United States. It is housing that households either purchase or rent at prices determined in the marketplace. Most of it is built by for-profit developers and then purchased and managed by owner-occupant households.[1] Large development companies produce most of the units built, but many of the producers are small. Private developers build a smaller amount of market-rate rental housing as well, sometimes to hold and manage as an investment, but more often to sell to for-profit investors or managers.

For-profit owners of rental property also provide housing for low- and moderate-income households who either (a) can afford market-rate housing because they receive federal housing subsidies or (b) cannot afford it (according to federal guidelines) and therefore must cope with some combination of high rent, overcrowding, and low-quality housing or neighborhood.[2] Since housing subsidies are available to only about 20 percent of the households that are income-eligible for them, many low- and moderate-income renter households fall into the second category. Unfortunately, this group is growing because the number of private, low-cost units removed from the housing inventory each year exceeds the number of new assisted units produced.[3] This means that most low-income households live in market-rate housing, albeit at relatively high rents or of poor quality.

Federal housing policy has responded to the nation's evolving housing problems in numerous ways over the years, starting in 1937 with the passage of legislation providing for the creation of public housing.[4] The construction and operation of public housing are subsidized by the federal government, but the housing is owned and operated by local (and occasionally state) public housing authorities. Although the earliest public housing developments were built to house working- and middle-class families hard-hit by the great depression, public housing has increasingly become the "housing of last resort." Some developments, built as elderly housing, now are home to low-income individuals with disabilities as well as to poor senior citizens. Others, called family developments, are open to all low-income households but are occupied primarily by very low-income, single-parent families.

Much public housing, especially the elderly housing and the family housing located in mid-size and smaller cities and towns, is decent and well maintained. However, the conspicuous physical and social deterioration of some large-scale family developments in large cities (often owned by troubled public housing authorities) has stigmatized this entire segment of the assisted housing market. Public housing authorities have had limited funds to construct new units since 1980 (and no such funds since 1995), although they have continued to receive federal support to modernize some severely deteriorated developments.

Since the end of World War II, a changing menu of other programs has provided public subsidies for the production or rental of privately held housing for low- and moderate-income persons. The federal government has provided the lion's share of such housing subsidy dollars.[5] Some of these programs have been available to both for-profit and nonprofit developers; others have been open to (or specifically designed for) one or the other exclusively. Some have supported production of rental housing; others have subsidized production of owner-occupied units. Some have targeted particular population groups, such as the elderly, homeless and formerly homeless individuals, or families and persons with physical or mental disabilities. Most of the early programs were supply-side programs that made resources available to housing producers in order to allow them to construct housing that could be occupied by low-income or special-needs persons. More recently, the federal government has adopted a demand-side approach that makes resources available to housing consumers. The chief program of this sort is the Section 8 lower-income rental assistance program, which provides certificates or vouchers that tenants can use to pay for rental housing of their own choice, provided it meets basic standards.[6]

In addition to the direct subsidy programs, several generations of the federal income tax code have provided incentives to stimulate development of low-cost rental housing. The current incentive is the low-income housing tax credit (LIHTC), which allocates tax credits to the states, which in turn allocate them to eligible housing developments. Typically, these credits are syndicated and purchased by private corporations, which use the credits to reduce their federal tax liability. The funds they pay in become the equity financing for the developments—a critical contribution since nonprofits (unlike their private for-profit counterparts) typically lack equity capital. This equity reduces the amount of debt the projects must carry and allows some units to be offered at rents that are below market rate, making them affordable for low- or moderate-income individuals and families.

In addition to the existing programs, federal housing policy also reflects the residual effects of a number of programs that have been phased out. Especially notable in this regard are the Section 236 and Section 8 new construction and substantial rehabilitation programs, all of which subsidized development of substantial inventories of affordable multifamily rental housing.[7] Nonprofits participated actively in these programs, and both for-profit and nonprofit organizations currently own and operate sizable stocks of this housing. The subsidy period has ended for the oldest of these developments, and the subsidies on significant numbers of them will expire over the coming years. When the subsidies expire, the projects' owners face the choice of trying to renew their subsidies or converting the developments to market-rate housing. Nonprofit owners are committed to keeping these units affordable (although a dependable source of the required subsidy dollars has not been identified); for-profit owners face mixed incentives, depending on the strength of the housing market in which their developments are located. Often called expiring-use properties, these apartment complexes constitute a major source of assisted housing that is at risk of being removed from the stock of affordable housing over the coming years. Carving out a role in preserving the affordability of these units is both an opportunity and a challenge for nonprofit developers—a topic discussed further below.

Structure of Community Development

While housing is fairly concrete, community development is more nebulous. It essentially concerns the broader community context within which housing operates. As one observor has put it, "Community development is asset building that improves the quality of life among residents of low- to moderate-income communities, where communities are defined as neighborhoods or multi-neighborhood areas."[8] Assets may take various forms—physical, human, intellectual, social, financial, and political. Assets generate a stream of benefits over time. For example, education and training improve an individual's ability to engage in productive work and to earn income; physical infrastructure improvements (streets, sidewalks, lighting) encourage homeowners to invest in their properties. Community assets provide benefits for members of the community. Thus a new park provides opportunities for recreation, exercise, and socializing and also produces aesthetic benefits. An active civic association may give neighborhood residents good access to their local city council member. In this sense, housing development is one aspect of community development, since housing is one of the many types of assets commonly found in neighborhoods.

Over at least the past four decades, private investors have typically avoided making new investments and maintaining existing assets in many low- and moderate-income neighborhoods. For example, manufacturing and retail facilities have shifted from central cities to suburbs. Individual households and entrepreneurs wanting to invest in lower-income communities, especially in minority neighborhoods, have consistently had greater difficulty gaining access to credit (such as mortgages to purchase homes) than individuals investing in other types of neighborhoods. In many lower-income communities, public sector investments—in streets and sidewalks, schools, and other public amenities—have not kept pace with the deterioration that comes with use. Hence the value of these assets—their ability to produce good services—has declined. This has made community development as important a part of the improvement of living conditions as the development of physical housing itself.

Role of Nonprofits in the Field

Nonprofit organizations are actively involved in both housing and community development, although their relative position in community development is clearly more dominant.

In the housing field, nonprofit providers focus almost exclusively on producing assisted housing. They are the only sponsors eligible for the Section 202 (elderly housing) program, which is now relatively small (6,000–8,000 units a year in recent years). They receive the vast majority of the funds available for housing and services for homeless persons and others with special needs. Nonprofit-sponsored developments make extensive use of the community development block grant program, which makes federal funds available to local communities for general community improvement; of the HOME program, which delivers federal support to state and local governments for affordable housing; and of the LIHTCs. For the latter two programs, in fact, nonprofit providers enjoy set-asides (15 percent of HOME funds and 10 percent of LIHTC funds).

Three types of nonprofit organizations are involved in housing development and management. The first and most numerous are community development corporations (CDCs), which are community-based organizations that emerged out of the war on poverty of the 1960s. CDCs tend to focus on a spatially defined target area, such as one or more urban neighborhoods or a cluster of rural counties, although some define their mission primarily in terms of a target population, such as Latinos. Housing is an important activity for the vast majority of these organizations, but most also engage in a variety of other community development activities, especially community economic development. Community economic development can include developing commercial and industrial real estate, providing loans and technical assistance to businesses, operating community development financial institutions, managing Small Business Administration and other revolving loan funds, sponsoring individual development accounts, and operating microenterprise loan funds. Other common community development activities include community organizing, advocacy, and general community improvement. Many CDCs also engage in workforce development and selected social service activities.

In addition to the CDCs, various area-wide nonprofit housing providers either operate across a significantly larger area (hence the label) or do not target their activities geographically. Some, such as the Metropolitan Boston Housing Partnership, work in many locations throughout a city or metropolitan region. Others, such as BRIDGE in California or Mercy Housing, work statewide or across the country. About sixty of the largest area-wide providers (including some that are not structured as partnerships) are now members of the Housing Partnership Network. In addition, a number of large faith-based groups, such as Catholic Charities and B'nai B'rith, while not specializing in housing, nevertheless have built substantial numbers of dwellings.

The area-wide nonprofit developers generally specialize strictly in housing and operate at a much larger scale of production than the CDCs. No systematic scan of their characteristics and operation has been done, although a few case studies of them exist. Nevertheless, they clearly are significant producers; for example, BRIDGE has built more than 8,500 units, Mercy Housing has built more than 10,000, and organizations affiliated with the Roman Catholic Church have built more than 50,000. Because of their scale and specialization, they are probably more efficient producers than many of the CDCs, and collectively they may have produced more housing units. Like the CDCs, their scale of operations has gradually been increasing in recent years.

The third broad group of nonprofit organizations operating in the housing development field is the nonprofit financial intermediaries: a small set of national and local nonprofits, umbrella organizations, and public-private partnerships that support the work of the CDCs and similar nonprofits, but that generally do not themselves develop or operate housing. The best-known intermediaries are the Local Initiatives Support Corporation (LISC) and the Enterprise Foundation, both of which work nationally. But the field also includes some more specialized national intermediaries and numerous local ones as well, often affiliated with one of the national entities. The intermediaries are one of the most distinctive features of the nonprofit housing and community development world. Their creation at the start of the 1980s effectively triggered the dramatic expansion in the number and productivity of CDCs over the subsequent two decades. Indeed, they provide a model that might be replicated or adapted in other fields.

Although assisted housing predominates in the nonprofit sector, the sector's share of that type of housing is modest. Walker estimates that over the past thirty-five years nonprofits have developed about 14 percent of the housing built or preserved with federal support, with the balance produced by for-profit developers.[9] Since assisted housing units are a relatively modest portion of the nation's overall housing, nonprofits are responsible for less than 2 percent of the nation's housing stock, despite the dramatic growth of the past two decades.

Nonprofit organizations also play a variety of roles in the housing field that go beyond housing development. In these roles, they both facilitate the creation of housing and support the preservation of existing housing assets. Such roles include the following:

—*Housing renovation and improvement.* Most notably, a national network of local neighborhood housing services organizations has renovated or financed the renovation or repair of more than 320,000 housing units since 1979.

—*Housing counseling.* CDCs, neighborhood housing services organizations, and other types of nonprofits provide housing counseling services to individuals seeking to become first-time homebuyers.

—*Provision of special-needs housing.* Some nonprofits provide temporary shelter and related services to homeless individuals and families. Others provide longer-term housing for other special-needs groups, for example, service-rich transitional housing for formerly homeless households or permanent housing for mentally disabled adults and their families.

—*Housing ownership and management.* In addition to the management that nonprofit developers do of their own units, some groups, such as the NHP Foundation nationally and Phipps Houses in New York City, specialize in managing low-cost rental housing developed by others (either nonprofit or for-profit).

—*Housing trusts and land trusts.* These organizations seek to acquire and hold housing in perpetuity for low- and moderate-income use.

—*Resident councils, mutual housing associations, and condominium associations.* These groups are concerned with project livability once housing is developed and, unlike the other types of organizations, can serve households at all levels of income.

Most CDCs and some of the other types of nonprofits that support the housing sector are also active in other aspects of community development. Among the CDCs, these activities include the development of commercial real estate and provision of support for private business development. In addition, going back to the settlement houses of the early twentieth century, community-based organizations have engaged in strengthening other types of community assets; they include the following:

—*Community organizing groups* that mobilize residents to build social relationships and cultivate political clout aimed at improving the community;

—*Community and neighborhood associations* (like the resident councils and others noted above) that protect community interests, for example, by fighting for proper zoning or safer streets;

—*Community development financial institutions*, specialized financing institutions that provide various forms of financing and banking services for businesses, real estate developers, and individuals (approximately 400 community development financial institutions have been certified nationally); and

—*Educational and workforce development organizations* that help residents in low-income communities to develop their human capital via activities that range from after-school tutoring for children to job training for adults.

Distinguishing Features of Nonprofit Involvement in the Field

Four central features distinguish the nonprofit producers of housing, particularly the CDCs, from their for-profit counterparts in the housing field. The first and most significant is that the CDCs generally engage in a range of community development activities that extend well beyond housing, whereas for-profit housing developers tend to specialize in housing alone. Thus for-profit developers deal with neighborhood influences by building in the best locations where they can identify development opportunities and by building at a large enough scale to create the type of neighborhood they seek to market. If they build rental housing, they typically limit their attention to maintaining their own properties. In contrast, CDCs commonly serve communities plagued by disinvestment. Housing development is, for them, part of a broader community development agenda. They tend to take a broad view of "community" and to be concerned about the full spectrum of community issues and needs. This inclination is reinforced by their organizational investments in housing, which create an incentive for them to be concerned about the behavior of residents and conditions in the surrounding neighborhood.

Second, the CDCs typically define their mission in terms of a geographic service area; in cities, a service area is commonly one or more neighborhoods. This has two effects. One is that it limits their development opportunities to those available within their target area. Although few CDCs have literally "run out" of housing development opportunities, this constraint often makes it more difficult (sometimes impossible) for them to develop at a large enough scale to maximize their economic efficiency. This is especially an issue in neighborhoods where infill housing is a priority.[10] The other effect is that focusing on a target area can also make CDC-sponsored developments more financially vulnerable than projects built by more mobile developers. LIHTC projects commonly require their owners to identify tenants with household incomes that fall within a fairly narrow range (say, a $2,000–$3,000 window) because the program puts a ceiling on income eligibility, and the limited subsidy available puts a floor on the income of households who can afford the rents. In some housing markets, households with incomes within the eligible income range can find better housing options in neighborhoods outside those that many CDCs serve. This makes some LIHTC developments in these markets vulnerable to higher than normal vacancy rates.

Third, the CDCs are typically smaller and less well capitalized than either the area-wide nonprofits or their for-profit counterparts. Most are highly vulnerable to the loss of key senior staff and have limited financial reserves either to respond to opportunities (for example, to acquire key properties when they become available) or to weather adversity. Developing at small scale, as many do, exacerbates this problem. In contrast, the area-wide producers are generally very sophisticated developers. Compared to the CDCs, they are larger, take on larger developments, and produce at higher levels. This makes them more likely to realize economies of scale and to have portfolios of rental properties that are large enough to manage efficiently. Because they are willing to build anywhere in the region, they are better positioned than the CDCs to build assisted housing in "hot" markets and attractive neighborhoods. This also means that they can better support the deconcentration of poor households outside of high-poverty neighborhoods. They generally do not complement their housing work with other community development activities.

Finally, nonprofit developers typically find themselves involved in much more complex financial arrangements than do for-profit housing developers. This is because the nonprofits seek to serve the lowest-income households, but no single existing public sector housing subsidy program provides deep enough assistance to make housing affordable for those families. As a result, nonprofits must resort to "patchwork financing" that layers as many sources of subsidy as possible into a single financing package in order to reduce rents.

In addition to being different from public and for-profit housing providers, nonprofit housing groups are also different from nonprofits in other fields in interesting ways. Perhaps the most unusual is the extent to which the nonprofits' role interacts with the operation of the market. In seriously disinvested neighborhoods, one of the CDCs' goals is to get the for-profit and public sectors to do their jobs better. Vis-à-vis the private sector, the challenge is to use sustained, strategic investments in housing and other community assets to recreate viable housing markets that will attract renewed flows of private investment. Accomplishing this requires significant, strategically placed investments in housing sustained over a period of years. In neighborhoods with very high concentrations of poverty, it sometimes requires the production of housing for moderate-income homeowners to give the neighborhood more economic diversity and strengthen its political influence. Corollary activities to strengthen neighborhood shopping districts, to encourage investments in public infrastructure (for example, streetscaping and parks), to improve safety, or to organize residents are also required. Conversely, in strong housing markets, such as neighborhoods experiencing gentrification pressure, the nonprofit role shifts to retaining as much affordable housing as possible, especially affordable homeownership opportunities, so that low-income residents are not forced out of the community as new investments make it a more desirable place to live.

A second distinguishing feature of nonprofit engagement in housing and community development as compared to other spheres of nonprofit activity is the success that has been achieved in addressing the financial challenges that pose such a serious obstacle to nonprofit activity in many other fields. This success has been strongly driven by the intermediary organizations mentioned earlier. The intermediaries' success stems from their ability to meet the particular needs of both the CDCs and their private financial supporters. The CDCs typically work in weak markets where property values and resident incomes cannot support market-rate debt. This makes their projects financially riskier than conventional developments. The intermediaries have established expertise and a track record in assessing risk and in structuring financial packages that both minimize risk and spread unavoidable risk across a sizable group of investors. They package philanthropic support (from both foundations and corporations), below-market-rate loans, and tax-induced corporate equity investments (syndicated via the LIHTC), and they make the proceeds available on a "retail" basis to CDCs and, to a lesser degree, other nonprofit developers. The intermediaries' demonstrated success in facilitating tangible improvements in poor communities while achieving repayment rates that rival those in conventional banking has made them attractive conduits for philanthropic and corporate support, especially from the nation's major banks and insurance companies. In essence, the intermediaries make it possible for funders who know little about assisted housing production or community development to support them effectively. In addition, the national intermediaries have made significant contributions to cultivating local funding partnerships and programs. For their part, the CDCs benefit from a much larger flow of funds into the industry.

Nonprofits in the housing field have also made important headway in resolving one of the other perennial challenges facing nonprofit organizations: training personnel and improving basic management systems. An important vehicle for this has been the National Community Development Initiative (NCDI) established in 1991. This unusual collaboration, which includes about a dozen national foundations, corporations, and the U.S. Department of Housing and Urban Development, has provided more than $250 million over ten years to support CDCs and their work. Although originally intended to sunset in 2001, this collaboration was extended at the initiative of the funders and transformed into a new nonprofit corporation. NCDI makes flexible dollars (channeled through LISC and the Enterprise Foundation) available to local intermediaries and partnerships to strengthen systems of local nonprofit housing production. It is currently active in twenty-three cities across the country. The use of NCDI funds is tailored to the needs of individual localities, but common uses include creating and supporting CDC capacity-building programs, providing general operating support, and developing new CDC-sponsored programs.

Factors Shaping the Position of Nonprofits in the Housing Field

The past two decades have been a period of enormous growth for nonprofit organizations in the housing and community development field. The number of CDCs has increased dramatically since 1980, and these organizations are gradually becoming larger and stronger. The same appears to be true of the area-wide nonprofit housing developers. Most standard indicators of the sector's health tell a consistent story—numbers of organizations (estimated to be about 3,600 CDCs in 1998 versus about 2,200 in 1987),[11] average staff size, average budget, number of housing units produced, public visibility, number of financial supporters, number and strength of local partners, and political influence have all increased, with growth coming especially rapidly during the 1990s.[12]

Nonprofit intermediaries, public-private partnerships, training and technical assistance organizations, and others that support the work of the CDCs have also blossomed during this period. The field has been self-conscious, especially in localities with numerous CDCs, about building human capital (for example, through training and improved benefit packages) and about building organizational capacity; localities where capacity-building programs are in place have seen steady improvements among the groups assisted.

The field's remarkable growth has been possible only because of significant expansion of the funding base. The central role of the national intermediaries in this regard has already been discussed. Their technical expertise enables them to offer funders both accountability and quality control, and the fact that the community groups they support produce (among other things) tangible products has been very attractive to banks and corporate contributors. NCDI provided another large-scale vehicle that attracted new private philanthropies to the field and encouraged the Department of Housing and Urban Development to increase its support for CDC-sponsored efforts. Stronger federal enforcement of the Community Reinvestment Act, which obliges financial institutions to devote a meaningful proportion of their lending to low-income neighborhoods, has made participation in nonprofit-sponsored developments, concentrated as they are in low-income neighborhoods and communities of color, more attractive to banks. It has also made it easier for low- and moderate-income households and entrepreneurs to access private financing. The institution of the low-income housing tax credit has facilitated the flow of corporate equity into assisted housing. Passage of the Stewart B. McKinney Homeless Assistance Act in 1987 and of the federal HOME program in 1992 increased the flow of subsidy dollars available for the production of assisted housing.

Despite this generally positive recent history, however, nonprofit organizations in the housing and community development field are confronting a number of important challenges. Six of these in particular deserve mention here.

Economic and Demographic Challenges

In the first place, nonprofit housing providers are affected by the broader economic and demographic trends shaping the cities and regions in which they operate, and these trends have complicated their work. For example, economic growth in the 1990s strengthened overall demand for housing in many urban markets. This made the development of assisted housing more costly by increasing the price of land and of housing suitable for rehabilitation. At the same time, increasing income inequality and the inability of poor unsubsidized households to afford market prices induced private owners to maintain low-cost units poorly or convert them to more profitable use. The results were a sustained loss of low-cost units from the national stock of housing and a heightened housing affordability crisis for low-income households despite the sustained production of nonprofit housing over the past two decades. That a growing proportion of the urban poor, particularly poor people of color, live in communities where poor people are highly concentrated complicates the problem further.

Also affecting the work of nonprofit housing organizations has been the increased flow of immigrants into American cities. As a consequence, nonprofits engaged in housing and community development face the challenges of providing housing, and sometimes a variety of other programs and services, to groups whose cultures and languages are unfamiliar. Many immigrants arrive with extremely limited resources, yet are often ineligible for the public subsidy and service programs that nonprofits rely on. Communication problems, differences in cultural norms (for example, about the use of residential space), and the newcomers' need for services that the nonprofit may not have provided previously all complicate the task further. This is particularly difficult in communities where tension develops between immigrant groups and the nonprofits' traditional constituents.

Growth of For-Profit Competition

A second challenge facing nonprofits in the housing field is the growth of competition from for-profit developers. Such competition has historically not been an issue in this field since nonprofits entered the field of housing and community development precisely because the market was not providing the housing and other amenities that poor communities needed. This has changed in at least two respects in recent years.

First, nonprofits have increasingly had to compete with private developers for LIHTCs. Congress initially authorized LIHTCs in 1986 as a temporary measure. Because the credits were temporary, for-profit developers were not willing to invest the time needed to learn how to use them. This changed in 1993, when Congress made the credits a permanent part of the tax code. Since then, private sector developers have become more interested in, and proficient at, using LIHTCs. Competition for the credits has intensified (since each state has a fixed supply to allocate each year). In states where demand for the credits is strong, the uncertainty about whether projects will go forward poses growing difficulties for nonprofit developers.

Second, the strong economy of the 1990s drove up housing prices in many cities and put pressure on neighborhoods once viewed as undesirable. In a growing number of communities, this forced nonprofits to compete with for-profits for development opportunities, driving up the costs and making low-income projects financially infeasible. As they became priced out of opportunities in their neighborhoods, nonprofits had to switch gears—for example, they had to help local families purchase homes so they could capitalize on rising prices and neighborhood improvements rather than be priced out as rents rose, to seek joint ventures with for-profit developers (either to improve local retailing or to build some affordable units into new market-rate housing developments in the community), or to broaden their initial target area.

Shifts in Public Policy

A third challenge confronting nonprofit organizations in the housing field has been caused by shifts in public policy. Starting in the early 1980s, federal policy began a dramatic shift from an emphasis on supply-side subsidies (supporting housing production) to demand-side subsidies (in the form of Section 8 vouchers and certificates). While potentially advantageous to the households that receive them, demand-side subsidies make life considerably more difficult for nonprofit developers. This is so because their developments become more vulnerable financially, since they must either attract and serve eligible moderate-income families or compete for the very limited supply of low-income certificate-holding households. This problem particularly affects nonprofits that work in relatively soft housing markets where vacancies in privately owned developments are plentiful.

Similar problems have arisen from the increased reliance on the LIHTCs. Affordable housing advocates, including nonprofit housing producers, fought hard in the early 1990s to make the LIHTC a permanent part of the tax code because, in the political climate at that time, it seemed highly unlikely that a better production subsidy mechanism would be achievable. Nevertheless, from the nonprofits' perspective, the LIHTC has its shortcomings. Chief among these is the fact that it provides a relatively shallow (that is, small) subsidy. Even when other sources of subsidy (such as community development block grants) are added to the financing package, LIHTC developments are not affordable to those households in greatest need. In addition, because the financing of these developments is complex, especially with other subsidies layered in, nonprofit developers and managers have had to become quite sophisticated technically. This requirement both limits the number of organizations that can become effective producers and makes it far more difficult for community members to exercise effective control over these supposedly community-based organizations.

On the plus side, steady funding of the HOME program, which provides flexible block grants to states and localities and encourages local government reliance on CDCs (called community housing development organizations, or CHDOs, in federal parlance), was very important in supporting the growth of the nonprofit housing sector during the 1990s. (However, the matching requirements have limited its use in some places, and the total amount of subsidy available still falls far short of meeting the federally defined housing needs of poor households.) Similarly, the 15 percent set-aside for nonprofit sponsors under this program has provided a very public vote of confidence for nonprofit providers as well as assuring nonprofit participation in these programs even in environments where competition for the subsidies is strong.

Funding Challenges

Notwithstanding the substantial growth of federal funding for low-income housing that occurred in the 1990s, nonprofit housing and community development organizations continue to confront significant funding challenges. These challenges arise on two fronts: first, the funding of actual housing projects and, second, the funding of the operational costs of the nonprofit agencies that help to develop the housing and assist with related community development tasks.

As far as project funding is concerned, sustaining the flow of federal housing subsidy dollars is the critical task. Absent those dollars, affordable housing production is not feasible since states and localities do not see the provision of affordable housing as their responsibility, corporate participation in assisted housing flows primarily through the federal LIHTC, and even at its height philanthropic support for housing development did not begin to make up for lost Section 8 new construction and substantial rehabilitation subsidy dollars.

Federal support for housing programs at a level that sustained the nonprofit role was not a problem in the middle to late 1990s, characterized as it was by sustained economic growth and budget surpluses. The most recent disputed issue was the need to increase the availability of LIHTCs to counteract the effect of inflation, and that was done. But with the reappearance of budget deficits in the aftermath of September 11 and the Bush administration tax cuts, the prospects for continued funding of low-income housing have become more problematic. More fundamentally, while the current level of federal support can sustain the nonprofit development sector at its current scale, it does not provide for renewed subsidies for expiring-use properties and does not even come close to enabling nonprofits to provide for all households with acute housing afford-ability problems.

The issue of operating support is much more challenging. In some localities, local intermediaries or public-private partnerships provide CDCs with some core operating support, often in exchange for the CDCs' increasing their organiza-tional capacity in some agreed-upon way or meeting other kinds of performance benchmarks. Some local governments use part of their community development block grant allocations for this purpose. On the whole, however, raising operat-ing support is an ongoing struggle for many groups, and the typical CDC remains small and undercapitalized. Some try to address the problem by develop-ing at a large enough scale to permit development fees to cover (or at least make a substantial contribution to) operating costs. This carries its own risks, however, since the loss of a single development (for example, because an LIHTC allocation is not obtained in a timely way) can threaten the organization's viability. Further, not all jurisdictions allow nonprofit builders a fee adequate to make this possible, and most CDCs (as opposed to the area-wide producers) cannot operate at this large a scale. Starting in the mid-1980s, philanthropic support for community development increased considerably—another factor supporting the rapid expan-sion in the number and size of organizations in the sector. Currently, spokesper-sons for the field have begun to voice concern that community development as practiced by the CDCs is no longer "the flavor of the month" and is at risk of los-ing essential foundation support to more fashionable causes, most notably com-prehensive community initiatives and so-called smart growth efforts.

Organizational and Management Challenges

The relatively limited funding available for the core operations of nonprofit housing organizations has, in turn, contributed to a number of organizational and management problems, three of which deserve special mention.

The first is attracting, developing, and retaining quality leadership and tech-nical talent. Although their size and capacity remain uneven, the typical CDC is still small, undercapitalized, and heavily reliant on a small number of key indi-viduals. Although they place substantial demands on staff, nonprofit housing agencies commonly offer comparatively low salaries, uncompetitive benefit packages, and limited opportunity for advancement. Major national founda-tions and national intermediaries and training organizations have made efforts to respond to this problem by conducting a national survey of CDC personnel and establishing a joint purchasing arrangement for the most important benefits identified. In addition, the same funders established the Human Capacity Development Initiative (a counterpart to the previously discussed National Community Development Initiative) to address staff development needs and create a career ladder in twenty-three cities.

Despite these self-conscious efforts to build human capital in nonprofit housing and community development organizations, the issue remains of concern for two reasons. First, the field is a victim of its own success: exponential growth generates an enormous demand for fresh talent—especially people of color—yet the pool of such people is highly restricted. Second, the technical skills required to develop and manage affordable housing are highly marketable. Unlike the case in other parts of the nonprofit sector, moreover, wage rates in the for-profit side of the industries in which nonprofits are involved—for-profit real estate and finance—can be very lucrative, creating a steady need to replenish the ranks of the nonprofit providers.

The expansion of the nonprofit housing and community development field has also created a need for broader organizational development assistance that goes beyond staff development. As nonprofits take on progressively more ambitious projects and activities, they both grow in size and become more complex internally. This creates the need for new financial management and reporting systems, client-tracking systems, more elaborate personnel policies, board development efforts, and similar organizational development activities. Such activities become all the more urgent as organizations take on new functions, as commonly occurs when a nonprofit developer builds rental housing that must then be managed.

Finally, nonprofit housing and community development organizations are under pressure to respond to these personnel and internal organizational challenges while maintaining their community roots and developing community leadership. This is the principal source of the CDCs' legitimacy in speaking for their neighborhoods, but many CDCs experience a tension between the desire to involve residents and the technical nature of housing development and management work. This work simply does not lend itself to resident participation and requires a different set of personal and professional staff skills than those that lead to success in initiating and managing group processes. Further, the financial aspects of the work are very complex, which increases the difficulty of enabling resident board members to "hold their own" in policymaking and decisionmaking conversations concerning the organization's investment decisions. This challenge is amplified by the fact that tenant and community organizing—the stock-in-trade method of stimulating and sustaining resident involvement and training new community leadership—are activities that many funders, both public and private, are reluctant to support.

Changes in Public Attitudes

A final challenge confronting nonprofit housing and community development organizations is the need to gain public recognition. In most places, CDCs and other nonprofit housing organizations are not on the general public's radar screen. Aside from a relatively brief period during the second half of the 1980s, when a sudden increase in homelessness—visible for the first time among families, not just single men—made this a high-profile national issue, affordable housing (like urban policy more generally) has not been a prominent focus of national attention. What is more, in the aftermath of the September 11 events, such domestic issues have been pushed even farther down the national list of priorities. Although the sector has worked hard at getting the word out and has become better known and more highly regarded as its numbers and accomplishments have grown, it remains one of the great untold tales of nonprofit inventiveness.

Future Directions and Next Steps

Against the backdrop of the substantial growth of the late 1980s and 1990s, the nonprofit housing and community development sector faces some important choices. On the one hand, the prospects for continued rapid growth appear dim. The return of budget deficits and alternative national priorities make this highly unlikely, although the organizations could continue to expand their partnerships with private corporate sponsors. On the other hand, however, three alternative lines of development are possible.

Beyond Housing

In the first place, while the production of affordable housing and the provision of related housing services remain critical, there is broad interest in developing systematic capacity to deal with community improvement in a more integrated, multifaceted way. CDCs have always thought about community development comprehensively and have taken up a variety of activities when they encountered opportunities. In cities with real depth of community development—that is, numbers of capable CDCs and well-developed systems of support for them— the national and local intermediaries have been working for a number of years to craft systems of support for a CDC agenda "beyond housing" (parallel to those being built to support housing). Prime targets of opportunity for this expanded agenda include greater involvement by the CDCs in (a) economic development (commercial development, support for small business development, workforce preparation) and (b) community-building activities (neighborhood planning and advocacy, community organizing, provision of community and childcare facilities).[13] Foundations, too, have increasingly become interested in this possibility, seeing the CDCs as community agents with demonstrated capacity in neighborhoods where such agents are sometimes in short supply. In addition, numerous foundations have undertaken intensive community improvement efforts in targeted communities—commonly called comprehensive community initiatives—that both strengthen existing community-based organizations and create new ones to pursue and support multifaceted community development. The upshot is the possibility of an expanded role for nonprofit housing agencies.

How such a strategy would play out will doubtless vary from place to place. In some places, CDCs will become more diversified, adding service functions to their developmental ones. In others, they could play a broker or intermediary role that identifies and works with other types of organizations that have experience providing the community benefits the CDC neighborhood needs.

Regardless of the approach, this expansion is likely to proceed at a measured pace. Funders are well aware that many CDCs remain small and financially fragile, and they want to guard against pressing them to become overextended. In addition, the new activities will be more difficult to support financially than housing, and they will require CDCs to acquire new skills and operating styles, most notably the ability to collaborate with organizations that have expertise in different fields, such as childcare.

Expiring-Use Property Management

Another prospective opportunity concerns the problem of expiring-use properties—that is, rental developments built under previous federal production programs whose owners will, over the next several years, have the option of converting their developments into market-rate housing. Concern about the fate of these units has grown with the strength of the economy, because the stronger local housing markets are, the greater are the financial incentives for for-profit owners to remove expiring-use properties from the stock of subsidized housing. Several hundred thousand assisted units are at risk of being lost over the next decade, a development that would greatly increase the housing costs of poor and near-poor families. Many in the housing field believe that capable nonprofit housing groups, including some very strong CDCs and the area-wide housing organizations, could become the buyers who would work with the Department of Housing and Urban Development and local jurisdictions to purchase these properties and maintain them as part of the stock of affordable housing (assuming that sources of subsidy can be identified).

Smart Growth Coalitions

A third, even more challenging, possibility would be for nonprofit housing organizations to make common cause with congregations, labor unions, environmental organizations, and others around issues like smart growth (now very fashionable in philanthropic circles) or living wages (decidedly less fashionable). There is little doubt that the nonprofits' constituents and communities would benefit from metropolitan or regional initiatives that emphasize reinvestment and redevelopment of core urban neighborhoods or from local government or union-led efforts that "make work pay" a family-supporting wage. There is little doubt that CDCs would find this difficult to do acting on their own: the scarce financial support for tenant and community organizing would be at risk of becoming even more scarce if it came to be seen as supporting serious political action. Groups of CDCs, especially acting through respected organizations such as their local or statewide membership and service associations, might weigh in on these broader issues with more success and less risk.

Next Steps

To make headway on these and related opportunities, nonprofit housing and community development organizations will need to make progress on four major fronts:

—First, extending the organizational capacity of existing organizations and developing reliable streams of operating support for them, with reasonable performance standards,

—Second, establishing similar organizations in additional cities and building strong local systems of support for them,

—Third, equipping themselves to play a leadership role in broader interorganizational collaborations that go beyond housing and address community problems in an integrated way, and

—Fourth, establishing coalitions and support organizations that can exert influence on public policy and on program development by foundations and intermediaries.

Conclusions

Nonprofit housing and community development organizations have enjoyed enormous growth over the past twenty years. Although the sector plays a very small role in the housing industry overall, it is a significant player in the production and management of assisted housing, and it predominates in the field of community development in disadvantaged neighborhoods. Although continued exponential growth in the number of nonprofit housing producers is unlikely, ample opportunities remain for the existing organizations and their supporters to become stronger and more effective in communities. And the sector may have an important role to play in helping the nation deal with the major upcoming challenge of retaining expiring-use properties in the stock of affordable housing.

Beyond this, the recent experience of nonprofit housing and community development organizations holds important lessons for nonprofit organizations in other fields. Especially important has been the success these organizations have achieved in tapping sizable pools of private capital and channeling them into nonprofit activities in this field. This success has been due to the availability of federal tax subsidies coupled with the presence of innovative nonprofit intermediary organizations that specialize in packaging these subsidies, marketing them to investors, and then using the proceeds to finance the work of local nonprofit housing producers. Although the special characteristics of housing make this function easier to perform in this sphere than many others, there surely are lessons here for nonprofits operating in other spheres where the demands for capital investment have recently escalated. More generally, this experience shows that significant private capital can be generated for the work of nonprofit organizations willing to build the necessary links. Indeed, nonprofit housing organizations and their affiliated intermediaries are exploring whether their model can be extended to fields beyond housing as well.

Notes

1. Although the home mortgage interest deduction is by far the nation's largest housing subsidy, homes whose owners take the deduction are not generally considered assisted housing.

2. Current federal policy deems housing "affordable" if it costs no more than 30 percent of a household's income.

3. U.S. Department of Housing and Urban Development, *Rental Housing Assistance— The Worsening Crisis: A Report to Congress on Worst Case Housing Needs* (Washington: U.S. Department of Housing and Urban Development, 2000).

4. Very modest efforts to move toward public housing date back to World War I, and some states made similar efforts during the 1920s, but serious federal policy was first established with the Wagner-Steagall Housing Act of 1937; see Lawrence M. Friedman, "Public Housing and the Poor," in Jon Pynoos and others, eds., *Housing Urban America* (Chicago: Aldine Publishing, 1973).

5. No systematic information exists about the magnitude of state and local housing subsidy programs or the number of dwelling units they have supported. The balance of this chapter deals only with federal programs.

6. Housing certificates enable income-eligible households that have them to rent any housing unit they can find that meets basic housing standards and rents for no more than a federally approved "fair market rent"; the certificate pays the difference between their actual rent and 30 percent of their income (that is, the amount they can officially "afford"). Housing vouchers permit households to pay more than 30 percent of their income as rent, but the households must pay the difference between the market rent and the federally approved fair market rent.

7. The Section 502 and 515 programs, both run by the Farmers Home Administration, also supported development of substantial housing inventories; they are not discussed further because nonprofit participation in these programs was low. Section 8 new construction and substantial rehabilitation funds are still available for federal use under special circumstances.

8. Ronald F. Ferguson and William T. Dickens, eds., *Urban Problems and Community Development* (Washington: Brookings, 1999), pp. 4–5.

9. Christopher Walker, "Nonprofit Housing Development: Status, Trends, and Prospects," *Housing Policy Debate,* vol. 4, no. 3 (1993): 369–414.

10. Infill developments are projects in urban areas that literally "fill in" buildings on land left vacant by previous development. Because most cities have few large parcels of land that are vacant, infill developments in residential areas are typically small in scale.

11. National Congress for Community Economic Development, *Against the Odds: The Achievements of Community-Based Development Organizations* (Washington: National Congress for Community Economic Development, 1989). National Congress for Community Economic Development, *Coming of Age: Trends and Achievements of Community-Based Development Organizations* (Washington: National Congress for Community Economic Development, 1998).

12. Christopher Walker and Mark Weinheimer, *Community Development in the 1990s* (Washington: Urban Institute, 1998).

13. Langley C. Keyes and Avis C. Vidal, *Beyond Housing: Growing Community Development Systems* (Washington: Urban Institute, forthcoming).

7

International Assistance

SHEPARD FORMAN AND ABBY STODDARD

Private voluntary organizations have come to play a crucial operational and advocacy role in the field of international relief and development assistance. Commonly referred to as nongovernmental organizations (NGOs), these entities not only undertake independent charitable activities but at times also serve as the operational arm of government and multilateral assistance agencies.[1] Over the past thirty years, NGOs have acquired a reputation for speed, flexibility, and programming innovation beyond the reach of official political or bureaucratic actors. In addition, their grassroots orientation and first-hand knowledge of local conditions have earned them the stamp of credibility and a measure of influence in national and international policy circles.

However, with the end of the cold war, the proliferation of complex humanitarian emergencies, and the widespread shrinking of the public sector role, relief and development organizations have found themselves literally and figuratively under fire. New forms of intrastate conflict, characterized by self-perpetuating illicit economies and heavy civilian tolls, have created hazardous working conditions and wrenching moral dilemmas for humanitarian organizations. They also have inflicted enormous damage on family livelihoods and national development efforts, most notably in Africa. Heightened visibility of NGOs, combined with inflated expectations as to what they can and should attempt to accomplish in such situations, has provoked a storm of criticism from both practitioners and outside observers. The critiques, some of them valid and some misplaced, are concerned with the negative by-products of assistance (prolonging war and creating dependencies) and the actual performance of NGOs (ineffectiveness, inefficiency, and poor accountability). In addition, there are economic forces to contend with. While effectively an oligopoly, the sector is characterized by intense competition due to a shrinking pool of public funding and the aggressive marketing of new private sector actors.

On the whole, the altered environment is forcing a rethinking of once steadfast principles of development and humanitarian assistance, and new dilemmas require new approaches beyond traditional activities. For one, the historical model of aid as a benevolent service from northern suppliers to southern recipients no longer seems relevant or workable. Similarly, it is increasingly clear that NGOs cannot hope to operate effectively or safely in the absence of applied political will and support of governments. Finally, the old organizational structures, management systems, and practices are proving increasingly inadequate to the new environment and tasks that confront NGOs. This chapter describes the unique characteristics of the international relief and development subsector that differentiate it from other nonprofits, explores the features of the current international context that have brought it to a crossroads, and discusses the steps that have already been taken and those that are still needed to equip the NGO community to meet the challenges ahead.

The Nonprofit Role in the Field

Between 10 and 20 percent of economic development assistance and relief aid from northern governments is now channeled through NGOs.[2] For humanitarian relief activities alone, the share of aid channeled through NGOs is 25 percent overall, and for some governments, including the United States, the percentage is much higher. Over 70 percent of U.S. foreign disaster relief aid is programmed through NGO grantees.[3] This reflects in part the credibility and legitimacy that have accrued to these nonprofit, nonstate actors in this area of international relations. Governments and multilateral organizations (such as the United Nations Children's Fund, the World Food Program, United Nations Development Programme, and United Nations High Commissioner for Refugees) rely on NGOs as implementing partners and as advisers on matters of policy.

Internationally oriented assistance organizations first appeared during the interwar period, and the field continued to grow slowly after World War II. The aim of these early organizations was to provide emergency relief supplies to war victims in Europe. The newly independent states emerging from decolonization after World War II saw the birth of the movement for economic development assistance, and throughout the 1960s and 1970s, the focus of NGOs shifted to poverty reduction efforts in the third world. Widespread disappointment with the initial government-to-government approach to development, which had resulted in high-profile, wasteful projects or outright diversion, shined a light on NGOs as an alternative vehicle for progress.[4] In contrast to the top-down approach, international NGOs working at the village level represented a strategy for development upward from the local communities, which donors embraced.

During this period, NGOs continued to respond to natural and conflict-related emergencies, but their access to victims was constrained by politics and limited technological and logistical capacity. The role of primary provider of aid in conflict situations was still the undisputed province of the Red Cross. The founding of Médecins sans Frontières in 1971 marked a turning point in relief assistance, forging a path of greater independent action by NGOs. Committing itself to the "humanitarian imperative," this new breed of organization sought to provide relief to victims wherever they happened to be, in direct opposition to the principles of sovereignty and noninterference. By the late 1970s, a boom had begun in the relief and development field, which was to gain increasing momentum through the next twenty years.[5]

As table 7-1 shows, the last decade of the twentieth century witnessed unprecedented levels of humanitarian crisis. Not only were there three times as many natural disasters in the 1990s as there were in the 1960s,[6] but the 1990s marked a high point for state fragmentation and violent civil conflicts. Only two of the world's twenty-seven major armed conflicts in 1999 were wars between nations.[7] Africa, in particular, was beset by the twin phenomena of "failed states" and "complex emergencies," where chronic environmental and food security problems are exacerbated by fighting or the outright collapse of central authority; Africa also had a higher incidence of new conflict than any other region in the world.[8] The mode of combat in such conflicts has been to inflict damage on civilian areas and populations rather than on the opposing forces directly, which has resulted in unprecedented numbers of civilian casualties, refugees, and internally displaced persons. The number of refugees more than doubled, and 100 million more people were affected by humanitarian crises in 1990 than in 1980.[9] In both natural and man-made disasters, the burden of post-crisis recovery has set back years of development progress in each country where it has occurred. The United Nations (UN) estimates the costs to the international community of dealing with humanitarian crises of the 1990s, not including the recovery costs for Kosovo or East Timor, at $675 billion.[10]

Along with burgeoning humanitarian need, the 1990s saw greatly increased access by independent relief agencies to victims. The end of the cold war ushered in a new era of cooperation on the Security Council and a willingness to take action on humanitarian grounds. By essentially loosening the principle of national sovereignty and promoting international "humanitarian intervention" to safeguard stability and individual human rights,[11] the Security Council's actions helped to legitimize the work of relief agencies even further. In addition,

Table 7-1. *Number of Humanitarian Emergencies, 1960s–70s*

Decade	Natural disasters		Armed conflicts[b]	
	Number of natural disasters[a]	Number of people affected (millions)[a]	Number of armed conflicts per year (average)[b]	Number of refugees per year (average in millions)[c]
1960s	521[d]	179[d]	23	2.5
1970s	1,203	784	30	3.5
1980s	2,435	1,420	42	11.8
1990s	4,864	1,959	43	14.7

Source: Figures are drawn from International Federation of Red Cross and Red Crescent Societies, *World Disasters Report 2000* (International Federation of Red Cross and Red Crescent Societies, 2000) and EM-DAT: the International Disaster Database of Office of U.S. Foreign Disaster Assistance and Center for Research on the Epidemiology of Disasters, available at www.cred.be. Both sources caution that the lack of systematic and standardized data measures and unified methodology for reporting on disasters results in "soft and noisy" data. Therefore, the authors have grouped them by decade in order to look at overall trends. Data on armed conflicts are drawn from the Monty G. Marshall, comp., *Major Episodes of Political Violence, 1946–1999* (New York: Center for Systemic Peace, 2001), available at www.members.aol.com/CSPmgm/warlist.htm [2001].

a. International Federation of Red Cross and Red Crescent Societies, *World Disasters Report 2000* and EM-DAT. Natural disasters refer to avalanches and landslides; droughts, famines, and food shortages; earthquakes; epidemics; floods; forest fires; cyclones, hurricanes, and storms; volcanoes; other weather- and tide-related disasters; and insect infestations.

b. Marshall, *Major Episodes of Political Violence.* Armed conflicts refer to international warfare, civil unrest, and ethnic violence resulting in the death of 1,000 persons or more over the course of the conflict.

c. United Nations High Commissioner for Refugees, *State of the World's Refugees 2000: Fifty Years of Humanitarian Action* (United Nations High Commissioner for Refugees, 2000), p. 310.

d. Data from 1964–69. Few major disasters are recorded before 1964. EM-DAT lists 1,183 major disasters, with 124.1 million people affected from the period 1900 to 1963.

these NGOs were now accorded the freedom to operate in formerly "closed" societies transitioning from communism.

The increased need and opportunity for humanitarian aid stimulated a doubling of relief funding from industrial countries and an explosion of new NGOs in the late 1980s and 1990s. Organizations already doing development work in the field found that their existing infrastructures and local knowledge made them well placed to respond to needs as they arose, while scores of new organizations were created in the wake of each new humanitarian disaster for the express purpose of launching a rapid-response delivery of relief aid. The number of international relief and development organizations based in the United States grew from fifty-two organizations in 1970 to more than 400 by 1994.[12]

It is not known exactly how many internationally operating NGOs based in northern countries currently exist, but the number is estimated to be around 4,000, delivering over $4.5 billion worth of assistance annually. (When southern

NGOs and community-based organizations are added, the number reaches the tens of thousands).[13] The United States Agency for International Development (USAID) currently registers 439 U.S.-based NGOs as funding partners, the largest number of such organizations in any OECD (Organization for Economic Cooperation and Development) nation.[14] In 1999 their combined revenue and in-kind support from public and private sources totaled over $12 billion—more than three-quarters the amount of the annual U.S. foreign aid budget.[15]

The U.S.-based NGOs represented on the USAID registry range widely in organizational size and scope of work, with the smallest maintaining budgets of under $10,000 and the largest maintaining budgets in the hundreds of millions. Some of these organizations focus on issues peripheral to development assistance, such as environmental conservation or political democratization, and others have chosen to focus on a single issue or activity, such as adoption, or a specific country or region. An untold number of other small NGOs exist outside the USAID partnership, and it is common for many to spring up around a particular emergency and then dissolve or reappear in a different institutional form. The largest U.S. consortium of relief and development organizations, the Washington, D.C.–based InterAction, narrows the field somewhat by requiring membership dues and imposing entry criteria. It counts roughly 170 members, still a sizable number. Yet even with this evident proliferation of aid organizations, the bulk of global aid dollars and materials continues to be channeled through an elite group of large and long-standing NGOs. Of a roughly estimated 4,000 northern industrial-nation NGOs, the ten largest account for approximately 20 percent of combined NGO revenue.[16] Among these giants are four of the largest American relief and development NGOs: CARE USA, Catholic Relief Services, Save the Children USA, and World Vision.[17]

These four organizations—two of them religious in orientation and two secular—are examples of broad-based, multisectoral relief and development agencies undertaking a wide range of programming. Such program activities are broadly defined below.

Economic Development

Development activities are geared toward long-term poverty reduction and aim to build local capacities and create sustainable improvements in quality of life. Such projects include technical assistance in agriculture, education, small business development and microcredit initiatives, and primary health care with an emphasis on maternal and child health, nutrition, and food security. In attempting to address the root causes of poverty and underdevelopment, the development field also has come to include activities focused on strengthening civil society, democratization, freedom of the press, reproductive health and family planning, and human rights.

Increasingly important are the contributions and independent activities of southern development NGOs, working to fight poverty at the grassroots level in their own countries and regions. The Grameen Bank in Bangladesh stands out as an example of the growing self-sufficiency of southern organizations in development efforts.[18]

Humanitarian Assistance

Humanitarian assistance refers to efforts to save lives and mitigate damage caused by natural disasters and complex political emergencies, including armed conflict. Often this takes place within the context of refugee movements or large-scale internal displacement of populations, where rapid provision of basic goods and services is required. The major subsectors in this field include emergency food aid, health care interventions, shelter, and water and sanitation services.

Most of the larger U.S.-based NGOs undertake both emergency relief and long-term poverty reduction activities in their areas of operation. These dual-mission organizations have discovered the strategic and cost advantages of launching emergency response in areas where they already maintain an operational presence, logistical infrastructure, and networks of contacts and partnerships in the community. Furthermore, there is now widespread recognition that the two sets of activities are functionally and conceptually interdependent. Just as poverty, overpopulation, and environmental degradation can increase a country's vulnerabilities to disaster, likewise disasters have an antithetical effect on development. Thus development seeks to reduce a country's vulnerability to disasters, and relief aid, appropriately targeted, can help to provide a solid foundation for rehabilitation and ongoing development.

During the 1990s, the relief and development community recognized a third set of needs to be met—those of post-crisis recovery and rehabilitation—along with the importance of a seamless transition from relief to recovery and onward to continued development assistance. Although many large donors continue to categorize activities into relief, recovery, and development, most practitioners have challenged this distinction as being outmoded and counterproductive. Since relief, recovery, and development activities are in reality all interrelated and overlapping, treating them as separate stages along a continuum results in funding and service gaps and poses the risk of backsliding into renewed crisis.[19]

NGOs and the Public Sector

For U.S.-based NGOs, the public sector refers not only to the U.S. government but also to national governments in the countries of operation and to the international public sector, meaning the United Nations and other multilateral, regional, and subregional organizations that provide transnational public goods. NGOs have historically had a complex relationship with local authorities. Designed to serve the people directly at the local community level, they have long been seen by some national governments as a threat to sovereignty. At times, NGOs have been accused of being covers for spies or simply pawns for furthering the cold war agenda of their own national donors. Conversely, some governments may lean too heavily on NGOs to provide the services that governments no longer provide. Whether in socialist countries transitioning to a market economy or in failing states with weak or corrupt governments, there is a global trend of weakened state capacity and political will to provide public goods.[20] NGOs have had to ask themselves whether they are providing a necessary stopgap or merely letting governments in recipient countries free ride on their services, perhaps creating greater dependencies on external assistance in the process.[21] And in extreme cases involving complete collapse of central authority, such as in Somalia and Haiti, NGOs and international agencies have had to step in to form a virtual public sector, providing everything from infrastructure maintenance to education and health care services.

With donor governments, the relationship is equally complex. NGOs require substantial funding for large-scale relief projects. For example, a typical six-month project grant from the Office of U.S. Foreign Disaster Assistance (USAID's relief wing) can easily top $1 million. Yet, with such large sums coming from government donors, the autonomy of the recipient organization may understandably be called into question. Similarly, political advocacy by an NGO may become problematic when the government that is being lobbied is also the organization's single largest donor. (The fact that some NGOs seem to have escaped this dilemma is explored in a later section).

The proportion of official government assistance that is channeled through NGOs is in fact understated, since a large percentage of what is given as a direct grant to an international agency such as the United Nations High Commissioner for Refugees is typically then farmed out to NGOs in the form of subgrants and implementing partnerships. These international agencies represent another important source of funding and cooperation for NGOs. NGOs look to the United Nations to provide interagency coordination and an umbrella of authority for their work in emergency situations (if not actual physical security) and strongly protest when it is not forthcoming. And UN agencies, like national governments, depend on NGOs to carry out much of the end-stage service delivery and to move quickly to identify and access populations in need. As with donor governments, there is a certain tension in the relationship between NGOs and international organizations, even as they recognize their mutual dependence. Donor funding patterns show a growing bilateralization of aid, meaning less and less is going as unrestricted grants to UN agencies and more is going to specific countries for specific purposes, often through NGOs. This bilateralization has in effect placed NGOs and UN organizations in a low-level competition with each other over donor resources. Another source of tension is that, while the UN agencies are mandated to set up operations in any and all areas of need, NGOs are free to pick and choose their countries of operation. This results, UN personnel argue, in an over-whelming number of actors responding in situations that attract media interest and in a dearth of agencies responding to the "forgotten emergencies," leaving gaps in basic service provision.

NGOs have pushed to make their voices heard in international forums and to a considerable extent have succeeded. Many UN agencies working in relief or development, such as the Office for Coordination of Humanitarian Assistance, the UN Development Programme, and the UN High Commissioner for Refugees, have established formal or semiformal structures for NGO participa-tion and consultation. In addition, the Security Council on occasion has invited NGO representatives to advise on matters related to ongoing humanitarian crises. Although some organizations have complained that the participation of NGOs tends to be more symbolic than real, the influence they have had in these intergovernmental forums has grown, as evidenced, for instance, by the success-ful passage of the international ban on land mines.

Characteristics of the Relief and Development Subsector

Clearly, the international relief and development organizations represent a unique subsector of U.S. nonprofits. Although a few also engage in some domestic programming, the bulk of their work is carried out overseas, in poor or war-torn countries. The majority of their employees are developing-country nationals, while senior management in the field and at headquarters remains predominantly northern. Also, unlike other nonprofits, these organizations, especially those engaged in relief efforts, face serious security risks and have suf-fered increasing casualties to their personnel. In recent years, NGOs have had to grapple with matters such as war-risk insurance and the effects of psychological stress and burnout of field staff.

Although the work of relief and development takes place largely outside the domestic public eye, it relies on public concern for foreign populations, in its efforts not only to solicit private donations but also to influence policymakers to take some sort of action in response to human suffering. Much has been written about the critical role of the news media—the so-called CNN effect—on gener-ating public interest, mobilizing giving, and even encouraging political action.

There are unique dynamics within the relief and development community as well. U.S. international relief and development organizations exist as part of a complex transnational community of NGOs and other international actors. Indeed, it may become a misnomer to speak of U.S., British, or French NGOs as more of them internationalize their membership and function in a global net-work where the players are not necessarily arranged along national lines. The NGOs are essentially private organizations, each following its own distinctive normative mandate in a highly politicized environment. But efforts have been, and continue to be, made to identify the common core principles of humanitarian assistance and to promote cooperation and coordination in assistance and advocacy efforts on behalf of the beneficiaries.[22] Despite NGOs' internationalization, cultural differences abound along both organizational and regional lines. Many of the French organizations place greatest emphasis on diversity and independence as the key to NGOs' operational advantage. A theme heard more often among British-based groups is that, to meet the current array of challenges, NGOs must strive to become a cohesive and rule-based community, something that thus far has proved impossible to achieve.

Factors Shaping the Position of Nonprofits in the Field and the Nature of Their Impact

The current international environment, characterized by economic globalization, on the one hand, and intrastate fragmentation and conflict, on the other, has thrust NGOs into more prominent roles than ever before in humanitarian relief and development assistance. At times, they find that these are roles for which they were neither intended nor adequately prepared. We look more closely first at the major drivers of change in the international and domestic arenas—globalization and the decline of national capacities, new forms of civil conflict, and trends in funding—and then at their effects on the international NGO sector.

Globalization and the Shrinking Public Sector

On the development side, the phenomenon of globalization has had both direct and indirect effects on the work of NGOs. It has opened new doors for fundraising and private sector partnerships. And technology suddenly available and affordable to NGOs (such as portable satellite communications systems, for example) has helped to increase their access to victims and their logistical capacity to provide assistance. At the same time, it may have created conditions that place the ultimate goals of their development mission further out of reach. In some corners, globalization has been hailed as a boon to developing countries, creating new jobs and educational opportunities, raising the standard of living, and building bridges to the modern industrial world. Others have argued, however, that globalization increases rather than decreases inequities within states, creating new forms of poverty and social tensions just as it creates new forms of wealth.[23] The ideological contest that characterized the cold war seems to have been decided firmly in favor of free market mechanics over government largesse, and states undergoing fiscal crisis have found an enabling philosophy in the "Washington consensus" for cutting back on social services. The public sector is shrinking, and social safety nets are fraying all over the world, including in many nominally socialist countries. For that reason, the international agencies (and local NGOs) are increasingly called on by national governments and the United Nations to meet these social needs and to fill ever widening gaps in places where they have been working for decades.[24]

Post–Cold War Conflicts

Relief agencies have found themselves in the unenviable position of representing the *primary* response of the international community to many of the emergencies resulting from the violent civil conflicts emerging in the post–cold war period. The break in the Security Council's long-standing deadlock between the veto powers of the United States and the former Soviet Union resulted in a spate of new peacekeeping activity. Thirty-six new missions were approved after 1988—nearly three times as many as were mandated in the first forty years of the United Nations' lifespan. However, these missions suffered from persistent underfunding and disputes over command and control. In fact, there remain strong disincentives to vigorous collective peacekeeping actions among the Security Council members. Governments without a cold war agenda find that they no longer possess a compelling national interest in most of these conflicts, and the United States, in particular, has been loath to run the risk of casualties to its personnel. Moreover, Russia, China, and a number of developing countries on the Security Council oppose the idea of humanitarian intervention on the grounds that it violates the principle of sovereignty. Yet the widely broadcast scenes of carnage and suffering create a moral and public pressure to do something. The western powers are thus inclined to support humanitarian aid operations, while eschewing deeper political or military commitments. Relief agencies, ever ambivalent about playing a role in military actions, have nonetheless protested the absence of an international military presence and objected to being used as a "humanitarian fig leaf." It is now a point of conventional wisdom that, without resolute political action, including security measures as necessary, relief work can become both dangerous and futile.

September 11 and Its Repercussions

The effects of the September 11 terrorist attacks on New York City and Washington, D.C., and the consequent refocusing of foreign policy are only just beginning to unfold. Many in the international assistance field expect that post–September 11 foreign assistance will become coupled more closely to political and security concerns, and they fear that attention and resources will be diverted away from emergencies and development efforts in areas outside the Middle East such as Angola and Congo. NGOs are steeling themselves for uncertain, yet assuredly tough, times ahead, as aid funding becomes more focused on specific geographic regions, competition between grantees increases, and organizations attempt to remain distinct from political-military agendas and operations.

Funding and Partnerships

The funding situation for relief and development NGOs shows a general tightening of the market in terms of government and individual contributions, on the one hand, and promising possibilities in private sector partnerships, which are only beginning to be explored, on the other.

Relief aid flows naturally tend to spike with the occurrence of major disasters (and, with them, the number and size of NGOs working in relief) and subsequently to decline again. Total annual national contributions for relief funding peaked at $5.7 billion in 1994 (reaching 10 percent of overall foreign aid) and then plateaued at around $4.5 billion to $5 billion a year.[25] That the NGO sector did not shrink correspondingly to this decline in funding may be a function of a greater portion of official aid going through NGOs as opposed to multilateral bodies. What it also means, however, is heightened competition among NGOs for the funding necessary to maintain their current level of activities. The United States is now second to the European Union as the largest humanitarian aid donor, and while the single most important funding relationship for most U.S. NGOs is still the United States, their increasingly global orientation is helping them to tap into European Union and other national government funding.

Official aid funding has not kept up with national economic growth. As a percentage of government expenditure, overall aid funding (for both relief and development) by OECD countries peaked in 1992 and then steadily declined through 1997, when it reached its lowest point in thirty years.[26] In 1998, aid rose again—for the first time in five years—by 8.9 percent in real terms.[27] However, the OECD Development Assistance Committee speculates that this is merely "a modest reversal of the downward slide."[28] Private charitable giving for international relief and development has not increased enough to offer a viable alternative to shrinking official aid flows. Traditionally, the portion of private giving in the United States that goes for international purposes is by far the smallest for all charitable recipients. Last year, out of $203.5 billion in private donations (including foundation and corporate grants, as well as individual donations and bequests), internationally operating organizations received $2.7 billion, or 1.3 percent. This percentage is roughly the same as it was in 1987, having peaked in 1994 at 1.6 percent of private giving overall.[29] Furthermore, this figure covers other types of international organizations besides relief and development NGOs, such as human rights and policy research organizations.

In contrast, commercial capital flows to developing countries have increased 500 percent over the past decade and now vastly outstrip official development assistance. By way of illustration, during the period 1983–88 net private capital flows totaled $15 billion, compared to $29 billion in official aid.[30] In 1990, private flows rose to $43.9 billion, and official aid reached $63.5 billion. But by

Table 7-2. *Source of Funding for Nongovernmental Organizations, 1997*
U.S. dollars unless otherwise noted

Organization	Total revenue or support	U.S. government[a]		Other governments and international organizations		Private contributions, revenue, and in-kind support	
		Amount	Percent	Amount	Percent	Amount	Percent
CARE	359,373,000	202,994,000	56	88,616,000	25	67,763,000	19
Catholic Relief Services	232,272,000	132,257,000	57	4,862,000	2	95,153,000	41
Save the Children	132,931,557	72,618,822	55	4,233,599	3	56,079,136	42
World Vision	141,653,940	53,502,320	38	1,304,498	1	86,847,122	61

Source: U.S. Agency for International Development, *VolAg Report 1999* (Washington: USAID, 1999).
a. U.S. Agency for International Development and other support; includes P.L. 480–donated food and freight costs.

1997, net private flows had risen to $299 billion, and official aid was down to $52.2 billion.[31] "Read large, it is capitalism—the for-profit sector—that is driving development in an area where heretofore the public and the nonprofit sector (NGOs), relatively recently allied with governments, had been in the driver's seat."[32] This sea change in development resources has NGOs making efforts to forge new partnerships with corporations and so far meeting with a willing audience, as is discussed below.

Notwithstanding the increase in private capital to the developing world, and NGOs' efforts to diversify funding and attract new donors and partners from the private sector, the largest NGOs (that is, those doing the bulk of the relief and development work in the world) remain heavily dependent on government funding. In its annual reports on its voluntary agency partners, USAID takes pains to point out that 75 percent of combined agency revenue comes from *private* sources, with the remainder more or less evenly split between USAID and other sources such as UN agencies and other governments.[33] Yet these figures belie the importance of public (government) funding to the small group of large organizations that constitute the major American players in the humanitarian field. Table 7-2 provides a snapshot of public versus private funding of these NGOs. Out of more than 400 U.S. organizations, the four listed in table 7-2 account for approximately 47 percent of total U.S. government annual support to NGOs, and all but one of the four (World Vision) rely on U.S. government sources for more than 50 percent of their funding.[34]

The reality is further obscured by the way NGOs report private in-kind contributions. Frequently these figures are inflated by cost estimates of donated goods and equipment that otherwise would have been disposed of or by hours worked by volunteers at pro bono or reduced rates calculated at their professional salary equivalents.

Prior to September 11, private individual contributions were generally considered to be stagnating.[35] Even as globalizing NGOs opened fundraising offices in new countries, they were finding that the domestic markets for direct mail and other fundraising activities had been saturated. The private funding situation post–September 11 seems considerably bleaker, at least in the short term. At the time of this writing, virtually no private funding is flowing to NGOs. Corporations, foundations, and other private donors, hit hard by the falling stock market, have channeled most of their diminished resources to post–September 11 domestic recovery and victim support efforts. Additionally, direct mail has dried up over the past year, with returns down 40 percent or more for many NGOs.

Another factor tightening the supply of aid funding is the rise of indigenous southern development organizations. Although many donors still prefer to work through northern-based NGOs for their reputation and accountability, northern NGOs are increasingly encouraged by donors, including USAID, to partner with, mentor, or subgrant to local organizations in their countries of operation. While many NGOs need no such encouragement and have already made strides in this direction in the interest of more effective and sustainable programming, others are struggling to adapt their mission to the reality of the burgeoning southern NGO sector and occasionally find themselves in the awkward position of competing with local counterparts for grants.

Finally, a long-standing financing problem for all but the very largest organizations is the general lack of endowments and reserve funds. This problem is particularly acute in the area of rapid humanitarian relief, where the nature of donor-agency financing results in costly and less effective outcomes.[36] The basic dilemma is that most emergency grants are negotiated and awarded *after* the onset of a disaster. NGOs wishing to respond in the critical early days and weeks of the emergency are forced to use their own funds, for which most have inadequate reserves. The dearth of unrestricted advance funding has also prevented NGOs from establishing organizational preparedness capacities such as standby personnel and relief supply stockpiles. Certain partnership mechanisms do exist among NGOs and donors to provide the necessary up-front funding to overcome this dilemma, but they are few, ad hoc, and underutilized.[37] The monetary and human costs associated with this northern-based, reactive stance to emergencies further underscore the utility of strengthening indigenous relief capacities and preparedness mechanisms.

The recent changes in international conditions and aid funding have brought about new challenges and adaptations in NGO operations, organizational governance, advocacy efforts, and public relations and created political and ethical dilemmas that have caused nothing less than an existential crisis for many agencies.

Operational Challenges

Some key concerns related to day-to-day operations of international NGOs include security, performance and accountability, and personnel issues.

SECURITY. Staff security has become an issue of vital importance to NGOs over the past decade. Although no accurate figures are available for the total number of NGO workers who have been killed or injured in the field (most agencies either do not keep or are unwilling to disclose such records), the widely held perception is that acts of violence against humanitarian workers are on the rise. A decisive juncture came during the Somalia crisis in the early 1990s when NGOs were forced to militarize themselves, traveling in armored vehicles or under the escort of heavily armed local mercenaries. A sobering discovery made around this time was that the insurance policies that NGOs had heretofore used for their overseas staff covered only accidents and medical conditions, not "acts of war" such as sniper fire or mine explosions. The murder of the Red Cross workers in Chechnya in 1996 was seen as a turning point in the operational reality of relief agencies.

There is a growing fear that humanitarian workers are no longer off-limits as targets and, worse, that harming them may come into vogue as a form of terrorism, as did airline hijackings in the 1970s. A growing body of literature on the utility of violence and "war economies" in modern-day conflicts suggests that such risks will not abate as long as there are parties to the conflict who benefit politically and economically from continued mayhem.[38]

These escalating risks of assassination, kidnapping, land mine detonation, harassment or arrest by local authorities, and road banditry come on top of the familiar risks of robbery, rape, traffic accidents, and health threats such as malaria and HIV. Another set of risks comes with the nature of the work, such as having large sums of cash on hand, transporting food or other material supplies, and hiring and firing local staff.

Beginning in the mid-1990s, NGOs began to look seriously at their security status, designing field security protocols and awareness-raising events for staff. Many hired in-house security professionals to oversee organizational training or serve as adjuncts to country offices. Conferences and seminars on the subject have proliferated, and the Office of U.S. Foreign Disaster Assistance and Inter-Action launched a comprehensive course on operational security management in 1998, offering sessions on a continuing basis to staff from all agencies in various field sites around the world. However, the NGOs walk a difficult line in their security planning and management. Some are reluctant to stress the security aspect too much for fear of scaring off scarce recruits.[39]

Security risks will continue to intensify for NGOs with the increased level of threat, particularly to U.S. expatriates, and general instability in the field during the military campaign against global terrorist networks. At the same time, the costs of insurance will rise, both as additional incidents occur and as a ripple effect of the September 11 attacks is felt.

PERFORMANCE AND ACCOUNTABILITY. In response to both internal evaluation and external criticism, NGOs have, in the past several years, put renewed emphasis on improving the quality, integrity, and measurable outputs of their programming. The various critiques, which peaked in volume in the 1990s, concern NGOs' overdependence on large government grants, donor-driven as opposed to need-based programming, poor accounting and evaluation practices, the lack of objective measures and quantifiable data on progress, and underinvestment in organizational learning and operations research.[40]

In both the development and humanitarian relief areas, impact measurement is increasingly emphasized. Most large donors now insist on results-oriented program design, illustrated by logical framework matrixes, to be clearly demonstrated in grant proposals. Interagency working groups on evaluation share empirical methodologies and develop software and other tools for field use. Increased attention to gender dynamics, cultural and religious factors, and community participation also has characterized the evolution of relief and development programming in the past two decades. Organizations such as CARE, Oxfam, and others have adopted a rights-based or justice-based approach to relief and development and have developed programming frameworks that focus on food and income security at the level of the individual household. These frameworks have had significant impact on the entire field.

NGO innovations notwithstanding, the ultimate reproach remains that "there are simply insufficient examples of a positive causal relationship between aid, growth, poverty reduction, and peace."[41] This may well be an example of inflated expectations vis-à-vis the scope of NGO capacities and objectives. It is not realistic to expect that the efforts of independent voluntary agencies could make a pronounced difference in the macroeconomic or political position of developing countries, especially given the complexities of the current international environment. As noted, natural disasters (for which the 1990s was the worst decade on record) have been known to set back development for years, today's civil wars have self-perpetuating economies and take their biggest toll on civilians, and the shrinking of the public sector has exacerbated the plight of the poor. To pin the blame on an underachieving NGO sector is naïve at best and unfairly overlooks the NGOs' many successes at the level of the individual community.

An example of unrealistic expectations encountering overwhelming difficulties may be seen in the Rwandan/Zaire refugee crisis of 1994. The humanitarian efforts in the camps in Zaire saw some significant achievements by aid organizations in containing a cholera outbreak and providing food and shelter to approximately 2 million refugees. At the same time, it witnessed a veritable "relief circus," with literally hundreds of NGOs scrambling for a piece of the action and competing for funds and airtime, legions of inexperienced and untrained international volunteers, and several examples of unsound health practices. Leaving aside the later controversy involving the takeover of the camps by individuals responsible for the Rwandan genocide, many practitioners felt that the initial response amounted to an operational and ethical failure on the part of the aid community. *The Joint Evaluation of Emergency Assistance to Rwanda*, a collaborative work by donors, NGOs, and UN bodies to document the crisis and relief efforts, found numerous shortcomings in preparedness, coordination, and quality of services.[42] That publication spawned an interagency standardization movement to improve the quality of aid by identifying best practices. The centerpiece of this movement, the interagency Sphere Project, put forth the *Humanitarian Charter and Minimum Standards in Disaster Response*.[43] The minimum standards cover the areas of water and sanitation, nutrition, food aid, shelter and site planning, and health services, and the charter addresses agency behavior and adherence to the basic principles of humanitarian assistance.

For its part, the U.S. NGO consortium InterAction has established a set of private voluntary organization standards—a "financial, operational, and ethical code of conduct"[44]—under which its NGO members are required to self-certify each year. This process is meant to encourage compliance and self-evaluation to identify areas for improvement.[45] Such standard setting has a great deal to do with "enhancing the public trust"[46] of relief and development agencies, which has been unquestionably damaged by recent scandals exposed in the press. These include the lucrative but controversial practice of child sponsorship, in which a 1998 series of articles in the *Chicago Tribune* uncovered widespread accounting discrepancies and misrepresentation to donors. (Other, moral, objections to child sponsorship, raised both within and without the aid community, are that it exploits children through graphic depictions of suffering and hopelessness and panders to a paternalistic desire for gratitude on the part of the donor.) Another blow to NGOs came when some agencies were charged with abetting the corporate "dumping" of expired pharmaceuticals and otherwise inappropriate aid commodities onto disaster victims.

A question that remains unresolved and contentious within the aid community is the extent to which it is possible and desirable to give real teeth to the standards now being set. Thus far, all standards and protocols established by the aid community are merely guidelines, and agencies are under no obligation to adhere to them (or even to learn of their existence).[47] Although many practitioners insist that standards must be vigorously upheld, others balk at the perceived infringement of independence, which presumably favors the large and well-established humanitarian organizations over the younger and smaller entrants to the field. In other words, the question is whether the aid regime should become tighter, more exclusive, and rule-based or remain subject to the competitive market forces that regularly overwhelm the cooperation ethic among NGOs.

NGO accountability once meant simply answering to donors on how their dollars were spent and to what effect. This practice resulted in donor-driven projects more concerned with fulfilling donor requirements than with addressing the actual needs of or offering long-term benefits to the target population. Increasingly, relief and development NGOs are attempting to be equally accountable to their "customers" or "clients" in developing countries. An independent Office of Humanitarian Accountability (formerly called the Humanitarian Ombudsman) has been proposed as one possible answer to the compliance question. An interagency initiative, this project seeks to establish an independent representative or organizational mechanism to act as a voice for the beneficiaries of emergency assistance and to promote and facilitate adherence to quality standards.[48]

PERSONNEL ISSUES. In some of their personnel concerns, the international NGOs probably do not differ much from other U.S. nonprofits. For instance, there is the eternal question of how to attract and retain qualified individuals at salary scales considerably lower than in the private sector. Yet there are also many issues unique to internationally oriented organizations, such as the inherent difficulty of managing field staff from great distances. Different NGOs have struck their own balance between "supervision" and "support" in the headquarters-field relationship, depending on how centralized they require their decision-making process to be. Another problem posed by maintaining expatriate staff in overseas missions is in trying to govern aspects of a staff member's private life that in the domestic setting would be considered strictly off-limits. In the field, staff members are never truly off-duty and must be cognizant that their public behavior, romantic relationships, and even privately expressed opinions may have an impact on the safety or success of their mission.

A host of issues also revolves around the employment of locally hired professionals and support staff. National staffers are the backbone of NGO operations in almost every country, and in many missions they hold all but the most senior positions. The disparity between the pay scales and benefits of national and international staff has long been a subject of debate. On the whole, NGOs pay their national staff at levels consistent with local salary levels, albeit at the upper end of the scale in order to attract skilled workers, who may be in short supply, and to remain competitive with other NGOs and UN agencies. The rationale holds that paying salaries equivalent to those of international staff would skew the local economy and contribute to "brain drain" from the local public and private sectors. Yet the ethically questionable result can be a situation in which a local and an international staff member are paid vastly different salaries for doing very similar jobs. Although hardly the worst offender when compared to the United Nations and bilateral agencies' payment practices, the NGO community has yet to confront this issue head on. The NGO Field Coordination Protocol deals with salary issues, but more with the purpose of preventing competitive outbidding of local staff among NGOs than addressing questions of equity between expatriates and locals. Health and life insurance benefits for local staff are also problematic, since many carriers that cover international staff will not offer policies for local hires or do so only at prohibitive rates. NGOs have dealt with the insurance problem through a variety of makeshift solutions that depend on the local circumstances, including purchasing local policies if available, making ad hoc arrangements with local health providers, devising self-insurance schemes, or, in many cases, simply not insuring their local staff at all. One proposed solution to both the salary and benefits issues is for NGOs to accept two common principles: (a) to provide all staff members performing comparable work with equal benefits and working conditions, while (b) paying salaries set "with reference to previous earnings and the prevailing rates in the country of origin."[49] NGOs have not yet seriously explored this or other options as a matter of joint policy.

As NGOs have grown and taken on more corporate-like structures and bureaucratic procedures, a culture clash of sorts has developed between the values of voluntarism and professionalism. Many U.S. NGOs were founded in a spirit of voluntarism and charitable giving rooted in the Judeo-Christian tradition. To lose this spirit, some say, would be to rob the NGOs of their unique role and motivation. NGOs worry about losing their organizational soul and succumbing to the global "commercial Zeitgeist"[50] or creeping "corporatization" of culture. However, it could conversely be argued that professionalization is not simply a measure of the inevitable bureaucracy and standardization that accompany organizational growth, but rather a moral imperative. If NGOs are truly to be accountable to their beneficiaries, then they are ethically obligated to provide the highest-quality, most cost-effective services possible. In circumstances where promoting the voluntaristic spirit is at odds with that obligation (for instance, sending volunteers on missions where their presence will be more of a logistical burden than a value), morality dictates that it be sacrificed in favor of a professionalized operation. In international health programming, this conflict can take the form of a clash between the divergent values of *public health* (raising the overall health status of the population), on the one hand, and *medicine* (treating individual patients with the highest level of care available), on the other. [51] Certain organizations that have built their reputation and public profile on sending volunteer physicians overseas feel compelled to continue this practice, under the rationale of "promoting voluntarism," even in cases where the more cost-effective (and ultimately more beneficial) alternative would be to retain the services of local health profession-als and simply provide them with the materials they need.

The increased security risk to NGO personnel also has contributed to the professionalization movement. Not only do NGOs feel a moral responsibility for the safety of their staff, and therefore insist that they be well-trained profes-sionals, but liability issues resulting from injuries and deaths have created a legal responsibility as well, particularly for NGOs based in the ultra-litigious United States.

Trends in Organizational Governance

It happens that the tumultuous changes and crises of the 1990s coincided with the approaching "middle age" of several of the oldest and largest relief and devel-opment organizations. These organizations, established in the wake of World War II or before, now find themselves with large and growing bureaucracies, outdated operational systems, and a perceived alienation from their original val-ues. The reengineering and restructuring processes many went through, or are going through still, represent a genuine, deep introspection on the part of these organizations. Some have undergone major overhauls of their financial, human resources, and information systems. The furthest reaching of these changes, however, are reflected in how the organizations are governed.

The organizational evolutions of individual NGOs are each unique and too complex to be labeled as simply centralization or decentralization of authority. Yet, broadly, for the largest, multicountry NGOs, there seems to be a conver-gence toward more coordinated, global forms of governance, with stronger rep-resentation and participation from developing countries. NGOs having separate national entities of the same name, such as Save the Children and Médecins sans Frontières, which at one time operated as independent national organiza-tions under loose umbrella structures, have over the years moved toward a con-federated model with a greater degree of central coordination. At the opposite end of the spectrum, NGOs such as CARE and World Vision have moved from a highly centralized, unitary corporate model to various forms of federation, where the national affiliates have more autonomy and a voice in the overall gov-ernance of the organization.[52] World Vision's "global bumblebee" structure seeks to devolve decisionmaking authority to local affiliates, while binding them under a single, coherent global mission strategy. The changes in governance reflect at once the need for tighter coordination and policy coherence among affiliates and the desire to increase southern participation. The language of inclusion and partnership has long been a part of the NGOs' mission state-ments, but decisionmaking for many years remained squarely in the north, as manifested in primarily northern boards of directors. Most of the large and long-standing relief and development NGOs now strive for mixed boards, proj-ects that are locally initiated and designed, resource acquisition in both north and south, and multiple partnerships and affiliates around the world. [53] Some NGOs, notably CARE, have begun to seek out (or create, when necessary) local NGO partners to mentor and support until such time as they are able to join the federation as equal members.

Public Attitudes and Advocacy

The decline in official government assistance in the latter half of the 1990s did not reflect a widespread public sentiment that foreign aid should be reduced, nor was it matched by a decline in voluntary giving by private individuals. On the contrary, private giving fluctuates independently of official flows, and around the world support for official foreign aid, according to opinion polls, remains strong. Although traditionally very little of Americans' private charitable giving has gone to international causes, Americans too tend to support a policy of foreign assistance by their government. A 1996 study of public perceptions of U.S. foreign aid conducted by the University of Maryland's Center for International and Security Studies finds that, while most Americans thought the United States was giving too much aid, this was based on the erroneous assumption that a far greater percentage of national spending went for aid than was actually the case.[54] Although the United States remains the largest single-nation donor after Japan, when expressed as a percentage of gross national product, it comes in last place among OECD donors, at 0.1 percent (and well below the UN target of 0.7 percent). In fact, the poll finds, most Americans support the provision of official foreign aid at a level five times higher than current levels of funding. The American public is generally unaware that Congress was moving to reduce relief and development assistance sharply over the past decade.

To reverse the downward trend of U.S. foreign assistance and bolster public generosity, NGOs engage in a variety of advocacy efforts on behalf of their developing-world clientele. NGOs consider development "education" of the public and policymakers to be a crucial element of advocacy efforts. This generally requires a more complex and nuanced discussion of poverty and development issues than that which makes for good sound bites, compelling grant proposals, or "tear-jerker" appeals for contributions. Avoiding the easy ploys has become a measure of integrity for some organizations. (One NGO even promised on its direct mail envelopes that the reader would not be subjected to pictures of starving children within.)

Despite international criticism over the large portion of their funding that comes from U.S. government sources, and the expectation that this would inevitably hinder independence in programming and policy stance, the major U.S. NGOs for the most part have not behaved in thrall to their largest benefactor and client. Two recent examples of NGOs' strong and decisive public opposition to U.S. government policy are the cases of the government's proposition to target aid directly to Sudanese rebel groups and the U.S. Export-Import

Bank's lending program to African nations to support the sale of U.S.-produced AIDS drugs (which, even at the reduced rate, are much more expensive than locally produced generic products). However, there remains some confusion among U.S. NGOs as to what forms advocacy and lobbying may legally take. Perhaps as a result, they have been more reluctant than their domestic counterparts to expand into a greater range of advocacy activities, in particular to engage the public in policy advocacy and build constituencies for relief and development issues.

Recently, NGO leaders have been cautioned by some in government not to exploit the events of September 11 by implying that poverty and underdevelopment led to the terrorist acts. Some practitioners respond that, while poverty may not have created the terrorist networks' leadership and agenda, it had a hand in creating receptive audiences for them in certain countries.

Advocacy undertaken with a developing-country government on behalf of its own citizens is a trickier matter, for NGOs essentially operate at the pleasure of the host government or local authorities. When faced with evidence of grievous government neglect or outright human rights abuses, NGOs must decide whether to remain silent and continue to work or to speak out and potentially jeopardize their programs and personnel. As a partial solution, many relief and development NGOs have established formal and informal partnerships with local and international human rights organizations whereby any information impugning the local government can be passed along discreetly to a human rights organization for public action.

Political and Ethical Dilemmas

In the camps for Rwandan refugees in Zaire in 1992–94, it became increasingly evident that interspersed with innocent civilians were a large number of ex-army and militiamen responsible for perpetrating the genocidal massacres in Rwanda that preceded the overthrow of the state and exodus of refugees. The NGOs working in the camps became aware that these men were still armed and were using the camps as a safe haven to regroup and launch periodic cross-border attacks into Rwanda. They were exercising control over the other refugees who served as their human shield, terrorizing them against returning to Rwanda, redistributing the food rations, and generally dictating daily life in the camp. As acts of violence inside the camp became commonplace, the NGOs appealed to the international community to provide funds for military protection to disarm and separate the *genocidaires* from the general population. When this was not forthcoming, the aid organizations had to decide whether their presence in the camps and their continued provision of material aid were doing more harm than good. Finally, the NGOs Médecins sans Frontières and International Red Cross, after much internal debate, took the difficult decision to halt operations and withdraw from the camps. Other organizations remained, concerned that the innocents in the camps would be left helpless if they withdrew.

Such are the agonizing dilemmas that now confront NGOs providing humanitarian assistance in complex emergencies. Over the past several years, much organizational soul-searching has attempted to clarify mission principles and political stances and find ways to incorporate themes of justice and human rights in relief work.

What exactly are humanitarian principles? Are they means or ends? In situations of state failure, civil strife, and war economies, the answers become murkier. Humanitarian organizations have always operated within a highly political environment, while espousing a normative value system intended to transcend politics. The classic archetype of a relief organization—for example, the Red Cross—is a purely neutral and apolitical agency providing impartial assistance and protection to civilian victims with the express consent of the parties to the conflict. The International Committee for the Red Cross (ICRC) was officially recognized in the Geneva Conventions as a neutral organization providing impartial aid in conflicts under a protected emblem. It thus derives its mission and operating principles and status from international law.

Owing to its unique history, structure, and legal status, the ICRC is a different sort of organizational entity than an NGO. Yet at least four of the ICRC's seven fundamental principles of humanitarian assistance are seen, with varying degrees of emphasis, in the mission statements and practices of NGOs working in humanitarian assistance. Those four concepts, sometimes referred to as core principles of humanitarian aid, are those of *humanity* (preventing and relieving suffering), *neutrality* (not taking sides), *impartiality* (providing aid indiscriminately, based on need alone), and *independence* (being free of influence of a foreign government and not pursuing a political or religious agenda). With these criteria satisfied, the reasoning once went, an agency could expect to deliver aid without interference from combatants. Naturally, any humanitarian action will in some way affect the course of conflict, so it cannot be said to be truly neutral, yet the guise of completely neutral, apolitical humanitarianism was a convenient "fiction,"[55] upheld by both sides, that allowed NGOs to operate.

The reality of modern conflict confounds these principles. Here the combatants are not opposing national armies, but more often loosely organized armed bands or paramilitaries. The belligerents flout the rules of war by deliberately targeting civilians (and occasionally aid workers) and manipulate assistance for strategic advantage or even as an end in itself. The fiction has largely unraveled, and NGOs have been forced to rethink their position. Some organizations have reworked their philosophies to place them in an underlying context of human rights and justice. A few NGOs have explicit human rights advocacy functions in their missions. Many organizations have adopted the "do no harm" approach,[56] which acknowledges aid's potential for negative impacts in conflicts and seeks to minimize them, while maintaining as neutral a stance as possible. Others have abandoned the concept of neutrality altogether, adopting a solidarity stance on behalf of the victims. This is the approach most commonly associated with organizations belonging to the "French doctors' movement," such as Médecins sans Frontières and Médecins du Monde. A third or middle-way course attempts to straddle the two, in that it strives to address the root causes and to use humanitarian aid toward peaceful outcomes, yet "resists taking sides."[57]

The urgency of providing aid in conflict situations means that organizations have had to shift their focus from the concept of "absolute" principles of humanitarianism to a utilitarian notion of operational guidelines.[58] Because there are no longer any absolutes, each situation must be decided on a case-by-case basis. There have been situations where the fundamental principles are internally contradictory, and different organizations may take opposite courses of action, each citing a humanitarian principle. As in Zaire, one NGO may withdraw assistance when criminal elements are misusing aid, while another may remain because they feel compelled by the humanitarian imperative to be of whatever small help they can be to the real victims. The problem NGOs face is a lack of guidance on how to make these judgment calls. Some practitioners have suggested that a legalistic model would be helpful: a compilation of "case law" or ethical history recounting NGOs' actual decisions and focusing on the process for making them.

At the end of the 1990s, relief and development practitioners were captivated for a brief period by the idea of active "political humanitarianism," that is, the idea that aid could be instrumental not only in recovery and peace*building* efforts but in peace*making* and conflict resolution as well. The watchword became "coherence" with the political actors, specifically the United Nations. Since then, the pendulum has swung back somewhat, and many practitioners, disillusioned with experiences in Afghanistan and Central Africa, have decided that integration with political actors requires too great a compromise of humanitarian ethics.[59] The talk is now more about "complementarity": finding ways to work in effective coordination with political and military actors, while maintaining independence and staying true to principles.

Overall, the notion of political "conditionality" on assistance—the withdrawal or threat of withdrawal of aid to achieve a particular political outcome—is widely disapproved among NGOs, but operational conditionality—the minimum criteria for an agency to be able to work effectively and in good conscience—is something most relief NGOs are now struggling to define for themselves.

The threat of withdrawing humanitarian assistance is perhaps the only leverage that NGOs wield in complex political emergencies, and it could conceivably be used in a decisive and strategic way.[60] Once again, however, achieving interagency consensus and coordination on a unified stance remains a sticking point. Although great strides have been made in setting common operational and performance standards, the community is still a long way from unanimity on operational principles and terms of engagement, suspension, and withdrawal.[61] This begs the question: Is unanimity required in every situation, or in some cases would it be desirable for certain organizations to disengage for the purpose of public condemnation, while others remain on the ground to ensure that the affected population receives at least some services? Would a unified strategy increase the leverage of NGOs, or would it play into the hands of belligerents by being predictable? There are naturally strong opposing viewpoints between practitioners seeking to tighten the rules of the NGO "club" and others wishing to protect its internal diversity. Those familiar with the complex and varied political conditions in the field are reluctant to sign onto something that may tie their hands in the future.

These dilemmas and debates are exacerbated in the general political vacuum that developed around intrastate and regional conflicts after the cold war. The major powers, in particular the United States, flirted briefly with armed "humanitarian intervention" in Somalia in the early days of what promised to be a "new world order," then sharply withdrew from this role after it became clear that casualties and protracted engagement were not acceptable risks in regions or crises where there was no compelling national interest. Most governments have followed the United States' lead, limiting themselves to funding humanitarian aid efforts. As Alex de Waal puts it, "Sending relief is a weapon of first resort: popular at home, usually unobjectionable abroad, and an excuse for not looking more deeply into underlying political problems."[62] The NGOs, along with the humanitarian agencies of the United Nations, have been thrown into the breach left open by the international political community, are expected to function without adequate protection for their workers or the populations they serve, and are often blamed for undesirable outcomes. NGOs have come to the reluctant realization that their options are in fact severely limited and that their role in protection and peacebuilding is essentially passive in the absence of the political will and concerted international action needed to achieve sustainable peace.

Likely Future Evolution of the Nonprofit Role in the Field and Factors Shaping It

Undoubtedly, the NGO landscape will look different five years from now than it did just five years ago. Several developments are probable in the near future.

Slower Growth of the NGO Sector

Some have predicted that the boom in NGOs of the 1980s and 1990s has plateaued,[63] for even if there were a new surge of complex humanitarian emergencies such as drove the sector's growth in the 1990s, the rising start-up costs and dwindling market share for new organizations would deter any further expansion. The oligopoly of large and reputable NGOs has solidified and controls an ever greater proportion of the resources for assistance. Many major donors, such as USAID, exhibit a preference for the larger NGOs with whom they have prior working relationships and in whom they have confidence. Donors are more wary of funding large numbers of international NGOs in a single area, having witnessed the effects of poor coordination, and are less willing to foot the bill for start-up costs for organizations without a preexisting operational presence in the area. Instead, they encourage mentoring and subgrant partnerships between their international NGO grantees and indigenous organizations. Therefore, as the large NGOs continue to build national affiliates and spin-offs, it becomes harder for new northern-based NGOs to penetrate the market. An additional barrier to entry for new NGOs may be the perception of higher security risks to personnel in the field. Continued security challenges will necessitate a greater emphasis on professional training and, in some circumstances, a more coordinated security stance.

Homogenization

Reflecting these pressures, a homogenization of sorts is taking place among the northern relief and development NGOs, and this process may threaten the diversity, vitality, and flexibility for which they first made their mark. The tide of professionalization and performance enhancement will not likely abate, as increasingly NGOs feel pressure to conform to the international standards. For smaller, younger NGOs especially, the desire for legitimacy and credibility with donors and counterparts will encourage them to adhere to such norms. Whether southern NGOs and regional organizations will agree to adopt and utilize these largely northern-created standards for their own operations is another question, one that will need to be addressed as NGOs increasingly go global and devolve responsibility onto local entities.

Partnerships

It is reasonable to expect increasing and tighter partnerships between NGOs and the private and public sectors. The private sector, in particular, has surged in importance to both development and relief efforts. Several large multinationals have explored opportunities for assisting populations in the developing world, where new markets for their products are emerging or anticipated. This movement, dubbed "global corporate citizenship," brings societal needs and concern for the public good within a firm's overall business strategy. Participating in development projects helps large firms to stay attuned to local cultures and conditions as a matter of good business sense, since in many cases "the company may be multinational, but its approach is multilocal."[64]

Acknowledging their lack of expertise in the area, the corporations are partnering with UN agencies and NGOs. Firms such as BP Amoco in Angola, Chevron in Kazakhstan, and many others have used such development partnerships to increase their standing with local governments, burnish their public image, and nurture growing markets. As Reynold Levy, International Red Cross president and former AT&T Foundation president, predicts, "More companies will join the early pioneers of overseas giving. To do otherwise isn't just uncharitable; it would deprive these companies of an important business asset."[65]

NGOs are approaching these new relationships thoughtfully and cautiously, with an eye toward the potential pitfalls as well as the benefits. A number of complex and strategic "cross-sector alliances" have sprung up in recent years, such as between CARE and Starbucks and between ACCION International and Citibank, where complementarities of mission and values are identified and utilized to the benefit of both parties. James Austin of Harvard Business School writes about a "collaboration continuum," in which these alliances may pass through three distinct stages: the philanthropic stage (where the NGO solicits a corporation for donations), the transactional stage (where resources are exchanged through specific activities, such as event sponsorship or cause-related marketing), and the integrative stage (where there is a higher level of engagement, communication, and integration between staffs, missions, and activities).[66] Within these multilayered relationships, NGOs can use their leverage with the multinational to push for business policies and practices they deem to be more developmentally sound.

Private sector actors are also increasing their presence in humanitarian relief. Corporate vendors have long been a fixture of emergency response, providing the relief commodities, equipment, and overseas transport for large and small aid agencies and doing billions of dollars a year worth of business with UN peace operations alone.[67] However, recent conflicts such as that in Bosnia-Herzegovina have seen the corporate sector moving beyond procurement and transport to actual implementation of aid activities. A group of five NGOs have partnered with Smithkline Beecham, earmarking portions of the firm's pharmaceutical inventory for emergency medical donations. And in the Kosovo crisis, NGOs such as the International Organization for Migration obtained the voluntary services of Microsoft, Hewlett Packard, and other corporations to create a simple, portable, computerized system for registering refugees.[68]

Short-Term Financial Hardship

The drying up of foundation and corporate donations after September 11 capped an already difficult period for NGO finances as the U.S.—and global—economy slipped into recession. Those NGOs who invested their endowments or reserves in the stock market lost a large portion of their buffer over the past year. Even the largest and most affluent organizations were not spared. CARE, for one, experienced its worst fiscal year in a decade and was forced to adopt budget austerity measures, even looking at the difficult choice between cutting the salaries of senior staff or laying off employees. NGOs as a whole appear to be hunkering down until the economy cycles upward, and most are not planning any major fundraising events until 2002.

Steps Needed

Various steps are needed to improve the position of the nonprofit sector in the field or to improve the capacity of nonprofits to make positive contributions. This section deals with the need to devolve responsibility to local actors, to involve regional organizations on a more significant level, to improve coordination and harmonization between NGOs and donors, to improve cooperation, and to reframe the public message of assistance.

Bringing in the South: Long-Term, Strategic Devolution of Responsibility to Local Actors

The future of the international system for relief and development lies not with the northern NGO sector, which for the moment has maximized its capacity for growth (although not for effectiveness and quality), but rather with the south. Devolution or "indigenization" of relief and development assistance has been happening piecemeal throughout the NGO sector. Whether this is done through training individual professionals, mentoring existing local organizations, or spinning off former country offices, the goal is to transfer responsibility and "ownership" of the assistance from international agencies to local authorities and organizations. The larger organizations, such as CARE and World Vision, have taken the greatest strides in this area, and the transfer has occurred mostly in the context of development activities as opposed to emergency assistance.

The prevailing model of humanitarian aid is one in which northern agencies and donors perform the bulk of the design, financing, implementation, and management of aid programs for affected populations in the south. While there is widespread support in principle for the idea of building local capacities and professional expertise in emergency relief, there has been very little in the way of concrete action toward this end. The participation of local organizations and professionals in the design and delivery of relief aid is minimal. Although many international NGOs will partner with local NGOs or community organizations in emergency situations, "they tend to be partnerships of necessity and the moment, with the local groups helping to target beneficiaries and acting as the last links in the delivery chain,"[69] as opposed to building capacity toward an eventual independent response. The reasons cited by field practitioners are related partly to the inherent complexities of providing relief, in particular in conflict situations. It is unreasonable, some argue, to expect that, among the chaos of a failed state such as Somalia or Sierra Leone, a developing country could muster the resources or organizational capacities required for an effective response.

In cases of civil conflict, the issue of impartiality of local staff is a particular stumbling block. Then, too, there are warnings of the potential brain drain of scarce professionals from local posts to better-paying NGOs. Finally, practitioners have voiced concern about the skills, financial acumen, and trustworthiness of local staffers. Each of these arguments has an equally persuasive counterargument,[70] and at the heart of the problem is the lack of relief agency resources to invest in the building of human capital and organizational capacity in the south.

Investment is the key concept in this regard. Successful devolution will not happen by itself; it requires the leap from reactive action to long-term strategic planning and capacity building. Scarce resources and inefficient funding arrangements make serious long-term planning nigh on impossible for all but the most well-endowed NGOs. However, if these organizations are genuine in their support for the idea of a lower-cost, locally based response capacity, they need to adopt a farsighted and proactive approach. A fundamental first step in this direction is to realign the governance structure so that the organization may draw on the diverse strengths of national, as well as regional and global, perspectives.

Exploring the Potential to Increase the Role of Regional Organizations in Relief and Development

One way of approaching the devolution issue is through "burden-sharing" with regional and subregional intergovernmental organizations.[71] The UN and various donor countries have called for these organizations to assume greater political and operational responsibility for humanitarian action. It is an appealing concept, since relief and development issues are rarely constrained by borders and the regional organizations have the potential to pool local resources and to coordinate action from a local political perspective.

There have been some initial successes with regional preparedness and mitigation efforts in the Americas and the Caribbean, and these have attracted international support. However, intergovernmental disaster management mechanisms in Asia are far less developed. And despite a number of planning initiatives, a survey of humanitarian capacities within Africa's regional and subregional organizations demonstrates that they possess "neither the institutional mechanisms nor sufficient financial resources required to undertake the comprehensive range of activities grouped under humanitarian action."[72]

NGOs, which have had very little to do with regional organizations in the past, may want to explore new capacity-building arrangements with these potential future partners. At the same time, there are valid concerns about relocating relief and development efforts to the regional organizations. There is the

fear, for instance, that the process will become overly politicized, with humanitarian concerns perhaps taking a backseat to the interests of a regional hegemon.
There are concerns also that the universal standards and codes of conduct, hard
won by the international NGOs, might be diluted or dismissed in the regional
context. Furthermore, the regional and subregional organizations may simply
not be interested in working with NGOs.

Improving Coordination and Harmonization among NGO and Donor Policies and Operations

The NGO community has always been distinguished by a blend of cooperation
and competition. For every example of destructive jockeying for funding and
turf, where a lack of coordination and transparency between agencies has caused
duplications and service gaps, there is another case where the NGOs have coordinated and rationalized their activities effectively (with or without prodding
from donors and UN agencies), sharing all manner of information and material
resources. On occasion, these opposing scenarios have occurred at different
phases of the same emergency. Redoubled efforts at coordination and complementarity, pooling of resources for greater efficiency, and perhaps even business-
style mergers of duplicative organizations should be explored.

Donors, for their part, need to recognize the power they possess to have positive and negative effects on NGO efficiency and effectiveness in the field. Many
of the major bilateral funders have already adopted quality-enhancing requirements of their grantees in the needs assessment and project design stages.
Although NGOs have complained that this sometimes results in donor micromanagement and infringes on programming independence, in some instances
the donors' requirements have improved the NGOs' project designs. Donors
such as USAID's Office of U.S. Foreign Disaster Assistance have also had some
success in compelling coordination among their implementing partners by
requiring that NGOs working in the same area present joint needs assessments
and proposals for projects with a rationalized division of labor. However, donor
coordination on substantive issues of relief and development is wanting. The
Development Assistance Committee of the OECD is a valuable forum for
donor dialogue and policy guidance and should be strengthened. Unfortunately,
most other donor forums and pledging conferences are used mainly as political
showcases rather than as forums for discussing technical matters and coordinating policy.[73]

Increasing Cooperative Efforts to Bridge the "Relief to Development Gap"

As further evidence of the need for enhanced coordination for greater effectiveness, NGOs and donors alike have begun to realize the danger of maintaining
an artificial separation between relief and development projects and funding. In
countries emerging from violent civil conflict or natural disaster, the recovery

period after the acute crisis (when emergency relief assistance has usually ended) is crucial. Without continued assistance throughout this period, such countries will not be able to get back on the development track, and crisis may easily erupt once again. The concept of a linear continuum from relief to development work in a post-crisis country must be supplanted by a more complex understanding of recovery, where relief, rehabilitation, and development activities coexist, overlap, and reinforce each other on a needs-driven basis, not according to an arbitrary timetable. To this end, NGOs that work in both development and relief have led the call for more sustained, consistent, and less fragmented funding. Donors and international organizations have begun to look seriously at the problem, with such recent efforts as the Brookings Roundtable on the Relief to Development Gap and proposals for new financing and coordinating mechanisms emerging from this process.[74]

Reframing the Assistance Message

At an impromptu meeting in the wake of the September 11 attacks, NGO leaders expressed the determination to stay true to their missions, in the conviction that relief and development priorities before September 11 are no less important now, and to distinguish themselves in the public eye from the "ambulance chasing" of some domestic groups that swarmed around the large sums of money raised for victims of the World Trade Center attack. NGOs' advocacy efforts will focus on urging the United States not to let geopolitical interests determine aid flows. At the same time, there is a sense among the organizations that the time may be propitious for reformulating the public relations message about assistance and for shifting from the western opportunity-based paradigm of development to one based on human rights. These sentiments among the NGO community are not new, however, and in the absence of such a coherent message, the domestic constituency for foreign relief and development assistance remains elusive. There is wide agreement among the NGOs that their most intractable problem is that no one has yet come up with a compelling story on the vital importance and effectiveness of foreign aid. In beginning to strategize around this problem, U.S. NGOs have called for the marshaling of hard facts and figures to better support their case. For example, new InterAction initiatives aim to gather empirical data supporting the positive effects of development assistance, on the one hand, while employing sophisticated polling techniques to probe public perceptions, on the other.

Conclusions

All in all, it has been a humbling few years for the international relief and development NGOs. David Rieff and other observers of the field have alluded to the "hubris" of humanitarian practitioners who refuse to recognize the limitations of their organizations in the face of the tremendously complicated situations in which they now operate. More realistic expectations of the proper roles and potential impact of NGOs are required of both policymakers and the NGOs themselves. This is especially true in complex emergencies, where humanitarian action without political action has proven ineffectual at best, disastrous at worst.

Fortunately, international relief and development have always been a highly introspective and self-critiquing field, with NGO members seemingly capable of innovation and adaptation in response to new challenges. And, unfortunately, the persistence of poverty and violent conflict in the developing world means that there is no shortage of opportunities for experiential learning and operations research at the field level. Indeed, the most far-reaching analyses on the issues of relief and development assistance tend to emanate from those individuals directly involved in its implementation. The era of well-meaning amateurs has given way to an epistemic community of well-trained professionals. Gone too is the old model of relief and development as northern charity to southern recipients. Development and, to a lesser degree, relief assistance are being slowly devolved into global networks of international affiliates and locally based capacities.

The U.S.-based NGOs represent some of the largest, oldest, and most highly regarded organizations in the field. Yet their ability and willingness to exercise leadership among NGOs in the search for common solutions have been hindered by an operational orientation that some European counterparts have criticized as excessively pragmatic and functional, politically shortsighted, and even isolationist. The issue is significant because the future of the U.S. NGO sector is inseparable from that of the international NGO community as a whole. Nonetheless, in that community there is currently no consensus on the degree to which NGOs should adopt a unified strategy on political principles, no charismatic leadership at the upper levels speaking persuasively for joint action, no peer review process, and no field-level compliance mechanisms for the international performance standards that have been set. The cooperation that does take place among NGOs has been purely voluntary, partially induced by the desire for legitimacy, and all the more remarkable for occurring within an essentially competitive environment. What makes this possible are the underlying values of the work, the unique spirit of the organizations, and their common commitment to humanitarianism.

Despite some images portrayed in the media, the current state of relief and development NGOs is not one of disarray and crisis, but rather one of a field at a crossroads, seeking to play a determinate role in its own evolution. The challenge now facing NGOs is to safeguard their independence, their principles as each organization defines them, and their comparative advantage, while at the same time forging closer partnerships with the public and private sectors and with their increasingly important southern counterparts.

Notes

1. The term *nongovernmental organization* encompasses a variety of organizations, including southern indigenous organizations and community-based groups. U.S. Agency for International Development (USAID) uses the term *private voluntary organization* to differentiate the northern-based, internationally operating organizations from other NGOs. This chapter uses the more universal designation of NGO, qualifying, when necessary, which type of organization is in question.

2. Thomas Dichter, "Globalization and Its Effects on NGOs: Efflorescence or a Blurring of Roles and Relevance?" *NonProfit and Voluntary Sector Quarterly,* vol. 28, no. 4 (1999), supplemental issue: "Globalization and Northern NGOs: The Challenge of Relief and Development in a Changing Context."

3. Office of U.S. Foreign Disaster Assistance, *Annual Report 2000* (www.usaid.gov/hum_response/ofda/00annnual/how.html [2001]).

4. Vernon Ruttan, *United States Development Assistance Policy: The Domestic Politics of Foreign Economic Aid* (Johns Hopkins University Press, 1996), pp. 476–77.

5. Marc Lindenberg and J. Patrick Dobel, "The Challenges of Globalization for Northern International Relief and Development NGOs," *NonProfit and Voluntary Sector Quarterly,* vol. 28, no. 4 (1999): 4–24.

6. Kofi Annan, *Facing the Humanitarian Challenge: Towards a Culture of Prevention* (New York: United Nations Department of Public Information, 1999), p. 2.

7. Taylor Seybolt, "Major Armed Conflicts," in *SIPRI Yearbook 2000: Armaments, Disarmament, and International Security* (Oxford University Press for the Stockholm International Peace Research Institute, 2000).

8. Seybolt, "Major Armed Conflicts."

9. International Federation of Red Cross and Red Crescent Societies, *World Disasters Report 1993* (Geneva: IFRC, 1993).

10. Annan, *Facing the Humanitarian Challenge*, p. 10.

11. Security Council Resolutions 688 and 794, pertaining to humanitarian intervention in northern Iraq and Somalia, have been seen as precedent-setting decisions, essentially eroding the principle of nonintervention in sovereign states in the interest of humanitarianism and human rights.

12. Marc Lindenberg, "Declining State Capacity, Voluntarism, and the Globalization of the Not-for-Profit Sector," *NonProfit and Voluntary Sector Quarterly,* vol. 28, no. 4 (1999): 147–67.

13. Dichter, "Globalization and Its Effects on NGOs," p. 39.

14. USAID, *2000 VolAg Report* (www.info.usaid.gov/hum_response/pvc/pvcpubs.html [December 2000]), p. 90; Dichter, "Globalization and Its Effects on NGOs," p. 40.

15. InterAction, "Final Budget Numbers for the FY2000 Foreign Aid Budget" (www.interaction.org/advocacy/leg/upd1122a99.html [June 14, 2000]).

16. Janet Salm, "Coping with Globalization: A Profile of the Northern NGO Sector," *NonProfit and Voluntary Sector Quarterly,* vol. 28, no. 4 (1999): 87–103.

17. USAID, *2000 VolAg Report*.

18. Established in the late 1970s as a microcredit program for the poorest of the poor, the Grameen Bank is now the largest rural lending institution in Bangladesh, with more than 2.3 million borrowers, primarily women.

19. Shepard Forman, Stewart Patrick, and Dirk Salomons, *Recovering from Conflict: Strategy for an International Response* (New York University, Center on International Cooperation, 2000).

20. Lindenberg and Dobel, "Challenges of Globalization."

21. Alex de Waal, *Famine Crimes* (Indianapolis: Indiana University, African Rights and the International African Institute, 1997).

22. Examples of NGO cooperation around principles of engagement include the Red Cross/NGO Code of Conduct, the Principles and Protocols of Humanitarian Operation (Liberia, 1995), and the Agreement on Ground Rules in South Sudan (1994). See Nicholas Leader, *The Politics of Principle: The Principles of Humanitarian Action in Practice* (London: Overseas Development Institute, Humanitarian Policy Group, March 2000).

23. See, for example, Dani Rodrik, *Has Globalization Gone Too Far?* (Washington: Institute for International Economics, 1997); Shashi Tharoor, "The Future of Civil Conflict," *World Policy Journal,* vol. 16, no. 1 (1999): 1–11.

24. Lindenberg, "Declining State Capacity."

25. *Global Humanitarian Assistance 2000,* an independent report commissioned by the Inter-Agency Standing Committee from Development Initiatives (Geneva: United Nations Office for the Coordination of Humanitarian Affairs, Inter-Agency Standing Committee, May 2000), p. viii; Shepard Forman and Rita Parhad, *Paying for Essentials: Resources for Humanitarian Assistance,* Policy Paper Series (New York: Center on International Cooperation, 1997).

26. Judith Randel, Tony German, and Deborah Ewing, eds., *The Reality of Aid 2000,* Development Initiatives (London: Earthscan, 2000).

27. Randel, German, and Ewing, *Reality of Aid 2000,* p. 4.

28. OECD Development Assistance Committee, *DAC News,* June 7, 2000 (www.devinit. org/dac.htm [October 2000]).

29. *Giving USA 2001* (Indianapolis: AAFRC Trust for Philanthropy, Indiana University, Center on Philanthropy, 2001), available at www.aafrc.org [September 2001].

30. Dichter, "Globalization and Its Effects on NGOs," p. 50.

31. Randel, German, and Ewing, *Reality of Aid 2000,* p. 4.

32. Dichter, "Globalization and Its Effects on NGOs," p. 51.

33. USAID, *1999 VolAg Report,* p. 90.

34. USAID, *1999 VolAg Report.*

35. Jean Bossuyt and Patrick Develtere, "Between Autonomy and Identity: The Financing Dilemma of NGOs," *Courier ACP-EU,* vol. 152 (July/August 1995).

36. Center on International Cooperation with Lester Salamon and Associates, *The Preparedness Challenge in Humanitarian Assistance* (New York: Center on International Cooperation, 1999), available at www.nyu.edu/pages/cic/projects/humanassist/publication.html [June 3, 2002].

37. Examples include prearranged rapid-response consortia, such as the Indefinite Quantities Contract signed between the Office of U.S. Foreign Disaster Assistance and the NGOs CARE, International Medical Corps, and IRC (International Rescue Committee), and earmarked advance funds for emergencies, such as the State Department Bureau for Population, Refugees, and Migration's memorandum of understanding with the International Red Cross. See Center on International Cooperation with Lester Salamon and Associates, "Preparedness Challenge in Humanitarian Assistance."

38. See Mats Berdal and David Keen, "Violence and Economic Agendas in Civil Wars," *Millennium,* vol. 26, no. 3 (1997): 795–818; William Reno, *Warlord Politics and African States* (Boulder, Colo.: Lynne Rienner, 1998).

39. Konrad Van Brabant, *Security Training: Where Are We Now?* RRN Discussion Paper (London: Overseas Development Institute with *Forced Migration Review,* 1999).

40. Michael Edwards and David Hulme, *Making a Difference: NGOs and Development in a Changing World* (London: Earthscan, 1992).

41. Edwards and Hulme, *Making a Difference*, p. 27.

42. Steering Committee of the Joint Evaluation of Emergency Assistance to Rwanda, *The International Response to Conflict and Genocide Lessons from the Rwanda Experience* (Steering Committee of the Joint Evaluation of Emergency Assistance to Rwanda, March 1996), available at www.reliefweb.int.

43. The Sphere Project was a collaboration of the major umbrella groups of aid organizations in Europe and the United States (Steering Committee for Humanitarian Response, InterAction, VOICE, International Committee of the Red Cross, and International Council of Voluntary Agencies). Phase I of the project culminated in the publication of the *Humanitarian Charter and Minimum Standards in Disaster Response*. The minimum standards cover the areas of water and sanitation, nutrition, food aid, shelter and site planning, and health services. The charter calls for agencies to adhere to humanitarian principles, such as those embodied in International Humanitarian Law, and reaffirms their commitment to the "Code of Conduct for the International Red Cross and Red Crescent Movement in NGOs in Disaster Relief" (1994). See Sphere Project, *Humanitarian Charter and Minimum Standards in Disaster Response* (London: Oxfam, 2000).

44. The private voluntary organization standards are available at www.interaction.org [August 22, 2002].

45. Barkely Calkins, "Improving InterAction's PVO Standards through the Pursuit of Excellence," *Monday Developments,* vol. 18, no. 19 (October 23, 2000): 4.

46. Calkins, "Improving InterAction's PVO Standards."

47. Abby Stoddard, "Background Paper on Issues in Humanitarian Aid" (New York: Center on International Cooperation—Ford Foundation Learning Initiative, May 1999).

48. John Mitchell and Deborah Doane, "An Ombudsman for Humanitarian Assistance?" *Disasters,* vol. 23, no. 2 (1999): 115–24.

49. Dirk Salomons, *Building Regional and National Capacities for Leadership in Humanitarian Assistance,* a report prepared for the Resources for Humanitarian Assistance Project (New York: Center on International Cooperation, 1999), www.nyu.edu/pages/cic/projects/humanassist/publication.html [June 3, 2002].

50. Dichter, "Globalization and Its Effects," p. 52.

51. Bradford Gray, "World Blindness and the Medical Profession: Conflicting Medical Cultures and the Ethnical Dilemmas of Helping," *Milbank Quarterly,* vol. 70, no. 3 (1992): 535–56.

52. Lindenberg and Dobel, "Challenges of Globalization."

53. Lindenberg and Dobel, "Challenges of Globalization."

54. Steven Kull, principal investigator, *Americans and Foreign Aid: A Study of American Public Attitudes* (University of Maryland, Program on International Policy Attitudes, March 1, 1995). See also U.S. Agency for International Development, "The Myth of Opposition to Foreign Assistance" (Washington: USAID, 2000), available at www.info.usaid.gov/about/polls.html [July 2000].

55. Leader, "Politics of Principle."

56. Mary Anderson, *Do No Harm: Supporting Local Capacities for Peace through Aid* (Cambridge: Collaborative for Development Action, 1996).

57. Leader, "Politics of Principle."

58. Leader, "Politics of Principle."

59. Paula Newberg, "Politics at the Heart: The Architecture of Humanitarian Assistance to Afghanistan," Working Paper (Washington: Carnegie Endowment for International Peace, July 1999).

60. A conference held in May 2000 by the Henri Dunant Center and Overseas Development Institute addressed this issue directly, asking whether common criteria could be

established among humanitarian actors on when to engage or disengage. The report is forthcoming.

61. The Humanitarian Policy Group at England's Overseas Development Institute has examined three interesting experiments in NGO coordination on operational principles: the "ground rules" negotiated in South Sudan and in Liberia and the Joint Policy of Operation and the Principles and Protocols of Humanitarian Operation. See Leader, "Politics of Principle."

62. de Waal, *Famine Crimes.*

63. Lindenberg, "Declining State Capacity," p. 155.

64. David Logan and Michael Tuffrey, "Striking a Balance between McStandardization and Local Autonomy," *@lliance,* vol. 5, no. 2 (2000): 6.

65. Reynold Levy, *Give and Take: A Candid Account of Corporate Philanthropy* (Harvard Business School, 1999), p. 187.

66. James E. Austin, *The Collaboration Challenge: How Nonprofits and Businesses Succeed through Strategic Alliances* (San Francisco: Jossey-Bass, 2000), pp. 20–26.

67. Ann Cooper, "To Vendors, the UN Is Just Another Customer," *Wall Street Journal,* September 26, 1997.

68. Logan and Tuffrey, "Striking a Balance," p. 18

69. Stoddard, "Background Paper."

70. Salomons, "Building Regional and National Capacities."

71. David O'Brien, *Regional Burden-Sharing for Humanitarian Action,* Discussion Paper (New York: Center on International Cooperation, 1999), available at www.nyu.edu/pages/cic/projects/humanassist/publication.html [June 3, 2002].

72. O'Brien, *Regional Burden Sharing.*

73. Shepard Forman and Stewart Patrick, eds., *Good Intentions: Pledges of Aid for Post-Conflict Recovery* (Boulder, Colo.: Lynne Rienner for the Center on International Cooperation, 2000).

74. See Forman, Patrick, and Salomons, *Recovering from Conflict.*

8

Religious Congregations

MARK CHAVES

There are more than 300,000 religious congregations—churches, synagogues, mosques, and temples—in the United States. More than 60 percent of American adults attended a service at a religious congregation within the
past year, and about one-quarter attend services in any given week. Although
their exact manner of legal incorporation varies across states and religious
groups, congregations, like most other kinds of membership organizations,
reside almost wholly within the nonprofit sector, if by nonprofit sector we mean
those organizations that do not distribute surplus income to their boards,
employees, or members. Although congregations' manner of incorporation
varies, and although at times they engage in for-profit activities, contemporary
American congregations do not span the nonprofit, for-profit, and government
sectors to the same extent as other types of organizations, such as hospitals,
childcare centers, social service providers, and schools.

Contemporary American congregations also do not span the boundary
between nonprofit and government to the same extent as congregations in other
times and places. In some other societies, and at earlier points in American history, religious congregations are, or were, at least partly under the auspices of
government in more or less officially established state churches. Today, however,

The author wishes to thank Peter Dobkin Hall, James P. Wind, and, especially, Lester Salamon
for very helpful comments on earlier drafts of this chapter.

contemporary American congregations are essentially voluntary membership organizations, and this fact fundamentally shapes their current situation and the nature of the challenges facing their leaders.

Assessing the overall health of religious congregations in the United States is greatly complicated by the dramatic variation that exists among congregations. One important dimension of that variation is size. Congregations and denominations define congregational "members" differently, making it difficult to examine congregations' size in terms of official membership. Other measures—the number of regular participants, for example, whether or not those participants are official members of the congregation—provide a better picture of congregations' size. The same picture emerges across several such measures. Most congregations are small: 59 percent of U.S. congregations, for example, have fewer than 100 regular participants, counting both adults and children; 71 percent have fewer than 100 regularly participating adults.

The smallness of most congregations represents only half the story, however, since the size distribution of American congregations is highly skewed. That is, there are relatively small numbers of very large congregations with sizable budgets and multiple staff, but there are many more small congregations with much more modest budgets and only one—or no—full-time staff person. This skewness is such that, although most *congregations* are small, most *people* are associated with medium-to-large congregations. The median congregation has only seventy-five regular participants, but the median person is in a congregation with 400 regular participants. David Horton Smith has pointed out that, like the natural universe, the nonprofit universe has much "dark matter" that is not visible through the usual lenses that focus on the largest organizations.[1] This certainly is true of congregations.

Resource distributions are similarly skewed. The average congregation has an annual budget of only $55,000, but the average person is in a congregation with an annual budget of $250,000. Forty percent of congregations, containing 15 percent of religious service attenders, have no full-time staff; 24 percent, with 7 percent of the people, have no paid staff at all. Only 25 percent of congregations have more than one full-time staff person, but 65 percent of the people are in those congregations. Clearly, congregations with no paid staff face challenges qualitatively different from those facing congregations with more than one full-time staff person.

Observers of American religion occasionally speculate about the amount of wealth controlled by religious organizations. Although some congregations hold very substantial endowments, the well-endowed congregation is a rarity. The median congregation has about $1,000 in a savings account, and even the median person's congregation has savings of only $20,000. Only 5 percent of congregations have endowments or savings that total twice their annual operating budget; only 11 percent have a one-year cushion. Although this might make congregations slightly more secure, on average, than other nonprofit organizations—one analyst estimates that only 2 percent of nonprofit organizations have endowments sufficient to cover at least two years of budget—it is clear that the well-endowed religious congregation is atypical.[2] As with income, the wealth distribution among congregations is highly skewed. Some congregations hold significant wealth, but the vast majority operate on the money raised each year.

Another major source of variation among congregations is their denominational affiliation or lack thereof. Individuals do not belong directly to denominations. They belong to congregations, most of which, in turn, are attached to umbrella religious organizations—denominations. The character of these attachments varies substantially. In some denominations, congregations are wholly independent local organizations, owning their own property, fully in charge of decisions about hiring clergy and other staff, and in no way subject to the authority of a denomination's regional or national bodies. In other denominations, congregational property is legally owned by a unit of the denomination, clergy are assigned to congregations by denominational officials, and congregational policies and practices are subject to denominational oversight. Many varieties and mixed forms exist between these two extremes.

However hierarchical or nonhierarchical the relations between congregations and denominations might be, denominations are, themselves, complex organizations. More accurately, denominations are sets of concrete organizations tied to each other in complex and variable ways. In addition to congregations, denominations might contain regional associations of congregations, regional or national representative assemblies, colleges, seminaries, foreign missions agencies, publishing companies, clergy pension companies, social service organizations, Washington lobbying operations, church development offices, and so on. The extent to which these concrete organizations are tightly or loosely connected to each other—and to congregations—varies substantially across denominations.

Congregations relate in very different ways to different parts of their denominations. For some denominational activities, such as periodic national assemblies or conventions, congregations are, on the one hand, sources of delegates and, on the other hand (in denominations in which such assemblies exercise religious authority over congregations), recipients of directives. For others, such as denominational publishing houses, congregations are the primary market for the denominational agency's products or services. Although this chapter does not fully catalogue the ways in which denominations might shape the challenges facing congregations, readers should keep in mind that denominations differ in ways that are relevant to congregational life, and broad developments might have variable consequences for congregations after they filter through different denominational structures.

Table 8-1 gives, in broad categories, the distribution of American congregations' denominational affiliations. The table shows this distribution from two

Table 8-1. *Denominational Distribution of U.S. Congregations, 1998*
Percent

Denominational affiliation[a]	Attendees in congregations with listed affiliation	Congregations with listed affiliation
Roman Catholic Church	29	6
Baptist conventions/denominations	18	25
None	10	18
Methodist denominations	10	14
Lutheran/Episcopal denominations	10	9
Denominations in the reformed tradition	8	8
Other Christian denominations[b]	6	9
Pentecostal denominations	6	8
Jewish	2	1
Non-Christian and non-Jewish	2	3
Total	101	101

Source: National Congregations Study, 1998.

a. Except for the Roman Catholic Church, these categories represent multiple distinct denominations. The largest Protestant denominations are the Southern Baptist Convention, with which 16 percent of congregations and 11 percent of churchgoers are affiliated, and the United Methodist Church, with which 12 percent of congregations and 9 percent of churchgoers are affiliated.

b. This category includes congregations affiliated with denominations but not elsewhere classified in this table.

perspectives. The first column gives the percentage of *people* in congregations associated with a particular denomination. The second column gives the percentage of *congregations* associated with each denomination without respect to how many people are in those congregations. These two percentages are most different for Roman Catholics. On the one hand, 29 percent of religious service attenders in the United States attend Catholic congregations; on the other hand, only 6 percent of U.S. congregations are Catholic. The difference between these two numbers reflects the fact that Catholic congregations are much larger, on average, than other congregations.

Another fact from table 8-1 is worth emphasizing: 18 percent of congregations, containing 10 percent of those who attend religious services, are formally affiliated with no denomination. Although it is not obvious from table 8-1—which collapses specific denominations, except the Roman Catholic Church, into religious families—if unaffiliated congregations were all in one denomination, they would constitute the third largest in number of participants (behind the Roman Catholic Church and the Southern Baptist Convention) and the largest in number of congregations. Although most congregations are attached to denominations, a noticeable minority of American congregations are not formally affiliated with any denomination. Some of these independent congregations even operate as sole proprietorships. We do not have national data to assess whether the number of independent congregations is increasing or decreasing, but research on congregations in one New England city finds that more recently established congregations were much more likely to be nondenominational than congregations established longer ago.[3] How independence from any denomination alters the challenges facing congregations and how the presence—perhaps the increasing presence—of large numbers of independent congregations creates challenges for the sector as a whole are open questions that this chapter does not attempt to answer.

Although size and denomination may be the most basic ways in which congregations vary, they are not the only important sources of variation. Some congregations draw their membership mainly from the immediately surrounding neighborhoods, others—which Nancy Ammerman calls "niche" congregations[4]—draw certain kinds of people from all over a city. Some are rural; others are urban. Congregations also vary in their ethnic, social class, and age composition. And so on.

This complexity notwithstanding, this chapter attempts to assess certain aspects of the state of America's religious congregations, paying special attention to four key challenges: maintaining a membership base, securing adequate financial resources, recruiting talented leaders, and finding the right balance between member- and public-serving roles. None of these challenges is new—indeed, they are all perennial challenges for American religion—but they take different forms at different times. The goal of this chapter is to describe the specific shape of these challenges at the beginning of the twenty-first century.

Unless otherwise noted, statistics reported in this chapter are from the National Congregations Study, a 1998 survey of a nationally representative sample of 1,236 religious congregations. The congregational sample was generated by asking respondents in a national survey of individuals to report the name and location of the religious congregation they attend, if they attend religious services. A one-hour survey was then administered to a key informant—usually clergy or other staff—within each named congregation. The response rate was 80 percent.[5]

Key Challenges for American Religious Congregations

American religious congregations are facing a variety of challenges. Four of these challenges seem especially significant: maintaining a membership base, securing adequate financial resources, recruiting talented leaders, and finding an appropriate balance between member-serving and public-serving roles. This section examines each in turn.

Maintaining a Membership Base

Religious congregations are voluntary membership organizations, and their fortunes are directly affected by demographic changes that influence participation in voluntary associations. Although conventional religious belief remains very high in the United States—more than 90 percent of Americans believe in some sort of higher power, more than 60 percent have no doubts about God's existence, almost 80 percent believe in miracles, 70 percent believe in heaven, and almost 60 percent believe in hell[6]—stable high levels of religious belief do not guarantee stable trends in participation.

Indeed, recent research shows that participation in organized religious activity has declined since the 1960s. One study, drawing on time-use diaries completed by individuals, finds that weekly attendance at a religious service declined continuously over the past three decades from about 40 percent in 1965 to about 25 percent in 1994.[7] Additional evidence comes from Robert Putnam's recent monumental book on civic engagement in the United States.[8] Putnam, using survey data from five sources, finds the same decline in religious participation evident in the time-use diaries. Although there are variations in this pattern across religious traditions, the pattern of decline is similar for both blacks and whites. African Americans are more religious than white Americans, but their religious participation shows the same sort of decline.

Putnam's findings on other sorts of civic engagement place the trends in religious participation in a broader context. These findings suggest that the decline in religious participation is but one part of a broader decline—one that began sometime in the last third of the twentieth century and continues into the present—affecting a whole range of civic and voluntary associations that are close cousins to religious congregations. In this light, it probably is a mistake to proceed as if the membership problems facing some congregations are peculiar to religion.

Evidence also converges on an important demographic aspect of this trend: recent generations attend religious services at lower rates than did previous generations when they were the same age. Putnam finds this pattern across a strikingly wide range of activities, including church attendance. Declining participation in all sorts of voluntary associations, including religious ones, is not occurring so much because individual people became less involved over the past three or four decades. Rather, younger cohorts of individuals do less of this activity than older cohorts, and those born earlier are inexorably leaving the scene, being replaced by less civically engaged recent generations. Even if not a single individual changes his or her behavior over time, it still is possible for widespread social change to occur via generational turnover, and this seems to be happening with civic engagement in general and with religious participation in particular.

There is, of course, variation in these patterns across religious groups, perhaps the most important of which is between evangelical and mainline Protestants. It is well known that evangelical or conservative Protestant denominations have grown in recent decades, while mainline and more liberal denominations have declined. While the percentage of American Protestants claiming mainline affiliation declined from 57 percent in the early 1970s to 47 percent in the late 1990s, conservative Protestant denominations grew from 43 percent of all Protestants to 53 percent in the same period. This shift is often attributed to people fleeing mainline denominations for the supposedly warmer confines of evangelical churches, but recent research shows that perhaps as much as 80 percent of this shift is produced by differential fertility rather than by religious switching. In every birth cohort for which we have the relevant data, women affiliated with conservative Protestant denominations have more children than women affiliated with mainline Protestant denominations.[9]

Nor is television evangelism successfully competing for members of traditional congregations. Research from the 1980s, at the height of televangelism's popularity, showed that, except for some elderly and infirm people who would not be able to attend conventional churches anyway, religious television is watched disproportionately by people who are regular churchgoers.[10] Religious television does not, in general, compete with congregations; it is better understood as a kind of entertainment that supplements, rather than substitutes for, congregation-based religious practice.

Religious switching is relevant to the different fortunes of evangelical and mainline Protestants, but not in the way many people think. The most important trend in religious switching is that conservative denominations lose fewer people to mainline denominations than they did in previous decades, perhaps because upward social mobility no longer prompts switching from being, say, Baptist, to being Presbyterian or Episcopalian. Evangelical denominations and congregations have, with their participants, become firmly middle class. Conservative denominations also lose fewer people to secularity. Conservative Protestant denominations have been doing better than mainline and liberal denominations in recent decades, but *not* because many people have switched from one to the other. The main dynamic is demographic, and this fact has implications for both mainline and evangelical congregations. For mainline congregations, evangelical competitors should not be a primary concern; the main membership challenge arises from low fertility rates and increasing losses to secularity. For evangelicals, birth rates also are declining (along with the gap between their fertility and mainline fertility), and the rate at which evangelicals lose people to secularity and to religions other than Protestantism, although still lower than for the mainline congregations, is increasing. The variations described here notwithstanding, both mainline and evangelical congregations face demographic challenges to their membership base in the coming years.[11]

Although variations within American religion are interesting and important, the key point in the current context is that the growth of evangelical denominations—with their higher levels of religious participation—is not sufficient to offset mainline losses and thereby change the general picture. This general picture is one in which fewer people engage weekly in religious activity, but without believing less in the supernatural and without becoming less concerned about spirituality. This pattern is not limited to the United States. On the contrary, it characterizes many countries around the world. Although the United States has more participation in organized religion than most other advanced industrial societies, and although advanced industrial societies vary widely in their aggregate level of religious participation and religious belief, many of these countries have experienced the same basic trends in recent decades: down on religious participation, stable on religious belief, and up on thinking about the meaning and purpose of life. (Some ex-communist societies show increases in both participation and belief, a subject for another time.)[12]

Although cohort differences in religious participation suggest that many congregations, in general, will have smaller pools of active members in coming years, another demographic trend will push in the opposite direction. Religious participation increases with age, and so the projected aging of the American population over the coming decades is good news for congregations. Whether the bump in overall participation produced by an aging population will offset the downward pressure exerted by the inexorable replacement of older people by their less civically engaged children and grandchildren remains to be seen.[13]

Increased immigration is another demographic development affecting the membership base of congregations. Recent immigrants may not be present in the majority of congregations, but they are noticeably shaping a minority of congregations. Fourteen percent of congregations—containing 24 percent of religious service attenders—held a worship service at which Spanish was spoken in the past year. Eleven percent—containing 19 percent of churchgoers—held a service within the past year in which a language other than English, Spanish, Hebrew, or Latin was spoken. The growing Hispanic population in the United States is especially consequential for Catholic churches. Within the past year, one-third of Catholic congregations held a worship service in which Spanish was spoken.

Although the current immigration wave is different from the wave in the early twentieth century in that recent newcomers are more likely to be from Latin America and Asia, there is continuity in that immigrant religion remains an important vehicle both for preserving ethnic identity and for facilitating assimilation. Recent immigration also is responsible for increasing numbers of non-Judeo-Christians in the United States. There probably are twice as many Muslims, Buddhists, and Hindus in the United States today as there were in the 1970s. The percentage of Muslims, Buddhists, and Hindus remains tiny—these three groups combined still make up less than 2 percent of the U.S. population—but their numbers are growing. It is safe to say that religious pluralism will continue to pose both opportunities and challenges for American religious congregations.[14]

Securing Adequate Financial Resources

The vast majority of congregational income comes from individual donations. Three-quarters of congregations receive at least 90 percent of their income from individual donations, and about 80 percent of all the money going to religious congregations comes from individual donations. This extreme reliance on individual donations sets congregations apart from the other types of nonprofit organizations examined in this volume, all of which rely much more heavily on government grants and fee-for-service income and for which individual donations constitute only a minor source of income. This contrast arises mainly because congregations are the only membership organizations examined in this volume. Like other membership organizations, congregations are much less affected by shifts in government funding or by competition from for-profit providers than are other parts of the nonprofit sector, and they are much more affected by trends in individual giving.

Because religious congregations depend almost entirely on donations from individuals, declining participation ought to produce declining revenue. But this does not seem to be happening. Although there is a long-term decline in the percentage of their income that Americans give to congregations, per capita religious giving among those individuals attached to congregations has increased in recent decades, outpacing inflation and producing an overall *increase* in the total amount of income received by congregations. An analysis of overall giving in twenty-nine denominations finds that total giving, adjusted for inflation, increased 63 percent between 1968 and 1998.[15] Evangelical giving is higher than mainline giving, but the trend is the same across the board. Those who remain in congregations are as generous as ever, perhaps more so, producing overall increases in the total number of dollars received by American congregations.

Although total giving to congregations has outpaced inflation in recent decades, congregations have been using more and more of their income to maintain their local operations. An analysis of spending in twenty-nine denominations finds that the percentage of congregations' income spent on maintaining the local operation rose from 79 percent in 1968 to 84 percent in 1998. In-depth studies of several denominations find a similar, or more dramatic, shift toward spending on congregations' internal operations.[16] Part of this trend probably is produced by higher clergy salaries. The median annual salary, in constant 1998 dollars, for full-time clergy with graduate degrees, rose from $25,000 in 1976 to $38,000 in 1999.[17] It also seems likely that increases in other expenses, such as health insurance and energy, have led congregations to spend more and more simply to maintain their basic operations. In recent decades, it seems that people remaining in congregations are giving more mainly in order to meet these internal budgetary needs.

If increased giving to congregations is mainly a response to the increased costs of organizational maintenance, then such increased giving should not be interpreted as an easing of financial pressure on American congregations. As mentioned, the median congregation has only about $1,000 in a savings account, and only 11 percent have as much as a one-year cushion of monetary savings. Moreover, the most common issues around which congregations seek help from their denominations or any other outside consultants are financial ones. In 1998, 16 percent of all religious service attenders were in congregations that sought outside consulting on financial matters. Of those congregations seeking outside consulting of any sort, 27 percent sought it about financial matters. Many congregations feel financially pressured, notwithstanding the aggregate increase in overall contributions.

It would be misleading to give the impression that financial pressure is new for American congregations. On the contrary, it would be difficult to find a moment in American religious history when there was no hand-wringing about the financial health of many congregations. Although there certainly is variation over time in the size of congregations' income streams—the 1930s, which is perhaps not surprising, was a particularly difficult decade for congregations—the fact of financial pressure for many congregations seems to change less than the typical strategies for relieving that pressure. Pew rents, dues systems, sales of goods, investment income—not to mention, in an earlier day, public support through taxation—all, in greater or lesser degree, have been part of congregations' funding streams.

Today, perhaps the most important source of secondary income for many congregations, after individual donations, is the sale or rent of property or space in their buildings. Although only a minority of congregations—23 percent, containing 38 percent of religious service attenders—received income from the sale or rent of buildings or property in 1998, this is substantially more than the number receiving income from their denominations (12 percent), from foundations (4 percent), or from government (3 percent). Congregations that received such income also received it in amounts that are not trivial for small organizations. In 1998, 30 percent of congregations with income from the sale or rent of buildings or property received at least $5,000 from this source, 20 percent received at least $10,000, and 10 percent received at least $25,000. Moreover, 30 percent of congregations receiving sale or rental income received at least 5 percent of their annual income from this source, and 15 percent received at least 10 percent.

It is difficult to know whether income from the sale or rent of property has become increasingly important for congregations over time. It seems safe to say, however, that, although income from this source remains small for the majority of congregations, for a notable minority it is an important way to make ends meet. More generally, we might expect congregations to respond to the financial pressures exerted by demographic changes by seeking to reduce their dependence on individual donations. More sales of auxiliary properties or buildings and more renting of building space seem likely. Congregations with valuable property or in desirable locations might, using this strategy, be able to sustain themselves for many years even in the face of dramatically dwindling memberships. The desirability of this sort of trajectory is, of course, another question.

Recruiting Talented Leaders

Perhaps the most important challenge raised for congregations by demographic trends, financial pressures, and other long-term social change is that of attracting quality leadership. Defining quality leadership is, of course, difficult, and it is especially difficult for clergy because there are qualitative differences among the employers of clergy—congregations and religious denominations—concerning which kinds of training, skills, and personal characteristics make for high-quality congregational leaders. Some congregations and religious traditions, for example, value religious zeal in clergy more highly than their level of formal education. This variation notwithstanding, some indicators suggest a long-term, and continuing, decline in the average talent of individuals choosing clerical careers. Of all individuals taking Graduate Record Examinations (GREs), for example, the number saying they were headed to seminary declined 20 percent between 1981 and 1987. Moreover, the average verbal and analytical GRE scores of prospective seminary students declined during the 1980s, a decade in which average scores rose for all test takers. Prospective seminary students score significantly lower than national averages on the quantitative and analytical sections of the GRE, although only male prospective Master of Divinity students score lower than the national average on the verbal section of the test. More generally, the gender differences in GRE scores among prospective seminary students are substantial, with females consistently outperforming males, a fact that perhaps is a basis for optimism, since clergy are increasingly female. In some denominations, recent cohorts of seminarians are 50 percent female, although only 10 percent of American congregations are led by females.[18]

Members of Phi Beta Kappa and Rhodes Scholars are, of course, a much more select group than all those who take GRE exams, but a similar trend is evident among both of these groups. Four percent of Phi Beta Kappa members who graduated from college in the late 1940s became clergy, dropping to 2 percent for early 1970s college graduates and to 1 percent for early 1980s college graduates. Eight percent of American Rhodes Scholars in 1904–09 became clergy, dropping to 4 percent in 1955–59 and to 1 percent in 1975–77.[19]

Neither GRE scores nor career choices of Phi Beta Kappa members or Rhodes Scholars are definitive measures of trends in the average talent level of America's clergy, and it certainly is true that many gifted individuals continue to enter the priesthood, ministry, and rabbinate. Still, it is noteworthy that all three of these measures, however imperfect, point in the same direction. Declining participation in congregations and other social changes influencing the status and authority of clergy seem to have reduced the attractiveness of spending one's life leading a religious congregation.

The challenge of attracting quality leadership is not shared equally by all congregations. As with participation, there are major differences across religious traditions. Jewish congregations—which pay their clergy much better, on average, than Christian congregations[20]—appear to be least affected by this challenge. The Roman Catholic Church, by contrast, appears most affected. In every tradition, however, the challenge of attracting quality leadership is most acute for rural congregations and, whether rural or urban, for the smallest and least well-off congregations. Although only the Catholic Church is widely perceived to have a severe shortage of clergy, Protestant congregations are in fact more likely than Catholic congregations to be without either clergy or full-time staff. Seven percent of Protestant congregations (with 5 percent of Protestants in them) are without a clergy person or religious leader in the congregation, compared with 1 percent of Catholic congregations (containing 2 percent of Catholics). Thirty-nine percent of Protestant congregations (containing 18 percent of Protestants) have no full-time staff, compared with 31 percent of Catholic congregations (containing 6 percent of Catholics).

Leaderless Protestant congregations are concentrated among Baptists, Pentecostals, and congregations with no denominational affiliation, but congregations within other major Protestant denominations, in general, are as likely as Catholic congregations to have neither clergy nor paid staff. Perhaps Protestant denominations, despite on-the-ground similarity with Catholics in the proportion of leaderless congregations, do not perceive themselves as experiencing a shortage of clergy because, in most denominations, the total number of clergy continues to exceed the total number of congregations. At the same time, however, many clergy do not work in congregations. The United Methodist Church, for example, reported 35,609 congregations in 1999 and 43,872 total clergy, but only 24,998 clergy were serving in congregations.[21] The same pattern is evident in many Protestant denominations. In other words, although there are sufficient qualified clergy to meet the labor needs of congregations, substantial numbers of congregations are unable to attract those clergy, mainly, it is safe to say, because they are unable to provide adequate compensation or because they are located in places where many clergy prefer not to live.

The demographic changes already described probably mean that a growing number of congregations will be too small to be able to employ a full-time clergy person. This clearly is occurring in at least one major denomination, the Evangelical Lutheran Church in America, which in 1998 had 270 more congregations with fewer than fifty attendees than it had in 1988. Consequently, the number of Lutheran congregations without pastors increased over this period from 10 percent in 1988 to 19 percent in 1998. Of the congregations in this denomination with fewer than 175 members, 38 percent had no pastor.[22] Part of the problem is a decline in absolute numbers of ordained clergy and new clergy recruits, but that decline is not sufficiently large to account wholly for the increase in congregations without a preacher. It seems likely that this kind of situation—in which the allocation of clergy is as problematic as the overall supply, and perhaps more so—characterizes other denominations as well.

Small and rural congregations long have been disadvantaged in the labor market for clergy, but this disadvantage is exacerbated by two recent developments. First, the growth of two-career families further constrains the geographic mobility of clergy, making rural congregations less attractive than they might be if meaningful employment for a spouse were not an issue. Second, the increasing number of individuals entering the ministry in mid-life, as a second career, enhances labor supply problems for small and rural congregations because such individuals often require higher salaries and are less geographically mobile than younger people.[23]

The main point here is that the challenges of attracting high-quality leadership are unequally distributed among congregations. The congregations hit hardest by demographic changes will be those crossing a threshold below which they can no longer attract the kind of leadership they would like to have. Several denominations recently approved ecumenical agreements making it easier for congregations to share a clergy person, even if they are in different denominations. These agreements were driven, in part, by recognition of this problem. It remains to be seen whether or not increasing numbers of small or rural congregations will take advantage of these administrative changes by pooling their resources for the purpose of jointly hiring a minister across denominational lines.

Finding the Balance between Member-Serving and Public-Serving Roles

A fourth challenge confronting congregations is emerging from the public policy realm. Policy analysts and policymakers have recently discovered the role played by inner-city congregations in running soup kitchens, homeless shelters, and other social service projects. In some quarters, this has given rise to the belief that religious organizations may hold the answer to the country's most severe poverty and human services problems. Indeed, a veritable movement— sometimes called the charitable choice movement—has emerged with roots in a resurgent evangelicalism and with the objective of encouraging new partnerships, including financial partnerships, between government and religious organizations doing antipoverty work. Visible in conferences and publications sponsored recently by prominent think tanks, government agencies, and religious organizations,[24] this movement has given new prominence to a longstanding tension within the world of religious congregations between their public-serving and member-serving functions.[25]

The charitable choice movement received a major boost when the Personal Responsibility and Work Opportunity Reconciliation Act of 1996—welfare reform—required states that contract with outside organizations for the delivery of social services using funding streams established by this legislation to include religious organizations as eligible contractees. It forbids states to require that a religious organization "alter its form of internal governance" or "remove religious art, icons, scripture, or other symbols" as a condition for contracting to deliver services, and it asserts that contracting religious organizations shall retain "control over the definition, development, practice, and expression of its religious beliefs."[26] Similar language has since been included in legislation affecting other funding streams.

The election of George W. Bush as president in 2000 gave these initiatives a further push. In the opening days of his administration, President Bush issued executive orders establishing offices of faith-based and community initiatives in the White House and five federal agencies, and he proposed legislation applying the charitable choice provisions to additional programs. These initiatives have been echoed as well in various federal agencies and at the state level. Indeed some attempts have been made to create public funding streams for which *only* religious organizations can apply. Included here are California's faith-based initiative and the U.S. Department of Health and Human Services' (DHHS) $4 million fund to support prevention of substance abuse and HIV infection, although the California initiative faces a court challenge and the DHHS fund has since been opened more broadly.

On one level, these initiatives break no new ground. Government agencies have long funded religiously affiliated organizations like Catholic Charities, Salvation Army, Lutheran Social Services, and many others to deliver social services. The legality of government funding for this sort of religious organization is well established and not affected by charitable choice legislation. Indeed, religiously based nonprofit organizations—what are sometimes called faith-based organizations—have always been significant players in our social welfare system, and many of them have long pursued and received government grants and contracts. Well before charitable choice became law, moreover, religious social service providers wishing to maintain a religious atmosphere or religious content in their programming—and not all, perhaps not even most, religious social service providers wish to do this—commonly did so openly and with little, if any, interference from their government funders.[27]

What is new about the charitable choice movement is its encouragement of government funding of organizations, like congregations, whose primary purpose is to provide religion to their members, not social services to their clients. In 1998, only 3 percent of religious congregations received government support for their social service activities, and only 11 percent reported any sort of collaborative relationship with a government agency on a congregational program or mission. If the charitable choice movement succeeds in directing meaningful amounts of public money to religious congregations, and in the process involves more than a very few in publicly funded human services work, this could constitute a notable change in the role of religion in our social welfare system.

How realistic such an expectation is, however, is open to considerable question. Most congregations are fundamentally focused on their religious activities, and they have neither the desire nor the capability to operate social service programs. Virtually all congregations produce worship services at least weekly, virtually all run religious education classes of some sort, and the vast majority of congregations' resources are devoted to these activities and to pastoral care for their own members. A recent national study of clergy in fifteen denominations, for example, finds that the top five time-consuming activities of clergy, in order, were sermon preparation and delivery, church administration, attendance at church meetings, visits with members, and education and teaching. Of the eleven activities that clergy were asked about, they spent the least amount of time serving on community boards or committees. A survey of clergy in one urban county finds that, in a work week of about fifty-five hours, about twenty hours were spent on worship or worship preparation, five on teaching, thirteen on counseling or visiting members, and thirteen on administration or congregational meetings. Clergy reported spending only about one hour each week in work with civic organizations. In short, the vast majority of congregational resources are spent producing religion and maintaining the congregation itself, not providing social services to a broader community.[28]

Only a minority of congregations engage in social service delivery in a serious way. Table 8-2 lists several types of social service activities and the percentages of congregations engaging in them. Although a majority of congregations (58 percent) engage in some sort of social service activity, only a minority engage in any particular kind of program, and fewer than 10 percent are involved in areas other than food, clothing, or housing. Moreover, social service activity is disproportionately engaged in by the largest congregations. The largest 10 percent of congregations, for example, account for more than half of all the money spent by congregations directly on social services.

The numbers in table 8-2 disguise a great deal of variation in the intensity with which congregations are involved in social service activity. The 33 percent of congregations supporting or participating in food programs, for example, encompasses a wide range of involvement levels, including donating money to a community food bank, supplying volunteers for a meals on wheels project, organizing a food drive every Thanksgiving, and operating independent food pantries or soup kitchens. Similar variety is evident among housing programs and programs to serve the homeless. Regarding housing, specific activities include providing volunteers to repair the homes of the needy, assisting first-time homebuyers with congregational funds, participating in neighborhood

Table 8-2. *Social Service Activity of U.S. Congregations, 1998*
Percent

Type of activity	Religious service attendees in congregations that have participated in or supported the activity	Congregations that have participated in or supported the activity
Social service projects of any sort	78	58
Food-related projects	50	33
Housing-related projects	34	20
Projects to collect or distribute clothing	19	12
Service provision for homeless people	16	8
Programs focused on health needs	12	5
Education programs (not including religious education)	10	6
Programs dealing with domestic violence	6	4
Programs dealing with substance abuse	5	2
Tutoring or mentoring programs	3	1
Job or work programs	3	1

Source: National Congregations Study, 1998.

redevelopment efforts, and building affordable housing for senior citizens. By far the most common housing-related activity engaged in by congregations is participation in Habitat for Humanity projects—projects in which groups of volunteers build or rehabilitate an apartment or house for a low-income family. Forty percent of the housing-related activities reported by congregations refer to Habitat for Humanity projects. Regarding serving the homeless, congregational involvement includes donating money to a neighborhood shelter, providing volunteers who prepare dinner at a shelter on a rotating basis with other congregations, and even providing shelter for homeless women and children in the congregation's building. Here, the most common activity is providing money or volunteers to shelters administered by other organizations.

Other measures also indicate the limited extent to which congregations are deeply engaged in social service activity. Only 6 percent of all congregations have a staff person devoting at least a quarter time to social service projects. Limiting attention to those congregations that report some sort of social service activity, only 12 percent of these more active congregations have a staff person devoting at least a quarter time to these activities. The median dollar amount spent by congregations directly in support of social service programs in 1998 was about $1,200. This level of spending, which does not take into account the value of staff time, volunteer time, or donations to denominations, represents a median of about 3 percent of congregations' total annual budgets.[29] Even volunteer involvement in social services is on a small scale for most congregations, with the median active congregation involving only ten volunteers in these efforts.

In a society in which the vast majority of services for the poor are funded by government, even when they are delivered by nonprofit organizations, and in which the median congregation has only seventy-five regular participants, an annual budget of only $55,000, and very limited current involvement in social service activity, substantially increased social service delivery by congregations can occur only via increases in government funding to congregations. Even if many more congregations are mobilized to participate in antipoverty work, it seems unlikely that engaging congregations is going to be a money-saving strategy for government.

It is too early to tell whether or not the charitable choice movement will succeed in significantly increasing congregational involvement in social services. On the one hand, only 24 percent of congregational respondents had heard of charitable choice in 1998, and a spring 2000 effort to exhaustively catalogue charitable choice efforts in nine states found only 125 post-1996 collaborations between government and religious organizations. More than 40 percent of these were simply new contracts with religious organizations, like Catholic Charities, that had long-standing funding relationships with government. Only one-third of the 125 collaborations (forty-five of them) were funding relationships with religious organizations that had not previously collaborated formally with a government agency.[30]

At the same time, some new collaborations involve dozens of congregations through a single grant to an intermediate organization, and a large minority of American congregations—about one-third—express willingness to apply for government money to support human services. This last number should be interpreted cautiously since it takes into account neither a congregation's collective will nor its administrative capacity to transform an inclination into an actual grant application. Still, given that today only about 3 percent of congregations receive government funds, there appears to be a sizable well of untapped interest among congregations in seeking government funds to support congregational social service activities. Moreover, public education and mobilizing efforts continue at both national and state levels, and these efforts have received wide publicity since the beginning of the Bush administration. It therefore remains possible that the charitable choice movement will, in the medium term, result in more congregations receiving government funds to deliver social services.

Whether this movement increases congregational involvement in the social service realm, however, will depend on how congregations respond to five important challenges. First, congregations will need to develop the expertise and management systems necessary to administer grant money and publicly funded work. Most experts recommend that congregations seeking government grants or contracts establish a separately incorporated nonprofit organization to administer such funds and make it easier to establish that public money is not inappropriately supporting worship or proselytizing.

Second, congregations will have to manage new dependencies that could be produced by new funding streams. We know that a nonprofit organization's mix of income sources influences its behavior in many ways.[31] A congregation wholly dependent on individual donations is likely to act differently than one whose income comes, say, 60 percent from donations, 30 percent from a contract with a state or county agency, and 10 percent from rental income. The resource dependency issues raised by charitable choice sometimes are described in terms of congregations moving from financial independence to dependence on government, but this is a misleading way to characterize the challenge. Congregations whose only source of income is individual donations are not without resource dependencies. Rather, they are dependent on the people who give the money. In most congregations something like 80 percent of the donations come from something like 20 percent of the people, which means that the typical congregation's financial livelihood depends on the minority of its people who are the best givers. The change in resources represented when a congregation receives a government grant or contract, then, is better described as a shift in the congregation's resource dependence—reducing somewhat its dependence on individual donors and increasing somewhat its dependence on government. The challenge for congregations moving in this direction is to manage the consequences of this sort of shift.

A third type of challenge is that government collaborations, with or without funding, might lead to program expansions that will then present additional challenges for congregations to manage. Ram Cnaan, for example, describes the challenges facing a Philadelphia congregation that was supporting several alcoholics anonymous (AA) and other substance abuse recovery groups. The city of Philadelphia, after cutting its own publicly funded AA program, began having its probation and parole officers refer offenders with substance abuse problems to the church's programs. This new partnership between government and a congregation did not involve a financial relationship. The consequence of this new partnership was that the church was overwhelmed with all the new clients and had great difficulty managing the expansion. Vandalism increased, thefts and damage to the building occurred, and volunteers who worked at the congregation complained of abusive behavior by clients.[32] The moral is that a congregation-based program or effort that is very successful at one level of operation may not be equally successful at an expanded level.

Fourth, and related, congregations engaging in social service activities may lack sufficient resources to sustain the desired activities or achieve the desired results. Beyond congregations' interests in protecting themselves from this sort of disappointment, important normative questions are raised by the prospect of their participation in social service initiatives that are not funded at adequate levels. The charitable choice movement has focused on redirecting existing social service funding so that more of it goes to funding religious organizations; it has *not* focused on expanding the overall size of the human service funding pool. Do congregations truly want to participate in collaborative initiatives that are not adequately funded, thereby encouraging the myth that small-scale, local efforts and volunteer labor can replace, rather than complement, comprehensive and well-funded social service systems?

Finally, if the charitable choice movement successfully increases the number of congregations pursuing social service projects in collaboration with government, this more visible religious presence in our social welfare system will likely raise new questions concerning congregations' public accountability. Some charitable choice proponents seem to believe that congregations delivering publicly funded social services ought to be subject only to minimal public accountability requirements and be exempted from many general rules regulating other social service deliverers, such as licensing requirements, building standards, and health, safety, and nondiscrimination laws. It seems more likely, however, that government agencies will want to subject congregations and other religious organizations to the same requirements as apply to secular social service providers.

Congregations moving in this direction should welcome the dual challenge of being accountable and of demonstrating that accountability to a wider public. In 1998, only 28 percent of Americans said that they had a great deal of confidence in those who run religious organizations. This is a higher vote of confidence than that received by some sectors, such as the press (10 percent) or Congress (11 percent). But it is less confidence than that expressed in some other institutions, such as medicine (45 percent) or the military (37 percent). Perhaps most important, this was significantly down from 1974, when 45 percent of people said that they had a great deal of confidence in those who run religious organizations.[33] It is not difficult to imagine that public confidence in religious organizations could be shaken further by only a few stories of malfeasance or substandard service on the part of religious organizations that receive public funds, much as the televangelism industry suffered from the 1980s sex and money scandals. Such stories already have begun to appear.[34] Religious congregations and other religious organizations that receive public money ought to welcome the opportunity to develop safeguards that will protect their reputations, while helping to ensure that public money is used for the public good.

In the end, if the charitable choice movement is consequential at all, it will probably affect religiously affiliated social service organizations more than congregations. Moreover, if there are new opportunities for congregations to seek government funds to offer social services, these opportunities will not be equally available to all congregations, and congregations will not be equally willing or able to take advantage of them. States vary in the extent to which they are reaching out to congregations, encouraging them to compete for available funds, and providing the technical assistance in grant writing that many congregations are likely to need if they are to move in this direction. Larger congregations, of course, are more likely to have the expertise, or the resources to purchase the expertise, necessary to write successful grant proposals. Theologically liberal congregations are more open than conservative congregations to pursuing financial collaboration with government. And, perhaps most important, African American congregations are much more likely than white congregations to respond favorably to opportunities to contract with government agencies for social service delivery. All this is to say that, although the charitable choice movement presents new opportunities—and, consequently, new challenges—to congregations, these opportunities and challenges will not engage the majority of congregations even though all congregations may be exposed to higher expectations.

Conclusions

Congregations are, in general, member-serving organizations that receive many of the tax privileges usually reserved for public-serving organizations. This chapter has sought to call attention both to demographic trends that pose challenges for congregations by virtue of their status as membership associations and to public policy changes that could encourage many congregations to serve the public more explicitly than they currently do. All in all, we should not lose sight of the reality that congregations mainly produce religion, serve their own members, and use the vast majority of their collective resources to maintain themselves as religious organizations. Only a small minority engage in any serious way in activities directly aimed at a wider public. The most significant challenges facing congregations are the ones most directly relevant to their core condition as religious membership associations.

That said, it would be a mistake to ignore the public-serving activities of religious congregations. Properly assessing congregations' contributions to communities—and the extent to which we should understand them as public-serving versus member-serving organizations—can best be done by comparing congregations' mix of member- and public-serving activities to the mix observed in other organizations, especially other membership organizations, whose main purpose, as for congregations, is something other than charity or social service. In what other population of membership organizations do the majority of units provide social services, however peripherally? In what other organizational population do as many as 33 percent of the units organize food donations, 12 percent distribute clothing, 8 percent engage in some sort of service to the homeless, or 6 percent have a staff person devoting quarter time to social service activities? From this comparative perspective, congregations appear to serve the public more than many other membership organizations.

Moreover, having a low percentage of congregations actively involved in social services does not necessarily imply trivial absolute levels of social service delivery. If only 0.5 percent of the approximately 300,000 congregations in the United States are deeply engaged in social service activity, roughly 1,500 congregations are so engaged. Especially when we consider that congregations in poor neighborhoods are more likely to be deeply engaged in social services, congregations emerge as a different sort of membership association, one that, although oriented primarily to serving the religious needs of its own people, at the same time seems to generate more public-serving activity—and more activity directed at serving the disadvantaged—than other membership associations. Indeed, maintaining a balance between serving the religious needs of members and serving the human needs of the community—and figuring out where that balance appropriately lies—are long-standing concerns in American religion. It is, perhaps, the perennial attention to this balance, rather than where it is struck at any particular time or place, that makes congregations, alone among membership associations, an appropriate topic of concern in a book about public-serving nonprofit organizations.

There are advantages to the current visibility of congregations and other religious organizations within the social service sector, not least of which is the possibility that this enhanced visibility may bring with it needed resources. But there also are risks, not the least of which is the possibility that these same opportunities will make congregations more vulnerable to demands for public accountability from which religious congregations have been largely exempt. This is why, after the ongoing and fundamental challenges of maintaining a membership base, securing adequate financial resources, and recruiting talented leaders, perhaps the most important challenge facing many congregations in the coming decades will be finding an appropriate balance between the member-serving and public-serving aspects of their identity and then managing the consequences of where this balance is struck.

Notes

1. David Horton Smith, "The Rest of the Nonprofit Sector: Grassroots Associations as the Dark Matter Ignored in Prevailing 'Flat Earth' Maps of the Sector," *Nonprofit and Voluntary Sector Quarterly*, vol. 26 (1997): 114–31.

2. The 2 percent estimate for nonprofits with endowments more than twice their annual budget is from note 62 in Evelyn Brody, "Charitable Endowments and the Democratization of Dynasty," *Arizona Law Review*, vol. 39 (Fall 1997): 873–948.

3. Peter Dobkin Hall, "Vital Signs: Organizational Population Trends and Civic Engagement in New Haven, Connecticut, 1850–1998," in Theda Skocpol and Morris P. Fiorina, ed., *Civic Engagement in American Democracy* (Washington: Brookings; New York: Russell Sage Foundation, 1999), pp. 211–48, especially p. 233.

4. Nancy Ammerman, *Congregation and Community* (Rutgers University Press, 1997).

5. For more detail about National Congregations Study methodology, see Mark Chaves, Mary Ellen Konieczny, Kraig Beyerlein, and Emily Barman, "The National Congregations Study: Background, Methods, and Selected Results," *Journal for the Scientific Study of Religion,* vol. 38 (December 1999): 458–76.

6. George Gallup Jr. and D. Michael Lindsay, *Surveying the Religious Landscape: Trends in U.S. Beliefs* (Harrisburg, Penn.: Morehouse Publishing, 1999).

7. Stanley Presser and Linda Stinson, "Data Collection Mode and Social Desirability Bias in Self-Reported Religious Attendance," *American Sociological Review,* vol. 63 (February 1998): 137–45.

8. Robert D. Putnam, *Bowling Alone: The Collapse and Revival of American Community* (New York: Simon and Schuster, 2000), especially chap. 4.

9. Michael Hout, Andrew Greeley, and Melissa J. Wilde, "The Demographic Imperative in Religious Change in the United States," *American Journal of Sociology,* vol. 107, no. 2 (September 2001): 468–500.

10. Steve Bruce, *Pray TV: Televangelism in America* (New York: Routledge, 1990), chaps. 5 and 6.

11. All the empirical facts in this paragraph are from Hout, Greeley, and Wilde, "Demographic Imperative in Religious Change."

12. Ronald Inglehart and Wayne E. Baker, "Modernization, Cultural Change, and the Persistence of Traditional Values," *American Sociological Review,* vol. 65 (February 2000): 19–51.

13. For additional discussion of an aging population's potential consequences for congregations, see Anthony E. Healy, "Picturing the 21st Century," *Visions,* vol. 3, no. 1 (January/February 2000): 4–8.

14. The observation that immigrant religion continues to be important for both ethnic preservation and assimilation is from Fenggang Yang and Helen Rose Ebaugh, "Transformations in New Immigrant Religions and Their Implications for Global Religious Systems," *American Sociological Review,* vol. 66 (April 2001): 269–88. For more on new immigrant religion, see R. Stephen Warner and Judith G. Wittner, eds., *Gatherings in Diaspora: Religious Communities and the New Immigration* (Temple University Press, 1998), and Helen Rose Ebaugh and Janet Saltzman Chafetz, *Religion and the New Immigrants: Continuities and Adaptations in Immigrant Congregations* (Walnut Creek, Calif.: AltaMira, 2000). The Muslim, Buddhist, and Hindu numbers and trends are from Darren E. Sherkat, "Tracking the 'Other': Dynamics and Composition of 'Other' Religions in the General Social Survey, 1973–1996," *Journal for the Scientific Study of Religion,* vol. 38 (1999): 551–60; Tom W. Smith, "Estimating the Muslim Population in the United States," unpublished paper (University of Chicago, National Opinion Research Center, October 2001).

15. Computed by Sylvia Ronsvalle using data from John Ronsvalle and Sylvia Ronsvalle, *The State of Church Giving through 1998* (Champaign, Ill.: empty tomb, inc., 2000). Personal communication from Sylvia Ronsvalle, July 3, 2001.

16. The twenty-nine-denomination result is from the same analysis cited in note 15. For studies of congregational spending in specific denominations, see, for example, Roger J. Nemeth and Donald A. Luidens, "Congregational vs. Denominational Giving: An Analysis of Giving Patterns in the Presbyterian Church in the United States and the Reformed Church in America," *Review of Religious Research,* vol. 36 (1994): 111–22; D. Scott Cormode, "A Financial History of Presbyterian Congregations since World War II," in Milton J. Coalter, John M. Mulder, and Louis B. Weeks, eds., *The Organizational Revolution: Presbyterians and American Denominationalism* (Louisville: Westminster/John Knox, 1992), pp. 171–98; and United Church Board for Homeland Ministries, *The State of the UCC, 1997* (Cleveland: United Church Board for Homeland Ministries, 1997).

17. Becky R. McMillan and Matthew J. Price, "At Cross Purposes? Clergy Salaries: Market and Mission," Working Paper (Durham, N.C.: Duke Divinity School, 2001).

18. The GRE results are from Jerilee Grandy and Mark Greiner, "Academic Preparation of Master of Divinity Candidates," *Ministry Research Notes: An ETS Occasional Report* (Princeton, N.J.: Educational Testing Service, Fall 1990).

19. The Phi Beta Kappa data are from Howard R. Bowen and Jack H. Schuster, *American Professors: A National Resource Imperiled* (Oxford University Press, 1986). The Rhodes Scholar data are the author's calculations using *A Register of Rhodes Scholars, 1903–1981* (Oxford: Alden, 1981).

20. Anthony Ruger and Barbara G. Wheeler, *Manna from Heaven? Theological and Rabbinical Student Debt,* Auburn Studies 3 (New York: Auburn Theological Seminary, 1995), p. 5.

21. *Yearbook of American and Canadian Churches, 2001* (Nashville: Abingdon, 2001).

22. Evangelical Lutheran Church in America, Division for Ministry, *Ministry Needs and Resources in the 21st Century* (Chicago: Evangelical Lutheran Church in America, Division for Ministry, 2000).

23. In the Evangelical Lutheran Church in America, the average age at ordination has increased from 29.5 in 1980 to 37.8 in 1998; see Evangelical Lutheran Church in America, Division for Ministry, *Ministry Needs and Resources.*

24. The Brookings Institution, for example, co-sponsored a Religion and Social Policy conference in January 1999; the Manhattan Institute included a session on successful church-state welfare-to-work partnerships in its April 1999, Next Steps in Welfare Reform conference; the U.S. Department of Health and Human Services sponsored a national Welfare Reform and the Faith Community conference in November 1999; the U.S. Department of Housing and Urban Development sponsored a Faith Communities and Community Building conference in June 2000; and Call to Renewal included a workshop on churches and charitable choice, along with many other sessions encouraging church-state collaborations to fight poverty, in its February 2000 national meeting, Poor No More! A National Summit on the Churches and Poverty.

25. Lester Salamon, *Holding the Center: America's Nonprofit Sector at a Crossroads* (New York: Nathan Cummings Foundation, 1997), p. 6, for example, distinguishes between member-serving and public-serving institutions and includes churches among the latter, along with "foundations, environmental groups, civic organizations, and a wide assortment of service agencies providing everything from health care to education to housing for the homeless to information on crucial unmet needs." This largely reflects the legal classification of congregations, unlike most other membership organizations, as eligible for tax-deductible gifts along with 501(c)(3) organizations.

26. *A Guide to Charitable Choice: The Rules of Section 104 of the 1996 Federal Welfare Law Governing State Cooperation with Faith-Based Social-Service Providers* (Washington: Center for Public Justice; Annandale, Va.: Christian Legal Society's Center for Law and Religious Freedom, 1997), pp. 28–29.

27. Stephen Monsma surveyed international aid agencies and child service agencies in 1993–94. For those organizations that both received government funding and reported that they engaged in religious practices, the majority of religious practices that they engage in—62 percent for the international aid agencies and 77 percent for the child service agencies—were done openly. Only a minority of religiously affiliated, government-funded, child service agencies—11 percent—reported having to curtail religious activities, and only a minority—22 percent—of publicly funded, religious, international aid agencies reported experiencing any sort of pressure or problem related to their religious activities. Most, perhaps all, of the activities about which problems were reported, such as requiring attendance at religious services, are the kind of sectarian worship, instruction, or proselytizing activities that are prohibited

even under charitable choice. See Stephen Monsma, *When Sacred and Secular Mix: Religious Nonprofit Organizations and Public Money* (Lanham, Md.: Rowman and Littlefield, 1996).

28. The facts in this paragraph are from Barbara Brown Zikmund, Adair T. Lummis, and Patricia Mei Yin Chang, *Clergy Women: An Uphill Calling* (Louisville: Westminster/John Knox, 1998); Sandi Brunette-Hill and Roger Finke, "A Time for Every Purpose: Updating and Extending Blizzard's Survey on Clergy Time Allocation," *Review of Religious Research,* vol. 41 (1999): 47–63.

29. Compare the estimates in Jeff E. Biddle, "Religious Organizations," in Charles T. Clotfelter, ed., *Who Benefits from the Nonprofit Sector?* (University of Chicago Press, 1992), pp. 92–133.

30. Amy L. Sherman, *The Growing Impact of Charitable Choice: A Catalogue of New Collaborations between Government and Faith-Based Organizations in Nine States* (Washington: Center for Public Justice, 2000).

31. Kirsten A. Grønbjerg, *Understanding Nonprofit Funding: Managing Revenues in Social Services and Community Development Organizations* (San Francisco: Jossey-Bass, 1993).

32. Ram A. Cnaan, with Robert J. Wineburg and Stephanie C. Boddie, *The Newer Deal: Social Work and Religion in Partnership* (Columbia University Press, 1999).

33. These numbers are from the General Social Survey. See James A. Davis, Tom W. Smith, and Peter V. Marsden, *General Social Surveys, 1972–1998: Cumulative Codebook* (Chicago: National Opinion Research Center, 1999).

34. For example, Hanna Rosin, "Faith and a Little Help from Friends," *Washington Post National Weekly Edition*, May 15, 2000, pp. 10–11; Carol D. Leonnig, "HUD Loses Faith in Housing Program," *Washington Post,* February 19, 2002, p. A-1.

9

Civic Participation and Advocacy

ELIZABETH T. BORIS AND JEFF KREHELY

A dvocacy is a vital, traditional role of nonprofit organizations. Throughout U.S. history, individuals have voiced their concerns and worked together in nonprofit associations to shape and reshape the country's political, economic, and cultural landscape. Nonprofit women's organizations promoted far-reaching political and social reforms, such as women's suffrage and child labor laws. Nonprofit civil rights organizations led the fight to tear down the legal and social structures of racial segregation. Organizations promoting environmental protection, family values, human rights, tax reform, and many other causes have fundamentally affected American society, sometimes in collaboration with business or government and at other times in conflict with them. Prominent organizations such as the Sierra Club, National Audubon Society, National Association for the Advancement of Colored People, Christian Coalition, American Association of Retired Persons, and National Organization for Women are known throughout the country, have large memberships, and are often in the news. They and other groups like them have had profound impacts on society, politics, and citizens, both in the United States and, increasingly, abroad.

The health and renewal of American democracy depend on the civic participation of individuals in local and national affairs and on the active role of the voluntary associations that facilitate it. Perhaps because of this dependency, freedoms of speech and association are constitutionally protected. At the same time, it is important to acknowledge that nonprofit advocacy can have costs as well as benefits. Opposing groups can cause polarization of attitudes, leading to conflict that fractures communities. Some may advocate for positions and activities that many will judge to be undesirable for society.[1] Advocacy groups can also add to information overload, especially through issue advocacy around elections.

The current status of civic participation and voluntary association advocacy is the topic of this chapter. This is a complex and multifaceted area with little empirical data. Scholars, observers, and journalists consequently come to different conclusions about whether nonprofit advocacy is flourishing, challenged, or in crisis.[2]

At the heart of the issue lies an interesting paradox that has become particularly evident in recent years. On the one hand, the role of money has grown increasingly important in American politics. Logically, this might suggest that nonprofit public interest advocacy is losing its influence. In fact, however, recent research by Jeffrey Berry and others suggests that nonprofit public interest organizations have gained more influence in recent years and exert considerable sway in the policy process.[3]

How can this be so? How can the influence of nonprofit advocacy be increasing at a time when monied interests are spending more to influence policy action? The answer, we suggest, lies in the growing sophistication of much nonprofit advocacy. Nonprofit advocacy has become highly professionalized, with complex organizations mobilizing hundreds of thousands of members, conducting expert research, and using sophisticated public relations techniques. Although such expertise is hardly evident in all policy spheres—and is generally concentrated within large, well-financed organizations—many groups have become effective and influential players in the political process. At the same time, smaller organizations or those that work for low-income constituencies often lack the resources, skills, and access that are needed to be politically successful. Also, while some nonprofit advocates have taken on the trappings of business, businesses are creating and using nonprofit organizations to advocate for their own positions.

The balance of this chapter develops the main features of this argument. The first section defines civic participation, identifies different types of nonprofit advocacy, and briefly examines the scale of one particular type—lobbying. The second section discusses recent forces shaping nonprofit advocacy. The third section zeros in on two particular types of nonprofit advocacy organizations: environmental organizations and civil rights and social action organizations, respectively. The conclusion summarizes the current status of nonprofit advocacy and offers ideas for improving its effectiveness and reach.

Civic Participation and Advocacy: Definitions and Scale

Among the roles that nonprofit organizations play in American life, few are as important as their role as structures for individuals to participate in civic life as volunteers, members, activists, and donors. Through associations, people interact, build organizational skills, and create networks of trust and affiliation—the social capital—that enable them to work together to solve community problems, promote causes, and seek redress or change through the policy process.

Associations may try to educate and inform the public in order to mold opinions and attitudes or change behavior—for example, about the use of tobacco. They may represent interests and values in the political system—for example, by lobbying for or against legislation and by litigating in the courts. Some organizations are involved in nonpartisan or partisan efforts to influence elections. All of these activities can be considered advocacy activities—organized efforts to shape public life.

While this chapter discusses the broad range of advocacy activities, it focuses on the public interest advocacy of public charities—classified by the Internal Revenue Service (IRS) as 501(c)(3) organizations, which are eligible for tax-deductible contributions—and social welfare organizations—classified as 501(c)(4) organizations, which are not eligible for tax-deductible contributions.

Defining Civic Participation and Advocacy

Civic participation refers to activities of individuals that relate to community life and public governance. Voting is the critical act of civic participation, but individuals participate in many other ways, from nonpartisan petitioning for better government services to political activities such as campaigning and running for public office. Voluntary associations often activate and mediate civic participation: "People learn grassroots skills and build relationships in community, religious, and workplace associations in ways that are transferable to politics."[4]

The nonprofit organizations that facilitate civic participation do so in a variety of ways. Traditional civic membership associations, such as the League of Women Voters, Parent Teacher Associations, Jaycees, and Kiwanis, have active members who work together on nonpartisan civic "good government" and service projects. Nonprofit service providers, such as hospitals, universities, and social service agencies, are professionally staffed and less likely to be advocates for broad public issues. When they advocate, they are likely to involve their clients, volunteers, and trustees in advocacy to promote their missions, to secure resources, and to weigh in on issues or policies that are likely to affect their work or constituents.

Advocacy is more focused than civic participation. Legal expert Bruce Hopkins defines advocacy as "the act of pleading for or against a cause, as well as supporting or recommending a position . . . Advocacy is active espousal of a position, a point of view, or a course of action."[5] According to J. Craig Jenkins, *policy* advocacy "is a specific form of advocacy that seeks to influence the decisions of any institutional elite on behalf of a collective interest."[6]

Advocacy can be for individuals, for specific populations or causes, for the self-interest of an organization or sector, or for broad public benefits. Citizen advocacy groups, such as the National Council of La Raza, Mothers Against Drunk Driving, National Rifle Association, and League of Conservation Voters, focus on changing public attitudes and public policies on specific issues, such as conservation, gun control, and drunk driving, or in specific issue areas, such as civil rights or environmental protection. The larger groups have professional staff and sophisticated organizational structures to mobilize members to advocate for their causes. Some public interest organizations like the Children's Defense Fund, Center on Budget and Policy Priorities, Conservation Fund, and most policy institutes do not have dues-paying members. However, volunteers and donors may play important advocacy roles in both types of organizations. Smaller advocacy organizations are often led entirely by volunteers.

Nonprofit organizations can engage in most types of advocacy and civic action without limit. However, some types are prohibited or subject to restrictions.

ISSUE IDENTIFICATION AND AGENDA-SETTING ADVOCACY. Nonprofit organizations can do unlimited research, education, and dissemination of information about social and economic problems as well as recommend solutions. They can send their information and analyses to the general public and to public policymakers. These activities form the core of advocacy for many nonprofit organizations.

LOBBYING. Lobbying is a particular type of advocacy. In its broadest sense, lobbying is "an attempt to influence the public policy and issue-making functions of a regulatory, administrative, or legislative body."[7] Virtually all nonprofit organizations are permitted to lobby, but for nonprofits that receive tax-deductible contributions—501(c)(3) public charities—lobbying to influence specific legislation cannot be their major activity, and private foundations may only lobby to protect their own interests.

Under IRS regulations, lobbying involves communications to influence specific legislation, and legislation is action that includes "introduction, amendment, enactment, defeat, or repeal of acts, bills, resolutions, or similar items." Legislative bodies are Congress, state and local legislatures, and the general public in referenda, initiatives, or proposed constitutional amendments. Also included are some agencies of the executive branch that have influence over legislation.

IRS regulations specify that charitable organizations cannot spend a *substantial* amount of time or money on lobbying. Unfortunately, the IRS does not define substantial, which causes concern among the charitable community since the penalty for violating this regulation is loss of 501(c)(3) tax-exempt status, including the right to receive tax-deductible donations. By completing a simple, one-page form available from the IRS, organizations can make the 501(h) election, which provides a formula they can use to calculate their lobbying expenditure limit. For groups that make the 501(h) election, total lobbying limits are currently set at 20 percent of the first $500,000 of exempt-purpose expenditures and are then calculated on a sliding scale based on total exempt-purpose expenditures, up to a cap of $1 million on total lobbying expenditures.[8]

Public charities that elect to come under the IRS 501(h) lobbying rules must report two types of lobbying: *direct* and *grassroots*. Direct lobbying refers to communication of a point of view on a specific piece of legislation to a legislator, an employee of a legislative body, or another government employee who may participate in the formation of legislation. It also includes lobbying activity directed at the general public in referenda, initiatives, or proposed constitutional amendments, as well as appeals asking members of the organization to contact legislators about a specific piece of legislation. Grassroots lobbying includes attempts to encourage the general public—beyond a group's membership—to contact legislators about specific legislation.[9] The cap on grassroots lobbying is set at 25 percent of an organization's total lobbying limit (because total lobbying is capped at $1 million, grassroots lobbying is effectively capped at $250,000).

NONPARTISAN ELECTORAL ACTIVITIES. Public charities may undertake voter education and voter registration drives and may sponsor nonpartisan candidate forums. They may also participate in referenda and initiative campaigns.

PARTISAN ELECTORAL ADVOCACY. Charitable nonprofit organizations— 501(c)(3)s—are prohibited from doing "express advocacy," that is, advocacy for the election or defeat of candidates for public office. Social welfare organizations—501(c)(4)s—may expressly advocate for or against candidates only to their members and, under some restricted conditions, may communicate to the general public.[10] These express advocacy activities must be reported to the Federal Election Commission.

Although most advocacy is unregulated, the regulations that do exist are complex and fragmented. The Internal Revenue Service and the Federal Election Commission regulate most lobbying and electoral activities at the national level, but the reporting requirements that different types of groups must adhere to for each agency are not always clear or consistent. State and local regulations only add to the confusion.

Scope of Nonprofit Lobbying

Data on nonprofit advocacy are difficult to find. Somewhat more accessible are data on nonprofit lobbying.[11] These data show that very few public charities actively lobby, and those that do spend only a tiny proportion of their resources specifically on legislative lobbying. Statistics collected by the National Center for Charitable Statistics (NCCS) from the Form 990s that charities are required

Table 9-1. *Expense Trends for Reporting 501(c)(3) Organizations That Lobby,*
1989–98

Indicator	1989	1992	1995	1998
Number of all reporting charities	137,799	165,181	190,844	228,011
Number of reporting charities with lobbying expenses	1,605	2,434	3,202	3,515
Percent of all reporting charities reporting lobbying expenses	1.2	1.5	1.7	1.5
Mean lobbying expenses (1998 U.S. dollars)	35,195	34,292	36,367	38,472
Median lobbying expenses (1998 U.S. dollars)	6,467	6,276	7,086	8,000
Total lobbying expenses (millions of 1998 U.S. dollars)	57	84	116	135
Total organizational expenses (millions of 1998 U.S. dollars)	64,672	96,504	135,462	160,400
Total lobbying expenses as a percentage of total expenses	0.09	0.09	0.09	0.08

Source: National Center for Charitable Statistics Core Files, 1990–99.

to file with the Internal Revenue Service reveal that only 1.5 percent of public charities reported lobbying expenditures in 1998 (see table 9-1). The amount of money devoted to lobbying (in constant dollars) was $57 million in 1989 and $135 million in 1998, a significant increase in dollars, but less than one-tenth of 1 percent of total public charity expenses in both years.

Organizations that report lobbying expenses tend to be larger than the average nonprofit; only thirty-five organizations spent more than $500,000 on this activity in 1998 (see table 9-2). Of those that reported lobbying expenses, 42 percent spent $5,000 or less. By 1998, about 1,500 of the 3,515 organizations that reported lobbying expenses elected to come under the more generous "expenditure test" lobbying provisions of section 501(h), which further suggests the small number of public charity organizations that actively lobby.

Environmental, civil rights, and social action organizations are usually considered the major advocacy organizations within the public charity universe. They spend a higher percentage of their budgets on lobbying than other types of organizations (see table 9-3). However, compared to environmental, civil rights, and social action groups, greater numbers of education, health, and human services organizations lobby, and they spend much more money on this activity. For example, education and health groups accounted for 18 and 40 percent, respectively, of all lobbying expenses in 1998. Human service organizations ranked third in lobbying expenditures (making up 12 percent of total lobbying expenses), although these groups made up a third of the entire charitable sector.

Table 9-2. *Ranges of Total Lobbying Expenses for Reporting 501(c)(3) Organizations That Lobby, 1998*

Amount spent on lobbying (1998 U.S. dollars)	Number of organizations	Percent of organizations
0–5,000	1,480	42.1
5,001–25,000	1,033	29.4
25,001–100,000	668	19.0
100,001–500,000	299	8.5
Greater than 500,000	35	1.0
Total	3,515	100.0

Source: National Center for Charitable Statistics Core Files, 1999.

Examining the top 100 501(c)(3) organizations that reported spending money on legislative lobbying in 1998 shows the diversity of groups represented. The leading spenders include the American Cancer Society, March of Dimes Birth Defects Foundation, Health Insurance Plan of Greater New York, Nature Conservancy, and Boston University (see table 9-4 for a list of the top ten). Other groups in the top 100 include the Council of Jewish Federations, Family Research Council, Paralyzed Veterans of America, Consumers Union of America, and American Foundation for AIDS Research. The top 100 organizations spent $47,336,226 on lobbying, a full 35 percent of all reported 501(c)(3) lobbying expenditures. Resources play an important role in legislative lobbying. Larger groups have the resources and the skills to be involved.

Further, not all environmental, civil rights, and social action organizations are highly visible advocates. Many are small and local in scope. A preliminary analysis of the programs that 501(c)(3) environmental organizations described to the IRS on their Form 990s reveals that many undertake public education, but most do not mention other types of advocacy activities or report legislative lobbying expenses.[12] In addition, the advocacy of informal and volunteer-led groups that do not report to the IRS is rarely documented.[13] Their activities, however, are critical for involving members in direct action, raising public awareness, and helping to shape public opinion.

Public interest advocates engage significant numbers of people in their activities, and they have impacts much greater than their resources might suggest. Jeffrey Berry estimates that citizen groups are less than 5 percent of all interest groups in Washington, D.C., yet they show up in the news and in congressional testimony at much higher rates than might be expected. He concludes that citizen groups have been very effective at setting and influencing the congressional agenda in recent years.[14] Susan Rees also finds citizen groups among the organizations rated most influential by congressional staff.[15] A closer focus on these

Table 9-3. *Total Lobbying and Organizational Spending by Reporting 501(c)(3) Organizations, by Type of Organization, 1998*

Type of organization	Number of organizations reporting	Percent of total organizations reporting	Number of organizations with lobbying expenses	Percent of total organizations with lobbying expenses	Percent of organizations in category that lobby	Total lobbying expenses Amount (1998 U.S. dollars)	As a percentage of total expenses	Percent of total lobbying expenses
Arts, cultures, and humanities	23,935	10.5	184	5.2	0.8	5,878,446	0.24	4.4
Education	37,928	16.7	576	16.4	1.5	24,411,841	0.07	18.1
Environmental and animal related	7,497	3.2	345	9.8	4.6	12,418,277	0.79	9.2
Health	33,623	14.7	934	26.7	2.8	53,619,362	0.06	39.7
Human services	78,448	34.4	824	23.5	1.1	15,969,938	0.23	11.7
International, foreign affairs, and national security	2,118	0.9	59	1.7	2.8	3,555,999	0.38	2.6
Public, societal benefit								
Civil rights, social action, advocacy	1,725	0.8	115	3.3	6.7	2,602,109	1.20	1.9
Community improvement, capacity building	9,687	4.3	138	3.9	1.4	4,186,015	0.47	3.1
Philanthropy and voluntarism	12,525	5.5	102	2.9	0.8	2,645,775	0.18	2.0
Research institutes/services	2,333	1.0	77	2.2	3.3	3,706,028	0.15	2.7
Public, society benefit, multipurpose, and other	1,827	0.8	77	2.2	4.2	3,407,385	0.64	2.5
Religion related, spiritual development	11,477	5.0	28	0.80	0.2	1,619,769	0.10	1.2
Mutual or membership benefit organizations	672	0.3	5	0.14	0.7	463,616	0.01	0.34
Unknown	3,936	1.7	51	1.5	1.3	743,468	1.50	0.55
Total	227,731	100.0	3,515	100.0	1.5	135,228,028	0.08	100.0

Source: National Center for Charitable Statistics Core Files, 1999.

Table 9-4. *Top Ten Reporting 501(c)(3) Organizations, Based on Total Lobbying Expenses, 1998*

Organization	Total expenses (1998 U.S. dollars)		Lobbying expenses as a percentage of total expenses
	Lobbying	Organizational	
American Cancer Society Divisions	2,077,495	511,815,145	0.41
March of Dimes Birth Defects Foundation	1,486,451	173,076,893	0.86
Health Insurance Plan of Greater New York	1,142,000	1,554,325,730	0.07
American Cancer Society	1,023,983	208,682,928	0.49
Nature Conservancy	993,396	274,403,216	0.36
Trustees of Boston University	845,986	920,571,303	0.09
Kaiser Foundation Health Plan	844,202	11,119,949,882	0.01
American Museum of Natural History	816,680	95,123,277	0.86
American Council on Education	746,077	21,067,615	3.50
Group Health Cooperative of Puget Sound	732,712	919,074,871	0.08

Source: National Center for Charitable Statistics Core Files, 1999.

organizations later in this chapter reveals the opportunities and barriers related to public interest advocacy.

Major Forces Shaping Nonprofit Advocacy

Public interest advocacy is pervasive and powerful. It has shaped public consciousness about nuclear weapons, tobacco use, gender, civil and human rights, and the environment. There are daily stories in the major print media about the activities of advocates on a broad range of current issues from charitable choice to global arms trafficking. Advocates are part of the give and take of the policy process. Although nonprofit advocacy organizations have grown in size and influence in recent decades, they will confront a number of challenges in the years ahead. Four in particular deserve special attention.

Civic, Social, and Economic Trends

In the first place, a number of social and demographic trends are posing new problems for nonprofit advocacy. For example, despite a flourishing nonprofit sector and impressive rates of giving and volunteering to nonprofit organizations, indicators of civic health such as voting levels, citizen involvement in politics, and trust in public institutions have declined in the United States. Robert Putnam's book *Bowling Alone* summarizes the data succinctly:[16]

Since the mid-1960s, the weight of the evidence suggests, despite the rapid rise in levels of education Americans have become perhaps 10–15 percent less likely to voice our views publicly by running for office or writing Congress or the local newspaper, 15–20 percent less interested in politics and public affairs, roughly 25 percent less likely to vote, roughly 35 percent less likely to attend public meetings, both partisan and nonpartisan, and roughly 40 percent less engaged in party politics and indeed in political and civic organizations of all sorts. We remain, in short, reasonably well-informed spectators of public affairs, but many fewer of us actually partake in the game.

Other analysts are not persuaded that there is a problem. They point to the growing number and variety of organizations, the high levels of giving and volunteering, and the fact that many people belong to multiple organizations. Recent surveys show that people are engaged in activities and believe that they can make a difference in their communities.[17] Berry argues that less personal types of civic participation, such as writing checks to support specific causes or groups, can represent civic commitment and that citizen groups are gaining access to the political system to represent their views on issues that their members care about. The ways people participate may have changed partly because the salient issues—environmental protection, human rights, and trade, for example—are global in scope and increasingly technical and therefore require different forms of organization, specialized skills, and new communications technology. "The problem with national citizen groups," Berry argues, "is not that they manifest an erosion of civic engagement or social capital, but that they empower only part of the population."[18]

One possible cause of the apparent decline in civic participation is the growing diversity of the American population. Greater diversity increases the need for nonprofit civil rights groups to protect and politically engage ever-broader and diverse communities. The growing number of advocacy organizations of all types, however, may lead to more contentious politics and civic discord.

Another important development is the growing income disparity in the country, which affects the capacity of disadvantaged groups to have their voices heard in an increasingly resource-intensive advocacy process. Research shows that poor and underserved populations are less likely to be heard than other groups.[19] They may have strong civic networks, but many organizations lack sufficient resources and access to the press, which are needed for political participation and success.

For example, the environmental justice movement and the living wage campaign are poorly funded and barely on the radar screen of national policymakers. Despite such challenges, some groups are successfully blocking chemical and garbage dumps in their neighborhoods by involving citizens whose lives would be negatively affected by these facilities. Other groups are winning victories for working families (for janitors in Los Angeles, for example) and new immigrant communities.

Changes in Management and Operations

A second challenge to nonprofit advocacy arises in the realm of management and operations. Many public interest advocacy groups have grown rapidly in the past two decades, hiring staff and professional fundraisers and revamping their administrative and advocacy operations in the process.[20] Such changes reflect the complexity and global nature of many issues and the extensive expertise and significant resources required to compete with well-financed corporate or government advocates. Professionalization can lead to efficiency gains but may have a negative impact on membership involvement and thus on the legitimacy of the organization. Building organizational capacity, mastering new technologies, learning how to make use of coalitions, and finding suitable organizational structures are all manifestations of this challenge.

CAPACITY. Some groups do not try to influence public policy even when it is clearly in their interest to do so because they lack the resources or skills to navigate the policymaking sphere.[21] A recent survey by Berry and colleagues reveals that inadequate financial resources are major barriers for nonprofit advocates.[22] Direct mail fundraising provides income to many groups, but at the price of simplifying messages and incurring huge fundraising costs. The ever-present challenge of raising general operating support, especially among smaller organizations, further limits their ability to advocate.

There is general agreement among many leaders, activists, and observers that nonprofit capacity to advocate needs to be strengthened. Meetings and discussions at the Advocacy Institute and Aspen Institute have generated suggestions for doing so.[23] These include encouraging foundations to provide support for both the general operations of advocacy organizations and for particular advocacy initiatives. Another suggestion is to educate nonprofit leaders about the current laws that regulate nonprofit advocacy and to educate the public and policymakers on the value of civic participation and nonprofit advocacy to American democracy.

TECHNOLOGY. New technologies, by most accounts, have expanded the capacity of nonprofits to advocate, as they provide a ready means of connecting organizations to constituents and members, the general public, policymakers, and other nonprofit organizations. Well-designed and maintained websites and e-mail listservs are inexpensive vehicles for disseminating reports, press releases, and other documents. In addition, this technology provides new ways for groups to receive feedback on their activities as well as to solicit contributions.

These technologies are an especially important component of efforts to build the capacity of smaller, grassroots service providers and social action organizations to be effective advocates, both domestically and worldwide.

There are, however, potential negative consequences in using these tools for civic and political work. First, there is a persistent digital divide in our country between the rich and poor. Low-income constituents and the groups that represent them may not have the resources needed to communicate broadly using these new technologies. Helping rural areas and inner cities become wired should be a priority of the nonprofit community, foundations, and the government.

A second negative impact is that mass advocacy communications to policymakers are likely to become ineffective as the outpouring of messages creates information overload. Blocking and tallying programs, and other devices to screen and keep out unwanted messages, will become more prevalent. Because of this drawback, the long-term and most valuable use for Internet technology may be as a way to link up groups with constituents and partner organizations.

COALITIONS AND COLLABORATIONS. Voluntary associations often join with other like-minded groups to undertake advocacy activities. Coalitions may shield organizations from unwanted exposure, leverage scarce resources, and mobilize significant cross-sector constituencies—government, business, labor, and other nonprofits. Collaboration, however, also requires organizing skills and financial resources that not all groups have. Sometimes organizations find themselves with strange bedfellows or on opposite sides of the same issue from like-minded groups. For example, some environmental organizations, such as the Environmental Defense Fund and World Wildlife Fund, supported the North American Free Trade Agreement, while others, such as the Sierra Club and Friends of the Earth, joined many unions in opposing it.[24]

It is rare to find broad coalitions of public interest nonprofits that take a stand on general issues, such as tax policy, an issue that is likely to galvanize business associations. However, led by Independent Sector, nonprofits have begun to coalesce around creating a better regulatory climate for all nonprofit organizations that is analogous to the role that trade associations play for various for-profit industries.

Additional research on coalitions is needed, for they are important actors in the public policy sphere and deserve more attention.[25] A quick scan of the Washington, D.C., area turned up more than thirty coalitions organized around diverse topics from education reform to homelessness, with varied memberships of secular, religious, neighborhood, business, and government interests. They clearly play a role in promoting civic participation and getting issues on the policy agenda.

ORGANIZATIONAL STRUCTURE. Although advocacy organizations vary in size and structure, a striking feature of the largest public interest nonprofits is that they are increasingly complex multiple-organization conglomerates. They are structured to take advantage of the specific legal benefits that different types of organizations receive—for example, tax-deductible gifts permitted to public charities, unlimited lobbying and indirect electioneering available to social welfare groups, and express advocacy permitted to political action committees. The resulting complex structures seem to be unintended consequences of the very complex regulatory framework for nonprofit advocacy, but they also have consequences for the management and legitimacy of organizations.

A Changing Regulatory Environment

Another set of changes shaping nonprofit advocacy is regulatory in character. Over the past few years, several attempts have been made to tighten the regulatory environment that shapes nonprofit advocacy. In an era of deregulation, it is noteworthy that nonprofit advocacy has been subjected to attempts at increased regulation.

CHARITABLE LOBBYING REGULATIONS. Concerns about whose interests are represented by nonprofits have led recently to efforts to limit their legislative lobbying. Legislation proposed by Representative Ernest Istook (and defeated five times) sought to limit the lobbying activities of nonprofit groups that receive government grants. Because nonprofits are already prohibited from lobbying with government funds (to avoid government-subsidized lobbying), many nonprofit leaders perceive that the civic, representative functions of nonprofits and their freedom of speech are under attack.[26] They believe that the legitimacy of nonprofit legislative lobbying, and ultimately the freedom of groups to communicate with government and play a role in the political system, is in jeopardy.

These attempts to limit the lobbying activities of public charities that receive government grants are partly based on the perception that these groups are advocates for larger government—an ideological argument—and that they represent their own organizational interests and not the "real" interests and needs of their constituencies. Ironically, most human service organizations, the group most likely to have been affected by these new restrictions, do not have the resources to lobby and thus are relatively poorly represented through legislative lobbying.[27] According to NCCS data, in 1998 human services groups made up 34 percent of the charities required to report to the IRS but were responsible for only 12 percent of the lobbying dollars spent by all reporting charities. Health organizations, in contrast, represented 15 percent of the organizations, but 40 percent of the public charity lobbying dollars.

In response to recent attempts to limit legislative lobbying by public charities, the nonprofit community has mobilized itself to assess the regulations and teach nonprofits how to defend their advocacy rights. The Let America Speak coalition, co-chaired by the Alliance for Justice, Independent Sector, and OMB Watch, was formed to rally nonprofits to defend their right to advocate. Several new research projects, training programs, and seminars have been created to study, promote, and improve the capacity of nonprofits to advocate. For example, Independent Sector, an umbrella group of nonprofit organizations, initiated Charity Lobbying in the Public Interest to educate nonprofits about the regulations and train them to take advantage of the opportunities to be involved in public policy.[28]

PAYCHECK PROTECTION. Prior permission proposals—the so-called paycheck protection ballot initiatives in recent elections in California and Oregon—reinforce the perception that nonprofit representational legitimacy is under attack. These ballot initiatives, usually championed by conservative groups such as Americans for Tax Reform, would require unions to receive permission from contributors to use their dues—or in the case of charities like United Way, their gifts—for planned advocacy expenditures every year. If passed, these initiatives would be an administrative nightmare and very costly. Unions and nonprofits have expended considerable resources trying to educate the public and defeat such initiatives.

CAMPAIGN FINANCE REFORM. After years of congressional debate, the president signed into law the Bipartisan Campaign Reform Act in spring 2002. The law is an attempt to stem the tide of unregulated "soft" money used for controversial election activities, such as issue advertising.

To take effect on November 6, 2002, after election day, the new law has several provisions that will affect tax-exempt organizations. It will alter the way politically active groups participate in the electoral process. Voter registration and voter identification campaigns, get-out-the-vote campaigns, support for political parties, and issue advertising are part of the repertoire of some tax-exempt organizations. These activities will be subject to new constraints regarding timing, coordination with other groups and individuals, communications with the public, and funding. For example, all types of nonprofit organizations, including labor unions, would be prohibited from giving "soft money" to political parties and from running "electioneering" issue ads (unless they channel their issue ad expenditures through a political action committee). Previously, ads that did not explicitly instruct the public to vote for or against a candidate, but merely suggested an organization's position on a candidate, were permissible. Also under Shays-Meehan, the amount of money a candidate may raise for a nonprofit organization's generic "get-out-the-vote" efforts, including those conducted by charitable organizations, would be limited to $10,000 per source. Further, candidates would not be able to raise this money from corporations or labor unions, as they did in the past.

There appears to be widespread support for reducing the amount of money that public and private interest groups pump into the electoral process. How to do this without jeopardizing valid public participation in the policy process will continue to be a challenge. These issues will be fought out in the courts.

Special Interest Advocacy

Also affecting nonprofit advocacy are the growing strength and sophistication of business advocacy. Nonprofits generally have fewer resources to devote to advocacy activities than businesses, and they must invest considerable time and money to raise their funds from multiple sources, including members, the public, foundations, and government. Donors must be educated about the cause and motivated to give and volunteer. This process may be cumbersome and in some respects inefficient, but public education and member involvement provide the legitimacy and potency of public interest campaigns.

ORGANIZATIONAL STRUCTURE. Like 501(c)(4) social welfare organizations, businesses and the 501(c)(6) trade associations that represent their interests are not constrained by regulations on the amounts they can spend on their lobbying activities, and they may spend substantial resources on election-related activities. They may also have affiliated political action committees. In contrast, 501(c)(3) public charity organizations, although they may undertake a wide variety of advocacy activities, are prohibited from electioneering—that is, engaging in activities on behalf of or in opposition to a particular candidate.

Business interests have also created organizations that mimic grassroots membership organizations in an effort to benefit from the legitimacy that comes with those kinds of entities.[29] Since donors are not disclosed, it is often difficult to discern who is behind some associations. For example, the Workplace Health and Safety Council (which consists of business groups that oppose efforts to increase workplace safety regulations) and the Coalition for Vehicle Choice (supported by Ford Motor Company and General Motors Corporation to "respond" to demands for higher fuel efficiency standards) appear to be citizens' groups but are really creations of business.[30]

FOR-PROFIT/NONPROFIT COOPERATION. Another important development is the formation of coalitions linking nonprofits and businesses in advocating for particular causes or policies. Both sides have something to gain from such collaboration. Businesses often have superior financial resources and public relations skills, while nonprofits often have social capital: visibility, public legitimacy, networks, and relationships. Combining financial and social capital can be a powerful tool for change.

The fight to reduce the sulfur content in gasoline in 1998 is a recent example of this partnering between the nonprofit and business sectors.[31] With the oil industry firmly opposed to lowering the sulfur content in gasoline, business groups, such as the Alliance of Auto Manufacturers and Engine Manufacturers of America, worked alongside nonprofits, such as the American Lung Association and Environmental Defense Fund, to lobby for lower sulfur levels.

Nonprofit standard setting within particular industries is another area of cross-sector partnerships that is gaining ground. For example, the Forest Stewardship Council (FSC) certifies timber producers that meet their standards for responsible forest management. Responsible producers can gain visibility with environmentally conscious buyers, as their products are identified with an FSC logo.[32]

Summary

Many of these forces, challenges, and trends are rooted in tensions surrounding two rather subjective and intangible characteristics of nonprofit advocacy: legitimacy and representativeness. At issue are two key questions: Whom do advocacy groups represent? And how are their policy positions established? The first question challenges the representation function of advocates and asks on what basis they legitimately speak for a constituency or for the public. The second question addresses the processes by which associations determine the issues and concerns of their constituencies and translate those concerns into policy decisions. These two questions can be thorny ones for public interest advocates, particularly for those that do not have active members or internal democratic decisionmaking processes.

Despite the cacophony of voices trying to influence policy and electoral outcomes within a complex regulatory environment, as well as the fact that public interest nonprofits are outnumbered and outspent by their for-profit, private interest opponents,[33] there is some evidence that nonprofits represent public interests with considerable success. They attract media attention, influence public opinion, convey voters to the polls, and provide valued information to decisionmakers.[34] To see this more clearly, however, it is useful to zero in on particular types of advocacy groups in more detail.

Nonprofit Advocacy in Operation: Two Examples

Two types of advocacy groups have had a particularly successful record of representing public interests in recent years: environmental organizations and civil rights and social action organizations. Many of these groups are familiar to most Americans, with several having the largest memberships among all organizations in the nonprofit sector. This section details the representational function, operations, resources, strategies, and organizational structure of each of these types in turn. The revenue streams and lobbying expenses of these organizations are also analyzed and discussed, based on data from the National Center for Charitable Statistics.

Environmental Organizations

Environmental organizations represent a variety of causes, from wildlife protection and species diversity to water quality, global warming, conservation, and many others. They include some of the most prominent organizations in America, including the Nature Conservancy, Sierra Club, and National Wildlife Federation. From 1989 to 1998, the number of 501(c)(3) environmental and animal organizations that reported financial information to the IRS increased from 3,504 to 7,497. Yet most environmental groups are small in terms of finances and staff. Only a relative handful has significant financial scale and large numbers of members. Yet these organizations have helped to change the national and global perception of the value of the environment to human life.

There is a growing sense of shared values and discourse on environmental issues that crosses national boundaries. International environmental associations have succeeded in promoting multinational meetings and international agreements that have strengthened the hands of national organizations. David John Frank argues that the creation of intergovernmental environmental organizations (113 by 1990) has led to a permanent and centralized domain and a top-down diffusion of environmental action, from the global to the nation and state levels.[35]

Although observers typically refer to the environmental movement, it is not a totally unified movement. There may be overarching agreement on the importance of the environment, but this is a diverse group of organizations that have different philosophies, organizational structures, strategies, and approaches. They often collaborate, but they also may oppose one another and compete for members and resources.

Some have chapters and active members; others have members whose only role is to write a check. A few, like the Sierra Club and National Audubon Society, have long histories and many thousands of members. Many, however, were created in the wake of environmental activism of the early 1970s, and quite a few were formed more recently, often in reaction to changing environmental regulations. The larger organizations have complex organizational structures that permit them to work effectively within the equally complex regulatory framework.

REPRESENTATION. Environmental organizations have the advantage of the moral high ground and broad public acceptance for their goals. Many have members who give them some legitimacy as they speak for the public interest. Some have respected scientists on advisory committees or boards who lend legitimacy to their research and policy positions. Low-income and minority-group interests are only weakly represented, however, among environmental groups. The environmental justice movement is seeking recognition and resources to bring those voices and unmet needs to the table. Environmental stewardship groups are beginning to bring a religious sensibility to the issues.

Market-oriented environmental organizations, as well as wise-use and legal action groups, largely funded by corporations and reflecting their interests, are a part of the mix. For example, business interests have organized groups like Citizens for Sensible Control of Acid Rain and National Wetlands Coalition to appear as if they had a grassroots constituency. They are sometimes called astroturf organizations, but despite their lack of grassroots legitimacy, they are often viewed as effective advocates for their constituencies and well-funded opponents of public interest advocates.

Representation is a significant issue for global environmental advocates. They face potential crises of legitimacy as they seek formal roles and recognition in international negotiations—for whom they speak and by what means they achieve that status are increasingly issues of concern. Michael Edwards has identified this as a general challenge facing nonprofit advocates, arguing that they need to put their houses in order to counter attacks on their legitimacy and on their representative functions.[36]

OPERATIONS. The question of whose interests are represented is an issue not only for the astroturf organizations but also for the highly professional organizations that have limited member involvement. Some environmental groups have begun to rethink their strategies and are organizing to attract and activate grassroots members. Grassroots lobbying and coalition building were reportedly the primary environmental strategies of the 1990s. One analyst reports that environmental organizations are becoming more staff intensive as groups open chapters and branches and reach out to constituencies.[37] These trends may be linked to the devolution of government activities to the state and local level. Monitoring public policies in a devolved system is much more difficult and expensive, and members are an important resource for keeping on top of local, state, and regional policies. Computer technology and Internet communications are facilitating outreach and connecting organizations more directly to members.

RESOURCES. Growing numbers of environmental groups and growing amounts of resources are being devoted to environmental issues. The global nature of environmental issues, combined with the devolution of powers to the states and the increasingly technical nature of challenges to environmental regulation, have undoubtedly increased expenses. Growing numbers of environmental organizations have also heightened the competition for resources. Organizations are challenged to be managed more efficiently and to use technology to cut costs, reach broader audiences, and produce measurable outcomes. Although many in the movement feel that working with increasingly complex issues and challenging well-financed opponents require much more money, some recent critics feel that the field has gotten too rich.[38]

Environmental organizations use a variety of fundraising techniques such as direct mail, foundation and corporate grants, government contracts, member and program fees, and for-profit subsidiaries. These multiple funding sources may permit them to advocate more freely. Some observers believe, however, that heavy reliance on direct mail may cause groups to shun unpopular causes, oversimplify their messages, and alienate their members. Yet direct mail and membership dues give groups discretionary revenues that are independent of the restrictions on advocacy that often characterize foundation, corporate, and government grants.

According to NCCS data, 501(c)(3) environmental and animal organizations rely primarily on contributions, gifts, and grants from the general public, their members, and foundations—approximately 50 percent of the total revenue of these organizations in 1998 came from these sources. Program revenues made up the next largest piece of total revenue, at 21 percent, while grants from the government made up 11 percent.[39] Sales of assets and other goods and services, as well as investment income, made up the remaining 18 percent of revenue.[40]

The revenue breakdown for environmental and animal organizations is very different from that of all reporting charities. In 1998, program revenues (including government voucher payments such as Medicaid) made up nearly 69 percent of revenue for all 501(c)(3) organizations. Contributions, gifts, and grants from private sources made up only about 10 percent of total revenue, while grants from the government made up about 9 percent. Again, sales of assets and other goods and services, as well as investment income, made up the remaining 12 percent of revenue.[41]

STRATEGIES. Strategies of environmental organizations have varied over time and across issues and organizations. Both conflict and cooperation have characterized their relationships with industry and government. Scientific research has been an important foundation for public education and litigation, and communications technology has been used to build national and global networks. Market incentives are among the current strategies to promote desirable corporate behavior, but government regulation is still an important, if less universally favored, tool.

Environmental groups use the full arsenal of advocacy techniques—research, communications, testifying, lobbying, litigation, monitoring, direct action, protests, demonstrations, and mobilizing voters. Yet very few of the environmental organizations eligible for tax-deductible gifts seem to engage in one of the central advocacy strategies—legislative lobbying. Fewer than 5 percent of environmental 501(c)(3) organizations reported legislative lobbying expenditures in 1998, and larger organizations were disproportionately represented among those that lobbied. Of the forty largest environmental groups in 1998, 45 percent reported legislative lobbying expenses, but fewer than 6 percent of the smaller organizations, which tend to be those most recently incorporated, reported such expenses.

Compared to a decade earlier, in 1998 environmental organizations spent a slightly larger proportion of their budgets, about 0.79 percent (compared to 0.70 percent in 1989), on lobbying (see table 9-5 for lobbying expenses of the top ten environmental and animal groups). Public interest environmental and

Table 9-5. *Top Ten Reporting 501(c)(3) Environmental and Animal Organizations, Based on Total Lobbying Expenses, 1998*

Organization	Total expenses (1998 U.S. dollars)		Lobbying expenses as a percentage of total expenses
	Lobbying	Organizational	
Nature Conservancy	993,396	274,403,216	0.36
Humane Society of the United States	632,685	36,633,759	1.70
Environmental Defense Fund	571,370	23,917,753	2.40
American Society for the Prevention of Cruelty to Animals	567,389	25,623,669	2.20
Trust for Public Land	534,321	44,253,998	1.20
National Parks and Conservation Association	377,396	16,621,574	2.30
Natural Resources Defense Council	348,747	25,950,396	1.30
Georgia Wildlife Federation	348,262	1,559,434	22.30
National Audubon Society	287,930	49,161,319	0.59
National Wildlife Federation	252,570	78,581,381	0.32

Source: National Center for Charitable Statistics Core Files, 1999.

animal advocates were responsible for 9.2 percent of reported lobbying expenditures of all public charities in 1998, compared with 13.2 percent a decade earlier. This decline may reflect the fact that environmental groups became increasingly complex amalgams of organizations that feature affiliated 501(c)(3), 501(c)(4), political action committee, and for-profit subsidiaries.[42]

Lobbying expenditures are only one piece of the advocacy puzzle. Groups continue to use strategies of protest and confrontation, and some have structured themselves so that they can take part in electoral politics. Only the Greens, however, have organized as a political party to try to change the U.S. political system, running Ralph Nader for president in 2000.

STRUCTURE. This section is based on a review of the environmental organizations described in *Public Interest Profiles*, a biennial publication of the Foundation for Public Affairs. This publication lists thirty-eight influential environmental and animal-related organizations in its 2001–02 edition, of which thirty-five are 501(c)(3) organizations and three are 501(c)(4) social welfare groups.

These leading environmental organizations have complex organizational structures and affiliated organizations that share the lobbying, advocacy, and representation functions. For example, fourteen of the groups have multiple offices, and twelve have chapters or similar divisions. Many of these offices and chapters are scattered around the country or the world. Ten organizations are affiliated with other 501(c)(3) organizations, and three indicate affiliations with

501(c)(4) groups that enjoy unlimited freedom to lobby. Three are affiliated with political action committees that permit them to be involved in partisan electoral activities. At least one is affiliated with nonexempt business entities.

The large environmental organizations have become sophisticated multidimensional entities. For example, the Sierra Club, a 501(c)(4) organization, has sixty-five chapters throughout the United States. It has 550,000 members and multiple affiliates, including the 501(c)(3) Sierra Club Foundation, which can receive tax-deductible contributions, and Sierra Club Political Committee, which conducts electoral activities. These affiliated organizations enable Sierra Club to carry out advocacy activities in the appropriate legal entity, according to the regulations that govern the legislative lobbying and electoral activities of nonprofits.

Similarly, Nature Conservancy, a 501(c)(3) organization, has among its related organizations five nonexempt and four exempt organizations, including the Nature Conservancy Action Fund, a 501(c)(4), as well as 300 state and program locations. Friends of the Earth, one of the newer and smaller organizations, founded in 1990, is affiliated with a network of fifty-seven international organizations, as well as Friends of the Earth Action, a political action committee. These examples indicate the wide, intertwined web of environmental organizations that span the nation and in some cases the globe.

Government regulation of advocacy activities clearly affects how these large environmental organizations structure themselves and organize their advocacy activities. The public charity affiliates can focus on public education activities, while the social welfare 501(c)(4) affiliates can conduct unlimited legislative lobbying, and the political action committees can engage in partisan campaign activities. For-profit subsidiaries earn taxable revenues to support programs. Whether this regulation-induced organizational structure is cost-efficient or the most effective strategy in terms of management, membership, or social capital building is an open question that requires in-depth research.

SUMMARY. The current status of environmental organizations is positive in terms of growth and impact, although their short-term successes are likely to vary with the political party in power. These organizations have changed national and international attitudes and expectations. Environmental issues are on policy agendas around the world, and complex webs of relationships on environmental issues cut across government, business, and nonprofit realms. Organizational revenues have grown over time, but so has the complexity of the scientific and economic problems, which makes the work more difficult to popularize and explain. Maintaining legitimacy and keeping members involved are difficult tasks. Resources continue to be an issue. Political access requires both money and professional expertise. Managing the large, complicated structures is also a challenge for strategic planning and outcome measurement.

Environmental organizations have forged mature, complex, related structures along with devolved memberships and networks that permit them to marshal resources and political clout. In the United States, a new political administration initially perceived as being more willing to favor economic development over environmental preservation may put environmental organizations on the defensive to preserve existing gains. Adversity, however, may help the organizations to strengthen coalitions and galvanize their memberships. The early decisions of President George W. Bush on global warming, arsenic levels in drinking water, and drilling for oil in Alaska have alarmed environmentalists and suggest contentious policy struggles over the course of this administration.

Civil Rights and Social Action Organizations

The civil rights and social action organizations of America are diverse in terms of causes, structures, and strategies. This diversity makes it difficult to generalize across organizations. Civil rights groups generally are focused on securing political rights or improving the circumstances of specific population groups. The National Association for the Advancement of Colored People (NAACP), for example, one of the oldest and best-known civil rights advocates, has been working on a wide range of issues to further the rights of African Americans since 1909. Social action groups, such as Citizens for Tax Justice, Family Research Council, and pro- and anti-abortion advocates, work to promote or oppose social causes or social change. Others try to make incremental changes in, for example, resources available for Head Start programs. Still others may sound the alarm and press government into action, as the AIDS Coalition to Unleash Power (ACT UP) and other advocates did during the early stages of the AIDS epidemic.

The activities of civil rights and social action groups may be directed toward changing or enforcing laws, as is the case with civil rights, toward changing corporate behavior, as is the case with consumer groups, or toward educating individuals or changing individual behavior, as is the case with campaigns to promote sexual abstinence for teens or discourage drunk driving.

From 1989 to 1998, civil rights and social action organizations grew in real numbers and as a proportion of public charities, but they are a small part of the nonprofit universe and command only a fraction of the sector's resources and a declining share of its lobbying expenditures. They range from very small volunteer entities working on local problems to very large membership groups with multimillion-dollar budgets. Some, such as the American Civil Liberties Union and NAACP, are known for their litigation; others, such as the National Rifle Association and Planned Parenthood, are known for their electoral activities. Regardless of their strategies, these organizations have had significant impacts on American life. Their research and policy advocacy attract the attention of the media, and policymakers often rely on them for information and support. These groups sometimes work together in coalitions on issues of common concern, and there are some long-term, strategic alliances, but little in the way of real cohesion.

REPRESENTATION. Civil rights groups that directly represent the rights and interests of particular populations have a certain prima facie legitimacy. Many of these groups started as small kitchen-table protest groups. The well-known ones have usually evolved into professionally staffed entities, often with members who may or may not meet on a regular basis, although they may have local chapters and offices in several locations. The larger and better-known organizations, such as the NAACP, League of United Latin American Citizens, and National Organization for Women (NOW), have broad agendas of advocacy and empowerment that may keep them relevant to their constituencies after the days of initial litigation and direct protest end.

These are the organizations most likely to represent the interests of the underserved and disenfranchised portions of society. But the mechanisms of representation and accountability vary from group to group. Many of these organizations are relatively small and poorly financed for their goals of changing the political system, social attitudes, and social mores. The degree to which they can mobilize their members for policy work is one measure of their representativeness. For example, the NAACP National Voter Fund in the 2000 national elections motivated many first-time minority voters to go to the polls. Reflecting the organization's effort, African American turnout increased by more than 1 million votes in the areas in which preelection organizing took place. The turnout increased 22 percent over 1996 in New York, 50 percent in Florida, and 140 percent in Missouri.[43]

Operations

Civil rights and social action groups are formed both as 501(c)(4) social welfare organizations and as 501(c)(3) public charities. Some are single-issue groups; others take on a cluster of related issues. Among the well-known social welfare organizations are some of the best-known single-issue advocates—for example, the National Rifle Association and National Abortion and Reproductive Rights Action League (NARAL), as well as the free speech advocate, American Civil Liberties Union.

These civic groups grew explosively during the civil rights and anti-poverty movements of the 1960s and 1970s. More recently, the conservative values movement fueled the creation of newer groups like the Christian Coalition, Promise Keepers, Focus on the Family, and others that endeavor to promote traditional Christian values at the individual, social, and political levels.

Promoting the kinds of changes these groups seek requires long-term commitments and sophisticated organizational strategies. Grassroots organizing, social marketing, communications technology, and sophisticated planning are required to raise the resources, get messages across, and make them stick in an environment that appears close to information overload. Yet there have been long-term successes—in changing attitudes toward spousal abuse and tobacco use; in securing legal rights for minorities, women, and disabled persons; and in securing greater government resources for breast cancer and AIDS research.

RESOURCES. According to the available data, the number of civil rights–oriented organizations has been steadily growing since the 1960s. The resources of these organizations seem to be increasing as well, with most relying on a combination of financial support from members, the general public, government, foundations, corporations, and the sale of goods or services.

Because most civil rights groups represent specific groups of people (Mexican Americans, the disabled, gays and lesbians, gun owners, and so forth), many make direct fundraising appeals to these targeted constituencies. Receiving funds from these populations serves two purposes. First, it provides the groups with unrestricted funds that may be used for general support or lobbying and political activities, unlike government, corporate, or foundation grants, which are often project-specific. Second, high levels of financial support from the people who stand to benefit from an organization's efforts translate into legitimacy in the political process.

NCCS data reflect this heavy reliance on contributions, as nearly 57 percent of the revenues of 501(c)(3) civil rights organizations derive from contributions, gifts, and grants from members, the general public, and foundations. Government grants provide about 23 percent of civil rights organizations' revenues, while program fees provide 13 percent. Investment income and sales from assets and general goods and services make up the remaining 7 percent of revenue.[44]

STRATEGIES. Civil rights organizations often use direct action strategies to gain attention and take advantage of the resources of the members they represent. Public demonstrations, marches, and marathons are favorite tools of action because they get the messages out and bring money in. Recent examples include the Million Mom March (gun control), Million Man March (family values), Race for the Cure (Breast Cancer), and pro-choice and anti-abortion rallies at the steps of the U.S. Supreme Court.

Research and public education are also used to good effect by social action organizations. Research funded by the American Cancer Society, for example, revealed the dangers of smoking and provided the foundation for the formation of the Coalition on Smoking or Health, with the American Heart Association and American Lung Association, to promote government action and changes in public attitudes toward tobacco use and the tobacco industry.[45]

Litigation is also favored for rights-based work.[46] This strategy can help to build a body of law around a particular issue as well as to keep an issue alive in

Table 9-6. *Top Ten Reporting 501(c)(3) Civil Rights Organizations, Based on Total Lobbying Expenses, 1998*

Organization	Total expenses (1998 U.S. dollars)		Lobbying expenses as a percentage of total expenses
	Lobbying	Organizational	
National Abortion and Reproductive Rights Action League Foundation	259,460	7,039,726	3.70
Women's Legal Defense Fund	173,242	2,750,304	6.30
Mexican American Legal Defense and Education Fund	168,170	4,802,169	3.50
Federation for American Immigration Reform	160,754	3,292,033	4.90
Anti-Defamation League of B'nai B'rith	149,319	45,479,769	0.33
Center for Reproductive Law and Policy	140,196	4,823,398	2.90
National Council of La Raza	138,567	13,667,353	1.00
American Civil Liberties Union Foundation	119,760	13,105,727	0.91
NOW Legal Defense and Education Fund	114,377	3,287,498	3.50
American Jewish Committee	99,617	24,686,844	0.40

Source: National Center for Charitable Statistics Core Files, 1999.

the public's mind. Since the *Roe* v. *Wade* decision in 1973, for example, anti-abortion advocates have used litigation strategies to make the nation's abortion laws more restrictive.[47]

Legislative lobbying seems less used by social action and civil rights groups than might be expected. While the number of such groups reporting lobbying expenditures more than doubled from fifty-three to 115 during the 1990s, this still represents less than 7 percent of such groups and only about 3 percent of all organizations that lobby. Further, although lobbying expenditures increased somewhat, from $2.3 million to $2.6 million, they declined as a percentage of all expenses from 2.1 to 1.2 percent (see table 9-6 for the lobbying expenses of the top ten civil rights groups). In 1998 median lobbying expenditures of 501(c)(3) civil rights and social action groups were only $5,500, compared with total median expenses of $478,000. The share of total 501(c)(3) lobbying expenditures attributed to civil rights and social action organizations decreased by half over the decade.[48]

STRUCTURE. Like environmental organizations, civil rights and social action groups tend to have complex organizational structures to carry out their strategies. Almost all of these groups have affiliated organizations, mainly either 501(c)(3)s or 501(c)(4)s. Many have offices and chapters throughout the United States. Eight of them have affiliated political action committees.

According to information contained in *Public Interest Profiles*, National Organization for Women, a 501(c)(4) organization, has a related 501(c)(3) organization, 500 local chapters, and two related political action committees (PACs)—the National NOW PAC (which supports candidates for national office) and the NOW Equality PAC (which supports state and local candidates). NARAL, a 501(c)(4), has an affiliated 501(c)(3) national foundation, as well as state-level 501(c)(3) foundations in ten states and a political action committee. The National Rifle Association has a similar structure, consisting of a 501(c)(3) foundation and the Political Victory Fund political action committee.

Twenty-three of the civil rights and social action groups featured in *Public Interest Profiles* have individual or organizational membership bases, with the National Rifle Association having the most members, at 2.8 million. In second place are NARAL, NAACP, and NOW, each having approximately 500,000 members.

SUMMARY. Civil rights and social action organizations represent a diverse mix of ideologies and identities. Collectively these groups represent the entire breadth of the political spectrum. Because they are especially sensitive to changes in the political climate, their influence in the policy process is constantly changing. Although a lack of data on these organizations hinders research on their current status, their presence and importance appear to have grown rapidly since the 1960s, and they remain an important force in representing diverse interests and bringing like-minded citizens together to achieve political goals.

The examples of both civil rights and environmental groups demonstrate how the large, visible advocacy organizations adapt to regulations that affect the attainment of their missions. A major question is the impact of the resulting structures on the accountability and effectiveness of the organizations. Is the separation of advocacy functions into affiliated organizations cost-effective? Does it lead to better representation of the public interest? Do business and industry groups also have to develop complicated organizational structures to advocate and lobby to achieve their missions? Analyses of the benefits, costs, and trade-offs of these complex structures should be undertaken. The implications for the organizations, for their stakeholders, and for the causes they represent are not self-evident.

Conclusions and Future Steps

Assessing the current status of nonprofit advocacy and civic participation is a challenging task. The various strategies, techniques, and organizations discussed in this chapter illustrate that nonprofit advocacy is multifaceted and that an archetypal advocacy organization does not exist. The changing civic, political, economic, and social realities, coupled with new technologies developed over the past decade, have resulted in new ways for organizations to advocate and for citizens to participate in the political process. The ultimate social benefit of these new forms of advocacy and civic participation may be debatable, but their influence is undeniable and deserves further research.

Building the capacity for advocacy is a relatively new and promising activity. Effective advocacy requires management as well as organizing skills and an understanding of the relevant laws and regulations. Many analysts and advocates believe that increasing funding for advocacy organizations and activities should be a top priority for the foundation community.

Several new initiatives have the potential to fill some research gaps, increase capacity to advocate, and educate the public, government, and foundations about the critical importance of nonprofit advocacy. For example, various commissions on civil society and civic renewal, and meetings at the Aspen Institute, Hauser Center at Harvard, Advocacy Institute, OMB Watch, and Urban Institute, to mention a few, have sought to come to grips with pressing and contested issues around civic participation and advocacy.

The roles played by public interest advocates in providing research, educating the public and policymakers, and fighting for policies that provide long-term, broad benefits are taken for granted. It is important to understand those roles and the impact of regulations, both current and proposed, that affect advocacy activities. The costs of advocacy, including information overload and polarization of the policy process, also deserve attention.

This suggests the need for better research on the advocacy activities of nonprofits. Precise definitions of advocacy are needed, as are regular tracking of activities, consistent measures of outcomes, and current case studies of different strategies and outcomes. Further, there is a dearth of information on non-501(c)(3) nonprofit organizations, such as 501(c)(4)s and 501(c)(6)s, as well as all types of organizations that are not required to file with the IRS. Understanding how small, informal groups connect citizens and effect change at the local level is critical if we are to assess fully and accurately the status of nonprofit advocacy, civic participation, and the health of American democracy.

The portrait of nonprofit advocacy is thus mixed. There is increased professionalism and use of technology, coalition building, and networking among major environmental, civil rights, and social action organizations. Although businesses and professional interests are reportedly better funded to get their messages across, citizen and environmental groups are by some measures better able to gain the ear of the media and Congress and may be more effective than others in achieving some of their goals. As the nation's political, social, and economic environments change, nonprofit groups will continue to fight to be heard in the policy process. They will continue to be flexible and opportunistic in their efforts to participate in democratic governance. Moreover, attempts to limit or regulate advocacy activities will continue, intimidating some organizations and mobilizing others.

A significant challenge is to articulate the core democratic values served by nonprofit advocacy and to understand the trade-offs between those values and competing ones. The dance of democracy is a tango, not a waltz. Negotiating and shaping change are ongoing, contentious processes, essential for renewal and innovation. They require an attentive public, an informed government, and an engaged nonprofit sector.

Appendix: Data Overview

The National Center for Charitable Statistics (NCCS), a project of the Center on Nonprofits and Philanthropy at the Urban Institute, is the national repository of data on nonprofit organizations in the United States. NCCS Core Files, on which this paper's analyses are based, are produced annually and are compiled from information that nonprofit organizations report to the Internal Revenue Service, primarily on Form 990 and Form 990's Schedule A. In particular, the Core Files combine descriptive information from the IRS Business Master Files and financial variables from the IRS Return Transaction Files, after they have been cleaned by NCCS.

The Core Files contain several variables that can be used to analyze lobbying. They are derived from Form 990's Schedule A, which all reporting 501(c)(3) organizations are required to file annually with the IRS. The lobbying variables are derived from responses to the following questions on Schedule A:

—Part III, line 1: "During the year, has the organization attempted to influence national, state, or local legislation, including any attempt to influence public opinion on a legislative matter or referendum? If 'Yes,' enter the total expenses paid or incurred in connection with the lobbying activities."

—Part VI-A, line 36: "Total lobbying expenditures to influence public opinion (grassroots lobbying)."[49]

—Part VI-A, line 37: "Total lobbying expenditures to influence a legislative body (direct lobbying)."[50]

—Part VI-A, line 38: "Total lobbying expenditures." (Calculated by adding the responses to lines 36 and 37, above.)

All organizations must respond to part III, line 1. However, part VI-A, lines 36, 37, and 38 are only answered by organizations that make the 501(h) election to lobby. In this chapter, most of the analyses of lobbying are based on responses to part III, line 1.

The IRS does not collect data on all organizations that are technically 501(c)(3) charities. For example, many religious organizations, including churches and associations of churches, are not required to register with the IRS. Organizations with less than $5,000 in annual gross receipts are also not required to register. Among those that must initially register, only organizations with more than $25,000 in annual gross receipts must file a Form 990 with the IRS (referred to as "reporting" organizations).

The National Taxonomy of Exempt Entities (NTEE) provides a system for classifying data on 501(c)(3) nonprofit organizations based on their purpose, type, or major function. The NTEE classification system divides nonprofit organizations into twenty-six major groups under ten broad categories. Table 9-3 adapts this system somewhat, as the seventh broad category (public, societal benefit) is broken into five major groups, allowing us to present data on the first major group in this category: civil rights, social action, and advocacy.[51]

Notes

1. Morris P. Fiorina, "Extreme Voices: A Dark Side of Civic Engagement," in Theda Skocpol and Morris P. Fiorina, eds., *Civic Engagement in American Democracy* (Washington: Brookings, 1999), p. 396.

2. See Nonprofit Sector Strategy Group, *The Nonprofit Contribution to Civic Participation and Advocacy* (Washington: Aspen Institute, 2000), for an overview of the debate.

3. Jeffrey M. Berry, *The New Liberalism* (Washington: Brookings, 1999).

4. Elizabeth J. Reid, "Nonprofit Advocacy and Political Participation," in Elizabeth T. Boris and C. Eugene Steuerle, eds., *Nonprofits and Government: Collaboration and Conflict* (Washington: Urban Institute, 1999), p. 292.

5. Bruce R. Hopkins, *Charity, Advocacy, and the Law* (New York: John Wiley and Sons, 1992), p. 32.

6. Craig Jenkins, "Nonprofit Organizations and Policy Advocacy," in Walter W. Powell, ed., *The Nonprofit Sector: A Research Handbook* (Yale University Press, 1987), p. 297.

7. Hopkins, *Charity, Advocacy, and the Law,* p. 104.

8. See Alliance for Justice, *Worry-Free Lobbying for Nonprofits; How to Use the 501(h) Election to Maximize Effectiveness* (Washington: Alliance for Justice, 2000), for more information on making the 501(h) election.

9. For more information on government regulation of charitable lobbying, see Gail M. Harmon and others, *Being a Player: A Guide to the IRS Lobbying Regulations for Advocacy Charities* (Washington: Alliance for Justice, 2000).

10. Holly B. Schadler, *The Connection: Strategies for Creating and Operating 501(c)(3)s, 501(c)(4)s, and PACs* (Washington: Alliance for Justice, 1998).

11. See the appendix for a detailed description of the data used for this analysis.

12. The National Center for Charitable Statistics will soon have a more detailed database of Forms 990 and a system for searching program descriptions that will permit more detailed analysis. At present, we are limited to identifying organizations by major sector of involvement. See National Center for Charitable Statistics and Foundation Center, *National Taxonomy of Exempt Entities Core Codes* (Washington: Urban Institute, 1998).

13. Mary Anna Culleton Colwell, "The Potential for Bias When Research on Voluntary Associations Is Limited to 501(c)(3) Organizations," Nonprofit Sector Research Fund Working Paper (Washington: Aspen Institute, 1997), pp. 3–4.

14. Berry, *New Liberalism*, p. 85.

15. Susan Rees, "Effective Nonprofit Advocacy," Nonprofit Sector Research Fund Working Paper (Washington: Aspen Institute, 1998), pp. 12–13.

16. Robert Putnam, *Bowling Alone: The Collapse and Revival of American Community* (New York: Simon and Schuster, 2000), p. 46.

17. See American Association of Retired Persons, *Maintaining America's Social Fabric: The AARP Survey of Civic Involvement* (Washington: American Association of Retired Persons, 1997); League of Women Voters, *Working Together: Community Involvement in America* (Washington: League of Women Voters, 1999); and Pew Research Center for People and the Press, *Trust and Citizen Engagement in Metropolitan Philadelphia: A Case Study* (Washington: Pew Research Center for People and the Press, 1997).

18. Jeffrey M. Berry, "The Rise of Citizen Groups," in Skocpol and Fiorina, eds., *Civic Engagement in American Democracy,* p. 391.

19. Sidney Verba and others, "Citizen Activity: Who Participates? What Do They Say?" *American Political Science Review,* vol. 87, no. 2 (1993): 303–18; see p. 314.

20. Ulf Hjelmar, *The Political Practice of Environmental Organizations* (Aldershot, U.K.: Ipswich Books, 1996), pp. 62–66.

21. See Lincoln Institute, "Annual Charitable Organizations Survey," (www.lincolninstitute.org/surveys/surv0100.htm [June 23, 2000]); and Maryland Association of Nonprofit Organizations, "Legal Needs of the Nonprofit Sector" (Baltimore: Maryland Association of Nonprofit Organizations, 1999).

22. Jeffrey M. Berry and David Arons, "Influencing Nonprofit Public Policy Participation: Factors and Findings from the Strengthening Nonprofit Advocacy Project," paper presented at the annual ARNOVA conference, New Orleans, November 15–18, 2000.

23. See Nonprofit Sector Strategy Group, "Nonprofit Contribution to Civic Participation and Advocacy"; Advocacy Institute, *Justice Begins at Home: Strengthening Social Justice Advocacy in the U.S.* (Washington: Advocacy Institute, 2000).

24. Peter Behr, "For Environmental Groups, Biggest NAFTA Fight Is Intramural," *Washington Post,* September 16, 1993, p. D10.

25. Hula has begun to examine this topic: Kevin W. Hula, *Lobbying Together: Interest Group Coalitions in Legislative Politics* (Georgetown University Press, 1999).

26. In May 1983 the Supreme Court, in *Regan, Secretary of the Treasury, et al. v. Taxation with Representation of Washington,* ruled that lobbying limits on charitable organizations do not violate First Amendment rights but instead serve to avoid government subsidization of charitable lobbying.

27. Jeff Krehely, "Assessing the Current Data on 501(c)(3) Advocacy: What IRS Form 990 Can Tell Us," in Elizabeth J. Reid and Maria D. Montilla, eds., *Exploring Organizations and Advocacy* (Washington: Urban Institute, 2001), p. 44.

28. Efforts to educate public charities about the benefits of taking the 501(h) election, which clarifies "substantial" lobbying by providing a formula for expenses related to total expenditures, seem to be having an effect. The number of 501(c)(3) organizations reporting their lobbying expenses under the 501(h) framework increased from 405, or 25 percent of all lobbying 501(c)(3)s, in 1989 to 1,510, or 43 percent of all lobbying 501(c)(3)s in 1998. In that year, these 501(h) "electors" spent $71,133,451 on lobbying, which represents 53 percent of all reported lobbying expenses.

29. O'Harrow has highlighted a recent attempt by the health industry to generate a "grasstops" movement. Robert O'Harrow, "Grass Roots Seeded by Drugmaker; Schering-Plough Uses 'Coalitions' to Sell Costly Treatment," *Washington Post,* September 12, 2000, p. A1. See also the National Hepatitis C Coalition's website (www.nationalhepatitis-c.org [August 19, 2002]) for more information.

30. Scott Shepard, "Deception in Lobbying: Are They 'Grassroots' or Astroturf?" *Atlanta Journal and Constitution,* December 8, 1994, p. A14.

31. As described by Berry and colleagues at lobby.la.psu.edu/Low_Sulfur_Gasoline/frame-set_sulfur.html [July 17, 2001].

32. Hank Cauley, comments made at the eighth seminar of the Center on Nonprofits and Philanthropy's Nonprofit Advocacy and the Policy Process seminar series, Urban Institute, Washington, May 18, 2001.

33. In an analysis of reports filed under the Lobbying Disclosure Act of 1995, Baumgartner and Leech find that businesses and trade associations "spent over nine times more money on lobbying than citizen groups and nonprofits." See Frank R. Baumgartner and Beth L. Leech, "Interest Niches and Policy Bandwagons: Patterns of Interest Group Involvement in National Politics," working draft (submitted to *Journal of Politics,* March 2001), p. 6.

34. Berry, *New Liberalism,* pp. 85–86.

35. David John Frank, "Science, Nature, and the Globalization of the Environment, 1870–1990," *Social Forces,* vol. 76, no. 2 (December 1997): 424.

36. Michael Edwards, *NGO Rights and Responsibilities* (London: Foreign Policy Centre, 2000), pp. 20–22.

37. Ronald G. Shaiko, *Voices and Echoes for the Environment: Public Interest Representation in the 1990s and Beyond* (Columbia University Press, 1999), p. 11.

38. See Tom Knudson, "Environment, Inc.," *Sacramento Bee,* April 22 and 26, 2001, for the *Sacramento Bee*'s recent series on the environmental movement.

39. Program revenues include fees for services and contract revenues, including government contracts and payments made through Medicare and Medicaid.

40. All revenue percentages are based on data from organizations that file the long version of IRS Form 990; 990 EZ filers are excluded from this analysis, as they are not required to break out government support from other sources of public support. Due to current data limitations, government payments for specific program services cannot be separated out of the aggregate program service revenue category.

41. See notes 39 and 40.

42. As part of our analysis, we examined the 501(c)(3) environmental organizations listed in the most recent issue of *Public Interest Profiles,* which catalogues the most prominent and effective interest groups in the United States. According to NCCS data on these organizations, these groups experienced a 17 percent decline in mean lobbying expenses over the past decade. Total lobbying amounts declined 1.9 percent, while organizational expenses increased almost 80 percent. This same pattern is seen among environmental groups as a whole, reinforcing the probability that they are strategically locating lobbying activities in 501(c)(4) affiliates or related entities.

43. Heather Booth, comments made at the fifth seminar of the Center on Nonprofits and Philanthropy's Nonprofit Advocacy and the Policy Process seminar series, Urban Institute, Washington, December 8, 2000.

44. See notes 39 and 40.

45. Christopher H. Foreman, "The Politics of Pleasure and Poison: Tobacco and Civil Society in the United States," *Civil Society in the United States* (Georgetown University Press, forthcoming), p. 35.

46. Comments made at the fourth seminar of the Center on Nonprofits and Philanthropy's Nonprofit Advocacy and the Policy Process seminar series, Urban Institute, Washington, September 22, 2000.

47. Kathryn Ann Farr, "Shaping Policy through Litigation: Abortion Law in the United States," *Crime and Delinquency,* vol. 39, no. 2. (April 1993): 168.

48. Analysis of NCCS data on the 501(c)(3) organizations listed in *Public Interest Profiles* as leaders in civil rights revealed that mean lobbying expenditures increased from $18,043 in

1989 to $27,300 in 1998 (in constant 1998 dollars). Total lobbying expenditures for these organizations nearly doubled during the period, from $541,293 to $1,064,684. However, the ratio of total lobbying expenditures to total organizational expenses held relatively steady over the period.

49. The IRS defines grassroots lobbying as "any attempt to influence any legislation through an attempt to affect the opinions of the general public or any part of the general public."

50. The IRS defines direct lobbying as "any attempt to influence any legislation through communication with any member or employee of a legislative body, or any government official or employee (other than a member or employee of a legislative body) who may participate in the formulation of the legislation, but only if the principal purpose of the communication is to influence legislation."

51. For more information on the NTEE classification system, see National Center for Charitable Statistics and Foundation Center, *National Taxonomy of Exempt Entities Core Codes.* Urban Institute, September 1998.

10

Infrastructure Organizations

ALAN J. ABRAMSON AND RACHEL McCARTHY

I n addition to the daycare centers, soup kitchens, hospitals, and universities with which most people are familiar, America's nonprofit sector also includes a variety of infrastructure organizations (IOs) that support these other organizations and seek to improve their effectiveness. Like similar organizations that support the business and government sectors, IOs serving the nonprofit sector are numerous and diverse. They include organizations that support nonprofits in particular fields (for example, American Hospital Association and American Symphony Orchestra League) as well as organizations that serve the entire nonprofit sector or at least large portions of it (for example, Independent Sector, Council on Foundations, and National Council of Nonprofit Associations).

As the nonprofit sector has grown in scale and importance in recent decades, the evolution and strengthening of the sector's infrastructure organizations have become a matter of increasing concern. Nevertheless, there has been little systematic analysis of these membership, advocacy, educational, research, management assistance, and other IOs that promote the health of the nonprofit sector. This chapter seeks to help fill this gap by examining the growth of nonprofit infrastructure over the past several decades, identifying the major challenges now facing infrastructure organizations, and suggesting priority directions for their future development.

The authors thank Audrey Alvarado, Robert Bothwell, Sara Engelhardt, Mark Rosenman, Lester Salamon, and Naomi Wish for comments on earlier drafts of this chapter.

To do so, the chapter focuses on the "nonprofit" portion of nonprofit infrastructure, with less coverage of the numerous government and for-profit entities that also support nonprofits and philanthropy. In particular, the focus is on IOs that reach across the entire charitable—501(c)(3) and 501(c)(4)—components of the nonprofit sector, or at least very large portions of it, rather than those that support a single subsector. Thus, not covered in this chapter are IOs seeking to strengthen organizations in a particular industry (for example, American Association of Museums) or those serving specific population groups or causes (for example, National Council of La Raza, which works with organizations serving Hispanic Americans).

The writing of this chapter was handicapped by significant gaps in the available information. With the exception of the Union Institute's 1996 study, *Mission Possible,* there are few data sources or previous studies on which to draw.[1] To help ground the discussion, therefore, the analysis supplements the available data and written material with a dozen interviews of infrastructure leaders and others that were conducted in the summer of 2000.[2] Even so, what follows should be considered a first step in assessing the world of nonprofit infrastructure that others will want to improve on.

The central thesis that emerges from this work is that nonprofit infrastructure organizations experienced a golden era of growth starting in the 1970s, but that this era is drawing to a close, with a major new challenge—the challenge of consolidating the gains of recent decades—demanding increased attention from nonprofit and other leaders. There is some concern that IOs are not serving the sector as effectively as they should. Of special concern are the quality of services that IOs are providing and their lack of vision and boldness in addressing the important challenges facing the sector. Inadequate financial support is an issue for some IOs and may underlie the other weaknesses. Now that a functional nonprofit infrastructure has been established, the biggest challenge for IOs, their leaders, members, funders, and others is to consolidate the gains achieved and to strengthen and extend in new ways what has already been created.

Overview of Nonprofit Infrastructure Organizations

Although nonprofit infrastructure organizations have recently mushroomed in number and size, such organizations have existed, in a limited form, for quite some time. By the late 1800s, for example, local organizations called charity organization societies, modeled after similar societies in Britain, were established in many U.S. cities to coordinate the efforts of independent charitable groups. Charity organization societies sought to maximize philanthropic results, avoid overlapping service provision, ensure accurate knowledge of all charity recipients, coordinate services to those in need, and expose impostor recipients as well as fraudulent institutions—all functions that echo those of nonprofit support organizations today.[3] The hope was that such information sharing and coordination would protect deserving recipients and legitimate institutions from the suspicion and scrutiny that occur in the absence of built-in safeguards and accountability measures.[4]

Besides the charity organization societies, many subsector infrastructure organizations have long histories. The American Hospital Association, Association of American Colleges (now the National Association of Independent Colleges and Universities), and American Association of Museums date from the turn of the nineteenth century. More relevant for this chapter, some sector-wide organizations have also been in existence for many decades: the National Charities Information Bureau (1918), which recently merged into the BBB Wise Giving Alliance, American Association of Fund-Raising Counsel (1935), Council on Foundations (1949), Foundation Center (1956), and National Society of Fund Raising Executives (1960), which was recently renamed the Association of Fundraising Professionals.

Despite their long history, IOs did not emerge as a discrete set of organizations with major roles in the sector and recognized public importance until the 1970s. Perhaps most significant was the establishment of Independent Sector in 1980. Independent Sector has come to be seen as the preeminent umbrella infrastructure organization, with an ambitious mission to represent, serve, and advocate for the whole nonprofit sector, or at least the 501(c)(3) and 501(c)(4) portions of it.

Since the 1970s, the scope and dimensions of the IO population have grown, almost commensurate with the expansion of the overall nonprofit sector. In the last two decades of the twentieth century, IOs multiplied in number and significantly increased their capacity to provide support and services to nonprofit organizations. To do so, however, they have had to overcome some special obstacles. In the first place, IOs that seek to serve the nonprofit sector as a whole must overcome the subsector orientation of many nonprofits. Subsector IOs serve many of the infrastructure needs of nonprofits, and sector-wide IOs must demonstrate their added value or they will not develop the needed client base. In the second place, IOs that seek to provide collective benefits that improve the nonprofit sector as a whole (for example, favorable tax treatment of charitable contributions or positive public attitudes toward charities) may have difficulty getting individual nonprofits to pay dues to defray the costs of collective benefits that they can enjoy whether or not they pay for them.

Overcoming the subsector orientation of nonprofits and the free rider problem remain difficult tasks for many IOs. However, IOs have found ways to address these two important challenges. In fact, the period since the 1970s has been a golden era for nonprofit infrastructure organizations. To better understand the scope of nonprofit infrastructure and the ways in which it has developed to respond to these organizational challenges, the following pages describe IOs, grouping organizations according to their key features:

—The clients they serve (the sector as a whole or individual nonprofits and their staff),

—The services they provide (advocacy, research, technical assistance, education and training, and other services), and

—Their program areas of focus (accountability, governance, fundraising, and other areas).

IOs Serving the Nonprofit Sector as a Whole

IOs that serve the nonprofit sector as a whole provide advocacy, public education, research, and other services.

ADVOCACY AND PUBLIC EDUCATION. Sector advocates represent the interests of the nonprofit sector as a whole in the policymaking process. At the national level the most prominent sector advocate is Independent Sector, a national coalition of more than 700 member organizations including both grantmakers and grantseekers. In the nonprofit community, Independent Sector is perceived as the voice of big nonprofits and foundations. Many Independent Sector members are themselves large, national associations of nonprofits (for example, YMCA of the United States, Girls Incorporated, Catholic Charities USA, and United Way of America). Among the large, nationally oriented foundation members are the Ford Foundation, Charles Stewart Mott Foundation, and Carnegie Corporation of New York.

Through its twenty-year history, Independent Sector's primary objectives have been to educate leaders and the public about the nonprofit sector, promote research on the nonprofit sector and philanthropy, improve the quality of executive leadership in the nonprofit sector, foster constructive relations between the nonprofit community and policymakers, and provide a common meeting ground for nonprofit leaders. Independent Sector recently approved a new strategic plan that will focus its activity in the areas of public policy, strategic partnerships, and research.

As a membership organization, Independent Sector confronts many of the same organizational challenges that confront other membership associations. An often-difficult challenge is the inability of membership associations to exclude nonmembers from enjoying the collective goods the associations provide.[5] In the case of Independent Sector, its successes in public policy are collective goods that are available to all nonprofits, whether or not they pay Independent Sector's membership dues.

Independent Sector and other membership organizations employ a variety of approaches to address this collective action problem. One strategy is to have a small group of concerned foundation members shoulder a disproportionate share of Independent Sector's budget. This allows other members to pay less than they otherwise would have to in order to sustain its sectorwide activities.

Thus grants and contributions made up the largest portion of Independent Sector's revenue during most of the past decade.

In addition to counting heavily on its foundation supporters, Independent Sector also relies on solidary incentives to get and keep dues-paying members.[6] While individual nonprofits may be tempted to forgo membership in Independent Sector and other umbrella organizations because they can free ride, the interest of many nonprofit organizations in being good nonprofit citizens and showing solidarity with other nonprofits can override their narrow cost-benefit calculations and lead them to join.

Another challenge for Independent Sector in attracting members is the strong pull that subsector associations exert on many potential joiners. Why should a nonprofit that belongs to a health, education, arts, or other subsector association that meets most of its needs also join Independent Sector? In fact, many organizations probably do not belong to Independent Sector for this reason. However, the public policy attacks on the nonprofit sector as a whole over the past several decades and the increasing consciousness of a unified, coherent sector have led more nationally oriented nonprofits and foundations to pay for multiple memberships, in both their subsector associations and Independent Sector.

While Independent Sector provides services to and advocates on behalf of both grantmakers and grantseekers, the Council on Foundations targets just grantmakers. The Council on Foundations seeks to promote organized philanthropy, improve its effectiveness, and enhance understanding of it. It also is a membership organization, with more than 2,100 foundation and corporate grantmaking members.

To address its free rider problems, the Council on Foundations employs some of the same strategies as Independent Sector but also makes heavier use of selective benefits that only members can obtain. For example, the Council on Foundations offers legal consultation, training sessions, an annual conference, and specialized information resources primarily to its members. Nonmembers can take advantage of some of these services, but generally only at much higher prices than members.

The Council on Foundations also enhances its attractiveness to potential members by supporting affinity groups, which are groups of funders with a common interest in a particular program area, population, or cause, such as health, children, Hispanics, HIV/AIDS, or national service. The Council on Foundations now recognizes thirty-eight affinity groups, up from sixteen in 1988.[7]

While the Council on Foundations speaks for a broad range of medium-size and large foundations, the Association of Small Foundations, which is one of the fastest-growing membership IOs, represents foundations with few or no paid staff. The National Network of Grantmakers advocates for progressive grantmakers, while the Philanthropy Roundtable brings together conservative funders.

The National Council of Nonprofit Associations and the Forum of Regional Associations of Grantmakers are national organizations that seek to expand the capacity of state-based and regional associations of nonprofits and grantmakers via public policy initiatives and the promotion of a cohesive vision that emphasizes the importance of nonprofits and philanthropy.

OMB Watch is a nonprofit research, educational, and advocacy organization that focuses on budgetary issues, regulatory policy, nonprofit advocacy, access to government information, and activities at the U.S. Office of Management and Budget. The Alliance for Justice provides legal information on the rules pertaining to advocacy, civic participation, and voter registration to nonprofits and foundations.

The National Committee for Responsive Philanthropy (NCRP) was founded in 1976 in response to concerns about the limited ability of low-income and disenfranchised populations to secure philanthropic support. Its mission is to make philanthropy more responsive to struggling populations, more relevant to public needs, and more accountable and transparent in order to create a more democratic society. The NCRP, together with OMB Watch, the Alliance for Justice, and Independent Sector, led the effort in 1995 to defeat the proposed Istook amendment that would have limited the lobbying activity of nonprofits that receive federal funding.

At the state and local level, state and regional nonprofit associations, such as the California Association of Nonprofits and Minnesota Council of Nonprofits, as well as regional associations of grantmakers, such as the Council of Michigan Foundations and Donors Forum of Chicago, perform many of the same advocacy and member assistance functions on sector-wide issues as do national advocates.

RESEARCH. Research conducted at universities and other institutions enhances the nonprofit sector by improving understanding of nonprofit activities. In the past two decades, the number of academic and other research centers dedicated to the study of the nonprofit sector has increased significantly.[8] Among the leading nonprofit research centers are the Center on Philanthropy at Indiana University, Center for Civil Society Studies at Johns Hopkins University, Center for the Study of Voluntary Organizations and Service at Georgetown University, Hauser Center for Nonprofit Organizations at Harvard University, and Center on Nonprofits and Philanthropy at the Urban Institute.

Along with the expansion in the number of nonprofit research centers and researchers has come corresponding growth in the organizations that serve the field of nonprofit research. The Association for Research on Nonprofit Organizations and Voluntary Action (ARNOVA), International Society for Third-Sector Research (ISTR), and Nonprofit Sector Research Fund at the Aspen Institute serve the sector by acting as clearinghouses for information on the nonprofit sector and promoting the expansion of knowledge about the sector. *Nonprofit and Voluntary Sector Quarterly, Voluntas,* and *Nonprofit Management and Leadership* are the leading academic journals focused on nonprofit research.

Infrastructure Organizations Serving Individual Nonprofits and Their Staff

Organizations that seek to strengthen individual nonprofits and their staff compose the other major category of IOs. Reflecting their missions and clientele, these organizations rely more heavily on fees for service than the sector-wide IOs, which depend more on foundation grants and membership dues.

EDUCATION. Universities and other educational institutions seek to provide nonprofit managers with appropriate skills and knowledge. The recent increase in education courses dealing with nonprofit management has been striking. While in 1990 only seventeen universities offered a graduate-level concentration in the management of nonprofit organizations, by February 2001 ninety-seven colleges and universities offered graduate degree programs with a concentration in nonprofit management.[9] The rapid increase in nonprofit management education programs reflects support for the development of specialized educational programs responsive to the particular needs of the nonprofit sector. The increase also indicates an emerging need for professional, highly trained nonprofit managers with various forms of technical expertise.

MANAGEMENT SUPPORT AND TRAINING. Management support organizations provide management assistance to nonprofit organizations with the goal of improving organizational effectiveness. Management support organizations were providing training for more than 250,000 nonprofit managers in 1997, and this was a conservative estimate.[10] Training, management consulting, and information programs compose the primary functions and services of management support organizations.[11]

The evolution of nonprofit management as a distinct field and the provision of nonprofit management assistance by specialized providers began in the late 1960s.[12] A 1979 study described the field of nonprofit management as small and fragmented.[13] More recent studies have identified almost 700 nonprofit management support organizations in the United States that receive philanthropic support.[14] Many additional management support providers are independent consultants, for-profit consulting firms, or government agencies.

Nonprofit management support organizations are a diverse group and themselves serve nonprofits with varied missions. Although these organizations are becoming more highly specialized and professionalized in accordance with overarching trends in the sector, they often act as multifunctional service providers for nonprofit organizations in a particular geographic region.[15] Comprehensive management support for all nonprofit organizations and communities is still not available, but the multiplication of management support organizations has helped to reduce the barriers to access, and their reported successes have led to higher demand for their services.[16] Indeed, management support organizations and professionals from around the country have established their own IO, the Alliance for Nonprofit Management, which was formed in the late 1990s from the merger of the Nonprofit Management Association and Support Centers of America.

United Way of America and its local affiliates are important sources of assistance for many nonprofits. Another major national management support organization is BoardSource, formerly the National Center for Nonprofit Boards, which was founded in 1988 by the Association of Governing Boards of Universities and Colleges and Independent Sector. BoardSource aims to increase the effectiveness of nonprofit organizations by strengthening their boards of directors. Its programs promote knowledge of effective board practices and advocate for the value of board service and the importance of effective governance.

PROFESSIONAL DEVELOPMENT. The Association of Fundraising Professionals (formerly the National Society of Fund Raising Executives), American Association of Fund-Raising Counsel, and American Society of Association Executives are all professional societies that seek to strengthen nonprofits and philanthropy by promoting the use of best professional practices and adherence to a code of ethics and accountability.

INFORMATION RESOURCES. The Foundation Center fosters public understanding of foundations by collecting, organizing, analyzing, and disseminating information about foundations and other grantmaking entities. The multitude of resources provided by the Foundation Center allows grantseeking organizations to obtain information on myriad potential funders in one place. The BBB Wise Giving Alliance, which recently formed from the merger of the National Charities Information Bureau and the Philanthropic Advisory Service of the Council of Better Business Bureaus' Foundation, promotes informed giving by providing information on organizations' activities, governance, staffing, and finances to grantmakers so they can make informed decisions about the organizations receiving their awards.

A variety of specialized nonprofit and for-profit periodicals report on the nonprofit sector and philanthropy. Major, general-audience journals are the *Chronicle of Philanthropy*, with about 45,000 paid subscribers; *NonProfit Times*, with a readership of 34,000; *Foundation News and Commentary*, published by the Council on Foundations; *Responsive Philanthropy*, the journal of the National Committee for Responsive Philanthropy; and *Nonprofit Quarterly*, formerly *New England Nonprofit Quarterly*.

A growing number of Internet sites also are serving the public, nonprofit practitioners, and researchers. A useful site for those seeking volunteer and giving opportunities is the Network for Good (www.networkforgood.org), which was recently joined by www.helping.org. Other online resources, such as Foundation

Directory Online (fconline.fdncenter.org) and GuideStar (www.guidestar.org) provide information for grantmakers or grantseekers to enhance the effectiveness of the philanthropic process. Others, such as Handsnet (www.handsnet.org), Internet Nonprofit Center (www.nonprofits.org), Philanthropy News Digest (fdncenter.org/pnd/), Nonprofit Online News (news.gilbert.org), and the Philanthropic News Network Online (www.pnnonline.org), provide general support and information about the nonprofit community.

Examples of research-oriented sites are the Literature of the Nonprofit Sector Online (lnps.fdncenter.org), Philanthropic Studies Index (cheever.ulib.iupui.edu/psipublicsearch), and Philanthropy.org, which are managed by the Foundation Center, Indiana University Center on Philanthropy, and Center for the Study of Philanthropy at City University of New York, respectively. The Nonprofit Sector Research Fund's www.NonprofitResearch.org includes summaries of research studies supported by it and contains the full text of many research reports.

Explaining the Growth of Nonprofit Infrastructure Organizations

Why has the nonprofit infrastructure grown in recent decades? As the nonprofit sector has grown, it has invited more attention—and challenge—from hostile policymakers and others; IOs are a vehicle for responding to these challenges. Moreover, with the overall growth of the sector, more nonprofit staff members have been concerned about their work and careers. IOs also are a vehicle for responding to this heightened professionalism.

Public Policy Challenges

Public policy challenges have been instrumental in fostering the growth of nonprofit IOs. As the nonprofit sector has grown, it has attracted increased attention from policymakers and others. However, this attention often has been hostile to nonprofits, especially foundations. The nonprofit community established IOs to lead the response to this negative attention.

EARLY POLICY CHALLENGES AND NONPROFIT RESPONSES: 1950–69. In response to concern over the accountability standards and influence of private foundations, including their possibly "un-American and subversive activities," the U.S. House of Representatives established the Cox Committee in 1952 to examine foundation activities.[17] When the Cox Committee's findings proved unsatisfying to foundation foes, the House created the Reece Committee in April 1954 to mount a comprehensive inquiry into the motives for establishing foundations as well as into the influence of foundations on public life. Although the investigation did not attract much attention and was discredited after the fall of rabid anticommunist senator Joseph McCarthy, it underscored the vulnerability of the tax-exempt world.[18]

As a consequence of these investigations, several large foundations recognized the need for greater preparedness to defend themselves in the event of future inquiries. The Ford Foundation distributed grants to encourage scholarly investigation of the role of philanthropy in American life, and the Carnegie Corporation and Russell Sage Foundation began planning for the establishment of the Foundation Library Center to serve as a strategic repository of knowledge about foundations.[19] However, other foundations, both large and small, resisted these efforts, and some of the small ones especially viewed with suspicion initiatives to gather information on their assets and activities.[20]

In the 1960s, Congressman Wright Patman launched a populist attack that challenged the very nature of philanthropy and nonprofit organizations in the United States. Patman's persistence, combined with rising taxes and government's search for additional revenue, resulted in intense inquiries into the tax-exempt status of nonprofit organizations.[21]

Despite this heightened scrutiny, "the defenders of charitable tax-exempt organizations were remarkably *un*unified in their efforts to defend themselves."[22] The Foundation Library Center was limited by its primary function as an information-gathering organization. The Council on Foundations, which was established in 1964 through a restructuring of the National Council on Community Foundations (formerly the National Committee on Foundations and Trusts for Community Welfare), continued to serve mainly smaller foundations, which had been the clientele of its predecessor organization. The council was not a unifying force for the foundation community as a whole and lacked the stature and resources to be influential in the congressional arena.[23] Beyond the Foundation Library Center and Council on Foundations, other organizations did not have the scope or capabilities to address the relevant issues.[24]

In the face of the continuing political vulnerability of foundations, Alan Pifer of the Carnegie Corporation wanted to move beyond just strengthening the foundation community and argued that, to survive, foundations and other components of the nonprofit community had to join together to fight for their common needs. He was concerned that nonprofits failed to understand that underlying the congressional attacks on foundations was the potential for an assault aimed at all private institutions.[25] Nonprofit organizations, with their diversity of goals and activities, did not see themselves as part of a unified sector with common needs. In a 1969 speech, Pifer urged that a "broad, national effort be made by private, charitable organizations generally, acting in concert, to reassert their basic unity and to reaffirm to the American people, to the Congress, and the Executive Branch their essential role in our national life."[26]

THE FILER COMMISSION AND THE EMERGING INFRASTRUCTURE: 1970–80. When the congressional hearings of the 1960s culminated in the Tax Reform Act of 1969, which imposed a variety of new restrictions on foundations, the foundation community was motivated to respond.[27] Among the philanthropic community's multipronged responses were the establishment of additional regional associations of grantmakers and the launching of the Commission on Private Philanthropy and Public Needs (the Filer Commission) chaired by John Filer, chief executive officer of the Aetna Life and Casualty Company.

The Filer Commission was organized in the mid-1970s by prominent philanthropists and foundation leaders. John D. Rockefeller III, who had become a leader of the Rockefeller family's philanthropic activities and who was especially concerned about the lack of unity in the foundation community, played a key role in organizing the effort.[28] The Filer Commission undertook a comprehensive, multidisciplinary assessment of the nonprofit sector and developed new information about nonprofit organizations and their role in American life.[29] This represented the first broad-scale effort to explain the societal role of nonprofits to the public as well as to the sector itself.

The positive reaction to the Filer Commission helped to improve the general standing of foundations and to create a perception of nonprofit organizations as part of a unitary sector and not just members of distinctive subsectors, like health and education.[30] Through its work, the Filer Commission forged a "security link" between foundations and the rest of the nonprofit world.[31] In addition, it helped to stimulate substantial amounts of research on the nonprofit sector, led to the creation of the first nonprofit academic center at Yale University, and set the stage for the founding of the National Center for Charitable Statistics.[32]

The Filer Commission also triggered the creation of the Donee Group, which consisted of representatives of advocacy and other nonprofits concerned about foundation responsiveness to disenfranchised populations. The Donee Group influenced the outcomes of the commission's work by demanding a more inclusive research agenda that was not focused only on grantmaker concerns. The work of the Donee Group was later picked up by the National Committee for Responsive Philanthropy, which continued to support advocacy groups and underrepresented populations.

Perhaps most important for our purposes here, the Filer Commission also outlined the need for an infrastructure that went beyond the subsector associations already in place. Among the Filer Commission's final recommendations was an initiative to establish a permanent quasi-governmental body "necessary for the growth, perhaps even the survival, of the sector as an effective instrument of individual initiative and social progress."[33]

When it became clear that there was insufficient support for this recommendation, two existing organizations, the National Council on Philanthropy and the Coalition of National Voluntary Organizations—the former founded in the mid-1950s and the latter created in the 1970s to focus on tax reform and cooperation across the sector—commissioned Brian O'Connell, former executive director of the Mental Health Association, to identify "ways in which they might collaborate to better address their mutual interests in philanthropy and voluntary action."[34] The upshot was that the two organizations merged in 1980 to form Independent Sector, whose membership included both grantmakers and grantseekers. The Filer Commission thus stimulated not only the development of sector identity and research on nonprofit activities but also the establishment of adequate infrastructure to support the growing sector.

RECENT POLICY CHALLENGES AND THE FILLING OUT OF THE INFRA-STRUCTURE: 1981–2002. Independent Sector's mission to promote the whole nonprofit sector was given added urgency by the inauguration of the Reagan administration in 1981. Nonprofits faced a "double whammy" in the Reagan era: federal funding of nonprofits was reduced at the same time that nonprofits faced greater demand for services from clients negatively affected by government cutbacks. Although the new administration supported adding a charitable deduction for taxpayers who were not itemizing their other deductions, it also proposed dramatic tax rate cuts that would reduce incentives to give.

The funding and regulatory crisis of the early 1980s finally sparked a larger-scale mobilization of the sector. According to historian Peter Dobkin Hall, the federal cutbacks in a time of recession, combined with other threats to the non-profit sector, drew nonprofits into a common defense.[35] Unlike the temporary coalitions mobilized against specific government initiatives in the late 1960s and 1970s, the mobilizations of the 1980s represented a shift toward less ephemeral, more established institutional responses to general threats against the sector.

In the early 1980s, Independent Sector stimulated research about the impact on nonprofits of budget cuts proposed by the Reagan administration, although it did not take a stand on the Reagan budget plans.[36] New IOs emerged in the 1980s and into the 1990s with the purpose of promoting the health of the non-profit sector by uniting nonprofit organizations and creating forums for research, communication, public education, and legislative defense. Moreover, previously established organizations extended their reach and activities during this period to address the new public policy issues more effectively.[37]

Beyond the Reagan budget reductions of the early 1980s and the Newt Gin-grich–inspired, Contract with America cuts of the mid-1990s, legislative chal-lenges for the nonprofit sector during this period included tax reform affecting the deductibility of charitable contributions, tax rate reductions that reduced incentives to give, and restrictions on lobbying by nonprofit organizations.[38]

Nonprofits were perhaps most united and vocal in opposing the attempts to limit their advocacy and lobbying activity that were led by Representative Ernest Istook Jr., Republican from Oklahoma.[39] The so-called Istook amendment and its numerous legislative cousins sought specifically to constrain the advocacy activities of nonprofits receiving government support. In response to this chal-lenge, some important infrastructure organizations and alliances emerged or were strengthened, including the Alliance for Justice, OMB Watch, Let America

Speak coalition, and Advocacy Institute. These entities have assisted nonprofits to become better advocates and helped to lead the nonprofit fight against the Istook amendment.[40]

Trends toward devolution—the shift of federal government authority to the state and local levels—also spurred the expansion of nonprofit infrastructure. In response to devolution, nonprofits have supported the establishment of state nonprofit associations to protect their interests at the increasingly important state level. State nonprofit associations have proven to be important monitors of state-level regulatory changes affecting nonprofits.[41] According to Dennis Young, federal devolution initiatives may "ultimately prove to be the same kind of catalyst for organizing nonprofits at the state level in the 1990s that congressional attacks on foundations in the 1960s were for galvanizing collective action by the sector at the national level."[42]

The lesson from the onslaught of legislative threats is clear: as one student of the field has put it, unrelenting "vigilance is needed to protect freedoms of voluntary association even in a democratic society."[43] IOs emerged in substantial part to provide that vigilance.

Professionalization

Also contributing to the growth of nonprofit IOs has been the professionalization of the nonprofit field. "Professionalization" refers to a shift away from amateur or personalized responses to needs or problems and toward technical and often standardized approaches to providing services that reflect expert knowledge gained through specialized training.

Moves toward professionalization began as early as the late 1800s but have accelerated sharply in recent decades. This recent trend contributed to the rapid expansion of the professional development infrastructure and further movement away from what Hall has called "methodless enthusiasm."[44]

The Tax Reform Act of 1969 played a major role in this trend. Much of the debate preceding enactment of the law focused on the perceived inefficiency and lack of accountability of nonprofits and foundations as well as a series of financial abuses by foundations in the 1960s. The Tax Reform Act expanded Internal Revenue Service oversight of nonprofit organizations in a variety of areas, including fiscal practices.[45] When the law was finally implemented, nonprofit organizations had to reconfigure their financial operations and management styles in order to conform.[46] Even leading foundations had to hire specialized staff to address the emerging procedural requirements.[47]

The expansion of government contracting with nonprofits was an additional spur toward professionalization. Nonprofits had to improve their internal management processes to meet government contracting requirements and were sometimes obligated to hire specially trained professionals to deliver government-funded services.[48]

However, government regulations were not solely responsible for the professionalization of the sector, nor was professionalization entirely forced on nonprofits. The push toward professionalization also came from within the sector.[49] Many nonprofit leaders embraced the movement toward professionalization in the interest of developing expert staff capable of handling the complicated challenges that nonprofits were being called on to address. Professionalization also served the interests of nonprofit staff members who themselves had received specialized training.

Increased professionalization also was a response to several scandals that roiled the sector over the past decade or more (for example, the Aramony scandal at United Way). The higher visibility and potency of nonprofit organizations, in conjunction with the publicized scandals involving inadequate reporting and misuse of funds, made nonprofits targets for public scrutiny and necessitated further responsiveness from the sector, which sought to standardize accounting practices, promote accounting transparency, and implement other professionalized processes.[50]

IOs established to provide a central voice for the sector also became vehicles for disseminating information on best practices, effective training methods, standards of accountability, and organizational effectiveness. Increases in professionalization required institutional mechanisms to dispense information and convene discussions on issues relating to the efficacy and accountability of the sector. IOs emerged, in part, to meet this need.

The expansion of the sector, the challenges of both increased government regulation and decreased government funding, and the public scrutiny of the sector and its processes created a propitious environment for the growth of IOs. Infrastructure organizations such as Independent Sector promised to provide common meeting grounds, resources to enhance professional development and organizational capacity, and permanent capacity to respond to public policy challenges. Nonprofit organizations, therefore, united under the auspices of infrastructure organizations to both defend and promote themselves and, by extension, to protect and enhance the health of the sector.

Current Challenges and Future Directions

Today, after an extended period of infrastructure growth, membership organizations represent nonprofits and foundations at the national, state, and local levels; management support organizations cover much of the country; nonprofit educational and research centers have multiplied; and media covering nonprofit issues are burgeoning. With the essential elements of infrastructure in place, the major challenge now and into the future is to fill in the remaining holes and strengthen the IOs that already exist.

Gaps: The Need to Strengthen IOs at the State and Local Level

Despite the recent growth of IOs, there are still some important holes, or weak spots, in the nonprofit infrastructure. Although existing data do not permit a simple comparison of nonprofit, business, and government infrastructure, it does seem likely that there is an underinvestment in the infrastructure of nonprofits relative to that of the other sectors. In any case, existing IOs do not entirely meet current needs.[51]

In the first place, management support is not obtainable in all locales and cannot be afforded by many nonprofits even when it is available. To remedy these problems, the National Council of Nonprofit Associations, its state affiliates, and other collaborators are seeking government funding for nonprofit management assistance modeled in part on the assistance that government provides to small businesses.

Another important gap at the state and local level is the absence of strong IOs focused on advocating for the nonprofit sector as a whole. This weakness is especially troubling in this devolutionary era when public policy decisions of importance to the nonprofit sector are increasingly being made at the state and local levels. It is appropriate that state nonprofit associations and regional associations of grantmakers have been established and are taking on more responsibility in many states and local areas. However, such associations are still missing in quite a few jurisdictions and remain weak in many of the places they do exist.

Most state and regional nonprofit associations are young organizations that are struggling to build membership bases and obtain financial support.[52] Like other membership associations, their advocacy activities are handicapped by the free rider problem. Potential members of state nonprofit associations can benefit from the policy work of the associations without joining them. To compensate for the lack of support from free riders, strong state nonprofit associations have developed grant support and other sources of revenue to supplement membership dues. However, these strong associations are few in number. Overall, nonprofit infrastructure is uneven at the state level, and the nonprofit sector has not adjusted adequately to devolutionary trends.

One promising approach to strengthening state and local IOs involves forming partnerships between the generally more well-established national IOs, on the one hand, and the more fragile state and local IOs, on the other. An example is the joint initiative of the National Council of Nonprofit Associations and Independent Sector—Building Capacity for Public Policy (BCAPP). BCAPP, which began in the summer of 2000, aims to "strengthen the public policy capacity of state associations and local coalitions of nonprofits; develop a comprehensive communication network to link organizations working on federal, state, and local policy issues; develop and strengthen expertise in state nonprofit associations on policy issues; and develop and promote an affirmative, public policy agenda for the sector."[53] Since bills affecting the nonprofit sector are introduced in state legislative bodies at significantly higher rates than they are in the federal Congress, enhancing the capacity of state-level policy infrastructure is imperative.[54]

While BCAPP and similar initiatives will help, the nonprofit community will need to redouble its efforts to strengthen state and local IO capacity if it wishes to establish an effective policy voice in this devolutionary era.

Overlaps: The Need for Collaboration

While there are still some holes or weak spots in nonprofit infrastructure, the recent period of growth has also produced overlap. State nonprofit associations provide some of the same services as management support organizations. Board-Source overlaps with local support centers. In the foundation world, the Council on Foundations, Forum of Regional Associations of Grantmakers, and the new Association of Small Foundations also overlap somewhat, as do regional associations of grantmakers and new state associations of community foundations. A plethora of nonprofit education and research institutes exists, many of which work on similar issues. Foundation Center data are increasingly becoming available from other sources.

Too much redundancy is wasteful of resources, and some funders are already expressing concern at having to support multiple IOs to do the same things. What should be done? Reducing redundancy by eliminating or cutting back turf-conscious IOs is obviously difficult. And eliminating all redundancy is probably not even desirable, since duplicative capacity and competition can be beneficial.

Collaborations, both formal and informal, are a promising way to minimize the negative consequences of the overlaps that are occurring with more frequency. The BCAPP initiative is a sensible partnership between Independent Sector and the National Council of Nonprofit Associations, both of which are active in the policy arena. BoardSource is partnering with state nonprofit associations to disseminate governance-related resources. A more informal mechanism for collaboration among IOs is the Infrastructure Exchange Group, which consists of the heads of six major IOs—Independent Sector, Council on Foundations, National Council of Nonprofit Associations, Forum of Regional Associations of Grantmakers, BoardSource, and Foundation Center. Currently, the women who head the six organizations meet every other month for lunch, informal conversation, and knowledge sharing. Whether these and other activities will overcome the obstacles to collaboration among IOs that still exist is difficult to predict, but they at least represent promising beginnings that deserve support.

Quality: The Need for Improved Performance

Perhaps it is not surprising that the rapid growth of nonprofit infrastructure has been accompanied by growing concerns about the quality of IO performance.

To be sure, evaluating IOs is difficult, and many judgments about IO quality are impressionistic. Developing better methods for assessing IO performance should be a priority for IOs and their stakeholders. However, until better information is available, nonprofit leaders will have to proceed on the basis of impressions, and these judgments now reflect growing concerns about quality in the areas of management assistance, nonprofit research, and elsewhere.

Today, almost anyone can hang out a shingle and claim to be a nonprofit management assistance provider. Beyond the market test, there is little or no assurance that assistance providers are delivering quality services. Many providers do not have relevant training and experience, the field lacks meaningful standards of practice, and the base of knowledge on which providers can draw is inadequate.[55] Moreover, management support providers too often give generic assistance that is inadequately customized to the needs of individual organizations.

To cope with concerns about the quality of management assistance being offered, IOs are initiating new programs to improve practice in this area. The Alliance for Nonprofit Management works toward "raising the bar" on organizational quality and effectiveness and convenes assistance providers to break down their isolation.[56] BoardSource sets standards for quality in management that can guide assistance providers. The Grantmakers for Effective Organizations Affinity Group was recently formed to "help grantmakers increase their effectiveness, to strengthen the overall practice of organizational effectiveness in grantmaking, and to focus on the broader foundation and nonprofit communities."[57] These organizations and others that are addressing issues of standards and accountability in the field of management assistance have produced significant reports and research. However, their analyses must be aggregated, analyzed, and properly disseminated and implemented to yield benefits for the sector.

In the area of nonprofit research, recent decades have been a period of tremendous growth, with dramatic increases in the number of nonprofit scholars and academic centers. Unfortunately, relatively few university-based scholars have won promotion or tenure because of their nonprofit research, and nonprofit academic centers generally receive only minimal financial support from their universities, relying heavily instead on soft money from foundations.

The failure of universities to fully embrace nonprofit scholars and academic centers results in part from the relative newness of the field of nonprofit research, and there is likely to be greater acceptance over time. However, nonprofit scholars are also being penalized for their too-frequent failure to meet accepted standards for research in the social sciences and other fields. One major concern, for example, has been the overuse of case studies that limit the generalizability of research findings.

To advance the field of nonprofit research, large databases are needed that will enable researchers to go beyond single case studies.[58] Nonprofit researchers must be trained to use the sophisticated methodologies that are now being employed in the social sciences to manipulate large data sets. In addition, to expand the pool of high-quality nonprofit researchers, funders and others must increase their outreach to promising scholars engaged in disciplinary networks (for example, American Political Science Association, American Sociological Association, American Economics Association) as well as interdisciplinary activities (for example, ARNOVA).

Another important concern about nonprofit research is its lack of relevance for and inaccessibility to policymakers and nonprofit practitioners. The lack of policy- and practice-relevant research is an important handicap for policymakers and nonprofit managers and leaders and hinders their job performance.[59] While building "basic" knowledge about nonprofit activities is important, scholars, practitioners, policymakers, and funders must also collaborate to build bridges between academic research and communities of practice and policy.[60]

All of these concerns about the quality and relevance of nonprofit research will become secondary if foundation support for nonprofit research declines, as it now appears may happen because of the depressed value of foundation stock portfolios and changes in foundation funding priorities. Replacing these funds is apt to be very difficult and to require coordinated efforts to persuade new funders of the importance of supporting nonprofit research.

Accountability: The Need for Standards, Education, Monitoring, and Enforcement

Spurred by recent declines in public trust of nonprofits, IOs are now seeking new ways of enhancing nonprofit accountability. Unfortunately, however, there is no clear consensus on exactly what "accountability" is or how it can be achieved. Under the rubric of accountability, IOs and others are seeking to increase the amount of financial and other information that nonprofits make available to the public, assure ethical behavior, improve organizational effectiveness, enhance board oversight, and secure compliance with relevant government laws and regulations. In pursuit of accountability, IOs are contemplating or actually undertaking a variety of initiatives, including the development of codes of ethics, governance-related education and training, and the certification of responsible behavior. For example, the Maryland Association of Nonprofit Organizations has developed a Standards for Excellence program that sets high standards and promotes excellence and accountability for nonprofits through self-regulation.

While IOs are increasing their efforts in the area of accountability, some argue that it is essentially impossible for the sector to regulate itself and that only government can really hold nonprofits accountable.[61]

The challenge to IOs to assure accountability is enormous. They have been called on to set standards, educate nonprofit leaders and boards, monitor compliance, and punish transgressions. Although this responsibility is immense, the ever-expanding nonprofit sector cannot increase its value to society simply by growing. If IOs and the sector fail to pay more attention to accountability, they will risk losing the public support that is critical to the health of the sector.

Voice: The Need for a Bolder, More Proactive Approach to Public Policy

In recent decades, IOs have advanced relatively modest public policy agendas. Rather than promote their own initiatives, IOs have often been in a reactive, defensive mode, fending off attacks, such as the proposed Istook amendment.

Although the reactive, crisis-oriented mode has had some payoff for IOs and the nonprofit sector has fared relatively well in recent times, there is growing sentiment that IOs should be bolder and more proactive in advancing sector interests regarding nonprofit-government relations, nonprofit advocacy, accountability, and other issues. For this to be possible, however, it will be necessary for IOs such as Independent Sector to overcome inertia and the lack of consensus among their constituent members. When members disagree, as they often do, it is difficult for IOs to resist the pull of the status quo and take bold initiatives.

IOs need to strike a better balance between their "servant" activities, in which they respond to the needs and wants of members, and their "leader" role, in which they forcefully promote the voice and health of the overall sector. Rather than paying strict heed to surveys of their member organizations, IOs must find ways to guide and synthesize member opinions and pursue initiatives that they, the IOs, believe will benefit the sector as a whole.

Another obstacle in the way of more aggressive policy work by sector-wide IOs is the subsector orientation of many nonprofits. Nonprofits are concerned primarily with policy developments in their own fields (that is, health, education, human services, and the arts). These subsector-specific interests are generally advanced by subsector associations, which may represent for-profits in the subfield as well as nonprofits. Only secondarily do individual nonprofits focus on cross-cutting nonprofit issues and turn to sector-wide IOs for assistance.

Fortunately, several of the IOs, including Independent Sector and the Council on Foundations, have begun to pay more attention to communications and public education on policy and other issues, and Independent Sector's new strategic plan explicitly calls for the organization to take a more proactive leadership position. These are promising developments, but more active steps are needed.

Financial Sustainability: The Need for a Secure Funding Base

Lack of funds has also limited the ability of IOs to advance nonprofit interests proactively. By most accounts, the nonprofit infrastructure does not have the resources it needs to support the sector properly.[62] The free rider phenomenon allows individual nonprofits to benefit from the public policy work of IOs without sharing the costs. This leaves IOs that depend on membership dues underfunded for policy work. Some IOs, including Independent Sector, have successfully raised grant funds to support their advocacy activity. However, IOs must have additional funds to support the policy work that is needed. IOs in the research field face similar funding problems because they also provide collective benefits.

Currently, only a relatively small number of foundations prioritize support of IOs in advocacy, research, and other fields. Many more foundations must educate themselves about the value of infrastructure activity and fund IOs. For their part, IOs must do better at communicating the importance of their work and attracting support not only from new foundations but also from individual donors. If the infrastructure is to assert a comprehensive, long-term, aggressive agenda to shape a better future for the nonprofit sector, it must engage a more diverse and extensive base of donors.

The need for IOs to diversify their resource base has become much more urgent in the past year because several of the few foundations that support them have announced reductions in their IO funding. Two of the largest, the Atlantic Philanthropies and the David and Lucile Packard Foundation, are dropping the infrastructure field as a major area of funding. Other foundations also plan to reduce their support because of shifting priorities and shrinking endowments. A major funding crisis may be looming. Unless IOs develop new funding sources to replace the lost dollars, they will have to reduce their activities or go out of business, with potentially significant negative consequences for the health of the nonprofit sector.

Vision: The Need for a Convincing Rationale for the Nonprofit Sector

IOs' funding problems and weak voice result in part from the uncertainty of their vision for the nonprofit sector. IOs cannot speak more strongly without a deeper understanding of what they stand for. The failure of IOs to articulate a clear rationale for the nonprofit sector invites others to question the need for the nonprofit sector and to try to constrain it. Ultimately, the lack of a compelling vision may threaten the future of the nonprofit sector as a vehicle for socially beneficial change.

The diversity of the sector complicates the development of a galvanizing, cohesive vision for the sector as a whole. On the one hand, sector leaders want to celebrate the expression—and protection—that the nonprofit sector gives to diversity, which is this country's special strength. On the other hand, these leaders also want to emphasize the underlying commonalities that bring these diverse organizations together in a single sector.

Major gaps in knowledge about the sector also hinder the development of a convincing sectoral vision. It is difficult to convey the importance of the nonprofit sector to the public, policymakers, or even people within the nonprofit sector using existing research. Although the research infrastructure has grown dramatically in recent years, basic information about the sector and its contributions to society still has not been uncovered. As an example, one major gap in knowledge relates to the vast world of small, informal grassroots nonprofit organizations, which may account for 90 percent of all nonprofits.[63]

In addition to the obstacle of insufficient research, nonprofit leaders do not have a good grasp of much of the research-based information that already exists. The culture gap between researchers and practitioners keeps much of the relevant research about the contribution of the nonprofit sector to society out of the hands of nonprofit leaders who could use the information in their work.

With sector blurring—the fading of distinctions between nonprofit and for-profit organizations—pressure is increasing on nonprofits to identify their unique contributions and justify their special tax treatment. If for-profits are increasingly providing services that nonprofits traditionally provided, the question becomes, Why do we need a nonprofit sector? One research-based effort seeking to answer this question is Independent Sector's Measures Project. This multiyear effort is surveying more than 1,000 nonprofits and employing other means to probe for the distinctive contributions that nonprofits make to society. The Union Institute's Changing Charity Project and the Aspen Institute's Nonprofit Sector Strategy Group and State of Nonprofit America Project, of which this volume is a product, are wrestling with the same issues.

One way for nonprofits to respond to sector blurring is to downplay their service-providing activities and emphasize their other, perhaps more distinctive, roles as builders of civil society and advocates. However, this approach, which seems to be gaining some currency, may be problematic. IOs are apt to have a difficult time distinguishing nonprofits from for-profits as long as program service fees, which are the natural source of revenue for for-profits, also constitute the largest portion of nonprofit revenues.[64]

The use of public discussions is a promising mechanism with which to articulate the special roles of the sector. Moreover, IOs must become better at telling the story of what nonprofits and foundations have accomplished.[65]

To articulate the importance of the nonprofit sector effectively to the public, infrastructure organizations need to enunciate clearly the correlation between the healthy functioning of the nonprofit sector and the healthy functioning of American society. In other words, a vital nonprofit sector must be understood as an essential building block of an engaged citizenry, a just society, and a healthy democracy. Nonprofit leaders have been drawn to the work of Robert Putnam for ideas about the role that nonprofits might play in building—or rebuilding— American civil society.[66] Even more than addressing the serious issues of gaps, overlaps, quality, accountability, and voice, the challenge of developing and communicating a compelling vision for the sector may be the most important task for nonprofit and IO leaders in the years ahead.

Notes

1. Union Institute, *Mission Possible: 200 Ways to Strengthen the Nonprofit Sector's Infrastructure* (Washington: Union Institute, 1996).

2. Alan Abramson conducted these interviews. In the interest of full disclosure, this analysis is also informed by his long involvement with many of the organizations discussed in these pages. In particular, he serves or has served on the boards of the Association for Research on Nonprofit Organizations and Voluntary Action and National Council of Nonprofit Associations and on advisory committees for Independent Sector and the Council on Foundations. He also has served as a consultant to Independent Sector on federal budget issues. His full-time job is director of the Nonprofit Sector and Philanthropy Program at the Aspen Institute.

3. Amos G. Warner, *American Charities* (New York: Arno Press and *New York Times*, 1971).

4. Warner, *American Charities*, p. 363.

5. See Mancur Olson, *The Logic of Collective Action: Public Goods and the Theory of Groups* (Harvard University Press, 1971), pp. 36–52, and James Q. Wilson, *Political Organizations* (New York: Basic Books, 1973), pp. 30–55, for detailed discussions of the organizational challenges of providing collective goods.

6. See Wilson, *Political Organizations*, pp. 39–45, for discussion of solidary incentives.

7. Marc Green, "Grantmaker Affinity Groups: Where Funders Go to Share," *Grantsmanship Center Magazine,* vol. 40 (Summer 2000): 21.

8. Dennis R. Young, "Games Universities Play: An Analysis of the Institutional Contexts of Centers of Nonprofit Study," in Michael O'Neill and Kathleen Fletcher, eds., *Nonprofit Management Education: U.S. and World Perspectives* (Westport, Conn.: Praeger, 1998), p. 119. The Nonprofit Academic Centers Council (NACC) has thirty-seven member academic centers; see www.independentsector.org/nacc/index.htm [September 25, 2002].

9. Naomi B. Wish and Roseanne M. Mirabella, "Curricular Variations in Nonprofit Management Graduate Programs," *Nonprofit Management and Leadership*, vol. 9, no. 1 (1998): 99. "Census of Nonprofit Management Programs" (pirate.shu.edu/~mirabero/kellogg.html [October, 24, 2001]).

10. Rick Smith, "Building the Nonprofit Sector Knowledge Base: Can Academic Centers and Management Support Organizations Come Together?" *Nonprofit Management and Leadership*, vol. 8, no. 1 (1997): 90.

11. Smith, "Building the Nonprofit Sector Knowledge Base," p. 90.

12. John McKiernan, ed., *Directory of Management Support Providers for Nonprofit Organizations* (Denver: Applied Research and Development Institute International, 1998), p. 23.

13. Cited in McKiernan, ed., *Directory of Management Support Providers*, p. 23.

14. McKiernan, ed., *Directory of Management Support Providers,* p. 15.

15. McKiernan, ed., *Directory of Management Support Providers,* p. 18.

16. McKiernan, ed., *Directory of Management Support Providers,* pp. 23–24.

17. See Eleanor L. Brilliant, *Private Charity and Public Inquiry: A History of the Filer and Peterson Commissions* (Indiana University Press, 2000), pp. 13–23, and Peter Dobkin Hall, *Inventing the Nonprofit Sector and Other Essays on Philanthropy, Voluntarism, and Nonprofit Organizations* (Johns Hopkins University Press, 1992), pp. 67–68.

18. Hall, *Inventing the Nonprofit Sector*, pp. 68–69.

19. F. Emerson Andrews, *Foundation Watcher* (Lancaster, Pa.: Franklin and Marshall College, 1973), pp. 175–94, as cited in Hall, *Inventing the Nonprofit Sector*, p. 69.

20. Hall, *Inventing the Nonprofit Sector*, pp. 69–70.

21. Hall, *Inventing the Nonprofit Sector*, pp. 70–71.

22. Hall, *Inventing the Nonprofit Sector*, p. 72.

23. Rockeller family associate Ray LaMontagne's memo dated September 21, 1964, to John D. Rockefeller III, as cited in Hall, *Inventing the Nonprofit Sector*, p. 72.

24. Darlene Siska, "Building a Sector," *Foundation News and Commentary*, vol. 40, no. 2 (1999): 50; Brilliant, *Private Charity and Public Inquiry*, p. 55; La Montange's 1964 memo to Rockefeller III, in Hall, *Inventing the Nonprofit Sector*, p. 72.

25. Alan Pifer, *Philanthropy in an Age of Transition: The Essays of Alan Pifer* (New York: Foundation Center, 1984), p. 44.

26. Pifer, *Philanthropy in an Age of Transition*, p. 53.

27. Among the new regulations aimed at foundations were a prohibition of self-dealing transactions, new payout rules, limits on excess business holdings, a tax on foundation investment income, reduction of the charitable deduction for contributions of capital gain property to most private foundations, and new restrictions to prevent foundation influence of campaign or legislation. See Thomas A. Troyer, *The 1969 Private Foundation Law: Historical Perspective on Its Origins and Underpinnings* (Washington: Council on Foundations, 2000), pp. 18–22.

28. See Brilliant, *Private Charity and Public Inquiry,* and Hall, *Inventing the Nonprofit Sector,* for discussions on the evolution of John D. Rockefeller III's views on the philanthropic community and its need for reform and unity.

29. Peter Dobkin Hall, "A Historical Overview of the Private Nonprofit Sector," in Walter W. Powell, ed., *The Nonprofit Sector: A Research Handbook* (Yale University Press, 1987), p. 20.

30. William G. Bowen, Thomas I. Nygren, Sarah E. Turner, and Elizabeth A. Duffy, *The Charitable Nonprofits* (San Francisco: Jossey-Bass, 1994), p. 41.

31. Paul N. Ylvisaker, "Foundations and Nonprofit Organizations," in Walter W. Powell, ed., *The Nonprofit Sector: A Research Handbook* (Yale University Press, 1987), p. 375.

32. Virginia A. Hodgkinson, "Creating a Third Sector of American Life," in *Toward a Stronger Voluntary Sector: The "Filer Commission" and the State of Philanthropy* (Indiana University Center on Philanthropy, 1996), p. 4.

33. Commission on Private Philanthropy and Public Needs, *Giving in America: Toward a Stronger Voluntary Sector* (New York: Commission on Private Philanthropy and Public Needs, 1975), p. 26.

34. Brian O'Connell, *Powered by Coalition: The Story of Independent Sector* (San Francisco: Jossey-Bass, 1997), p. 21.

35. Hall, "A Historical Overview," p. 21.

36. For discussion of the federal budget's impact on the nonprofit sector in the early 1980s, see Lester M. Salamon with Alan J. Abramson, *The Federal Government and the Nonprofit Sector: Implications of the Reagan Budget Proposals* (Washington: Urban Institute, 1981), and Lester M. Salamon and Alan J. Abramson, *The Federal Budget and the Nonprofit Sector* (Washington: Urban Institute Press, 1982).

37. Hall, "A Historical Overview," p. 21.

38. Dennis R. Young, "Complementary, Supplementary, or Adversarial? A Theoretical and Historical Examination of Nonprofit-Government Relations in the United States," in Elizabeth T. Boris and C. Eugene Steuerle, eds., *Nonprofits and Government: Collaboration and Conflict* (Washington: Urban Institute, 1999), p. 60.

39. See Carol De Vita, "Nonprofits and Devolution: What Do We Know?" in Boris and Steuerle, eds., *Nonprofits and Government*, pp. 229–30.

40. Elizabeth J. Reid, "Nonprofit Advocacy and Political Participation," in Boris and Steuerle, eds., *Nonprofits and Government*, p. 316.

41. Reid, "Nonprofit Advocacy," p. 316.

42. Young, "Complementary, Supplementary, or Adversarial?" p. 61.

43. Brilliant, *Private Charity and Public Inquiry*, p. 157.

44. Hall, *Inventing the Nonprofit Sector*, p. 91. On the origins of professionalization among nonprofits, see Eleanor L. Brilliant, *The United Way* (Columbia University Press, 1990), pp. 20–21; Warner, *American Charities*, pp. 402–03; Roy Lubove, *The Professional Altruist: The Emergence of Social Work as a Career, 1880–1930* (New York: Atheneum, 1980).

45. Hall, *Inventing the Nonprofit Sector*, p. 91.

46. Hall, *Inventing the Nonprofit Sector*, p. 91.

47. Brilliant, *Private Charity and Public Inquiry*, p. 101.

48. Lester M. Salamon, "Partners in Public Service: The Scope and Theory of Government-Nonprofit Relations," in Walter W. Powell, ed., *The Nonprofit Sector: A Research Handbook* (Yale University Press, 1987), pp. 114–15.

49. Salamon, "Partners in Public Service," p. 115.

50. Robert O. Bothwell, "Trends in Self-Regulation and Transparency of Nonprofits in the U.S.," *International Journal of Not-for-Profit Law*, vol. 2, no. 3 (2000), available at www.icnl.org/journal/vol2iss3/Arn_bothwell.htm [September 25, 2002].

51. Hodgkinson, "Creating a Third Sector of American Life," p. 44; Union Institute, *Mission Possible*, pp. 37–46.

52. National Council of Nonprofit Associations, *Strategic and Operational Plan: 2000–2002* (Washington: National Council of Nonprofit Associations, December 1999), p. 2.

53. "IS and NCNA Announce Recipients of Building for Public Policy Grants to Nonprofit Organizations, August 29, 2000" (www.independentsector.org/media/bcap_release.htm [September 25, 2002]).

54. National Council of Nonprofit Associations, *Strategic and Operational Plan*, p. 2.

55. Thomas E. Backer, "Strengthening Nonprofits: Foundation Initiatives for Nonprofit Organizations," in Carol J. De Vita and Cory Fleming, eds., *Building Capacity in Nonprofit Organizations* (Washington: Urban Institute, 2001), pp. 44, 64, 66–67, and 89.

56. "The Alliance: Raising the Bar on Quality" (www.allianceonline.org [September 25, 2002]).

57. "Organizational Effectiveness Affinity Group Formed" (www.cof.org/newsroom/newsletters/corporateupdate/spring99/page05.htm [September 25, 2002]).

58. See, for example, Colin B. Burke, "Nonprofit History's New Numbers (and the Need for More)," *Nonprofit and Voluntary Sector Quarterly*, vol. 30, no. 2 (June 2001): 174–203.

59. Smith, "Building the Nonprofit Sector Knowledge Base," p. 91; Thomas J. Billitteri, "Research on Charities Falls Short," *Chronicle of Philanthropy*, November 27, 1997, p. 33.

60. The W. K. Kellogg Foundation's $12.5 million Building Bridges Initiative, launched in 1998, is an example of such an effort.

61. Joel Fleishman, "Public Trust in Not-for-Profit Organizations and the Need for Regulatory Reform," in Charles T. Clotfelter and Thomas Ehrlich, eds., *Philanthropy and the Nonprofit Sector in a Changing America* (Indiana University Press, 1999), pp. 188–91.

62. Union Institute, *Mission Possible*, pp. 37–46.

63. David Horton Smith, "The Rest of the Nonprofit Sector: Grassroots Associations as the Dark Matter Ignored in Prevailing 'Flat Earth' Maps of the Sector," *Nonprofit and Voluntary Sector Quarterly*, vol. 26, no. 2 (1997): 126–29.

64. Elizabeth T. Boris, "The Nonprofit Sector in the 1990s," in Clotfelter and Ehrlich, eds., *Philanthropy and the Nonprofit Sector*, p. 14.

65. Dorothy S. Ridings, "Once Upon a Time . . . ," *Foundation News and Commentary*, vol. 40, no. 2 (1999): 17.

66. Robert D. Putnam, *Bowling Alone: The Collapse and Revival of American Community* (New York: Simon and Schuster, 2000); Robert D. Putnam, "Bowling Alone: America's Declining Social Capital," *Journal of Democracy*, vol. 6, no. 1 (1995): 65–78; Robert D. Putnam, *Making Democracy Work: Civic Traditions in Modern Italy* (Princeton University Press, 1993).

11

Foundations and Corporate Philanthropy

LESLIE LENKOWSKY

W riting more than twenty years ago, John D. Rockefeller III observed, "The invisible sector [the private nonprofit sector] is eroding before our eyes." Philanthropic giving, he wrote, "has steadily lost ground in recent years," forcing churches, universities, and other institutions to curtail services, if not close altogether. Americans appeared to be losing faith in their ability to deal with the nation's social problems. No less than the future of democracy seemed to be at stake.[1]

Rockefeller's worried assessment was especially relevant for the type of giving with which his family had long been identified: institutional philanthropy, the awarding of funds through an organization set up for that purpose rather than directly from a donor. Although providing only a small share of what Americans contribute to charitable causes, foundations, corporate giving programs, charity federations, and other vehicles for managing the flow of charitable donations have frequently been among the philanthropic world's most visible and prestigious sources of support. Because of their ability to mobilize resources and expertise, they have often been seen as among the most influential as well.

Yet for institutional philanthropy the period that preceded Rockefeller's comment was a difficult one. The Tax Reform Act of 1969 imposed new restrictions on private foundations. Partly in response, foundation assets and grants barely

Emily W. Spencer assisted in the preparation of this paper.

kept pace with inflation, and the rate at which new foundations were being formed declined. Federated giving organizations, such as United Ways, experienced similar problems; their outlays increased, but not much more than the cost of living. At business-sponsored philanthropies, donations went up and down with the state of the economy, which, in the 1970s, was notably volatile.

Today, however, institutional philanthropy looks to be in much better shape. Since Rockefeller sounded his alarm, the number of foundations has tripled to nearly 47,000. Their grants and assets have increased far more rapidly than inflation. Nearly fifty foundations now have endowments of more than $1 billion, compared with just one—the Ford Foundation—when Rockefeller made his gloomy appraisal. Barring a decline in its assets, the largest of them—the Bill and Melinda Gates Foundation—will have to give away more than $1 billion annually in grants just to meet the federally mandated payout requirement.

Corporate philanthropy has also been growing, partly the fruit of nearly a decade of economic expansion and partly the result of new ways of providing support for charities, such as corporate-community partnerships and various kinds of business activities that also aid charities, such as cause-related marketing. New kinds of pooled giving, such as alternative funds and gift funds, have also come into existence, supplementing (or even competing with) the more traditional federations.

As a result of these changes, according to the most recent figures compiled by the American Association of Fund-Raising Counsel, the growth rate of institutional philanthropy is outstripping that of individual giving. Foundations and corporations now account for more than one-sixth of all gifts to charity (and better than one-quarter to secular groups), growing from 12.5 percent to more than 17 percent in the 1990s, their highest share for more than thirty years.[2] Since this figure does not include federated charities, the newer pooled funds, or contributions whose value is difficult to measure (such as several kinds of business support), the actual portion may be even higher.

Yet this expansion has given rise to a host of questions for institutional philanthropy. Some people, for example, wonder whether, in view of their rapidly growing endowments, foundations should be required to spend more. Others ask if foundation grants are really doing enough to reduce the gap between the haves and the have-nots. From the new dot-com philanthropists comes the charge that foundations are too bureaucratic and unimaginative, unable to do much of anything effectively. And from a variety of quarters can be heard complaints that they are not sufficiently accountable for what they do or even that they are up to no good.

Despite their increased generosity, corporations have come under fire for tying their support too closely to business objectives. However, others fault them for not tying it closely enough. A new generation of donors seems to be challenging the relevance of the more traditional charity federations, like the

United Ways, to what they view as the most urgent problems. But some of the competing models, such as the gift funds and donor-advised funds at community foundations, have prompted questions about whether they are really just disguised types of individual giving that do not deserve the special tax incentives created for publicly supported grantmakers.[3]

These questions go to the heart of institutional philanthropy. Although grantmaking organizations have been used for a variety of purposes, an important motive for the creation of foundations, corporate-giving programs, federated charities, and the like has been to improve "efficiency in giving," as the first John D. Rockefeller once put it.[4] By drawing on sizable sums of money, usually with the assistance of professional staff or advisers and on an ongoing basis, these organizations were presumed to be able to have an impact greater than that of individual contributors acting on their own. Indeed, as Barry Karl and Stanley Katz have noted, the early foundations were almost governmental in scope, possessing not just the resources but also the ability to affect major areas of life throughout the United States at a time when the public sector was either weak or in disrepute.[5] Much the same could be said about United Ways and corporate philanthropy in many communities.

Institutional philanthropy was never entirely "institutional." It always reflected the personal motives of donors, trustees, staff, member charities of federations, and corporate executives as well, such as providing a vehicle for family unity, a way of holding funds for future charitable gifts, a living memorial, a tool for reducing taxes, an instrument for improving one's image in the eyes of others, and a worthwhile career. Indeed, the suspicion that they were not as public serving as they should be fueled much of the criticism of grantmaking organizations in the past and, in the case of foundations, led in 1969 to a variety of restrictions on their activities. But for the most part, their accomplishments earned legitimacy for the institutional model as a distinctive and effective approach to philanthropic work.

That may be changing. The growing interest in—and acceptance of—donor-directed giving, grantmaking funds that combine personal involvement with financial payments, corporate support that provides business benefits as well as charitable ones, and other forms of hands-on philanthropy raises the possibility that the institutional model (as it had been understood) is entering a new stage in its history, one marked by a growing variety of forms and ways of operating, some of which look distinctly uninstitutional. Equally telling are the complaints of critics that organized grantmakers have become better at accumulating wealth than spending it, are not sufficiently accountable for their actions, and may even be hindering efficient giving, rather than enhancing it, implying that the more traditional expressions of institutional philanthropy need to be altered. And with government spending far more than the largest foundations, even those who have been associated most closely with the institutional model have begun to wonder how much of a difference institutional philanthropy should really be expected to make.[6]

All of this makes the time ripe for taking a fresh look at the state of institutional philanthropy in America. The aim in doing so is neither to celebrate nor to deplore the changes taking place, but rather to identify the challenges that grantmaking bodies are facing in an era of new organizational forms, new donor interests, and new developments in government and the for-profit sector. While grantmaking organizations are not about to go away, the question is whether they will look and act differently in the future than they did in the past. And if so, how and to what effect? This chapter aims to sketch the basic contours of this component of America's nonprofit sector, to identify what is happening to it, and, finally, to speculate on how it is likely to evolve.

The World of Institutional Philanthropy

From Benjamin Franklin's junto to the latest click-to-give website, the history of American philanthropy has been marked by innovations aimed at enhancing the ability of charities to obtain resources and of people to support organizations serving their social or personal goals. Many of these, such as direct mail fundraising and telemarketing, have sought to improve the ability of individuals to contribute directly to nonprofit organizations (or nonprofits to solicit help more efficiently from individuals). But another set—what in this chapter is called institutional philanthropy—consists of intermediary organizations that collect money from individual donors and then grant it to charities, following procedures that are independent of the original donors to some degree. Foundations, corporate giving programs, charity federations, and other kinds of organizations fall within this category. They are, in effect, the bankers of the charitable world, collecting money from depositors (donors) and paying it to borrowers (charities) based on criteria they have established.

Rationale

Why should donors use these banks when they could just as easily make contributions directly to charities? As noted, some of their objectives are undoubtedly personal, although many of these—for example, creating a lasting memorial, deferring giving to the future, or reducing the tax consequences of large increases in income or capital—can sometimes be attained without using an intermediary group. But just as banks help to make their depositors' funds more productive by investing them, what distinguishes institutional philanthropy is the value it potentially adds to donors' gifts to the nonprofit sector.

Some grantmaking organizations may provide reservoirs of expertise and other kinds of help to people who think they would be unable to contribute responsibly on their own (perhaps because they lack information or have too many resources to dispense without assistance). Others may enable donors to be more confident that their gifts are going to high-priority uses (whether in a community or in the treatment of a disease), because a trustworthy organization can weigh them against the alternatives.

Grantmaking organizations can also produce economies of scale, as they do when they aggregate relatively small sums of money that might otherwise go to shareholders and deposit them into a corporate foundation (or the modest savings of a local businessman and entrust them to a community foundation). And some institutions can create economies of time by allowing funds contributed in one period to be available (with fewer limits than are usually placed on trusts) in another period when they might do more good. By establishing and administering substantial funds that are controlled by neither their donors nor government, grantmaking organizations can also provide the equivalent of a venture capital fund for the nonprofit world that can be used for innovative, risky, or unpopular causes.

Regardless of the personal motives of contributors, in other words, what makes institutional philanthropy attractive and important for donors is the possibility that it will improve their ability to support charities. For that reason, public policy encourages it, such as by exempting from taxation the returns on assets donated to an intermediary. (If the assets had been left in the donor's bank account to appreciate for direct giving, the returns would have been taxed until they were contributed to a charity.) And because of their potential to have greater impact than individual philanthropy, public policy has carefully watched grantmaking organizations, sometimes even limiting what they can do, such as by restricting their ability to support political activities more tightly than charitable activities.

Major Components

What are the contours of institutional philanthropy? And how is it evolving? This section describes the major components of institutional philanthropy: foundations, corporations, federations, and gift funds.

FOUNDATIONS. The most prominent among the grantmaking organizations are foundations. Approaching 50,000 in number and spending more than $25 billion in 1999, they are what most people think of as institutional philanthropy (although they are by no means all of it). Even among foundations, there are differences, and although they share some features, they are probably best understood as comprising four separate types: independent, operating, community, and corporate.

Foundations arose out of two parallel but largely unrelated developments in the late nineteenth century: the growth of industrial wealth and the scientific charity movement. As vast fortunes were amassed, personal giving seemed increasingly inadequate as a way of supporting charity, especially to those, such as Andrew Carnegie, who believed that the wealthy should dispose of their surplus during their lifetime. At the same time, the desire to do more than merely dispense alms, but instead to address the causes of personal or social problems, suggested a need for applying expertise to giving. The independent foundation (as it is now known) emerged as a means of doing both.

Although it was not the first, the Rockefeller Foundation, established in 1913, was the quintessential foundation. As Ronald Chernow suggests in his recent biography of John D. Rockefeller, the Rockefeller Foundation was for charitable giving what the Standard Oil Company was for American industry.[7] The Rockefeller Foundation was a product of its founder's interests, enabling him to increase the already sizable amount of his donations to charity and spread his wealth into fields not previously tapped. It also allowed him to employ advisers and professional staff who could draw on the latest scientific advances to identify public problems needing attention and solutions needing money, in much the same way as the industrial laboratories of Standard Oil turned crude oil into useful products.

But like Standard Oil, the Rockefeller Foundation occasioned considerable suspicion. When it was initially proposed, both public officials and the press charged that it was simply a way of extending and perpetuating its founder's influence, then widely regarded as something less than salutary. Even after it began giving out money, critics accused it of helping its founder's business interests more than the public interest. The controversy died down only after the Rockefeller Foundation made a name for itself in medicine, public health, and other areas (and when its founder was no longer a presence).[8]

Notwithstanding this rocky start, foundations continued to be created. Of today's approximately 17,000 larger foundations (those that have at least $1 million in assets or make $100,000 annually in grants), slightly more than 200 were already in existence by the end of World War I.[9] By the end of the 1920s, nearly 400 had been created, and the birth rate continued during the 1930s. The establishment of sizable new foundations slowed in the 1970s but picked up again afterward.

These larger foundations are only about one-third of the foundations estimated to exist in the United States. The rest are small, usually unstaffed, sometimes little more than an account in a bank trust department. (Many are family foundations, created largely to facilitate charitable giving by a one- or two-generational family.) Moreover, the larger ones hold most of the assets (98 percent of the approximately $450 billion held in 1999), make most of the grants (almost 96 percent of the $23 billion granted), and employ most of the staff (more than 90 percent of the some 14,000 professional and support positions in foundations with staff).[10] For the most part, these are the foundations that seek the advantages of institutionalization for their philanthropic work.

Most foundations are grantmaking bodies, using their resources to provide support for other charitable organizations, such as universities, museums, hospitals, and social service agencies. However, about 6 percent—roughly 2,800—are operating foundations, which principally conduct their own programs, rather than provide support for other nonprofit groups. Among the best known are the Open Society Institute and the J. Paul Getty Trust. The larger ones (which account for 25 percent of all operating foundations but make 97 percent of total expenditures) typically have sizable, highly professional staff, well-developed organizations, and long-standing missions.[11] While rooted in their donor's concerns, they normally develop institutional features (such as specialized departments and programs) that bring them closer operationally to publicly supported charities than to grantmaking intermediaries.

In addition to independent and operating foundations, two other types of foundations receive their resources not from a wealthy individual or family, but from a broader group of people. One is the community foundation, which obtains its assets from contributors in a particular community. Developed in Cleveland at about the same time Rockefeller was creating his foundation, these organizations pool the funds of smaller givers into larger endowments, which can exist indefinitely and employ staff or consultants to advise on giving. The Cleveland Foundation, for example, pioneered the use of social surveys to gauge local conditions.[12] In effect, community foundations seek to extend the benefits of institutional philanthropy to those who lack the means to establish their own grantmaking foundation.

Over 500 community foundations exist today, more than half of which were established after 1980. Although they compose less than 1 percent of grantmaking organizations, in 1999 they held about 6 percent of foundation assets and made more than 7 percent of all grants. As with independent foundations, the larger ones (such as the New York Community Trust and the San Francisco Foundation) account for well over 90 percent of assets and grants.[13] Community foundations are also far more likely to have staff than are other grantmaking foundations.[14]

A new and important type of foundation that is a kind of hybrid of the operating and community types of foundations is the conversion foundation. Typically created after a publicly supported nonprofit institution, such as a hospital, insurance plan, or higher education financing agency, is acquired by a for-profit company, these organizations use the proceeds of the sale for their endowments (ostensibly on the grounds that the money was partly the fruit of donations and tax exemptions and thus should be put to community-serving purposes). Their programs usually combine grantmaking with the provision of services, often under the leadership of professionals from the predecessor institution.

Although they did not really begin to appear until the early 1980s, the number of health care conversion foundations now exceeds 120, with endowments totaling more than $15 billion. Slightly fewer than half are organized as private foundations, principally engaged in grantmaking, but they have 60 percent of the assets. The rest mostly run various kinds of health-related programs.[15] Since they are of more recent vintage, estimates of the number and size of conversion foundations outside health care are hard to come by. However, the creation of a $770 million foundation from the sale of student loan guarantor USA Group to SLM Corporation in mid-2000 suggests that such conversions are likely to yield substantial new resources for institutional philanthropy.

At the end of the 1970s, one of the authors of a Council on Foundations study on the future of foundations judged the prospects for large, independent foundations to be bleak.[16] Although this was a reasonable extrapolation of the trend in foundation births and growth during that decade, it turned out to be far from the mark, for reasons discussed later.

CORPORATIONS. For-profit companies occupy their own niche in the world of institutional philanthropy. Among the nation's 50,000 foundations, more than 2,000 are sponsored by businesses. In 1999, although they held just 3 percent of the assets of foundations, they made more than 12 percent of the grants, totaling approximately $2.5 billion. Not all companies create endowed foundations. Those that do so aim to ensure that their grantmaking will not suffer too much from business downturns; the rest completely or partially support their foundations through annual grants from corporate earnings. Although the corporate share of institutional philanthropy has declined since the 1980s, this has occurred largely because giving by other kinds of foundations has risen more rapidly. Corporate foundation grants have risen steadily since 1995, with the growth rate of the past three years being exceptionally strong. Their assets have grown at a record pace too, partly because investment returns have been robust, but also because businesses have been paying more into their foundations than the foundations have been paying out.[17]

Along with other kinds of institutional philanthropy, modern corporate giving programs originated in the early decades of the twentieth century. As American industry became larger and more prosperous, leaders such as Edward Filene, John Patterson, and Gerard Swope encouraged it to take a more expansive, long-term view of its social responsibilities, especially toward its employees and communities. To them and others, establishing a private welfare state seemed not only necessary in light of the weakness of public programs and services, but also desirable as a way of forestalling government intervention. Advocates of scientific management also emphasized the importance of efficiency in these corporate social activities, no less than in manufacturing.[18]

By the depression, American businesses had already begun to institutionalize their giving in foundations. (In 1935 the first tax deduction for corporate charitable contributions became law.) Of the larger corporate foundations, one-quarter were established before the 1960s.[19] During the 1970s, their numbers rose rapidly, before the growth rate trailed off in the late 1980s, owing primarily to the recession at the end of the decade. The 1990s saw a new surge in large corporate foundations, but it was offset by the termination of older ones as a result of mergers or acquisitions.[20] Accompanying these organizational developments has been the emergence of corporate staff specializing in philanthropy. Indeed, except for community foundations, business foundations are more likely to have professional and support staff than any other kind.[21]

Foundation giving probably accounts for less than one-quarter of corporate philanthropic activity. The rest of the nearly $11 billion that businesses gave in 1999 went directly to charities, often through company units specializing in public affairs or human resources and sometimes in goods or services rather than in cash. (The most generous givers are typically those, such as pharmaceutical and computer companies, whose products make up a large share of their donations.) Many corporations also devote a sizable portion of their contributions—both from their foundations and directly—to matching employee gifts to colleges, universities, charity federations, and other kinds of nonprofit organizations rather than develop their own philanthropic programs. Although in a sense these donations reflect individual rather than institutional priorities, businesses often justify them as a way of enhancing employee morale, productivity, or other corporate goals.

In addition to the contributions of cash and in-kind products, corporations make donations in the form of free publicity, meeting space, marketing assistance, loaned executives and other help for charities, corporate sponsorships of special events and other nonprofit activities, royalty and licensing fees paid to charities in connection with product marketing, and political contributions to issue-oriented advocacy groups. Although rarely included in most tallies of corporate philanthropy, by some estimates, the value of these contributions may be at least as great as what companies contribute in cash and products.[22] Including them would thus make the contributions of institutional philanthropy—corporate style—approximately the same as those of independent, operating, and community foundations combined.

FEDERATIONS. Businesses have also played a central role in another form of institutional philanthropy: charity federations. In 1913, in order to make fundraising more efficient and expand the number of contributors to the city's charities, the Cleveland Chamber of Commerce persuaded fifty-three organizations to coordinate their appeals for support through an annual campaign. Unless the giver designated a particular group, the money raised was allocated by a governing board, composed of representatives of the participating charities, business leaders, and other philanthropists, based on their assessment of Cleveland's priorities.[23]

This was the first modern United Way. (Earlier efforts, such as one launched in Denver in 1887, were linked to the charity organization societies and sought to improve how contributions were raised and distributed.) Within a few years, the idea had spread to a dozen more cities, and by the end of the 1920s joint appeals in more than 129 communities raised close to $60 million.[24] By the end of World War II, more than 1,000 United Ways were in existence, and the number has continued to grow, totaling roughly 1,400 locally based organizations by the end of the century. Despite a series of problems in recent years, their fundraising drives still brought in $3.6 billion in contributions in 1998–99.

United Ways are only one kind of charity federation. A number of religious groups have long maintained organizations to raise money from their members and distribute it among denominational charities according to priorities determined by the group's board and staff. Among the most successful have been Jewish federations, operating in about 200 localities and raising collectively more than $1.5 billion in gifts and endowment funds annually for Jewish charities.[25] As with the United Ways, a national organization sets policies, provides support, and loosely coordinates their efforts. Most local federations also engage in planning around religious needs and direct their contributions accordingly.

The so-called alternative funds are another type of charity federation. Created mostly since the 1980s, they conduct fundraising campaigns, often in the workplace, on behalf of small groups of charities usually linked by a common interest, such as the arts, the environment, education, health care, or disaster relief, or by a common group of beneficiaries, such as women or minorities. According to the National Committee for Responsive Philanthropy (which has promoted them as an alternative to United Ways), more than 200 such funds existed in 1997, and together they raised nearly $200 million.[26] Although practices vary widely, they normally distribute the funds they raise based on requests from member agencies or other eligible groups.

Finally, a number of health and relief organizations, such as the American Cancer Society, American Lung Association, March of Dimes, and American Red Cross, operate as federations. Using a variety of methods, local chapters raise money, a portion of which supports the work of the affiliates and the rest of which is allocated according to national priorities, such as research or public information efforts. These organizations typically rank among the nation's most successful charities in fundraising.

Altogether, Americans probably give between 5 and 10 percent of their charitable contributions through federations like these.[27] That is more than corporate, community, and all but the larger independent foundations donate to charity.

GIFT FUNDS. The most recent innovation in institutional philanthropy is also the most controversial. In 1992 a Massachusetts mutual fund company, Fidelity Investments, began offering its clients the opportunity to create a charitable gift fund. In exchange for agreeing to use it only for philanthropic contributions, the donor could immediately receive a tax deduction for the money deposited in the fund, since the Internal Revenue Service classified it as a publicly supported charity—or 501(c)(3) organization. While Fidelity's trustees and staff reviewed and set certain limits on the grants (such as restricting them to organizations located in the United States) and also retained the right to disapprove them, the fund's donor (or his successor) could determine where and when the contributions would be made.

Although community foundations have used donor-advised funds for years, the adoption of this technique by for-profit investment firms was an innovation and one that turned out to be an immediate success. Within four years, more than 6,000 donor-advised accounts, worth more than $500 million, had been established in Fidelity's Charitable Gift Fund; four years later, the number of accounts topped 16,000 and assets, $1.7 billion. In its 1998–99 fiscal year, the organization made nearly $374 million in grants, three times as much as the largest community foundation did. Other financial companies, including the Vanguard Group, Merrill Lynch, PNC Bank, and American Guaranty and Trust, set up similar funds.[28]

To many in the world of institutional philanthropy, Fidelity's Charitable Gift Fund looks more like a collection of bank accounts for individual donors than a grantmaking organization. Although it provides the same tax advantages as giving to a community foundation or charity federation, it makes no pretense of trying to pool and allocate the contributions to it according to priorities determined by the fund's trustees or staff. Nor are donors even required to give any of the money they put in their accounts to charity each year, as would be the case if they had created their own foundations instead. As the Charitable Gift Fund grew and spawned imitators, demands began to be heard for regulations requiring it to act more like a grantmaking organization or even for revoking its 501(c)(3) status.[29]

In response to these concerns, Fidelity and the other funds have moved modestly toward the institutional philanthropy model. The Charitable Gift Fund, for example, now aims to distribute to charity an amount equal to at least 5 percent of its net assets each year. If necessary to reach this goal, it can draw on individual accounts that give less to make up a special fund, controlled by its trustees. (In fact, since it was established, the Charitable Gift Fund has spent an average of more than 20 percent of its assets annually.)[30] If a donor dies without naming a successor, the money in his account goes to the trustees' fund too.

These steps are not likely to change the minds of those who believe gift funds are really disguised forms of individual giving and that donors to them do not deserve the same tax benefits they would get by giving their money to a foundation or federation. Even so, their popularity raises the question of whether they are harbingers of what institutional philanthropy is likely to look like in the future.

Patterns

What difference does it make if a donor uses a grantmaking organization rather than giving directly? One way of assessing this is to examine how institutional philanthropy actually spends the money deposited with it. Although the possibility that those people who give to foundations, federations, or other intermediaries allocate their personal gifts the same way cannot be ruled out, the pattern of grants made by these organizations (and even gift funds) looks very dissimilar from charitable giving as a whole (which is heavily dominated by individual contributions).

So far as the gift funds are concerned, in the 1998–99 fiscal year only one-quarter of the Fidelity Charitable Gift Fund's grants went to religious groups, compared to 43 percent of total gifts, as shown in table 11-1; 28.0 percent of its donations supported education, in contrast to just 14.4 percent from all donors.[31] To be sure, these differences may be due chiefly to differences between the preferences of people who set up accounts with the Charitable Gift Fund and those who contribute to charities directly. But people who use an organization for their grantmaking, even one as loosely organized as Fidelity, may use different aims or methods than they use for their personal giving.

The contrast with overall giving patterns is even sharper for other forms of institutional philanthropy. The larger foundations, for example, gave little more than 2 percent of their grant funds to religious groups in 1998, but nearly 25 percent to education. Community foundations donated a slightly larger share (4 percent) to religion and a slightly smaller one to education, but corporate foundations did just the opposite.[32] Most United Way grants go to well-established health and social service agencies, while religious federations typically specialize in supporting secular charities with a denominational background, such as those providing educational and welfare services to members or international relief. Although they underwrite many traditional charities too, alternative funds are more likely to support groups whose activities involve considerable political advocacy.

These funding priorities changed little in the past decade. Although some varied by a few percentage points from year to year, each of the major categories of support tallied in the Foundation Center's annual review of larger foundations received approximately the same share of grant dollars in 1998 as in 1991.[33] (Important shifts have occurred within some categories, such as education, where foundations now devote a larger share of their gifts to precollegiate schooling than they used to.) By contrast, over the same period, the percentage of individual giving to religion has declined substantially, while giving to most of the other categories has risen.[34]

Grantmaking organizations also give different types of support than individual donors do. During the 1990s, only a small fraction—usually around 12 per-

Table 11-1. *Individual and Institutional Giving as a Percentage of Grant Dollars, by Destination, 1999*

Source	Religion	Education	Health	Community services[a]	Other
All sources[b]	43.0	14.4	9.4	14.9	18.2
Independent foundations	2.3	24.3	17.8	24.7	30.9
Community foundations	4.1	22.5	18.1	34.0	21.4
Corporate foundations	1.1	28.0	6.5	39.9	24.5
Fidelity Charitable Gift Fund	25.0	28.0	5.0	34.0	8.0

Source: Foundation Center, *Foundation Giving Trends: Update on Funding Priorities, 2000* (New York: Foundation Center, 2000); Ann E. Kaplan, ed., *Giving USA 2000: The Annual Report on Philanthropy for the Year 1999* (Indianapolis: American Association of Fund-Raising Counsel Trust for Philanthropy, 2000); Fidelity Charitable Gift Fund, *Annual Report, 98–99* (Boston: Fidelity Investments, 1999).

a. Includes human services and public or society benefit.

b. 75 percent individual.

cent—of grant dollars from the top 1,000 foundations went for general support of charities, while nearly half was earmarked for program support. Roughly one-quarter paid for capital expenditures, such as buildings and equipment.[35] Although no comparable tallies exist for individual donors, most personal gifts are used for general support (although a not insignificant share also funds endowments and capital investments). Donors who give through institutional philanthropy, in other words, perceive either the needs of charities or what they can most advantageously contribute differently than do individuals who give directly.

The biggest institutional givers are even more likely to finance particular programs than to provide general support. In 1998, for example, the 100 largest foundations in the Foundation Center's review (which accounted for nearly 60 percent of the funds donated) devoted 55 percent of their grant dollars to program support, compared to 27 percent among the other 909 large organizations studied. Corporate foundations were less programmatic and more likely to renew their gifts regularly (although more than half of the dollars expended by business-sponsored philanthropies could not be categorized). The same is true for charity federations (although religious federations obtain considerable sums for capital funds as well).

Community foundations allocate a bigger share of their grants to health and human service programs than do other kinds of foundations. They also give a larger portion for activities aimed at children and youth, while other foundations and corporate philanthropies provide more funds for minority groups. In the past ten years, the share of grant dollars for children and youth, as well as for the economically disadvantaged, has grown steadily, while that for the elderly and the disabled has grown more slowly.

However, as with the type of support, these trends are heavily influenced by the activities of the largest grantmaking organizations, which are far more likely than the smaller ones to be interested in minorities and the economically disadvantaged. Upward of 60 percent of foundation grants, moreover, either are not directed at identifiable groups or are reported as intended for the public as a whole.[36] Who benefits from the other forms of institutional philanthropy is even less well documented.

If institutional philanthropy was meant to be more than the lengthened shadow of the people (or businesses) whose contributions support it, it clearly has succeeded. At the very least, it has diversified the pattern of support for charitable endeavors, thus reinforcing the central rationale for charitable intermediaries. A key question for the future is whether institutional philanthropy will continue to be able to perform this role.

The Changing Face of Institutional Philanthropy

Like individual giving, institutional philanthropy is affected by changing economic and demographic conditions, legal rules, and popular attitudes. In addition, ideas about how grantmaking organizations should operate—what one might call philanthropic strategies—also play an important role. In recent years, the growth of new foundations, corporate giving programs, and other kinds of grantmaking organizations has brought with it new (or in some cases revived older) perspectives about the strategies institutional philanthropy should use.

Economic, Demographic, and Institutional Changes

When John D. Rockefeller III offered his worried prognosis of the state of philanthropy, the American economy was stagnant, mired in high unemployment and double-digit inflation. In the twenty years since then, it has been growing, with unemployment and inflation mostly declining until relatively recently. Institutional philanthropy has been a principal beneficiary of this change in the economic winds, although the change has had as much impact on the growth of new organizations as on that of existing ones.

Since 1981, total foundation assets have more than quadrupled in inflation-adjusted dollars.[37] This is as much due to the creation of 24,000 new foundations as to the appreciation of (or additional gifts and bequests to) the endowments of preexisting ones. (In real terms, the average assets per foundation have "only" doubled.) During the mid-1990s, the growth rate of foundation wealth was especially high, tracking closely the performance of the stock market. Larger foundations did relatively better at riding the booming economy than did smaller ones.[38]

Corporate philanthropy also profited from prosperous times. The assets of the larger corporate foundations tripled in constant dollars between the early

1980s and the late 1990s, despite declines during the recession of the early 1990s. However, until recently, much of the growth in corporate giving was due more to the larger number of companies engaged in philanthropy than to greater contributions to business foundations or higher returns on their investments.[39] Indeed, corporate philanthropy has not kept up with the growth of corporate profits, declining from 1.4 percent of pretax net income at the beginning of the 1990s to 1.3 percent at the end, although this may reflect more the numerous other ways in which companies now support charities besides foundation and direct giving than a lessening of the amount.[40]

Community foundations have followed a similar path. Since the early 1980s, assets of the larger ones have grown sixfold, but, since 300 new ones were created, the average endowment per organization has increased much more slowly. In constant dollars, the average gift per community foundation has risen 16 percent, half as fast as the average for all foundations.[41]

Traditional charity federations generally have not fared as well. After doubling during the 1980s, in the 1990s total gifts to the United Ways fell in constant dollars, as did their share of all giving, despite nearly a decade-long economic expansion.[42] (Since the total includes donor-designated gifts, even this overstates the additional amount available for institutional purposes.) Major religious federations, such as the United Jewish Appeal, reported virtually no growth.

By contrast, although they started out at a much lower level, the alternative funds have posted impressive gains. A group of environmental federations, for example, had a 55 percent increase in contributions between 1995 and 1999.[43] And Fidelity's Charitable Gift Fund became one of the nation's largest grant-making bodies in 1999.

Other economic factors also benefited the newer components of institutional philanthropy more than the old. Conversion foundations partly owed their existence to the discovery by entrepreneurs and investors that money could be made running health, education, and human service agencies. According to a Conference Board study, traditional corporate restructuring led to a reduction in philanthropy when the firms involved were located in the same region, but an increase when they were based in different ones or when a company had to move away from a long-time home.[44] Far from diminishing business generosity, in other words, at least some kinds of mergers or acquisitions apparently increased it.

Indeed, contrary to any fears about how the shift of industry and jobs away from their traditional concentration in the Northeast and Midwest might affect philanthropy, the South and West are proving to be fertile soil for institutional givers. Since the beginning of the 1980s, the number of foundations has grown more rapidly in the two regions than in the rest of the country. Differences in the growth rate of foundation assets have been even more pronounced.[45] Likewise, instead of diminishing corporate philanthropy, economic globalization may have spurred it, especially for businesses active in foreign countries.[46]

Notwithstanding the attention paid to younger philanthropists, such as Bill Gates, the aging of the population is having an impact on the growth of institutional giving too, and only partly because as people grow old, they become wealthier and more generous. In 1999 bequests to charities exceeded $15 billion, a 15 percent increase over the previous year; throughout the decade, in fact, only the growth rate of foundation grants exceeded that of bequests among sources of giving.[47] Much of this money undoubtedly went directly to charities, but some also was used to create or enlarge grantmaking organizations as well, thus increasing the resources for institutional philanthropy. With an unprecedented share of the nation's population moving into the latter stages of the life cycle, bequests are likely to continue playing a significant role in shaping institutional philanthropy in the future.[48]

To be sure, just as the new economy has a long way to go before it replaces the old, the landscape of institutional philanthropy will continue to be dominated by foundations and federations that were created when manufacturing was king. Despite the growth rate of foundations since the 1980s, three-quarters of their assets are still held by organizations founded earlier, sometimes much earlier. And even though grantmaking bodies have been springing up rapidly in the West and the South, most are still located in the Northeast and Midwest.[49]

Yet the economic and demographic changes of the past two decades have helped to produce a plethora of new banking options, and they are bringing forth new kinds of charity bankers as well, who often claim to have new ideas about how to run foundations, align corporate social responsibility with business strategies, and allocate donated funds. Whether the impact on institutional philanthropy will be as profound as it has been on financial services remains to be seen.

Legal Environment

Another factor contributing to John D. Rockefeller III's despair about the prospects for philanthropy in the late 1970s was the legal environment. In 1969, after a frequently acrimonious decade of studies and hearings, Congress enacted a set of new rules that were regarded at the time as punitive toward independent foundations and likely to discourage their growth. Among the rules were expanded reporting obligations, restrictions on investments and grants, a requirement to pay out a certain amount of money each year, and even a special excise tax on endowment income.[50] To many, the decline in the formation of new foundations during the 1970s seemed to bear out their fears about what Congress had done.

Yet, although the 1969 rules have not been substantially modified, they have posed a much less formidable barrier to those interested in setting up foundations than earlier feared. Moreover, in contrast to the earlier legislative climate, Congress took a number of steps in the past two decades to encourage the growth of grantmaking organizations. For example, it made donating property (such as stock or real estate) to a foundation more attractive by enacting a permanent rule allowing contributors to deduct the property's appreciated value, rather than its cost, as had previously been routinely permissible for gifts only to publicly supported charities. It also raised the amount that corporations could deduct for charitable gifts and resisted calls to declare sponsorships and other new ways in which companies underwrote charities as business activities (which could have made taxable the income the charities received). After a series of court cases, Congress also expanded the participation of alternative funds in the federal government's workplace fundraising campaign.

Other branches of government took similar steps. Despite some second-guessing, the Internal Revenue Service concluded that Fidelity's Charitable Gift Fund and similar grantmaking organizations were entitled to be designated as publicly supported charities, enabling their account holders to claim tax deductions for their gifts even before selecting nonprofit groups to receive them. Both federal and state officials (such as state attorneys general) had to develop procedures for valuing and protecting the assets of nonprofits whose sale produced conversion foundations.

Still, especially for upper-income people, tax rates are lower now than they used to be, making the deductibility of gifts to a grantmaking organization (or even giving directly to charity) less valuable than it once was. In addition, many analysts believe that efforts to eliminate the federal inheritance tax will sharply reduce the incentive to make bequests to foundations (or other kinds of charities), which have been fully deductible from the taxable value of estates.[51] Despite the impressive growth of institutional philanthropy in the past two decades, no one knows if it might have expanded even more rapidly if the legal rules pertaining to it had been different, such as by allowing foundations to retain larger holdings in high-growth companies.[52]

Nonetheless, in a legal environment that was once thought to be sounding a death knell for grantmaking organizations (and especially foundations), institutional philanthropy has not only adapted but also flourished. Indeed, the more pressing question looks to be not whether the laws governing this type of giving are too restrictive, but whether they are restrictive enough in view of the increasing mix of philanthropic and commercial interests in some of the newer forms of institutional grantmaking.

Public Attitudes

Part of the reason the Rockefeller Foundation was so controversial when it was created was that its founder was popularly seen as a ruthless competitor who had engaged in unscrupulous business practices to make his fortune. At the time he was proposing to put a large share of his wealth into a grantmaking organization, in fact, his company was in the midst of the first major federal antitrust prosecution, which it would eventually lose. Nearly a century later, another business leader with a vast fortune, but a terrible public reputation, began to make large gifts to his foundation. His company, too, was embroiled in an antitrust case that it would ultimately lose, at least at the trial stage. But rather than being denounced, Bill Gates was widely praised for his generosity.

Although this comparison partly reflects the fact that institutional philanthropy is no longer the novelty it was in Rockefeller's day, it may also signify an important, if not definitively provable, change in public attitudes. "We expect rich men to be generous with their wealth and criticize them when they are not," Robert H. Bremner has written, "but when they make benefactions, we question their motives, deplore the methods by which they obtained their abundance, and wonder whether their gifts will not do more harm than good."[53] Although this may have been true in the early years of the twentieth century and for several decades afterward, it seems less true now.

The past three decades have seen a decline in public confidence in most American institutions. But trust in government has fallen further than trust in nonprofit organizations and business.[54] The public overwhelmingly believes that charities play a major role in enhancing communities.[55] Younger people are more inclined to put their faith in service activities than in government for dealing with the nation's problems.[56] Since the mid-1990s, a growing number of Americans have judged charities to be more effective than they were previously.[57]

These positive attitudes carry over to institutional philanthropy as well. According to a Wirthlin Worldwide survey for the Council on Foundations, Americans believe strongly that "maintaining permanent charitable endowments is critical to the long-term viability of communities."[58] Another Wirthlin study has found that consumers ranked responsiveness to community as being an important component of a corporation's reputation.[59] Of those responding, 76 percent told a 1997 Cone-Roper survey that they would change to a product associated with a good cause (an increase of 10 percentage points since the question was asked four years earlier). When price and quality are the same, two-thirds of American consumers said they would choose the one identified with a good cause.[60]

Not all grantmaking organizations have fared as well in the public's eyes. After a well-publicized scandal in the early 1990s involving its national president, United Way suffered a slump in confidence. Some religious federations—notably those in the Jewish community—have encountered waning support as their members first lost their faith, then their interest, in its charities. Moreover, as the Council on Foundations survey revealed, although they generally thought well of them, most Americans knew little about foundations. This suggests that a scandal or two like the one that embroiled United Way could lead, without much opposition, to a new round of efforts to investigate foundations and other institutional grantmakers. Indeed, the flap created by the Red Cross's handling of its September 11 fund suggests the tenuousness of the situation.

In the always somewhat adversarial relationship between donors and grantees, suspicions about how institutional grantmakers are discharging their responsibilities are not uncommon. From time to time, public officials, including the Internal Revenue Service, have expressed concerns about how accountable and open to oversight institutional philanthropy is. However, wider use of new technologies, such as the Internet, which improves access to information about foundations and other organizations, may eventually dampen them.

For now, at any rate, institutional philanthropy seems to enjoy more esteem than it ever has. Ironically, its sharpest critics may be those, such as the new philanthropists from the dot-com industries or the leaders of the alternative funds, who think they know it best.

Changing Philanthropic Strategies

Grantmaking bodies inevitably reflect views current at the time of their creation about what makes for an effective organization. The Rockefeller Foundation, for example, resembled the modern industrial corporation, with its bureaucracy, specialist staff, and policy-setting duties for the donor and trustees.[61] Likewise, the early United Ways and community foundations owed much to the formal and informal networks through which businessmen and professionals, especially in the Midwest, built consensus in their communities.

As the new economy has begun to replace the old, it comes as no surprise that new ideas about how philanthropic institutions should operate are emerging as well. In keeping with the current thinking about management, philanthropic institutions are emphasizing less formal organizational structures, fewer subject matter specialists, and more individual involvement by the donors as the keys to success.

These ideas appear to be particularly appealing among philanthropists coming out of the high-tech industries. Foundations, according to Paul Brainerd, a founder of Aldus Corporation, are no longer as attractive to people in his community. Instead, high-tech entrepreneurs want to develop a venture capital model of philanthropy that involves a long-term, direct relationship between the donor and the recipient, focused on investing rather than giving.[62] Other successful dot-com entrepreneurs fault traditional philanthropy for spending too much on administration and accomplishing too little. They vow that their foundations will be streamlined, rely on people with business backgrounds as staff, and take seriously the notion of obtaining a social return on investment.[63]

Not all of them will actually do so, of course, nor do all the high-tech-industry philanthropists even necessarily agree on what grantmaking organizations should look like and how they should operate in the future. Moreover, the venture capital analogy is hardly a new one; it was central, for example, to the thinking of the Commission on Foundations and Private Philanthropy (the Peterson Commission), which sought to defend institutional philanthropy against congressional criticism thirty years ago.[64] The older grantmaking organizations have also been making an effort to encourage the newer ones to adopt (and adapt) traditional grantmaking strategies. The economic shakeout in the high-tech world will undoubtedly affect how quickly the industrialists of the digital age develop their own philanthropic identities. But it would be surprising if they wound up looking like those of the grantmaking organizations rooted in the manufacturing era.

Questions have also been raised about long-standing practices in other parts of the world of institutional philanthropy. Although no one seems to be keeping track of the numbers, community foundations are reporting an upsurge in donor-advised funds. Rather than being applied to address local priorities as determined by the organization's staff and trustees, the uses of these gifts are specified by the contributor, albeit sometimes in such broad terms that the foundation has considerable discretion over them.[65] The appeal of creating such funds and the often sizable amounts of money they contain raise the possibility that community foundations are looking, especially to living donors, more like holding companies than organizations for helping them to improve their giving.

The United Ways are facing a similar challenge. Of the $3.6 million they raised in 1998, contributors designated one-fifth for charities that were not United Way members (and in some cities the share was even greater). In 1990 that figure was only 14 percent, suggesting that federated giving, despite its value for generations of donors, was less attractive for newer ones.[66]

Corporate giving has begun to change as well. Whether as strategic philanthropy or as a component of its marketing efforts, businesses are increasingly gearing their relationships with charities toward being more like commercial investments or synergistic collaborations and less like expressions of enlightened corporate citizenship (to use one of the many phrases common a generation ago). In addition to giving grants, they are also offering company expertise in areas such as publicity and finance to nonprofits that need it. Perhaps not coincidentally, when corporations started moving in these directions, their share of institutional philanthropy—including sponsorships—began to rise.

Not least important, these new strategies have gained wide and growing intellectual credibility. In its 1997 report, *Giving Better, Giving Smarter,* the National Commission on Philanthropy and Civic Renewal, an organization funded by the Lynde and Harry Bradley Foundation, urged philanthropists to become more directly involved with the causes they want to support. They should stop spending so much time and money studying problems or networking with other grantmakers too, the commission advised.[67] In the same year, the *Harvard Business Review* published "Virtuous Capital: What Foundations Can Learn from Venture Capitalists," a widely discussed article that called on donors to give themselves as well as their money to charity and to do so for a longer period than most were accustomed to.[68]

A steady stream of conferences, studies, consulting groups, and new training programs has arisen to promote venture philanthropy as well. And the most successful recent innovations in institutional philanthropy—the gift funds established by Fidelity and other investment companies—depend so much on the involvement of individual donors and so little on specialist staff or organizational structures that some believe they ought not to be considered grantmaking intermediaries at all (or to receive the benefits that go with that status).

If these new approaches to institutional philanthropy are the wave of the future, no one knows for sure how many grantmakers are riding it. Some of the largest and most prominent foundations created by high-tech entrepreneurs look and behave much like traditional grantmaking organizations, although perhaps a little less top-heavy in staff (which may simply be due to their newness). While donor designation and new allocation formulas clearly have had an impact on contributions to community foundations and charity federations, they may not have made much difference in the charities receiving their gifts.[69]

As might be expected, corporations seem to show the most enthusiasm for philanthropic strategies that make a virtue of getting involved with causes that directly interest the donor. But for business, this is, in a way, going backward to the future, for nineteenth-century views held that charitable giving should be limited to situations where the company receives a tangible benefit.[70]

Even if the new philanthropic strategies have yet to leave a major mark on the face of institutional philanthropy, they harbor an implicit criticism of it. Those advocating these new approaches are, in essence, saying that, even though they may be more extensive and wealthier than in the past, grantmaking intermediaries are not fulfilling society's expectation that they should make giving more effective.

Four Questions Facing Institutional Philanthropy

At a time when the gap between the resources available to the nonprofit sector and the demands being placed on it appears to be growing, such a conclusion would be serious indeed. For as Harvard Business School guru Michael Porter and Mark Kramer observe in a widely noted article, institutional philanthropy, especially that of foundations, involves an implicit trade-off: by allowing contributions to go into grantmaking organizations, rather than directly to charity, society is supposed to reap greater benefits.[71] But what if there is reason to doubt that it does? Critics of institutional philanthropy argue that there are at least four bases for such doubts.

Payout

Perhaps the most important—certainly the most widely discussed—basis for doubting the value of institutional philanthropy concerns how much money existing charitable institutions are actually giving to charity.

Since the 1969 rules were enacted, foundations have been required to dispense a specific percentage of their endowments annually—currently 5 percent of the average market value of their assets during the preceding year. Some commentators have charged that most of the larger foundations act as if this were not just a minimum standard, but also a maximum one. According to Peter Frumkin's calculations, for example, seventeen of the twenty largest independent foundations in 1995 gave less than 5 percent of their assets in grants, with eight totaling between 2 and 4 percent. The reasons, he argues, were chiefly that staff and administrative costs (including a special tax paid on investment earnings) also count toward the payout requirement and that the number of people employed by these foundations has risen substantially since 1969.[72]

With grantmaking organizations growing wealthier, especially during the stock market boom of the 1990s, the 5 percent standard began to look to some as too low. In an analysis done in the market boom year of 1999 for the National Network of Grantmakers, for example, Barnard College economist Perry Mehrling argues that the typical foundation could perhaps spend as much as 8 percent without reducing the value of its endowment. For such an organization, this would have meant nearly 20 percent more spending over the period from 1975 to 1994.[73]

Others dispute this. In a report prepared for the Council on Foundations, DeMarche Associates concluded that, although a higher payout rate would have resulted in more money going to charity in recent years, it would have diminished the total over the long term (meaning, in this study, from 1950 to 1998).[74] A Cambridge Associates examination of the record of thirty-three Michigan foundations between 1973 and 1999 discovered that the inflation-adjusted return on their assets was barely enough to sustain a 5 percent payout without diminishing their endowments.[75]

Even if one could reconcile these different findings (which depend heavily on the assumptions and time frames used), the real issue they raise is more normative than empirical: How much *should* grantmaking organizations be expected to distribute? The payout requirement was adopted in response to critics such as Texas Congressman Wright Patman and Tennessee Senator Albert Gore Sr., who claimed that foundations were being set up to allow wealthy people to protect and accumulate assets without using much, if any, of the income earned on grants. After rejecting efforts to require foundations to dissolve after a period of time (rather than exist in perpetuity, as most do), Congress mandated a minimum percentage of giving each year, thereby hoping to ensure that institutional philanthropy would be used for charitable purposes.[76]

Those who want to raise the payout rate are suggesting that, at its current level, it is not having this effect and, furthermore, that spending additional money in the present would be more beneficial than deferring it to the future. But if so, why stop at 8 percent? If more grants now are likely to be more useful than funds saved for later, why create grantmaking organizations at all? Or why *not* require them to dissolve after a certain number of years, as some of the newer philanthropists, such as George Soros, say they intend to do with their own foundations?

Those who speak on behalf of institutional philanthropy argue not only that a higher payout rate (or a limit on the foundation's lifetime) is likely to produce less giving but also that the administrative and staff costs of grantmaking institutions add value to what they do. Moreover, although the new donors may be willing to forgo permanent staff for their grantmaking efforts, they do not seem to shy away from retaining consultants and others to give them advice. In any case, judging from the high growth rate of new foundations, most of which do not have limits on their lifetime, the personal and social appeal of perpetual endowments obviously is still considerable.

The question of whether grantmaking bodies should go on forever or put their funds into charities as rapidly as possible is an old one. Those who favor permanency emphasize the advantages of institutionalizing philanthropy, such as continuity, pluralism, and experience. Those who prefer high payouts, or even eventual dissolution, point to institutionalized philanthropy's supposed disadvantages, such as excessive caution and bureaucracy.[77] Since both viewpoints have some validity, the desire of the coming generation of philanthropists to rely less on the traditional model of intermediaries might be good for the nonprofit sector.

Accountability

The second charge against grantmaking organizations is that they are not sufficiently open to public scrutiny. This criticism normally would not be lodged against an individual giver. What charities a person supports is usually deemed to be a private matter, even though the individual might receive a public benefit, such as a tax deduction.[78] But institutional philanthropy has always been subject to greater oversight, partly to ensure that the funds directed through foundations, corporate giving programs, federations, and other intermediaries ultimately do go to charities and partly because these organizations can potentially exert greater influence than individuals because of their ability to accumulate resources (both money and staff) over many years. As charitable giving organizations have grown more extensive and wealthier in the past two decades, efforts to make them more accountable to the public have grown too.

In 1997, for example, foundations were required to make their Internal Revenue Service information returns more easily available for public inspection. (This led to the growth of services, such as GuideStar, that put these documents on the Internet.) The Securities and Exchange Commission has considered requiring corporations to report on their contributions (and even to give shareholders the right to approve them). United Way has faced calls for including a wider range of charities in overseeing the distribution of the money its affiliates raise. And the new gift funds and alternative federations have presented an ongoing series of novel issues for charity watchdogs and regulators.

Although the more demanding reporting rules established after the congressional investigations of the 1960s were thought to have contributed to the slowdown in the growth of foundations in the 1970s, no signs of a similar result are apparent from the recent efforts to increase public accountability. Instead, donors themselves are insisting on a different kind of accountability—what one might call personal accountability—by tying their gifts more closely to their own interests. Implicit in this view is the notion that earmarking contributions to a community foundation or federation for a specific charity should lessen a donor's concerns about how the money will be used. Likewise, getting directly involved with a charity, rather than doing so indirectly through an intermediary, should reduce any worries a donor might have that trustees and staff will allocate grants in some unwanted way. Corporations that measure their philanthropy by its contribution to the bottom line or to corporate reputation may also feel that they would have less explaining to do to profit-minded shareholders than corporations that see themselves as pursuing the more nebulous goal of social responsibility.

In the past, demands for more accountability typically sought to prevent grantmaking organizations from serving the interests of individual benefactors (or member charities) rather than the broader needs of society. Today, with Congress and regulators seemingly less troubled by issues of accountability, donors are worried about their own accountability and are seeking to assure greater expression of their own goals and ideas.

If these are creative and worthwhile, that might not be so bad. However, sometimes they are not (and it is easy for someone who has been successful at making money to assume that he will be equally adept at giving it away), with the result being not only wasted grants but possibly also calls for heightened public scrutiny. That is why grantmaking intermediaries come in handy, and we may ultimately be sorry if too many philanthropists decide to do it on their own.

Philanthropic Competition

A third challenge facing institutional philanthropy is the growing competition it is encountering from operating charities. The case of Mrs. Mildred Othmer is illustrative in this regard. In April 1998 Mrs. Othmer passed away, leaving an estate of $750 million that she and her husband, Donald, a professor at the Polytechnic Institute of Brooklyn, had amassed (with a bit of investment advice from Warren Buffet). However, instead of using this fortune to endow a new grantmaking foundation, her will provided for a series of gifts, including several exceeding $100 million, to a number of hospitals and universities.[79]

Her actions were by no means unusual. According to annual lists of multimil-lion-dollar donations, such as the one created by *Slate* magazine, contributions directly to charities on such a large scale are no longer as uncommon as they used to be. If, as Andrew Carnegie discovered when he tried unsuccessfully to give all his money to charity before he died, creating a grantmaking organization (or making a large gift to a community foundation) used to be almost as inevitable as death and taxes for very wealthy people, that is no longer the case today.

What has happened is not that philanthropists have become less enamored of the institutional model. To the contrary, they are still setting up foundations or giving to other intermediaries at record-setting rates. However, the growth of grantmaking organizations would have been even greater if charities themselves had not become better at competing with them. If the social case for setting up a foundation or giving to a federation or community fund once rested on the ability of such institutions to improve giving, growing numbers of charities now can argue that they can use large sums of money effectively too—and without the intermediaries' overhead. Judging from the Othmers and others, their argu-ment seems to be increasingly persuasive.

Moreover, even the lines that once separated grantmaking organizations have blurred. Community foundations used to be the means for pooling local resources into an endowment and addressing problems on a long-term basis. Charity federations—typically United Ways—specialized in raising money for operating expenses and allocating it to member agencies as current needs dic-tated. Yet, today, with more of their incomes designated for nonmember agen-cies, many United Ways are seeking to build up assets and giving greater empha-sis to long-term community planning. As more of their gifts become donor-advised, community foundations are more often finding themselves sup-porting the operations of local health and human service agencies selected by the donors (albeit sometimes with considerable advice from the foundations' staff), rather than serving chiefly as a source of funds and expertise for tackling more systemic issues.

In a way, these shifts are just the latest turn in what is now a familiar saga of adaptation by American nonprofits to changing legal incentives and donor pref-erences. They attest to the extraordinary resilience of the nonprofit sector as social, economic, cultural, and political circumstances change.

However, this time, rather than developing grantmaking organizations to offer an alternative to individual giving, the nonprofit world is coming up with new ways of attracting personal gifts directly to charities, including the kinds of gifts that in past years might have gone to charitable intermediaries.[80] Those who value getting funds to where they can be put to immediate use might applaud this change. But those who wonder whether donors, like investors, should have their own advisers might worry that philanthropic speculation and day trading will become more frequent.

Effectiveness

Notwithstanding all that grantmaking organizations accomplish or the difficulties of making broad generalizations about so varied a group, there is more than a little anxiety, particularly among those who know it well, that evidence of the effectiveness of institutional philanthropy has been hard to come by lately.

On the Council on Foundations' list of philanthropy's great grants, for example, none of the more recent ones deals with issues, such as inequality, poverty, or health care, that are often cited among the matters most urgently in need of philanthropic attention, especially from the larger, well-endowed organizations. The list was undoubtedly not meant to be scientific or comprehensive, and many of the grants on it—such as the money that several organizations provided to promote the concept of designated driver—have been valuable. Nonetheless, at the very least, the list symbolizes how difficult it is to determine what spending by foundations has actually contributed to remedying the nation's most critical problems.

Independent foundations are not alone in facing this problem. Corporate giving programs continue to be bedeviled by the difficulties of showing what they have contributed to their companies and in some areas, such as education, to the communities they have been trying to help. United Ways and other federated givers have just begun trying to measure rigorously the impact of the charities they support—and, which has been controversial, to adjust their allocation formulas accordingly. Even some of the champions of the newer approaches to grantmaking, such as venture philanthropy, are acknowledging that, as a recent report puts it, "despite very strong expressions of interest in measuring outcomes and 'return on investment,' very few of the [investment] funds have established concrete measures for doing this."[81]

Why is it so difficult to determine the effectiveness of institutional philanthropy? Part of the reason may be that the problems themselves are complex and not as readily solvable—by philanthropy or any other part of society—as they were when the Rockefeller Foundation, for example, was able to cure hookworm by identifying the responsible parasite.[82] Part also reflects the fact that in its heyday the resources available to institutional philanthropy were at least the equal of what government spent; today, not even the most efficient grantmaker will have as much money—let alone influence—as the head of just a modest-size public agency. On some issues, such as welfare reform and health care, rightly or wrongly, some grantmakers were pursuing approaches that many thought were unlikely to solve the problems needing to be addressed or were so far removed from the public's views that they stood little chance of having the widespread impact their supporters desired.[83]

Whatever the reasons, the probability that institutional philanthropy can play the influential role that it did in its formative era seems slim. This does not mean that foundations, charity federations, and the like are not useful in any number of ways; the sums that donors continue to invest in them strongly suggest otherwise. Nor does the likelihood they will play a more limited role imply that these organizations do not undertake socially beneficial activities, including many that are creative and make important contributions to American life (although there are undoubtedly foolish ones too). But after a period in which the nation's non-profits have seen contributions decline as a share of their revenues, the fact that the accomplishments of institutional philanthropy are difficult to demonstrate weakens the case for directing billions of dollars annually to them.

Conclusions

Perhaps adopting the new models championed by the new philanthropists will provide the basis for a stronger case on behalf of institutional philanthropy. Yet apart from the fact that these models are still largely undefined, unproven, and fraught with practical and policy issues,[84] they are ultimately a step—in some versions, a large step—in the direction of individually directed giving, rather than a reassertion of the value of using intermediaries for grantmaking. So too are the fastest growing kinds of philanthropic organizations: donor-advised funds at community foundations and gift funds such as the one at Fidelity. Under the rubric of strategic philanthropy, corporations have become more dependent on self-interested motives for their charitable activity as well. Even major foundations have been experimenting with grant programs that look more like the activities of charities (for example, funding scholarships, individual development accounts, homeownership loans, and the like) than the research-driven, far-reaching, time-consuming efforts at social, educational, public health, and other kinds of change that were once their hallmark.

However, just as the early twentieth-century industrial corporation provided a successful model for the Rockefeller Foundation and its imitators, perhaps today's decentralized and entrepreneurial businesses will offer the right starting place for the grantmaking organization of the future. Nor is the desire of today's high-tech givers to be more involved with their charities, rather than leave them to the specialized professionals of institutional philanthropy, necessarily a bad idea, especially if they can bring with them the kinds of abilities they have displayed in their careers. Indeed, technology itself has undoubtedly made such donor involvement more feasible—and organizational structuring more flexible.

Institutional philanthropy is not going to disappear. It is going to continue a century-long pattern of innovation and diversification. New models are coming on the scene, and the existing grantmaking organizations are already beginning to operate differently than they did in the past. Some things may be lost, but others may be gained in the process.

Notwithstanding frequently expressed worries that institutional philanthropy will allow the dead hand of long-departed donors to determine the charitable priorities of today, the truth is that nothing goes on in the same way forever, not even large grantmaking endowments.

Notes

1. John D. Rockefeller III, "The Third Sector," in Brian O'Connell, ed., *America's Voluntary Spirit: A Book of Readings* (New York: Foundation Center, 1983), pp. 355–62.

2. Melissa Brown, ed., *Giving USA 2001: The Annual Report on Philanthropy for the Year 2000* (Indianapolis: Center on Philanthropy at Indiana University and American Association of Fund-Raising Counsel Trust for Philanthropy, 2001), p. 151.

3. For example, even though a donor retains control over money placed in a gift fund and does not need to make any payments to a particular charity for several years, he is eligible to claim a tax deduction immediately.

4. See John D. Rockefeller, "The Difficult Art of Giving," in O'Connell, ed., *America's Voluntary Spirit*, pp. 109–17.

5. Stanley Katz and Barry Karl, "The American Private Philanthropic Foundation and the Public Sphere 1860–1900," *Minerva*, vol. 19, no. 2 (1981): 236–70.

6. See Carnegie Foundation President Vartan Gregorian's comment on Annenberg grants in Meg Sommersfield, "What Did the Money Buy?" *Chronicle of Philanthropy*, May 4, 2000, p. 8.

7. Ron Chernow, *Titan: The Life of John D. Rockefeller, Sr.* (New York: Random House, 1998).

8. Robert Bremner, *American Philanthropy*, 2d ed. (Chicago University Press, 1988).

9. Foundation Center, *Foundation Yearbook of Facts and Figures on Private, Corporate, and Community Foundations, 2000,* Foundations Today Series (New York: Foundation Center, 2000), p. 75. Assets and grant amounts are based on 1997–98 dollars. The total number of foundations was undoubtedly larger than this, since an unknown number either had dissolved or did not have enough assets or make enough grants to be included in the Foundation Center survey from which the historical data are drawn.

10. Foundation Center, *Foundation Giving: Yearbook of Facts and Figures on Private and Community Foundations, 1999* (New York: Foundation Center, 1999), p. 22. Staff figures are not reported for foundations with less than $5 million in assets.

11. Foundation Center, *Foundation Yearbook, 2000*, pp. 70–72.

12. Peter Dobkin Hall, "The Community Foundation in America, 1914–1987," in Richard Magat, ed., *Philanthropic Giving: Studies in Varieties and Goals* (Oxford University Press, 1989): 180–99.

13. Foundation Center, *Foundation Yearbook, 2000*, pp. 64–70.

14. Foundation Center, *Foundation Giving, 1999*, p. 22.

15. Grantmakers in Health, *Philanthropy's Newest Members: Findings from the 1999 Survey of New Health Foundations* (Washington: Grantmakers in Health, 2000).

16. Teresa Odendahl, ed., *America's Wealthy and the Future of Foundations* (New York: Foundation Center, 1987), p. 24.

17. Foundation Center, *Foundation Yearbook, 2000*, pp. 55–64.

18. For an account of this period, see Edward Berkowitz and Kim McQuaid, *Creating the Welfare State*, 2d ed. (University Press of Kansas, 1992).

19. With 1997–98 assets larger than $1 million or annual grants exceeding $100,000.

20. Foundation Center, *Foundation Yearbook, 2000,* pp. 63–79.

21. Foundation Center, *Foundation Giving, 1999,* p. 22.

22. Ann E. Kaplan, ed., *Giving USA 1999: The Annual Report on Philanthropy for the Year 1998* (New York: American Association of Fund-Raising Counsel Trust for Philanthropy, 1999), pp. 68–69; Ann E. Kaplan, ed., *Giving USA 2000: The Annual Report on Philanthropy for the Year 1999* (Indianapolis: American Association of Fund-Raising Counsel Trust for Philanthropy, 2000), pp. 70–71.

23. Hall, "Community Foundation in America, 1914–1987," pp. 185–86.

24. Hall, "Community Foundation in America, 1914–1987," p. 186. United Way of America reports that 353 federations existed by 1929.

25. Meg Sommerfeld, "A New Era for Jewish Giving," *Chronicle of Philanthropy,* November 18, 1999, p. 1.

26. National Committee for Responsive Philanthropy, *Charity in the Workplace* (Washington: National Committee for Responsive Philanthropy, 1997).

27. In *Giving USA*'s annual estimate of charitable contributions, donations to federations are included principally in the categories of public and society benefit, health, and religion.

28. Mary Williams Walsh, "Philanthropy Is Good Business for Gifts Fund," *Los Angeles Times,* December 30, 1999. Banks also have long operated "trusts" that enable clients to dedicate a portion of their resources for charitable gifts. However, these have been neither marketed on as wide a scale nor set up legally as public charities as the newer gift funds have.

29. Harvey Lipman, "Survey Finds Rapid Rise in Assets and Grants of Donor-Advised Funds," *Chronicle on Philanthropy,* May 31, 2001, pp. 10–11.

30. Fidelity Charitable Gift Fund, *Annual Report, 98–99* (Boston: Fidelity Investments, 1999), p. 3.

31. Fidelity Charitable Gift Fund, *Annual Report, 98–99,* p. 12; Kaplan, ed., *Giving USA 2000,* p. 23.

32. Foundation Center, *Foundation Giving Trends: Update on Funding Priorities, 2000* (New York: Foundation Center, 2000), p. 52.

33. Foundation Center, *Foundation Giving: Yearbook of Facts and Figures on Private, Corporate, and Community Foundations, 1997* (New York: Foundation Center, 1997), p. 66; Foundation Center, *Foundation Giving Trends, 2000,* p. 8. The sample consisted of 1,009 foundations that had assets of at least $1 million or made grants of at least $100,000.

34. Ann E. Kaplan, ed., *Giving USA 1992: The Annual Report on Philanthropy for the Year 1991* (New York: American Association of Fund-Raising Counsel Trust for Philanthropy, 1992), p. 11; Kaplan, ed., *Giving USA, 2000,* p. 23.

35. Foundation Center, *Foundation Giving, 1997,* p. 86; Foundation Center, *Foundation Update, 2000,* p. 48. The remaining support went for research, student aid, and unspecified uses.

36. Foundation Center, *Foundation Update, 2000,* pp. 49, 59.

37. Foundation Center, *Foundation Yearbook, 2000,* p. 11.

38. Foundation Center, *Foundation Yearbook, 2000,* p. 9. According to the Council on Foundations' survey of foundation management practices, the larger foundations typically invest more of their portfolios in stocks than the smaller ones do.

39. Foundation Center, *Foundation Yearbook, 2000,* p. 63.

40. Kaplan, ed., *Giving USA, 2000,* p. 145. These figures normally do not include corporate sponsorships and other kinds of business-driven partnerships with charities, partly because determining their value to the charity is sometimes more problematic than it is for gifts of cash or goods and partly because statistics on them are not systematically kept.

41. Foundation Center, *Foundation Yearbook, 2000*, pp. 8, 9, 69.

42. Nicholas Varchaver and Irene Gashurov, "Can Anyone Fix the United Way?" *Fortune*, November 27, 2000, p. 170.

43. Numbers of various state federations for 1999 were compiled by William Borden, executive director, Earth Share of Washington.

44. Sophia Muirhead and Audris Tillman, *The Impact of Mergers and Acquisitions on Corporate Citizenship* (New York: Conference Board, June 2000).

45. Foundation Center, *Foundation Yearbook, 2000*, pp. 32, 34.

46. Debra E. Blum, "Corporate Giving Rises Again," *Chronicle of Philanthropy*, July 13, 2000, p. 16.

47. Kaplan, ed., *Giving USA, 2000*; Kaplan, ed., *Giving USA, 1999*, p. 131.

48. Paul G. Schervish, "The New Physics of Philanthropy: The Supply-Side Vectors of Charitable Giving," paper presented at the Taking Fund Raising Seriously Thirteenth Annual Symposium, Indiana University Center on Philanthropy, August 25–26, 2000.

49. Foundation Center, *Foundation Yearbook, 2000*, pp. 32, 79.

50. John Edie, "Congress and Foundations: Historical Summary," in Odendahl, ed., *America's Wealthy and the Future of Foundations*, pp. 43–64. Because they are classified legally as public charities, community foundations and federations were treated more leniently, receiving, for example, an exemption from the payout requirement.

51. For a balanced discussion of the issues, see Patrick M. Rooney and Eugene R. Tempel, "Repeal of the Estate Tax and Its Impact on Philanthropy" (Center on Philanthropy at Indiana University, June 15, 2001). In 2001 Congress voted to eliminate the inheritance tax as of 2010, but to restore it in 2011 to its 2001 form.

52. The Tax Reform Act of 1969 generally prohibited foundations from owning more than 20 percent of the shares in any company.

53. Bremner, *American Philanthropy*, p. 2.

54. Lester Salamon, *Holding the Center: America's Nonprofit Sector at a Crossroads* (New York: Nathan Cummings Foundation, 1997), p. 42.

55. National Commission on Philanthropy and Civic Renewal, *The National Survey on Philanthropy and Civic Renewal, 1997–1998: Americans on Giving, Volunteering, and Strengthening Community Institutions* (Washington: National Commission on Philanthropy and Civic Renewal, 1998), p. 77. Everett C. Ladd conducted the survey.

56. Peter D. Hart Research Associates, "New Leadership for a New Century: Key Findings from a Study on Youth, Leadership, and Community Service," No. 5128 (Washington: Public Allies, July 1998). But the public as a whole is equally divided. See National Commission on Philanthropy and Civic Renewal, *National Survey on Philanthropy and Civic Renewal*, p. 78.

57. Independent Sector, *Giving and Volunteering in the United States, 1999* (Washington: Independent Sector, 1999), p. 14.

58. Council on Foundations, "New Study Reveals Attitudes, Perceptions about American Foundations," press release, December 16, 1998.

59. Wirthlin Worldwide, "Maximizing Corporate Reputation," *Wirthlin Report*, vol. 10, no. 1 (April 2000): 2.

60. Sophia A. Muirhead, *Corporate Contributions: The View from Fifty Years* (New York: Conference Board, 1999), p. 54.

61. Perhaps not coincidentally, one of the most influential shapers of the modern corporation, Chester A. Barnard, served as president of the Rockefeller Foundation.

62. Paul Brainerd, "Social Venture Partners: Engaging a New Generation of Givers," *Nonprofit and Voluntary Sector Quarterly*, vol. 28, no. 4 (December 1999): 502–07.

63. For a sample of these views, see "The New Philanthropists," *Time*, July 24, 2000, pp. 48–59. The idea of measuring a social return on investment was popularized by Jed Emerson of the Roberts Enterprise Development Fund in San Francisco.

64. Commission on Foundations and Private Philanthropy, *Foundations, Private Giving, and Public Policy* (University of Chicago Press, 1970).

65. In theory, donors may advise, but not control, the funds they establish. How to distinguish between the two—and whether or not the money should ultimately revert to the foundation's general fund—are sometimes difficult to determine.

66. Debra E. Blum, "Moving Away from Donor Designation," *Chronicle on Philanthropy*, October 7, 1999, p. 33.

67. John W. Barry and Bruno V. Manno, *Giving Better, Giving Smarter: Renewing Philanthropy in America: Final Report* (Washington: National Commission on Philanthropy and Civic Renewal, 1997).

68. Christine Letts and William Ryan, "Virtuous Capital: What Foundations Can Learn from Venture Capitalists," *Harvard Business Review*, vol. 75, no. 2 (March/April 1997): 36–43.

69. Kirsten A. Grønbjerg and others, "The United Way System at the Crossroads: Community Planning and Allocation," *Nonprofit and Voluntary Sector Quarterly*, vol. 25 (1996): 428–52. Also see Donald Haider, "The United Way System," in National Commission on Philanthropy and Civic Renewal, *Giving Better, Giving Smarter*, pp. 147–68.

70. Joel Schwartz, "Corporate Philanthropy Today," in National Commission on Philanthropy and Civic Renewal, *Giving Better, Giving Smarter*, pp. 131–46.

71. Michael E. Porter and Mark R. Kramer, "Philanthropy's New Agenda: Creating Value," *Harvard Business Review*, vol. 77, no. 6 (November/December 1999): 121–30.

72. Peter Frumkin, "Three Obstacles to Effective Foundation Philanthropy," in National Commission on Philanthropy and Civic Renewal, *Giving Better, Giving Smarter*, pp. 84–104. One-year payment figures can be misleading since foundations are permitted to carry over unspent funds to subsequent years.

73. Perry Mehrling, *Spending Policies for Foundations: The Case for Increased Grants Payout* (San Diego: National Network of Grantmakers, 1999), p. 9.

74. Carter R. Harrison Jr., "It's How You Slice It," *Foundation News and Commentary*, vol. 40, no. 6 (November/December 1999): 33.

75. Cambridge Associates, *Sustainable Payout for Foundations: A Study Commissioned by the Council of Michigan Foundations* (Grand Haven: Council of Michigan Foundations, 2000).

76. Initially, the payout was set at 6 percent of average assets or the income earned by the foundation, whichever was higher.

77. The classic statement of the case against perpetuity was made by Julius Rosenwald, a contemporary of John D. Rockefeller. See Rosenwald, "Principles of Public Giving," in O'Connell, ed., *America's Voluntary Spirit*, pp. 119–28.

78. The principal exceptions involve political candidates and certain kinds of issue-oriented political groups. The identities of their supporters have to be disclosed to the public.

79. Kaplan, ed., *Giving USA, 1999*, p. 51.

80. The high growth rate of operating foundations provides further evidence, since they combine grantmaking and service provision. Likewise, the shift in corporate support for charity from corporate foundations and giving programs to sponsorships, licensing agreements, and the like reflects a similar dynamic.

81. Community Wealth Ventures, *Venture Philanthropy 2001: The Changing Landscape* (Reston, Va.: Morino Institute, 2001), p. 13.

82. James Smith has called on today's foundations to think of social problems as viruses that need to be managed, rather than germs that can be eradicated, as early grantmaking organizations did. See James Smith, "The Evolving Role of American Foundations," in Charles Clotfelter and Thomas Ehrlich, eds., *Philanthropy and the Nonprofit Sector* (Indiana University Press, 1999), pp. 34–51.

83. Mark Greenberg and Michael C. Laracy, "Welfare Reform: Next Steps Offer New Opportunities: A Role for Philanthropy in Preparing for the Reauthorization of TANF in 2002," Public Policy Paper 4 (McLean, Va.: Neighborhood Funders Group, June 2000), p. 8.

84. For a discussion, see Nonprofit Sector Strategy Group, *The Nonprofit Sector and the Market: Opportunities and Challenges* (Washington: Aspen Institute, 2001).

12

Individual Giving and Volunteering

VIRGINIA A. HODGKINSON
WITH KATHRYN E. NELSON AND EDWARD D. SIVAK JR.

Volunteerism is crucial to a functioning democracy because it mobilizes enormous energy. The more citizens involve themselves as volunteers in all areas, the closer they come to making the ideals of democracy real.[1]

The modern fundraising campaign, carefully organized, shrewdly promoted, and aimed at broad segments of the citizenry, had made American philanthropy a people's philanthropy . . . in total sum, popular philanthropy in the United States is a great democratic strength.[2]

Neighbor helping neighbor is part of the American mythology. Reflecting the national and religious heritage of Americans, self-reliance and dependence on local government characterized how average citizens handled their public business well into the twentieth century. Citizens as much as government were responsible for building their communities. With the rise of urban America, the great depression, and two world wars, however, the federal government became more important to the health of the nation. No longer could citizens solve their problems alone at the community level; neither could private giving alone solve the overwhelming problems of a nation in economic crisis.

Despite the increasing role of the federal government in social welfare, private giving and volunteering have remained a vibrant part of American culture. At the close of the twentieth century, volunteering and individual giving are higher than they have ever been, in large part due to the growth of organized management of volunteers, the establishment of a fundraising profession, and the expanded role of both government and the corporate sector and their respective partnerships with nonprofit organizations. However, other major developments have emerged in the last decade, and these could fundamentally change the market and the means through which Americans give and volunteer.

This chapter examines the relative health of giving and volunteering by individuals in the context of recent social, political, and economic changes. More specifically, the chapter argues seven points:

—While individual giving has increased markedly over the past two decades, it has not kept pace with the growth in personal income.

—Even though individual giving has remained an important source of financing for nonprofit organizations, its share has declined as a proportion of total revenue for the nonprofit sector.

—Giving has increased not only due to the overall growth of personal income but also due to the professionalization and growth of the fundraising profession and the creation of a host of new giving instruments developed in both the nonprofit and for-profit sectors.

—Individual giving might have been greater, but tax policies have had an impact on the amount of total giving.

—After some years of stagnation and decline, the rate of volunteering among adults and youth has surged recently, largely because of the dedicated effort of organizations and leadership in all three sectors and the growth of volunteer management.

—Volunteering also is important to the financing of the nonprofit sector and doubles the role that philanthropy plays when the value of contributed time is added to individual giving.

—The overall trends of the past two decades suggest that both giving and volunteering could continue to increase substantially and probably reach new peaks in the decades ahead if adequately encouraged by public policy.

These seven observations are explored in seven sections, focusing on current giving, current volunteering, the role of giving and volunteering in financing the nonprofit sector, key trends in giving, key trends in volunteering, future prospects, and conclusions.

Current Giving

No single source of data is regularly available on the scale of private charitable giving. Nevertheless, it is possible to piece together a reasonable estimate of such giving from a variety of different sources.[3] This section draws on these sources to provide an overall picture of the scale of current giving and the major forms of giving. It focuses on the share of giving by income level, the distribution of giving among types of organizations, the broader meaning of giving in the national culture, and its limitations.

Giving by Level of Income

Overall, in 2000, total charitable giving in the United States was estimated at $203.5 billion, of which living individuals gave $152.1 billion (75 percent), bequests totaled $16.0 billion (8 percent), private foundations provided $24.5 billion (12 percent), and corporations contributed $10.9 billion (5 percent). Remarkably, most private giving thus came from individuals (83 percent), while institutional giving accounted for less than 20 percent of total contributions.[4]

Although a majority of Americans contribute to causes of their choice, the bulk of individual and bequest giving comes from *wealthy* individuals and households. In 1998, the Internal Revenue Service (IRS) estimated that 27 percent of taxpayers (33.8 million returns) gave $109.2 billion to charity, or about 65 percent of all individual giving. Of this group, 23 percent (about 7.3 million returns) had adjusted gross income of over $100,000 and reported contributions of $58.5 billion, or 34 percent of total individual giving. Within this group of wealthy citizens, there were 151,583 returns with adjusted gross income of $1 million or higher, representing less than 0.5 percent of the group that took charitable deductions. This group reported more than $21 billion in contributions, or 12 percent of the total.[5] The balance of giving, about one-third of the total, came from all other households, which did not itemize their deductions.[6]

The Distribution of Giving by Type of Charity

As figure 12-1 illustrates, religious organizations capture by far the largest portion of individual giving. According to calculations of individual giving taken from *Giving USA*, religious institutions receive 44 percent of this giving.[7] The remaining individual giving is split among a variety of purposes, with human services (8 percent), health (8 percent), education (11 percent), and other purposes (primarily giving to foundations, 23 percent) receiving the largest shares.

Democratization of Individual Giving

During the twentieth century, individual giving became a pervasive activity among most Americans. Household contributions are reported by more than 70 percent of American households.[8] Before the twentieth century, individual giving to secular causes was primarily limited to wealthy individuals. However, during the twentieth century a whole new set of fundraising organizations, such as the American Lung Association, the Community Chests, and the March of Dimes, demonstrated that many small donations could add up to a large amount of fund support for various causes. Out of these early efforts emerged a fundraising profession and many new techniques for reaching a large proportion

Figure 12-1. *Giving by Individuals as a Percentage of Dollars Contributed,
by Type of Charity, 2000*

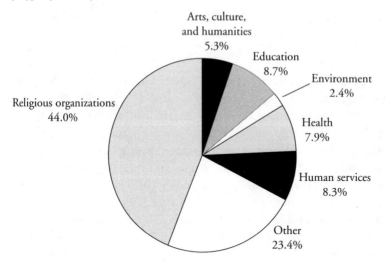

Arts, culture,
and humanities
5.3%

Education
8.7%

Environment
2.4%

Religious organizations
44.0%

Health
7.9%

Human services
8.3%

Other
23.4%

Source: AAFRC Trust for Philanthropy, *Giving USA 2001* (Indianapolis Center on Philanthropy, 2001). Authors' estimates of distribution of individual giving and bequests estimated at
$168.07 billion in 2001.

Note: Religious organizations include religion-related and spiritual development groups
(includes giving to churches, synagogues, seminaries, and so forth; does not include giving to
parochial schools and faith-based human services, which are included in education and human
services, respectively). Other includes international/foreign, private/community foundations,
public/societal benefit, and other types of charities.

of the population. By the end of the century, most Americans contributed to
one or more charitable causes. Thus individual giving was "democratized,"
moving from the province of the "few" to most of the adult population. Such
behavior was demonstrated amply after the September 11, 2001, terrorist
attacks on New York and Washington, D.C., when an estimated 58 percent of
Americans reported that they donated money to a charity or nonprofit organization within a few weeks after the disaster.[9] In fact, total donations generated
after September 11 have been estimated at $1.13 billion.[10]

While individual giving serves many functions, it also has limitations. Private
giving does not assure equitable distribution of resources, either by income class
or by type of charity. Even within subsectors, certain institutions attract greater
support because of their reputation, not necessarily because they are meeting
greater need. Both private giving and volunteering are inherently limited by
donor choice and geography. Philanthropic particularism (the way nonprofits
and their donors and volunteers choose to focus on particular causes or societal

needs) and philanthropic disparity (the charitable differences among communities) invariably affect the role that individual giving and volunteering play in financing the nonprofit sector.[11] Homogeneous communities that are somewhat more affluent are more generous than heterogeneous communities where there are wider variations in income.[12] In his history of charitable fundraising, Scott Cutlip observes that such particularism can cause fundraising to exacerbate the mismatch between society's needs and available resources: "In the 1980s the American Cancer Society and the American Heart Association, both dealing with major threats to our health, are the giant fundraisers. Yet, the nation's fourth biggest killer, kidney disease, ranks at the bottom in health fundraising efforts. . . . These facts illustrate the need for more widely available knowledge to guide our generous citizens in their contributions to charitable causes."[13] Although charitable giving performs many necessary functions, it cannot guarantee equity of support for a variety of institutions, causes, and citizens. Such equity can only be provided by government with the force of law.

Current Volunteering

Volunteering, or the giving of time to various organizations and causes, is very robust in the United States. Recent estimates indicate that nearly 56 percent of the population (109 million adults eighteen years of age or older) volunteered nearly 20 billion hours in 1998, or the equivalent of more than 9 million full-time employees.[14] In fact, the estimated value of volunteer time—$226 billion to all institutions—exceeded the *Giving USA 1998* estimates of total giving ($172.1 billion) and far exceeded the total giving by individuals ($146.7 billion).[15]

While volunteering is found among all ages and incomes, participation rates increase with household income and education. In 1999, 43 percent of adults with a high school degree volunteered compared with 68 percent of adults with a college degree. Respondents with household incomes of $20,000 volunteered at a rate of 42 percent, compared to 68 percent for respondents with household incomes between $40,000 and $50,000 and 71 percent for those with incomes of $100,000 or above. Volunteer rates also varied by race, with 59 percent of whites volunteering compared to 47 percent of blacks and 46 percent of Hispanics. The rate of volunteering among adults working part-time was higher (67 percent) than the rate among adults working full-time (57 percent). Those who were married also had a higher volunteering rate (62 percent) compared with those who were single (45 percent). Those who attended religious services during the year were far more likely to volunteer (61 percent) than those who did not attend (38 percent). Adults born in the United States were more likely to volunteer (58 percent) than adults not born in this country (34 percent). Finally, persons between the ages of thirty-five and sixty-four years were more likely to volunteer (60 to 67 percent) than those sixty-five to seventy-four years (49 percent) or those seventy-five years and older (43 percent).[16]

Understandably, most volunteer time (73 percent) is donated on behalf of charitable causes and the nonprofit sector; however, the government and for-profit sectors together secure 27 percent.[17] Even so, the assigned value of volunteer time to just the nonprofit sector, at $159 billion in 1998, still exceeded the total value of individual giving to the sector that year ($146.7 billion). Although volunteers are spread widely across the nonprofit sector, volunteering, like charitable giving, goes disproportionately to religious congregations. In particular, slightly more than half of total volunteer hours (52 percent) were contributed to religious institutions and 48 percent were given to other private, nonprofit organizations.[18]

Beyond its estimated economic value as a measure of labor, volunteering is a powerful mechanism for leveraging social change and empowering citizens. Recent studies suggest that volunteers are more likely than others to believe that they have it in their power to improve the lives of others and that individuals can make a difference in the quality of life in their communities. Volunteering is also strongly associated with other types of civic behavior. For example, adults who volunteer are more likely to join organizations and vote than adults who do not.[19]

The Role of Private Giving and Volunteering in Financing the Nonprofit Sector

While private giving and volunteering are quite substantial in the United States, they are far from the only, or even the major, source of revenue of America's nonprofit sector. As figure 12-2 shows, even with religious congregations included, private giving from all sources—including foundations and corporations—accounted for only 20 percent of nonprofit income in 1997. By contrast, dues, fees, and charges accounted for 38 percent, and government accounted for 31 percent. With religious congregations excluded, private giving accounted for an even smaller 9 percent of nonprofit income, compared to 42 percent for dues, fees, and charges and 35 percent for government.

This picture changes significantly when the value of volunteer time is included in the revenue of the sector, especially in view of the extensive volunteering for religious congregations. Thus, with religion included, giving and volunteering composed 36 percent of combined nonprofit cash and volunteer income. By comparison, dues and charges accounted for 30 percent of this expanded total and government for 25 percent. With religion excluded, however, and attention focused on the remaining nonreligious organizations, even with volunteering included, private philanthropy remained the third most important source of nonprofit income, at 20 percent, compared to 37 percent for dues and charges and 31 percent for government.

This picture varies considerably by type of organization, however. Revenue from giving provided the largest source of income for religious institutions (95 percent) and for arts and cultural organizations (40 percent). For private foundations, giving ranked a close second as a source of income (46 percent), behind investment earnings (51 percent). Giving was also the second largest source of revenue for social service organizations and civic, social, and fraternal organizations, but here it accounted for only 20 and 21 percent, respectively, behind government support at 51 and 33 percent, respectively. The total amount of giving to the health sector ($13 billion) equaled giving to civic, social, and fraternal organizations ($6.3 billion) and arts and cultural organizations combined ($6.7 billion). However, this giving to the health sector represented only 4 percent of total health organization revenue.[20]

The value of charitable giving goes well beyond its monetary value, however. Charitable support provides risk capital, developmental funds for investment in institutions' future, and a crucial source of organizational independence from either governmental priorities or the dictates of the market. For example, even in education, where giving in 1997 represented only 13 percent of total revenue, these private funds provided a good source of risk capital for new programs and development.

The role of volunteer effort also varies by subsector. For example, in the religious organization subsector, 71 percent of the full-time-equivalent employment consisted of volunteers in 1997. Likewise, arts and cultural organizations and civic, social, and fraternal organizations relied on volunteer time for more than 50 percent of their total employment needs. Clearly, without the efforts of the volunteer labor force, some nonprofit organizations would have to curtail their activities substantially.[21]

Key Trends in Giving

Measured in absolute terms, individual giving has increased substantially over the last several decades. *Giving USA 2001* reports that giving by individuals grew from $71.86 billion in 1970 to $152.07 billion in 2000 in inflation-adjusted dollars. The growth in giving was particularly robust during the 1990s, increasing at twice the rate of inflation during the second half of the decade, before slowing down with the faltering stock market in 2000.

Behind these encouraging figures, however, lies a more complicated reality. While individual giving has grown in absolute terms, it has declined as a share of national wealth and as a share of the income of the nation's nonprofit organizations, and this has occurred despite a dramatic professionalization of the fundraising field and the emergence of a variety of innovative fundraising techniques. To understand the dynamics of giving and volunteering, therefore, it is necessary to unpack these divergent trends and examine them in turn. In particular, we focus here on six key trends that have characterized individual giving in recent decades.

Decline in Individual Giving as a Share of Income

Perhaps the most significant trend in private giving in recent decades has been the lag in the growth of private giving behind the growth in personal wealth. Put simply, Americans are giving a smaller share of their personal income to charity than they were in the past. Data generated by the AAFRC Trust for Philanthropy, for example, reveal that even after a significant run-up of giving during the heyday of the late 1990s, individual giving as a share of personal income stood at only 1.8 percent, compared to 2 percent in 1969.[22] A new historical data series on the nonprofit sector to be published in the millennial edition of *Historical Statistics of the United States* reveals, in fact, a steady decline in the share of personal income going to charitable giving since the 1960s. According to this series, individual giving as a percentage of personal disposable income rose from 1.3 percent in 1929 to a high of 2.7 percent in 1963, before declining steadily to reach 1.8 percent in 1996.[23] In 1990, the average American donor was giving half of what the average American gave in the 1920s.[24]

Reflecting this, the share that charitable giving represents of the total income of nonprofit organizations has also been in decline. According to one estimate, private contributions as a share of all funds received by charitable and social welfare organizations declined from 37 percent in 1943 to 18 percent in 1992. More recent data paint a similar picture. As shown in figure 12-2, whether we focus on the entire sector or on the service portion excluding religious congregations, the overall picture is the same: giving declined as a share of nonprofit income even between 1987 and 1997, a period during which government support was also constrained. While volunteer effort mitigated some of this effect, it did so only in part.

What many find especially troubling about these data is that the drop in generosity seems to have been greatest among the most affluent, who benefited most from the economic boom of the 1980s and 1990s and from the tax policies enacted during this period. Statistics provided in the millennial edition reveal that during the great depression, wealthy individuals gave very generously at a time when the average American had little to give. However, during the 1980s, the newly wealthy were not as generous. Among the super rich, defined as taxpayers with incomes of $1 million or more, using an index of 100 for 1980, giving declined to 29 on the index by 1994. In other words, this wealthy group was giving at just more than a quarter of what it gave in 1980, taking into account its increased wealth in constant dollars. At the same time, giving by the middle class, defined as those with between $35,000 and $50,000 in gross income, declined from an index of 100 in 1980 to 91 in 1994. In short, "The group least rewarded (in fact, most burdened) by the new economy and tax

Figure 12-2. *Sources of Revenue in the Nonprofit Sector*
1997 constant dollars

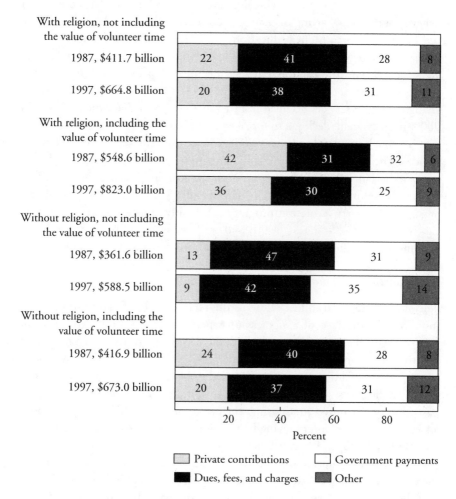

Source: Tables 3.15, 4.2, and 4.4 in prepublication release data from *The New Nonprofit Almanac and Desk Reference* (Washington: Independent Sector, 2001) and author's calculations.

Note: Without religion excludes approximately $8.4 billion of contributions for religious organizations donated to other nonprofit organizations.

structure of the 1980s seems to have been the one carrying the post-1970 version of the voluntary benevolent society."[25] In an era of new wealth, where the number of households with net worth of $1 million or more (exclusive of primary residence) has grown from 3.5 million in 1994 to an estimated 8.3 million in 2000, what is surprising is not that giving has grown in absolute terms, but that the increases have not been more substantial.[26]

Decline in Share of Benevolent Giving

A second notable trend in individual giving is the decline that has occurred in benevolent giving, or giving to charitable causes that serve people in need. Since the 1970s, giving to higher education, the arts, and private foundations has increased as a percentage of total individual giving, while giving to human services, health, and international aid has declined. For example, total private giving to the arts increased from 3 percent in 1965 to 7 percent in 1995, while giving to human services declined from 14 to 8 percent in the same period.[27] In 2000, the arts' share declined to 6 percent, and human services captured 9 percent, although it is hard to have confidence that this represents a reversal of the trend.[28] The watershed for the change in patterns of giving by type of charity seems to have occurred in the 1970s, when the economy stagnated and the federal government increased social welfare spending to individuals in need and engaged in poverty reduction programs. Arguably, once government significantly entered the arena of health and welfare, shifts occurred in both the amount of individual giving and the distribution of giving by type of charity.[29]

The Growth of a Fundraising Profession

The shift in the focus and decline in the relative scale of giving took place, moreover, in the face of a significant expansion and professionalization of fundraising in the United States. Indeed, the decline might have been far greater had these developments not taken place. Until the beginning of the twentieth century, new philanthropic ventures tended to be funded by a small number of wealthy individuals who gave in response to appeals.[30] However, throughout the past century, organized fundraising, the evolution of a fundraising profession, and the democratization of giving by individuals have changed the face of individual philanthropy. As Scott Cutlip argues, "The modern fundraising campaign, carefully organized, shrewdly promoted, and aimed at broad segments of the citizenry, has made American philanthropy a people's philanthropy."[31]

When Arnaud Marts assessed the growth of charitable giving in 1952, he observed that in 1900 total gifts to charitable causes amounted to $500 million. By 1952, that figure was well over $4 billion, which "was all out of proportion to the increase in population and wealth."[32] Marts attributed this tremendous growth in charitable giving to the creation of a new way to persuade people to give, the modern fundraising campaign.[33] As the country became more urbanized, philanthropic fundraising adopted the new methods of organization that had emerged during the two world wars.

In 1905, Lyman Pierce and Charles S. Ward, both secretaries of the YMCA, initiated the first modern fundraising campaigns. Working in different cities, both men came up with creative ways to raise money. Lyman Pierce established the first membership campaign, while Charles S. Ward convinced his directors to close down the YMCA in Grand Rapids for a month so that he could raise enough money through solicitations to run the organization for a year. Building on their efforts, the mass campaign for small donations came into widespread use, democratizing philanthropy. Pioneers in this area include the National Christmas Seals' tuberculosis appeal and the March of Dimes' campaigns to eliminate polio. Another factor was the establishment of Community Chests, later the United Way, which set the stage for organized federated giving using payroll deductions.[34]

As fundraising appeals became more organized, so did the individuals conducting these appeals. A new fundraising profession emerged as colleges and universities, hospitals, and churches appointed staff focused solely on the task of fundraising. Recognizing that fundraising had evolved into a legitimate profession, the American Association of Fund Raising Counsel (AAFRC) was formed in 1935, leading the development of professional standards for fundraisers.[35] Since then, several other organizations have been established to promote excellence and accountability in fundraising practices: the Association of Fundraising Professionals (1960), previously the National Society of Fund Raising Executives; the Association for Healthcare Philanthropy (1967), previously the Association for Hospital Development; the Council for the Advancement and Support of Education (1974); and, most recently, the National Committee for Planned Giving (1988).

Although no firm data are available to confirm the rate at which the fundraising profession is growing, several fundraising associations have reported a growing membership base. In 1997, AAFRC listed twenty-six members, the Council for the Advancement and Support of Education reported having members from 2,800 institutions of education, and the Association for Healthcare Philanthropy served 2,500 members from hospitals and health care associations.[36] Founded in 1960, the Association of Fundraising Professionals (AFP) started keeping membership records in 1979 and reported 1,899 members at that time. Today, AFP serves more than 20,000 members in 154 chapters, with most members working on behalf of education, health, or social service organizations.[37] With the growth of wealth in the 1980s and the desire to increase giving among affluent Americans, the National Committee on Planned Giving was founded in 1988. By 2000, it included 11,000 members from nonprofit and for-profit organizations and firms. A 1998 profile of its members indicates that most members work for charitable organizations (76 percent), while the rest (24 percent) work for a variety of for-profit firms. Survey results also suggest that planned giving fundraisers, on average, have worked in the area of planned gifts for six years.[38]

Overall, Margaret Duronio and Eugene Tempel estimate that there were 25,000 fundraisers affiliated with major fundraising organizations and roughly 25,000 others who were not part of fundraising associations in 1997.[39] This estimate may be conservative, since members of religious organizations are not typically represented in fundraising associations. While membership may be increasing, diversity in the field of fundraising has yet to keep pace. The National Society of Fundraising Executives' 1999 survey found that more than 60 percent of fundraisers were female, up from 57 percent in 1995, and that minorities were poorly represented, at roughly 5 percent. This survey also found that, although 90 percent of the respondents held a college degree and more than 40 percent had a master's degree or higher, only 23 percent were professionally certified as fundraisers.[40] The National Committee on Planned Giving's recent survey also suggests that the field has not become fully "professionalized." While many respondents indicated that they had received short-term training in the field, only 25 percent of those working in charitable organizations reported any formal academic course work. This figure is slightly lower than the 36 percent of planned giving fundraisers working in for-profit organizations who reported such formal academic training.[41]

The growth of the fundraising profession in recent decades helped to expand giving beyond the wealthy to the population more broadly. Although this was not sufficient to keep giving growing on a par with personal income, it seems likely that without it private giving as a percentage of personal income would have been even less than it was. The proliferation of fundraising appeals through the mail, telemarketing, telethons, payroll deduction, and special events helped to make individual giving a national habit among typical Americans who previously might have given solely to their religious organizations.

That the expansion of the fundraising profession has contributed to the democratization of giving is due in important measure to the role that "being asked" seems to play in charitable giving. The Independent Sector national surveys on giving and volunteering consistently indicate that being asked is by far the greatest determinant of giving or volunteering behavior. Simply put, adults are most likely to give when asked. In 1999, 65 percent of respondents reported that they or members of their household were asked to give in the last year, and 81 percent actually contributed. Among the 33 percent who were not asked, only half reported contributions.[42]

Asking also is a particularly effective way to engage members of minority or ethnic groups, the youth and the elderly, single people from low-income households, and persons who are not employed. An independent analysis of the 1998 Independent Sector survey data indicates that blacks and Hispanics are more than twice as likely to give if they are asked than if they are not asked. Survey findings also reveal that certain populations, such as young people, older adults, those in lower-income households, and people from minority or ethnic groups, are not asked at the same rate as whites. These findings also suggest that, as income increases, so does the likelihood that households or individuals are asked to give.[43]

After asking, membership has the most powerful effect on participation in giving. Association with others provides incentives to support a variety of causes. In 1999, more than 80 percent of survey respondents reported that they were members of a religious or secular organization. Of these, 77 percent reported household contributions compared with 40 percent among the 20 percent who reported no membership in any organization. In other words, members were twice as likely to give as nonmembers.[44] This finding gives special meaning to the recent concerns about a decline in organizational membership raised in the work of Robert Putnam.[45] To the extent that civic participation is declining in America, giving could also be at risk. The expansion of fundraising efforts, and hence of asking, may have offset these effects, but the underlying trend in participation may pose a problem in the future.

For now, however, the data on household giving and the pervasiveness of giving in the American population seem contrary to the "bowling alone" thesis that describes a decline in civic engagement in America. Most survey data suggest that this century has generated a tremendous increase in participation in giving, although there does seem to be a decline in generosity, particularly among wealthy individuals. The outpouring of giving that emerged after September 11 bears witness to the depth of American generosity during times of crisis and reveals the ingrained nature of the American habit of giving.

The Proliferation of New Vehicles for Giving

Also important has been the creation and popularization over the past twenty years of a variety of new vehicles for giving that serve affluent families and newly affluent young adults. These vehicles provide tax deductions during the donor's lifetime and estate exclusions on gifts at death, permitting families to engage in estate planning and avoid, or reduce, tax obligations on their estates. The largest class of planned giving instruments are called "split income" or "charitable remainder trusts." There are three major types:

—The pooled-income fund, which is created and maintained by a charitable organization or mutual fund and pays a lifetime income to as many as two beneficiaries while the remaining interest goes to charity.

—The charitable lead trust, which pays a fixed amount to a charity for a period of time, after which the remainder goes to a beneficiary.

—The two types of charitable remainder trust: the charitable remainder unitrust and the charitable remainder annuity trust. Each of these trusts pays the donor a fixed amount annually that is either a percentage share of the market value of the net assets placed in the trust (the charitable remainder trust) or a fixed amount of the net assets valued annually (the unitrust). In both cases, the remainder goes to charity and cannot be less than 10 percent of the value of the assets initially paid into the trust.

According to the IRS, 85,060 charitable remainder trust returns were filed in 1998, with a value of $64.3 billion. These trusts earned $11.1 billion in income, of which $5.1 billion was distributed to noncharitable beneficiaries, and the remaining $6 billion was added to the value of the trusts.[46] These various vehicles thus allow donors to provide for charity either currently or at death, while retaining income from the assets they have contributed. As these trust funds grow, they could provide a sizable addition of funds to charitable organizations.

In addition to the charitable remainder trusts, significant growth has also occurred in two other planned giving instruments: private foundations and donor-advised funds. Individual giving to foundations has grown sevenfold, from $4.25 billion in 1978 to $29.73 billion in 1999, after adjusting for inflation.[47] The growth in giving to private foundations in the last decade suggests that the foundation as an instrument of individual giving is growing in popularity. Gifts to community foundations increased even faster than gifts to private foundations, up 125 percent between 1995 and 1999, from $13.3 billion to $29.9 billion. Notably, much of this growth occurred in the newest vehicle for giving, the donor-advised fund, which gives donors the opportunity to designate the uses to be made of assets they contribute to a foundation.[48]

The popularity of donor-advised funds has, in fact, attracted a number of for-profit mutual funds into the charitable field. In 1992, for example, Fidelity Investments, a for-profit investment management firm, launched a donor-advised fund with 160 accounts. Initial gifts to the fund started at $10,000. By the end of its 1998–99 fiscal year, Fidelity had 16,458 accounts with assets worth $1.7 billion. The Fidelity Charitable Gift Fund, a 501(c)(3), has given more than 263,000 grants worth over $1 billion. According to Fidelity, nearly four out of five gifts given in 1998–99 were from appreciated assets. Along with its donor-advised fund, Fidelity offers a pooled-income fund, which provides payments from fund income for up to two beneficiaries and then distributes the remaining assets to as many as ten charities after the death of the last beneficiary. The number of pooled income accounts grew from 137 with $10.2 million in assets in 1993 to 467 with nearly $48 million in assets in 1998.[49] The $578.6 million that Fidelity's Charitable Gift Fund distributed in fiscal 1999–2000 earned Fidelity a spot among the top ten charities in both the Chronicle of Philanthropy 400 and the Nonprofit Times 100.[50] The distribution of Fidelity's charitable grants was also promising, with 34 percent going to community and human services, 25 percent to religion, 28 percent to education, 7 percent to arts and culture, 5 percent to health research, and 1 percent to the environment. In 2000, Fidelity announced that its Charitable Gift Fund had opened two more programs with on-line account access, one for corporate giving and the other for corporate executives. In other words, Fidelity is offering financial services to corporate giving programs or foundations.[51]

Not to be outdone, Vanguard, another mutual fund, started its Charitable Endowment Program in 1997. Initial gifts to the program must be at least $25,000. After a little more than two years in operation, the program grew from 550 donors giving $59.8 million and total assets of $72.2 million in fiscal 1999 to 1,258 donors giving $114.4 million in contributions and total assets of $171.4 million in 2000. In fiscal 2000, Vanguard's Endowment, a 501(c)(3) charity, gave 3,653 grants totaling nearly $20 million. The bulk of the grant dollars (75 percent) were given to human services organizations, schools, and religious institutions in fairly equal proportions. Another 16 percent went to arts and culture, and the rest went to civic organizations and environmental and wildlife organizations.[52]

The incursion of large financial firms into the area of charitable giving has increased giving and created a professional financial alternative for young affluent givers. Increasingly, corporations and community foundations are also working with such institutions for their own giving programs.[53] Thus, for example, more than 200 community foundations have entered into an agreement with Merrill Lynch to steer donors to community foundations. Foundations secure the gifts, and the firm manages the assets and earns interest. Other banks and major financial institutions are entering this arena as well, including the Bank of New York, Comerica Bank in Detroit, the Pitcairn Trust Company in Pennsylvania, Legg Mason in Baltimore, and Credit Suisse Asset Management in New York. Moreover, financial advisers are using these financial service companies and getting fees for finding customers or managing funds. Fidelity even opened the Advisor Charitable Gift Fund for donors who use financial advisers.

A major concern regarding this type of advised fund is where the money goes: what percentage is spent on adviser fees and what percentage actually results in charitable contributions. What is clear is that the lines are blurred between nonprofit fundraisers in charities and those working as advisers, investors, or employees in financial services corporations. The competition is growing between the two sectors, and charities and community foundations are working to find ways to serve their clients and to improve their financial services.[54] In an increasingly complex financial environment, smaller charities, which may not be able to invest in a planned giving officer, might find ways to increase their giving through engaging such firms. These firms also provide the donor with experienced financial advice that smaller charitable organizations and community foundations cannot afford.

Changes in Tax Policy

If the professionalization of fundraising and the emergence of new techniques of giving have generally had a positive influence on charitable giving, recent changes in tax policy have likely worked in the opposite direction. To be sure, tax policy is only one of many factors that affect giving levels, but it can have an effect by determining the "price" of giving. As a general rule, the higher are the tax rates, the lower is the out-of-pocket "price" of any charitable gift since the taxpayer would have to pay a portion of any forgone gift to the government as taxes. For example, if a taxpayer faces a tax rate of 50 percent, the cost of giving a dollar to charity is really fifty cents, since the taxpayer would have to pay taxes of 50 cents on that dollar if she did not give it to charity. If the tax rate is 70 percent, however, the cost of giving that same dollar to charity would be only 30 cents, since the taxpayer would have to pay 70 cents in taxes if she kept the dollar.

Beginning with the Reagan tax cuts of 1981, Congress has generally acted over the past two decades to lower income tax rates, capital gains tax rates, and estate tax rates. In the estate tax area, for example, (1) the amount of estate giving subject to taxation dropped from 70 to 55 percent, (2) the exemption level was raised to $600,000 for a single person and to $1.2 million for a married couple (which is gradually being increased to $2 million over the next several years as an offset to inflation), and (3) full estates may now be passed on to the living spouse. These changes are estimated to reduce the incentive to give at death by increasing the cost of such giving.[55] Perhaps reflecting this, according to IRS data, the proportion of decedents filing estate tax returns who gave a charitable bequest fell from 19 percent in 1989 to 17 percent in 1998, and the average size of the charitable bequests declined from 10 percent of the total value of the estate in 1989 to 6 percent in 1998.[56] More generally, the changes in tax policy over the past twenty years may help to explain why the percentage of income given by very wealthy individuals has dropped despite the growth of the economy and of personal wealth.

Recent changes in tax law suggest, moreover, that these trends are likely to persist. In May 2001, at the behest of newly elected President Bush, Congress passed and the president signed into law a new tax law that reduces the top tax rates for individuals from 39 to 33 percent. This law also gradually eliminates the estate tax in 2010, although it would be reinstated in 2011 unless there is renewal legislation. Taken together, these changes seem likely to reduce the incentives to give among the wealthy even further. Experts recently estimated that the elimination of the estate tax alone could decrease bequest giving to charities by 12 percent a year and significantly reduce the incentives to create charitable remainder trusts.[57]

Although the overall thrust of recent tax policy has been to lower tax rates and increase the cost of giving, several pro-giving tax changes have been discussed, but not yet passed. One of these is a provision that would allow households that do not itemize their deductions, and therefore receive no tax incentive to give, to claim a deduction for charitable contributions. Former president Clinton advocated such a deduction to start at 50 percent of charitable contributions over $1,000, and the Bush administration has indicated its support for a similar measure, although no action has been taken as of this writing. Pricewa-terhouseCoopers has estimated that such a provision, if enacted without a floor, would increase giving by nearly $15 billion if the law were in effect in 2000 and would lead to an increase of nearly 12 million new donors, most of them among low- and lower-middle-income taxpayers.[58]

A second proposal now under consideration would allow individuals to give direct gifts to charity out of their retirement accounts without incurring tax lia-bilities on the increased value of the assets. Such a proposal passed the House of Representatives in 2001 but has not passed the Senate.

Growing Inequality of Income

Another factor affecting levels of charitable giving in recent years has been the growing inequality of income in the United States. To be sure, economic growth during the 1990s helped to fuel an expansion of individual giving. Although many Americans have done well in recent years, however, a substan-tial proportion of the society has not benefited from the new economy. Indeed, the gap between rich and poor Americans grew dramatically over the last twenty years and reached new heights during the 1990s. Between 1977 and 1999, the average income of the wealthiest 1 percent of households grew nearly 120 percent, while the bottom 40 percent of households lost income in real terms. Furthermore, the top 1 percent of income earners took home half of all national income, which is more than the collective income of the poorest 100 million people in the United States. While median weekly wages increased slightly over 2 percent in 1997 and 1998, these were the first real increases since the 1970s, and the recession of 2000–01 very likely reversed them. Moreover, in spite of the increase in median wages, wages for females were still below their 1989 level.[59]

This inequality has significant implications for household giving. Indepen-dent Sector national surveys of giving and volunteering show that financial worry is the most prevalent reason individuals cite for *not* giving. In 1998, 67 percent of respondents reported worrying about money, a slight decrease from 74 percent in 1996. Among those individuals who reported having serious financial concerns, 55 percent reported contributing and 43 percent reported volunteering. By contrast, among the 30 percent who did *not* worry about money, 71 percent reported contributing and 54 percent reported volunteering.[60] As in the past, these trends reveal that individuals who have seri-ous economic worries do not participate at the same rate as others.

Key Trends in Volunteering

While giving and volunteering are closely linked today, they do not share a com-mon history. Before the turn of the century, the American populace gave more time than money, since Americans lived in small communities and few Americans were wealthy. Volunteering tended to be informal and community-based; a few individuals would join together to start a fire department, a library, a school, or a local government. Examples of organized volunteering also permeate American history: colonists and then citizens helped to establish local governments, finance the American Revolution, create the abolitionist movement, and serve as caregivers to soldiers in the Civil War on both sides. Volunteering expanded during the progressive era and the two world wars.[61] After further proliferation during the civil rights era and the peace movements of the 1960s, the rate of volunteering declined, particularly among college students, during the 1980s.[62] In the 1990s, the rate of volunteering among young people recovered, and volunteering among adults rose steadily, remaining above 50 percent at the close of the twentieth century.

Several factors contributed to the steady rise in volunteering: (1) the professionalization of volunteer management, (2) efforts to boost volunteering among youth, (3) changes in public policy, particularly in the area of youth service, and (4) other identified motivations for volunteering.

The Professionalization of Volunteer Management

Volunteers have long been able to identify emerging needs and offer solutions to address them, either temporarily or on a long-term basis. Organizations such as the Red Cross and numerous religious organizations have provided the first line of help in emergencies until government could supply significant financial and other logistical assistance. This also has been the case with the major "disease" organizations, such as the March of Dimes and the American Lung, Cancer, and Heart Associations founded earlier in the century by volunteers and the food kitchens and homeless shelters founded in more recent decades. Voluntary action has always been available to address public needs; however, as the country grew larger and the problems more complex and demanding, it became necessary to supplement the involvement of volunteers and informal action with the involvement of paid professionals and formal institutions.

Although many institutions created by volunteers are now managed and staffed by paid professionals, they still depend on volunteer service and volunteer leadership. For example, while hospitals and schools now rely predominately on paid staff, these institutions also depend on volunteers serving in various capacities, from candy stripers and tutors to board members and trustees. The professionalization of public services does not, therefore, necessarily lead to the replacement of community volunteers. In some fields, such as fire fighting, volunteers remain a dominant presence. In others, they work in tandem with paid professional staff.[63] From helping individuals with AIDS to preserving the local environment, citizens continue to band together voluntarily to improve the quality of life in their communities.

Just as the management of nonprofit organizations became more professional during the twentieth century, so did the management of volunteer recruitment. To accommodate the rapid growth in voluntary services provided for the mentally ill during the 1940s, the American Association of Volunteer Services Coordinators was founded. This organization became the Association for Volunteer Administration (AVA) in 1979 and boasted 1,800 members in 1999. AVA offers a competency-based credentialing program for volunteers and volunteer managers, organizes an annual conference, and collaborates with university programs providing such programs. In the 1940s, local volunteer bureaus also emerged to help organize volunteers. In 1951 these bureaus formed the Association of Volunteer Bureaus, which later became VOLUNTEER, the National Center, in 1981.[64] More recently, the Points of Light Foundation, founded in 1990 during the first Bush administration, incorporated VOLUNTEER's network of 500 volunteer centers into its programs. The Points of Light Foundation offers a range of services to these volunteer centers in cities and communities across the country, including technical assistance, training and consulting, a range of publications, and leadership training.[65] Other training is offered under government-sponsored programs for volunteers, including VISTA, the Peace Corps, the Senior Service Corps, and AmeriCorps. Large voluntary organizations like the Girl Scouts of the USA, the American Red Cross, and the Salvation Army, which depend on volunteers for their workforce, have had major training programs for their volunteers for a long time. The attention to volunteer training and management has led to an increase in volunteers and volunteer retention over the past decades as well as a growing recognition by nonprofit organizations that volunteer programs need managers and opportunities for professional development.

Efforts to Boost Volunteering among Youth

In light of declining volunteer rates among college students during the 1980s, policymakers and education advocates initiated several programs to stimulate and encourage youth volunteerism and civic engagement. Organizations like City Year and Teach for America advanced the cause of youth service, focusing attention on youth at greatest risk. Umbrella organizations like Youth Service America worked with major youth development organizations like the Boy Scouts, Girl Scouts, and Boys and Girls Inc., and partnered with Campus Compact, a coalition of university presidents, and the student-led Campus Outreach Opportunity League (COOL) to increase community service among young people and encourage schools to include community service as part of the education experience. As evidence of their success, Campus Compact grew from twenty-five public and private college members in 1985 to 620 members in 2000.[66] COOL also reported significant growth and now is operating in 107 colleges.[67] Combined, these efforts ultimately led to a national service program, as detailed below.

Public Policy Changes Supportive of Volunteering and Their Effects

Arguably, more progress has been made to broaden the base of volunteers than to broaden the base of donors in the United States. In part, this can be explained by the strong public policy emphasis on volunteering as a way to solve community problems for the past two decades. Each president since Jimmy Carter has focused on the importance of volunteering. George H. W. Bush supported the founding of the Points of Light Foundation in May of 1990. Working through a network of 500 volunteer centers, every day the Points of Light Foundation recognizes one volunteer as a "point of light" for his or her community. President Clinton followed with AmeriCorps in 1993 and legislation for the Corporation for National Service. In 1997, the Points of Light Foundation and the Corporation for National Service launched the President's Summit on Volunteering. Bearing witness to the history of a national commitment to volunteering, all living presidents either attended or, in the case of President Reagan, were represented at the summit.

The AmeriCorps program provides an excellent example of how public policy can increase volunteering. In 1993, the National Community Service Trust Act established AmeriCorps by merging Volunteers in Service to America (VISTA) and the National Community Service Corps. In that same year, Congress enacted legislation with broad bipartisan support to establish the Corporation for National Service (CNS). CNS serves as the umbrella organization that manages AmeriCorps, VISTA, and other programs related to community service. Other volunteer programs also managed through CNS include the National Senior Service Corps, the Retired and Senior Volunteer Program, and the Foster Grandparents Program. AmeriCorps embodies the ideal that those who provide community service empower themselves. AmeriCorps envisions that "service will become a common expectation and experience as [an] integral part of civic responsibility."[68] Attempting to kill many birds with one stone, AmeriCorps seeks to meet community needs through public service, to engage low-income young people in service, and to provide incentives for youth to continue their education. Similar to Peace Corps volunteers, AmeriCorps volunteers receive a stipend for one or two years of service and a scholarship for education beyond their service. In 1998–99, the Corporation for National Service reported that 33,854 young people were actively serving through 593 grants awarded to state and national grantees and that well over 100,000 young people had served in AmeriCorps since its inception.[69]

To date, independent evaluations suggest that AmeriCorps has been successful. Aguirre International's 1997 and 1999 evaluations found that communities were able to leverage additional time and money from enlisting the service of AmeriCorps volunteers: eight volunteers and a return of $1.66 per dollar of investment were generated in communities for each AmeriCorps volunteer. The breadth of services provided by AmeriCorps volunteers also confirms the program's success. In 1997–98, volunteers taught nearly half a million students in primary and secondary school, recruited or trained 41,000 peer tutors, administered prenatal screening and health services to half a million people, and distributed health information to nearly 1.6 million. Volunteers also provided shelter for the homeless, planted trees, repaired community buildings, and trained students in conflict mediation and violence avoidance activities. Interviews in twelve communities found overwhelming majorities confirming the need for AmeriCorps services.[70]

The program also has been successful in attracting volunteers who themselves can benefit from the program. While 51 percent were white, 27 percent were black/African American, nearly 15 percent were Hispanic, and 8 percent were Asian/Native Hawaiian or Pacific Islander, American Indian or Alaskan Native, or other. The vast majority (65 percent) had not completed even community college. Additionally, an overwhelming 78 percent had income below $20,000. To date, AmeriCorps has provided 102,000 volunteers with educational awards. While the number of AmeriCorps volunteers is small compared to the estimated number of unpaid volunteers nationwide, the AmeriCorps program has significantly reinforced the importance of community service among young people nationwide.[71] By the end of 2000, President Clinton's AmeriCorps, which sustained significant criticism from the Contract with America's 104th Congress, had secured bipartisan support for its continuation.

Volunteer effort has been encouraged as well by private sector actors. IBM, AT&T, and Timberland are some of the more visible companies involved in promoting volunteerism and youth service. While IBM and AT&T established traditional corporate volunteering programs, Timberland entered into an innovative, broad-based partnership with Boston-based nonprofit City Year. In addition to providing substantial financial support, Timberland is the official uniform outfitter for the City Year corps and Timberland chief executive officer Jeff Schwarz sits on City Year's board of trustees. According to the Timberland website, "The City Year/Timberland partnership is in every way a relationship—a relationship between two like-minded organizations wanting to create lasting change in the views of people and in the landscape of the urban environment."[72]

Recent studies suggest that these public and private efforts to encourage volunteering have had a positive impact. The Cooperative Institutional Research Program at the University of California, Los Angeles reported, for example, that 75 percent of freshmen entering college in 1999 reported volunteering.[73] This is up considerably from 1989, when 62 percent of entering freshmen reported volunteering.[74] In 1996, the Independent Sector teen volunteering survey found that 59 percent of young people between twelve and seventeen years of age volunteered an average of 3.5 hours a week. This translates into 2.4 billion hours of effort, the equivalent of nearly 1.1 million full-time employees.[75]

In that same year, the National Education Household Survey (NEHS) reported high participation among young people in student service in grades six through twelve. Although the NEHS survey asked about volunteering over a shorter period of time (three months) than the Independent Sector survey did, nearly half of the respondents reported engaging in some form of community service. In both surveys, large numbers of students indicated that their schools encouraged such service.[76] Among students who attended schools that encouraged community service, 71 percent volunteered, compared with 44 percent who volunteered in schools where there was no encouragement. Although only 37 percent of students reported taking a course requiring community service, those taking a civics or service learning course were more likely than those who did not take such a course to be aware of human-service programs in their community (36 versus 25 percent), to know how to solve community problems (32 versus 19 percent), and to understand how government works (27 versus 19 percent).[77]

A 1999 survey by the National Center for Education Statistics (NCES) showed, moreover, the substantial extent of service learning in public elementary and secondary schools. According to this survey, over 64 percent of all public schools reported students participating in community service, although the percentages were higher in high schools (83 percent) than in middle schools (77 percent) or elementary schools (55 percent). Service learning activities were also extensive, with 32 percent of public schools offering such instruction. However, the data also show that schools with more than 50 percent of their students on free or reduced-price school lunches were somewhat less likely than schools with fewer poor children to have students participating in community service (50 versus 67 percent). Schools with more than 50 percent minority enrollment also were less likely than schools with fewer minority students to have students participating in community service (67 versus 72 percent). Although data on community service in schools have not been collected regularly, this survey does point to a significant increase in schools involving students in community service activities. In 1984, 27 percent of high schools reported offering community service curriculum compared with 83 percent in 1999.[78]

Impressive though the record of increased community service involvement on the part of young people is, it does not seem to have translated into greater civic awareness or civic interest. The National Assessment of Educational Progress recently has found, for example, that students tested in grades four, eight, and twelve did not show great proficiency in civic knowledge, although the students in grade twelve who reported that they volunteered scored higher than those who did not volunteer. But so did those who worked for pay between five and fifteen hours per week.[79] Similarly, although volunteering increased throughout the 1990s among children in elementary and high school, the Cooperative Institutional Research Program's survey of entering college freshmen showed a continuing disconnect between young people and government. Only 16 percent of entering freshman reported frequently discussing politics in 1996, the lowest level ever recorded in an election year. The percentage of students who reported ever having voted in a student election dropped from nearly 32 percent in 1992 to 23 percent in 1996.[80] The Fall 1999 survey results indicate that, while 75 percent of freshmen performed volunteer work, students' long-term goals for social activism were declining. In 1999, incoming freshman were less interested in becoming community leaders or participating in community action programs than previous cohorts. The latter measure hit a ten-year low of 21 percent of respondents.[81] Evidently, the growth in volunteering has not been sufficient to offset other factors encouraging civic disengagement. This may explain why some analysts argue that we are in the midst of a civic decline,[82] while others contend that the growth in volunteering among young people may signal the emergence of a new civic generation and a new progressive era in the early decades of the twenty-first century.[83] Combined, this evidence underscores the importance of understanding why young people become involved in their community and what factors contribute to lifelong civic participation.

Motivations for Volunteering

The professionalization of volunteer management and the growth of publicly encouraged efforts to promote volunteerism are important in view of research findings on the factors that contribute to volunteering. The most powerful determinant of volunteering for both adults and youth is being asked. Among young people who were asked to volunteer, 93 percent became involved, whereas only 24 percent of those *not* asked actually volunteered.[84]

After being asked, membership in an organization is another important factor in motivating volunteering. More than 80 percent of respondents in the 1999 survey were members of a religious or secular organization. Of these, 63 percent reported volunteering, well above the 24 percent volunteering rate among people who reported not belonging to any organization.[85] These findings apply across racial and ethnic groups, although among blacks church membership in particular is most closely associated with volunteering. This finding is especially important in light of recent research showing a general decline in civic participation among Americans.

Youth participation is another important factor influencing adult volunteering. Independent Sector surveys consistently find that adults who reported belonging to a youth group, being active in church volunteering, or participating in student government regularly show a much higher level of volunteering as adults than those who did not have these experiences as children.

Furthermore, certain personal motivations are also associated with volunteering. Respondents volunteer at much higher rates if they feel they have the power to improve the welfare of others, they feel compassion and want to help people in need, and they believe that by giving or volunteering they can improve the moral basis of society. In a recent analysis of these attitudes, Eleanor Brown finds that volunteering can, in turn, affect these attitudes: individuals who volunteer turn out to be more trusting of others.[86]

In sum, research over the past decade has indicated that membership in religious and secular organizations, regular attendance at church, socializing with friends, volunteering during youth, and most important, simply being asked to participate are the most important factors contributing to volunteering. Although participation also increases with household income and education, being asked may mitigate the power of these characteristics. One possible theoretical explanation for these accumulated findings might be that active participation over a life cycle and particularly when young encourages a lifetime of engagement.

The Future of Giving and Volunteering

The future prospects for increased participation in giving and volunteering are bright in the long term, but not so bright in the short term. This prediction is based largely on an analysis of the following major forces that will shape giving and volunteering in the decades ahead: (1) the 2000–01 recession, (2) the growing inequality in income distribution, (3) changes in tax policy, (4) the proliferation of new vehicles and approaches for philanthropy, (5) the changing demography of the population, and (6) the potential of a new civic generation.

The Changing Economy

The recession that struck the American economy in the first year of the new millennium seems likely to be even more prolonged than the one in the early 1980s. Unemployment, which could rise to 7 percent, will disproportionately affect lower-income workers, who tend not to have employee benefits. Those workers who have exceeded the five-year limit for welfare benefits will have nowhere to go, and demands on charities may exceed their ability to provide services in an era of declining federal and state government support. The U.S. recession comes at a time when the world economic growth rate has declined to its lowest rate in over three decades, suggesting that this recession may be deeper than originally predicted. Before September 11, the Nasdaq had lost 75 percent of its value since it peaked in spring 2000, and the Dow Jones Industrial Average had declined 30 percent. After a precipitous drop in the stock market following September 11 and the loss of 415,000 jobs in the following month, the stock market rebounded somewhat, but economists remain uncertain about how long the recession will last. With world economic growth highly uncertain, the short-term economic future looks troubling.[87]

Although individuals do not stop giving during economic hard times unless they become unemployed, findings from the Independent Sector survey covering the recession in the early 1990s reveal that individuals gave less during that period.[88] Since a great deal of wealth has been lost in the past year, we can expect giving by the wealthy to decline. In the short term, while people will not stop giving, we can expect a lower or negative real growth rate in individual giving over the next few years. Already there is evidence that many donors who contributed generously to the various funds set up after September 11 substituted these contributions for their regular charitable donations, leaving many charities in need of money.[89] According to one recent survey, 29 percent of respondents with income below $15,000 and 23 percent of those with income between $15,000 and $30,000 reported that they would not have much more to give to other charities this year. Nearly half of all respondents reported that the downturn in the economy would cause them to stop their charitable giving altogether (9 percent), greatly reduce their giving (11 percent), or somewhat reduce their giving (28 percent).[90] Since foundations have also suffered losses in their investment portfolios, moreover, we can expect that the amount of payout from foundations and gifts to foundations will decline in the near term as well. Although individual giving seems likely to grow again when the economy resumes its growth, in the meantime giving seems likely to lag.

Growing Income Inequality

With the growth of the new economy in the 1980s and 1990s, a small percentage of Americans made extraordinary gains in personal wealth. These gains were aided by reduced rates of income and capital gains taxes. The 2001 Tax Act, which lowered tax rates and eliminated the estate tax, will only serve to increase the gap between the rich and poor in American society. While lower-income workers began to see higher income in the late 1990s, the current decline in the economy will offset these gains. On the one hand, the after-tax income of the top 1 percent of Americans has increased 157 percent since 1979. This group will get 52 percent of the new tax cuts. On the other hand, the after-tax income of the poorest fifth of Americans has increased less than 1 percent over this same period. This group will get 2 percent of the new tax cut. The middle fifth of Americans have seen an increase of 10 percent in their after-tax income since 1979 and will share 4 percent of the new tax cut.[91] Should the economy continue to decline and the rate of unemployment continue to increase, declines in both giving and volunteering seem likely, as previous surveys have shown.[92]

Growing income inequality also affects the ability of many Americans to solve community problems. In a recent survey by the Pew Partnership for Civic Change, 75 percent of Americans felt connected to their communities, but admitted that the largest problems that their communities faced were lack of living-wage jobs (42 percent) and lack of affordable health care (39 percent).

Furthermore, many organizations that seek donations and volunteers seek out higher-income families.[93] Increasing income inequality thus could slowly erode the last century's efforts to democratize giving and volunteering, as fewer and fewer families are asked, further isolating the nation's poorest citizens and weakening American civil society.

Understandably, people with limited income have a limited capacity to give. This capacity to give did not increase for a majority of Americans during the 1990s and will be diminished further by a declining economy and current tax policy favoring the wealthy.

Changes in Tax Policy and the Capacity to Give

In addition to exacerbating the growing divide between the rich and poor, recent and proposed changes in tax policy, coupled with the crash of the stock market in 2001, promise to depress giving by the wealthy further at a time when they have the greatest capacity to give. Recent estimates by Newtithing Group indicate that during the 1990s wealthy individuals gave far below their capacity, in spite of large gains in after-tax income. Based on calculations of annual surplus income after expenses and the net worth of assets, the Newtithing Group estimates that taxpayers with income of $100,000 or above could have given over $170 billion more than the $152 billion in total individual giving actually recorded without negatively affecting the value of their assets.[94] These estimates suggest that, while the middle class continues to give at capacity, wealthy individuals are not motivated to do likewise, and this was true even before the further reductions in tax rates and elimination of estate taxes enacted in 2001. Much more, therefore, needs to be done by the fundraising profession to increase giving among this group.

The Potential of the Intergenerational Transfer of Wealth

Before the 2001 Tax Act, estimates of the potential for increased charitable bequests at death were quite favorable. John Havens and Paul Schervish estimate that the transfer of wealth over the next half century from 1998 to 2052 could total anywhere from $41 trillion to $136 trillion.[95] Furthermore, they assert that 15 percent of the $41 trillion, or $6 trillion, could be bequeathed to charity. If this transfer occurred, it would double or triple the current percentage of estate funds contributed to charity. Eleanor Brown also estimates that there could be an additional increase in bequest giving from the baby boom generation. Furthermore, she contends that since philanthropy increases with level of education and each generation since 1900 has attained a higher level of education, such bequests could increase in future generations.[96]

Although the potential is there, the 2001 Tax Act, which would phase out taxation of estates, makes it increasingly unlikely. This is the lesson emerging from an earlier reduction of estate taxation in the 1980s. Following this reduction, while bequest giving increased in absolute terms, reflecting the substantial growth in income, it declined as a percentage of total estate value. To realize the potential that the growing intergenerational transfer of wealth has created, it will be necessary to build a stronger culture of philanthropy among wealthy individuals.

New Approaches and Vehicles for Philanthropy

With the growth of new wealth, primarily from the new high-tech economy, new ways of giving have emerged, from venture philanthropy to e-philanthropy. These trends reflect the desire of new donors to exercise more control over their contributions and to become more involved with the beneficiary organizations. The newest form of giving is called venture philanthropy, where donors build venture funds similar to venture capital funds, but use them to invest in nonprofit organizations. Among the most notable examples are Social Venture Partners, founded by Paul Brainerd in Seattle, Washington; the Marino Institute in Reston, Virginia, founded by Mario Marino; the Roberts Enterprise Development Fund; the Silicon Valley Social Venture Fund; and Social Venture Partners of Arizona. Most of these venture funds are small. The donors, having benefited from the new high-tech economy, are considerably younger than the average philanthropist and focus on measurable outcomes, following a business investment model. Typically, these donors set up portfolios in which individuals can invest or donate funds and then decide together what causes and organizations they will support. Although no figures are available on the size of this type of philanthropy, it is emerging as the model of choice for many new, young philanthropists.[97]

According to a recent study by Community Wealth Ventures, two distinct models of such venture philanthropy have surfaced. One, the social venture fund model, involves investments in traditional nonprofits, but with the expectation of a measurable social return on the investment. The second model involves investments in organizations that generate a financial return to investors in addition to their social return. Community Wealth's study also identified a number of traditional foundations that are engaged in social venture philanthropy as part of their larger portfolio, including the Edna McConnell Clark Foundation, the W. K. Kellogg Foundation, the Milwaukee Foundation, and the Charles Stewart Mott Foundation.[98]

Another major trend spurred by changes in technology is e-philanthropy, or on-line giving. While only 1 percent of respondents reported giving on-line in the 1999 Independent Sector Survey of Giving and Volunteering, several organizations and charities offer opportunities for people to give in this way. The Red Cross has been successful with giving on-line when it calls for emergency funding. Helping.org, now Network for Good, created by the AOL Foundation, has established a portal for on-line giving that is protected against fraud and requires no transaction costs. AOL also offers a similar on-line portal to match volunteers with various causes across the country. Many nonprofits are not yet able to offer these options since they are unable to maintain privacy for their donors and volunteers. However, since September 11, use of the Internet for donations and information has increased exponentially. The Red Cross raised the most money this way, about 10 percent of the $676 million raised for relief efforts ($10 million), perhaps signaling somewhat wider usage in the future.[99] Indeed, it is expected that e-philanthropy will grow in the decade ahead to accommodate the habits of the younger generation of donors. Most likely, this expansion will not occur at the hand of nonprofits directly, but rather through secure portals run by reliable intermediary organizations. As outlined earlier in this chapter, moreover, other new vehicles for giving, such as commercial donor-advised funds and adviser charitable funds, also will continue to change the way Americans give and ultimately increase charitable giving overall.

A New Focus on Civic Education, Community Service, and the Next Civic Generation

In response to the findings of the 1998 National Assessment of Educational Progress that only 25 percent of students were proficient in civics, several efforts have been launched to increase and broaden civic education in the schools. These include a Center for Civic Education campaign to increase the effectiveness of civic education and the formation of a new initiative, the National Alliance for Civic Education, to promote youth civic engagement in a variety of settings, from schools to neighborhoods and voluntary organizations.[100]

Coupled with the attention given to youth volunteering and community service over the past decade, these efforts could lead to a new civic generation. What is more, the proposed Younger Americans Act (HR17 and S1005) and the McCain-Bayh "AmeriCorps" bill could measurably increase youth service in the future. Responding to the September 11 tragedy, the McCain-Bayh bill proposes to increase AmeriCorps participation from 50,000 to 250,000 a year by 2009, so that 1 million young people would serve their country every four years.

The increases in youth and adult volunteering in the 1990s are changing American attitudes about involvement in community. In the four weeks after September 11, 70 percent of adults either gave monetary donations, donated blood, or volunteered.[101] While some analysts attribute this increase simply to this event and indicate that other events in history such as Pearl Harbor led to increased civic activism that did not persist, there is encouraging evidence that the "bowling alone" scare, while perhaps somewhat exaggerated, may have stimulated actions that are already producing a civic revival.[102]

Conclusions: Challenges and Opportunities for Giving and Volunteering

The tremendous technological and economic changes over the past two decades have significantly boosted people's capacity to give in the United States. These changes include the strong growth in the U.S. economy and the new opportunities created by the Internet. The new wealth created by this growth spurred both fundraisers in the traditional nonprofit community and the corporate financial services sector to create a number of new vehicles to encourage people to give more. These included expanded use of donor-advised funds in community foundations, the creation of new private foundations, increased use of planned giving instruments, and the creation of commercial donor-advised and pooled-income funds by mutual fund companies such as Fidelity and Vanguard. The overall results were increases in giving of 7 to 11 percent annually in inflation-adjusted dollars from 1996 to 1999.

With the major declines in the stock market during 2000, however, individual giving only increased 1.5 percent, suggesting that giving is vulnerable to economic circumstances. The subsequent recession in 2001 and 2002 seems likely to depress giving even further. What is more, although the growth in individual giving has been substantial, it could have been far better. Giving by the wealthy could have tripled without affecting the asset position of affluent families. Even with all of the growth in giving, giving as a percentage of personal income remained below 2 percent. In fact, it took the extraordinary efforts and creativity of fundraisers to maintain giving even at this level.

Indeed, a significant challenge lies ahead for fundraisers to maintain giving at this level in the face of continuing declines in individual and estate tax rates and a slowing economy. A more positive public policy to encourage giving is therefore needed. The proposed "above-the-line" charitable deduction for individuals who do not itemize deductions is an example of the form such encouragement could usefully take.

Not only the aggregate amount but also the distribution of giving among households is a cause for some concern. The growing gap between rich and poor Americans, coupled with the new forms of charitable solicitation, threaten to reduce the philanthropic participation of the poor. Lower-income earners often do not have access to personal computers that could link them to on-line charitable websites or provide them with solicitable e-mail addresses. Since being asked is one of the most influential factors in individual giving, the digital divide could affect the proportion of the population asked to contribute, the economic diversity of donors, and the charitable causes supported. In sum, many of these new trends may result in some erosion of the last century's democratization of giving. Thus a major challenge to nonprofits will be to develop mechanisms for retaining involvement of a broad segment of the population.

Participation in giving has become part of the American culture. The tremendous outpouring of generosity from individuals of all incomes after September 11 reveals how important giving is as an act of participation among Americans. Despite some evidence that giving to local charities has declined since the terrorism attacks because individuals sent their donations to the September 11 funds, the challenge facing the nonprofit sector is the recession-bound economy.

If the past is any indication of what to expect in the future, rapid increases in unemployment and uncertainty about the economy will not necessarily lead to fewer individuals making charitable donations, but may result in lower levels of giving. A decline in the amount of individual giving will challenge nonprofit organizations, particularly those that serve people in need, whose demand for services will only increase with the economic downturn.

The nonprofit sector, the corporate sector, and recent public policy changes have helped to shape a public climate supportive of volunteering from preschool through retirement, regardless of level of education or income. These efforts have led to an extraordinary increase in community service offerings by elementary and secondary schools, to the creation of AmeriCorps, and to expanded support for volunteering by corporations and youth organizations. The result has been a substantial increase in the percentage of young people and adults who volunteer.

In fact, a new civic generation seems to be emerging. The overwhelming volunteer response from individuals from all occupations and incomes after September 11 is a testament to the civic spirit of Americans. Organizations still have long waiting lists of volunteers. Reports indicate that volunteers lined up to volunteer over Thanksgiving to help others in need. Since September 11, many Americans are reevaluating their life goals, staying home, and getting involved in their communities. The challenge for society is to maintain this spirit of service by expanding opportunities for young people and others to serve. The work of many organizations over the past decade has demonstrated that Americans have a deep concern about their communities and other people and that they respond with great generosity. This is not a nation that "bowls alone," but rather a nation that pulls together in crisis and remains together for the long haul. The challenge for the future will be to maintain this effort and to provide volunteers with meaningful opportunities.

In conclusion, while individual giving and volunteering will never replace government *of* the people, it can lead to fuller participation *by* the people. Since democracy depends on citizen participation *at all levels*, the positive trends that have led to increased attention to volunteering and community service need to continue in the decade ahead. Similarly, efforts must be made to ensure fuller participation in charitable giving. Now is the time to build on the achievements of the past two decades. American democracy can only be strengthened by such efforts.

Notes

1. Susan J. Ellis and Katherine H. Noyes, *By the People: A History of Americans as Volunteers,* rev. ed. (San Francisco: Jossey-Bass, 1990), p. xii.

2. Scott M. Cutlip, *Fundraising in the United States* (New Brunswick, N.J.: Transaction Publishers, 1990), p. 3.

3. The only available sources of annual data on giving are the IRS summary reports of individual income tax returns, but these reports only include taxpayers who itemize their

deductions (just under 31 percent of taxpayers in 1998). Of this group, 32.6 million, or 27 percent of taxpayers, reported a charitable deduction. The kinds of data reported are from household surveys, estimates of total giving from a variety of sources, and the IRS data for individuals reporting charitable deductions and bequest giving from the 2 percent of Americans who must file estate tax returns. Trends in household data come from the Independent Sector surveys commissioned every two years, and figures on total giving are provided by the AAFRC Trust for Philanthropy, which has been providing annual reports on giving since 1955. Taken together, these reports provide enough data to discern trends. Information is reported in current dollars unless otherwise noted.

4. AAFRC Trust for Philanthropy, *Giving USA 2001: The Annual Report on Philanthropy for the Year 2000* (Indianapolis Center on Philanthropy, 2001), p. 20.

5. Statistics calculated using data from the Internal Revenue Service, *Statistics of Income Bulletin*, vol. 20, no. 3 (Winter 2000–01): 9–57.

6. Susan K. E. Saxon-Harrold, *Giving and Volunteering in the United States: Findings from a National Survey*, 1999 Edition (Washington: Independent Sector, 1999), p. 6.

7. Household surveys may overstate the extent of giving to religion since they do not provide a full picture of giving by the wealthy, which accounts for the bulk of individual giving. Overall, religion receives 36 percent of all giving, including giving by individuals, foundations, and corporations. Assuming that corporations do not give to religion, religion likely accounts for 44 percent of individual giving.

8. Saxon-Harrold, *Giving and Volunteering in the United States*, p. 2.

9. Stephen G. Greene, "Most Americans Plan No Decrease in Their 2001 Donations, Poll Finds," *Chronicle of Philanthropy*, November 1, 2001, p. 55.

10. Ian Wilhelm, "Gifts Continue to Pour in for Recovery Efforts; Other Disaster News," *Chronicle of Philanthropy*, November 1, 2000, p. 23.

11. Lester M. Salamon, *Partners in Public Service: Government-Nonprofit Relations in the Modern Welfare State* (Johns Hopkins University Press, 1995), pp. 45–47; Julian Wolpert, "Communities, Networks, and the Future of Philanthropy," in Charles T. Clotfelter and Thomas Ehrlich, eds., *Philanthropy and the Nonprofit Sector in a Changing America* (Indiana University Press, 1999), p. 238.

12. Wolpert, "Communities, Networks, and the Future of Philanthropy," pp. 238–39.

13. Cutlip, *Fundraising in the United States*, p. xvi.

14. Saxon-Harrold, *Giving and Volunteering in the United States*, p. 2.

15. AAFRC Trust for Philanthropy, *Giving USA 2001*, p. 151.

16. Author's analysis of unpublished data from the Independent Sector's 1999 Giving and Volunteering Survey.

17. Independent Sector, pre-publication data release from the *New Nonprofit Almanac*, 2001.

18. Independent Sector, pre-publication data release from the *New Nonprofit Almanac*, 2001.

19. Eleanor Brown, "The Scope of Volunteer Activity and Public Service," *Law and Contemporary Problems*, vol. 52, no. 4 (Autumn 1999): 17–42; see pp. 32–36. See also Virginia A. Hodgkinson and Murray Weitzman, *Giving and Volunteering in the United States: Findings from a National Survey*, 1996 edition (Washington: Independent Sector, 1996), pp. 87–121.

20. Independent Sector, pre-publication data release from the *New Nonprofit Almanac*, 2001.

21. Virginia A. Hodgkinson and Murray Weitzman, *Nonprofit Almanac: Dimensions of the Independent Sector, 1996–1997* (San Francisco: Jossey-Bass, 1996), p. 311, and Independent Sector, pre-publication release data.

22. AAFRC Trust for Philanthropy, *Giving USA 2001*, p. 159.

23. Colin C. Burke, "Nonprofit History's New Numbers (And the Need for More)," *Nonprofit and Voluntary Sector Quarterly*, vol. 30, no. 2 (June 2001): 174–203; see pp. 186–87.

24. Colin Burke, "Establishing a Context: The Elusive History of America's Nonprofit Domain—Numbers Count—If Someone Counted," Working Paper 261 (Yale University Press, Program on Non-Profit Organizations, November 2000), p. 88.

25. Burke, "Establishing a Context," p. 94.

26. Kathleen Day, "Where the Money Is," *Washington Post*, November 26, 2000, pp. H-1, H-6.

27. Burke, "Establishing a Context," pp. 84–85.

28. AAFRC, Trust for Philanthropy, *Giving USA 2001*, p. 21.

29. Burke, "Establishing a Context," pp. 46–47. Cutlip, *Fundraising in the United States*, p. 3.

30. Cutlip, *Fundraising in the United States*, p. 3.

31. Cutlip, *Fundraising in the United States*, p. 3.

32. Arnaud C. Marts, *Philanthropy's Role in Civilization* (New York: Harper and Row, 1953), p. 108.

33. Marts, *Philanthropy's Role in Civilization*, p. 108.

34. Cutlip, *Fundraising in the United States*, pp. 38–39.

35. Cutlip, *Fundraising in the United States*, pp. 220–224.

36. Harland G. Bloland, "The Role of Association in the Professionalizing Process," *New Directions for Philanthropic Fundraising*, vol. 15 (Spring 1997): 97–110; see pp. 99–102.

37. National Society of Fundraising Executives, "Profile of NSFRE Members" (Alexandria, Va.: National Society of Fundraising Executives, 1999).

38. National Committee on Planned Giving, "Employer Characteristics" (www.ncpg.org/employer.html [January 11, 2001]).

39. Margaret A. Duronio and Eugene R. Temple, *Fundraisers: Their Careers, Stories, Concerns, and Accomplishments* (San Francisco: Jossey-Bass, 1997), p. xvi.

40. National Society of Fundraising Executives, "Profile of NSFRE Members."

41. National Committee on Planned Giving, "Employer Characteristics."

42. Saxon-Harrold, *Giving and Volunteering in the United States*, p. 8.

43. Author's analysis of unpublished data from the Independent Sector's 1999 Giving and Volunteering Survey.

44. Author's analysis of unpublished data from the Independent Sector's 1999 Giving and Volunteering Survey.

45. Robert Putnam, *Bowling Alone: The Collapse and Revival of American Community* (New York: Simon and Schuster, 2000).

46. Melina J. Belvedere, "Charitable Remainder Trust, 1998," *501 Bulletin*, vol. 20, no. 3 (Winter 2000–01): 58–76; see p. 58.

47. AAFRC Trust for Philanthropy, *Giving USA 2001*, p. 151.

48. AAFRC Trust for Philanthropy, *Giving USA 2001*, pp. 72–74.

49. Fidelity Investments Charitable Gift Fund, "Charitable Gift Options 1998–2000" (www.charitablegift.org [August 15, 2002]).

50. "The Philanthropy 400," *Chronicle of Philanthropy*, November 1, 2001, p. 37; Matthew Sinclair, "Top 100 Revenues Zoom to $49 Billion," *Nonprofit Times*, November 1, 2001, pp. 31–32.

51. Fidelity Investments Charitable Gift Fund, "Charitable Gift Options, 1998–2000."

52. Vanguard, www.vanguardcharitable.org/VGApp/vcep/home.jsp [August 22, 2002].

53. Nicole Wallace, "Online Giving Soars as Donors Turn to the Internet Following Attacks," *Chronicle of Philanthropy*, October 4, 2001, p. 22.

54. Debra A. Blum, "Chasing Charitable Assets," *Chronicle of Philanthropy,* November 15, 2000, pp. 1, 23, 27.

55. Alan J. Abramson, Lester M. Salamon, and C. Eugene Steuerle, "The Nonprofit Sector and the Federal Budget: Recent History and Future Directions," in Elizabeth T. Boris and C. Eugene Steuerle, eds., *Nonprofits and Government* (Washington: Urban Institute, 1999), pp. 99–139.

56. AAFRC Trust for Philanthropy, *Giving USA 2001,* pp. 61–62.

57. Iris J. Lav and James Sly, "Estate Tax Repeal: A Costly Windfall for the Wealthiest Americans" (Washington: Center on Budget and Policy Priorities, 2000 [revised, May 24, 2002]), www.cbpp.org/5-25-00tax.htm [July 17, 2002].

58. National Economic Consulting Practice, "Incentives for Nonitemizers to Give More" (PricewaterhouseCoopers UP, January 2001).

59. Lawrence Mishel, Jared Bernstein, and John Schmitt, *The State of Working America 2000–2001* [advance copy]. (Washington: Economic Policy Institute, 2000), p. 2.

60. Saxon-Harrold, *Giving and Volunteering in the United States,* p. 13.

61. Ellis and Noyes, *By the People,* p. 333.

62. A. W. Astin and others, *The American Freshman: Thirty Year Trends* (University of California, Los Angeles, Higher Education Research Institute, 1997), p. 45.

63. Ellis and Noyes, *By the People,* pp. 350–51.

64. Ellis and Noyes, *By the People,* pp. 350–51.

65. Points of Light Foundation, "About Us" (www.pointsoflight.org [2001]).

66. College Compact, "What We Do" (www.compact.org [2000]).

67. Campus Outreach Opportunity League, "Membership 2000" (www.cool2serv.org [August 16, 2002]).

68. Corporation for National and Community Service, "Fiscal 1999 Performance Report" (Washington: Corporation for National and Community Service, March 2000), p. 12.

69. Corporation for National and Community Service, "Fiscal 1999 Performance Report," pp. 18–20.

70. Corporation for National and Community Service, "Fiscal 1999 Performance Report," p. 6.

71. Corporation for National and Community Service, "Fiscal 1999 Performance Report," pp. 18–20.

72. Timberland, www.timberland.com [2001], pp. 44–72.

73. Linda J. Sax and others, *The American Freshman: National Norms for Fall 1999* (University of California, Los Angeles, Higher Education Research Institute, 1999).

74. Astin and others, *The American Freshman,* p. 45.

75. Virginia A. Hodgkinson and Murray Weitzman, *Volunteering and Giving in the United States among Teenagers 12 to 17 Years of Age: Findings from a National Survey, 1996 Edition* (Washington: Independent Sector, 1997), p. 2.

76. Rebecca Skinner Westat and Chris Chapman, "Service Learning and Community Service in K–12 Public Schools," *Statistics in Brief,* NCES 1999-043 (Jessup, Md.: U.S. Department of Education, National Center for Education Statistics, September 1999).

77. Hodgkinson and Weitzman, *Volunteering and Giving in the United States among Teenagers,* p. 6.

78. Westat and Chapman, "Service Learning and Community Service in K–12 Public Schools."

79. Anthony D. Lutkus and others, *NAEP Civics Report Card for the Nation, National Assessment of Educational Progress* (Jessup, Md.: U.S. Department of Education, National Center for Education Statistics, November 1999).

80. Astin and others, *The American Freshman,* p. 45.

81. Sax and others, *The American Freshman.*

82. Putnam, *Bowling Alone.*

83. See E. J. Dionne Jr., *Community Works: The Revival of Civil Society in America* (Washington: Brookings, 1998), p. 13; Everett C. Ladd, *The Ladd Report* (New York: Free Press, 1999).

84. Hodgkinson and Weitzman, *Volunteering and Giving in the United States among American Teenagers,* p. 44.

85. Virginia A. Hodgkinson and Arthur Kirsch, "The Characteristics of Citizen Participation and Generosity with Implications for Public Policy," paper delivered at the ISTR conference, Dublin, Ireland, July 2000, pp. 23–25.

86. Brown, "The Scope of Volunteer Activity and Public Service," pp. 39–41.

87. "Lengthening Shadows," *Economist,* November 10–16, 2000, p. 32.

88. Hodgkinson and Weitzman, *Giving and Volunteering in the United States,* p. 20.

89. Jacqueline L. Salmon, "Sept. 11 Donations, Economy Leave Many Nonprofits Strapped," *Washington Post,* October 9, 2001, pp. B1, B5.

90. Wirthlin Worldwide, "A Survey of Charitable Giving after September 11, 2001," prepared for Independent Sector (Washington: Independent Sector, October 23, 2001).

91. "Who's Working the Class War," *Too Much,* vol. 7, no. 1 (Summer 2001): 1.

92. Hodgkinson and Weitzman, *Giving and Volunteering in the United States,* pp. 20, 21–30.

93. Pew Partnership for Civic Change, "Ready, Willing, and Able: Citizens Working for Change" (Philadelphia: Pew Partnership for Civic Change, June 2001), pp. 1–6.

94. AAFRC Trust for Philanthropy, *Giving USA 2001,* p. 57.

95. John J. Havens and Paul G. Schervish, "Millionaires and the Millennium: New Estimates of the Forthcoming Wealth Transfer and the Prospects for a Golden Age of Philanthropy," unpublished paper (Boston College, Social Welfare Research Institute, 1999), pp. 6–8.

96. Eleanor Brown, "Patterns and Purposes of Philanthropic Giving," in Clotfelter and Ehrlich, eds., *Philanthropy and the Nonprofit Sector in a Changing America,* pp. 224–26.

97. Thomas K. Reis and Stephanie J. Clohesy, *E-Philanthropy, Voluntarism, and Social Changemaking: A New Landscape of Resources, Issues, and Opportunities* (Battle Creek, Mich.: W. K. Kellogg Foundation, 2000).

98. Community Wealth Ventures, *Venture Philanthropy: Landscape and Expectations* (Reston, Va.: Mornio Institute, 1999).

99. Nicole Wallace, "Surge in Online Giving Lifts Hopes for Some Charities," *Chronicle of Philanthropy,* December 13, 2001, p. 12.

100. Center for Civic Education, "Campaign to Promote Civic Education" (Calabasas, Calif.: Center for Civic Education, November 18, 1999).

101. Wirthlin Worldwide, "A Survey of Charitable Giving after September 11, 2001."

102. Putnam, *Bowling Alone,* pp. 54–55.

PART III

Major Challenges

13

Commercialization, Social Ventures, and For-Profit Competition

DENNIS R. YOUNG AND LESTER M. SALAMON

The end of the twentieth century witnessed a fundamental questioning of the traditional welfare state in western industrial countries, the fall of communism in Central Europe and the states of the former Soviet Union, and the disappearance of dominating authoritarian regimes in many developing countries. Underlying all of these events has been a profound disaffection with government that has helped to create new opportunities and responsibilities for the private sector—both for-profit and nonprofit—to address societal problems and improve the welfare of citizens. The free market holds center stage in this unfolding drama. Powered by vast new opportunities created by the revolution in technology, the free market is now seen as the primary engine of progress and growth in societies around the world. Entrepreneurship, competition, new wealth creation, efficiency, and consumer sovereignty are the prevailing values of this market revival. These values now dominate private commerce, stimulate globalization of the economy, and strongly influence public policy in countries throughout the world.

Nonprofit organizations have not been immune from this widespread marketization of social and economic life. To the contrary, they have been profoundly affected. Indeed, as this chapter argues, many nonprofits have enthusiastically embraced the new market impulses and found ways to integrate them creatively into their operations. As a consequence, a significant commercialization or marketization of the nonprofit sector appears to be under way, although with consequences that are far from clear.

This development is not, of course, wholly new. Nonprofit organizations have been involved in commercial transactions from the sector's earliest days. Religious orders, for example, have long marketed wine, and orphanages have taken in laundry to help cover their costs. But the scope, scale, and variety of the commercial engagement of the nonprofit sector appear to have undergone a quantum leap over the past decade or more. This is apparent in the substantial growth of fee income as a source of nonprofit revenue, in the expanded involvement of nonprofits in the sale of ancillary goods and services, in the considerable proliferation of business-nonprofit partnerships, and in the widespread growth of an enterprise culture within nonprofit organizations. Indeed, the whole concept of a separate nonprofit sphere has come under serious question as interest has grown in a new kind of entity—the social enterprise—that marries business means to nonprofit ends through the creation of social-purpose business enterprises.

This chapter explores this important trend toward commercialization within the nonprofit sector in more detail, identifying the forces that are giving rise to it and assessing its implications for the sector's operation and role. To do so, the discussion falls into three parts. The first part examines the forces that seem to be propelling nonprofits into greater engagement with the private market economy. The second part explores how nonprofits have responded to these forces, documenting the extent of nonprofit adoption of the dominant market culture. The third part assesses the implications of these developments for the role and character of nonprofit organizations.

The central conclusion emerging from this analysis is that nonprofits have accommodated themselves quite well to the commercial pressures they are confronting, reinventing themselves in often creative ways. At the same time, this development is posing a variety of new challenges and dangers for the sector. Nonprofit organizations seem to be finding ways to deal with these dangers, although egregious counterexamples do exist. At the same time, it is far from clear whether public understanding, or approval, has kept pace with the scope of the changes under way, with the result that the sector's most precious asset of all—the public's trust—may increasingly be at risk.

The Pressures for Commercialization

The fact that nonprofit organizations have turned increasingly to the market over the past two decades should come as no surprise given the pressures under which these organizations have been operating and the opportunities to which they have been exposed. Broadly speaking, six factors seem to be propelling nonprofit organizations toward greater integration with the prevailing market system.

Fiscal Squeeze

In the first place, nonprofits have long confronted a significant fiscal squeeze as a result of the relatively limited level, and generally tepid growth, of their traditional form of financial support—charitable giving—and the significant cutbacks that occurred in the early 1980s in government support, which had fueled the sector's substantial growth in the previous two decades. While charitable giving is probably higher in the United States than in most other nations, it has rarely exceeded 2 percent of the nation's gross domestic product, and only about half of these contributions are available for social welfare purposes (health, education, and welfare).[1] What is more, the level of private giving has been declining as a share of national income in recent decades—from an average of 1.86 percent in the 1970s to 1.78 percent during the 1980s and to 1.72 percent in the early 1990s. Although there was hope in the late 1990s that this pattern had been reversed, the stock market decline of 2000 and the recession of 2001 have significantly dimmed this optimism.

Although their charitable support remained limited, nonprofits benefited enormously in the 1960s and early 1970s from a significant expansion of government involvement in the field of social welfare, much of which was channeled through nonprofit organizations. The result was a massive surge in nonprofit activity and substantial growth in the scale and reach of the sector. By 1980, government accounted for well over 30 percent of a considerably larger base of nonprofit income.[2] But with the election of Ronald Reagan in the early 1980s, this expansion of government support slowed considerably and, in some fields, was completely reversed. Nonprofits therefore found themselves in a fiscal squeeze. Although, as Salamon shows in chapter 1 of this book, public sector support for nonprofit organizations subsequently resumed its growth, that support changed significantly in form. Instead of grants and contracts to nonprofit providers, which were cut, the available government support increasingly came through programs such as Medicaid and Medicare that provide reimbursement "vouchers" to the "customers" that nonprofits serve. As a consequence, nonprofit organizations more and more found themselves in a commercial-type relationship even to secure government support.

Expanded Demand

While experiencing a significant squeeze in their charitable and government support, nonprofit organizations have faced higher demand for their services. In part, this demand has originated with the poor and disadvantaged, long an important constituency of the nonprofit sector. But social and demographic changes have also generated demands from other segments of the population, many of whom can afford to pay for the services they receive, either on their own or with the aid of public subsidies.

The continued rapid aging of the population, for example, has significantly increased the demand for a variety of elderly care services, from nursing home care to home health services. By 2025 the number of people over age sixty-five is expected to be four times higher than it was in 1960. Similarly, the changing role of women in American society has substantially increased the demand for childcare and related services. Between 1960 and 1996, the labor force participation rate for women with children under six years of age rose from less than 20 percent to more than 60 percent. Changes in the structure of American families have also ratcheted up the need for various types of counseling and supportive services. With one out of three marriages ending in divorce by the mid-1990s, up from 5 percent in the early 1960s, childcare, psychiatric counseling, crisis intervention, and associated activities are in much higher demand.[3]

Taken together, these and related social and demographic developments have put a premium on the kinds of services that nonprofit organizations have traditionally provided. In the process, they have helped to create a much broader market for nonprofit organizations to serve.

Increased For-Profit Competition

One important effect of this growing market for nonprofit services has been to attract for-profit competition into fields once dominated by nonprofit providers. This has turned on its head the long-standing small business concern about unfair competition from nonprofits in traditional for-profit fields. An overriding concern now is the increased competition from for-profits in traditional nonprofit fields. In many of these fields, moreover, for-profits have certain structural advantages. For example, for-profits can focus more easily than nonprofits on the most profitable segments of particular service markets, neglecting the populations unable to pay or at most severe risk, whereas nonprofits often retain a mission-oriented focus that obliges them to serve those in greatest need. In some fields, such as health care, this can drive up the costs of care for the remaining clients because it increases the level of risk involved. In addition, for-profits have access to sources of capital that are unavailable to nonprofits—most particularly equity capital generated through the sale of stock. Equity capital tends to be cheaper since it involves an ownership stake in a company. Because nonprofits do not have owners who can share in any profits earned, this source of capital is not accessible to them. The more important access to capital is in a field (for example, to build new facilities or acquire technology), the greater is the comparative advantage of for-profit businesses.

Reflecting this, for-profit firms have been expanding more rapidly than nonprofits in a variety of traditional fields of nonprofit endeavor. As Salamon shows in chapter 1, between 1982 and 1997 the nonprofit share of childcare jobs declined from 52 to 38 percent, and that of home health care jobs declined from 60 to 28 percent.[4] Similarly, as Gray and Schlesinger show in chapter 2, the nonprofit share of health care facilities declined substantially between the mid-1980s and the late 1990s in a number of fields: from 58 to 32 percent among kidney dialysis centers, from 70 to 35 percent among rehabilitation hospitals, from 65 to 26 percent among health maintenance organizations, and from 89 to 76 percent among hospices.

The federal welfare reform legislation of 1996 recently opened a new arena for for-profit involvement in the areas of employment counseling, job training, and placement services, all of them traditionally nonprofit markets. Large corporations such as Lockheed Martin IMS have entered the social services market as master contractors, exploiting their access to high-speed computing technology to manage large caseloads and process clients through complex networks of nonprofit and for-profit service providers. For-profit firms have even penetrated the field of charitable giving, as financial service firms such as Fidelity and Merrill Lynch have begun offering donor services similar to those originally developed by community foundations.[5] In less than five years, the Fidelity Charitable Gift Fund alone has attracted more capital than is held by the nation's largest community foundation.

To be sure, the competition between nonprofits and for-profits is not a one-way stream. Rather, it ebbs and flows over time. In the 1960s and 1970s, non-profit nursing homes lost ground to for-profit homes as Medicaid increased its coverage and for-profits were better positioned to tap into the capital markets to construct the facilities required to respond. Similarly, in the early 1990s nonprofit hospitals and health maintenance organizations lost ground to their for-profit counterparts that were able to invest in the information-processing equipment needed to make managed care work. In each of these fields, however, nonprofits have regained ground in more recent years, as reductions in the reimbursement rates under Medicare and Medicaid and pressures from private insurance companies have squeezed profit margins to the point where for-profit providers no longer find it so attractive to operate. Nevertheless, the growing prominence of for-profits in a number of traditionally nonprofit fields has called into question the competitive advantages and disadvantages of the nonprofit form.[6]

Growing Competition among Nonprofits

Not only are nonprofits encountering increasing competition from for-profit firms, they also are facing increasing competition from other nonprofits. Such competition has long been at least implicit in a number of service fields, such as higher education and the arts, where nonprofits compete for clients and patrons among themselves as well as with for-profits. But the pressures of rivalry and competition have long been balanced by expectations of collaboration and pursuit of broader community interests, expectations that have been reinforced by the funding community—especially community foundations and federated fundraising organizations—which encourages both improved individual organizational performance as well as collaboration and consolidation in the interests of achieving greater overall efficiency and effectiveness.

Currently, however, the balance between collaboration and competition may be tipping toward competition. In health care and higher education, in particular, nonprofit institutions now invest heavily in advertising and marketing so as to outpace their competition, whether the competition be from for-profits or other nonprofits. The competition is not only for clients, moreover. It extends as well to competition for charitable contributions. With the development of the Internet and services such as GuideStar, donors are being empowered to become active shoppers in the arena of charitable giving, requiring nonprofits to make their cases more forcefully to distinguish themselves from their peers. Nonprofits also are having to compete for affiliations with for-profit corporations that offer their websites for Internet giving. Cisco Systems and America Online are two corporations that have made significant investments in on-line giving services, an area likely to experience explosive growth in the near future.[7]

Traditional institutions for coordination of charitable giving, especially at the community level, are themselves experiencing the forces of disaggregation and competition. United Ways, which once enjoyed monopoly access to corporate payroll deduction systems, are now forced to share that access with alternative funds and even individual charities. Moreover, donors have insisted on having more say over the allocation of their charitable dollars to federated fundraising organizations, resulting in donor-choice systems that allow donors to designate their gifts to particular charitable causes.[8] This, in turn, increases the pressure on individual nonprofits to promote themselves vis-à-vis their nonprofit competitors. Finally, the entire corporate economy has become more decentralized after the downsizing of large corporations in the 1980s and the growth of entrepreneurial small businesses. The new small business economy has undermined both the payroll deduction system and the domination of community fundraising by a few large corporations. Individual nonprofits must therefore target a broader field of business ventures for their fundraising appeals.

Broader Availability of Corporate Partners

In addition to the push of expanding competition from for-profit enterprises, nonprofits are also being drawn into the commercial orbit by the pull of increasing corporate willingness to cooperate in a host of joint undertakings. This development is part of the broader transformation of the corporate economy during the past several decades, as corporations have come to emphasize quality and identity—traditional nonprofit concerns—and not simply cost and efficiency as central values in an increasingly competitive global economy. To retain skilled staff and attract dedicated customers, corporations have found it desirable to bolster their corporate image by identifying their organizations with socially useful undertakings. Forging partnerships with nonprofit organizations is one effective way to do this. Cause-related marketing, collaborative projects, and related undertakings are all manifestations of this phenomenon as corporations have increasingly made themselves available to nonprofit organizations not simply as donors, but as full-fledged partners, and have integrated such partnerships into their overall corporate strategies.[9]

Increased Demands for Accountability

Finally, the pressures nudging nonprofit organizations in the direction of the market arise as well from the increased attention to performance on the part of the various stakeholders of the nonprofit sector. One consequence of the growing competition from for-profit providers is to force nonprofit organizations to pay more attention to efficiency and effectiveness in order to compete successfully for customers. Potential corporate partners and other institutional donors, including government agencies, are also seeking concrete measures of nonprofit performance as a condition of continued support. Thanks to new technologies, individual donors, too, are able to shop around and are demanding information on how nonprofits spend their money and do their work before parting with their charitable dollars.

These demands for accountability are arising, moreover, against the backdrop of an important shift in public philosophies about the causes of social problems. Where formerly such problems were perceived as the product of lack of opportunity and skills, increasingly they are viewed as the product of lack of initiative and will. This shift has put nonprofits, with their traditional "helping" orientation, on the defensive and moved employment-oriented organizations into an advantaged position.[10] To remain relevant in this climate, nonprofits have had to put more emphasis on demonstrating results in order to justify and protect the benefits they enjoy under public policy.[11]

The Response: The Move toward the Market

In response to this combination of pressures and opportunities, nonprofit organizations are drawing far closer to the market economy than perhaps at any time in their history. To be sure, not all components of the nonprofit sector are responding to these developments in the same way, and even within particular fields there are immense differences among individual organizations. The growing market involvement of nonprofit organizations is a complex and multifaceted phenomenon, with various strands interwoven into a rich tapestry. Nevertheless, a new picture of a "social sector" is slowly coming into focus—a self-propelled social problem–solving sector, loosened from its original moorings in charity or its role as a passive agent of government and much more tightly connected to the market system, while still tied, however tenuously, to the pursuit of public benefit. The picture remains blurred and filled with crosscurrents, but the emerging pattern seems clear enough to describe in general terms. This section considers a number of its most tangible manifestations.

The Growing Reliance on Earned Income

Perhaps the most salient aspect of the growing involvement of nonprofit organizations with the market has been the steady growth of nonprofit reliance on fee income. As Salamon reported in chapter 1, as of 1997, the most recent year for which data are available, 49 percent of the revenue of nonprofit agencies, including religious congregations, came from commercial sources—fees, charges, and investment earnings. By comparison, government provided 31 percent of total income, and charitable giving provided only 20 percent.[12] Between 1977 and 1997, in fact, fees and other commercial income accounted for half of the sector's overall growth, compared to 32 percent for government and less than 20 percent for charity.

Even this understates the commercial involvement of the nonprofit sector, however, since the character of government support has changed markedly over this twenty-year period, as noted in previous chapters. In particular, a much larger share of government support is reaching nonprofits through voucher programs that deliver their assistance directly to consumers rather than to the nonprofit producers of services. As a consequence, nonprofits are increasingly having to compete for clients in the market even for government support. According to Burton Weisbrod, with such voucher payments included, reliance of U.S. public benefit—501(c)(3)—nonprofits on essentially commercial income increased from 69 percent in 1987 to 74 percent in 1992.[13] Such dependence on fees increased particularly sharply in education, health, human services, and environmental and animal-related services and was stable in the arts over this period of time.

Nonprofit reliance on fees and charges is evident outside the United States as well. Salamon and associates found that, on average, 49 percent of the revenue of nonprofits in twenty-two countries scattered widely around the world derived from fees and charges, compared to 40 percent from government and 11 percent from philanthropy in 1995.[14] Some thirteen of the twenty-two countries' nonprofit sectors were found to be fee dominant, that is, more dependent on fees and charges than on any other source of income.

Most of this earned income takes the form of fees and charges for the mission-related services that nonprofits provide: tuition in education, box office receipts in the arts, charges for hospital stays and services, fees for counseling in social services, and so on. Some, however, also emanates from ancillary commercial activities not necessarily associated with core mission–related activities. For example, museums run gifts shops in shopping centers and airports, colleges offer travel services for their alumni, and YMCAs rent out their facilities for private parties. Determining the extent of such unrelated business income is difficult, however. By law, nonprofit organizations are obligated to pay taxes on such unrelated business income and to file a special tax form, the 990-T unrelated business income tax (UBIT) return, if they receive at least $1,000 in gross unrelated business income in a given year. Unfortunately, the data resulting from such returns are a poor indicator of the extent of unrelated business income, for several reasons. First, certain categories of earned income are excluded from UBIT, including passive investment income, royalties, and activities performed by volunteers or for the convenience of the nonprofit's clientele (such as on-campus conveniences for students). Second, the rules on unrelated business income are liberal and allow nonprofits to declare income as related rather than unrelated within very broad boundaries. Revenue generated by Girl Scout cookie sales and on-premises museum gift shop sales are considered related income, for example, although one might argue that they are peripherally related to the organizations' missions. Reflecting this, Segal and Weisbrod found that only a small percentage of nonprofits—ranging between 1 and 10 percent depending on the field—file the required Form 990-T.[15] Third, nonprofits have broad discretion in allocating costs between related and unrelated activities so as to minimize their liabilities for profit tax on unrelated income activity. Thus Margaret Riley finds that in 1997 only half of the 39,302 organizations filing an unrelated business income form reported any net income from their unrelated business activities, and the total net income for UBIT filers as a whole was actually negative, as total expenses allocated to unrelated activities exceeded total revenues![16]

Despite these limitations, the data on unrelated business activity are still revealing. As of 1997, for example, gross unrelated business income reported by nonprofit organizations reached $7.8 billion, an increase of 7 percent over the previous year. During this same period, net income from such businesses increased 18 percent, and this was on top of increases of 31 and 35 percent, respectively, for 1996 and 1995.[17] Looking at the period from 1990 to 1997, the *Chronicle of Philanthropy* found that the number of charities reporting unrelated business income increased 35 percent and the amount of income they reported more than doubled.[18] This suggests that the significant growth in the scale and nature of enterprise activities and in the number of institutions engaged in such activities, which Crimmins and Keil had already identified in the early 1980s, has accelerated in recent years.[19]

Social-Purpose Enterprise

Not only have nonprofit organizations turned to the market to supplement their incomes, but they also are integrating the market into the pursuit of their social missions in a more fundamental way.[20] For example, rather than training disadvantaged individuals and sending them out cold into the private labor market, some nonprofit training agencies have begun creating their own small business ventures to help reintegrate their disadvantaged or structurally unemployed clientele into the mainstream economy. The venture is thus not a sideline or a mere source of revenue, but an integral component of the agency's program, directly related to the pursuit of its mission.

This development has given rise to a new type of social institution known variously as social-purpose enterprises, social ventures, or community wealth enterprises.[21] Such enterprises can take at least four forms.[22] These include traditional sheltered workshops of the sort long operated by Goodwill Industries and that often enjoy government preferences, open-market enterprises that compete in the marketplace without governmental preference, franchises that operate within the context of a national corporation, and program-based enterprises that grow out of a nonprofit organization's social service programs.

Many of these enterprises function largely to provide protected employment opportunities to disadvantaged populations. For example, Asian Neighborhood Design employs low-income individuals in a furniture manufacturing business, Barrios Unidos employs Latino youth in a screen-printing business, and Community Vocational Enterprises employs people with psychiatric disabilities in janitorial, food service, clerical, and messenger service businesses. Other examples include the Greyston Bakery in Yonkers, New York, a for-profit subsidiary of the Greyston Foundation, which trains and hires unemployable workers in its gourmet bakery business; the New Community Corporation in Newark, New Jersey, which provides job training and employment to inner-city residents as well as needed retail services to underserved neighborhoods through its various for-profit business enterprises such as franchised grocery and convenience stores, restaurants, and print and copy shops; and Pioneer Human Services, a nonprofit in Seattle, Washington, which operates a variety of business enterprises, including an aircraft parts manufacturer, food buying and warehousing services, and restaurants, in which it trains, employs, and rehabilitates ex-offenders, chemically dependent individuals, and persons on probation or under court supervision.[23] In these cases, the business ventures are logically connected to the mission of the nonprofit only as a means to provide training and employment opportunities for their clientele, not because their particular products are especially relevant to that mission. The point of the ventures is to create commercial opportunities as the best possible environment in which to nurture client success and (at least incidentally) to generate resources to sustain the organization.

The concept of social-purpose enterprise has also been extended beyond the employment sphere to include business ventures that contribute directly to nonprofit mission-related outputs as well as to revenues and mission-related employment. In Mexico, for example, social-purpose enterprises emphasize the relief of poverty rather than the provision of employment per se.[24] Other social-purpose enterprises address social issues such as the environment and community transportation. For example, the Orange County Community Distribution Center in Florida serves an environmental conservation mission by warehousing discarded materials and providing them to local nonprofits at reduced cost, employing and training inmates on work release in the process. Similarly, Bikeable Communities in Long Beach, California, promotes bicycle use to address community transportation and environmental objectives by offering various services to cyclists, including valet bicycle parking, changing rooms, and repair services.[25]

These various experiences with commercial enterprise on the part of nonprofit organizations are beginning to put nonprofit commercial activity into a new light. No longer conceived simply as a revenue generation strategy, these ventures treat market engagement as the most effective way to pursue a nonprofit organization's mission, to provide marketable skills to the structurally unemployed, or to change behavior in an environmentally sensitive way.

The concept of a social venture has taken an even broader form in Europe and elsewhere, where it includes cooperatives and worker-owned or worker-controlled enterprises. Clearly, such ventures do not adhere to the central criterion of a nonprofit entity in the American setting—that is, one that does not distribute its profits to its members or owners. Reflecting this, some analysts are finding the nonprofit form too restrictive a category with which to capture the scope of new social enterprise activity. In Mexico, for example, social enterprise is not restricted to a particular sector but rather refers to "efforts of government, nonprofit organizations, and businesses directed toward the creation of novel schemes that take into consideration the global frame of a free-market economy to induce programs to help alleviate regional development lags and poverty."[26] Even in the United States, proponents of the new social entrepreneurship chafe against the strictures of the nonprofit form and are beginning to claim that some new type of structural classification may be needed to capture their socially driven business ventures. Perhaps the broadest generic definition of social enterprise is offered by the Organization for Economic Cooperation and Development, stressing intent rather than a particular organizational form: social enterprise is "any private activity conducted in the public interest, organized with entrepreneurial strategy, but whose main purpose is not the maximization of profit but the attainment of certain economic and social goals, and which has the capacity for bringing innovative solutions to the problems of social exclusion and unemployment."[27]

In Europe, the notion of social enterprise focuses more heavily on the way an organization is governed and what its purpose is rather than on whether it strictly adheres to the nondistribution constraint of a formal nonprofit organization.[28]

A social enterprise in these terms is thus any organization that is private, that enjoys managerial autonomy, that produces and sells collective goods, that earns income partly from sales and not solely from donations, and that grants some meaningful degree of control to key stakeholders, such as workers, users, volunteers, and consumers, regardless of whether the organization distributes profits to them.

While the social enterprise movement has not overturned conventional notions of the nonprofit sector in the United States, a stream of opinion is emerging that characterizes the nonprofit sector and its related business ventures as a continuum of activity between market and philanthropy, arguing for a more general understanding of social enterprise than a strict divide between nonprofits and for-profits would comfortably allow.[29] This argument is centered on the observation that some socially focused enterprise activity takes places outside the formal nonprofit realm as well as through interactions and combinations of nonprofit and for-profit activity. According to Reis and Clohesy, "There are hundreds—and perhaps thousands—of examples throughout the U.S. of organizations that are experimenting with enterprise or market-based approaches for solving problems that are weaving together profitmaking activities with social change purposes."[30] Clearly, the relationship between the nonprofit sector and the market seems to be entering a new phase of development.

Nonprofit-Business Collaboration

A third important manifestation of the penetration of the market into the operations of nonprofit organizations takes the form of nonprofit-business partnerships. Even nonprofit organizations that are not engaged in enterprise activity or fee-for-service operations may still engage the market indirectly through cooperative relationships with for-profit corporations. As noted, the pressures of global competition have put a premium on reputational capital in order for corporations to attract customers, retain high-level staff, and ensure the kind of public support they need to operate. For a variety of reasons, these pressures have led corporations to see nonprofit organizations as important strategic partners. As one practitioner notes, "A company's relationship to the Third Sector is only partly charitable in impulse. In varying measure, nonprofits represent markets, sources of employees, pools of research and expertise, and sources of community goodwill for companies."[31]

Just as corporations have discovered the strategic value of working with nonprofits, nonprofits have come to understand how relationships with corporations can be helpful programmatically as well as financially. As a consequence, over the past decade, the old stereotypes of corporate altruism, on the one hand, and nonprofit suspicion of business, on the other, have all but evaporated.[32] In their place have come new concepts of strategic fit and new forms of interaction that go well beyond simple philanthropic giving.[33] Corporate involvement with nonprofit organizations now also involves the provision of equipment, space, and contacts; employee volunteer programs; loaned executives; event sponsorship; cause-related marketing; complex royalty and licensing arrangements; and even joint ventures.[34] Underlying these relationships is the belief that corporate-nonprofit ties, properly conceived, can serve the strategic missions of both the corporation and the nonprofit so that both sides gain something of value. Examples of such strategic partnerships include the following:[35]

—The Merck Corporation provides scholarship funds to the United Negro College Fund and provides mentors and internships to recipients of these scholarships. In return, Merck gains access to bright minority students with an interest in science.

—Ralston Purina provides support to the American Humane Association for the pets for people program, whose purpose is to encourage the adoption of pets. In addition to gaining reputation within its industry, the corporation helps to increase the market for its pet foods.

—Under growing criticism that its packaging was creating environmental problems, McDonald's teamed up with the Environmental Defense Fund to design packaging and processes that were more environmentally friendly. McDonald's fended off environmental criticism, and Environmental Defense Fund made a significant breakthrough in its environmental mission.

—American Express entered into a partnership with Share Our Strength under which American Express agreed to contribute 2 cents from every use of an American Express card to Share Our Strength for use in relieving international hunger. American Express gained increased use of its credit card, and Share Our Strength gained access to significant new resources.

—MCI WorldCom partnered with the National Geographic Society to support the Marco Polo geography website, which promotes the integration of Internet content in the K–12 curriculum. Both organizations stand to benefit from expanded use of the Internet in education.

—The Nature Conservancy works closely with Georgia Pacific to manage wetlands owned by the corporation. Through this arrangement, Nature Conservancy advances its mission of helping to protect large and important environmental resources, while Georgia Pacific gains access to the Nature Conservancy's expertise and improves its relationship with the general public.

The potential benefits to business corporations of collaborating with appropriate nonprofit partners fall along several possible lines. Corporations polish their public images, gain access to special expertise or future talent, create demand for their products, and motivate their employees by providing opportunities for volunteering and community service. In turn, their nonprofit partners gain access to substantial financial, personnel, and other corporate resources, obtain wider forums in which to broadcast their messages and appeals, and in some cases influence consumers in ways that directly support the nonprofit's mission. For example, when the American Cancer Society associates itself with the Florida citrus industry and offers the use of its name and logo on citrus products and commercials, it helps to increase the consumption of citrus fruit, a contributor to cancer prevention. Similarly, the affiliations between the American Lung Association and the American Cancer Society with manufacturers of smoking patches and the affiliation between Prevent Blindness and makers of protective eyewear directly contribute to the health-related missions of those organizations.[36]

Gauging the extent of such corporate-nonprofit partnerships is difficult. Clearly not all nonprofits have equal access to them, nor are all corporations fully engaged. Indeed, the globalization of the economy, while increasing the pressures on corporations to attend to their corporate images, paradoxically has also distanced many corporations from the communities they serve as a consequence of the extensive mergers and acquisitions that globalization has also encouraged. Nevertheless, something fundamental has happened to the relationship between corporations and nonprofit organizations over the past decade or more; the change is in the direction of closer working relationships, and the scope of the change is quite extensive.

A Changing Nonprofit Culture

The expanded engagement of nonprofits with the dominant market culture has not been limited to increased reliance on fee revenues, experimentation with commercial ventures, and partnerships with for-profit firms. It now pervades the very manner in which nonprofits conduct their day-to-day affairs. Nonprofits are no longer bashful about aggressively advertising their services or competing for charitable contributions. They are more forthright in paying the going wage rate in labor markets to secure the talent they need to operate or to hire fundraising consultants or development staff in order to secure greater shares of gifts and grants. They administer a variety of planned giving options, sometimes competing with for-profit financial institutions to secure the investments of older donors; and they are increasingly preoccupied with performance, with demonstrating their ability to serve their missions efficiently and effectively.

In short, in response to the challenges they are facing from the market, nonprofits are internalizing the culture and techniques of market organizations and making them their own. This is resulting in changes in internal processes, in organizational structures, and ultimately in the culture and ethos of the organizations. Management practices, organizational values, and the very language that nonprofits use have been changing dramatically, signaling that nonprofits are becoming very different kinds of organizations than they were in the past and that their market involvement is likely to continue unabated into the indefinite future.

One manifestation of this change is the transformation that has occurred in nonprofit attitudes toward entrepreneurship and management. Twenty years ago, the term *entrepreneurship* was virtually unknown in the nonprofit sector, and where it was applied, it was thought to be irrelevant or even pejorative. Entrepreneurship was something that pertained to the for-profit sector, not to nonprofits. People in the nonprofit world never fully separated the generic idea of entrepreneurship from its association with for-profit activity, even when research stressed the generic character of entrepreneurship and linked it to nonprofit organizational success.[37] Similarly, nonprofits traditionally put little emphasis on management or on hiring people with special management expertise. Nonprofit managers were normally professionals in their various service fields—the arts, social work, health care, education, and so on—who incidentally took on administrative responsibility as their careers evolved.

Growing competition from the for-profit sector, declining public revenue, and increased calls for accountability beginning in the early 1980s have changed this markedly, however.[38] In response, nonprofits have firmly embraced "managerialism."[39] As a consequence, attention to nonprofit management education has soared. Some ninety universities now operate nonprofit management degree or certificate programs, and numerous others offer nonprofit management courses within traditional public administration, business administration, or other degree programs.[40] In the process, nonprofit management has become a respected career path, and nonprofit manager, a legitimate profession.[41]

One by-product of this development has been a further infiltration of the language and the practice of the market into nonprofit operations. Nonprofit organizations are increasingly encouraged to identify their market niches, to maximize their comparative advantages, to think of their clients as customers, to devise marketing plans, and to engage in strategic planning.[42] Pressured by both public and private funders, nonprofit organizations have had to become much more focused on measurable outcomes and impact, on assessing their performance and demonstrating their cost-effectiveness.[43]

The particular difficulties of United Way are of special interest in this connection. The Aramony scandal of the early 1990s gave impetus to reforms that have moved the nonprofit sector further in the direction of the market culture. Measuring performance and social impact became a theme for United Way in this decade, stressed by the national organization for adoption by local United Way affiliates.[44] Moreover, more heed was taken in the United Way system of demands by donors to have more say over the allocation of the funds they contribute through payroll deduction systems.[45] Donor choice has thus surfaced in the charitable realm as a manifestation of the concept of consumer sovereignty in the market paradigm. So has the fact that the United Way monopoly has been broken in the payroll deduction systems of many private and public sector employers. Charitable giving through payroll deduction is now a choice among alternative charitable mutual funds that have assembled different portfolios of charitable investments for donors to choose from and even offer donors a choice of investments within those portfolios.

In response to these pressures, nonprofits, through federated fundraising systems or as individual organizations, have taken to promoting particular aspects of their programming to suit donor preferences. Admittedly, this may simply represent a contemporary example of a long-standing nonprofit practice of identifying particular aspects of an organization to "sell" to particular donors for a given "price." But nonprofits seem to be moving more and more to taking a product differentiation approach to solicitation, allowing donors to designate their gifts, and often affix their names, to particular initiatives or assets that suit their preferences. This is yet another aspect of market culture that has become firmly rooted in contemporary nonprofit organizations.

Elements of this market culture have also spread to the world of foundations, perhaps the chief institutional embodiment of organized philanthropy. A new generation of philanthropists, many associated with the burgeoning technology-based economy of the 1990s, have pushed for a more activist and cost-effective approach to charitable giving modeled on the operations of venture capitalists.[46] Central to this venture philanthropy approach is an emphasis on measurable results, on achievement of a positive rate of return on charitable investments, and on engagement of the donor in helping to ensure the effective management of the funded organization. Indeed, some advocates of this approach now talk of a full-blown nonprofit capital market in which funders manage portfolios of social investments that exhibit varying degrees of diversification for risk and return, use a combination of grant and loan instruments to implement their investments, try to maximize the social returns on their investments, and use rating services to carry out the social return assessments.[47] Clearly, this is a new language, and a new conception, of what philanthropy is all about.

Not only is the cultural transformation under way in the nonprofit sector evident in the changing language and practice of agency *management*; it also is evident in a significant transformation of agency *structures.* A major restructuring of nonprofit organizations appears to be under way. In part, this has manifested itself in complex interconnections among agencies. Under pressure to collaborate, coordinate, and consolidate their operations as competition increases, as greater size becomes advantageous in order to stand out in the more competitive landscape, and as major funders seek ways to allocate their funds strategically for greatest impact, nonprofits have responded with a variety of restructuring initiatives, sharing, transferring, or combining services, resources, or programs among agencies in a variety of ways.[48] Such restructuring includes simple one-time programmatic collaborations, longer-term administrative consolidations and joint ventures, and out-and-out mergers. The upshot is a much more dense and complex network of relationships among nonprofit agencies.

At the same time, the internal structure of individual nonprofit organizations has also become increasingly complex. Here the pressures are partly legal and partly managerial. Advocacy organizations that combine education with lobbying are establishing separate 501(c)(3) and (c)(4) organizations to ensure that they can attract tax-deductible gifts for their advocacy work while still being free to engage in lobbying when this becomes necessary. Similar pressures are convincing service agencies to segment their various services into separately incorporated entities in order to shield them from liability in case of challenge or to separate funding streams in order to simplify cost accounting. A family and children's service organization that operates a residential treatment home financed in part by Medicaid as well as a daycare center and a counseling center supported largely by private fees might therefore choose to restructure its service activities into separately incorporated 501(c)(3)s and to manage the resulting conglomerate as a holding company with separate boards for the individual subsidiaries. The expanding involvement of nonprofit organizations in for-profit ventures has naturally accelerated this development as nonprofits find it desirable to organize separately incorporated for-profit subsidiaries to handle their venture activities. Although solid data on the scope of such organizational restructuring are not available, what evidence exists suggests a considerable elaboration of the internal structure of nonprofit agencies, with numerous programs and funding streams, multiple organizational components, and complex combinations of nonprofit and for-profit activity. Increasingly, this is clearly not the traditional nonprofit sector.

Summary: The New Governance

In short, the market system and the market culture are penetrating nonprofit organizations in many different ways. Growing reliance on fee income, expanded experimentation with enterprise activities, broader partnerships with for-profit companies, growing adoption of management practices characteristic of business enterprises, and increasing organizational complexity all signal a fundamental shift in orientation that will be difficult to reverse.

This shift has been encouraged by major changes in the world's political landscape and in technology, all of which have contributed to the ascendancy of the market as the primary institutional framework for organizing social and economic activity. Inevitably, this ascendancy has infiltrated the nonprofit sector and the manner in which it conducts its business. Not only has this infiltration changed the character of the nonprofit sector, but more fundamentally it has called into question the categories through which society previously organized its work. In the old order, business, government, and charitable enterprise all had their particular places, and although there was much interaction among them, they remained relatively distinct in organizational terms, in motivational values, in their sources of support, and in the work they carried out.

That appears to be changing now. The new market orientation of nonprofit organizations is driven not so much by changes in ideology as by pragmatism. Given the political changes, especially the withdrawal of government from a dominant role as public service provider, nonprofits have sought, generally with success, other means of support. Given the revolution in technology, nonprofits are adapting to the demands for information and donor empowerment. Given increasingly sophisticated and intense competition in the business world, nonprofits are responding to the needs of business for closer relationships with charitable and community-based enterprises.

As these pragmatic initiatives have been pursued, the boundaries between sectors have broken down and become less meaningful. Nonprofits and business have become intertwined along many different lines. Hence classical sectoral distinctions have become less important and less inhibiting as nonprofit sector leaders and present-day social entrepreneurs consider new approaches to social problem solving. It is now more natural to think outside the box, both in business and in the nonprofit sector, especially when it comes to persistent problems such as poverty, education of minority groups, community development, social justice, and other issues that have not responded to old programs and old solutions. The criterion for organizing solutions to social problems is moving away from sectoral mandates—the "government should do it" theme of the war on poverty, "the voluntary sector should do it" notion of the Reagan administration, or the "business will take care of it" posture of some free-market enthusiasts. Rather the new clarion call is "whatever works"—a non-formulaic, non-legalistic, non-political, non-categorical approach to getting the job done.

This suggests the emergence of a "new governance," a new approach to solving public problems.[49] The heart of this approach is an emphasis not on the differences among the sectors, but on the opportunities for collaboration among them. It is in this context that business, markets, and nonprofits are becoming intertwined and that new organizational forms are emerging.

Implications and Conclusions

The commercialization and marketization of the nonprofit sector detailed here offer important opportunities but also carry enormous risks for the nonprofit sector, for those it serves, and for American society. How the balance between the opportunities and the risks plays out may well determine the future of this set of institutions and its ability to continue making its distinctive contributions to our national life. Indeed, this may well determine whether the existing legal definition of a nonprofit organization, with its stress on the nondistribution of profits, still makes sense.

The potential opportunities are enticing, if not yet clearly defined. By engaging market forces and strategies in a more substantial way, marketization offers the nonprofit sector access not only to more resources but also to the energy and creativity that the market system has long represented. Empowered with earned income, nonprofits may become more fully independent than either government support or reliance on the whims of wealthy donors has ever made possible. Beyond this, engagement with the market opens possibilities for leveraging enormous private resources and talents for social sector purposes. The record of nonprofit low-income housing organizations detailed in chapter 6 provides a powerful lesson in this regard. Finally, and not inconsequentially, given the ascendance of the norms of efficiency and effectiveness in our society, adoption of the trappings of business management may help to erase popular images of nonprofit ineffectiveness and establish instead the image of organizations that have learned how to bring the most efficient means to the service of the most valued ends.

Set against these opportunities, however, are substantial risks and uncertainties. First, and most obvious, is the distinct possibility that the pressures of the market will entice the nonprofit sector to lose its way and surrender precisely those values that make it so vital—its commitment to quality, to free expression, to serving those in greatest need, and to doing what is right as opposed to what is popular or commercially viable. This concern has already arisen forcefully in several areas of nonprofit activity, including health care and higher education. A recent article in the *Atlantic Monthly* talks about the "kept university," a reference to the fact that the research and teaching agendas of private, nonprofit universities are now being influenced by the commercial needs of private corporations, which not only skew those agendas toward work of commercial value (to the neglect of basic research and less applied activities) but also influence longstanding mission-related practices and institutional values such as public access to research-generated knowledge.[50] Inevitably, the more the nonprofit sector is forced to rely on fees and charges, the more it will be tempted to orient its services to those able to pay.

Many of the cause-related marketing and joint venture arrangements between nonprofits and for-profit firms discussed in this chapter raise these issues in stark form. The more closely a reputable nonprofit is willing to identify itself with a particular product or company, the more the arrangement will be worth to that company and the more that company will be willing to remunerate the nonprofit. But such exclusive arrangements can compromise a nonprofit's objectivity. The American Cancer Society receives substantial grants from the Florida citrus growers and from Smith-Kline Beecham in exchange for understandings that it will not associate itself with other producers of citrus or smoking patches. By comparison, the American Heart Association receives much more modest fees for attaching its "heart-healthy" seal to various food products that meet its nutritional standards.

The growing closeness of nonprofits and corporations, while creating many benefits, is not without risk to participating nonprofits. In particular, a nonprofit may be perceived as neglecting or harming its mission if it identifies itself with questionable products, with disreputable organizations, or exclusively with products that may not be the very best for its intended beneficiaries. In the recent case of the American Medical Association and the Honeywell Corporation, leaders of the American Medical Association lost their jobs for entering an exclusive relationship that appeared to offer advanced endorsements of yet-to-be-tested medical devices. Similarly, the American Association of Retired Persons has been questioned for entering special relationships with health insurers that may not always assure the best coverage for older people. In response to similar concerns, the American Association of Museums recently issued a code of ethical standards for museums entering arrangements with owners and dealers of art collections to protect against situations where private parties would stand to benefit financially from the display of their art in a museum and where they might use financial incentives to influence the museum's decisions regarding the art to be exhibited. Many nonprofits, particularly smaller ones, remain leery of such involvements because they lack the expertise or sophistication to avoid such pitfalls. Other nonprofits have yet to identify corporations that provide the appropriate strategic fit with their own particular cause. Finally, issues of organizational size influence the propensity to partner on both sides of the market. Smaller nonprofits may not be well enough known or may not represent large enough constituencies to be attractive to corporate sponsors. Nonprofits with unpopular constituencies, such as ex-offenders or the mentally ill, might similarly be unattractive to corporations. To the extent that the nonprofit sector becomes dependent on the market for its sustenance and legitimacy, crucial functions and values could be lost. Indeed, there is a danger that nonprofits will find themselves smothered in the corporate embrace.

Equally significant is the impact that the marketization of the nonprofit sector can have on the sector's public support. To be sure, the public seems to be demanding higher standards of performance from nonprofit organizations, and the adoption of market-oriented management techniques may help to achieve this. But to the extent that adoption of business methods—including competitive salaries, charges for services, and marketing to paying customers—obscures the distinction between nonprofit and for-profit firms, it opens the nonprofit sector to serious charges of neglecting its social mission. This is particularly true given the limited effort that so far has been put into educating the public and key opinion leaders about the changes under way. In this kind of setting, the nonprofit sector could easily find itself exposed to cheap shots in the press and the public policy arena, jeopardizing its special tax and other advantages in the process.

These issues naturally arise most sharply in relation to the new social ventures that have gained popularity in recent years both in this country and in Western

Europe. Such ventures consciously blur the distinction between nonprofit and for-profit forms. Indeed, in their European incarnation, these ventures relax or eliminate what has long been the principal defining feature of nonprofit organizations in the American setting—their inability to distribute profits to their owners or members. Instead, such organizations are granted special tax and other privileges so long as they serve socially useful ends and provide meaningful opportunities for input to employees and other stakeholders.

Controversial though this approach may be, it may hold useful lessons for the American nonprofit scene. It has long been recognized in the United States that the nonprofit form per se does not guarantee responsible behavior or effective performance. The nondistribution constraint must always be carefully policed to avoid inurement, and even then it is difficult to guarantee that nonprofits are truly driven by mission rather than self-serving goals.

This does not mean that we can ignore organizational form and simply embrace the market as a suitable vehicle for serving social objectives. The evidence is strong that nonprofits serve different groups of clientele and provide different varieties of service than for-profits.[51] They also promote other important values related to diversity, expression, and innovation.[52] Preserving a set of institutions that adheres to incentives that are not wholly market-driven thus seems essential.

But what the European social enterprise experience suggests is that we may be looking in the wrong place to ensure socially responsible and effective behavior, that a prohibition on the distribution of profits may not be the most effective means to this end, and that more direct measures of performance and more direct mechanisms of control may be desirable—measures that spell out expected performance and mechanisms that empower key stakeholders, such as those for whom the benefits of a social venture are intended, to make sure that this performance is achieved. Indeed, by limiting access to market incentives that would otherwise be available, American nonprofit laws may limit the achievement of the socially desirable outcomes that social ventures promise.

The growing integration of the nonprofit sector into the market economy thus opens a Pandora's box of challenges and risks. But it also unleashes important energies and creates significant new opportunities to pursue long-standing social goals. Although it is essential to keep the challenges clearly in view, it would be foolhardy to let the opportunities go unexplored.

Notes

1. U.S. Social Security Administration, *Annual Statistical Supplement to the Social Security Bulletin* (Washington: U.S. Department of Health and Human Services, Social Security Administration, 2000), p. 120.

2. Lester M. Salamon and Alan J. Abramson, *The Federal Budget and the Nonprofit Sector* (Washington: Urban Institute, 1982), p. 44.

3. Lester M. Salamon, *America's Nonprofit Sector: A Primer.* 2d ed. (New York: Foundation Center, 1999), pp. 161–62.

4. Based on data from U.S. Census Bureau, *Census of Service Industries, 1997* (Washington: U.S. Census Bureau, 1997).

5. Thomas K. Reis and Stephanie Clohesy, "Unleashing New Resources and Entrepreneurship for the Common Good," paper prepared for the International Society for Third Sector Research conference, Dublin, Ireland, July 2000, p. 9.

6. John H. Goddeeris and Burton A. Weisbrod, "Conversion from Nonprofit to For-Profit Legal Status," in Burton Weisbrod, ed., *To Profit or Not to Profit* (Cambridge University Press, 1998), pp. 129–48.

7. Reis and Clohesy, "Unleashing New Resources," p. 16.

8. Sharon M. Oster, *Strategic Management for Nonprofit Organizations* (Oxford University Press, 1995), pp. 272–86.

9. Reynold Levy, *Give and Take: A Candid Account of Corporate Philanthropy* (Harvard Business School Press, 1999), pp. 3–15; Jane Nelson, *Business as Partners in Development* (London: Prince of Wales Business Leaders Forum, 1996), pp. 52–54; David Logan, Delwin Roy, and Laurie Ruggelbrugge, *Global Corporate Citizenship: Rationale and Strategies* (Washington: Hitachi Foundation, 1997), pp. 6–18.

10. Lester M. Salamon, *Partners in Public Service: Government-Nonprofit Relations in the Modern Welfare State* (Johns Hopkins University Press, 1996), pp. 211–13.

11. Elaine Morley, Elisa Vinson, and Harry P. Hatry, "Outcome Measurement in Nonprofit Organizations: Current Practices and Recommendations" (Washington: Independent Sector, 2001); Paul C. Light, *Making Nonprofits Work* (Washington: Brookings, 2000).

12. Computed from data in Murray S. Weitzman and others, *The New Nonprofit Almanac and Desk Reference* (San Francisco: Jossey-Bass, 2002). With religious congregations excluded, the share of philanthropy drops to 12 percent, the share of government grows to 35 percent, and the share of business grows to 53 percent.

13. Weisbrod, ed., *To Profit or Not to Profit,* p. 17.

14. Lester M. Salamon and associates, *Global Civil Society* (Johns Hopkins Center for Civil Society Studies, 1999), p. 27.

15. Lewis M. Segal and Burton A. Weisbrod, "Interdependence of Commercial and Donative Revenues," in Weisbrod, ed., *To Profit or Not to Profit,* pp. 105–28.

16. Margaret Riley, "Unrelated Business Income of Nonprofit Organizations, 1997," *Statistics of Income Bulletin,* vol. 20, no. 4 (Spring 2001): 127.

17. Riley, "Unrelated Business Income," p. 102.

18. Harvey Lipman and Elizabeth Schwinn, "The Business of Charity: Nonprofit Groups Reap Billions in Tax-Free Income Annually," *Chronicle of Philanthropy,* October 18, 2001, p. 25.

19. James C. Crimmins and Mary Keil, *Enterprise in the Nonprofit Sector* (New York: Rockefeller Brothers Fund, 1983), p. 11.

20. Edward Skloot, "Enterprise and Commerce in Nonprofit Organizations," in Walter W. Powell, ed., *The Nonprofit Sector: A Research Handbook* (Yale University Press, 1987), pp. 380–93; Edward Skloot, ed., *The Nonprofit Entrepreneur* (New York: Foundation Center, 1988); Jed Emerson and Faye Twersky, eds., *New Social Entrepreneurs* (San Francisco: Roberts Enterprise Development Fund, 1996); Dennis R. Young, "Commercialism in Nonprofit Social Service Associations," in Weisbrod, ed., *To Profit or Not to Profit,* pp. 195–216.

21. Roberts Enterprise Development Fund, *Social Purpose Enterprises and Venture Philanthropy in the New Millennium,* 2 vols. (San Francisco: Roberts Enterprise Development Fund, 1999); see vol. 1, p. 2.

22. Emerson and Twersky, *New Social Entrepreneurs,* pp. 6–7.

23. For additional discussion of these and other examples of social ventures, see Roberts Enterprise Development Fund, *Social Purpose Enterprises,* and www.independentsector.org/pathfinder, a website created by the pathfinder project of Independent Sector and the University of Maryland.

24. Gabriela Perez-Yarahuan, "Social Enterprises: Who Benefits?" paper prepared for the International Society for Third Sector Research conference, Dublin, Ireland, July 2000.

25. See the Nonprofit Pathfinder website: www.independentsector.org/pathfinder.

26. Perez-Yarahuan, "Social Enterprises," p. 12.

27. Organization for Economic Cooperation and Development, *Social Enterprises in OECD Countries* (Paris: OECD, 1998), p. 10.

28. Carlos Borzaga and Alceste Santuari, eds., *Social Enterprises and the New Employment in Europe* (Trento, Italy: University of Trento, 1998), p. 75.

29. J. Gregory Dees, "Enterprising Nonprofits," *Harvard Business Review,* vol. 76, no. 1 (January/February 1998): 55–67.

30. Reis and Clohesy, "Unleashing New Resources," p. 7.

31. Levy, *Give and Take,* p. 17.

32. Dwight F. Burlingame and Dennis R. Young, eds., *Corporate Philanthropy at the Crossroads* (Indiana University Press, 1996).

33. James R. Austin, *The Collaboration Challenge* (San Francisco: Jossey-Bass, 2000).

34. For discussions of this mode of corporate engagement with nonprofits, see Craig Smith, "The New Corporate Philanthropy," *Harvard Business Review,* vol. 72, no. 3 (May/June 1994): 105–16; Levy, *Give and Take,* pp. 39–57; Austin, *Collaboration Challenge.*

35. These examples are drawn from Austin, *Collaboration Challenge,* pp. 20–34; Logan, Roy, and Regelbrugge, *Global Corporate Citizenship,* pp. 19–39; Nelson, *Business as Partners,* pp. 211–82.

36. Dennis R. Young, *Commercial Activity and Voluntary Health Agencies: When Are Ventures Advisable?* (Washington: National Health Council, 1998), p. 13.

37. Dennis R. Young, *If Not for Profit, for What?* (Lexington: D.C. Heath, 1983), pp. 21–41.

38. Crimmins and Keil, *Enterprise in the Nonprofit Sector;* Skloot, "Enterprise and Commerce in Nonprofit Organizations," pp. 380–93.

39. On the concept of managerialism and the managerial revolution in American business, see Alfred D. Chandler Jr., *The Visible Hand: The Managerial Revolution in American Business* (Harvard University Press, 1977), pp. 1–12, 484–98. Managerialism here refers to the emergence of complex, multiple-unit organizations and emphasis on management and managers, as opposed to owners or boards, to ensure organizational performance.

40. Roseanne M. Mirabella and Naomi Bailin Wish, "University-Based Educational Programs in the Management of Nonprofit Organizations," *Public Performance and Management Review,* vol. 25, no. 1 (September 2001): 30–41.

41. Michael O'Neill and Kathleen Fletcher, eds., *Nonprofit Management Education* (New York: Praeger, 1998), pp. 1–10.

42. For a useful summary of these concepts as they apply to the nonprofit sector, see Kevin P. Kearns, *Private Sector Strategies for Social Sector Success: The Guide to Strategy and Planning for Public and Nonprofit Organizations* (San Francisco: Jossey-Bass, 2000).

43. Paul Light, *Making Nonprofits Work,* pp. 68–77; Patricia Patrizi and Bernard McMullan, "Realizing the Potential of Program Evaluation," *Foundation News,* vol. 40, no. 3 (May-June 1999): 30–35; Gary Walker and Jean Grossman, "Philanthropy and Outcomes," in Charles Clotfelter and Thomas Ehrlich, eds., *Philanthropy and the Nonprofit Sector in a Changing America* (Indiana University Press, 1999), pp. 449–60.

44. Light, *Making Nonprofits Work*, pp. 19–22.

45. Oster, *Strategic Management for Nonprofit Organizations*, pp. 277–86.

46. Christine Letts, William P. Ryan, and Allen Grossman, "Virtuous Capital: What Foundations Can Learn from Venture Capitalists," *Harvard Business Review*, vol. 75, no. 2 (March/April 1997): 2–7; Roberts Enterprise Development Fund, *Social Purpose Enterprises*, vol. 2.

47. Jed Emerson, "The U.S. Nonprofit Capital Market: An Introductory Overview of Developmental Stages, Investors, and Funding Instruments," in Roberts Enterprise Development Fund, *Social Purpose Enterprises*, vol. 2, pp. 187–216; Michael E. Porter and Mark R. Kramer, "Philanthropy's New Agenda: Creating Value," *Harvard Business Review*, vol. 77 (November/December 1999): 121–30.

48. Amelia Kohm, David LaPiana, and Heather Gowdy, *Strategic Restructuring: Findings from a Study of Integrations and Alliances among Nonprofit Social Service and Cultural Organizations in the United States*, Discussion Paper (Chicago: Chapin Hall Center for Children), p. 1; Jane Arsenault, *Forging Nonprofit Alliances* (San Francisco: Jossey-Bass, 1998).

49. For further elaboration, see Lester M. Salamon, "The New Governance and the Tools of Government Action: An Introduction," in Lester M. Salamon, ed., *The Tools of Government: A Guide to the New Governance* (Oxford University Press, 2002), pp. 1–18.

50. Eyal Press and Jennifer Washburn, "The Kept University," *Atlantic Monthly*, vol. 285, no. 3 (March 2000): 39–54.

51. Burton A. Weisbrod, *The Nonprofit Economy* (Harvard University Press, 1988).

52. Bradford H. Gray, *The Profit Motive in Patient Care* (Harvard University Press, 1991), pp. 332–33.

14

Devolution, Marketization, and the Changing Shape of Government-Nonprofit Relations

KIRSTEN A. GRØNBJERG AND LESTER M. SALAMON

Relations between the nonprofit sector and government—always complex, multifaceted, and in flux—have undergone significant changes in the United States over the past two decades. In the process, the implicit partnership that has characterized these relations during much of American history, and that was fundamentally expanded during the 1960s and 1970s, has been substantially redefined, with results that are still not wholly clear, but that seem increasingly problematic for the sector and those it serves.

More specifically, as partly reflected in the chapters on major nonprofit fields in section II of this volume, five changes in the policy environment facing nonprofit organizations are particularly noteworthy. First, funding for many of the government programs that had fueled the growth of the nonprofit sector in the 1960s and 1970s declined in the early 1980s in both absolute and constant dollars, at least outside the health arena. Especially notable was the decline in discretionary grant and contract spending.

Second, despite this, overall government spending and government support to nonprofit organizations have grown substantially, but have taken a different form. In particular, government support has shifted substantially away from producer-side subsidies provided directly to nonprofit service providers and toward consumer-side subsidies provided to potential recipients of their services. This shift, which was already evident with the G.I. bill in the 1940s for education, and with Medicare and Medicaid in the 1960s for health, has now spread to the human service arena more broadly, making it necessary for nonprofits across a broad front to compete in the market not only for private fee income but for government assistance as well. The result has been a deepening "marketization" of nonprofit operations that has had a broad impact on the character of these organizations.

Third, this shift toward consumer subsidies has reinforced other government policies that have jeopardized the preferred-provider status of nonprofit organizations in many government programs and increased the relative advantages of for-profit providers. Although characterized as "privatization," these policies have shifted public resources not from government agencies to private ones, but from *nonprofit* private ones to *for-profit* private ones. Coupled with more recent proposals to advantage faith-based organizations, the result has been to subject nonprofit service agencies, particularly in the human services field, to increasing competitive pressures.

Fourth, nonprofits are facing growing regulatory pressures from government at all levels. Particularly noteworthy here are recent legislative and administrative efforts to discourage nonprofit advocacy. But other mission-critical nonprofit functions are also at risk, such as the commitment to serve those in greatest need, to promote teaching and research, and to value quality and community benefit over efficiency and responsiveness to market pressures.

Finally, changes in tax policy, whether intentionally or unintentionally, have reduced the financial incentives to make charitable contributions both out of current income and at death. At the same time, continuing battles over nonprofit property tax exemptions have added further to the fiscal uncertainties of nonprofits in many locales.

Several caveats are in order, of course. These developments are not necessarily new to the last two decades since most have important historical precursors. Nor are they uniformly in evidence, since there are important variations by field and by locality. What is more, the generally negative developments detailed here need to be seen in the context of a number of more supportive actions that have also occurred. These include the increased attention and visibility accorded the nonprofit sector by the Reagan administration and the two Bush administrations, the "national service" initiative developed by the Clinton administration, and the encouragement of faith-based organizations promoted by President George W. Bush. Despite these caveats, however, there seems to have been a general shift in government-nonprofit relations over the past two decades, and that shift, on the whole, has intensified the challenges facing the sector.

This chapter examines these recent developments in greater depth. To put the discussion into context, it begins by outlining the multiple arenas of government-nonprofit interaction and the historical pattern of government-nonprofit ties. It then investigates the recent changes that have occurred in each of the arenas of government-nonprofit interaction. A concluding section, finally, examines the implications of the recent changes and offers some recommendations for improving the relations between government and the nonprofit sector in the years ahead.

Background: Arenas and Patterns of Government-Nonprofit Relations

Government-nonprofit relations in the United States are complex and dynamic and have been from the very beginning. These relations are embedded in the economic and political structures of American society and in the political ideologies that have come to guide our national consciousness, shaping our concepts of the proper role of government, the virtues of markets, and the role of private initiative. Disentangling the realities from the myths in this field is consequently very difficult, but also essential. Simplistic explanations that fail to capture critical dimensions are poor guides for interpreting new developments and making choices about the future.

Major Arenas of Government-Nonprofit Interaction

A useful starting point for such an exercise is to recognize that nonprofit-government relations operate on more than one level and in multiple arenas. What is more, variations also exist across localities and across components of the sector. It is quite possible, therefore, that different perceptions of these relations can result from focusing on different levels, arenas, localities, or components.

Perhaps most important for our purposes is the conflict that has long existed between the ideological or normative perception of government-nonprofit relations and the empirical or factual perception. For better or worse, the nonprofit sector has been the ideological battleground for a long-running debate in American thinking about the appropriate role of government in responding to social and economic needs. Much of the discussion of government-nonprofit relations has thus occurred at the ideological level. Advocates of a limited state have championed the nonprofit sector as an alternative mechanism for responding to social ills and consequently have emphasized strict separation between government and voluntary groups. Advocates of greater governmental involvement, on the other hand, have downplayed the presence of nonprofit organizations and emphasized instead the need for government action to cope with social and economic problems. Neither side, therefore, has had an ideological interest in emphasizing the possibilities for cooperation between the sectors, so an image of separation and conflict has come to dominate our rhetoric even when it has failed to resonate with actual realities on the ground.

Even at the empirical level, however, government and nonprofit organizations interact in a variety of arenas, and this can cause added confusion and misperception. One of these arenas, for example, is the arena of *government spending*.

Government spending decisions affect nonprofit organizations indirectly by affecting the need for nonprofit services. But they also affect nonprofit organizations directly since government is an important source of nonprofit revenues.

Nonprofit organizations are also affected both directly and indirectly in the arena of government *taxation policies*. Nonprofits are typically exempted from taxation in the United States, but the range of activities so exempted and the range of taxes—income, sales, property—from which exemptions are provided can vary over time and among jurisdictions. Tax policies also affect the donations that nonprofits receive from individuals and corporations. Donations to charities eligible for exemption under Section 501(c)(3) of the tax code are deductible from the taxable income of individual taxpayers and corporations within certain limits, which means that the value of these deductions varies with the tax rate. Similarly, contributions to such organizations have also been deductible from estates in computing estate taxes, which have historically been fairly high in the United States to avoid the creation of an aristocracy of wealth.

A third arena in which government and nonprofit organizations interact is *regulatory* in nature. Government regulations determine the types of organizations eligible for tax-exempt status, the procedures under which they secure this status, the types of activities they can undertake, and the kinds of public disclosure they must make. Thus, for example, religious congregations have historically not been required to seek official designation as tax-exempt entities, whereas other types of organizations typically are required to file for such status with the Internal Revenue Service. Similarly, constraints of various sorts have been placed on the political and legislative activity of organizations receiving tax-deductible gifts.

Finally, nonprofit organizations have a deep stake in the broader *policies* that governments pursue. As noted in chapters by Salamon and Boris and Krehely of this book, policy advocacy is one of the principal functions of the nonprofit sector and one of the major contributions these organizations make to American society. Indeed, one of the great strengths of the American democratic system is the freedom it affords individuals to come together in organizations to promote the common good, including pressuring government to respond to disadvantaged groups or attend to unresolved problems.

Given these multiple arenas, it is quite possible for government and nonprofit organizations to be at odds in one arena, while cooperating in others. For example, it is quite reasonable to expect government and the nonprofit sector to be at odds on certain policy issues, while cooperating intensively in the spending, tax, and regulatory arenas.

A Heritage of Cooperation

Although it is consequently difficult to generalize about government-nonprofit relations across all arenas and all fields, it seems fair to conclude that the general tenor of these relations at the operating level has been cooperative throughout most of our history, even though a rhetoric of conflict and separation has dominated at the ideological and rhetorical level. Historian Waldemar Nielsen put it as well as anyone when he noted in 1979, "Throughout most of American history government has been an active partner and financier of the Third Sector to a much greater extent than is commonly recognized. . . . [C]ollaboration, not separation or antagonism, between government and the Third Sector . . . has been the predominant characteristic."[1]

Although some early colonies resisted the formation of nonprofit institutions, and such institutions were outlawed for a time in the early history of Massachusetts, government has generally protected the right of citizens to associate. The first nonprofit organization on American soil, Harvard College, was not only chartered by the Commonwealth of Massachusetts but also made the recipient of a dedicated commonwealth tax, the "colledge corne." This pattern was replicated in the design of other venerable nonprofit educational institutions, such as Columbia, Dartmouth, and Yale.[2] As state governments expanded their functions in the late nineteenth century in response to the twin challenges of urbanization and industrialization, this pattern of government support of private institutions was extended as well, at first into the health field and later into social services more broadly. A 1901 survey found, in fact, that "except possibly two territories and four Western states, there is probably not a state in the union where some aid [to private charities] is not given either by the state or by the counties and cities."[3] The federal government followed the same approach in its dealings with the District of Columbia. By 1892, half of the funds that Congress allocated for aid to the poor in the district went to private charities, and these private institutions also absorbed two-thirds of the funds the district allocated for the construction of charitable facilities.[4]

None of this is to say that the relationships between government and the nonprofit sector were without tensions. Nonprofits vigorously challenged public neglect of poverty and distress, and governments at various points challenged the accumulations of wealth that nonprofit institutions sometimes amassed.[5] Yet even when protests were most in evidence, the objective was typically not to replace government but to energize and enlist it. And the result quite often was to mobilize government to finance initiatives that nonprofits were then empowered to carry out. The upshot was the development of a distinctive, but by no means unique, American approach to addressing public problems, an approach that Lester Salamon has termed "third-party government."[6] The central feature of this approach is the reliance by government on a variety of "third parties" to carry out functions that the public wants to be performed, whether it be the extension of loans to home buyers, the provisioning of the military, the construction of roads and bridges, or the pursuit of scientific research. These third parties have included commercial banks, industrial corporations, highway construction companies, and nonprofit colleges and universities.

Table 14-1. *Sources of U.S. Nonprofit Organization Revenue,*
Exclusive of Religious Congregations, 1977
Percent of total

Type	Government	Fees, investments	Private giving
Health	32	53	14
Education and research	18	67	15
Social and legal services	54	13	33
Civic and social	50	19	31
Arts and culture	12	47	41
Total	31	51	18

Source: Authors' estimates based on data in Murray S. Weitzman, Nadine Tai Jalandoni, Linda M.
Lampkin, and Thomas H. Pollack, *The New Nonprofit Almanac and Desk Reference* (San Francisco:
Jossey-Bass, 2002).

When the federal government was finally persuaded to address the health,
employment and training, community development, and social service problems of the nation during the Great Society era of the 1960s and 1970s, therefore, it was only natural that it would use this same approach. The upshot was a
substantial enlargement of the existing pattern of government-nonprofit cooperation. Although it is not widely recognized, most of the Great Society programs
operated with and through nonprofit organizations. In the process, government
helped to stimulate a massive expansion of the nonprofit sector. Indeed, much
of the nonprofit sector as we know it today took shape as a result of this growth
in government support. In some cases, government stimulated the creation of
such organizations where none existed (for example, the community action
agencies fostered by the war on poverty, area agencies on aging, community
mental health centers, and regional planning agencies in health and metropolitan development). Elsewhere, government relied on existing nonprofit hospitals,
higher education institutions, family service agencies, and daycare centers.
Between 1960 and 1980, as a consequence, the operating expenditures of American nonprofit organizations increased nearly tenfold in current dollar terms and
more than doubled in constant dollar terms, jumping from less than 4 percent
of the nation's gross domestic product to nearly 6 percent.[7] Outside of religious
congregations, government easily surpassed private giving from individuals, corporations, and foundations combined as a source of nonprofit income (see table
14-1). Among social service organizations, government moved into first place.

For the most part, this newly expanded government support flowed directly to
the nonprofit agencies themselves. While much of it took the form of grants or
contracts for particular services rather than the general-purpose funding of earlier
eras, the grants or contracts were often on terms highly favorable to the nonprofit
organizations. Thus, for example, expanded federal funding of university-based

scientific research during and after World War II operated through project grants to researchers that were controlled largely by the academic research community and carried with them substantial overhead support to the host institutions.[8] Other support was provided for the capital construction needs of universities and hospitals. Even the consumer-side vouchers created during this period, such as Medicare and Medicaid, utilized cost-based reimbursement systems that were highly advantageous to the recipient institutions, essentially committing the federal government to reimburse them for their costs.[9]

Not only did federal funding of nonprofit organizations blossom during this period, but so did other facets of government-nonprofit relations. Most notable here was the federal government's encouragement and subsequent responsiveness to nonprofit advocacy and promotion of social and political rights. This was evident in the passage of the civil rights and voting rights acts and in the opening of greatly expanded opportunities for class action suits in fields such as consumer rights and environmental protection. Thanks to these openings, nonprofit organizations representing African Americans, Native Americans, Hispanics, welfare recipients, migrant farm workers, women, gays and lesbians, people with disabilities, consumers, and environmentalists were able to push for much fuller participation in the nation's social, political, and economic life.

This is not to say that the resulting relationships between government and the nonprofit sector were without their tensions and strains. The more numerous and substantial funding relationships inevitably created the need for greater formality and structure. The result was a loss of flexibility for both parties.[10] What is more, the sheer number and variety of government programs created major coordination problems for both the recipient organizations and the government agencies, increasing the transaction costs for both sides.[11] Nevertheless, this period represented, in many respects, a golden era of government-nonprofit cooperation.[12]

Retrenchment, Marketization, Devolution, and Regulation

Set against this backdrop, the years since 1980 have witnessed a significant deterioration in government-nonprofit relations. To be sure, not all the developments have been negative. What is more, at least some of the negative impacts have been inadvertent, a result of misunderstanding the real relationships that exist. Yet, even with these caveats it is hard not to view this recent period as one of growing tension and uncertainty. What is more, tension and uncertainty have been evident in more than one of the arenas of government-nonprofit interaction.

The Arena of Government Spending

Perhaps most striking has been the shift that has occurred in the arena of government spending.

RETRENCHMENT. The signal development here was the sharp reversal in the growth of direct government support of nonprofit organizations ushered in by the Reagan administration in the early 1980s. In a sense, the Reagan administration took the rhetoric of conflict and competition between government and the nonprofit sector that has long dominated the ideological picture of this relationship as an accurate portrayal of reality and proposed to strengthen the nonprofit sector by getting government out of its way, overlooking the extent to which these two sectors had forged mutually supportive bonds. Although only a portion of the budget cuts the administration proposed were enacted, the result was a significant decline in government spending in fields where nonprofit organizations are active, at least outside of health, and a considerable reduction in the real value of government support to nonprofit organizations. Such support declined approximately 25 percent in real dollar terms in the early 1980s and still had not returned to its 1980 level in real dollar terms as of 1994, when the Contract with America Congress ushered in a new round of cuts. As of the mid-1990s, the real value of federal support to nonprofit organizations was 19 percent below its 1980 level in the fields of education and social services, 17 percent below in the field of international assistance, and 42 percent below in the field of community development.[13]

MARKETIZATION. In addition to reducing the level of government support to nonprofit organizations, at least outside of the health field, the Reagan administration also took measures to promote for-profit involvement in government contract work, including that for human services. Thus a 1983 Office of Management and Budget circular established an elaborate process requiring federal agencies to open even more of their activities to "the competitive market-place," meaning particularly private businesses.[14] Although these moves were characterized as "privatization" and were justified by "public choice" economic theories, their real impact, given the widespread government reliance on private nonprofit organizations, was to increase for-profit competition for many of the grants and contracts that nonprofit organizations were already receiving. At the same time, earlier preferences for nonprofit organizations in key fields were weakened or phased out. Thus, for example, in the health field, the Medicare licensure requirement for for-profit (but not nonprofit) home health facilities and the start-up assistance to nonprofit health maintenance organizations were eliminated.

SHIFT TO CONSUMER-SIDE SUBSIDIES. As important as the reduction in government spending in many fields has been the significant shift that has occurred in its basic forms. Most of the reductions in government support to nonprofit organizations were focused on "producer-side" subsidies—that is, programs that deliver their assistance directly to the producers of services. Meanwhile, most of the federal entitlement programs, which generally took the form of consumer-side vouchers, continued to grow, often at exponential rates. As Salamon noted in chapter 1 of this volume, part of this was due to the natural escalation of costs and growth of the existing eligible populations. But a far larger part was due to the considerable expansions that occurred in the late 1980s and throughout the 1990s in the services and populations covered by these programs. For example, Medicaid coverage was extended to fifty distinct subgroups during this period, boosting the program's coverage from 21.6 million people in 1980 to 40.6 million by 1998.[15] Also at work were successful state attempts to shift more of their human service spending from declining federal grant and contract programs to the growing Medicaid voucher program, which provides a more generous federal matching rate and a more open-ended funding stream. Despite the budgetary stringency, therefore, overall federal spending in fields where nonprofits are active continued to grow rather robustly, particularly after the mid-1980s. In the process, the balance between producer-side subsidies and consumer-side subsidies shifted decisively toward the latter, with over 70 percent of federal support to nonprofit organizations taking this form by 1986. This, in turn, made it easier for for-profit firms to enter markets formerly dominated almost exclusively by nonprofits.

Also working in the same direction was the increased reliance on a variety of other indirect tools of government action, such as loan guarantees and tax subsidies. These tools gained popularity in the prevailing anti-government, anti-tax climate of the 1980s and 1990s.[16] Indeed, the price of securing support for government efforts to deal with child poverty, daycare services, low-income housing, and a host of other problems in the late 1980s and into the 1990s was to utilize such indirect tools. This is hardly entirely new, of course. The tax deduction for medical expenses and the exclusion of scholarship aid from taxable income, for example, have long been established features of the tax code. But the use of such tools in fields where nonprofits are active expanded considerably over the past decade or more with the addition or extension of programs such as the childcare tax credit, the credit for student loan interest payments, and the low-income housing tax credit. As table 14-2 shows, by fiscal 2001 these alternative tools represented another $315.2 billion in federal assistance in fields where nonprofits are active. This represents a 123 percent increase in constant dollar terms over what was available through these tools a decade earlier, a rate of increase that exceeds even that achieved by spending programs in these same fields (see table 14-3). In many fields, therefore, the value of activities supported through these off-budget tools exceeds the value of the outright spending programs. In daycare, for example, the $3.56 billion in subsidies made available to middle-income and lower-middle income families through the daycare tax credit exceeds the roughly $3 billion in subsidies provided to poor families through the childcare and development block grant.

Table 14-2. *Major Federal Tax Expenditure and Loan Programs of Relevance to Nonprofit Organizations, 2001*

Program	Amount (millions of U.S. dollars)
Tax expenditures (outlay equivalent)	
Insurance companies owned by nonprofits	300
Low-income housing credit	4,360
Empowerment zone	380
New markets tax credit	20
Scholarship income exclusion	1,330
HOPE tax credit	5,300
Lifetime learning tax credit	3,030
Student loan interest deduction	460
State prepaid tuition plans	250
Student loan bond interest deduction	330
Nonprofit education facilities bond interest	770
Parental exemption for students	1,120
Charitable contribution deduction	53,260
Employer educational assistance	320
Employer-provided child care	950
Adopted foster care assistance	220
Adoption credit	160
Child credit	26,460
Child care credit	3,560
Employer medical insurance contributions	106,750
Self-employed medical insurance	1,900
Workers compensation insurance premiums	5,900
Medical expense deduction	4,990
Hospital construction bond interest	1,580
Public-purpose state and local bond interest	33,100
Parsonage allowance deduction	400
Subtotal, tax expenditures	257,200
Loan guarantee commitments	
Health center guaranteed loan	7
Family education loan program	34,705
Community development loan guarantees	244
Student Loan Marketing Association	3,819
Subtotal, loan guarantees	38,775
Direct loan obligations	
Historically black college capital financing	16
Direct student loan program	19,219
Community development financial institutions fund	12
Community development credit union revolving fund	10
Subtotal, direct loans	19,257
Total	315,232

Source: *Analytical Perspectives, Budget of the United States Government, Fiscal Year 2003* (Washington: Government Printing Office, 2002), pp. 99–101, 213–33.

Table 14-3. *Growth in Federal Tax Expenditure and Loan Programs of Relevance to Nonprofits, 1990–2001*

Type of program	Amount (billions of constant 2001 dollars)		Percentage change, 1990–2001
	1990	*2001*	
Tax expenditures	114.4	257.2	125
Direct loan commitments	0.1	19.3	17,000
Loan guarantee commitments	26.9	38.8	44
Total	141.4	315.3	+123

Source: *Special Analyses, Budget of the U.S. Government, FY 1990,* pp. F70–87, G44–49 (Washington: Government Printing Office, 1989); *Analytical Perspective, Budget of the U.S. Government, Fiscal Year 2003* (Washington: Government Printing Office, 2002), pp. 99–101, 212–33.

This shift in government support from producer-side grants and contracts to consumer-side vouchers, tax credits, and loan guarantees has been justified on grounds that it gives consumers more choice and fosters efficiency by forcing providers to compete for clients in an open market. In the process, however, this shift has injected a much higher degree of uncertainty into nonprofit operations, intensified the pressures on nonprofits to market their services, brought new for-profit competitors into the field, and generally narrowed the range of criteria on the basis of which competition occurs. Of particular concern to nonprofits is that mission-critical functions such as research or teaching have been rendered more difficult to support and that for-profit firms can siphon off the clients that are least costly to treat, leaving nonprofits to handle the rest despite government reimbursement rates that are insufficient to cover the costs.

PERFORMANCE MEASUREMENT AND MANAGED CARE. Not only have the instruments being used to channel public support to nonprofit organizations changed, but so too have the internal operations of some of the existing instruments, often in ways that have made them more challenging for nonprofits. Thus, for example, the retrospective cost-based reimbursement system long used to finance the Medicare and Medicaid programs was replaced in the early 1980s by a prospective payment system that established fixed rates for particular medical procedures and required institutions to meet these costs or suffer losses on their publicly subsidized services. In many cases, nonprofits charged that the new rates took too blanket an approach and failed to cover the special costs incurred by nonprofits as a result of their mission-critical activities, such as teaching and research for university-based hospitals.

A related challenge is represented by the growth of managed care systems in several service fields, most notably health and now also human services, as detailed in chapters 2 and 4 of this volume. Under these systems, both public and private third-party payers, such as insurance companies, establish set fees for coverage of particular classes of clients for particular ranges of service and then negotiate with nonprofit and for-profit providers to provide the services at the lowest possible cost. The growth of managed care presents profound challenges for nonprofits. Successful operation of managed care systems requires large pools of clients in order to balance risks. But this requires sophisticated information-processing equipment that nonprofits often lack the investment capital to acquire. Inevitably, therefore, these developments have attracted for-profit competitors into key service fields. What is more, nonprofits have had to find ways to reconcile their missions of providing quality care with reimbursement structures that frequently drive them toward lowest-cost service.

Passage of the Government Performance and Results Act of 1993 has had a similar effect. The thrust of this legislation has been to inject a greater concern for tangible performance into government operations at all levels. However, since cost and efficiency considerations are easier to measure than quality or equity ones, the overall result has been to give an implicit advantage to for-profit providers who tend to focus on these more market-oriented criteria.

All of this has fundamentally changed the ground rules for many nonprofit service providers. The momentum has moved away from mission-driven efforts to deliver effective services and toward cost-control, efficiency, and minimum standards of care. In the process, this has increased the competitive advantage of for-profit providers who are accustomed to competing on precisely these terms.

WELFARE REFORM AND CHARITABLE CHOICE. A final major factor affecting the public sector funding environment for nonprofit organizations has been welfare reform and its accompanying expansion of so-called charitable choice. The impacts here have been complex and by no means unidirectional.

In its basic design and thrust, the welfare reform legislation that passed in 1996 appeared largely hostile to nonprofit organizations. This legislation put a lid on federal payments to states for welfare assistance and stipulated that states had to move welfare recipients off the welfare rolls into work within a five-year time span. It thus shifted the focus of this major federal income support program from services and income support to work readiness and employment, not fields where traditional nonprofit social service agencies have had a particular comparative advantage. Reflecting this, many states moved early in the implementation of welfare reform to enlist for-profit companies, including a number of defense contractors such as Lockheed Martin, to assist them in managing the complex process of moving welfare recipients into jobs, thus intensifying the competition between nonprofit agencies and for-profit companies in the human service arena. Thus Nathan and Gais report that almost one-third (31 percent) of the states have contracted out their administrative design of employment and training programs, and one-fifth have contracted out the policymaking responsibilities for this field.[17] The corresponding percentages for pregnancy prevention services are 21 and 15 percent. As Frumkin and Andre-Clark report, a growing number of these administrative contracts are with for-profit entities, so nonprofits may no longer interact directly with government when they deliver publicly financed services, but rather contract with a for-profit party.[18]

Additional competition for nonprofits resulted from the so-called charitable choice provisions in the welfare reform bill. These provisions specifically authorized the funding of so-called faith-based organizations—religious congregations and other avowedly sectarian organizations—in the efforts to help welfare recipients overcome dependence and secure paying jobs. The arguments advanced for these provisions were similar to those that underlay the marketization initiatives of this period—that sacramental organizations are more cost-effective than traditional nonprofit agencies in achieving the objectives of welfare reform. This is so, advocates argued, both because they mobilize the power of faith to change human behavior and because they have access to religiously inspired volunteers, making it possible for them to avoid payments to nonprofit professionals.[19] These arguments have since been expanded beyond the welfare reform arena through the Bush administration's "faith-based charity" initiative, which would open more of the federal funding stream to faith-based organizations, increasing the competition for the available public dollars and drawing the most mission-based segment of the nonprofit sector into the competition for public funds.

Although the basic structure of the welfare reform posed significant challenges to the nonprofit sector, however, the actual evolution of the program also turned out to produce some important windfall gains. This was so because the economic boom of the late 1990s created extraordinary employment opportunities for welfare recipients, leading to an unexpected drop in welfare rolls from 5 million families in 1995 to 2 million in 2000.[20] Since the welfare reform legislation guaranteed that federal payments to states would remain at their pre-1996 levels for at least five years, this drop in the rolls translated into a fiscal windfall for the states. Thus Gais and others report that by 1999 the median state spent only 54 percent of its combined federal temporary aid to needy families (TANF) money and state "maintenance of effort" funds on cash assistance, a quarter of the states spent less than 45 percent, and Wisconsin, which had implemented its welfare reform program very early, spent only 28 percent.[21] The remaining funds could therefore be channeled into a variety of supportive services. Thus Geen reports that state TANF spending for child welfare services increased by $1.5 billion, or 170 percent, over the 1996–2000 period, so that by 2000 states were spending $9.9 billion in federal funds (including federal TANF dollars) on child welfare services, up 36 percent from 1996.[22] More in-depth analysis for four states (California, Georgia, Missouri, Wisconsin) shows that cash assistance declined between 29 and 51 percent over the 1995–99 period, while expenditures for most types of services increased during the same period, in most cases significantly.[23]

Unfortunately, neither of the two major ongoing projects to analyze the impact of welfare reform is designed to determine the impact on the nonprofit sector. Thus while Nathan and Gais show that 79 percent of states use private providers to deliver employment and training and 73 percent use them to deliver pregnancy prevention services, we do not know whether these providers are nonprofit or for-profit.[24] Frumkin and Andre-Clark note that for-profits have gained significant footholds in several fields as a consequence of welfare reform.[25] But, as noted in chapter 4 of this volume, the increases in state spending for child welfare and other welfare-related services are likely to have benefited nonprofits, since they are dominant in these fields.

IMPLICATIONS FOR NONPROFIT FUNDING. If the funding environment for nonprofit agencies has grown more challenging and complex during the past twenty years, however, the agencies seem to have found ways to cope with the resulting challenges. At the very least, despite the retrenchment with which this period began, the nonprofit sector has managed to boost its revenues from public sector sources—and to do so massively. Thus, as Salamon reports in chapter 1 of this volume, nonprofit receipts from government grew 195 percent between 1977 and 1997 alone, before the full effects of the welfare reform windfall had even been felt. Welfare reform doubtless boosted these gains in subsequent years. Although health organizations were prime beneficiaries of this growth, social service agencies were not far behind. Overall, government accounted for a striking 42 percent of the dramatic growth of the nonprofit sector during this period. Among social service providers, it accounted for 51 percent. Clearly, nonprofit organizations mastered the new market-oriented funding streams that came to dominate public sector funding during this period.

Harder to determine is the cost of this success in terms of the traditional functions of the nonprofit sector. What is more, there is serious question about whether these gains can be sustained into the foreseeable future. The mid- to late-1990s was a boom period for the economy and hence for government revenues. The early years of the new century, by contrast, have been a period of lagging economic growth. Coupled with significant tax cuts, the result has been to turn budget surpluses into budget deficits for both the federal government and an increasing number of states. Pressures are mounting as of this writing, therefore, to constrain the growth of Medicaid spending, to reduce Medicare and Medicaid reimbursement rates, to scale back welfare payments to states, and generally to limit federal government spending in fields where nonprofit organizations are active.

States, too, have been feeling the fiscal pinch. Recent reports by the National Governors' Association indicate significant budget shortfalls in forty-five of the fifty states, with collective deficits approaching 10 percent of state budgets.[26] Most seriously, the shortfalls seem to be structural rather than cyclical: that is, they are a product of changes in state economic and tax structures rather than simply temporary fluctuations in economic activity. Given the anti-tax political climate that exists, this increases the likelihood that states will seek to restrict the spending side rather than to increase their revenues. The result seems likely to eliminate the one positive element in the generally negative picture of government policy toward nonprofit organizations over the past two decades: the fact that the overall volume of government support has been rising, even while its basic forms have been changing and the nonprofit sector's access to it has been growing more difficult.

The Taxation Arena

Accompanying the changes in government spending during the past twenty years have been dramatic changes in taxation policies that have also had significant, and generally negative, implications for nonprofit organizations. These changes have taken many forms and have shifted somewhat over time. What is more, they have affected the taxation of both nonprofit organizations themselves and the donations they receive from the public.

INCOME TAX RATE CHANGES. Most dramatic, perhaps, have been the changes in individual income tax rates. Income tax rates determine not only how much money taxpayers have to contribute to charity (the income effect) but also the out-of-pocket cost of such gifts (the price effect). Generally speaking, the price effects are thought to be stronger than the income effects. This means that lowering the tax rate is likely to reduce charitable giving since it increases the out-of-pocket cost of the gift—that is, the net cost of the gift after taking account of what the taxpayer has to pay in taxes if she does not make the gift.[27]

Generally speaking, tax rates have been in decline over the past twenty years, especially for upper-income taxpayers, who make the bulk of the charitable donations, at least outside of giving to religious congregations.[28] Thus the Reagan administration pushed through significant income tax rate reductions in 1981, and these were extended in 1986. Although these reductions were partly reversed during the first Bush administration, the second Bush administration successfully pushed through further deep cuts in tax rates for upper-income taxpayers in 2001. In addition, a 1993 act tightened administration of the charitable contribution provisions by requiring written substantiation for gifts of $250 or more. While other detailed changes in tax legislation increased the incentives to give (for example, the institution for a short period in the early 1980s of a special charitable deduction for those who do not otherwise itemize their deductions and the elimination in 1993 of gains on appreciated property from the alternative minimum tax base), the overall effect of the changes has been to reduce tax rates, especially for better-off taxpayers, and thereby to increase the out-of-pocket costs of charitable giving.

ESTATE TAXES. Also significant have been changes in estate taxes. Such taxes have historically been fairly high in the United States in order to avoid the creation of an aristocracy of wealth in the country. As a consequence, wealthy individuals have had strong incentives to make charitable bequests and to create charitable foundations rather than see their estates go to the government at their death.

Beginning in the early 1980s, however, steps have been taken to reduce these taxes. Thus the 1981 Economic Recovery Tax Act reduced the maximum tax on estates from 70 to 50 percent over a period of years, increased the exemptions from this tax, and permitted a complete exemption for spouses. The Tax Act of 1997 further increased the estate tax exemption, and the tax act enacted in 2001 as part of the Bush administration's tax program began a full phase-out of this tax. Although the full implementation of this provision is still some years away and ultimately may be reversed, the impact on nonprofit revenues and capital resources seems likely to be negative.[29]

PROPERTY AND SALES TAX EXEMPTIONS. Other forces are challenging the direct tax exemptions that nonprofit organizations enjoy, at least at the state and local level. These exemptions cover all three major forms of state and local taxes: income, sales, and property. The nature and extent of these exemptions vary widely, however, among states and localities.[30] Perhaps because of this, little is known about the extent to which they subsidize nonprofit activity.[31] As state and local fiscal circumstances deteriorate, as they appear to be doing, however, pressures are likely to mount for reconsidering the exemptions that nonprofit organizations receive from these various taxes, particularly given the growing scale of nonprofit operations and the increasing nonprofit reliance on commercial fees and charges.

The opening salvo in this assault has already been fired in the property tax arena. Brody's recent edited volume *Property-Tax Exemption for Charities: Mapping the Battlefield* suggests the contentiousness that has surrounded this exemption in recent years.[32] The battle has been joined most strikingly in Pennsylvania, where a 1985 Supreme Court decision narrowed considerably the criteria under which nonprofit organizations could claim exemption from local property taxes as "purely public" charities. This emboldened local property tax assessors to threaten nonprofit organizations with loss of property tax exemptions unless they made "payments in lieu of taxes" (PILOTs). In the late 1980s and early 1990s, therefore, the scope and scale of these PILOT programs expanded considerably in Pennsylvania, attracting increased attention from other jurisdictions and from the nonprofit sector. This challenge subsequently receded considerably as nonprofit groups turned up the political heat and local politicians came to understand the limited revenue likely to come from this source. Recent research has thus shown that only a small fraction (seven out of fifty-one) of the largest cities in the nation were soliciting payments in lieu of taxes from non-profit organizations in the late 1990s, and most of these focused only on certain portions of the sector.[33] Still, it seems clear that the fate of this and other exemptions hinges critically on public perceptions of the sector and the circumstances of state and local revenue. What is more, states and localities are increasingly relying on user charges rather than taxes to finance various municipal services (for example, water and sewer), and exemptions typically are not available for these.

The Regulatory Arena

The third arena of nonprofit-government interaction has also witnessed a considerable squeezing of nonprofit freedom of action in recent years. This is somewhat ironic given the overall deregulation climate in national policy. While substantial parts of the business sector have been deregulated, however, nonprofits have confronted an increase in regulation in certain crucial spheres. Two of these spheres deserve particular mention: charitable fundraising and advocacy.

REGULATION OF FUNDRAISING. Nonprofit access to charitable donations, one of the distinctive features of the nonprofit sector, is, according to one leading expert, "under siege" at the present time.[34] In response to growing concerns about charitable misbehavior, all but four states now have some form of regulation of charitable solicitations, with some local jurisdictions having their own ordinances. These regulations usually cover the use of professional fundraisers; commercial co-ventures; permits, licenses, or registrations for fundraising activities; and financial reporting. These provisions vary considerably from state to state, making it necessary for any charity operating in more than one state to alter its mode of operation in each state. Thus, for example, any organization seeking charitable donations or managing charitable trusts must be registered with the Attorney General's Office in Illinois. Next door in Indiana, only professional fundraisers or others raising funds *on behalf of* another organization need to register.

There are also more aggressive efforts to regulate the ways in which nonprofits raise funds. Indiana nonprofits, for example, may now only use their own volunteers or staff, not contractors, to seek donations via telemarketing techniques from the roughly one-third of the state's households who have signed up for a "no-calls" service through the Attorney General's Office. Other states have also imposed restrictions on the use of telemarketing, sometimes including, sometimes excluding, charitable solicitations.

Federal regulation of fundraising also has tightened and now includes requirements that charitable gifts be substantiated in writing, that quid pro quo contributions be reported, and that the organization's application for exempt status and its annual financial information returns be available to the general public on request.[35] In addition, a number of court cases have clarified or complicated applicable rules at both the federal and state level. While these regulatory provisions potentially serve the salutary purpose of buttressing public confidence in nonprofit institutions, they nevertheless have increased substantially the legal and regulatory burdens under which organizations labor.

REGULATION OF ADVOCACY. Nonprofit organizations have also been under increased regulatory pressures with regard to their policy advocacy activities, another crucial function of the nonprofit sector. Restriction of nonprofit lobbying has long been a part of the basic federal tax exemption law, which bars charitable nonprofit organizations—that is, 501(c)(3) organizations—from lobbying as a substantial part of their activities. However, lobbying in the tax law is defined rather narrowly to mean directly or indirectly attempting to influence the passage of particular pieces of legislation or administrative actions. Beginning in the early 1980s, however, efforts have been made to broaden this restriction. The first of these was an Office of Management and Budget circular (A-122) on nonprofit cost accounting developed by the Reagan administration in 1982–83 and ultimately promulgated in 1984. This circular essentially prohibited nonprofits from using federal grant dollars to support "political advocacy," a concept that embraced more than the relatively narrow concept of "lobbying."[36] A subsequent Office of Management and Budget circular (A-133) issued in 1990 then tightened the audit process that nonprofits must use in order to ensure that this prohibition is enforced.

The Lobbying Disclosure Act of 1995 imposed additional restrictions on nonprofit organizations in the political advocacy arena. Most seriously, the act prohibits nonprofit 501(c)(4) organizations, the ones specifically permitted to engage in lobbying, from engaging in such activity if they receive any federal grants, loans, or awards. In addition, the act requires nonprofit organizations that employ at least one person who spends at least 20 percent of his or her time on lobbying activities to register with the secretary of the Senate and the clerk of the House of Representatives.

Notwithstanding these restrictions, additional legislation was introduced by Representative Ernest Istook (Republican, Oklahoma) and his colleagues beginning in 1995 to put further restrictions on nonprofit advocacy activity. Under the Istook amendment, as it came to be called, nonprofits that receive federal funds would be barred from using more than 5 percent not only of their federal funds but also of their overall funds for a wide range of policy advocacy activities. This provision passed the House of Representatives in 1996 but ultimately was dropped in conference. Since then, variants have been introduced as amendments to a variety of other bills and pursued at the state level as well.

Some of these proposals would define political advocacy so broadly as to prevent nonprofits from engaging in litigation or participating in administrative agency proceedings, activities that have long been considered fundamental forms of expression in a free society.

Side by side with the Istook-type proposals, moreover, have been a raft of so-called paycheck protection measures that seek a similar goal. These provisions would require nonprofit organizations to obtain permission from their members before using membership dues, or payroll deductions, for political activities, a term that is defined quite broadly in these proposals. Attempts have been made to pass such provisions in more than twenty-five states and at the federal level as well. Although aimed specifically at labor unions, they would affect many other types of nonprofit organizations as well, including workplace solicitation organizations such as the United Way.[37]

The nonprofit sector has responded to these challenges vigorously, and a small cottage industry has emerged to track the proposals and mobilize the sector to respond. Although highly successful, this battle has put a chill on at least some nonprofit engagement in policy deliberations and has left nonprofits that choose to engage in policy advocacy with considerably expanded paperwork burdens. The recently enacted campaign finance law, the Bipartisan Campaign Reform Act of 2002, promises to complicate nonprofit political advocacy further, although the full impact of these provisions is still not clear, since the act leaves a number of issues unspecified.[38]

The Policy Arena

These regulatory developments have naturally complicated nonprofit involvement in the policy arena. But they are hardly the only source of such complication. The shift in forms of government action detailed earlier has also played a part. As government has come to use an increasingly broad range of tools to carry out its mandates, especially structures that involve less direct action and more complex network structures, it has become more difficult to track who is involved and how or to assess the outcome of policy initiatives. For nonprofits, this has meant mastery of a much wider array of forms of interaction with the public sector and often a much wider array of agencies. Thus child welfare agencies formerly accustomed to dealing with social service grant programs must now find their way through the complex intricacies of the health field to tap funding that is now available only through Medicaid. Indeed, these new forms of public action have produced what Salamon in a recent volume has termed a "new governance" characterized by complex collaborations among a variety of public and private actors and requiring new activation, orchestration, and modulation skills on the part of both government and its for-profit and nonprofit partners.[39] Neither public administration theory and practice nor nonprofit management training has yet caught up fully with these developments, so there are few guidelines for how to carry out public policy initiatives under these new structures and no well-established principles for analyzing their operations.

Nonprofits are increasingly immersed in policy issues well beyond those that affect the organizations directly, however. And these debates, too, now occur across a much broader array of policy arenas and have more diverse participants than ever before. From the evidence available, nonprofits have managed to hold their own in this shifting policy environment,[40] but the task has become more demanding.

Illustrative of the new challenges is the set of changes ushered in by the welfare reform legislation of 1996. This act, which, as noted, eliminated the largest cash assistance program for low-income families (Aid to Families with Dependent Children) and replaced it with a program of temporary assistance that imposed lifetime limits (generally five years) on welfare benefits, has raised the prospect of large unmet needs once families exceed the lifetime limits, as they are beginning to do. Nonprofit service providers worry that they will be called on to meet these needs and that they will lack the resources to do so, especially if the recession that began in 2001 continues to linger.

The ability of nonprofits to cope with the resulting challenge has been hindered, however, by the significant devolution of policymaking authority that the welfare reform legislation also triggered. Indeed, policymaking and service delivery systems have been decentralized to the point that the state may no longer be the most appropriate unit of analysis. Rather, much of the decisionmaking has moved to the community level.[41] This has naturally made the task of responding to the changes all the more difficult and all the more demanding. Although the rise of state-level nonprofit associations detailed in chapter 10 of this volume doubtless helps nonprofits to deal with this fragmented policy playing field, the need for coalitions, policy analysis capability, and lobbying to influence the growing array of decision points has grown far beyond what these infrastructure organizations can offer. Nonprofits are therefore having to run harder to stay in the same place, and this at a time of growing restrictions on, or at least scrutiny of, their policy advocacy activities.

Conclusions: Toward a New Government-Nonprofit Compact

The past twenty years has thus been a time of enormous tension for the nonprofit sector in its pivotal relations with government. After a period of rapidly expanding cooperation, nonprofits have had to deal with a significant retrenchment in public funding, a widespread diversification of the forms of public assistance, a shift from producer-side to consumer-side subsidies, the loss of their preferred-provider status in many government programs, greater demands for efficiency, less favorable tax regimes, increased regulatory pressures, and a far more fragmented policy arena.

From the evidence at hand, it appears that nonprofits have responded effectively to these challenges, but at some cost to their basic character and operations, as suggested in chapter 1 of this volume. Among other things, this set of changes has contributed to the increased competition nonprofits are experiencing from for-profit providers, a growing marketization and commercialization of the sector, a shift in the locus of decisionmaking in a number of crucial fields to levels of government that lack the resources to cope with them, increased scrutiny and regulation of some crucial nonprofit functions, and a squeezing out of important mission-critical functions.

Given the crucial role that nonprofit organizations continue to play, and should continue to play, in both the operation and design of public policies, it seems highly desirable to move beyond the growing conflict that has characterized government-nonprofit relations in recent years. To do so, a new paradigm of government-nonprofit interaction is needed, one that treats the collaboration between government and the nonprofit sector not as a regrettable necessity but as a highly positive feature of a modern, pluralistic society that encourages active engagement by all sectors in the resolution of societal problems.

At its base, this new paradigm will require a better balance between the legitimate performance requirements of government and the distinctive role requirements of nonprofit organizations. More concretely, nonprofits must accommodate the public sector's growing need to be able to demonstrate effective performance in its programs. But government policymakers and program managers must acknowledge the special role that nonprofits play in maintaining a channel for citizen input into policy decisionmaking, mobilizing dedicated volunteers and staff (as well as donors), humanizing the service system, achieving high standards of quality, promoting equity, and calling attention to unmet needs.

At a minimum, this will require greater government acceptance of the right of nonprofit organizations to advocate on public policy issues and to conduct research (with related training activities) on topics consistent with their missions and norms. These functions are easily compromised under pressure, but are essential to a democratic, open society. Also important will be the protection of a level playing field between nonprofits and for-profits. At the present time, the playing field tilts heavily toward the for-profit sector by virtue of the criteria used to evaluate program progress and the uneven access to capital—and hence to technology—that results from the inability of nonprofit organizations to generate equity capital. Tax-exempt bond financing has been used in some spheres to counteract this problem, but this solution is not available to smaller, community-based organizations. A much broader facility for giving nonprofit organizations access to capital at reduced rates would go a long way toward relieving this problem.

Finally, we urge new efforts to ensure greater stability in funding streams that support nonprofit activity. This will require sustained efforts by government and for-profit procurers of nonprofit services to cooperate with nonprofits in the design of how policies are implemented and payment systems are structured, so that the predictability and manageability of nonprofit revenue streams can improve. Otherwise, nonprofit missions and special capacities may be subverted or derailed. More generally, this will require greater government acceptance of multiple definitions of the public good, including definitions emanating from the nonprofit sector, not just the corporate world. It also will require more sustained efforts by government to activate and modulate the network structures under which public policy initiatives now are carried out. While efficiency and manageability are important goals, so are equity, effectiveness, and legitimacy.

If the late twentieth century marked the resurgence of the market as the mechanism for addressing public problems following an era of much heavier reliance on the state, it also demonstrated that sole reliance on the market is no more a panacea for societal ills than is sole reliance on the state. We can therefore hope that the twenty-first century will bring a new climate of realism that recognizes instead the virtues of collaboration, not only between government and the nonprofit sector but with the business sector as well. The challenge before us is to confront this reality and build systems that can take advantage of what each sector has to offer without subverting what makes them distinctive. This is a significant challenge, to be sure, but one that simply must be met.

Notes

1. Waldemar Nielsen, *The Endangered Sector* (Columbia University Press, 1979), pp. 14, 47.

2. John S. Whitehead, *The Separation of College and State: Columbia, Dartmouth, Harvard, and Yale, 1776–1876* (Yale University Press, 1973), pp. 3–16.

3. Frank Fetter, "The Subsidizing of Private Charities," *American Journal of Sociology* (1901/02): 360.

4. Amos Warner, *American Charities: A Study in Philanthropy and Economics* (New York: Thomas Y. Crowell, 1894), p. 337.

5. For a discussion of these conflicts, see Peter Hall, *Inventing the Nonprofit Sector and Other Essays on Philanthropy, Voluntarism, and Nonprofit Organizations* (Johns Hopkins University Press, 1992), pp. 20–36.

6. See Lester M. Salamon, "Rethinking Public Management: Third-Party Government and the Changing Forms of Public Action," *Public Policy*, vol. 29 (1981): 255–75; Lester M. Salamon, *Beyond Privatization: The Tools of Public Action* (Washington: Urban Institute, 1989); Lester M. Salamon, "The New Governance and the Tools of Public Action," in Lester M. Salamon, ed., *The Tools of Government: A Guide to the New Governance* (Oxford University Press, 2002).

7. Murray S. Weitzman, Nadine Tai Jalandoni, Linda M. Lampkin, and Thomas H. Pollack, *The New Nonprofit Almanac and Desk Reference* (San Francisco: Jossey-Bass, 2002), p. 26.

8. Donald K. Price, *The Scientific Estate* (Harvard University Press, 1965); David Guston and K. Keniston, *The Fragile Contract: University Science and the Federal Government* (Massachusetts Institute of Technology Press, 1994).

9. For an excellent analysis of the design of the Medicare program and its accommodation of the concerns of hospitals, see Herman Miles Somers and Anne Ramsay Somers, *Medicare and the Hospitals: Issues and Prospects* (Washington: Brookings, 1967).

10. See, for example, Harold W. Demone Jr. and Margaret Gibelman, eds., *Services for Sale: Purchasing Health and Human Services* (Rutgers University Press, 1989); Steven Rathgeb Smith and Michael Lipsky, *Nonprofits for Hire: The Welfare State in the Age of Contracting* (Harvard University Press, 1993).

11. Kirsten A. Grønbjerg, *Understanding Nonprofit Funding: Managing Revenues in Social Services and Community Development Organizations* (San Francisco: Jossey-Bass, 1993).

12. For further detail, see Lester M. Salamon, "Partners in Public Service: The Scope and Theory of Government-Nonprofit Relations," in Walter W. Powell, ed., *The Nonprofit Sector: A Research Handbook* (Yale University Press, 1987), pp. 99–117; Lester M. Salamon, *Partners in Public Service: Government-Nonprofit Relations in the Modern Welfare State* (Johns Hopkins University Press, 1995).

13. Lester M. Salamon and Alan J. Abramson, "The Federal Budget and the Nonprofit Sector: Implications of the Contract with America," in Dwight F. Burlingame, William A. Diaz, Warren Ilchman, and associates, eds., *Capacity for Change? The Nonprofit World in the Age of Devolution* (Indianapolis: Indiana University Center on Philanthropy, 1996), p. 8.

14. Office of Management and Budget, *Enhancing Governmental Productivity through Competition: A New Way of Doing Business within the Government to Provide Quality Government at Least Cost* (Washington: Office of Management and Budget, 1988), p. 15, quoted in Donald Kettl, *Shared Power: Public Governance and Private Markets* (Washington: Brookings, 1993), p. 46.

15. U.S. House of Representatives, Committee on Ways and Means, *2000 Green Book: Background Material and Data on Programs within the Jurisdiction of the Committee on Ways and Means,* 106 Cong., 2 sess. (Washington, October 6, 2000), pp. 892–93; Teresa A. Coughlin, Leighton Ku, and John Holahan, *Medicaid since 1980: Costs, Coverage, and the Shifting Alliance between the Federal Government and the States* (Washington: Urban Institute Press, 1994), p. 2.

16. For a general discussion of these "alternative tools" of public action, see Lester M. Salamon, "The New Governance and the Tools of Public Action: An Introduction," in Salamon, ed., *Tools of Government*, pp. 1–47. For a discussion of tax expenditures and loan guarantees, see Christopher Howard, "Tax Expenditures," in Salamon, ed., *Tools of Government*, pp. 410–44; and Thomas H. Stanton, "Loans and Loan Guarantees," in Salamon, ed., *Tools of Government*, pp. 381–409.

17. Thomas L. Gais, Richard P. Nathan, Irene Lurie, and Thomas Kaplan, "The Implication of the Personal Responsibility Act of 1996: Commonalities, Variations, and the Challenge of Complexity" (Albany, N.Y.: Nelson A. Rockefeller Institute of Government, 2000).

18. Peter Frumkin and Alice Andre-Clark, "When Missions, Markets, and Politics Collide: Values and Strategy in the Nonprofit Human Services," *Nonprofit and Voluntary Sector Quarterly*, vol. 29, no. 1 (2000): 141–63.

19. Sheila Suess Kennedy, "Constitutional Competence of Nonprofit Managers," paper presented at the annual meetings of the Association for Research on Nonprofit Organizations and Voluntary Action (ARNOVA), Miami, Fla., 2001.

20. Sheila Zedlewski, *Are Shrinking Caseloads Always a Good Thing?* Assessing the New Federalism: Short Takes on Welfare Policy 6 (Washington: Urban Institute, 2002).

21. Gais and others, "Implication of the Personal Responsibility Act of 1996," p. 16.

22. Rob Geen, *Shoring up the Child Welfare-TANF Link,* Assessing the New Federalism: Short Takes on Welfare Policy 7 (Washington: Urban Institute, 2002).

23. Gais and others, "Implication of the Personal Responsibility Act of 1996."

24. Richard P. Nathan and Thomas L. Gais, *Implementing the Personal Responsibility Act of 1996: A First Look* (Albany, N.Y.: Nelson A. Rockefeller Institute of Government, 2000).

25. Frumkin and Andre-Clark, "When Missions, Markets, and Politics Collide."

26. Dan Balz, "States' Budget Outlook Remains Bleak: Even Tougher Measures May Be Needed to Make up for Revenue Shortfall," *Washington Post,* July 15, 2002, p. A5; Adam Nagourney, "In Sharp Change, Governors Share Woes on Budgets: Shortfalls for 45 States," *New York Times* July 15, 2002, p. A15; David E. Rosenbaum, "States Make Cuts and Increase Fees as Revenues Drop," *New York Times,* May 16, 2002, p. A1.

27. To illustrate, for a taxpayer in a 50 percent tax bracket, the out-of-pocket cost of making a gift to charity is $0.50, since the taxpayer has to pay $0.50 in taxes if she does not make the gift. If the tax rate falls to 33 percent, the out-of-pocket cost of the gift goes up to $0.67, since the taxpayer has to pay only $0.33 in taxes if she does not make the gift.

28. For a detailed discussion of these changes, see Alan J. Abramson, Lester M. Salamon, and C. Eugene Steuerle, "The Nonprofit Sector and the Federal Budget: Recent History and Future Directions," in Elizabeth T. Boris and C. Eugene Steuerle, eds., *Nonprofits and Government: Collaboration and Conflict* (Washington: Urban Institute Press, 1999), pp. 114–26.

29. See, for example, Patrick M. Rooney and Eugene R. Tempel, "Repeal of the Estate Tax and Its Impact on Philanthropy," *Nonprofit Management and Leadership,* vol. 12, no. 2 (2001): 177–92.

30. John L. Mikesell, "Sales Taxation of Nonprofit Organizations: Purchases and Sales," in William F. Fox, ed., *Sales Taxation: Critical Issues in Policy and Administration* (Westport, Conn.: Praeger, 1992), pp. 121–30.

31. John L. Mikesell, "Tax Expenditure Budgets, Budget Policy, and Tax Policy: Confusion in the States" (Bloomington, Ind.: School of Public and Environmental Affairs, 2002).

32. Evelyn Brody, ed., *Property-Tax Exemption for Charities: Mapping the Battlefield* (Washington: Urban Institute Press, 2002).

33. Pamela Leland, "PILOTs: The Large-City Experience," in Brody, ed., *Property Tax Exemption for Charities,* pp. 202–06.

34. Bruce Hopkins, *Starting and Managing a Nonprofit Organization: A Legal Guide* (New York: John Wiley and Sons, 2001), p. 131.

35. Hopkins, *Starting and Managing a Nonprofit Organization,* p. 139.

36. Harmon, Curran, and Spielberg, "Regulation of Advocacy Activities for Nonprofits That Receive Federal Grants" (Washington: Alliance for Justice, June 2002), available at www.afj.org/regula.thml [June 24, 2002].

37. OMB Watch, "Paycheck Protection Proposals in Congress and the States: Varying Impacts on Charities" (Washington: OMB Watch, June 1998), available at www.ombwatch. org/las/1998/paypro.html [June 24, 2002].

38. Michael B. Trister and Holly B. Schadler, "Bipartisan Campaign Reform Act of 2002: Provisions Affecting Nonprofit Advocacy Organizations" (Washington: Alliance for Justice, 2002), available at www.afj.org/bcrabriefingfinal.html [June 24, 2002].

39. Salamon, "New Governance and the Tools of Public Action," pp. 1–47.

40. See, for example, Jeffrey Berry, *The New Liberalism: The Rising Power of Citizens' Groups* (Washington: Brookings, 1999); Elizabeth J. Reid, *Structuring the Inquiry into Advocacy,* Nonprofit Advocacy and the Policy Process: A Seminar Series 1 (Washington: Urban Institute Press, 2000).

41. See, for example, Gais and others, "The Implication of the Personal Responsibility Act of 1996"; Thomas L. Gais and B. Kent Weaver, *State Policy Choices under Welfare Reform,* Welfare Reform and Beyond Brief 21 (Washington: Brookings, April 2002); Nathan and Gaise, *Implementing the Personal Responsibility Act of 1996;* Sheila R. Zedlewski, Pamela Holcomb, and Amy-Ellen Duke, *The Story of 13 States: Assessing the New Federalism* (Washington: Urban Institute Press, 1998).

15

Accountability and Public Trust

EVELYN BRODY

E ven before the events of September 11, 2001, calls for greater nonprofit accountability were coming from myriad sources, among them funders, governments (at all levels), the press, and the nonprofit sector itself. Front-page news stories called attention to fundraising inaccuracies, mismanagement, embezzlement, public funding clashes, and associational disputes.

These concerns intensified in the aftermath of the terrorist attacks. The charitable sector gained new prominence after September 11, but with prominence came heightened scrutiny, raising some uncomfortable questions despite the sector's generally positive response to this tragedy. First, more than 250 new nonprofit organizations were formed to handle the outpouring of September 11 contributions, and the Internal Revenue Service (IRS) announced expedited review of new applications for federal tax exemption.[1] Yet these new organizations—along with existing major charities like the Red Cross and Salvation Army—found themselves tripping over each other, unable to ensure that the more than $1.5 billion in contributions was being distributed wisely, fairly, and expeditiously.[2] Second, the fundraising practices of some of the charities, notably the American Red Cross, brought charges of deceptive charitable

The author is grateful for comments and suggestions from Lisa Berlinger, Margery Heitbrink, Elizabeth Keating, Lester Salamon, Judith Saidel, Russy Sumariwalla, Bennett Weiner, and Burton Weisbrod and for additional support from the Chicago-Kent College of Law.

471

solicitation practices, culminating in several days of embarrassing congressional hearings, the departure of the Red Cross's executive director, and the Red Cross's appointment of former Senate majority leader George Mitchell to develop a plan to distribute its Liberty Fund receipts to victims of the attacks.[3] Third, the allegation that a number of Muslim charities may have been acting as collection agencies for terrorist groups revealed an especially dark side of the philanthropic sector.

For all the concern over nonprofit accountability, however, the meaning of the term is not self-evident. To the contrary, it means different things to different people. This poses a particular challenge to charities because they, perhaps more than other social institutions, depend on public trust, and this trust involves multiple—sometimes conflicting—demands from a variety of stakeholders.

This chapter seeks to unpack the complex accountability challenge facing nonprofit organizations. It discusses how the term is used to embrace several distinct concepts, from narrow questions of sound internal governance, fiscal honesty, and avoidance of fraud to broad notions of adherence to mission and demonstrated effectiveness. As the chapter moves into these broader questions, the idea of accountability grows increasingly subjective. One stakeholder's mission drift might be another's appropriate responsiveness, and each of these conflicting characterizations is correct from that constituent's perspective. In sum, moving the discussion beyond narrow issues of accountability makes it difficult to resolve accountability conflicts. Nevertheless, the nonprofit sector clearly must address accountability concerns. Some reforms should not be difficult for individual charities, like adopting safeguards against self-dealing. Even when ultimate goals are contested, charities must seek to improve—and explain—the effectiveness and social benefits of their operations.

To a large degree, nonprofits are now paying the price of their success. The nonprofit sector's claims to exist for the public good are no longer taken on faith, and more people believe they have a stake in the accountability of nonprofits. The sector is growing, moving into commercial fields, and more vocally defending its competitive position in traditional fields. Like other powerful societal forces, the nonprofit sector now has an obligation to justify itself to the public at large. More worrisome, a growing confidence in the market (if not in government) is feeding the idea that the nonprofit sector is not even the best, let alone the only, guardian of public worth. Indeed, the nonprofit structure intensifies the problems. A charity's inability to sell stock or impose taxes drives it to search for new revenues, its desire to serve the public good increases the multiplicity of its stakeholders, and dependence on funders and contractors risks altering the original mission.[4] Moreover, with greater scrutiny comes greater criticism, even if not based on any departure from past practice. Having grown up, nonprofit organizations must now devote more care and resources to earning the trust of their constituents and the public.

Framing the Issues

Accountability involves three fundamental questions: (1) To whom is someone accountable, (2) for what, and (3) how? In the case of charities, these are not straightforward issues. Because of the difficulty of categorizing even the questions, this chapter examines spheres of accountability. This section begins by assessing the scope of the problem and setting out a framework for analysis. The second section focuses on the classical model of nonprofit accountability, which emphasizes the central role of a board of directors acting under a prohibition against taking profits. Because this structure alone cannot assure internal and external accountability, the third section addresses the "to whom, for what, and how" questions for four alternative spheres of accountability: (a) the *government regulator* through the legal process, (b) the *nonprofit sector* or *industries* through peer regulation, (c) the *charity's constituents* (donors, members, staff, clients, and contract funders) through struggles for control over the charity's mission and endeavors to ensure program effectiveness, and (d) the *general public* (as taxpayers and as citizens) through disclosure of information and attempts to measure the social value of charitable activity. Complicating nonprofit management, each of these stakeholders has its own mechanisms for pursuing its own conception of accountability. Indeed, some of these players might not want an active role in accountability. Often those providing support seem to recognize the conflicts under which the nonprofit labors: "Accrediting agencies, boards of trustees, government agencies, and individuals accept at face value the credentials, ambiguous goals, and categorical evaluations that are characteristic of ceremonial organizations."[5] To look too closely might upset the accommodation that the parties have reached. Thus some of the loudest critics are outside the sector, such as the press and the public at large. Finally, the fourth section offers some recommendations about how individual nonprofit organizations, and the sector as a whole, might best cope with their accountability challenges.

Scope of the Accountability Problem

As a first step in this analysis, it is important to establish the severity of the problem of accountability in the nonprofit sector. This is not an easy task. Because regulators focus on serious wrongdoing, and even then often settle rather than litigate, it is difficult to assess the number of merely mediocre— much less "good"—charities.[6] Certainly by one measure—public behavior—the sector's standing seems secure. Public support for philanthropy continues to grow and to grow in new ways. Some 40,000 organizations a year apply for recognition of their section 501(c)(3) tax-exempt status from the IRS, on top of more than 725,000 existing exempt charities.[7] Contributions to charity surpassed $200 billion in 2000 (although the sector is keeping a nervous eye on the plummeting stock market). The number of volunteers has increased (although total hours have fallen slightly). Commercial donor-advised funds have surged to the top of the giving charts; boomers are making their way onto boards; and the young rich demand hands-on involvement through venture philanthropy. For future executives, the nonprofit sector has become a "destination of choice for graduates of the nation's top public policy and administration graduate schools."[8]

Survey data similarly provide a generally favorable impression of the sector. In the Independent Sector's 1999 survey on giving and volunteering, 62 percent of respondents agreed that "most charitable organizations are honest and ethical in their use of donated funds." Although 32 percent agreed that "most charitable organizations are wasteful in their use of funds," 62 percent agreed that "charitable organizations are more effective now in providing services than five years ago" (up from 58 percent in 1996 and from 55 percent in 1994).[9]

Recent legislative and administrative actions, however, provide evidence of increasing public concerns over nonprofit accountability. Although the fundamental benefits of autonomy and tax exemption remain undisturbed, federal law now requires tax-exempt organizations to make their tax information returns (IRS Forms 990) available on demand. Legislative staffers have recommended that Congress require disclosure of additional information, including advocacy spending and the returns of taxable affiliates.[10] In 1996, in the most important charity law since the Tax Reform Act of 1969, Congress enacted intermediate sanctions (penalty taxes) on excess benefits paid to insiders of charities and social welfare organizations. Congress was moved to act by a few isolated cases of favorable management buyouts of nonprofit health maintenance organizations and the Bishop Estate's exorbitant trustee compensation,[11] yet all charities engaging in a potentially excess-benefit transaction must now worry about the new law. In July 2001 Senate Finance Committee ranking member Charles Grassley asked the General Accounting Office to study IRS data to determine what percentage of donations is being spent on fundraising and the extent to which charities are engaging in deceitful and fraudulent practices.[12] The post–September 11 hearings by the Oversight Subcommittee of the House Ways and Means Committee might be followed by closer scrutiny in 2002, with possible federal legislation.

At the state level, twenty-two states have adopted an enhanced role for the attorney general (and sometimes the public) in the conversion of nonprofit hospitals to for-profit status. State and local governments evince an increasing desire to regulate charitable solicitations, most recently on-line solicitations. Some municipalities condition zoning variances on, or simply demand, payments in lieu of taxes from otherwise exempt commercial-type charities, such as hospitals and schools. San Francisco requires charities with which it enters into large contracts to open some of their board meetings to the public.

Also of importance, finally, is the perception of those in the nonprofit sector itself. Here the picture is mixed. National and state associations of charities and foundations, as well as charity watchdog organizations, have begun a high-level dialogue on the issue of nonprofit accountability.[13] At the 1999 annual meeting of Independent Sector, 74 percent of the attending senior officials of many of the country's most prominent charities and foundations answered "yes" to the question "Do you think there is a problem of openness and accountability in the sector as a whole and therefore vulnerability?" Only 42 percent believed that nonprofits deserve a B or better for their ability to maintain public trust.[14] Many operating-level charity workers, by contrast, view the issue as an abstraction and a distraction and worry about drawing scarce resources away from program services and toward make-work reporting. To a large degree, the accountability movement within the sector is driven from the top down rather than the bottom up.

Concepts of Accountability: To Whom, For What, and How?

One reason that it may be so difficult to gauge the extent to which an accountability "problem" exists in the nonprofit sector is that nonprofit organizations involve a variety of stakeholders, each with its own needs and desires. Relationships—some voluntary, some contractual, and some political (in the broad sense)—exist within and between organizations and between nonprofit organizations and business, government, and the public at large.[15] As Paul Light describes, these concerns lead to counter-tugging tides for reforming nonprofit management. Funders seek accounting standards and adherence to best practices ("scientific management"), clients seek responsiveness and sensitivity ("liberation management"), donor and consumer advocates seek disclosure ("watchful eye"), and the media feed off scandals of inefficiency ("war on waste").[16]

Given this complexity, the "To whom?" and "For what?" questions inevitably overlap. Nevertheless, it is useful to identify four broad meanings of nonprofit accountability.

FINANCIAL PROBITY. In the dictionary sense, to be accountable means having to answer to another for one's actions; specifically, the root of the word suggests a reckoning for a sum of money. Thus the term clearly embraces fiscal responsibility. Financial fraud and abuse are the easiest types of accountability problems for the law and practitioners to address, although even here controversies exist.[17]

GOOD GOVERNANCE. Sound nonprofit operations depend primarily on the structure of internal governance. The law imposes on nonprofit fiduciaries the twin duties of loyalty and care and makes trustees or directors responsible for overseeing officers and staff. Best practice guides supplement minimal legal requirements. Broad consensus exists about the basic structure for an organization's policy and decisionmaking processes, even if in practice many charities fall short. In general, best practices "enable directors to efficiently gather and absorb

. the relevant information in helping make good decisions, and . . . help to insure that directors have the right set of incentives in making those decisions."[18] Increasingly, though, beneficiaries, staff, donors, the community, and the public at large have begun demanding a role in organizational decisionmaking. How far should we go in giving these stakeholders a role in charity governance— indeed, what degree of transparency is appropriate?

ADHERENCE TO DONOR DIRECTION AND MISSION. We commonly think of responsiveness to the donor as the classic example of accountability, but the use of accountability to include faithfulness to the mission of the organization is more contested and political (in the broad sense). A charity's constituents, both at the outset and over time, consist of more than those who formed the organization. For every person concerned about the prudent stewardship of charitable assets and maintenance of purpose, another is worried about keeping older charities relevant. What happens if the wishes of potential donors differ from the wishes of the initial donors? Do we want nonprofits to grow into new ventures or to close their doors when their missions are accomplished? Who should resolve these disputes among multiple stakeholders? In the debate over "How private is private philanthropy?" too much legislation and regulation could jeopardize the independence of the sector.

EFFECTIVENESS AND PUBLIC TRUST. The broadest conception of the term *accountability* relates to a charity's effectiveness. This is also the most problematic usage. No agreement exists over what constitutes effectiveness—both in terms of the ultimate public good and in terms of the charity's activities to further that good. Consider, for example, the debates over bilingual education, school vouchers, affirmative action, welfare reform, teenage pregnancy, and abortion. Even where consensus exists as to the goal, is an organization effective if it concentrates on treatment rather than prevention? How can a single organization claim success when other societal factors, over which it has no control, influence the outcome? Is competition by multiple charities for the same funds and clients good or bad? In light of the recent legal requirements to disclose information on nonprofit operations, charities will increasingly find themselves justifying their decisions and actions to all constituencies, including the general public.

The Classical Model of Nonprofit Accountability

At the heart of the concern about accountability is the growing conviction that the classical model of nonprofit accountability—relying on a disinterested board and prohibiting the distribution of profits—cannot adequately achieve any but the most narrow version of accountability and even then only imperfectly. Unlike the boards of business corporations, which must answer to the shareholders, and elected representatives, who must answer to the voters, the nonprofit board is seemingly accountable only to itself.

In theory, donors could be empowered with the legal authority to hold a charity to account. In general, though, the law denies a donor *as a donor* (that is, as distinct from his or her role as a trustee or director) any authority over the funds or property once the gift is made. Donors cannot sue for misuse of their donations. The law quite clearly has determined that "despite the fact that the organization is legally bound by specific terms of the gift, *legally* it is not the donor's concern. It is *society's* concern, to be pursued (or not) by society's representative, the attorney general."[19] Given the general disinclination of law enforcers to interfere with charity operations, donors have developed a range of self-help mechanisms and vehicles that allow for differing levels of donor control, but these are only partial solutions.

The law imposes on nonprofit directors and charitable trustees only two fiduciary duties: the duty to be loyal to the organization and the duty to act with care (prudence). Within broadly bounded charitable purposes, no laws tell the entity or its managers how to "do" charity. In general, moreover, the same rules apply to fiduciaries throughout the range of charitable institutions, from a small neighborhood soup kitchen to a major university.

The existence of a (traditionally) voluntary board unable to profit from charity operations (the so-called nondistribution constraint), in theory, eliminates the need for additional mechanisms to protect the public interest.[20] To proponents of the classical model, the legal prohibition against distributing profits both explains the existence of the nonprofit sector and keeps it honest, ensuring the dedication of assets and effort toward performing good deeds. Yet the classical model of a disinterested board often fails to deliver. Compensation scandals, fundraising abuses, conflicts of interest, and poor management all reflect failures of internal control. Regarding the level of quality, the prohibition on profit distribution does not alone guarantee that nonprofits are *worthy* of trust, because the model also posits that nonprofits form when the public cannot judge the quality of services being provided. Under this model, then, a donor or client cannot tell if the nonprofit wastes its resources or uses the funds to cross-subsidize other services desired by its managers. Accordingly, accepting nonprofit status as a signal of trustworthiness bestows a halo on any nonprofit organization regardless of merit, and organizational form is of no help in comparing competing nonprofits.

The environment in which a nonprofit operates can help with these accountability challenges, but it also can intensify them. Nonprofits form and operate in social networks, such as a city's business community.[21] These ties can be both good and bad for the sound functioning of charities. On the one hand, when the same people see each other in a variety of capacities, they develop reputations and can substitute trust for direct monitoring. On the other hand, an inbred group is prey to lapses in judgment, such as the virus that swept the Philadelphia nonprofit sector in the form of the Foundation for New Era Philanthropy.[22] In sum, while coordinated philanthropy allows for more efficient and effective allocation of resources, control of charities by a homogeneous elite raises worries of philanthropic orthodoxy, paternalism, and particularism.[23] The most important constituent of the charity—the beneficiary—is often the least empowered.

Within the organization, some observers believe that the absence of shareholders reverses the power relationship between the board and the officers. In most of the highly publicized scandals, the nonprofit board is caught flat-footed, having been lulled or simply kept in the dark by charismatic or domineering executives. The situation often is not qualitatively better in organizations with shareholders—indeed, the business sector has originated proposals to improve board operations such as the use of audit committees and appointment of a greater proportion of outside directors (board members who are not also officers).[24] Nevertheless, nonprofit executives can fear and resent boards that ask too many questions, initiate new policy, or "interfere" with operations. Many boards, at least of the elite institutions, require no more of their directors than that they "give, get, or get off"; and many directors seem to want the honor of board membership without the work and responsibility.[25]

At the operational level, as bad as lapses of fiscal responsibility and governance look on the front page of the newspaper, nothing unique to the nonprofit form bars reform. Good governance, of course, is not easy and requires an investment in time and training. More worrisome, the explosion in the number and complexity of nonprofit organizations—all of which must staff their boards—suggests that the problem of fiduciary inexperience will only get worse. Nevertheless, good governance in the nonprofit sector requires the same types of oversight and checks and balances that exist in the business and public sectors: a strong and independent board, active committees, an enforced conflicts-of-interest policy, audited financial statements, and financial controls. For boards as a whole, as the universe of constituents with authority over the charity grows, the traditional role of the board shrinks.

Alternative Spheres of Accountability

In addition to the board of directors, four other mechanisms, or sets of constituents, exercise accountability over nonprofit organizations: government regulators, peer regulators, charity constituents, and the general public. Each of these has its own concerns, advantages, and weaknesses, and all spheres operate simultaneously (and sometimes in conflict) on charities.

Government Regulation: State Attorneys General and the Internal Revenue Service

Under our system of federalism, two levels of general regulation apply to charities.[26] First, state attorneys general are responsible for ensuring that charity boards carry out their fiduciary duties of loyalty and care, for enforcing donor-imposed restrictions on gifts, and for regulating charitable solicitations. Second, the Internal Revenue Service regulates nonprofit governance through its administration of congressional requirements for federal income tax exemption. However, these regulators hold nonprofits to minimum (and in practice minimal) legal standards. While enjoying nearly exclusive authority and discretion to challenge the actions of a charity fiduciary, attorneys general do not want to take over the business of running charities.[27] Similarly, the IRS uses its powers sparingly. Funding for charity enforcement has never been high, at either the state or federal level, and law enforcers generally feel more comfortable focusing on improper distribution of profits to insiders. Moreover, while intoning tough-sounding legal standards, regulators and courts tend to treat charity fiduciaries leniently in order not to discourage charity service. Thus, in the absence of inappropriate self-dealing, fiduciaries generally have little to fear from the regulators.

In theory, volunteer directors should worry about exposure to personal liability. To allay these concerns, however, charities purchase D&O (director and officer) insurance policies and provide indemnification for directors and officers. Such policies are inexpensive, reflecting the reality that monetary liability is rare. In practice, the desire to save directors from financial ruin leads regulators and courts to degrade the legal standards by avoiding findings of liability. In one admittedly extreme case, a state court absolved the founder and dominating manager of one foundation of any breach of duty in running up a $300 million loss through poor investments. The court asserted that, if the defendant had mismanaged his wealth before making the contribution, "Would anyone be so crazy and cruel as to assert a claim against him for his carelessness in not holding intact the fortune which he intended to bestow on others?"[28] The chief drafter of both the current California nonprofit law and the American Bar Association's revised model act observed that the law—out of concern for attracting "sensible people" to nonprofit boards—allows volunteer directors "to almost be asleep at the gate."[29]

In their role as guardians against consumer fraud, state regulators concentrate on the fundraising activities of charities. Many states and localities tried imposing caps on fundraising percentages and point-of-solicitation disclosure requirements, but in the 1980s the Supreme Court declared these types of laws unconstitutional under First Amendment free-speech protection.[30] Such limits disproportionately affect new charities (which have low name recognition and no established donor base) and unpopular causes (which require a greater expenditure to raise a dollar). After the fact, states may, of course, punish fraudulent fundraising (such as when charitable solicitations are used for private purposes or for purposes other than those represented)—if they can find the wrongdoer. Multiple-state charitable solicitation has always been a problem for state regulators, and enforcement has grown exponentially more difficult with Internet solicitations.[31]

Moreover, state attorneys general and the IRS have an accountability problem of their own. Lack of transparency in their regulation of charities makes it impossible to assess whether regulators truly improve charity governance—or even whether they are acting at all. Few cases involving nonprofit fiduciary issues have reached the courts. Reform rather than punishment is generally the goal of the charity regulator, and charities as well prefer a chance to improve their behavior while avoiding embarrassment and personal liability. Closing agreements between the regulator and the charity to end an enforcement action can be quite detailed, often spelling out specific terms dealing with future governance. Although regulators occasionally condition settlement on the charity's assenting to public disclosure of the agreement, most agreements are kept confidential. Finally, state attorneys general can act out of parochial motives, such as the recent action by the attorney general of Illinois that effectively forced the board of the struggling Terra Museum to keep its assets in Chicago, even though the museum's articles of incorporation did not include a geographic restriction in the purposes clause.[32] Perhaps the sector should call on the state charity officials and the IRS to publish annual reports explaining, at least in general terms, both the level and types of enforcement and the outcomes achieved.

In view of the generally disappointing performance of traditional charity regulators, proposals have emerged from time to time to create some type of charities board, at either the state or federal level.[33] Law professor Joel Fleishman recently asserted that for "the long-run good of the sector," society cannot continue to rely on "an inadequately staffed and insufficiently powerful IRS, the vagaries of inadequately staffed and usually not-very-interested offices of state attorneys general, . . . the limited scope and vision of voluntary watchdog agencies, the new information-providing organizations, and the investigatory, inflammatory press."[34] Fleishman's proposal echoes calls made twenty-five years ago, in reports compiled by the influential Filer Commission, for a regulatory body as concerned with sound charity operations as with the often-minimal legal requirements.[35] Proposals for a national body raise difficult issues of state sovereignty in our federal system, and any expansion of regulatory authority enlarges the realm of sanctionable behavior at the expense of nonprofit autonomy.

Self-Regulation and Private Standards and Accreditation

A second alternative mechanism of nonprofit accountability takes the form of private review and standard-setting boards. Such private regulation takes many forms, which vary in their degree of compulsion and attendant sanctions. Over the decades, private regulation of charitable activity has occurred through religious institutions, scientific philanthropy, federated philanthropy, charities bureaus, community foundations, and state and national associations of nonprofit organizations. Private regulation of the nonprofit sector as a whole overlaps, moreover, with private regulation of particular industries—such as hospitals, higher education, and daycare—regardless of organizational form. In addition, private regulation and public regulation often complement each other, as when governments condition funding or eligibility on private accreditation. On occasion, public regulation is deflected or spurred by private regulatory action or inaction.[36]

One long-time charity regulator, the donor-focused BBB Wise Giving Alliance, recently proposed new standards for responding to public requests about specific charities. These standards cover board membership, activity and policies, accuracy of public information such as solicitations and websites, openness about relationships with commercial entities, use of funds, annual report and budget, and, for established charities, the percentage of revenues spent on fundraising and other administrative costs. However, rating systems that employ formulas or grades are the most controversial.[37]

More systematically, state nonprofit associations have begun to design variously named accountability codes and standards of practice.[38] Two of the most thorough—adopted by the Maryland Association of Nonprofit Organizations and by the Minnesota Council of Nonprofits in substantially similar form—cover mission and program evaluation, governance, human resources, financial management, fundraising, public accountability and communications, and public policy and advocacy. (Indeed, these best practices might be too prescriptive for some.) In light of the new federal penalty scheme for excess-benefit transactions with insiders, charities will increasingly need to adopt conflict-of-interest policies, and these guidelines explain what such policies should require. Finally, the Maryland association offers a peer-review certification program for nonprofits seeking to demonstrate that they abide by its principles.[39]

To skeptics, the idea of private regulation (or, worse, self-regulation) is an oxymoron—think of the role of the accounting profession in the Enron meltdown. Others believe that peer standards and pressure can elevate practice, even if only voluntarily. Each legal and private regulatory scheme has its advantages and disadvantages, its benefits and costs, and no single approach is "best" from either the organization's or society's perspective. While public regulation of nonprofits is compulsory but minimal, organizations have some discretion in orienting themselves toward particular types of private regulation and standard setting. Some private bodies are poorly funded, and impartiality can be questioned if the body relies on member dues for its operations. However, an organization seeking accreditation might be called on to make major structural sacrifices. Indeed, the relationship between the private regulator and the regulated organization can become just as complicated as that between government agencies and their regulated industries, with concerns that the regulatory process will be captured by elite, vested interests. Moreover, calls arise for the accrediting process to be opened up and made more accountable to the public, particularly where government funds are conditioned on accreditation.[40]

The real test of the effectiveness of private regulation comes when the body must expel or otherwise sanction a nonconforming nonprofit, but institutional pressures often induce timidity (even the prospect of field visits makes the members of many nonprofit associations decidedly uncomfortable). The question "Who guards the guardians?" thus asks how the private process can send not just an image of trustworthiness but also a credible and legitimate signal. Moreover, a proliferation of watchdogs and industry or sector associations with different tests could either unnecessarily burden compliant charities or cause charities lacking the sophistication or resources to conform to appear unworthy of donor support.

Accountability to Other Charity Constituencies

Beyond the relatively narrow mechanisms and spheres of accountability discussed so far, a much broader array of stakeholders also has claims on the performance and operation of nonprofit organizations. Included here are institutional funders, organizational members, professional staff and volunteers, contract funders, and clientele. Charity managers often try to satisfy these multiple stakeholders by failing to specify—or by adopting fuzzy or even conflicting—goals. Because there is no objective measure of a charity's effectiveness, each participant's attitudes become part of the social structure in which a charity, and indeed all charities, operates.[41]

These multiple forces inevitably exert a pull on a charity's methods, if not on its conception of its mission. A constituent can further his or her goals by exercising voice (such as imposing conditions on the donation or contract) or exit rights (such as withholding future donations or dealings). But attempts to influence performance—even a funder's simple mandate that the charity conduct an assessment of its outcomes—can create tension within an organization and within the nonprofit sector. As an example of the frequently "irresolvable tension in questions of accountability," a hospital seeking a disciplined bottom line for bond-rating purposes might fail to provide sufficient community benefit for tax-exemption purposes.[42] However, if a charity board tries to insulate itself financially from these problems, issues of public legitimacy arise. Commercial activities and large endowments could bring charges of empire building and betrayal of the nonprofit ethos.

INDIVIDUAL AND INSTITUTIONAL DONORS. As we have seen, restrictions placed by the donor on the charitable purpose of a gift are binding on the charity. A difficult legal issue can arise if it later becomes impossible or impracticable to carry out that purpose. If the charity takes the form of a trust, the venerable doctrine of cy pres allows the trustees to seek court approval for applying the assets to another purpose as close as possible to the one originally designated. Courts in some states have also applied the cy pres doctrine (or a modified version of it) to nonprofit corporations and require court approval before allowing an amendment to the charitable purposes in the articles of incorporation. Similarly, some believe that all charity boards (trust or corporate) owe a duty of obedience to the original mission of the organization.[43]

The inherent conservative nature of this legal structure pleases those who fear the prospect of unfettered discretion by current trustees and frustrates those who believe, like Thomas Jefferson, that "the land belongs to the living." Some reformers believe that this focus on donor direction so permeates the legal regulation of charities that it infringes on the ability of charity fiduciaries to govern. In the absence of restrictions on gifts, they ask, who is in a better position to decide whether to alter a charity's historic purposes: the charity's board or the state attorney general or court? As a practical matter, the issue rarely arises because most charities were formed with missions broad enough to accommodate evolving needs, and restricted gifts do not ordinarily constitute a large percentage of assets. The real battles occur when other stakeholders (such as students, foundation grantees, or beneficiaries) seek to influence the institution within the confines of its purposes.

For those organizations whose missions have become jeopardized, the bigger problem often is not fiduciaries who are overly zealous but rather those who are overly timid. Regulatory structures already lock assets into the nonprofit sector, but what stops languishing charities from selling their assets and redeploying the funds for other charitable purposes is again the cy pres doctrine and the general expectation that charity managers must keep the purposes of the charity alive through thick and thin.[44] Recent legal proposals would also allow cy pres where the donor's purpose becomes "wasteful," but some view such an expansion as too open-ended; a separate question is whether charity fiduciaries would take advantage of greater flexibility.

The institutionalization of philanthropy creates as well as solves accountability problems and does so in both directions. Private foundations and United Ways have recently shifted from a policy of general grants to grants defined by output or methods. Like the United Way, foundations have begun promoting performance measurements.[45] In response to criticism about inappropriate micromanagement of grantee charities, foundations have begun to make capacity grants for general overhead and for self-assessments by grantees and to urge more cooperation (if not mergers) between charities.[46] In a development that some grantees (and observers) view as crossing the line, some of the new venture philanthropists are even demanding seats on the boards of the charities they fund. In general, though, foundations (like other donors) seem little accountable to the charities they support.[47]

Institutionalized philanthropies separately face criticism for the level of wealth maintained in the charitable sector rather than spent currently. Here the question is not what charities do with the wealth they command, but rather when they do it. According to tax records, as of 1997 the nonprofit sector held over $1 trillion in nonoperating assets, and this figure does not include most church assets.[48] In addition, many charities with significant savings continue to seek and attract contributions—in the 1990s Harvard University, leading the collegiate pack, closed out a fund drive for over $2 billion (nearly $1 million a day for seven years!). The recent explosion in donor-advised funds (the middle-class philanthropist's foundation) has brought hundreds of millions of dollars more into the charitable sector.

Do individual charities spend much time considering *when* they want to spend their funds? Under the law, only a donor can require a charity to maintain the principal of a gift; not all charitable assets constitute "endowment" that must be preserved. Charitable funds surged with the stock market returns of the latter half of the 1990s, yet a conservative (generally 5 percent) payout rate continues to guide the spending decisions of both the largest private foundations (which generally make grants at the legal minimum payout rate) and universities (which face no legal minimum payout requirement).[49] Perpetual charitable endowments and other forms of charity savings appear to persist as the happy coincidence of donors' desire for immortality for themselves and for their cultural beliefs, the professional staff's desire for employment and authority, and society's (apparent) desire for narrowly controlled investment capital.[50]

As the post–September 11 experience of the American Red Cross reminded us, donors sometimes want their gifts to be spent currently in situations where charities might prefer that charitable expenditures take place over time. As a general policy matter, society might want to ensure not only that a charity performs good deeds but also that those good deeds are performed within a certain period of time from when the charity receives donations or earns income. Ironically, though, entity-level income tax exemption encourages charities to save because the assets of exempt organizations grow at a pretax rate of return. This encourages charities to believe that they can and therefore should do more good for future generations than for the current one.[51] It would be difficult, however, to require a meaningful minimum level of current or planned spending for operating charities.[52]

MEMBERS. The law of nonprofit corporations often views members as serving the monitoring function that shareholders are expected to perform in for-profit corporations. State statutes permit—but do not require—nonprofit organizations to have members with rights to elect the board of directors and to exercise other extraordinary powers set forth in the statute or the articles of incorporation. For example, members might be granted the right to vote on the corporation's decision to merge, sell substantially all of its assets, or dissolve.

This monitoring device rarely applies in the charitable sector, however, because most charities have no members or have members only in the ceremonial sense.[53] Membership is more common in the "mutual" nonprofit, such as a labor organization, social club, or business league. For national charities with local affiliates, those affiliates, rather than individuals, might be the formal members. Common in the health care area is the structure where a nonprofit (such as a religious organization) is the sole member of other nonprofits (such as hospitals). A nonprofit corporation without members, by negative definition, has a self-perpetuating board of directors.

Moreover, the rights of members of a particular nonprofit generally can be determined by the organization. After all, so long as membership is voluntary, a member whose voice has failed to influence the organization is free to leave and to start a new organization. Some commentators worry about the lack of democratic powers in many nonprofit organizations.[54] Others worry about forcing democratic congruence onto the internal governance structure of voluntary associations.[55] As a practical matter, too, it would be difficult to force constituents (whatever the type) to exercise better oversight.

The membership policies of certain organizations could be affected by legal protections relating to nondiscrimination. These protections apply to all public accommodations, which include many nonprofits, but the U.S. Supreme Court has held that the constitutional rights of expressive associations override these laws. Thus the Supreme Court unanimously held that the Jaycees, which barred women from full voting membership, can be made subject to nondiscrimination laws applicable to public accommodations. Recently, though, the court only narrowly ruled that the Boy Scouts of America—determined by the New Jersey Supreme Court to be a public accommodation—operates in part for expressive purposes and thus can expel a gay troop leader for violating the organization's prohibition on homosexuality.[56] Although this decision greatly upset and frustrated many within and outside the Boy Scouts, numerous charities filed friend-of-the-court briefs on the side of the Boy Scouts, defending the right of private associations to control their memberships.

STAFF. Within the organization, employees and volunteers can provide different degrees and types of oversight, with their own advantages and disadvantages. Staff and volunteers can hold charities accountable by choosing to work with them or to leave. The danger in relying on mobile labor as a monitoring (or even signaling) device, however, is that the goals of the workers and volunteers may diverge from those of the organization. For example, staff might focus on the paycheck or working conditions, and volunteers might focus on the résumé value or social linkages of the assignment. Additional tensions arise, moreover, from the norms that can develop within particular professions.[57] Peter Dobkin Hall, for example, observes that some view the increasing professionalism of nonprofit managers as "a sort of Trojan horse" by tending to shift policymaking from the governing board to the staff.[58] Eventually, he concludes, activities by the manager to achieve legitimacy beyond the organization can "fundamentally alter the direction of an institution, the composition of its board, and the nature of its membership."

In many cases, professionalism homogenizes firms within an industry and diminishes the influence of organizational form on the good or service provided. This is especially true when government is enlisted to impose professional standards through legally required licenses and practices, transforming the organizations operating within an industry.[59] Moreover, excessive professional standards can disqualify volunteers from effective participation, further challenging one of the distinctive features of charities.

CONTRACT FUNDERS AND INSTITUTIONAL GRANTORS. Also prominent among a charity's external stakeholders are institutional "purchasers" of nonprofit services. The relationship between charities and government, in particular, has undergone two profound shifts. First, as documented in chapter 14 of this volume, unrestricted grants have fallen and purchases of services have increased. Welfare reform has brought a revolution in the type of entities with which government is willing to contract, explicitly including not just religious organizations but also for-profit providers. Second, in contrast to subsidies to nonprofit producers, government third-party payments and tax benefits increasingly channel subsidies directly to consumers, who are then free to purchase services from the organizations of their choice, be they public, business, or nonprofit. This shift from trust to market production requires charities to adopt more commercial and competitive strategies and operations.

Not only is the nonprofit provider subject to government review of the contract performance, but in many cases it also is subject to scrutiny by government auditors.[60] In addition, the federal government often conditions its grants on conformance to government personnel standards, such as affirmative action requirements. The proposed Istook amendment would have conditioned federal grants on the charitable recipient's agreement not to engage in lobbying and certain other advocacy activity. State-level as well as municipal-level requirements can also apply. For example, San Francisco recently adopted an ordinance requiring any nonprofit organization that receives more than $250,000 in city contracts to allow the public to attend one board meeting a year.[61]

Government contracting—and government standards—brings both advantages and disadvantages.[62] On the upside, the activity is run in a manner specified by a sector accountable to a broad constituency, and, presumably, the greater is the government's financial stake, the more it invests in monitoring performance. On the downside, though, the dictation of standards and practices reduces the heterogeneity of the private sector. Finally, if a nonprofit depends for its funding on a single-source contract (or a few contracts), accountability may be high, but a change in the political climate might threaten its funding or even its survival.

BENEFICIARIES AND CLIENTELE. As described under the classical model, the nonprofit form is itself a proxy for client control, providing a trustworthy vehicle for serving client needs. Viewed from this perspective, empowering beneficiaries becomes neither necessary nor helpful.

This paternalistic approach clashes directly with capitalism's veneration of consumer sovereignty. Indeed, the trend toward using demand-side vouchers in public programs demonstrates a faith in the ability of consumers to select the best service provider. In programs for simple goods—like food stamps—the beneficiary needs no assistance in spending wisely. By contrast, in programs for complex services, another party (not necessarily nonprofit) with superior monitoring abilities might act as a "broker." For example, a doctor is a Medicare patient's gateway into a hospital, and state licensing bodies can condition access to nursing homes.

These mechanisms do not address criticisms that beneficiaries rarely participate in the governance of nonprofit organizations. This is more than a matter of service recipients. Recall the discussion of efforts by grantee charities to hold foundations more accountable for their decisions. Generally, such user empowerment has made little headway in the American nonprofit sector, although it is a matter of active debate in other countries.

TAXPAYERS AND THE PUBLIC. The final sphere of accountability is the broadest: many of the concerns already described affect the reputation of charities in society at large. Indeed, the general public as taxpayers and as citizens is, to a significant degree, one of the largest groups of stakeholders of the nonprofit sector. Public support is crucial to the tax and other privileges that nonprofit organizations enjoy. Tax laws already limit the advocacy and political activity of charities. In addition, debates continue over the role of nonprofits in foreign (as opposed to domestic) activities and over the appropriateness of corporate (as opposed to individual) philanthropy. For example, the Securities and Exchange Commission recently considered a proposal to give shareholders of public companies approval rights over contributions (or, at least, to require companies to disclose major donations).

Lester Salamon has observed that the "growing mismatch between the actual operation of the voluntary sector and popular conceptions of what this sector is supposed to be like" has increasingly opened the sector to "cheap shots," exposés, and political attack.[63] The public often believes that nonprofits should not charge more than the cost for a service or good or run a surplus from year to year (that is, should not make a profit), should not be run in a "business-like" way, should not pay a market wage to employees, should not compete, and should not take "tainted" money—even that a charity can ignore laws that interfere with its mission.[64] The public occasionally expresses ambivalence about philanthropy—sometimes because of the tax benefits that redound to the donors and sometimes because of uneasiness about the effectiveness of charities.

Accountability Devices

To address these public concerns, two additional accountability devices developed: government-mandated public disclosure and performance measurement techniques.

GOVERNMENT-MANDATED PUBLIC DISCLOSURE. Helping the public to understand charity operations, as well as reducing the potential for fraud and abuse in fundraising, has led to a broad movement for increased public disclosure of charity operations. At the state level, government regulators have come to rely on public vigilance by requiring charities to make increased public disclosure on standardized forms.[65]

At the federal level, Congress, too, views sunshine as an important disinfectant. Nonprofit organizations have long been required to file a financial report, the so-called Form 990, with the Internal Revenue Service each year, reporting details of their expenses, revenues, activities, and staff compensation. Recent legislation obligates a charity to make any of its last three Form 990 filings, as well as its application for tax exemption, available to members of the public on request. A private organization, GuideStar, now maintains a database on the World Wide Web through which the public can access all filed Forms 990, and the Foundation Center makes the forms filed by private foundations available in hard copy at its regional offices throughout the country.[66]

Although Form 990 is the most widely available uniform document on the finances of individual charities, it is not a complete solution. Because of statutory filing exemptions, it can be difficult, if not impossible, to obtain information on charities with less than $25,000 in gross receipts and on churches. Moreover, many of the forms as filed contain errors, some materially misleading.[67] However, compliance should improve as charity boards recognize the visibility of these filings. More substantively, this document cannot provide much insight into the nature and quality of charity activities, and charity advisors debate the relative merits of the Form 990 and audited financial statements or other vehicles for adequate disclosure.[68]

The federal tax exemption regime mandates a range of other filings, which currently are protected by privacy laws, but which Congress recently directed the Joint Committee on Taxation to consider making publicly available. In response, the committee staff issued a report in January 2000 calling for the public disclosure of a variety of exemption-organization items: (1) complete private letter rulings and technical advice memoranda, without removal of information identifying the tax-exempt entity and its transactions; (2) the results of all audits of tax-exempt organizations; (3) applications for exemption, not just exemptions once issued; (4) Forms 990-T (reporting taxable unrelated business income) and the returns of taxable affiliates; and (5) a description of lobbying activities and amounts spent on self-defense lobbying and certain nonpartisan research and analysis.[69] Because of the perceived threat to charities' privacy rights, many of the committee staff's recommendations have attracted strong criticism. Nevertheless, a congressional hearing into the post–September 11 charity response might spur enactment of some of the committee staff's recommendations.[70]

Charities resist increased standardized disclosures because they are justifiably concerned that the public might misunderstand or misinterpret the information released. The public fails to appreciate the fiscal needs of charities, with people often expressing surprise that nonprofit managers are paid at all, that charities have legitimate overhead costs or fundraising expenses, and that charities compete. A survey conducted by the charity watchdog BBB Wise Giving Alliance suggested, for example, that the public does not accept fundraising costs over 15 percent, much lower than the 35 percent cap that the alliance has proposed in its newly revised standards of conduct. Clearly, a public that does not understand the demands on nonprofit organizations or that focuses on inappropriate or unrealistic considerations cannot perform effective oversight and can induce inefficient and ineffective behaviors. One of the great lost opportunities of the September 11 experience was the failure of charities to defend the costs entailed in wisely allocating charitable resources. If any charity had the reputation to explain overhead costs, it was the American Red Cross. However, once the public outcry grew over how the Red Cross intended to distribute the money contributed to its Liberty Fund, the charity was forced to retreat, finally announcing that the overhead costs of the Liberty Fund's activity would be covered only from interest earned on the fund resources and not from public contributions themselves.[71]

The solution to the problem of a misinformed public is more disclosure— nothing prevents an organization from providing a more positive narrative of its goals and accomplishments. The voluntary disclosure of information also serves those charities that do not solicit donations. An educated public is, one hopes, a sympathetic public, and all nonprofits will benefit from a climate of transparency.

BROADER MEASURES OF SOCIAL BENEFIT. Separate from disclosure of financial and other regulatory data, individual charities (sometimes under pressure from funders) and the sector as a whole have sought to develop mechanisms to demonstrate not only their financial probity but also their broader value to society. The United Way of America has been a pioneer in such work, seeking to develop measures of the outcomes, as opposed to the outputs, of the charities its local affiliates fund.[72] As of November 1999, nearly 400 local United Ways—at least one in every state—reported being involved in or planning to implement program outcome measurement. In a survey conducted in early 2000 of nearly 400 funded agencies in six metropolitan areas (with a 76 percent response rate), the United Way of America identified overall satisfaction with the enterprise, but also some concerns.[73] Most recently, the United Way of the Bay Area began working with the consulting company McKinsey, as well as with the business schools of Harvard and Stanford universities, to develop objective standards for identifying charities that outperform their peers.

More generally, in an attempt to make their case in financial terms, nonprofit associations in California, Maryland, Minnesota, and elsewhere have attempted to assess the monetary value of the sector by producing geographically based economic impact studies. Recently, using a socioeconomic approach called social return on investment—which blends traditional stock reporting with an assessment of social costs and benefits—the Roberts Enterprise Development Fund examined specific nonprofit social enterprise organizations, such as thrift stores, bakeries, and bicycle repair shops. The fund's website asserts, "The true impact of the collective work taking place in the nonprofit sector is undervalued by those both within and outside the sector due to an absence of appropriate metrics by which value creation may be tracked, calculated, and attributed to the philanthropic and public 'investments' financing those impacts." It concludes, "As the nonprofit sector continues to compete for limited charitable dollars it becomes increasingly important that we be able to understand not simply that a program is a 'good cause,' but rather that its social returns argue for increasing our investments in their work."[74] A similar push for social auditing or social accounting has begun in the United Kingdom.[75]

Unfortunately, although attempts to introduce qualitative assessments into evaluation have obvious appeal, the effectiveness of any given organization is difficult to determine.[76] As a society, we want to be able to assess whether charities are producing good outcomes, but often we cannot even measure outputs because quality can be subjective. What is more, focusing on outputs (such as patient stays or unemployed persons trained) can lead to de facto quotas, while focusing on outcomes (such as good health or jobs) holds nonprofits responsible for factors beyond their control. Finally, the quest of nonprofits to "do good"— the assessment of which involves "societal values about which there may be little or no consensus"—adds another layer of measurement difficulty.[77] Richard Hoefer's study of self-evaluations finds that organizations usually use only a simple post-test or pre-test/post-test design rather than a comparison-group design, making the results of questionable value and difficult to compare. Hoefer also finds that, although almost all charities used the results to improve operations— and many would use the results to seek more resources from funders—none considered shifting funding away from an unsuccessful program.[78] The examination (to the extent that it can be validly constructed and conducted) not only costs time and labor but also could call into question the efficacy of a charity's current practices or even the very value of the charitable enterprise.[79]

These and other difficulties suggest that performance measurement is hardly the panacea for accountability that many have hoped. Indeed, as Paul Light notes, outcomes measurement "is already beginning to fade at the federal level and has been only marginally effective in the states."[80] Perhaps reflecting this, the United Way of America's website emphasizes, "United Ways are independent organizations, incorporated and governed locally. Not all United Ways that are implementing outcome measurement are using the resources or approach developed by United Way of America." Even many local United Ways bridled when the national body sought to require them to conduct a self-assessment every four years and "share a summary of the findings with United Way of America."[81] Paul Light praises less coercive networks and resources for improving nonprofit management.[82]

Whatever the method of evaluation used, individual charities, their institutional supporters, and the public need to appreciate the limits of what charities can do and avoid suggesting that effectiveness requires success in the sense of single-handedly solving underlying social problems. As Roger Lohmann warns, these "ideals of measurable performance, and specifically of outcomes of social service," miss "how utterly incidental and unimportant the program evaluation ideal really has been in national social policy over the past thirty years."[83]

Recommendations and Conclusions

Given the various spheres of accountability, there can be no single solution to the wide-ranging issue of nonprofit accountability. Lack of accountability in the nonprofit sector, in historian David Hammack's useful phrase, is the problem "that the United States chose to have" by favoring diverse private philanthropies over established churches and big government.[84]

Still, certain reforms would have a salutary effect on nonprofit operations and reputation. To improve financial practices and internal governance, the nonprofit sector could benefit from adopting standards and best practices and offering training to individual charities. Progress made voluntarily could forestall unwise tighter legislation and regulation.

For problems of broader accountability—such as determining a charity's mission and effectiveness—the nonprofit sector could benefit from fuller disclosure to its constituents and the general public. Granted, disclosure makes many charities uncomfortable. Signs of wealth, high fundraising costs, and dependence on earned income could chill donations and possibly tax benefits; yet a charity often must appear successful in order to merit support. Accordingly, most annual reports lack specifics about finances and rarely mention projects that failed; where fundraising information is described, many charities try to minimize the share of resources reported as paid for fundraising. Nonprofits today, however, operate in a society that demands greater transparency. Every filing tax-exempt organization should assume that its IRS Form 990 is (or soon will be) available on the Internet and that someone will be examining it. Individual charities, and the sector as a whole, should take the lead in providing more and better information than the tax collector and state regulator require. Although the competing demands of the various stakeholders cannot always be reconciled, all involved will better appreciate the challenges faced by a charity that reveals rather than hides its costs of fundraising and administration, explains why its executives merit their pay and why its reserves are necessary, and describes its limits as well as its potential in delivering services and addressing social needs.

Reforming financial and governance practices, improving effectiveness, and helping the public to understand the contributions nonprofits make to society will not be easy or costless. However, occupying the least-understood sector of American society, charities (and their supporters) must be willing to pay the price—by investing time, money, and reputation—for improving accountability.

Notes

1. See IRS News Release IR-2001-82, September 18, 2001, posted at ftp.fedworld.gov/pub/irs-news/ir-01-82.pdf [March 17, 2002]. As of June 11, 2002, the IRS had recognized the exempt status of 284 new organizations formed for this purpose. See www.irs.gov [June 11, 2002].

2. See, for example, David Barstow, "Charities: Driven by Need, Not Centrally Monitored," *New York Times*, October 11, 2001, p. B1.

3. Among a flood of newspaper coverage, see Lena H. Sun, "Red Cross to Give All Funds to Victims: Contrite Charity Changes Course on September 11 Donations," *Washington Post*, November 15, 2001, p. A1; Mary Pat Flaherty and Gilbert M. Gaul, "Red Cross Has Pattern of Diverting Donations," *Washington Post*, November 19, 2001, p. A1.

4. See Evelyn Brody, "Agents without Principals: The Economic Convergence of the Nonprofit and For-Profit Organizational Forms," *New York Law School Law Review*, vol. 40, no. 3 (1996): 457–536.

5. John W. Meyer and Brian Rowan, "Institutionalized Organizations: Formal Structure as Myth and Ceremony," in Walter W. Powell and Paul J. DiMaggio, eds., *The New Institutionalism in Organizational Analysis* (University of Chicago Press, 1991), pp. 41–62; the quote is on p. 60.

6. See Stephen G. Greene, "Getting the Basics Right," *Chronicle of Philanthropy*, May 3, 2001, p. 1.

7. This includes approximately 105,000 churches, but the IRS estimates that there are several hundred thousand more.

8. Paul G. Light, *Making Nonprofits Work* (Washington: Aspen Institute and Brookings, 2000), p. 9.

9. Independent Sector, *Giving and Volunteering in the United States, 1999* (Washington: Independent Sector, 2000). A similar survey, conducted in 1999 by Michigan State University, finds that 85 percent of respondents agreed somewhat or strongly that most charities are honest and ethical in their use of donated funds. For the executive summary, go to www.cmif.org/MichiganGives.pdf [March 17, 2002]. According to a 2001 Maryland survey, while 70 percent of Maryland residents agreed that recent scandals at some national organizations have hurt the public image of the state's charities, 89 percent agreed that most charities are trustworthy. See www.mdnonprofit.org/cromerweb.pdf [March 17, 2002].

10. Joint Committee on Taxation, *Study of Present-Law Taxpayer Confidentiality and Disclosure Provisions as Required by Section 3802 of the Internal Revenue Service Restructuring and Reform Act of 1998,* Vol. 2: *Study of Disclosure Provisions Relating to Exempt Organizations,* JCS-1-00 (Washington: Joint Committee on Taxation, January 28, 2000).

11. The Kamehameha Schools/Bishop Estate paid its trustees hundreds of thousands of dollars in fees each year while running what the IRS and the Hawaii attorney general considered an indifferent charitable program. See Evelyn Brody, "The Limits of Charity Fiduciary Law," *Maryland Law Review,* vol. 57, no. 4 (1998): 1400–501; Evelyn Brody, "A Taxing Time for the Bishop Estate: What Is the I.R.S. Role in Charity Governance?" *University of Hawaii Law Review,* vol. 21 (Bishop Estate symposium issue, Winter 1999): 537–91; Evelyn Brody, "Administrative Troubles for the Intermediate Sanctions Regime," *Tax Notes,* vol. 92 (July 16, 2001): 423–32.

12. See "Grassley Launches Investigation of Misleading Charities," press release, June 12, 2001 (www.senate.gov/~finance/prg071201a.pdf [March 17, 2002]). See also Harvey Lipman, "Senator Seeks Review to Find Out Whether Charities Defraud Taxpayers," *Chronicle of Philanthropy,* July 26, 2001, p. 31.

13. See, for example, www.independentsector.org/programs/leadership/Accountability_Report.pdf [March 17, 2002].

14. Marina Dundjerski, "Non-Profit Officials Admit Weaknesses in Leadership," *Chronicle of Philanthropy,* November 4, 1999.

15. See, for example, Kevin P. Kearns, *Managing for Accountability: Preserving the Public Trust in Public and Nonprofit Organizations* (San Francisco: Jossey-Bass, 1996), pp. 65–90.

16. Light, *Making Nonprofits Work,* p. 7. See also Roger A. Lohmann, "Has the Time Come to Reevaluate Evaluation? Or, Who Will Be Accountable for Accountability? [book review]," *Nonprofit Management and Leadership,* vol. 10 (Fall 1999): 93–101.

17. Financial accountability requires not only standardization but also adherence to a particular philosophy of financial health, which explains why the auditing rules of the American Institute of Certified Public Accountants and the Financial Accounting Standards Board sometimes are controversial. For example, a charity might believe that uncollected pledges should not yet be reported as income, contrary to FAS-117, or that more of the joint costs of a fundraising letter should be allocated to its educational mission, contrary to the American Institute of Certified Public Accountants' Statement of Position (SOP) 98-2.

18. Alan G. Hevesi and Ira Millstein, *Nonprofit Governance in New York City* (www.comptroller.nyc.gov/bureaus/opm/Nonprofit Governance in New York City.pdf [March 17, 2002]), p. 17.

19. Laura B. Chisolm, "Accountability of Nonprofit Organizations and Those Who Control Them: The Legal Framework," *Nonprofit Management and Leadership,* vol. 6, no. 2 (1995): 141–56; quote is on p. 147 (emphasis in original).

20. The prohibition does not bar reasonable compensation of directors, although the practice is rare.

21. Joseph Galaskiewicz, "Making Corporate Actors Accountable: Institution-Building in Minneapolis-St. Paul," in Walter W. Powell and Paul J. DiMaggio, eds., *The New Institutionalism in Organizational Analysis* (University of Chicago Press, 1991), pp. 293–310; Elaine V. Backman and Steven Rathgeb Smith, "Healthy Organizations, Unhealthy Communities?" *Nonprofit Management and Leadership*, vol. 10, no. 4 (2000): 355–73.

22. In this scandal, hundreds of charities and donors fell for the "double your money" offer from the Foundation for New Era Philanthropy. But the promised anonymous matching donors never existed, and the collapse of the Ponzi scheme threatened the stability of dozens of charities, ranging from small Bible colleges to mainstream Philadelphia cultural institutions.

23. David C. Hammack, "Accountability and Nonprofit Organizations: A Historical Perspective," *Nonprofit Management and Leadership*, vol. 6, no. 2 (1995): 127–39; see pp. 133–35.

24. See Brody, "Agents without Principals."

25. In addition, board members and officers seem to have different conceptions of how to assess an effective organization. Robert D. Herman and David O. Renz, "Multiple Constituencies and the Social Construction of Nonprofit Organization Effectiveness," *Nonprofit and Voluntary Sector Quarterly*, vol. 26, no. 2 (1997): 185–206; Lester Salamon and Peter Berns, "Ethics and Accountability," in Lester M. Salamon, ed., *Private Action/Public Good: Maryland's Nonprofit Sector in a Time of Change* (Baltimore: Maryland Association of Nonprofit Organizations, 1997), pp. 73–82.

26. Industry-focused regulation—for example, of hospitals or daycare centers—can also apply to organizations regardless of their organizational form.

27. Harriet Bograd, "The Role of State Attorneys General in Relation to Troubled Nonprofits," Working Paper 206 (Yale University Program on Non-Profit Organizations, August 1994), p. 6.

28. *George Pepperdine Foundation* v. *Pepperdine*, 271 P.2d 600 (Cal. App. 1954). Although California later reversed this standard, according to Fishman, the "*Pepperdine* attitude causes one of the larger difficulties in achieving effective supervision over charities." James J. Fishman, "Standards of Conduct for Directors of Nonprofit Corporations," *Pace Law Review*, vol. 7 (Winter 1987): 389–462; see p. 413.

29. Michael Hone, "Aristotle and Lyndon Baines Johnson: Thirteen Ways of Looking at Blackbirds and Nonprofit Organizations: The American Bar Association's Revised Model Nonprofit Corporation Act," *Case Western Reserve Law Review*, vol. 39, no. 3 (1988–89): 751–63; see p. 772.

30. *Riley* v. *National Federation of the Blind of N.C., Inc.*, 487 U.S. 781 (1988); *Maryland* v. *Joseph H. Munsun Co.*, 467 U.S. 947 (1984); *Village of Schaumburg* v. *Citizens for a Better Environment*, 444 U.S. 620 (1980). See also Bruce R. Hopkins, *Charity under Siege: Government Regulation of Fund-Raising* (New York: Wiley, 1980), pp. 96–97.

31. National Association of Attorneys General–National Association of State Charities Officials, September 2000 draft "Charleston Principles" on Internet solicitations; see www.nasconet.org [March 17, 2002].

32. See, for example, Alan G. Artner, "Terra Founder's Deeds May Not Reflect Desires," *Chicago Tribune*, February 25, 2001, p. 1; Jon Yates, "Judge to OK Museum Accord," *Chicago Tribune*, July 25, 2001, Metro sec., p. 1.

33. For state-level boards, see Kenneth L. Karst, "The Efficiency of the Charitable Dollar: An Unfulfilled State Responsibility," *Harvard Law Review*, vol. 73, no. 3 (1960): 433–83; Avner Ben-Ner, "Who Benefits from the Nonprofit Sector? Reforming Law and Public Policy towards Nonprofit Organizations [book review]," *Yale Law Journal*, vol. 104, no. 3 (1994):

731–62. For federal-level proposals, see Filer Commission, "Commentary on Commission Recommendations," in U.S. Treasury Department, *Filer Commission Research Papers*, vol. 1 (Washington: U.S. Treasury Department, 1977), p. 38; David Ginsburg, Lee R. Marks, and Ronald P. Wertheim, "Federal Oversight of Private Philanthropy," in U.S. Treasury Department, *Filer Commission Research Papers*, vol. 5, pp. 2575–696; Adam Yarmolinsky and Marion R. Fremont-Smith, "Preserving the Private Voluntary Sector: A Proposal for a Public Advisory Commission on Philanthropy," in U.S. Treasury Department, *Filer Commission Research Papers*, vol. 5, pp. 2857–68; Regina E. Herzlinger, "Can Public Trust in Nonprofits and Governments Be Restored?" *Harvard Business Review,* vol. 74 (March-April 1996): 97–107; Elizabeth K. Keating and Peter Frumkin, "Reengineering Nonprofit Financial Accountability: Toward a More Reliable Foundation for Regulation," *Public Administration Review,* forthcoming.

34. Joel L. Fleishman, "Philanthropy and Outcomes: Dilemmas in the Quest for Accountability," in Charles T. Clotfelter and Thomas Ehrlich, eds., *Philanthropy and the Nonprofit Sector in a Changing America* (Indiana University Press, 1999), pp. 172–97.

35. See U.S. Department of Treasury, *Filer Commission Research Papers*; Ginsburg, Marks, and Wertheim, "Federal Oversight of Private Philanthropy"; and Yarmolinsky and Fremont-Smith, "Preserving the Private Voluntary Sector."

36. Peter G. Meek, "Self-Regulation in Private Philanthropy," in U.S. Treasury Department, *Filer Commission Research Papers*, vol. 5, pp. 2781–855. The absence of satisfactory peer regulation of private foundations led to the Tax Reform Act of 1969, while Billy Graham and other religious leaders created the Evangelical Council for Financial Responsibility in 1979 under threat by Congress to toughen laws against religious charities, particularly televangelists; see www.ecfa.org [March 17, 2002].

37. See www.give.org [March 17, 2002]. The American Institute of Philanthropy, available at www.charitywatch.org [March 17, 2002], issues letter grades. MinistryWatch applies a five-star rating system for assessing the financial efficiency of "400 of the largest national parachurch [Christian] ministries in the United States," having annual revenues of an estimated $7 billion. See www.ministrywatch.org [March 17, 2002], in particular, the lengthy essay "In Defense of Ratings" by the parent organization, Wall Watchers; see also Harvy Lipman, "By the Book?" *Chronicle of Philanthropy*, June 28, 2001, p. 46.

38. For management-focused membership groups, see the Evangelical Council for Financial Accountability, *Seven Standards of Responsible Stewardship*, at www.ecfa.org [July 18, 2002]; Maryland Association of Nonprofit Organizations, *Standards for Excellence: An Ethics and Accountability Code for the Nonprofit Sector*, II.B.6 (Baltimore: Maryland Association of Nonprofit Organizations, 1998), available at www.mdnonprofit.org/ethicbook.htm [March 17, 2002]; Minnesota Council of Nonprofits, *Principles and Practices for Nonprofit Excellence* (St. Paul: Minnesota Council of Nonprofits, 1998), available at www.mncn.org/pnp_doc.htm#intro [March 17, 2002]; and the Association of Fundraising Professionals (formerly the National Society of Fund Raising Executives), which requires those applying for certification to adhere to its Code of Ethics and Standards of Professional Practice in addition to its Donor Bill of Rights, available at www.afpnet.org [March 17, 2002].

39. In 1999 the Maryland body certified its first "class" of seven charities (www.mdnonprofit.org/standards_PR.htm [March 17, 2002]).

40. Meek, "Self-Regulation in Private Philanthropy," pp. 2842–44.

41. Herman and Renz, "Multiple Constituencies."

42. See Chisolm, "Accountability of Nonprofit Organizations," p. 150.

43. See Daniel L. Kurtz, *Board Liability: Guide for Nonprofit Directors* (Mt. Kisco, N.Y.: Moyer Bell and Association of the Bar of the City of New York, 1988), pp. 84–90.

44. Henry Hansmann, *Ownership of Enterprise* (Belknap Press of Harvard University, 1996), pp. 295–96. Indeed, recent years have brought a wave of nonprofit hospital conversion statutes, which make it even harder for a struggling nonprofit hospital to liquidate its assets and redeploy the proceeds to a more socially useful purpose.

45. See, for example, Garth Nowland-Forman, "Dangerous Accountabilities: Remaking Voluntary Organizations in Someone Else's Image," paper presented at the twenty-ninth annual conference of the Association for Research on Nonprofit Organizations and Voluntary Action, New Orleans, November 16–18, 2000.

46. See Greene, "Getting the Basics Right."

47. But see Darlene Siska, "Accountability, Updated," *Foundation News and Commentary,* vol. 42 (March/April 2001), available at www.foundationnews.org/CME/article.cfm?ID=282 [March 17, 2002].

48. Specifically, in 1997, more than 55,000 private foundations reported total investment assets worth almost $325 billion; in addition, the 199,000 filing public charities reported almost $823 billion in savings ($91.4 billion), securities ($600.4 billion), and other investments ($131.6 billion). See Melissa Whitten, "Private Foundations and Charitable Trusts, 1997," *[IRS] Statistics of Income Bulletin,* vol. 20 (Fall 2000): 150–90; Paul Arnsberger, "Charities and Other Tax-Exempt Organizations, 1997," *[IRS] Statistics of Income Bulletin,* vol. 20 (Fall 2000): 47–61.

49. Publicly supported charities (public charities, for short) have no statutory annual minimum spending requirement. By contrast, the tax law mandates that narrowly funded private foundations must pay out for charitable purposes each year at least 5 percent of the net value of their investment assets.

50. See Evelyn Brody, "Charitable Endowments and the Democratization of Dynasty," *Arizona Law Review,* vol. 39 (Fall 1997): 873–948.

51. See Evelyn Brody, "Charities in Tax Reform: Threats to Subsidies Overt and Covert," *Tennessee Law Review,* vol. 66 (Spring 1999): 687–763.

52. See Brody, "Charities in Tax Reform."

53. As Theda Skocpol has noted, this applies even to advocacy organizations. Theda Skocpol, "Advocates without Members: The Recent Transformation of American Civic Life," in Theda Skocpol and Morris P. Fiorina, eds., *Civic Engagement in American Democracy* (Washington: Brookings, 1999), pp. 461–509.

54. These issues are explored in Evelyn Brody, "Entrance, Voice, and Exit: The Constitutional Bounds of the Right of Association," *U. C. Davis Law Review,* vol. 35 (April 2002): 821–901. Avner Ben-Ner has suggested that *all* charities be required to be run by active members, who would acquire their interests in proportion to contributions (defined as monetary donations, purchases, and volunteer time). Ben-Ner, "Who Benefits from the Nonprofit Sector"; Avner Ben-Ner and Theresa Van Hoomissen, "The Governance of Nonprofit Organizations: Law and Public Policy," *Nonprofit Management and Leadership,* vol. 41, no. 4 (1994): 393–414; see pp. 408–10.

55. *Boy Scouts of America* v. *Dale,* 530 U.S. 640 (2000).

56. See Nancy L. Rosenblum, *Membership and Morals: The Personal Uses of Pluralism in America* (Princeton University Press, 1998), pp. 36–41. See also Julian N. Eule, as completed by Jonathan D. Varat, "Transporting First Amendment Norms to the Private Sector: With Every Wish There Comes a Curse," *UCLA Law Review,* vol. 45, no. 6 (1998): 1537–634.

57. Paul DiMaggio finds the nonprofit sector particularly receptive to administrative professionalism because of "the affinity between the legitimizing accounts of professionals and of nonprofit organizations—both based on claims to expertise, a service ethos, and disinterest in pecuniary gain." Paul J. DiMaggio, "Constructing an Organizational Field as a Professional Project: U.S. Art Museums, 1920–1940," in Walter W. Powell and Paul J. DiMaggio, eds.,

The New Institutionalism in Organizational Analysis (University of Chicago Press, 1991), pp. 267–92; see p. 288.

58. Peter Dobkin Hall, *Inventing the Nonprofit Sector* (Johns Hopkins University Press, 1992), p. 91.

59. See Meyer and Rowan, "Institutionalized Organizations," p. 48.

60. See Keating and Frumkin, "Reengineering Nonprofit Financial Accountability."

61. See Vince Stehle, "San Francisco Passes 'Sunshine' Law, but Critics Say It Shines Little Light," *Chronicle of Philanthropy*, June 18, 1998, p. 45.

62. Steven Rathgeb Smith and Michael Lipsky, *Nonprofits for Hire: The Welfare State in the Age of Contract* (Harvard University Press, 1993); Lester M. Salamon, *Partners in Public Service: Government-Nonprofit Relations in the Modern Welfare State* (Johns Hopkins University Press, 1995).

63. Karen W. Arenson, "As Woeful Year Nears an End, Charities Are Led to Introspection," *New York Times*, December 10, 1995, p. A15.

64. See Evelyn Brody, "Institutional Dissonance in the Nonprofit Sector," *Villanova Law Review*, vol. 41, no. 2 (1996): 433–504.

65. Many states require registration and annual filings by charitable trusts and nonprofit corporations that solicit charitable contributions in their states (as well as by fundraisers and counsel). A charity soliciting in more than one state will welcome the Uniform Registration Statement accepted in most states requiring registration. Specifically, Version v2.11 supports thirty-three jurisdictions (thirty-two states and the District of Columbia) and includes supplemental forms required by six states. See www.nonprofits.org/library/gov/urs [March 17, 2002].

66. See www.guidestar.org [March 17, 2002].

67. "Charities' Zero-Sum Filing Game," *Chronicle of Philanthropy*, June 15, 2000, p. 1; Keating and Frumkin, "Reengineering Nonprofit Financial Accountability."

68. See Karen Froelich, Tom Pollak, and Terry Knoepfle, "Financial Measures in Nonprofit Organizational Research: Comparing IRS 990 Return and Audited Financial Statement Data," *Nonprofit and Voluntary Sector Quarterly*, vol. 29, no. 2 (2000): 232–54. See also Russy D. Sumariwalla and Wilson C. Lewis, *Unified Financial Reporting System for Not-for-Profit Organizations* (San Francisco: Jossey-Bass, 2000).

69. Joint Committee on Taxation, *Study of Present-Law Taxpayer Confidentiality and Disclosure Provisions.*

70. See Elizabeth Schwinn, "Uphill Battle for Charity Tax Breaks," *Chronicle of Philanthropy*, January 24, 2002, p. 1.

71. See November 14, 2001, press release at www.redcross.org/press/disaster/ds_pr/011114libertyfund.html [March 17, 2002].

72. See United Way of America, *Measuring Program Outcomes: A Practical Approach* (Alexandria, Va.: United Way of America, 1996), excerpt from "Introduction to Outcome Measurement."

73. United Way of America, *Agency Experiences with Outcome Measurement: Survey Findings* (Alexandria, Va.: United Way of America: 2000), p. 11, fig. I; p. 8, fig. G-2.

74. See www.redf.org/about_sroi.htm [March 17, 2002]; Jed Emerson, Jay Wachowicz, and Suzi Chun, "Social Return on Investment: Exploring Aspects of Value Creation in the Nonprofit Sector," *Social Purpose Enterprises and Venture Philanthropy in the New Millennium* (San Francisco: Roberts Enterprise Development Fund, 2000), vol. 2, chap. 8, available at www.redf.org/download/boxset/REDF_vol2_8.pdf [March 17, 2002].

75. See www.neweconomics.org [August 18, 2002].

76. For an annotated bibliography on measuring impact (including methodological issues, social indicators, and impact assessment), go to www.independentsector.org/pathfinder/impact/indepsec_res/method_issues.html [March 17, 2002].

77. Rosabeth Moss Kanter and David V. Summers, "Doing Well While Doing Good: Dilemmas of Performance Measurement in Nonprofit Organizations and the Need for a Multiple-Constituency Approach," in Walter W. Powell, ed., *The Nonprofit Sector: A Research Handbook* (Yale University Press, 1987), p. 154. See also David Campbell, "Outcomes Assessment and the Paradox of Nonprofit Accountability," *Nonprofit Management and Leadership,* vol. 12, no. 3 (2002): 243–59.

78. Richard Hoefer, "Accountability in Action? Program Evaluation in Nonprofit Human Service Agencies," *Nonprofit Management and Leadership,* vol. 11, no. 2 (2000): 167–77. See also Allison H. Fine, Colette E. Thayer, and Anne Coghlan, "Program Evaluation Practice in the Nonprofit Sector," *Nonprofit Management and Leadership,* vol. 10, no. 3 (2000): 331–39.

79. See Gary Walker and Jean Grossman, "Philanthropy and Outcomes: Dilemmas in the Quest for Accountability," in Charles T. Clotfelter and Thomas Ehrlich, eds., *Philanthropy and the Nonprofit Sector in a Changing America* (Indiana University Press, 1999), p. 449.

80. Light, *Making Nonprofits Work,* p. 21.

81. Nicholas Varchaver, "Can Anyone Fix the United Way?" *Fortune,* November 27, 2000, p. 170.

82. Light, *Making Nonprofits Work,* pp. 32–34.

83. Lohmann, "Has the Time Come to Reevaluate Evaluation?" p. 100.

84. Hammack, "Accountability and Nonprofit Organizations," p. 137.

16

Demographic and Technological Imperatives

ATUL DIGHE

W̶e are in the midst of a historically unique demographic, technological, and cultural transformation. While this transformation has implications for all of our institutions, its implications may be especially pronounced for the country's nonprofit institutions given their commitment to innovation, their vulnerability to shifts in other sectors, and their involvement in many of the fields, such as health care and education, where the pace of change is especially fast.

It used to be possible to know a great deal about the future, because in slower times the future was bound to be similar to the present and the recent past. Now, however, prediction beyond a few years ahead is less and less possible for most important things because technological change is creating so much discontinuity and novelty. But the need for foresight, problem prevention, and anticipatory problem solving is greater than ever before. There are unprecedented dangers ahead that we need to head off and unprecedented opportunities that we can only grasp if we see them clearly.

We can be better prepared for whatever the future may bring by scanning for trends and emerging developments and exploring alternative futures. Given the accelerating pace of change, nonprofit organizations, like their counterparts in business and government, need to reshape their structures, cultures, stakeholder interactions, and information systems to foster continuous learning and a capacity for rapid self-organization.[1]

It is critical that nonprofit organizations have a sense of the most important questions to raise about the future as well as a sense of the likely answers to them. The future is fundamentally uncertain, yet there are potential directions, even if they may be conflicting and multiple in nature. Without a concerted effort to remain focused on the future, nonprofit organizations run the risk of losing importance in the fluctuating world of the early twenty-first century.

One appropriate approach is to focus on areas where trends can be forecast fairly confidently. Projecting the racial, gender, and ethnic makeup of the work force of a particular region or country is straightforward and relatively accurate. Demographic statistics have proven to be generally stable over time. However, exploring the possible implications of demographic trends often leads to new and occasionally surprising insights into the future.

Another area for study is technological trends. Perhaps more so than ever before, technology is shaping the future. Like demographic trends, technological trends can be forecast, and, which is more important, their potential impacts can be explored.

A final area for study is cultural trends. Often spurred by demographic and technological changes, cultural trends shape who we are and how we interact.

Identifying existing trends and emerging developments sets the stage for thinking about the future. This chapter explores key demographic, technological, and cultural trends affecting the nonprofit sector. The information is meant to serve as a starting point for a constructive conversation about the future. The trends discussed here are by no means comprehensive; rather they illustrate the types of dynamic change the future holds.[2]

Demographic Destinies

Perhaps the most easily identifiable, demographic trends provide us with quantifiable glimpses into the future. However, along with the comfort of "knowing" the numerical shape of the future comes a high level of discomfort in not being able to know how these demographic destinies will play out. For example, we know that minority populations in the United States will continue to grow in the future; however, we do not know how this emerging "minority majority" will affect our collective society. We know that we soon will have four major generational cohorts interacting in the marketplace; we do not know whether generational synergies will develop or whether generational outlooks will divide us. We know that life expectancy in the developed world is increasing; we do not know how our social institutions will adapt to this challenge. So, although we can seek to understand our demographic destinies, we also must use this new understanding to inform our human choices.

A Minority Majority

The census 2000 snapshot of America shows that Latino American, Asian American, African American, Native American, and other ethnic groups jumped from 23 to 30 percent of the total U.S. population between 1990 and 2000.[3] But that was only a foretaste of things to come. Our society has a "diversity generation gap": more than 40 percent of our nation's young people are minorities.[4] As those young people grow up, we will experience the most dramatic demographic transition in our history. More than five-sixths of all new employees in the next generation will be women and non-Euro Americans. Demographers forecast that, by mid-century, America will have a minority majority.[5]

Dramatic evidence of the change our society is experiencing is the fact that immigrants, and even first-generation Latino Americans, no longer need to learn English to function and thrive in our economy. In the past, immigrants who left home were "gone for good." Today, with global telecommunications and travel, the reinforcement of home values is just a phone call or e-mail away. Even in the wake of the trauma of September 11, people have less need to be apologetic about their cultural differences. Many people, in fact, are rediscovering their cultural roots, others are trying hard to preserve the best of their cultures, and still others are learning to delight in cultural diversity. The latest census figures show a large increase in the number of people who identify themselves as multiracial or multiethnic and reject conventional demographic categories.

A process of mutual adaptation is under way in which the mainstream culture is itself in flux, trying to accommodate the entire mixture of diversity and the growing desire to maintain much of that diversity. The most fascinating developments to watch will be the cultural fusions, where new forms of everything from food and entertainment to business practices and worldviews emerge as the United States innovates at the intersection of multiple cultures.

Indeed, the blending is even occurring *within* individuals. Golfer Tiger Woods describes himself as "Cablinasian," an amalgam of Caucasian, African American, and Native American from the side of his father and Asian from the side of his mother, a Thai partly of Chinese ancestry. Singer Mariah Carey proudly tells people that she has a half Venezuelan, half African American father and an Irish mother. The 2000 census for the first time gave people an opportunity to choose more than one race to describe themselves, and nearly 7 million people did. Intermarriage rates are soaring, and the number of multiracial children is growing accordingly. By 2050, 21 percent of Americans will be claiming mixed ancestry, according to projections by demographers Jeffrey Passel and Barry Edmonston.[6]

Most Americans view a multiracial future optimistically. In a recent poll sponsored by *USA Today*, Cable News Network (CNN), and Gallup, 64 percent said that it would be "good for the country" to have more Americans "think of themselves as [being] multiracial rather than as belonging to a single race." While only 47 percent of people over sixty-five hold this view, 74 percent of people eighteen to twenty-nine believe that a multiracial future is good. This outlook is almost certain to grow over time.[7]

To optimize differences, we need to understand what differences actually make a difference. Many of the old categories we place people into are now irrelevant. For example, in *The History and Geography of Human Genes*, Paola Menozzi and Alberta Piazza set out a genetic atlas of the world that demonstrates the genetic absurdity of traditional concepts of race. Their findings virtually eliminate the category of Caucasians. Most European Caucasians are a genetic combination of roughly 35 percent African and 65 percent Asian, even in populations whose gene pools were in place in 1500, before the Americas were colonized.[8]

Race is obsolete as a meaningful biological distinction, but racial and ethnic differences still matter at a cultural and personal level. But our old categories often blur important differences and keep us from seeing the diversity within diversity. Americans with Cuban, Puerto Rican, and Mexican heritage may all be called Hispanics, for example, but the culture of each group is appreciably different from that of the others.

Seeing that the meaningful differences between people are not biological but cultural and personal reaffirms the importance of defining diversity to encompass cultural background, age, values, outlooks, and many other dimensions. Nonprofit organizations can facilitate this type of dialogue in society at large and serve as the nexus for this new blended society. In helping minority groups to preserve the best that their unique cultures have to offer, while learning from the best of others, nonprofit organizations can help to build a productive multiracial society. Nonprofit organizations focused on serving a specific segment of the minority population need to pay special attention to these trends. As multiethnic identities grow in number and acceptance, organizations focused on a single ethnic group will need to change and adapt in order to stay relevant. In bridging the gap of cultural misunderstandings by promoting the common good for society, nonprofit organizations can help to create a better society for us all.

Understanding the Generational Constellation

Generational labels rankle something fundamental within us because they are inevitably oversimplifications.[9] Each generation can be broken into many subgroups. Even the labels and the years used to define them vary from analysis to analysis. People born on the cusp of two generations often blend the experiences of both. The rich of each generation have very different life experiences than the poor. As more people live longer lives, and patterns of education, work, and leisure become more flexible, the life experiences of different generations may blur together. Ultimately, everyone is a unique individual. Nevertheless, generational labels can serve as a starting point from which to explore the specifics of an individual or group of people.

THE SILENT GENERATION (BORN 1925–42). Sandwiched between the two dominant generations of GIs (named for those born between 1900 and 1924 because of their dominant role in World War II) and baby boomers, members of the silent generation often developed strong negotiation skills.[10] The silent generation produced many of the twentieth century's greatest legislators. Their distinctive leadership role has often involved fine-tuning the institutional order and negotiating between the larger generations around them. They have excelled at bringing people together and modifying the extremes on either side of divisive controversies. The flexible, consensus-building leadership of the silent generation opened many of the paths that baby boomers traveled, providing leaders ranging from Martin Luther King Jr. and Gloria Steinem to Colin Powell.

THE BABY BOOM GENERATION (BORN 1943–60). The baby boom after World War II gave rise to the largest generation in American history, a generation destined to be influential if for no other reason than its size.[11] The social movements for civil rights, women's rights, ecology, and other causes that took place in the formative years of many baby boomers created a sense of idealism that placed individuals over institutions. Even the baby boomers who embraced evangelical religion and the political right had a sense of idealism. The coming-of-age passions of the baby boom generation calmed as its members took on jobs, started families, and pursued the material comforts of an affluent society. Now many members of this generation are dealing with both their aging parents and their children of all ages, from older generation Xers to budding millennials. Older baby boomers are moving toward their career peaks. People who, in their youth, flouted their individualism and challenged the moral vacuity of America's institutions now find themselves spending much of their time attending consensus-oriented meetings and managing the types of institutions against which they once rebelled.

GENERATION X (BORN 1961–81). Generation Xers constitute the first wave of the baby boom generation's offspring.[12] They are a highly diverse generation, with one in three belonging to an ethnic minority compared to one in four in the total population. Generation Xers are a smaller generation than their parents, as reflected in another term used to describe them: the baby bust generation. The sheer numbers and cultural dominance of the baby boom generation can be disheartening to a small generation trying to stake out its own identity. Some of their ranks are emerging as the hard-driving entrepreneurs behind the development of new high-tech companies. But having experienced the consequences of their parents' hectic work lives, many generation Xers intentionally seek balance, looking for flexible jobs with tangible outcomes that leave them time to "have a life."

THE MILLENNIAL GENERATION (BORN 1982–TO BE DETERMINED). The millennial generation includes children born from 1982 up to the present day.[13] These were the "babies on board" of the early Reagan years, the "Have you hugged your child today?" sixth graders of the early Clinton years, the teens of Columbine, and most recently the high school class of 2000. They are beginning to make their presence felt on college campuses, and by 2004 they will start entering the work force. William Strauss, co-author of *Millennials Rising*, describes seven important traits of the millennial generation: sheltered, confident, group oriented, special, achieving, pressured, and conventional.

Millennials offer a sharp contrast to the perceptions of their predecessors, generation X. Where generation Xers are ironic and cynical, millennials are enthusiastic and idealistic. The drive and passion of the millennial generation will become increasingly important for nonprofit organizations, since millennials are inclined to build and support institutions. Baby boomers tried to tear down dominant cultural institutions, generation Xers ignored them, but the millennial generation is going to want to rebuild and reform them.

GENERATIONAL SYNERGY. To make their best contributions, these age groups or generations need to work together effectively. To do that, people in each generation need to know something of the life experiences, outlooks, and motivations of each of the other generations around them in the workplace. Each of these generations brings a distinctive culture to the workplace, and their unique needs will evolve over time. The challenge for nonprofit organizations is twofold: to identify and fill the unique needs of each generation and to develop generational synergies among the four cohorts.

Each generational cohort will rely on the nonprofit sector in different ways. For example, the silent generation may need assistance to deal with all of the issues related to aging (for example, health care, retirement finances, advocacy for government benefits), while baby boomers will continue to advocate for social justice issues. Both the silent generation and the baby boomers could serve as a prime source of funding as well as a large pool of volunteers for nonprofit organizations. Meanwhile, generation Xers and the millennial generation could view nonprofit organizations as vehicles to bridge the gap between haves and have-nots and to advocate for environmental issues.

In addition to meeting the unique needs of each generational cohort, non-profit organizations, because of their relatively small scale and value orientation, could serve a larger, and perhaps more important, purpose—modeling as well as fostering intergenerational synergy. Facilitating mentoring relationships between the silent generation, generation Xers, baby boomers, and the millennial generation could help each generation to build on its strengths and experiences for the greater good. Fostering intergenerational synergy may, in fact, prove to be one of the nonprofit sector's major contributions to society.[14]

The Changing Definition of Aging

Aging will be a key demographic trend for the foreseeable future. Average life expectancy (in the developed world) is rising dramatically. A child born today can expect to live nearly thirty years longer than a child born in 1900. Reflecting this, between 2010 and 2030 in the United States the size of the sixty-five-plus population will grow more than 75 percent, while the population paying payroll taxes will rise less than 5 percent.[15] Indeed, with breakthroughs in anti-aging medicine and a greater knowledge of disease prevention, living to a healthy 100 years old may not be as rare as it once was. As a result, the number of centurions is expected to grow from around 100,000 today to 5 million over the next fifty years.[16]

The challenges to society are vast. Never before has such a high proportion of people been living such long, healthy lives. There has never before been a generation moving toward old age that is so large in proportion to the total population as are the baby boomers. And, finally, there has never before been an older generation whose life experience has so little relevance to emerging realities because the rate of change is so high.[17]

Nonprofit organizations that focus on elder care, such as nursing home care, home health care, and retirement or residential care, will experience a growth in demand as a consequence. However, with this growth in demand will come more for-profit competitors. Organizations attuned to the unique needs of aging baby boomers will enjoy success in the future. For example, over the past few years, small to mid-size college towns have become one of the most popular locations for retirement communities because they combine access to high-quality health care with cultural and educational opportunities.

In fact, the very definition of "old" is changing, with baby boomers authoring the new definition with their life-style choices over the next thirty to fifty years. A new paradigm of life will develop, replacing the old linear paradigm of education-work-retirement with a new cyclical one of learn-contribute-reflect. People will cycle in and out of different learning experiences, different careers, and different forms of reflection.

Nonprofit organizations can play a key role in helping people to reinvent themselves repeatedly. Today's commonly held assumptions about what is "old," "retirement," and "a student" will no longer hold true. Adult education—providing people with meaningful volunteering opportunities and facilitating the development of society's potential—will be key areas for nonprofit involvement.

Fusion Family

The pace of life is accelerating, and free time is becoming one of the most precious commodities for working adults. This acceleration, which some pundits have dubbed "the great blur," is a key force driving life-style changes in the American family. Family life-styles are increasingly being defined by the way in which families approach this critical issue. What is emerging is a range of family life-styles bounded by two extreme approaches: *outsourcing* and *downshifting*.[18]

Outsourcing in family life uses money—often from two-career couples—to purchase essential but time-consuming family services. Daycare and home childcare are the primary family functions that are commonly outsourced, with cleaning and laundry services to a somewhat lesser extent. However, in recent years the scope of family activities that are being subcontracted has expanded considerably. Private tutoring for children is available at Sylvan Learning Centers. Personal assistants will come to your house and precook meals for your family. Services will plan your child's birthday party or assemble family albums from a box of random pictures. As these services become more common and inexpensive, the line between family and family services will grow less distinct.

Downshifting involves limiting the material consumption of the family in order to gain more time to pursue wider personal interests or a more extensive family life. Whether it is a desire to quit the rat race, live a more holistic and sustainable life-style, or allow a parent to stay at home with a child full-time, downshifters are willing to trade material wealth for a better quality of life. Families are beginning to move beyond the suburbs to rural small towns to enjoy the peaceful and unhurried life-style of the country. A movement toward voluntary simplicity provides advice and justifications for stepping off the treadmill of the corporate career path. Growing numbers of children are being home-schooled by full-time parents, who are willing to forgo a free public school education for their children. The rising popularity of telecommuting, temping, and independent consulting will enable growing numbers of dissatisfied workers to choose a new balance between work, play, and home.

While a range of family life-styles is emerging, the very structure of the modern family is changing as well. The traditional two-parent nuclear family is becoming increasingly rare in American society, due to a combination of premarital sex, single parenthood, and no-fault divorce. Three new family structures are in the process of joining the two-parent nuclear family as recognized family structures:

—*The gay and lesbian family.* Vermont has sanctioned the establishment of domestic partnership benefits for gay couples, and other states are poised to do likewise. Ironically, gay and lesbian couples are fighting for the legal rights of traditional marriage, while heterosexual couples seem to be moving away from that ideal.[19]

—*The extended family.* It is increasingly common for multiple generations to be housed under one roof. Reasons can include using grandparents for child-care, providing home care for an aging parent, and housing a child unable to afford an apartment after college. In a postindustrial era, these extended families are mimicking preindustrial family structures.[20]

—*The single-parent family.* The single-parent family is already a common family structure, and it spans the entire range of income level—from the single mother on welfare, to the successful, single career woman who decides to start a family.[21]

These new types of family structures will challenge nonprofit organizations to reevaluate the mix of stakeholders they serve. Although some family needs, such as child advocacy, will exist regardless of the form of family, nonprofit organizations might discover that new types of families also have new, unmet needs. Furthermore, due to an expansion in the demand for family services, nonprofit organizations, more than ever before, will meet with stiff competition from the for-profit sector.

Technology Breakthroughs

In addition to these demographic shifts, nonprofits also face a series of dramatic technological shifts. Technology drives and alters our commerce, our way of learning, our impact on the environment, and our understanding of life itself. This section explores three technological trends that are shaping our future.

Distributed Learning

There is growing recognition that the days of the "sage on a stage" model of face-to-face education are numbered. Schools and training institutions are scrambling to develop new capacities in distance education or are setting up new virtual universities. Lifelong learning and the need to retrain for new career opportunities are creating a large new segment for education—adults from ages nineteen to ninety-nine. These initial steps will eventually bring about the next paradigm for education and training—distributed learning.[22] In the future, learning will be distributed across time, location, age, subject matter, teaching or learning style, and the nonprofit, for-profit, and government sectors.

Many in the education community have already discovered that face-to-face interaction places strict limitations on the scope of learning. Such interaction is restricted to predetermined times, predetermined places, and predetermined materials. The new paradigm of distributed learning relies on new communication technologies to overcome these limitations. Asynchronous communication allows education to be distributed across time through the use of e-mail and online discussion forums. The ubiquity of Internet access transcends any geographic limitations on participation and allows education to occur among a geographically dispersed body of students. Arriving shortly on the scene will be technological breakthroughs such as artificial intelligence tutors, high-quality voice synthesis, information appliances, and biofeedback input devices.

Although we are still years away from a fully immersive learning simulation environment along the lines of the holodeck in "Star Trek," advances in technology are revolutionizing education. New discoveries in the field of neurosciences are helping us to understand how we learn on an individual basis. Wireless technologies such as personal digital assistants, two-way text messaging cell phones, and electronic books and paper have redefined communication and hence redefined education. The expectations of a generation of schoolchildren who have grown up with a ubiquitous World Wide Web, computers in every classroom, and Power Point slides for every lecture are very different than those of previous generations. In short, the information age has placed its permanent stamp on education—from this point forward education must make full use of available technology not just to supplement the learning experience but to be an integral component of it. Terms used in the Internet world, such as *twenty-four/seven, anytime/anyplace, customizable,* and *user-friendly interface,* will be key descriptors of learning in the twenty-first century.

As educational models evolve toward distributed learning, nonprofit organizations will need to engage their stakeholders in a dialogue about their educational and training needs and the best ways in which those needs can be fulfilled. Keeping in mind issues such as equity and access to technology, nonprofit organizations can help their stakeholders to navigate the increasingly diverse set of educational options available in the marketplace.

As innovation reinvents the education process itself, nonprofits that lack access to technological resources may find themselves at a severe disadvantage in the marketplace. Distributed learning will attract a whole host of new competitors from both the nonprofit and for-profit sectors. Rapid innovation will lead to experimentation with a mixed set of successes and failures. The successful educational and training organization (nonprofit or otherwise) will be able to integrate the best new technologies and innovations with timeless educational principles.

Good Technology: Influencing Technological Change

Technology is not simply an external force to which we must respond. It can also be molded and shaped. Inventors, visionaries, entrepreneurs, employees, investors, consumers, politicians, regulators, and environmentalists are all involved in this molding and shaping, but nonprofit organizations can be also.

One potential example of this is the shift to *green buildings*—energy-efficient buildings with healthy indoor environments and high levels of visual, thermal, and acoustic comfort.

In the United States, buildings use one-third of our total energy and two-thirds of our electricity. Greening our buildings is one of the highest-impact strategies available for reducing the environmental effects of economic growth and heading off global warming.

Patricia Griffin, president of the Green Hotels Association, points out that nonprofit organizations can easily and simply influence the evolution of the whole lodging industry by consciously placing their meeting dollars with hotels that are working to green their properties.[23] Going green can be as simple as the sheet changing card now found in thousands of hotel guest bathrooms, which asks guests to consider using their linens more than once. Or it can involve more ambitious renovations like the one recently undertaken by the Boston Plaza hotel. Occupancy rates increased and brought in an additional $2 million in business after the hotel installed energy-efficient lighting, water-efficient showerheads, thermopane windows, and a comprehensive recycling program.[24]

New construction provides an opportunity to show what can be done. For example, the Olympic Village at the 2000 Summer Olympics in Sydney, Australia, had such a good passive cooling design that its rooms were comfortable without conventional air conditioning. The money saved on cooling was used to install a kilowatt of solar cells on the roof of each unit.[25]

A growing body of case studies shows that green designs usually cost no more to build than conventional designs and have much lower operating costs. The most surprising finding is the savings that result from the satisfaction and performance of the people who use the buildings. Better indoor air quality, daylight that reaches into the interior of buildings, and other aspects of green design reduce absenteeism, improve worker productivity, and boost occupancy. In offices, a 1 or 2 percent increase in labor productivity produces the same bottom-line benefit as *eliminating* the entire energy bill.

Green buildings are a good example of an area in which nonprofit organizations can save money while acting in an environmentally conscious manner. Nonprofit organizations can use their collective clout to raise awareness of important environmental issues, while at the same time advocating and using energy-efficient, cost-savings techniques.

Biomolecular Convergence

The most far-reaching scientific and technological advances sometimes can be found at the intersection of disparate industries or disciplines. Walter Truett Anderson observes in his book *Evolution Isn't What It Used to Be* that we are now witnessing a convergence between the biosciences and electronics—a bionic convergence.[26]

The biosciences, also known as life sciences, are any of the several branches of science, such as biology, medicine, anthropology, or ecology, that deal with living organisms and their organization, life processes, and relationships to each other and their environment. Electronics is the field of engineering and applied physics dealing with systems and devices that depend on the flow of electrons for the generation, transmission, reception, and storage of information. As biosciences and electronics converge, the advancement of each is accelerated as developments in one domain are applied to the other. Today, electronics has the strongest influence on the biosciences. For example, the planet is now enveloped by an electronic skin of sensors that collect, store, and interpret information about our planet and its living creatures. The human genome project—which Paula Gregory of the National Center for Human Genome Research estimated was 40 percent an information technology project—would not have been possible without powerful computers.

In the future, the tide of influence will likely shift, and the biosciences will become the stronger force. For example, the future of electronics may include computers that metaphorically and literally are biological: for example, artificial limbs or organs that have direct connections to the brain and biosensing "smart skin" that can monitor blood sugar levels of people with diabetes and administer insulin if needed.

Many sciences are operating at smaller and smaller scales and are converging on the molecule and the atom as a focal point. The end result may be the development of nanotechnology, which is manufacturing at the scale of a nanometer or one billionth of a meter. If such technology proves feasible, molecular-size machines called assemblers may one day build objects atom by atom. Nanotechnology would radically alter our world. We could literally change the molecular nature of waste products and pollution and transform it into useful fuels and structures. We could create new materials that are molecularly flawless and fifty times stronger than steel. Manufacturing could actually become a "desktop" process with nano-machines constructing and deconstructing items one atom at a time. We could develop airborne artificial immune systems that could be programmed to recognize and eliminate all known threats.

Much less fanfare has welcomed in MEMS—microelectromechanical systems. MEMS are microchips that not only think, like those in personal computers, but also sense and act. Incorporating tiny sensors, probes, lasers, and actuators, these micromachines may underpin the next generation of medical, electronic, and communication devices and spawn entirely new technologies.

MEMS are being developed in more than 600 laboratories worldwide, and the technology is already in widespread use (for example, in automotive airbags). MEMS technology is also being used to create biosensors that offer "hospital labs on a chip" and gene chips that rapidly and efficiently acquire, analyze, and manage genetic information.[27] While these advances could have dramatic positive impacts on the treatment of disease as well as the prevention of illness, they also will significantly affect the nonprofit health community. The biomolecular convergence will fundamentally alter the current health system. Testing and diagnostic processes that currently need a lot of time, money, and equipment could be completed instantly by biosensors the size of a postage stamp. Nanotechnology would allow us to attack disease on the molecular level as opposed to the microscopic level. Self-regulating artificial limbs and organs can be created that will open entirely new possibilities for the handicapped as well as those seeking performance enhancements. Parallel breakthroughs in nanotechnology and MEMS coupled with a better understanding of genomics could render our current paradigm of health care (and the institutions that support it) completely obsolete.

Furthermore, scientific exploration and discovery in the biosciences are far ahead of any societal dialogue about the ethics and appropriate uses of those types of technologies. "Can we do it?" instead of "Should it be done?" is the driving question in our scientific community. The nonprofit sector could serve as a needed resource in this case. By providing a safe space in which to discuss the implications of these types of scientific advances, nonprofit organizations can promote a much-needed, yet largely nonexistent, dialogue about our future. In helping society to think through (and policymakers to plan for) the emerging technological breakthroughs, nonprofit organizations can fill a vital need.

Internet-Enhanced Voluntary Social Activism

Networked computing and global telecommunications are making possible truly global markets and global companies. The digital revolution is also giving rise to new kinds of civic accountability that impose novel checks and balances on the power of global corporations. For example, when Nike's Vietnamese labor practices were exposed to the world, first in cyberspace and then on CNN, a global firestorm of public opinion was unleashed demanding change. An Internet- and e-mail coordinated campaign led by the Rain Forest Action Network and Greenpeace, but involving hundreds of environmental organizations and grassroots groups around the world, led Home Depot to commit itself publicly to stop sourcing timber from endangered forests. In a world of radically expanding connectivity, there appears to be no way for companies in any industry to shield themselves from initiatives of this kind.[28]

Internet-enhanced social activism is also proving effective in influencing international policies and structures, which in turn affect the operations of corporations. For example, an informal network of more than 700 human rights groups around the world coordinated online to formulate and push forward a global treaty to ban land mines—over the opposition of many governments—and their effort was recognized with the Nobel Peace Prize. Less well known are the efforts of a similar network of nongovernmental organizations that played a major role in establishment of the International Court of Justice in 1999.[29] Initiatives of this nature are proving so powerful that they deserve to be viewed as an important aspect of the emerging processes of global governance.

We appear to be evolving toward a situation where virtually all private sector companies of any significant size will be under constant scrutiny by hundreds of nongovernmental organizations around the world. The cost to companies that become targeted by global social activism networks can be extremely high, including the loss of brand value, the disappointment of major stakeholders, and the loss of market share.

Understanding the dynamics of Internet-enhanced voluntary social activism will be crucial to the success of any nonprofit organization wishing to effect societal change. Harnessing the ability to influence global citizens, corporations, and governments can give the nonprofit community the ability to overcome any resource disadvantages. The nonprofit organizations that best understand this trend will be able to exert a tremendous amount of leverage on behalf of their particular viewpoints and agendas.

Culture of Tomorrow

While demographics and technological trends shape how and what our future might look like, cultural trends help us to understand the most important question of all—Why? Cultural trends reflect society's ability to adapt to its changing environment and our ability as individuals to create something greater than ourselves. Cultural trends inform us of what values we might hold highest in the future and how we might choose to interact and influence each other. They speak of how we will define ourselves and about our highest aspirations for the future.

Cultural Creatives: An Emerging Subculture

So-called cultural creatives are emerging as a new demographic subculture in America and other developed nations.[30] In extensive surveys and focus groups conducted over the past decade, sociologist Paul Ray has identified a large cluster of Americans who embrace core values that set them apart from their peers. These values include a preference for holistic thinking, cosmopolitan attitudes, integrated lifestyles, and social activism.

Ray estimates that there are upward of 50 million of these cultural creatives in America. The cultural creatives may share rather similar values, yet they often have little awareness that they share their deeply held values with so many others. This lack of self-awareness as a subculture is understandable because cultural creatives are identical to mainstream Americans in most respects. They range in income from lower middle class to rich, with few being very poor or very rich. Age, education, and residence also vary widely. In short, their demographics are not very different from those of the country as a whole: their values are what sets them apart.

Cultural creatives directly contrast with the two other cultural groups that hold sway in contemporary America: *moderns* and *traditionals*. The modern mind-set is the dominant worldview in America and is shared by close to 90 million American adults; it pervades the mainstream press, civic institutions, and commercial sector. The modern ideology places a premium on personal success, consumerism, materialism, and technological rationality. In contrast, about 56 million adults share the traditional mind-set. Tradtionals embrace small-town life and value the traditional conceptions of family, church, and nation, which they perceive as threatened by modern culture. Much of the heated rhetoric about the "culture wars" is the result of moderns and traditionals squaring off against one another in the political arena.

The cultural creatives have rejected elements of both the modern and traditional worldviews and have blazed a trail in a new direction. They have become disenchanted with conventional beliefs in materialism, greed, and progress at any cost. They reject the intolerance and narrowness of social conservatives and the religious right. They are moving away from the extremes that each of these cultures represents and are shaping their lives around alternative values:

—*Holistic thinking*—a viewpoint that encompasses whole systems, rather than just one facet of a problem in isolation,

—*Globalism*—the practices of other cultures,

—*Integrated practice*—the integration of the demands of the workplace with personal values and aspirations,

—*Activism*—a commitment to working for a better world, reflecting the fact that many cultural creatives had their awakening during the ideological struggles of the 1960s.

Although the cultural creatives are a subculture of 50 million Americans, they have yet to recognize their own prevalence and shape a new self-identity around being cultural creatives. However, all the signs indicate that they are poised to awaken as a force in our culture, an event that will have consequences for decades to come.

Cultural creatives may well become the financial and human backbone of nonprofit organizations over the next twenty years. With tightly aligned values and a predisposition to "do well by doing good," cultural creatives are likely already entrenched in leadership roles within the nonprofit community. A growing awareness of an important trend such as this could help to mobilize the collective energies of a significant cohort of the population.

Learning Culture

Over the past decade, learning has emerged as one of the key skills that individuals and institutions will need in order to cope with the opportunities and challenges of the twenty-first century.[31] The old models of education are becoming increasingly irrelevant in an economy that places a higher value on skills and ability than on formal credentials. New communication technologies are putting vast quantities of educational resources online, enabling learning activities to escape the confines of schools and classrooms. We are beginning to evolve toward a learning society that extends learning far beyond classrooms, transforming learning into an activity pursued throughout our institutions and throughout the course of our lives.

The need for continuous learning has never been greater. We live in an era where skills are constantly evolving in order to adapt to the rapid changes in technology and the economy. The great challenges we face as a society, from stopping global warming to fostering equitable and sustainable global development, can only be met by collectively "learning our way into the future." As we move toward a model of lifelong learning, nonprofit organizations are in an opportune position to provide educational resources to support continuous leaning. Schools are at a competitive disadvantage because of their orientation around a formal curriculum, not around offering extended learning support services. Nonprofit organizations can play a central role in the learning society, shaping environments that are supportive of learning communities.

Learning facts and being able to repeat them on tests are still the dominant approaches to education, and some significant degree of attention will always have to be given to factual learning. But several forces are undermining the relevance of fact-based education. Continual technical innovation has created a situation where entire scientific fields are in a state of perpetual flux from new breakthroughs. Fact-based education is increasingly irrelevant when new facts are constantly emerging and being recognized as socially constructed.

With fact-based educational styles becoming obsolete, if not yet in decline, there has been a gradual movement toward styles of learning that place much greater emphasis on the process of learning. From this perspective, learning is a form of active mental work that involves the internal mental construction of new ideas and associations, not the passive reception of teaching. Learners are not simply empty, passive vessels into which knowledge can be poured. They are active agents who construct their understanding of the world, validating and cross-checking their images of reality through social negotiations with peers.

These "constructivist" theories of learning have been integrated into the curriculum of some primary and secondary schools, and certain aspects of this approach are becoming widely popular. High schools across the nation have begun to adopt law school–style study circles and make them a part of the curriculum. In some cases, final essay questions are given out weeks in advance, and students are explicitly encouraged to collaborate together in formulating their answers. These study groups allow students to discover the answers through a collective process of exploration and allow students to have first-hand exposure to the learning strategies and mental models of their peers. Under the old paradigm of fact-based learning, this sort of cooperation would be regarded as cheating, but under the new paradigm it is a powerful technique for promoting group learning and the sharing of mental models.

One of the greatest benefits of this approach to learning is that it facilitates finding common ground between divergent ideas. Instead of dwelling on who is right and who is wrong, or arguing facts back and forth, embracing the idea that knowledge is a mental construction makes it possible to get additional perspective on the issues at stake. If we are willing to accept that *our* understandings of the world are a constructed mental model, it becomes possible to see that the people we disagree with are operating from an entirely different mental model. Nonprofit organizations can dramatically influence the future direction of society by fostering the growth of a learning culture.

Conclusions

All of our experience is with the past, but all of our decisions are about the future. Leaders at every level have usually assumed that their past experience is a fairly reliable guide to the future. This can no longer be taken for granted. In area after area today, we are confronted by true uncertainty: we do not know what will happen, but we know that it will happen quickly.

Demographers can tell us about our future ethnic and age mix, but we must decide if we will use these changes to unite and advance our society or to divide and retard it. We must decide how we can use new technologies to strengthen our society. By definition culture changes, but we must decide if it will be a culture oriented around love and acceptance or around hate and exclusion.

If we are to create a future that narrows the gap between the haves and the have-nots, addresses environmental issues, eliminates poverty and disease, and allows each individual an unencumbered opportunity to maximize his or her unique contribution to society, then nonprofit organizations must lead the way. To do so, they must first understand the underlying forces with which they will have to contend.

Notes

1. For more information on scanning for trends, see Robert Olson and Atul Dighe, *Exploring the Future: Seven Strategic Conversations That Could Transform Your Association* (Washington: American Society of Association Executives, 2001).

2. Futurists Robert Olson, Mark Justman, Marsha Rhea, and William Rowley of the Institute for Alternative Futures all heavily contributed to the work in this chapter.

3. "Census 2000 Shows America's Diversity" (www.census.gov/Press-Release/www/2001/cb01cn61.html [July 2001]).

4. "Hispanic Heritage Month 2001: September 15–October 15: U.S. Census Bureau" (www.census.gov/Press-Release/www/2001/cb01fff13.html [September 2001]).

5. "Back to School: U.S. Census Bureau" (www.census.gov/Press-Release/www/2001/cb01fff11.html [August 2001]).

6. Barry Edmonston and Jeffrey Passel, *Immigration and Ethnicity: The Integration of America's Newest Arrivals* (Washington: Urban Institute, 1994).

7. "Gallup Poll Topics: Race Relations" (www.gallup.com/poll/indicators/indrace2.asp [May 2001]).

8. Paola Menozzi and Alberta Piazza, *The History and Geography of Human Genes* (Princeton University Press, 1994).

9. For more information on the generational constellation, see Olson and Dighe, *Exploring the Future.*

10. William Strauss and Neil Howe, *Generations: The History of America's Future, 1584 to 2069* (New York: William Morrow, 1992).

11. Strauss and Howe, *Generations.*

12. Strauss and Howe, *Generations.*

13. William Strauss and Neil Howe, *Millennials Rising: The Next Great Generation* (New York: Vintage, 2000).

14. For more information on intergenerational synergy, see Olson and Dighe, *Exploring the Future.*

15. "Older Americans Month Celebrated in May: U.S. Census Bureau" (www.census.gov/Press-Release/www/2001/cb01ff07.html [June 2001]) and "Back to School: U.S. Census Bureau" (www.census.gov/Press-Release/www/2001/cb01fff11.html [August 2001]).

16. "Americans Hold Great Expectations for Their Personal Aging, New National Survey Reveals Research Has Far-Reaching Potential for Human Health: Alliance for Aging Research" (www.agingresearch.org/news/061301survey.html [June 2001]).

17. Ken Dychtwald, *Age Power: How the 21st Century Will Be Ruled by the New Old* (San Francisco: JP Tarcher, 2000), available at www.dychtwald.com/index2.html [January 2001].

18. "The Change Agent" (www.thechangeagent.com/pdfs/chng6_1.pdf [August 2001]).

19. Kate Terwilliger, "Census: Same Sex Couples Increased" (www.denverpost.com/Stories/0,1002,169%257E56795,00.html [July 2001]).

20. "Grandparent's Day 2001: September 9: U.S. Census Bureau" (www.census.gov/Press-Release/www/2001/cb01fff12.html [September 2001]).

21. "Mother's Day 2001: May 13: U.S. Census Bureau" (www.census.gov/Press-Release/www/2001/cb01ff05.html [May 2001]).

22. Chris Dede, "Distance Learning to Distributed Learning: Making the Transition" (www.educause.edu/nlii/articles/dede.html [January 2001]).

23. "What Are Green Hotels? Green Hotels Association" (www.greenhotels.com/whatare.htm [February 2001]).

24. "What Are Green Hotels?"

25. "Eco-Friendly Olympics" (www.dfat.gov.au/australia2000/olympics.html [April 2001]).

26. Walter Truett Anderson, *Evolution Isn't What It Used to Be* (San Francisco: Freeman, 1997).

27. "MEMS Clearinghouse" (www.memsnet.org [August 2001]).

28. "Rainforest Action Network: Action Center" (www.ran.org/action/ [June 2001]).

29. Allan Hammond and Jonathan Lash, "Cyber-Activism: The Rise of Civil Accountability and Its Consequences for Governance" (www.cisp.org/imp/may_2000/05_00hammond.htm [January 2001]).

30. Paul Ray and Sherry Ruth Anderson, *Cultural Creatives: How 50 Million People Are Changing the World* (San Francisco: Harmony, 2000).

31. For more information on learning culture, see Olson and Dighe, *Exploring the Future.*

17

For Whom and for What?
The Contributions of the Nonprofit Sector

WILLIAM DÍAZ

W*ebster's New World Compact School and Office Dictionary* defines charity as "giving of help to those in need." Reflecting this, Americans have generally associated the charitable or nonprofit sector with service to those most in need, namely the poor and other groups in economic or social distress, such as immigrants and other historically disadvantaged groups, including communities of color. This close association of charity with aid to the poor finds its roots in the country's Judeo-Christian religious heritage. In the book of Isaiah, God threatens to judge those who plunder the poor and grind their faces.[1] The New Testament places an even greater emphasis on charity toward the poor: "For when I was hungry, you gave me food, when thirsty, you gave me drink; when I was a stranger you took me into your house, when naked you clothed me; when I was ill you came to my help; when in prison, you visited me."[2] One reason that Americans continue to support the nonprofit sector is their belief that it largely benefits the poor and most disadvantaged among us.

This chapter is concerned with issues of equity. Whom does the nonprofit sector actually serve? How well does it address the issues of poverty, disadvantage, and social injustice faced by communities of color, immigrants, and others in need? What implications do current trends in the sector have for its ability to serve the disadvantaged? Statistics on the distribution of nonprofit services and charity are difficult to come by. However, studies of the distributional effects of the nonprofit sector indicate that it generally has not done a good job of serving either the poor or minorities.[3]

Charitable donations go primarily to religious organizations, private higher education, and the arts and culture.[4] Although the institutions that receive these funds may include the disadvantaged in their service populations, by and large, except for religious organizations, these are elite institutions that serve mostly non-Hispanic whites (termed Anglos in the remainder of this chapter). Furthermore, although grantmaking foundations have, on occasion, played an important role in advancing the interests of the disadvantaged (for example, in their support for the civil rights movement), on the whole, only a small share of foundation grants support minority concerns. For example, in 1995, the last year for which data are available, only 2 and 1 percent of foundation giving were designated for African Americans and Latinos, respectively.[5] Because these figures include grants to Anglo organizations serving these groups, an even smaller proportion went to minority-affiliated organizations representing them. In other words, contrary to the conventional wisdom, by and large, the nonprofit sector has answered the question "For whom?" with "Not for the poor or minorities."

The remainder of this chapter reviews the nonprofit sector's service to the poor, sector by sector, and the impact of current trends, as analyzed in earlier chapters of this book, on the sector's capacity to serve those most in need. This leads to a discussion of the role of indigenous agencies—those established and controlled by the disadvantaged themselves—which play perhaps the most important role in supporting disadvantaged communities. This is followed by a discussion of both private and public opportunities and strategies for expanding support to indigenous and other agencies that serve the poor.

The Continuing Need

The need for special assistance to the poor and disadvantaged did not disappear during the economic boom of the 1990s. Although the strong economy of the 1990s boosted the incomes of families throughout the income scale, the gap between the haves and have-nots grew wider. Indeed, the incomes of the bottom fifth of the income distribution remain more than 7 percent below where they were at the end of the 1970s.[6] Although the national poverty rate dropped to 12 percent in 1999—the lowest rate since 1979—it remained much higher for African Americans and Hispanics, at 24 and 23 percent, respectively. The rate for Hispanics was about three times the poverty rate for Anglos (8 percent).[7] Furthermore, the percentage of children in poverty remained at about 20 percent, and immigration flows were close to reaching historically high levels.[8]

Nonprofit Responses to Social Services for Disadvantaged Populations

One would expect that the social service industry of the nonprofit sector would be the one most concerned with serving the poor and disadvantaged. Historically, as Stephen Smith discusses in chapter 4 of this volume, social services refer to services provided to the deprived, neglected, handicapped, children and youth, needy elderly, mentally ill, and developmentally disabled and disadvantaged adults. These services include daycare, counseling, job training, child protection, and foster care. But as Smith notes, changes in federal policy have blurred the distinction between traditional social services and other services, including health care, housing, corrections, and public assistance. This change has shifted the focus of nonprofits from a narrow goal of reducing poverty to a wider goal of providing appropriate services to a broad cross section of the population.[9] The effect of this shift can be seen in data collected by Lester Salamon in a survey of local social service agencies throughout the country in 1982 (first round) and 1984–85 (second round). Of 1,474 agencies reporting on whether they served poor clients (family income below the official poverty line), only 27 percent indicated that most of their clients were poor. Another 20 percent indicated that they serviced some poor clients (between 21 and 50 percent of the total client base), suggesting that the remaining 53 percent had few poor clients (below 20 percent).[10]

The trends described in Smith's chapter provide little basis for believing that social service agencies are expanding their attention to the poor and disadvantaged. Among other things, the devolution of social service funding and management to the state level has resulted in states encouraging (a) more managed care arrangements in a variety of fields and (b) accountability and performance evaluation—neither of these encourages the expansion of services to high-cost clients among the very poor. Further, an expansion of government funding for social services has attracted new for-profit service deliverers into the field, a group unlikely to jeopardize profit margins by providing services to the very needy. The pressure to be entrepreneurial pushes nonprofit managers away from assuming responsibility for costly services. And, although Smith suggests that this entrepreneurship has led some to greater success at fundraising from foundations and local affiliates of the United Way, it is unclear how many of these funds have been earmarked for services to the poor.

The one ray of hope in this picture is the expansion of Medicaid funding to cover a new array of social services. Because it is targeted to the poor, Medicaid funding encourages service deliverers to serve the poor. But this ray of hope is dimmed by changes in Medicaid provisions that allow for-profit providers to receive Medicaid reimbursement. These agencies are not likely to jeopardize their bottom line by serving the poor.

Health

In their review of the health sector for the book *Who Benefits from the Nonprofit Sector*, Salkever and Frank note, "There is some evidence that nonprofit hospitals serve larger fractions of the uninsured and Medicaid patients."[11] In addition, nonprofit teaching hospitals devote more resources to serving the uninsured and Medicaid patients than for-profit hospitals. Yet, as we learn from Bradford Gray and Mark Schlesinger in chapter 2 of this volume, several trends are pushing nonprofit hospitals away from service to the poor.

—Increasing commercialization and the tendency to see health services as market goods mean that nonprofit hospitals are less likely to serve the poor.

—The third-party payment system that characterizes the financing of the health care industry means that the interest of the payer does not always coincide with the interest of the communities served.

—The change in Medicare from a cost-reimbursement system to a fixed-payment system makes it harder for hospitals to serve charity cases.

The trend toward managed care includes many plans that are focused on profitability and thus may avoid contracting with providers who serve the indigent and other patients likely to be expensive to treat. Gray and Schlesinger also note two counterpressures to these trends. One is the emerging practice of state and local governments to hold nonprofit hospitals to their charitable mission. Another is the opportunity that third-party purchasers, insurers, and public programs (Medicare, Medicaid) have to hold nonprofit hospitals to some standard of community benefit. Neither of these trends has developed sufficient momentum to overcome the trends militating against service to the poor.

Housing and Community Development

Nonprofit organizations focusing on housing and community development may do a somewhat better job of assisting the poor and disadvantaged. As Avis Vidal notes in chapter 6 of this volume, these organizations focus exclusively on "assisted" housing, which is generally available only to low- and moderate-income households.

At the same time, Salamon found in the 1980s that among a sample of social service agencies that provided housing assistance, 47 percent served "few or no poor" clients, where "poor" is defined as those with income below the federal poverty level. In addition, just over 30 percent of the expenditures of social service agencies that were focused on housing were dedicated to poor clientele.[12]

A possible explanation for these figures may be that homeownership, even with government assistance, requires a certain level of initial capital and continuing income. The barriers to homeownership may simply be too steep for the very poor so that those most in need are not eligible for assistance from a social service agency or community development corporation. As Vidal notes, although nonprofit involvement in the housing field has grown in recent years, it still accounts for only 14 percent of all assisted housing, and assisted housing is only available to at most 20 percent of the families eligible for it. Moreover, nonprofit housing organizations must often serve moderate-income families in addition to low-income ones in order to make their projects, and the neighborhoods in which they are located, viable.

Nonprofit Higher Education

In their 1992 analysis of the distributional effects of nonprofit higher education benefits, Schwartz and Baum conclude, "Students from high-income families are more likely than students from low-income families to attend secondary and post-secondary schools in the private nonprofit sector."[13] In examining subsidies to students in the form of scholarships and loans, they note that total educational subsidies are notably "pro-poor" in the private sector, although the level of subsidies is higher in the public sector.[14] However, if the basis is shifted from average subsidies *per student* to average subsides *per young person* (student or not), then the distribution of average subsidies becomes markedly pro-rich instead of mildly pro-poor.

As with other nonprofit institutions, current trends in private higher education, as discussed by Donald Stewart, Pearl Rock Kane, and Lisa Scruggs in chapter 3 of this volume, are likely only to exacerbate this private education gap between the rich and poor. Stewart, Kane, and Scruggs describe a tuition squeeze for private institutions of higher education that is likely to make private colleges and universities less likely to subsidize poor students. Private institutions rely heavily on tuition for their income. For example, 76 percent of the income of private liberal arts colleges comes from tuition. Any significant effort to enroll more low-income students would represent a steep opportunity cost for them.

Publicly subsidized scholarships and grants could provide an alternative way to support the enrollment of disadvantaged students in private colleges and universities. However, according to Stewart and his co-authors, the principal vehicle for dispensing federal student aid support—the basic education opportunity grants, also called Pell grants—can hardly cover the cost of community college, let alone four years of tuition. Moreover, in 1995–96 federal funding for student aid sank to its lowest level since the 1980s.

Finally, the assault on affirmative action in higher education mounted both in Congress and in the courts has limited the access of minority students to private higher education because of a chilling spillover effect from public colleges and universities to the private sector.

Arts and Culture

A similar situation exists with regard to the nonprofit arts and culture world. As Margaret Wyszomirski details in chapter 5 of this volume, the 24,000 operating nonprofit arts, culture, and humanities organizations in the United States spent $36.8 billion and employed an estimated 1.3 million workers as of the mid-1990s.

Who are the beneficiaries of arts spending, in addition to artists and related staff themselves? In the early 1990s, Dick Netzer established, through statistical analysis of various surveys, that persons with relatively higher incomes attend, and thus benefit more directly from, more arts events than persons with lower incomes.[15] Netzer writes,

> Those with incomes of $50,000 [in 1985 dollars] or more were 32 percent of all those who attended classical music performances even once, but they accounted for 41.5 percent of total attendance. Predictably, opera attendance is more concentrated at the top of the income scale than is the case for any other of the activities, but classical music and theater are not much less concentrated. Ballet attendance and visits to art museums both are noticeably less concentrated, especially the latter. . . . The output of the arts and culture subsector of the nonprofit sector is consumed mainly by individuals and households whose income, wealth, and social attributes are well above the national averages.[16]

Regarding subsidization of ticket prices, Netzer concludes, "There is little or no redistribution from the upper to the lower half of the income distribution, but significant redistribution from the highest-income receivers to the one-third just above the median."[17]

Netzer is also skeptical of the argument linking the arts and culture to local economic development and to the theory advanced by Frey and Pommerehne to the effect that "artistic activities . . . may help a society to foster creativity, to improve the capacity for cultural evaluation, and to develop aesthetic standards, aspects that benefit all persons in a society."[18] Wyszomirski's findings provide a more sanguine view of the contribution that arts organizations make to society at large. As she notes in chapter 5, "Virtually all local arts organizations encourage and fund collaborations with other public and community agencies, especially school districts, parks and recreation departments, libraries, convention and tourism bureaus, neighborhood groups, and chambers of commerce."

By the end of the 1990s, the nonprofit arts community had become more involved in the public education of youth in general and "had extended its efforts to a targeted concern with at-risk youth, often through after-school programs." Further, she describes the increasing awareness of museums and orchestras of their public role and their need to become more relevant to a broader cross section of the public in order to survive. She cites an American Assembly report that provides four public roles for the arts: (1) helping to define and project an American identity, (2) contributing to the quality of life and to economic growth, (3) helping to foster an educated and aware citizenry, and (4) enhancing individual life.

Wyszomirski notes that the American Association of Museums' data in particular show that 62 percent of art museums offer family programs in which parents or caregivers interact with preschool or school-age children and 44 percent offer programming targeted to at-risk youth. According to Wyszomirski, museums must move "from inward-directed establishment whose prime responsibility is its collection to outward-oriented, outcome-based social enterprise that is accessible, unpretentious, and lively." The fact that 85 percent of art museums had a web presence in 1999 and 20 percent of the art museums that have websites provide educational material formatted for use in the classroom provides further evidence that these institutions are coming to understand their broader social role.

Institutional Philanthropy

Robert Mango, analyzing the distributional effects of foundation grants in the early 1990s, finds that, of the four foundations he studied, allocations for low-income minority grants ranged from a low of 5 percent of allocated amounts (in 1989) to a high of 46 percent.[19] Based on these and other data, he concludes that, while only a minority of foundation grants can be readily classified as pro-poor, it would be premature to conclude that foundations are regressive in their impact. For example, low-income households also benefit from foundation grants for medical and scientific research, and some foundations are more pro-poor than others.[20]

Current trends in institutional philanthropy, as Leslie Lenkowsky describes in chapter 11 of this volume, have increased its potential, at least, to address the needs of the poor more aggressively. Since the 1970s, the number of foundations has doubled. Since 1981, foundation assets have more than quadrupled in inflation-adjusted dollars. Foundations, moreover, are under pressure to spend more of their assets. New kinds of endowments have emerged such as alternative funds and gift funds, providing new sources for poverty-related grantmaking. Moreover, the new dot-com millionaires are adding new capital into philanthropy and encouraging new formats for giving. These include venture philanthropy and social enterprise giving, which could choose to address poverty. The creation of new charitable gift funds also has injected a new competitiveness into the field and may lead some foundations to pursue new grantmaking initiatives, possibly targeting the poor.

Whether the new sources of wealth in philanthropy will choose to target poverty or the income gap is the central question. As Lenkowsky's analysis shows, foundations are slow to change funding priorities, and for some foundations a new focus on poverty could take a long time to emerge.

The Promise of Indigenous Agencies

Although the nonprofit sector may serve the needs of the poor and other disadvantaged populations far less than popular beliefs might lead us to expect, it would be ludicrous to say that it has played no role in advancing the interests of these groups. We know, for example, that nonprofit organizations like the National Association for the Advancement of Colored People (NAACP) and Southern Christian Leadership Conference were at the forefront of the struggle for civil rights. Over the past two decades, nonprofit community development corporations have sprung up in almost every inner-city poor neighborhood to address housing and other local needs. More recently, faith-based nonprofit groups are receiving new attention for their efforts to address youth and welfare problems in poor communities. This suggests that the only portion of the nonprofit sector that pays consistent attention to the neediest communities is the portion created and led by members of those communities themselves. These organizations focus on community problems or aspirations, were created or are led by community members, and have directors and chief executives who come from the community.[21] What share of the nonprofit service sector do these indigenous agencies represent? Although we do not have precise data on how many of these agencies there are or whom they serve,[22] Lester Salamon's national survey of local nonprofit service agencies in the late 1980s discovers that 15 percent focused on serving a particular ethnic, social, or special needs group.[23] This 15 percent may well constitute the indigenous nonprofit sector—that is, agencies created by disadvantaged groups themselves to provide comfort and succor to their members. These would include mutual aid associations organized by immigrant groups, black churches, and numerous community-based agencies created under the war on poverty in the 1960s under the "maximum feasible participation" clause of the Economic Opportunity Act of 1964.[24]

In 1999 there were 85,257 social service nonprofits nationally (filing Form 990s with the Internal Revenue Service).[25] If 15 percent of these were indigenous agencies, then there were 12,789 indigenous social service agencies nationally. Despite the small share of the nonprofit sector they represent, private indigenous nonprofit organizations promote the social and political integration of disadvantaged populations into the larger society. As Stokely Carmichael and Charles Hamilton note, "Before a group can enter your society, it must first close ranks."[26] According to Lawrence Fuchs, "The history of Americanization for immigrant groups has shown that groups first form associations for fraternal or religious solidarity, then organize for economic success and political power."[27] In this sense, indigenous nonprofits provide a platform from which a group, or at least its leaders, can launch its integration into society's mainstream political and social institutions. Populations that have been barred from active political participation, either by law or by practice, have used nonprofit organizations to establish alternate power structures designed both to provide their basic needs and advance their interests.[28] As immigrant groups, particularly people of color, entered the United States along with African slaves, they were introduced to a culture in which government laws and institutions were often used to limit their full and active participation in society. For example, poll taxes were used to prevent African American freemen from voting in the late nineteenth and early twentieth centuries.[29] In some cases, it was not the explicit government policy that created inequalities, but rather the lack of policy: for example, Hispanic immigrants in the Midwest and Southwest, excluded from many of the white labor unions, were faced with racial wage differentials. In response, many ethnic communities developed an indigenous nonprofit sector, one that was tailored to their specific needs and worked to provide equal rights in the absence of government protection.[30]

This is not to imply that the ability of disadvantaged minorities to form nonprofit associations as a means to provide and advocate for their needs has restored a level playing field. Indeed, as David Hammack notes, "The fact that the nonprofit organizational form made it possible to create alternate power structures did not make it easy to do so, nor did it grant equal rights to the disenfranchised. The nonprofit form is a legal structure, designed to protect rights to property and to the control of policy: those who can understand and make use of legal skill make the best use of nonprofits."[31]

The important point is that disenfranchised groups established their own philanthropic and activist organizations to provide for their needs as a grassroots response to the conditions they faced in U.S. society and, in many cases, in advance of widespread and effective government intervention. This set the stage for the huge growth in the number of government- and foundation-funded organizations and programs that has occurred since the 1960s. The development of nonprofits within the African American and Mexican American communities illustrates the development of this form of organization as a response to the status of marginalized groups within U.S. society.

The Early Development of African American and Mexican American Organizations

The roots of the African American philanthropic tradition can be traced back to the colonial period and the establishment of black churches, mutual aid societies, and social and fraternal organizations. Many of these organizations were closely linked, with the societies and mutual aid organizations serving, in many ways, as the secular arm of the church.[32] These groups encompassed a wide variety of purposes and activities in response to the needs of the black community during this era, providing moral and political leadership, fulfilling community service activities, as well as creating opportunities for socializing and networking.

One of the earliest black-established benevolent societies was the Free African Society, which was established in Philadelphia in 1786. Benefits of membership included weekly financial assistance to the needy, death benefits to widows, as well as occupational and educational assistance to the children of deceased members. In addition to serving its members, the Free African Society also reached out to the broader Philadelphia community in times of trouble. During the great plague of 1793, for example, members volunteered to perform duties such as nursing and burial services. Richard Allen and Absalom Jones, the founders of the society, also founded two churches, the Bethel African Methodist Episcopal Church and the St. Thomas Protestant Episcopal Church. This link between social action and the church, begun at the end of the eighteenth century, continued into the civil rights movement and the 1960s, where it flourished into a social movement.

Neither the early black mutual aid societies nor the black fraternal organizations were molded completely in the image of their counterparts serving the white community. They developed and evolved to meet the distinctive needs of their founders, black freedmen who, although they were not slaves, were nonetheless relegated to second-class status by society. African Lodge No. 459, founded by Prince Hall, provides another example of the early mutual aid societies and the services they performed for their members. In addition to creating a forum for socialization and fellowship, the lodge also provided financial protection in order to prevent enslavement for past-due debts, participated in the abolitionist movement, and supplied goods to the poor such as firewood and food.

As the status of black people in U.S. society changed over time, so did the organizations founded to meet the needs of their community. In the period after the Civil War, many mutual aid societies were founded, both in the North and in the South. Some of this growth can be attributed to the need for economic security among newly freed slaves.[33] Also contributing to the increase was the Hayes-Tilden Compromise, in which President Rutherford B. Hayes restored a significant amount of autonomy in race relations to the southern states. As Emmett Carson notes, "For Blacks, the Hayes-Tilden compromise meant a return to second-class citizenship, a status they were determined to fight through racial solidarity and education."[34] Thus, for example, the Grand United Order of Odd Fellows grew from 89 lodges and 4,000 members in 1868 to 1,000 lodges and 36,858 members in 1886 and to 2,047 lodges and 155,537 members in 1896. By 1904 the group had more than 4,000 lodges and almost 300,000 members. Like their predecessors, most of the mutual aid societies founded after the Civil War were small in scope and linked to a church or group of churches in the same community. In addition to helping families in distress, many of these groups provided educational opportunities to African Americans.

The Mexican American community has a similar tradition of establishing mutual aid organizations to meet the needs of their community. The Treaty of

Guadalupe Hidalgo, signed in 1848, ceded much of what is the present south-western area of the country to the U.S. government. Mexicans who chose to remain in this area soon found themselves citizens of the United States and, as such, were promised equal protection under the U.S. constitution. In reality, "dispossessed of their lands through legal and extralegal means, disenfranchised from the new political institutions brought by Americans, relegated to the lower class of workers in the new labor market, and maligned socially and culturally by Anglo newcomers to the region, Mexican Americans emerged as a racial/ethnic minority with attendant negative associations."[35]

Mexican Americans began to form mutual aid societies, or *mutualistas*, in an effort to satisfy their community's growing need for economic assistance, political advocacy, and civil rights protection. In addition to serving the economic needs of increasingly impoverished working-class Mexican Americans across the Southwest, many *mutualistas* also worked to maintain the sociocultural traditions that bound the community together and to Mexico. One example of such a comprehensive mutual aid association was La Alianza Hispano Americana, founded in Tucson in 1894. In addition to providing sickness and death benefits to its members, the organization provided a variety of other functions designed to meet both the cultural and social needs of Mexican Americans. It promoted ethnic pride by sponsoring events celebrating Mexican national holidays, and it promoted and protected the political representation of Mexican Americans in local government. By the beginning of the early twentieth century, the Alianza Hispano Americana represented more than 10,000 members from across the Southwest.

In addition to mutual aid societies, other organizations formed in response to the increasing economic and political uncertainty. The sudden cultural shift away from Mexican traditions and toward U.S. capitalism threatened Mexican Americans' customary ways of life. In 1889 a group of villagers in New Mexico formed Las Gorras Blancas (White Caps) in response to the increasing threat posed to ancestral lands by Anglo speculators, ranchers, and the railroads. Las Gorras Blancas rode through their region at night, ripping up railroad ties and cutting down barbed wire fences in an effort to prevent further encroachment.

The number of mutual aid societies in the Mexican American community exploded at the beginning of the twentieth century as the number of immigrants from Mexico increased. Recent immigrants patterned their mutual aid societies largely after their predecessors, providing sickness and death benefits to their members as well as opportunities for celebrating Mexican heritage and culture. Albert Camarillo notes that these *mutualistas* played two key roles: (a) assimilating the growing number of recent arrivals into the United States by providing them with both social networks and economic assistance and (b) preserving and passing down traditional folk dances and songs to new generations of Mexican Americans.

By the 1920s and 1930s, Mexican Americans further adapted the *mutualistas* to meet the changing needs of their community. As large numbers of immigrants became employed in the labor market in the Southwest, the large labor unions made it clear that they would not work to unionize Mexican workers. Some unions even actively opposed the entry of immigrant workers into the labor market. During this era, Mexican workers were subject to a number of exploitative practices, including racial wage differentials, deportation for unionizing activities, payment in credit or in script good only at the company store, and placement in jobs labeled specifically for Mexicans. *Mutualistas* took the lead in organizing Mexican and Mexican American workers by hosting a conference in Los Angeles in 1928 that gave rise to the first labor union dedicated to protecting the rights of Mexican workers.

As the twentieth century progressed, civil rights organizations were formed in both the African American and Mexican American communities, setting the stage for the civil rights movement. The National League on Urban Conditions, later renamed the Urban League, and the NAACP were both founded between 1909 and 1910. In 1939 the Congreso de Pueblos de Habla Española (Congress of Spanish Speaking People) was formed. These organizations marked the start of organizing for civil rights at the national level and represented a new style of nonprofit organization. Although the names and styles of the organizations serving these communities, and other traditionally disadvantaged communities, have changed over time, the basic principles have not. Mutual aid societies, fraternal groups, and other similar organizations have provided disadvantaged communities with indigenous nonprofit organizations through which to meet their own socioeconomic and cultural needs. In the modern era, these organizations grew rapidly in number as the result of the federal government's war on poverty and great society programs. As Stephen Smith discusses in chapter 4 of this volume, the war on poverty was the first time that the federal government provided funding directly to nonprofit organizations rather than through state and local governments. The Economic Opportunity Act of 1964 mandated the "maximum feasible participation" of local residents in the creation and implementation of the war on poverty program, thereby giving prominence to local indigenous organizations. This was the last great growth spurt for indigenous organizations.

The Contribution of Indigenous Agencies

Indigenous nonprofits play several important roles for disadvantaged communities.

—First, they serve as the *first line of defense* against economic, social, and political adversity. For example, in the late nineteenth century, burial societies, orphanages, and other social service programs sprang up in African American communities in the North to provide charitable services to these communities and to newcomers from the South.[36]

—Second, they perform *a public education function*. In recent years, for example, the Urban League has published an annual report *The State of Black Americans*.

—Third, they serve as *advocates* helping to promote the participation of community members in government. A primary example of this is the NAACP's Legal Defense Fund's sponsorship of the *Brown* v. *Board of Education* case of 1954 that resulted in the Supreme Court's order desegregating the nation's public schools.

—Fourth, they contribute to *leadership development*. The examples are numerous. Thurgood Marshall went from the NAACP Legal Defense Fund to the Supreme Court. Vernon Jordan, formerly president of the Urban League, now serves on several corporate boards and was an advisor to President Clinton. Federico Peña was a lawyer for the Mexican Education Project in Colorado before becoming mayor of Denver and then energy secretary.

—Finally, by mobilizing individuals in nonprofit associations and organizations, indigenous organizations contribute to the greater political participation of these communities and ultimately their integration into American society.[37]

The absence of national data on indigenous agencies makes it difficult to evaluate their current place and position within the larger nonprofit sector. Indeed, the lack of attention paid to these agencies by scholars of the nonprofit sector itself indicates how much these agencies are undervalued by the larger society and suggests an important opportunity for research.

Perhaps the most thorough recent analysis of these agencies is a study by Michael Cortes of Latino nonprofit organizations.[38] Focusing on organizations "whose missions focus on Latino community problems or aspirations" and that "are controlled or led by Latino community members," Cortes identifies 2,757 Latino agencies registered as 501(c)(3) organizations in the Internal Revenue Service Exempt Organizations Business Master File.[39]

Cortes discovers that these Latino nonprofits have some distinct characteristics.[40] First, most are new, with half being less than ten years old. Second, they have limited income and assets (62 percent have no reported income). Third, more than four-fifths (82 percent) have no affiliation with any national, regional, or geographic group. Moreover, their distribution into functional areas leaves important community needs uncovered. Many Latino agencies are involved in veterans' activities, scholarships, educational activities, and promotion of business and commerce. As Cortes notes, "Activities notably lacking among Latino organizations include emergency preparedness, consumer advocacy, endowments, environmental conservation, legislative and political activities, litigation and legal aid, fundraising, and advocacy attempting to influence public opinions about social problems or public policy."[41]

One cannot, of course, generalize to all indigenous agencies from Cortes's analysis of Latino agencies alone. However, *if* his portrait does in fact reflect the larger universe of indigenous agencies, then these agencies are relatively new, unaffiliated, poorly funded, and generally quite fragile. They do not function in important areas for the betterment of their communities, notably advocacy, litigation, and public policy.

Factors Shaping the Nonprofit Sector's Impact on Disadvantaged Populations

Against this backdrop, what are the prospects for increased attention to the poor and disadvantaged on the part of America's nonprofit organizations and philanthropy? Several factors seem relevant here.

Demographic and Economic Changes

In the first place, the growing number of ethnic Americans, especially new African, Latino, and Asian immigrants, provides a potent argument for the continued need for nonprofit organizations to play a role in assisting in the economic and social integration of disadvantaged populations, especially in the areas of advocacy and legal services. Immigration continues to grow and will soon match the historically high levels experienced in the early twentieth century.[42] Today, however, most legal immigrants are not from Europe, but from Latin America and Asia. For example, the Hispanic or Latino population (of any race) grew 58 percent between 1990 and 2000.[43] As these populations grow, so does the need for services.

The Potential for Private Support

The environment of private support for anti-poverty and advocacy agencies is difficult to ascertain. On the one hand, as Virginia Hodgkinson suggests in chapter 12 of this volume, levels of charitable giving are rising, foundation coffers are full, and we may be in the midst of a new golden age of philanthropy. Since 1996, the assets of independent foundations have grown by $100 billion due largely to the rising stock market.[44] Because of this prosperity, grantmaking among all foundations grew to $22.8 billion between 1998 and 1999, or 17 percent. In addition, there is some evidence that foundations are boosting their payout rates above the required 5 percent minimum.[45] The growth of foundation assets and grantmaking presents an opportunity for nonprofit anti-poverty agencies.

Although the endowments of private grantmaking foundations have grown rapidly, private support can only make up a small portion of the government revenue that nonprofits have lost as a result of recent budget cutbacks. Salamon and Abramson have estimated that the budget compromise between President Clinton and the Republican Congress in 1996 in effect reduced "spending on discretionary programs of interest to nonprofit organizations by 12 percent, or some $8.5 billion, below what was spent in fiscal year 1995."[46] Moreover, following the conservative criticism of social programs, many foundations have grown suspicious of the effectiveness not only of such programs but also of nonprofit organizations generally as compared to informal family networks and greater individual responsibility. Finally, many private donors are reluctant to support identity-based organizations for fear of contributing to social divisions, while foundations are reluctant to provide general support grants, preferring project support instead. A positive development is the increasing use of social venture partnerships between businesses and nonprofits to address social needs. Such partnerships put an array of corporate resources to work for nonprofits. And new trends in foundation programming indicate some hopeful signs for poverty alleviation. These include a renewed attention to families and children, especially children in poverty, and a growing interest in comprehensive community initiatives that attempt to address the needs of whole communities in a vertically integrated systems approach. But these remain piecemeal efforts, well below the scale of national need. In fact, foundation support for human services was one of the slowest growing areas of grantmaking between 1997 and 1998.[47]

More promising is the increase in representation of minority communities on the boards and staff of local and national funding agencies and the formation of affinity groups within the foundation world made up of minority representatives. Such identity-based associations of grantmakers have begun to lobby within their foundations for greater support of their same-identity nonprofit service organizations. For example, Hispanics in Philanthropy recently created a collaborative of national and regional funders to address the needs of Hispanic nonprofits across the country.[48]

Also promising has been the formation of funding collaborations among organizations serving particular minority communities in order to counter the increasingly competitive funding environment that now exists. In New York City, for example, Hispanic agencies have grouped themselves into the Hispanic Federation of New York. Similarly, African American agencies have created Associated Black Charities modeled on the Jewish federations of social service agencies. These "minority" federations provide technical assistance to member agencies and are a convenient way for funders to assist their agencies through a form of one-stop shopping. Community-based agencies also are likely to heighten their efforts to raise funds in their own communities. The booming economy of the 1990s raised the personal incomes of people of color, and, although poverty still characterizes many of these communities, each group has a growing class of entrepreneurs and professionals that can now be tapped for charitable contributions. If the dominant philanthropic sector is unresponsive, perhaps this new professional and entrepreneurial class will not be. Indeed, several so-called diversity funds attached to community foundations have developed across the country to raise funds among this new class of entrepreneurs for permanent endowments devoted to community needs.[49]

Government Support

Although it is unrealistic to believe that a targeted funding strategy for poverty alleviation along the lines of a war on poverty will emerge from the Bush administration, at least in the president's faith-based nonprofit service initiative there lies a ray of hope for federal support for this small sector of community-based social service programs.

A case also can be made for a new strategy on immigrant adjustment to American society. Politically, such a policy would appeal both to the left and to the right. To the left, it would appeal to traditional concerns for social justice and the reduction of need and distress. To the right, it would appeal to concerns for the social and political integration of immigrant aliens. Economic conservatives have long supported liberal immigration policies to satisfy the labor needs of American industry and provide downward pressure on wages. Although the primary focus of U.S. immigration policy lies at the federal level, it is focused exclusively on quota issues (how many and who). It does not address issues of adjustment. Adjustment issues are left largely to the states, which must address the education, health, and welfare needs of new immigrants. As such, federal immigration policy becomes another unfunded federal mandate. A federal immigrant policy is needed that provides states and, through them, nonprofit agencies with assistance to help with the adjustment of new immigrants particularly in the areas of English language training, job training, and health needs. To make it more politically appealing, the policy could focus on the immigrant family and its adjustment to American society. Although this policy would only address the needs of immigrant-serving agencies, immigrants are an increasing proportion of the disadvantaged population of the United States, so the policy might meet the needs of a large share of community agencies. In the wake of September 11 and the war on terrorism, however, such initiatives seem unlikely indeed.

Conclusions

Contrary to the conventional wisdom, by and large, the nonprofit sector does not address the needs of the poor and disadvantaged very well, and current trends, as discussed in other chapters in this book, suggest that this situation will not improve much in the foreseeable future. Nevertheless, indigenous nonprofits, although accounting for only a small share of the nonprofit service sector, play a role for their communities and the nation as a whole that is disproportionate to their numbers. They provide the first line of defense against poverty and other economic and social problems facing the most disadvantaged among us: people of color and new immigrants. They also advocate for these communities and are important vehicles for leadership development and the integration of their communities into the political and economic mainstream. Yet because many are relatively new and their leaders are inexperienced, they are the most vulnerable nonprofit agencies to the winds of change affecting the sector. When the nonprofit sector catches a cold, these agencies get pneumonia. This should concern the larger society, not only out of a sense of charity but also out of self-interest. A healthy civil society depends, at least in part, on the health of this subsector of agencies.[50] For this reason, if no other, funders should again be paying particular attention to the needs of indigenous agencies. Diversity funds within community foundations and funding collaboratives targeted on the needs of disadvantaged communities provide new models for mobilizing resources for these agencies. It is to be hoped that such mechanisms will grow in number and scale in the years ahead.

Notes

1. Isaiah 3:14–15, *New American Standard Bible* (Nashville: Broadman and Holman, 1997).

2. Matthew 25:35–36.

3. See, for example, Charles T. Clotfelter, ed., *Who Benefits from the Nonprofit Sector?* (University of Chicago Press, 1992); Lester M. Salamon, *Partners in Public Service: Government in Nonprofit Relations in the Modern Welfare State* (Johns Hopkins University Press, 1995), pp. 115–44.

4. American Association of Fund-Raising Counsel Trust for Philanthropy, *Giving USA 1999* (Indianapolis: American Association of Fund-Raising Counsel Trust for Philanthropy, 2000).

5. Foundation Center, *Foundation Giving 1997* (New York: Foundation Center, 1997).

6. Gary Burtless, "Growing America Inequality," in Henry J. Aaron and Robert D. Reischauer, eds., *Setting National Priorities: The 2000 Election and Beyond* (Washington: Brookings, 1999).

7. U.S. Bureau of the Census, "Poverty in the United States" (Washington: U.S. Bureau of the Census, 1999).

8. Isabel V. Sawhill, "Families at Risk," in Aaron and Reischauer, eds., *Setting National Priorities;* Jeffrey S. Passell, *Immigration and the New Work Force* (Washington: Urban Institute, 2000).

9. Lester M. Salamon, "Social Services," in Clotfelter, ed., *Who Benefits from the Nonprofit Sector?*

10. Salamon, "Social Services."

11. David S. Salkever and Richard G. Frank, "Health Services," in Clotfelter, ed., *Who Benefits from the Nonprofit Sector?* pp. 24–54.

12. Salamon, "Social Services," pp. 149–50.

13. Saul Schwartz and Sandy Baum, "Education," in Clotfelter, ed., *Who Benefits from the Nonprofit Sector?* pp. 9–86.

14. Salamon, "Social Services," p. 87.

15. Dick Netzer, "Arts and Culture," in Clotfelter, ed., *Who Benefits from the Nonprofit Sector?* pp. 182–87.

16. Netzer, "Arts and Culture," p. 186.

17. Netzer, "Arts and Culture," pp. 199–200.

18. Netzer, "Arts and Culture," pp. 189–90; Bruno S. Frey and Werner W. Pommerehne, *Muses and Markets: Exploration in the Economics of the Arts* (Oxford, U.K.: Basil Blackwell, 1989), p. 19.

19. Robert Mango, "Foundations," in Clotfelter, ed., *Who Benefits from the Nonprofit Sector?* p. 228.

20. Mango, "Foundations," p. 233.

21. Michael Cortes, "A Statistical Profile of Latino Nonprofit Organizations in the United States," in Diana Campoamor, William A. Díaz, and Henry A. J. Ramos, eds., *Nuevos Senderos* (Houston: Arte Público, 1999).

22. Elizabeth Boris, 2001, personal communication with author.

23. Salamon, "Social Services," p. 62.

24. Daniel P. Moynihan, *Maximum Feasible Misunderstanding: Community Action in the War on Poverty* (New York: Vintage, 1969).

25. Boris, personal communication, 2001.

26. Stokely Carmichael and Charles V. Hamilton, eds., *Black Power: The Politics of Liberation in America* (New York: Random House, 1967), p. 44.

27. Lawrence H. Fuchs, *The American Kaleidoscope: Race, Ethnicity, and the Civic Culture* (Wesleyan University Press, 1995), p. 343.

28. David C. Hammack, "Nonprofit Organizations as Alternative Power Structures," in David Hammack, ed., *Making the Nonprofit Sector in the United States* (Indiana University Press, 1998).

29. Hammack, "Nonprofit Organizations as Alternative Power Structures."

30. Albert Camarillo, "Mexican Americans and Nonprofit Organizations: A Historical Overview," in Herman E. Gallegos and Michael O'Neill, *Hispanics and the Nonprofit Sector* (New York: Foundation Center, 1991); and Hammack, ed., *Making the Nonprofit Sector.*

31. Hammack, ed., *Making the Nonprofit Sector,* p. 222.

32. The discussion of black philanthropic organizations is drawn from the following work by Emmett Carson, unless otherwise noted. Emmett D. Carson, *A Hand Up: Black Philanthropy and Self-Help in America* (Washington: Joint Center for Political and Economic Studies, 1993).

33. Susan Greenbaum, "A Comparison of African American and Euro American Mutual Aid Societies in 19th Century America," in Hammock, ed., *Making the Nonprofit Sector.*

34. Carson, *A Hand Up,* p. 17. The following numbers on the growth of members and lodges are also from Carson.

35. The discussion of Mexican American mutual aid societies is drawn from Camarillo, "Mexican Americans and Nonprofit Organizations," unless otherwise noted. The quote is found on p. 17.

36. W. E. B. DuBois, "Economic Cooperation among Negro Americans," in Hammack, ed., *Making the Nonprofit Sector.*

37. Sidney Verba and Norman Nie, *Participation in America: Political Democracy and Social Equality* (University of Chicago Press, 1972).

38. Michael Cortes, "Statistical Profile," p. 17.

39. Cortes, "Statistical Profile," p. 21.

40. This discussion is based on analysis found in Cortes, "Statistical Profile," pp. 26–32.

41. Cortes, "Statistical Profile," p. 32.

42. Passell, *Immigration and the New Work Force.*

43. U.S. Census Bureau, *2000 Census of Population* (Washington: U.S. Census Bureau, 2000).

44. Foundation Center, *Foundation Growth and Giving Estimates* (New York: Foundation Center, 2000).

45. Foundation Center, *Foundation Growth and Giving.*

46. Lester M. Salamon and Alan J. Abramson, "The Federal Budget and the Nonprofit Sector: Implications of the Contract with America," in Dwight F. Burlingame and others, eds., *Capacity for Change? The Nonprofit World in the Age of Devolution* (Indianapolis: Indiana University Center on Philanthropy 1996), p. 17.

47. Foundation Center, *Foundation Giving Trends* (New York: Foundation Center, 2000).

48. Campoamor and others, eds., *Nuevos Senderos.*

49. Joint Affinity Groups, "Diversity Practices in Foundations: Findings from a National Study" (Santa Fe: Joint Affinity Groups, 2001).

50. Cortes, "Statistical Profile."

Contributors

Alan J. Abramson is director of the Aspen Institute Nonprofit Sector and Philanthropy Program.

Elizabeth Boris is director of the Center on Nonprofits and Philanthropy at the Urban Institute.

Evelyn Brody is professor of law at the Chicago-Kent College of Law, Illinois Institute of Technology.

Mark Chaves is professor of sociology and department head at the University of Arizona.

William Díaz was senior fellow at the University of Minnesota's Hubert H. Humphrey Institute of Public Affairs.

Atul Dighe is a senior futurist with the Institute for Alternative Futures.

Shepard Forman is director of the Center on International Cooperation at New York University.

Bradford H. Gray is director of the Division of Health and Science Policy at the New York Academy of Medicine and editor of *The Milbank Quarterly*, a journal of public health and health care policy.

Kirsten A. Grønbjerg holds the Efroymson Chair in Philanthropy at the Center on Philanthropy and is professor of public and environmental affairs at Indiana University.

Virginia A. Hodgkinson is research professor of public policy at the Center for Voluntary Organizations and Service, the Georgetown University Public Policy Institute.

Pearl Rock Kane is the Klingenstein Family Professor in the Department of Organization and Leadership at Teachers College, Columbia University, and director of the Esther A. and Joseph Klingenstein Center.

Jeff Krehely is special assistant to the president of the Atlantic Philanthropies.

Leslie Lenkowsky is on leave from Indiana University where he was professor of philanthropic studies and public policy at the Indiana University Center on Philanthropy when he wrote the chapter on foundations and corporate philanthropy. He is currently chief executive officer of the Corporation for National and Community Service.

Rachel McCarthy is a program coordinator in the Aspen Institute Nonprofit Sector and Philanthropy Program.

Lester M. Salamon is a professor at Johns Hopkins University and director of the Johns Hopkins Center for Civil Society Studies.

Mark Schlesinger is associate professor at Yale University's School of Medicine, a fellow at Yale's Institution for Social and Policy Studies, and a visiting research professor at Rutgers University.

Lisa Scruggs is an associate at the law firm Jenner and Block.

Steven Rathgeb Smith is associate professor at the Daniel J. Evans School of Public Affairs at the University of Washington.

Donald M. Stewart is president and chief executive director of the Chicago Community Trust.

Abby Stoddard is a research associate at New York University's Center on International Cooperation.

Avis Vidal is professor of urban planning and chair of the Department of Geography and Urban Planning at Wayne State University.

Margaret J. Wyszomirski is professor of both art education and public policy and director of the Arts Policy and Administration Program at Ohio State University.

Dennis R. Young is professor of nonprofit management and economics at Case Western Reserve University and chief executive officer of the National Center on Nonprofit Enterprise.

Index

AAFRC. *See* American Association of Fund-Raising Counsel

AARP, 301, 442

Abortion issue advocacy, 321–23

Abramson, Alan J., 530

Academic health centers. *See* Health care

ACCION International, 265

Accountability, 16–17, 29, 471–98; and adherence to donor direction and mission, 476, 482–84; arts and culture, 198, 213; to beneficiaries of services, 487; classical model of, 29, 476–78; and commercialization of nonprofits, 429, 437; congressional investigations of nonprofits, 474; devices for, 488–91; donors' rights, 477, 482–84; and effectiveness, 476; factors in, 473–76; and fiduciary duty of nonprofit directors and trustees, 475–78; and financial probity, 475; foundations and corporate philanthropy, 166, 377–78; GAO study of deceitful and fraudulent practices, 474; government regulation for, 479–80, 488–89; health care organizations, 77–80; infrastruc-ture organizations (IOs), 347–49; members' rights, 484–85; nondiscrimination protections, 485; nongovernmental organizations (NGOs), 254–56; to public at large, 487–88; public disclosure to ensure, 474, 488–89; and public trust, 19–21, 476; to purchasers of nonprofit services, 486–87; scope of problem for nonprofits, 473–75; self-regulation, 480–82; social return on investment as measure of, 490; social services, 151, 166–67, 175; to staffs, 485–86; to stakeholders, 17, 475, 482–88; standards and accreditation, 349, 481–82; state attorneys general role, 474, 479–80; tax returns, public disclosure of, 474, 488; to taxpayers, 487–88; value to society, demonstration of, 489–91; to volunteers, 485–86; workforce development and training, 135–36

Accreditation and standards, 349, 481–82

Activism, 513

Advocacy. *See* Civic participation and advocacy